The Economics of Exchange Rates

Lucio Sarno

and

Mark P. Taylor

with a foreword by

Jeffrey A. Frankel

CAMBRIDGE
UNIVERSITY PRESS

PUBLISHED BY THE PRESS SYNDICATE OF THE UNIVERSITY OF CAMBRIDGE
The Pitt Building, Trumpington Street, Cambridge, United Kingdom

CAMBRIDGE UNIVERSITY PRESS
The Edinburgh Building, Cambridge CB2 2RU, UK
40 West 20th Street, New York, NY 10011-4211, USA
477 Williamstown Road, Port Melbourne VIC 3207, Australia
Ruiz de Alarcón 13, 28014 Madrid, Spain
Dock House, The Waterfront, Cape Town 8001, South Africa

http://www.cambridge.org

First published 2002
Fourth printing 2006

Printed in the United Kingdom at the University Press, Cambridge

Typeface Times Roman 10/13 pt.   *System* LaTeX 2_ε [TB]

A catalogue record for this book is available from the British Library

ISBN 0 521 48133 3 hardback
ISBN 0 521 48584 3 paperback

To my parents
L.S.

To my mother and the memory of my father
M.P.T.

Contents

Foreword

Research is supposed to proceed according to what is called the scientific method. Hypotheses are proposed, tested, and enthroned if consistent with the evidence. The accretion of knowledge is supposed to be cumulative over time, discarding what is at odds with evidence and retaining what works. The ability to answer questions about the real world is supposed to be the ultimate motivation.

Unfortunately, economics does not always work that way. Intellectual fads and the effort to demonstrate mathematical prowess sometimes dominate the research agenda. Everyone becomes more specialised, and few seek to synthesise. Some even forget that the ultimate goal is to design models consistent with the real world and that, for example, the derivation of behaviour from principles of optimisation should be considered only a tool to that end.

After the rational expectations revolution of the 1970s, the study of exchange rates turned nihilistic in the 1980s. It was discovered that a decade or two of experience with floating currencies had not provided enough data to verify some of the systematic patterns of movement in real or nominal exchange rates that the theories of the time had predicted. Statistical tests failed to reject the hypothesis that the nominal exchange rate followed a random walk, or that the real exchange rate followed a random walk. This meant, embarrassingly, we had nothing to say that would help predict changes in such variables. But these demonstrations of the state of our ignorance were misleadingly labelled as evidence in favour of theories, versions of the random walk 'theory'. More elaborate models were then designed, based on optimising behaviour, so as to have no testable implications, and thereby to correspond superficially to the empirical findings of no statistical significance. Never mind that the random walk proposition was in fact a proclamation of lack of knowledge rather than a proclamation of knowledge. Never mind that there was in any case excellent reason to believe that the failures to reject were due to low power – insufficient data – rather than the truth of the null hypothesis. (Never mind that the hypothesis of a random walk in the nominal exchange rate was inconsistent with the hypothesis of a random walk in the real exchange rate, given sustained inflation differentials. One can write about them in separate papers.)

The state of affairs improved a lot in the 1990s. Big data sets, based on long time series or panel studies, now allowed higher levels of statistical confidence, including rejections of random walks at long horizons. Geography reappeared in international economics after a strangely long absence. The old question of exchange rate regimes was reinvigorated with theories of dynamically inconsistent monetary policy, credibility and target zone dynamics. New areas of research focused on specific real world questions, such as the study of pricing to market in exports, of monetary unions, of speculative attacks and of microstructure in the foreign exchange market. The 'new open-economy macroeconomics' managed to accomplish the craved derivations from micro-foundations of optimisation in dynamic general equilibrium *without* at the same time sacrificing the realism of imperfect integration, imperfect competition or imperfect adjustment, and without sacrificing the ability to address important questions regarding the effects of monetary policy.

What, then, is the current state of knowledge regarding exchange rate economics? Who can synthesise it all and present it clearly? For years, Mark Taylor has been pursuing the research of international money and finance in the way science is supposed to be done. The work is patient and careful. The accumulation of understanding is cumulative. Old theories are discarded when shown to be inconsistent with the evidence, and retained if supported by the evidence. New theories are incorporated when they too pass the hurdles. Occam's razor is wielded. It all has to fit together. Above all, the enterprise is empirical, in the best sense of the word: the motivation is to explain the world. More recently, Lucio Sarno has been seen as a promising new researcher in the field.

Sarno and Taylor's book is a *tour de force*. The exposition is comprehensive, covering contributions from all corners of the field, and covering the range from the seminal models of the 1970s to the latest discoveries on the theoretical and econometric frontiers of the 2000s. There is no excess verbiage or mathematics. Everything is there to serve a purpose. This is the current state of knowledge.

Jeffrey A. Frankel
Harvard University

Preface

The economics of exchange rates is an area within international finance which has generated and continues to generate strong excitement and interest among students, academics, policy-makers and practitioners. The last fifteen years or so in particular have seen a great flurry of activity in exchange rate economics, with important contributions to exchange rate theory, empirics and policy. Much of this activity has been so revolutionary as to induce a significant change in the profession's way of thinking about the area. In this book – part monograph, part advanced textbook – we seek to provide an overview of the exchange rate literature, focusing largely but not exclusively on work produced within the last fifteen years or so, expositing, criticising and interpreting those areas which, in our view, are representative of the most influential contributions made by the profession in this context. Our overall aim is to assess where we stand in the continuing learning and discovery process as exchange rate economists. In doing so, we hope to provide a framework which will be useful to the economics and financial community as a whole for thinking about exchange rate issues. The monograph is intended to be wide-ranging and we have attempted to make chapters easy to follow and largely self-contained.

The primary target for the book is students taking advanced courses in international economics or international finance at about the level of a second-year US doctoral programme in economics or finance, although students at other levels, including master's degree students and advanced undergraduates, should also find the book accessible. The book should also prove useful to our professional colleagues, including researchers in international finance in universities and elsewhere, and specialists in other areas requiring an up-to-date overview of exchange rate economics. Last, but by no means least, we very much hope that the book will be of interest and use to financial market practitioners.

The intellectual history behind this monograph is long and tortuous. At one level it began while Mark Taylor, freshly graduated from Oxford in philosophy and economics, was working as a junior foreign exchange dealer in the City of London whilst simultaneously pursuing graduate studies part-time at London University in the early 1980s. At another level, it began while he was a senior economist at the International Monetary Fund (IMF) during the first half of the 1990s, in that his survey article on exchange rate economics, largely prepared at the IMF and published in the *Journal of Economic Literature* in 1995, initially prompted Cambridge University Press to commission the book. Returning to academia, Taylor subsequently recruited one of his most promising graduate students at the time, Lucio Sarno, as a co-author, in order to ease the burden. Given, however, the large amount of material that we intended to cover, the high productivity of the area, and our other research commitments, it took us several further years to complete the book. One advantage of this long gestation period is that we have had the opportunity to test much of it in advanced graduate courses at Warwick, Oxford and Columbia, and to get valuable feedback from colleagues while we have held visiting positions at institutions such as the IMF, the World Bank and the Federal Reserve Bank of St Louis.

More generally, in preparing the book, we have become indebted to a large number of individuals. In particular, we are grateful for helpful conversations through the years of gestation, as well as for often very detailed comments on various draft chapters, to the following people: Michael Artis, Andrew Atkeson, Leonardo Bartolini, Tam Bayoumi, Giuseppe Bertola, Stanley Black, William Branson, Guillermo Calvo, Yin-Wong Cheung, Menzie Chinn, Richard Clarida, Giuseppe De Arcangelis, Michael Dooley, Rudiger Dornbusch, Hali Edison, Martin Evans, Robert Flood, Jeffrey Frankel, Kenneth Froot, Peter Garber, Charles Goodhart, Gene Grossman, Philipp Hartmann, Robert Hodrick, Peter Isard, Peter Kenen, Richard Lyons, Nelson Mark, Bennett McCallum, Paul Masson, Michael Melvin, Marcus Miller, Ashoka Mody, Maurice Obstfeld, Paul O'Connell, Lawrence Officer, David Papell, David Peel, William Poole, Kenneth Rogoff, Andrew Rose, Nouriel Roubini, Alan Stockman, Lars Svensson, Alan Taylor, Daniel Thornton, Sushil Wadhwani, Myles Wallace, Axel Weber and John Williamson.

Naturally, we are solely responsible for any errors that may still remain on these pages.

We must also offer our thanks, as well as our public apology, to Ashwin Rattan and Chris Harrison, our editors at Cambridge University Press. They patiently worked with us through the extensive preparation of the manuscript and quietly tolerated our failure to meet countless deadlines. The phrase 'the manuscript will be with you by the end of the month' will be as familiar to Ashwin and Chris as 'the cheque is in the mail'.

Finally, albeit most importantly, we owe our deepest thanks to our families and friends for providing essential moral support throughout this project.

The publisher has used its best endeavours to ensure that the URLs for external websites referred to in this book are correct and active at the time of going to press. However, the publisher has no responsibility for the websites and can make no guarantee that a site will remain live or that the content is or will remain appropriate.

1 Introduction

In the last few decades or so exchange rate economics has seen a number of important developments, with substantial contributions to both the theory and the empirics of exchange rate determination. Important developments in econometrics and the increasing availability of high-quality data have also been responsible for stimulating the large amount of empirical work on exchange rates published over this period. Nevertheless, while our understanding of exchange rates has significantly improved, a number of challenges and open questions remain in the exchange rate debate, further enhanced by important events in this context such as the launch of the euro as the single European currency in January 1999 and the large number of currency crises which occurred during the 1990s.

In this book – part monograph, part advanced textbook – we provide a selective coverage of the literature on exchange rate economics, focusing particularly but not exclusively on contributions made during the last fifteen years or so. Throughout the book our aim is, in addition to giving a clear exposition, to provide constructive criticism of the literature and to suggest further avenues for research and analysis. The survey article by Taylor (1995) on 'The Economics of Exchange Rates', which provides a comprehensive review of the post-war literature on the subject until the early 1990s, may be seen as useful groundwork preliminary to the study of this book, although readers with a good general background in economics should be able to tackle the book head on. In this brief introduction, we provide a guide to the following chapters.

Chapter 2 covers the literature on foreign exchange market efficiency. In an efficient speculative market prices should fully reflect information available to market participants and it should be impossible for a trader to earn excess returns to speculation. Academic interest in foreign exchange market efficiency can be traced to arguments concerning the information content of financial market prices and the implications for social efficiency. In its simplest form, the efficient markets hypothesis can be reduced to a joint hypothesis that foreign exchange market participants are, in an aggregate sense, endowed with rational expectations and are risk-neutral. The hypothesis can be modified to adjust for risk, so that it then becomes a joint hypothesis of a model of equilibrium returns (which may admit risk premia) and rational expectations. In particular, the chapter covers the literature relating to the covered and uncovered interest rate parity conditions which have direct implications for market efficiency, and provides an account of the recent econometric methods employed in testing the foreign exchange market efficiency hypothesis. Regardless of – or indeed perhaps because of – the increasing sophistication of the econometric techniques employed and of the increasing quality of the data sets utilised, one conclusion emerges from this literature relatively uncontroversially: the foreign exchange market is not efficient in the sense that both risk neutrality and rational expectations appear to be rejected by the data.

Chapter 3 is devoted to recent studies on purchasing power parity (PPP) and the behaviour of the real exchange rate. Under PPP, price levels are the same across countries if expressed in a common currency. Academic opinion concerning the validity of PPP as a realistic description of exchange rate behaviour over both the short run and the long run has shifted quite significantly over time. A long list of studies suggests that deviations from PPP are characterised as conforming to martingale or random walk behaviour, indicating the violation of PPP in the long run. However, increasing support for PPP as a *long-run equilibrium* condition has emerged during the last decade or so. We survey much of the influential literature on testing the validity of the law of one price (the hypothesis that individual traded goods prices should be equal once expressed in a common currency at the going exchange rate) and of PPP, covering the tests of the random walk real exchange rate model, the cointegration literature on PPP and the most recent developments in econometric techniques applied to PPP testing, which include using long-span data, multivariate unit root tests and the recent state-of-the-art nonlinear econometric models of deviations from PPP. Overall, arguably the main conclusion emerging from the recent relevant literature appears to be that PPP might be viewed as a valid long-run international parity condition when applied to bilateral exchange rates obtaining among major industrialised countries and that, because of the effects of international transactions costs and other factors, real exchange rate adjustment displays significant nonlinearities.

Chapter 4 is devoted to an overview of the theory and evidence relating to standard macroeconomic models of exchange rate determination, namely the flexible price monetary model, the sticky price monetary model, equilibrium models and liquidity models, and the portfolio balance model. The exposition of the theoretical foundations of these theories is followed by an analysis of their empirical formulations and an account of the relevant empirical literature. We also assess the validity of asset-market-based exchange rate models on the basis of the evidence on their out-of-sample forecasting performance. In fact, we discuss selected articles on exchange rate predictability, recording the difficulties encountered in using standard empirical models of exchange rate determination to predict the nominal exchange rate. We conclude that, although there seems to be increasing evidence that empirical models of exchange rate determination may be helpful for forecasting exchange rates at long horizons, it is still difficult to beat a simple random walk forecasting model in the shorter run. This is an area of research where more work is very much warranted.[1]

Chapter 5 offers an introduction to the recent literature on the 'new open economy macroeconomics'. This literature reflects an attempt by researchers to formalise theories of exchange rate determination in the context of dynamic general equilibrium models with

---

[1] See Clarida, Sarno, Taylor and Valente (2001) and Kilian and Taylor (2001) for recent contributions on forecasting
exchange rates and attempts to beat a random walk forecast.

explicitly defined microfoundations and allowing for both nominal rigidities and imperfect competition. This literature has been growing exponentially since the appearance of Obstfeld and Rogoff's (1995) seminal 'redux' paper. The increasing sophistication of stochastic open economy models allows rigorous welfare analysis and provides new explanations of several puzzles in international macroeconomics and finance. Whether, however, this approach will become the new workhorse model for open economy macroeconomics, whether a preferred specification within this class of models will be reached, and whether this approach will provide insights on developing better-fitting empirical exchange rate models remain, at present, open questions. Nevertheless, this is clearly an exciting area of research.

Chapter 6 is devoted to the literature on monetary integration and target zones. The literature on monetary integration is largely dominated by the theory of optimum currency areas, developed in the 1960s and refined over the last few decades. The theory of optimum currency areas has increasingly attracted the interest of academics and policy-makers in the transition towards Economic and Monetary Union (EMU) and in the aftermath of the birth of the euro. A related literature, discussed in some detail in this chapter, is related to modelling exchange rate behaviour under target zone arrangements. Since the collapse of the Bretton Woods system, most of the major exchange rates have not in fact been officially pegged but have been allowed to float freely for the longest period of time in recent economic history. Many smaller central banks, however, have adopted policies of pegging their exchange rates to major currencies and the Exchange Rate Mechanism (ERM) of the European Monetary System (EMS) offers an important recent example of a pegged exchange rate system amongst major currencies.

Chapter 7 surveys and discusses the theoretical and empirical literature on foreign exchange market intervention. We start by examining the rationale for exchange rate management, and then discuss a number of relevant specific issues such as the secrecy of intervention, the role of international co-ordination, the profitability of intervention operations, and the availability and nature of data on official intervention. We describe the mechanics of official intervention through the portfolio balance channel and the signalling or expectations channel, and also provide a review of the empirical literature on the effectiveness of official intervention. We briefly present the simple positive theory of exchange rate intervention used by the literature to derive estimatable reaction functions and discuss the empirical evidence on central bank reaction functions.

Chapter 8 is devoted to an exposition and survey of the literature on speculative attacks and currency crises. In large part, this literature is a reaction to the relatively large number of currency crises which affected the international financial markets during the 1990s. The three strands of the literature we cover – so-called first-generation, second-generation and third-generation models of currency crisis – were largely developed, moreover, as a reaction to the apparently disparate nature of the various crises which have occurred. In particular, economies affected by speculative attacks and crises ranged from a number of Latin American economies, where economists were quick to point out apparent inconsistencies between the stance of domestic macroeconomic policy and a commitment to a fixed exchange rate; to advanced European economies where there appeared to be no inconsistency between the stance of macroeconomic policy but instead a perceived *temptation* of the authorities to pursue a more expansionary domestic policy; to the 'tiger economies' of East Asia, where, prior to the crisis, the economic fundamentals appeared very strong and macroeconomic policy appeared entirely consistent with the fixed exchange rate rule.

In Chapter 9 we discuss the very recent literature on the microstructure of the foreign exchange market. As a reading of the first eight chapters of the book, and in particular of Chapter 4, will reveal only too clearly, an emerging stylised fact is that, while macroeconomic fundamentals appear to be an important determinant of exchange rate movements over relatively long horizons and in economies experiencing pathologically large movements in such fundamentals (such as during a hyperinflation), there seem to be substantial and often persistent movements in exchange rates which are largely unexplained by macroeconomic fundamentals. The recent and emerging literature on foreign exchange market microstructure in some measure reflects an attempt by researchers in international finance to understand these deviations from macroeconomic fundamentals. In addition, the microstructure literature is also concerned with other issues which are seen to be of interest in their own right by international financial economists, such as the transmission of information between market participants, the behaviour of market agents, the relationship between information flows, the importance of order flow, the heterogeneity of agents' expectations and the implications of such heterogeneity for trading volume and exchange rate volatility. We conclude that, to date, the foreign exchange market microstructure literature appears to shed light most strongly on issues such as the transmission of information between market participants, the heterogeneity of agents' expectations and the implications of such heterogeneity for trading volume and exchange rate volatility.

Although the sequence of presentation of the various chapters is, we hope, logical, it is not necessary to read the book in sequence from beginning to end, although this would be our preference. In particular we have attempted to make the chapters largely self-contained so that, if reference is made to results discussed in earlier chapters, it is brief enough to be easily remedied.

We very much hope that you enjoy using this book.

References

Clarida, R.H., L. Sarno, M.P. Taylor and G. Valente (2001), 'The Out-of-Sample Success of Term Structure Models as Exchange Rate Predictors: A Step Beyond', *Journal of International Economics*, forthcoming.

Kilian, L. and M.P. Taylor (2001), 'Why is it so Difficult to Beat the Random Walk Forecast of Exchange Rates?', *Journal of International Economics*, forthcoming.

Obstfeld, M. and K. Rogoff (1995), 'Exchange Rate Dynamics Redux', *Journal of Political Economy*, 103, pp. 624–60.

Taylor, M.P. (1995), 'The Economics of Exchange Rates', *Journal of Economic Literature*, 33, pp. 13–47.

2 Foreign exchange market efficiency

In an efficient speculative market prices should fully reflect information available to market participants and it should be impossible for a trader to earn excess returns to speculation. Academic interest in foreign exchange market efficiency can be traced to arguments concerning the information content of financial market prices and the implications for social efficiency. In its simplest form, the efficient markets hypothesis can be reduced to a joint hypothesis that foreign exchange market participants are, in an aggregate sense (a) endowed with rational expectations and (b) risk-neutral. The hypothesis can be modified to adjust for risk, so that it then becomes a joint hypothesis of a model of equilibrium returns (which may admit risk premia) and rational expectations.

If the risk-neutral efficient markets hypothesis holds, then the expected foreign exchange gain from holding one currency rather than another – the expected exchange rate change – must be just offset by the opportunity cost of holding funds in this currency rather than the other – the interest rate differential. This condition, generally referred to as the uncovered interest rate parity (UIP) condition, represents the cornerstone parity condition for testing foreign exchange market efficiency:

$$\Delta_k s_{t+k}^e = i_t - i_t^*, \tag{2.1}$$

where s_t denotes the logarithm[1] of the spot exchange rate (domestic price of foreign currency) at time t, i_t and i_t^* are the nominal interest rates available on similar domestic and foreign securities respectively (with k periods to maturity), $\Delta_k s_{t+k} \equiv s_{t+k} - s_t$, and the superscript e denotes the market expectation based on information at time t. Most often, however, discussions of foreign exchange market efficiency have taken place in the context of the relationship between spot and forward exchange rates. Implicitly, researchers have used a link between spot and forward rates and interest rates, known as covered interest rate parity. Prior to discussing the uncovered interest rate parity condition in detail, therefore, we shall first examine covered interest rate parity.

---

[1] See Appendix B to this chapter for a discussion of the use of logarithmic transformations with exchange rates.

2.1   Covered interest rate parity

... forward quotations for the purchase of the currency of the dearer money market tend to be cheaper than spot quotations by a percentage per month equal to the excess of the interest which can be earned in a month in the dearer market over what can be earned in the cheaper (Keynes, 1923, ch. 3).

If there are no barriers to arbitrage across international financial markets, then arbitrage should ensure that the interest rate differential on two assets, identical in every relevant respect except currency of denomination, adjusted to cover the movement of currencies at the maturity of the underlying assets in the forward market, be continuously equal to zero, so that covered interest rate parity (CIP) should hold.

Algebraically, the CIP condition may be expressed (ignoring transactions costs) as:

$$\frac{F_t^{(k)}}{S_t} = \frac{1 + i_t}{1 + i_t^*} \tag{2.2}$$

where S_t is the spot exchange rate (domestic price of foreign currency) and $F_t^{(k)}$ is the k-period forward rate (i.e. the rate agreed now for an exchange of currencies k periods ahead).

A standard story as to why CIP should hold is that market deviations from (2.2) will result in arbitrage activity which will force the equality to hold. Suppose, for example, (2.2) did not hold at time t because of a relatively low domestic interest rate:

$$i_t < \frac{F_t^{(k)}}{S_t}(1 + i_t^*) - 1. \tag{2.3}$$

If (2.3) held, arbitrageurs could make a riskless profit by borrowing the domestic currency for k periods at the interest rate i, selling it spot for the foreign currency (yielding $1/S$ units of foreign currency for every unit of domestic currency), lending the foreign currency for k periods at the interest rate i^*, and selling the foreign currency proceeds (principal plus interest) in the k-period forward market against the domestic currency. At the end of k periods, the arbitrageur will have to repay $(1 + i_t)$ for every unit of domestic currency borrowed, but will receive $(F_t^{(k)}/S_t)(1 + i_t^*)$ units of domestic currency for every unit of domestic currency borrowed and used in the arbitrage. Hence, the arbitrageur will make a net profit of $[(F_t^{(k)}/S_t)(1 + i_t^*) - (1 + i_t)]$ which, from (2.3), is positive. The simple laws of supply and demand imply that such arbitrage will induce movements in i, i^*, S and F until (2.2) holds.

On reflection, however, it should be clear that no such arbitrage need logically occur for (2.2) to hold, since any lender of domestic funds at an interest rate which satisfies (2.3) must be either irrational or ill-informed, or both. This follows because either a higher rate could have been extracted (demand for domestic funds should be perfectly elastic so long as (2.3) holds), or else a return equivalent to:

$$\left(F_t^{(k)}/S_t\right)(1 + i_t^*) - 1 \tag{2.4}$$

could have been risklessly earned by selling the domestic funds against foreign currency spot, lending the foreign currency and selling the proceeds against domestic currency forward. Clearly, similar reasoning could be applied to any of the four arguments of (2.2) – i.e. $F_t^{(k)}$, S_t, i_t^* and i_t.

A logarithmic approximation to (2.2) is often used:

$$f_t^{(k)} - s_t = i_t - i_t^* \qquad (2.5)$$

where $f_t^{(k)} \equiv \log_e F_t^{(k)}$, $s_t \equiv \log_e S_t$ and use has been made of the conventional approximation $\log_e(1 + x) \approx x$ for small x – in our case $x = i_t, i_t^*$.

In any computation of CIP, it is clearly important to consider home and foreign assets which are comparable in terms of maturity and in terms of other characteristics such as default and political risk (Aliber, 1973; Dooley and Isard, 1980; Frankel and MacArthur, 1988). For this reason, empirical analyses of CIP have most often employed interest rate data on Euro-deposits: 'Since Euro-currency deposits are comparable in terms of issuer, credit risk, maturity and all other respects *except* currency of denomination, they offer a proper test of [CIP]' (Levich, 1985, p. 1027). A typical barrier to arbitrage would be capital controls, and deviations from CIP using domestic security interest rates (or the spread between off-shore and onshore rates) have often been used as an indirect indicator of the presence and effectiveness of capital controls (Dooley and Isard, 1980).

In practice, two approaches have been taken by researchers in testing CIP empirically. The first approach relies on computing the actual deviations from interest parity to see if they differ 'significantly' from zero. The significance of departures from CIP is often defined with respect to a neutral band, which is determined by transactions costs. For example, Frenkel and Levich (1975, 1977), for a selection of currencies, demonstrate that around 80 per cent of apparent profit opportunities lie within the neutral band when Treasury bills are used and almost 100 per cent when Euro-rates are considered. Furthermore, in Frenkel and Levich (1977) it is demonstrated that in periods of turbulence a much smaller percentage of deviations from CIP may be explained by transactions costs; this is interpreted as reflecting higher financial uncertainty in such periods. Clinton (1988) also demonstrates that deviations from CIP should be no greater than the minimum transactions costs in one of three markets: the two underlying deposit markets (e.g. Euro-marks and Euro-dollars) and the foreign exchange swap market (i.e. the market in which a currency can be simultaneously bought and sold forward against another currency). On the basis of analysis of data for five major currencies against the US dollar 'taken from mid morning quotes on the Reuter Money Rates Service from November 1985 to May 1986', Clinton finds that the neutral band should be within + 0.06 per cent per annum from parity and that, although the hypothesis of zero profitable deviations from parity can be rejected, 'empirically, profitable trading opportunities are neither large enough nor long-lived enough to yield a flow of excess returns over time to any factor'.

By questioning the quality of the data used by Frenkel and Levich, various researchers have often arrived at different conclusions. For example, McCormick (1979) finds, using higher-quality data, that most of the deviations from CIP (70–80 per cent) lie *outside* the neutral band for UK–US Treasury bills. Taylor (1987, 1989), however, goes further than McCormick and argues that in order to provide a proper test of CIP it is important to have data on the appropriate exchange rates and interest rates recorded at the same instant in time at which a dealer could have dealt. Taylor uses high-quality, high-frequency, contemporaneously sampled data for spot and forward dollar–sterling and dollar–mark exchange rates and corresponding Euro-deposit interest rates for a number of maturities and makes allowance for bid–ask spreads and brokerage costs in his calculations. He finds, *inter alia*, that there are few profitable violations of CIP, even during periods of market uncertainty and turbulence. One interesting feature of Taylor's work is the finding of a *maturity effect* – the frequency, size and persistence of profitable arbitrage opportunities appear to be an increasing function of the length of the period to maturity of the underlying financial instruments. A rationale is offered for this in terms of banks' prudential credit limits. Since banks impose prudential limits on the amount of outstanding liabilities they have with other parties, arbitraging at the shorter maturities will result in limits being filled for shorter periods, leaving dealers on average freer to take advantage of other profitable opportunities as they arise.

A second approach for testing the validity of CIP is based on regression analysis, generally inspired by equation (2.5). In fact, if CIP holds, in the absence of transactions costs, estimation of the following equation:

$$f_t^{(k)} - s_t = \alpha + \beta(i_t - i_t^*) + u_t \tag{2.6}$$

(where u_t is the regression error) should result in estimates of α and β differing insignificantly from zero and unity respectively and a non-autocorrelated error. Equation (2.6) has been tested by a number of researchers for a variety of currencies and time periods (see, for example, the early study by Branson, 1969). The main conclusion to be drawn from this line of research is that, broadly speaking, CIP is supported in that although there are significant deviations of α from zero (reflecting perhaps non-zero transactions costs) the estimates of β differ insignificantly from unity in the majority of cases. As noted by Taylor (1989), however, it is not clear what regression-based analyses of CIP are actually testing. For example, it may be that a researcher cannot reject the hypothesis that $\alpha = 0$ and $\beta = 1$ in equation (2.6) but that the fitted residuals themselves represent substantial arbitrage opportunities. Put another way, such a test may suggest strongly that CIP held *on average* over a period when in fact it did not hold *continuously* during the period. Thus, although regression-based tests may be useful for testing the broad stylised fact of CIP (which may be of interest, for example, for exchange rate modelling), they can say virtually nothing about market efficiency.

Some recent empirical work on testing CIP and modelling the spot–forward relationship has also taken into account the importance of transactions costs. Balke and Wohar (1998) examine the dynamics of deviations from CIP using daily data on the UK–US spot and forward exchange rates and interest rates over the period January 1974 to September 1993. Balke and Wohar find a substantial number of instances in the sample in which the CIP condition exceeds the transactions costs band, implying arbitrage profit opportunities. While most of these implied profit opportunities are relatively small, Balke and Wohar also provide evidence of some very large deviations from CIP in their sample. In order to examine the persistence of these deviations, they estimate a threshold autoregression in which the dynamic behaviour of deviations from CIP is different outside the transactions costs band than it is inside the band. They also find that while the impulse response functions when inside the transactions costs band are nearly symmetric, those for the outside the bands are asymmetric and suggest less persistence outside of the transactions costs band than inside the band.

More recently, Peel and Taylor (2002) have applied a threshold model to test CIP on weekly data for US–UK rates during the 1920s exchange rate float. Peel and Taylor provide support for the conjecture advanced by Keynes (1923) and Einzig (1937) that, during the 1920s, deviations from CIP were not be arbitraged unless the arbitrage opportunity yielded a substantial profit of a half of one percentage point on an annualised basis. Their results suggest that the no-arbitrage bandwidth is indeed insignificantly different from plus or minus fifty basis points and that deviations from CIP are moderately persistent even outside of the band. A neutral bandwidth of plus or minus fifty basis points on an annualised basis is very large by modern standards, so that these results raise further issues, in particular the issue of why the minimum covered interest rate differential needed for international arbitrage activity should have been so high in the inter-war period. One obvious possibility is simply that markets were to this extent inefficient, which indeed seems to be a modern interpretation of the explanation given by Keynes (1923) and Einzig (1937). An alternative but related view, also developed by Einzig (1937) as well as Hawtrey (1932), would be that banks were unwilling to place large deposits in pursuance of covered interest arbitrage unless the resulting profit were large enough in percentage terms, because of the effect this would have had on their overall liquidity.

This, however, only raises a further question, namely why should banks care about liquidity in this fashion, over and above any issues of political risk? As noted above, Taylor (1987, 1989) suggests that banks may wish to retain liquidity in order to be ready to exploit other arbitrage opportunities which may arise (although a fifty basis points deviation would still seem large). It is also possible that banks may have wished to retain liquidity because of the fear of a run on the bank, and that this effect may have declined in the post-war period because of the growth in the asset base of large investment banks and the general deepening of the forward exchange markets (Einzig, 1962). Yet another possibility may be related to the assumed risklessness of covered interest arbitrage. Covered arbitrage is only riskless if all of the transactions – the taking of a deposit, the placing of a deposit, a spot foreign exchange transaction and a forward foreign exchange transaction are effected simultaneously. In a modern foreign exchange dealing room, equipped with highly sophisticated communication equipment and served by a sophisticated system of foreign exchange and money market brokers, prices can be obtained and orders carried out literally within seconds (and may even be automated and synchronised), so that covered arbitrage will indeed be virtually riskless. Although poorly documented, the dealing room environment of the 1920s must have been quite different, with communication between London and New York banks taking place by cable and 'long-distance trunk calls' (Einzig, 1937, p. 57) and therefore being much slower. In this environment, it may have been prudent to wait for a sizeable deviation from CIP to arise before arbitraging in order to be sure of effecting the necessary transactions before prices moved against the arbitrageur.

The 1920s experience apart, however, an overall reading of the literature on CIP provides strong empirical support in favour of CIP, especially as applied to Euro-deposit interest rates.

2.2   Testing foreign exchange market efficiency: uncovered interest parity

As noted above, any test of market efficiency is a joint test of several composite hypotheses. The best that can be done in practice is to define what one means by market efficiency and test statistical hypotheses conditional upon the given definition, generally using additional assumptions on the statistical properties of the data (see Fama, 1970, 1976). The most widely tested and, as noted above, simplest form of market efficiency (which we shall therefore term the *simple efficiency hypothesis*) is a joint hypothesis that market agents are risk-neutral and endowed with rational expectations.

Also, some confusion is present in many tests of foreign exchange market efficiency due to an incorrect application to foreign exchange markets of ideas formulated by, among others, Samuelson (1965) and Fama (1970) on the efficiency of stock markets (see e.g. Kohlhagen, 1978; Levich, 1985; Hodrick, 1987 for discussion of these issues). The argument is that in an efficient market prices fully reflect all available information and consequently speculators cannot make above-normal profits using publicly available information. This does not imply, however, either equality of equilibrium expected returns for different assets – since different assets have different risky prospects – or constancy of the equilibrium expected return on an asset over time. These presumptions expand the concept of efficient markets and make testing the concept more difficult. Further, Kohlhagen (1978) and Levich (1985) argue that one cannot neglect the activities of central banks in foreign exchange markets in conventional tests of efficiency since these activities may have a very strong, decisive effect upon the movements of exchange rates as well as on the efficiency of the market relative to the activities of arbitrageurs and speculators.

The literature usually distinguishes between three different forms of market efficiency (Fama, 1970):

   (i) *weak form*: the current price incorporates all the information contained in past prices;
  (ii) *semi-strong form*: the current price incorporates all publicly available information, including its own past prices;
 (iii) *strong form*: prices reflect all information that can possibly be known.

The strong form of market efficiency is, in theory, expected not to hold, mainly because secret non-random intervention by central banks occurs in exchange markets. Semi-strong form efficiency is perhaps the version of efficiency closest to the rational expectations hypothesis since it is assumed that economic agents know the true model of the economy and use all publicly available information in forming expectations.[2]

As mentioned above, the basic relationship which is used to assess foreign exchange market efficiency is the uncovered interest rate parity or UIP condition (2.1). Early efficiency studies tested for the randomness of exchange rate changes. For example, Poole (1967) finds significant first-order serial correlation for many of the exchange rates examined during the

---

[2] Geweke and Feige (1979) also distinguish two categories within the semi-strong form of market efficiency:
   (a) *single-market efficiency*: all publicly available information concerning a single exchange rate is contained in the information set;
   (b) *multi-market efficiency*: information on all other exchange rates and all available economic information is included in the information set.

1920s, also providing evidence that simple trading rules could potentially yield large profits. Little evidence supporting the presence of serial correlation is provided, however, by other early studies (e.g. Giddy and Dufey, 1975). Nevertheless, only if the nominal interest rate differential is identically equal to a constant and expectations are rational, does (2.1) imply a random walk in the exchange rate (with drift if the constant is non-zero). Generally, the random walk model is inconsistent with the UIP condition.

Cumby and Obstfeld's (1981) analysis is a logical extension of this work since they test for – and reject – the randomness of deviations from UIP. Notwithstanding this, it remains true that time series for the major nominal exchange rates over the recent float are extremely hard to distinguish empirically from random walks (Mussa, 1984).[3]

Another method of testing market efficiency is to test for the profitability of simple filter rules. A simple j-percent filter rule involves buying a currency whenever it rises j per cent above its most recent trough and selling the currency whenever it falls j per cent below its most recent peak. If the market is efficient and UIP holds, the interest rate costs of such a strategy should on average eliminate any profit. A number of studies do indicate the profitability of simple filter rules (see e.g. Dooley and Shafer, 1984; Levich and Thomas, 1993), although it is usually not clear that the optimal filter rule size could have been chosen *ex ante*, and there are often important elements of riskiness in that substantial sub-period losses are often generated. Further, indirect evidence on the profitability of trading rules is also provided by Engel and Hamilton (1990), who show that the dollar, from the early 1970s to the late 1980s, displayed 'long swings' (largely uninterrupted trends), which were susceptible to mechanical ('trend-following') trading rules.

More often, researchers have tested for efficiency using regression-based analysis of spot and forward exchange rates. Given that the forward rate is the rate agreed now for an exchange of currencies at some agreed future point in time, the forward premium at a certain maturity is the percentage difference between the current forward rate of that maturity and the current spot rate.[4] Assuming covered interest parity, uncovered interest parity implies that the forward premium should be equal to the market expectation of the exchange rate depreciation. To see this, use (2.1) and (2.5) to eliminate the interest rate differential and obtain:

$$s_{t+k}^e - s_t = f_t^{(k)} - s_t. \tag{2.7}$$

Equivalently, covered and uncovered interest parity together imply that the forward rate should be equal to the market expectation of the future spot rate, since (2.7) implies directly:

$$s_{t+k}^e = f_t^{(k)}. \tag{2.8}$$

Under rational expectations, the expected change in the exchange rate should differ from the actual change only by a rational expectations forecast error. Hence, assuming

---

[3] Note that the martingale model of changes in asset prices has slightly different implications from the random walk model. The former simply postulates that only expected yields or price changes describe a market equilibrium, whereas the random walk model – which is a special case of the martingale model – implies that yields or price changes are independently and identically distributed.

[4] Some authors term this the forward discount rather than the forward premium. The choice is essentially arbitrary, since a premium is just a negative discount.

covered interest rate parity, the uncovered interest rate parity condition (2.1) can be tested by estimating a regression of the form:

$$\Delta_k s_{t+k} = \alpha + \beta \left(f_t^{(k)} - s_t \right) + \eta_{t+k}, \tag{2.9}$$

where η_{t+k} is a disturbance term. If agents are risk-neutral and have rational expectations, we should expect the slope parameter β to be equal to unity and the disturbance term η_{t+k} – the rational expectations forecast error under the null hypothesis – to be uncorrelated with information available at time t. This property of the disturbance term follows from a standard property of rational expectations forecast errors that $E\left[\eta_{t+k} \mid \Omega_t\right] = 0$, where $E\left[\cdot \mid \Omega_t\right]$ denotes the mathematical expectation conditioned on the information set available at time t, Ω_t. Empirical studies based on the estimation of (2.9), for a large variety of currencies and time periods, generally report results which are unfavourable to the efficient markets hypothesis under risk neutrality (e.g. Frankel, 1980; Fama, 1984; Bekaert and Hodrick, 1993). Indeed it constitutes a stylised fact that estimates of β, using exchange rates against the dollar, are generally closer to minus unity than plus unity (Froot and Thaler, 1990). A number of authors have interpreted the stylised fact of a negative coefficient in this regression – the so-called 'forward discount bias' – as evidence that the forward premium mispredicts the direction of the subsequent change in the spot rate, although such statements may be misleading because they ignore the constant term in the regression (Hodrick, 1992). What the negativity of the estimated slope coefficient does imply, however, is that the more the foreign currency is at a premium in the forward market at a certain term k, the less the home currency is predicted to depreciate over the k periods to maturity.[5] This may imply an expected appreciation of the home currency, but the constant terms are relatively large and often it does not.

Early regression-based tests of simple foreign exchange market efficiency regressed the logarithm of the forward rate onto the lagged logarithm of the spot rate (e.g. Frenkel, 1976), and usually found an estimated slope coefficient close to unity. It was subsequently realised, however, that standard regression analysis (or at least standard inferential statistical theory) was invalid with such a relationship, because of the nonstationarity of the series. Moreover, it should be noted that the two relationships (2.9) and

$$s_{t+k} = \alpha + \beta f_t^{(k)} + \eta'_{t+k} \tag{2.10}$$

are identical only under the null hypothesis $\beta = 1$. In particular, suppose (2.9) holds with $\beta \neq 1$. Then (2.9) may be reparameterised as:

$$s_{t+k} = \alpha + \beta f_t^{(k)} + \left[(1 - \beta) s_t + \eta_{t+k} \right], \tag{2.11}$$

so that the error term in (2.10), η'_{t+k}, is seen to be $\left[(1 - \beta) s_t + \eta_{t+k} \right]$. Now, if s_t is nonstationary (in particular, if it is a realisation of a unit root process)[6], then its sample variance

---

[5] Equivalently, via the covered interest arbitrage condition, these findings indicate that the more domestic interest rates exceed foreign interest rates, the more the domestic currency tends on average to appreciate over the holding period, not to depreciate so as to offset on average the interest differential in favour of the home currency.

[6] See Appendix D to this chapter.

will be very high. But the ordinary least squares (OLS) estimator works by minimising the residual variance in a regression relationship. Thus, OLS applied to (2.10) will tend to drive the estimated value of β towards unity, regardless of the true value of β, in order to reduce the influence of the unit root in the error term.

As noted above, a stylised fact concerning major exchange rates over the recent float is that they are not only nonstationary but extremely hard to distinguish from simple random walks. If the exchange rate did literally follow a random walk, then the estimated value of β in (2.9) should be close to zero, regardless of whether the market is efficient. Moreover, since the best predictor of future values of the spot rate is, under the assumption of a random walk, simply the current spot rate, then the simple efficiency hypothesis (i.e. rational expectations plus risk neutrality) combined with the random walk hypothesis would imply $f_t^{(k)} = s_{t+k}^e = s_t$, so that the regressor in (2.9) should be close to zero, in which case β would be unidentified. In practice, the observed variation in $(f_t^{(k)} - s_t)$ would almost certainly be non-zero, even under these assumptions, if only because of measurement errors.

Thus, regressions of the form (2.9) or (2.10) as tests of simple efficiency are seriously confounded by the near-random-walk behaviour of spot exchange rates. Given these problems, perhaps a better approach for testing the simple efficiency hypothesis is to test the orthogonality of the forward rate forecast error (the error made in forecasting the future spot rate using the current forward rate)[7] with respect to a given information set by imposing the restriction $\beta = 1$ in (2.9) and testing the null hypothesis that $\Gamma = 0$ in regressions of the form:

$$s_{t+k} - f_t^{(k)} = \Gamma \Psi_t + \eta_{t+k}, \tag{2.12}$$

where $\Psi_t \subset \Omega_t$ is a vector of variables selected from the information set available at time t, Ω_t. Orthogonality tests of this kind, using lagged forecast errors of the exchange rate in question in Ψ_t (a test of weak-form efficiency), have generally rejected the simple, risk-neutral efficient markets hypothesis. Moreover, even stronger rejections are usually obtained when additional information is included in Ψ_t (tests of semi-strong-form efficiency – e.g. Hansen and Hodrick, 1980).

A discernible trend in the efficiency literature since the 1970s has been towards increasing econometric sophistication. Thus, early tests of efficiency, which involved simple tests for a random walk in the spot rate, were supplanted by basic linear regression analyses of uncovered interest parity, which were in turn supplanted by application of the use of sophisticated rational expectations estimators which allowed the use of data sampled more finely than the term of the forward contract involved (Hansen and Hodrick, 1980).[8] Hansen and Hodrick (1980) concentrate on testing the orthogonality of the forecast error $s_{t+k} - f_t^{(k)}$

---

[7] This term, $(s_{t+k} - f_t^{(k)})$, may alternatively be thought of as the return to forward speculation. Some authors term it the 'excess return' because no allowance is made for risk.

[8] Hansen and Hodrick (1980) and Hayashi and Sims (1983) also discuss the problems caused by the use of overlapping data. In general, the use of overlapping data, while causing econometric complications, prevents the loss of information involved in discarding the data in order to match the maturity of the forward contract. Discarding the data, in fact, may exclude from the econometric analysis short periods of turbulence and speculative action in the foreign exchange markets, thereby presenting a misleading picture of the markets.

to lagged forecast errors. Because Hansen and Hodrick use overlapping data – the sampling of the data is finer than the maturity of the forward contract – serial correlation is introduced into the forecast errors, even under the assumption of rational expectations. This can be seen intuitively as follows. The k-period forward rate $f_t^{(k)}$ will typically fail to forecast the k-period-ahead spot rate s_{t+k}, even under the null hypothesis of efficiency, because of unforeseen events – 'news' – occurring in each of the k intervening periods. By the same token, one period later, $f_{t+1}^{(k)}$ will fail to forecast s_{t+k+1}. Indeed, the forecast errors $s_{t+k} - f_t^{(k)}$ and $s_{t+k+1} - f_{t+1}^{(k)}$ will have $k - 1$ news items in common. Proceeding in this way, it is then seen that any forecast errors where the forward rates are dated (i.e. quoted) at points in time less than k periods apart will be correlated, so that there will be serial correlation of order $k - 1$.[9] Hansen and Hodrick (1980) note that this serial correlation cannot be dealt with using the standard approach of generalised least squares (GLS) estimation because of a failure of strict exogeneity. Intuitively, many of the variables in Ψ_t are such that knowledge of their future value is powerful in predicting s_{t+k}, which implies that the strict exogeneity requirement:

$$E\left(\eta_{t+k} \mid \ldots, \Psi_{t-1}, \Psi_t, \Psi_{t+1}, \ldots\right) = 0 \qquad (2.13)$$

is not satisfied. Hansen and Hodrick (1980) therefore suggest using OLS, which will still yield consistent parameter point estimates, together with a method-of-moments correction to the estimated covariance matrix (see Appendix C to this chapter). Using this adjusted covariance matrix, they test the null hypothesis that $\Gamma = 0$ in (2.12). Overall, the Hansen and Hodrick results suggest rejection of the null hypothesis for six of the seven currencies examined in the 1970s and for five of the six currencies examined using 1920s data.

Another econometrically sophisticated method for testing the simple efficient markets hypothesis – which has also generally led to rejections of the hypothesis – has involved testing the nonlinear cross-equation restrictions which the simple efficiency hypothesis imposes in a bivariate vector autoregression (VAR) comprising time series for spot and forward rates. This was originally suggested in the context of foreign exchange rates by Hakkio (1981) and Baillie, Lippens and McMahon (1983) although, as the subsequent cointegration literature revealed, a VAR in first differences alone – as in these early papers – may not be appropriate for spot and forward rates (see e.g. MacDonald and Taylor, 1991). This approach is based on modelling spot and forward rates as a bivariate stochastic process and testing the cross-equation restrictions implied by the efficient markets hypothesis. A crucial assumption in this approach is that the series examined are covariance stationary; this is why first-difference transformations of the spot and forward exchange rates were first used. First-differencing does not allow, however, the imposition of all rational expectations restrictions since these have implications for the levels of the variables (Shiller, 1979; Campbell and Shiller, 1987; MacDonald and Taylor, 1991). Most importantly, if spot and forward exchange rates are both integrated of order one, or $I(1)$, and cointegrated, then a bivariate model with the variables in first differences is misspecified due to the omission of the error correction term (Engle and Granger, 1987).

---

[9] In fact, this pattern of serial correlation is consistent with the overlapping forecast errors following a moving average process of order $k - 1 : \eta_t = u_t + \sum_{i=1}^{k-1} \theta_i u_{t-i}$, where u_t is a white-noise error.

This problem can be handled by appropriately modelling the forward premium $f_t^{(k)} - s_t$ and the rate of depreciation Δs_t, as a bivariate VAR of the form:

$$z_t = \sum_{i=1}^{m} \Phi_i z_{t-i} + \omega_t, \tag{2.14}$$

where $z_t' = [\Delta s_t, \ f_t^{(k)} - s_t]$, the Φ_i's are (2×2) matrices of coefficients and ω_t is a bivariate vector of white-noise processes for an appropriately chosen lag specification m. Equation (2.14) may be reparameterised in companion form as:

$$Z_t = \Phi Z_{t-1} + \varphi_t, \tag{2.15}$$

where $Z_t' = (z_t, z_{t-1}, \ldots, z_{t-m+1})$, $\varphi_t' = [\omega_t, 0, \ldots, 0]$ and Φ is a $(2m \times 2m)$ matrix of the form:

$$\Phi = \begin{bmatrix} \Phi_1 & \Phi_2 & . & \Phi_m \\ I & O & O & O \\ O & I & O & O \\ O & O & . & O \\ O & O & I & O \end{bmatrix}$$

where I and O are the (2×2) identity and null matrices respectively.

Consider two $(2m \times 1)$ selection vectors – say g and h – containing unity in the first and second elements respectively and zeros elsewhere and define Θ_{t-1} as an information set including only lagged z. Then, using the chain rule of forecasting, it follows that:

$$E\left(s_{t+k} - s_t \mid \Theta_{t-1}\right) = g' \sum_{j=1}^{k} \Phi^{j+1} Z_{t-j} \tag{2.16}$$

$$E\left(f_t^{(k)} - s_t \mid \Theta_{t-1}\right) = h' \Phi Z_{t-1}. \tag{2.17}$$

Thus, the efficient markets hypothesis orthogonality condition, given the information set Θ_{t-1}, may be written as follows:

$$E\left(s_{t+k} - s_t \mid \Theta_{t-1}\right) = E\left(f_t^{(k)} - s_t \mid \Theta_{t-1}\right). \tag{2.18}$$

Using (2.16)–(2.18) the set of nonlinear, cross-equation restrictions required by the efficient markets hypothesis on the parameters of the vector autoregression can be derived (Hodrick, 1987; MacDonald and Taylor, 1991):

$$g' \sum_{j=1}^{k} \Phi^{j+1} - h' \Phi = 0. \tag{2.19}$$

The restrictions in (2.19) can be tested by estimating the unrestricted vector autoregression and constructing a Wald test statistic.[10] All studies employing this approach – e.g. Hakkio (1981); Baillie, Lippens and McMahon (1983); MacDonald and Taylor (1991) – strongly reject the joint null hypothesis of rationality and risk neutrality.

---

[10] MacDonald and Taylor (1991) also employ a likelihood ratio test statistic to strengthen the findings suggested by the Wald statistic, since the latter is known to be sensitive to the form in which the nonlinear restrictions are parameterised (see Gregory and Veall, 1987).

McFarland, McMahon and Ngama (1994) circumvent some of the problems typical of the estimation of regressions of the spot and forward rates in levels by employing Phillips and Hansen's (1990) fully modified regression analysis to construct appropriate Wald tests to analyse whether or not the forward rate is an unbiased predictor of the future spot rate for the 1920s. Using daily data for five UK sterling exchange rates (German mark, Belgium franc, French franc, Italian lira and US dollar), McFarland, McMahon and Ngama reject the forward unbiasedness hypothesis for three (Belgian franc, French franc and German mark) of the five exchange rates, and argue that this result may be due to the presence of a risk premium for the Belgian and French francs and to market failure in the case of the German mark. The results also indicate that, with the exception of the German mark, the forward rates and future spot exchange rates are cointegrated.[11]

More recently, Clarida and Taylor (1997) have revisited the question of whether the forward exchange rate contains relevant information about the future path of the spot exchange rate, developing an empirical framework that is able to accommodate rejection of the pure efficiency hypothesis (i.e. that the forward rate is the optimum predictor of the spot rate) while still allowing forward premia to contain information about future spot rate changes. As noted above, it is a stylised fact that nominal spot exchange rates between the currencies of the major industrialised economies are well described by random walk processes. A slight generalisation of a random walk process is a unit-root process, which may have higher-order autoregressive properties than a pure random walk, but which nevertheless lacks a constant mean and finite variance, although the first difference of the series has a constant mean and finite variance (and is therefore covariance stationary). Beveridge and Nelson (1981) and Stock and Watson (1988) have shown that any unit-root process can in fact be decomposed into the sum of a pure random walk process (possibly with drift) and a stationary process. Clarida and Taylor therefore start by writing the spot exchange rate as the sum of two components:

$$s_t = m_t + q_t, \tag{2.20}$$

where m_t is a unit-root process evolving as a random walk with drift, and q_t is a stationary process having mean zero and a finite variance. They then define general departures from the simple efficiency hypothesis, due either to the presence of risk premia or to a failure of rational expectations, or both, as follows:

$$\gamma_t \equiv f_t^{(k)} - E\left(s_{t+k}|\Omega_t\right). \tag{2.21}$$

From (2.20) and (2.21) we can obtain:

$$f_t^{(k)} = \gamma_t + k\theta + E_t(q_{t+k}|\Omega_t) + m_t, \tag{2.22}$$

where θ is the drift of the random walk process m_t. Subtracting (2.20) from (2.22), we achieve an expression for the forward premium at time t:

$$f_t^{(k)} - s_t = \gamma_t + k\theta + E_t\left(q_{t+k} - q_t|\Omega_t\right). \tag{2.23}$$

---

[11] See also the futher evidence provided on this data set by Phillips, McFarland and McMahon (1996).

Equation (2.23) says that if γ_t, the departure from the simple efficiency hypothesis, is stationary (i.e. $I(0)$), given that q_t is stationary, the forward premium ($f_t^{(k)} - s_t$) must also be stationary, or $I(0)$. This implies that forward and spot rates exhibit a common stochastic trend and are cointegrated with cointegrating vector $[1, -1]$ (Engle and Granger, 1987; see Appendix D to this chapter). Moreover, since this is true for any k, if we consider the vector of m forward rates of tenor 1 to m periods, together with the current spot rate, $[s_t, f_t^{(1)}, f_t^{(2)}, f_t^{(3)}, \ldots, f_t^{(m)}]'$, then this must be cointegrated with m unique cointegrating vectors, each given by a row of the matrix $[-\iota, I_m]$, where I_m is an m-dimensional identity matrix and ι is an m-dimensional column vector of ones. Further, by the Granger representation theorem (Engle and Granger, 1987) the same set of forward and spot rates must possess a vector error correction (VECM) representation in which the term structure of forward premia plays the part of the equilibrium errors (see Appendix D to this chapter). Clarida and Taylor (1997) exploit this framework and, employing a VECM in spot and forward rates and using data on the spot dollar exchange rate and one-, three-, six- and twelve-month forward dollar exchange rates for Germany, Japan and the UK, they provide evidence suggesting that the information content of the term structure of forward premia is in fact considerable. In fact, their parsimonious VECMs significantly reduce the root mean square error and the mean absolute error relative both to unrestricted VARs and to a simple random walk model. Indeed, the evidence presented by Clarida and Taylor may perhaps be viewed as the strongest evidence to date in favour of an empirical exchange rate model that is able to beat a random walk model in out-of-sample forecasting. The essence of the Clarida–Taylor analysis is that, although the simple (risk-neutral) efficiency hypothesis may be strongly rejected by the data, it is nevertheless true that forward rates – and the whole term structure of forward rates – may contain information useful for forecasting future spot exchange rates.[12]

In general, therefore, the increasing sophistication in the econometric techniques employed has generated increasingly strong evidence against the simple, no-risk-premium speculative efficiency hypothesis, although empirical exchange rate models have been developed which are able to outperform a random walk model in out-of-sample forecasting exercises.

2.3   Rethinking efficiency I: risk premia[13]

The rejection of the simple, risk-neutral efficient markets hypothesis may be due to risk aversion of market participants or to a departure from the pure rational expectations hypothesis, or to both of these reasons. If foreign exchange market participants are risk-averse, the uncovered interest parity condition (2.1) may be distorted by a risk premium, ρ_t say, because agents demand a higher rate of return than the interest differential in return for the risk of holding foreign currency. Thus, arbitrage will ensure that the interest rate cost of

---

[12] Clarida, Sarno, Taylor and Valente (2001) have recently shown how the Clarida–Taylor forecasting results may be improved upon using a nonlinear Markov-switching VECM.

[13] See Lewis (1995) for a survey of the literature on the foreign exchange risk premium and departures from the rational expectations paradigm. See also Frankel (1988) for a survey of the empirical work on risk premia.

holding foreign currency (i.e. the interest rate differential) is just equal to the expected gain from holding foreign currency (the expected rate of depreciation of the domestic currency) plus a risk premium:[14]

$$i_t - i_t^* = \Delta_k s_{t+k}^e + \rho_t. \tag{2.24}$$

Equivalently, using the covered interest rate parity condition (2.5) in (2.24), the forward premium may be thought of as composed of two parts – the expected depreciation and the risk premium:

$$f_t^{(k)} - s_t = \Delta_k s_{t+k}^e + \rho_t. \tag{2.25}$$

The existence of risk premia has interesting implications for regressions of the rate of depreciation onto the forward premium, of the kind (2.9), which were first spelt out by Fama (1984). In addition to a regression of the form (2.9), Fama also considers the related regression of the excess return from taking an open forward position, $f_t^{(k)} - s_{t+k}$, onto the forward premium:

$$f_t^{(k)} - s_{t+k} = \gamma + \delta\left(f_t^{(k)} - s_t\right) + v_{t+k}, \tag{2.26}$$

where v_{t+k} denotes the regression error. Under appropriate regularity conditions, the probability limits of the OLS coefficient estimates of β and δ in the regressions (2.9) and (2.26) respectively are given by:

$$\beta = \frac{cov\left(\Delta s_{t+k}, \, f_t^{(k)} - s_t\right)}{var\left(f_t^{(k)} - s_t\right)} \tag{2.27}$$

$$\delta = \frac{cov\left(f_t^{(k)} - s_{t+k}, \, f_t^{(k)} - s_t\right)}{var\left(f_t^{(k)} - s_t\right)}, \tag{2.28}$$

where cov and var denote covariance and variance respectively. If we assume rational expectations, then we can replace $\Delta_k s_{t+k}$ with its expected value plus a forecast error which must be orthogonal to all information dated time t or earlier, $\Delta_k s_{t+k} = \Delta_k s_{t+k}^e + \eta_{t+k}$. Similarly, we can write $f_t^{(k)} - s_{t+k} = f_t^{(k)} - s_t - \Delta_k s_{t+k} = f_t^{(k)} - s_t - \Delta_k s_{t+k}^e - \eta_{t+k}$. Using these expressions and (2.25) to solve for the forward premium, equations (2.27) and (2.28) can be manipulated to yield:

$$\beta = \frac{var\left(\Delta_k s_{t+k}^e\right) + cov\left(\rho_t, \Delta_k s_{t+k}^e\right)}{var(\rho_t) + var\left(\Delta_k s_{t+k}^e\right) + 2cov\left(\rho_t, \Delta_k s_{t+k}^e\right)} \tag{2.29}$$

$$\delta = \frac{var(\rho_t) + cov\left(\rho_t, \Delta_k s_{t+k}^e\right)}{var(\rho_t) + var\left(\Delta_k s_{t+k}^e\right) + 2cov\left(\rho_t, \Delta_k s_{t+k}^e\right)}. \tag{2.30}$$

---

[14] Our use of the term 'premium' rather than 'discount' is again arbitrary and follows standard usage in the literature; risk premia can, however, be negative. Note also that (2.24) is an arbitrage condition rather than a behavioural relationship. In particular, (2.24) could just as well be written with ρ_t on the left-hand side, in which case it would have to be redefined as -1 times its present implicit definition, $\rho_t = i_t - i_t^* - \Delta_k s_{t+k}^e$.

Hence, the two regression coefficients measure roughly the relative contribution of the two components of the forward premium – i.e. the expected depreciation and the risk premium – to the variability of the forward premium, given the maintained hypothesis of rational expectations. In fact, if the two components are orthogonal, the decomposition is exact. It is also clear from (2.29) that if, as is often found, β turns out to be negative, this implies negative covariation between the risk premium and the expected rate of depreciation of the domestic currency, $cov(\rho_t, \Delta_k s^e_{t+k}) < 0$.

Suppose, however, that we make the weaker assumption that β is less than $1/2$ (which of course is also true if it is negative). Then we have:

$$\beta = \frac{var(\Delta_k s^e_{t+k}) + cov(\rho_t, \Delta_k s^e_{t+k})}{var(\rho_t) + var(\Delta_k s^e_{t+k}) + 2cov(\rho_t, \Delta_k s^e_{t+k})} < \frac{1}{2} \qquad (2.31)$$

or:

$$2var(\Delta_k s^e_{t+k}) + 2cov(\rho_t, \Delta_k s^e_{t+k}) < var(\rho_t) + var(\Delta_k s^e_{t+k}) + 2cov(\rho_t, \Delta_k s^e_{t+k})$$

$$(2.32)$$

which implies:

$$var(\rho_t) > var(\Delta_k s^e_{t+k}). \qquad (2.33)$$

Inequality (2.33) says that the variance of the risk premium is greater than the variance of the expected depreciation. From (2.25) we can also see that the predictable component of the excess return is just the risk premium, so that (2.33) also implies:

$$var\left[\left(f^{(k)}_t - s_{t+k}\right)^e\right] > var(\Delta_k s^e_{t+k}), \qquad (2.34)$$

i.e. the predictable component of the excess return has a greater variance than the expected depreciation itself. Both of these inequalities follow from the finding of a small estimated slope coefficient (less than $1/2$) in the regression of the rate of depreciation on the forward premium. Overall, therefore, regression evidence based on this approach suggests both that significant excess returns exist in the foreign exchange market, which can be predicted using current information, and that the variance of these predicted returns is larger than that of expected changes in the exchange rate.

What is very clear from this analysis, however, is that a time-varying risk premium will confound simple efficiency tests of the kind outlined above. An earlier strand of the literature attempted to understand the foreign exchange risk focused on simple extensions of the static version of the capital asset pricing model (CAPM) (see e.g. Frankel, 1982; Adler and Dumas, 1983; Domowitz and Hakkio, 1985; Lewis, 1988; Engel and Rodrigues, 1989; Giovannini and Jorion, 1989; Engel, 1992). Most of these studies provide evidence that the risk aversion parameter is very large but not significantly different from zero and also that the restrictions imposed in the model are rejected. Nevertheless, the assumed lack of variability in the conditional variance of exchange rates and the fact that the model is static and a partial equilibrium one, in addition to the assumption that the exchange rate and the interest rate are exogenous with respect to the risk premium, represent strong theoretical weaknesses, which made this approach succumb over time to analyses involving dynamic general equilibrium models. In the next sub-section we use a dynamic, two-country, general equilibrium model due to Lucas (1982) to derive risk premia in the foreign exchange market.

2.3.1 The Lucas model

The Lucas model is a theoretical model in which representative agents in two countries are provided with identical preferences over two consumption goods but different stochastic endowments of the two goods. In period t, each agent of the domestic country is endowed with $2Y_t$ units of the domestic good and no units of the foreign good, while each agent in the foreign country is endowed with $2Y_t^*$ units of the foreign good and no units of the domestic good. The Lucas model assumes that securities markets are complete so that there is complete pooling of risks. This, together with identical preferences, means that agents will consume exactly one-half of the endowment of each good in each period, i.e. Y_t and Y_t^*. Agents in each country maximise their expected infinite lifetime utility function:

$$E_0 \left[\sum_{t=0}^{\infty} \gamma^t U(Y_t, Y_t^*) \right],$$ (2.35)

where γ is the common discount factor, $U(.)$ represents single-period utility and E_0 denotes the mathematical expectation, given information at time 0. We assume the function $U(.)$ to be bounded, twice differentiable, increasing in both arguments and strictly concave.

Assume that the two goods are produced exogenously and therefore the production side of the economy is described by the bivariate process (Y_t, Y_t^*), assumed to be drawn from a unique stationary Markov distribution $F(Y_t, Y_t^* \mid Y_{t-1}, Y_{t-1}^*)$ that gives the probability of Y_t and Y_t^* for given values of Y_{t-1} and Y_{t-1}^*. Every period, each country's agents receive the current per capita output of the home good and are also endowed with money (M_t and M_t^* for domestic and foreign per capita money respectively). Money is required because of cash-in-advance constraints requiring the good of each country to be bought only with the money of that country. We also assume that the endowments of money are drawn from a known Markov process $G[M_t, M_t^* \mid M_{t-1}, M_{t-1}^*, F(Y_t, Y_t^* \mid Y_{t-1}, Y_{t-1}^*)]$ that gives the probability of M_t and M_t^* for given values of M_{t-1} and M_{t-1}^* and given probabilities of Y_t and Y_t^*. If P_t is the domestic-money price of the domestic good and the foreign-money price of the foreign good is P_t^*, then the cash-in-advance constraints can be written as follows:

$$P_t = M_t/2Y_t \text{ and } P_t^* = M_t^*/2Y_t^*.$$ (2.36)

Note that the relative price of the good Y^*, expressed in terms of good Y, say π, is:

$$\pi_t = U_{Y_t^*}/U_{Y_t}$$ (2.37)

where U_{Y_t} and $U_{Y_t^*}$ denote the agent's marginal utilities at time t with respect to Y and Y^* respectively. This follows from the first-order conditions for the maximisation of (2.35). In fact, π may be thought of as the real exchange rate in this model.

But this relative price or real exchange rate must be equal to the ratio of the foreign to the domestic price level, each expressed in a common currency:

$$\pi_t = S_t P_t^* / P_t, \tag{2.38}$$

where S_t is the spot exchange rate – the domestic price of foreign currency. Equation (2.38) is, in fact, how the real exchange rate is normally defined. Given preferences and endowments of domestic and foreign output and money, we can then solve for the nominal exchange rate:

$$\begin{aligned} S_t &= \pi_t P_t / P_t^* \\ &= \left[U_{Y_t^*} / U_{Y_t} \right] P_t / P_t^* \\ &= \left[U_{Y_t^*} / U_{Y_t} \right] M_t Y_t^* / M_t^* Y_t. \end{aligned} \tag{2.39}$$

It should be noted that a weakness of the Lucas model is that the exchange rate does not depend upon any forward-looking variables. This is because it is assumed that all information relevant for period t consumption is received prior to trading taking place in that period. Since, however, we are not concerned with exchange rate determination *per se*, this may be viewed as a simplifying assumption. For simplicity, we shall assume that the domestic and foreign goods have identical characteristics, so that their relative price must be unity, and from equation (2.38) we can write:

$$S_t = P_t / P_t^*, \tag{2.40}$$

which is the purchasing power parity (PPP) condition. (Note that a relative price of unity also implies, via (2.36) and (2.38), that the spot exchange rate is determined by relative monetary velocity. As we shall see in Chapter 4, this is a feature of the monetary model of exchange rates.)

Having derived an expression for the spot rate in the Lucas model, we now need to derive an expression for the forward rate in order to solve for the forward exchange risk premium. Our strategy is to use CIP and PPP to derive an expression for the real interest rate differential and then to use the Euler equations for intertemporal consumption smoothing to solve for the wedge between the forward rate and the expected future spot rate.

Let the *ex post* real rate of return on a one-period domestic asset held during period t be r_t and the corresponding *ex post* real return on a foreign asset be r_t^*. If i_t and i_t^* are the nominal rates of return on these assets, then the real return differential may be written as follows:

$$r_t - r_t^* = \frac{(1 + i_t) P_t}{P_{t+1}} - \frac{(1 + i_t^*) P_t^*}{P_{t+1}^*}. \tag{2.41}$$

Using the CIP condition (2.2) and the PPP condition (2.40), this real differential can be written as:

$$r_t - r_t^* = \frac{(1 + i_t) P_t}{F_t^{(1)}} \left[\frac{F_t^{(1)} - S_{t+1}}{P_{t+1}} \right]. \tag{2.42}$$

Now the Euler equation relating to the return on the domestic asset can be written:

$$U_{Y_t} = \gamma E_t[(1 + r_t)U_{Y_{t+1}}]. \tag{2.43}$$

If agents attempt to increase future consumption by reducing current consumption by a small amount, their current-period utility will fall by U_{Y_t}. If they invest this in the domestic asset for one period they will be able to increase their consumption of the domestic good next period by $1 + r_t$, leading to an increase in utility of $(1 + r_t)U_{Y_{t+1}}$ or, in expected present value terms, $\gamma E_t[(1 + r_t)U_{Yt+1}]$. Now, if agents have optimised their consumption plans, these two should be equal – which is what the Euler equation says. A similar Euler equation must hold with respect to the real return on the foreign asset:

$$U_{Y_t} = \gamma E_t[(1 + r_t^*)U_{Y_{t+1}}]. \tag{2.44}$$

– note that the asterisk appears only for the real interest rate in (2.44); this is because we are considering *real* returns, so that we can think of the payoff as units of the foreign good, and assuming perfect substitutability between the domestic and foreign good, marginal utilities with respect to the domestic and foreign goods will be identical. From (2.43) and (2.44) we can derive:

$$E_t[(r_t - r_t^*)U_{Yt+1}/U_{Yt}] = 0. \tag{2.45}$$

Using (2.42)–(2.45) and the fact that $E_t[(1 + i_t)P_t/F_t^{(1)}] = (1 + i_t)P_t/F_t^{(1)} \neq 0$, we can then derive:

$$E_t\left[\frac{F_t^{(1)} - S_{t+1}}{P_{t+1}}\frac{U_{Yt+1}}{U_{Yt}}\right] = 0. \tag{2.46}$$

The term $(U_{Y_{t+1}}/U_{Y_t})$ can be thought of as a subjective discount factor, since it values next period's marginal utility in terms of this period's marginal utility. Hence, equation (2.46) effectively says that the expected current-period value of the real return from taking an open forward position must be zero, and this is intuitive since it involves no commitment of funds and no risk in the current period. Equation (2.46) can, however, be solved for the wedge between the forward rate and the expected future spot rate and hence the risk premium. Suppose, for example, that the instantaneous utility function is of the constant relative risk aversion form:

$$U(Y_t, Y_t^*) = U(C_t) = (1 - \phi)^{-1}C_t^{1-\phi}, \tag{2.47}$$

where ϕ is the coefficient of relative risk aversion and $C_t = Y_t + Y_t^*$ (since we have assumed that the domestic and foreign goods have identical characteristics, agents must only care about their total consumption of them). Equation (2.47) now becomes:

$$E_t\left[\frac{F_t^{(1)} - S_{t+1}}{P_{t+1}}\left(\frac{C_t}{C_{t+1}}\right)^\phi\right] = 0$$

or:

$$C_t^{\phi} E_t \left[\frac{F_t^{(1)} - S_{t+1}}{P_{t+1}} \left(\frac{1}{C_{t+1}} \right)^{\phi} \right] = 0$$

since C_t is known at time t. And since C_t is non-zero, this implies:

$$E_t \left[\frac{F_t^{(1)} - S_{t+1}}{P_{t+1}} \left(\frac{1}{C_{t+1}} \right)^{\phi} \right] = 0. \tag{2.48}$$

If all variables in (2.48) are joint log-normally distributed, conditional on information at time t, then we can write (2.48) in logarithmic form as[15]:

$$E_t s_{t+1} - f_t^{(1)} = \phi cov_t(s_{t+1}, c_{t+1}) - \frac{1}{2} var_t(s_{t+1}) + cov_t(s_{t+1}, p_{t+1}), \tag{2.49}$$

where lower-case letters denote natural logarithms and var_t and cov_t denote the conditional variance and covariance based on information at time t. Note that, if agents were completely risk-neutral then $\phi = 0$ and (2.49) would reduce to:

$$E_t s_{t+1} - f_t^{(1)} = -\frac{1}{2} var_t(s_{t+1}) + cov_t(s_{t+1}, p_{t+1}). \tag{2.50}$$

There is still a wedge between the spot and forward rate even in the risk-neutral case. This is because we have log-linearised a nonlinear first-order condition. This effectively involves taking a Taylor series expansion and uses the fact that distribution moments above the second moments vanish for the normal distribution – we are still left with the second moments, however.[16] The first term on the right hand side of (2.50) is the proper risk premium, for $\phi \neq 0$, i.e. $\phi cov_t(s_{t+1}, c_{t+1})$. Thus, for the risk premium to explain a significant portion of the forward rate forecast error or excess returns, either there must be a very large coefficient of relative risk aversion ϕ, or consumption must be highly correlated with the exchange rate. The intuition for the fact that high correlation between consumption and the exchange rate raises the risk premium is that forward exchange positions provide less of a hedge against variations in consumption the greater is this covariation. The fact is, however, that consumption tends to be fairly smooth in any advanced economy, while the nominal exchange rate – at least under floating rate regimes – is typically a lot more volatile, so that this covariation will be quite small.

Mark (1985) assumes a constant relative risk aversion utility function and tests the intertemporal restrictions with consumption. His study reports a very large and significant estimate of the risk aversion parameter, consistent with the high variance of the predictable returns in the risk premium model. A number of researchers, including Hansen and Hodrick (1980), Hodrick and Srivastava (1984, 1986), Giovannini and Jorion (1987) and, more

---

[15] A standard result in statistical theory is that, if a variable Z has a log-normal distribution, i.e. $z = \log Z \sim N(\mu_z, \sigma_z^2)$, then $E(Z) = E[\exp(z)] = \exp(\mu_z + \frac{1}{2}\sigma_z^2)$ – see Appendix A to this chapter. If we write (2.48) as:

$$E_t[\exp(f_t^{(1)} - p_{t+1} - \phi c_{t+1})] = E_t[\exp(s_{t+1} - p_{t+1} - \phi c_{t+1})]$$

then, by applying this result, noting that $var_t(f_t^{(1)} - p_{t+1} - \phi c_{t+1}) = var_t(-p_{t+1} - \phi c_{t+1})$ (since $f_t^{(1)}$ is known at time t), and using the standard formulae for the variance of sums, we can derive (2.49) straightforwardly.

[16] These terms are another way of viewing Siegel's paradox – see Appendix B to this chapter.

recently, Bekaert and Hodrick (1992) and Bekaert (1994), also derive testable restrictions relating forward exchange rates and expected spot exchange rates from the first-order conditions of the Lucas model or similar general equilibrium models. These risk premium models have generally met with mixed and somewhat limited success, and have not been found to be robust when applied to different data sets and sample periods (Lewis, 1995). Sibert (1996) investigates whether non-standard consumption behaviour, such as habit persistence, is able to account for excess returns but is unable to replicate actual data even under the assumption of extreme values of risk aversion.[17]

The message which emerges from empirical analysis of the Lucas model is that it is hard to explain excess returns in forward foreign exchange by an appeal to risk premia alone: either ϕ, the coefficient of relative risk aversion, must be incredibly large, or else the conditional covariance of consumption and the spot rate must be incredibly high.

2.4   Rethinking efficiency II: expectations

An alternative explanation of the rejection of the simple efficient markets hypothesis is that there is a failure, in some sense, of the expectations component of the joint hypothesis. The literature identifies in this group at least four possible issues: rational bubbles; learning about regime shifts (Lewis, 1989a, 1989b); the 'peso problem', originally suggested by Rogoff (1979); or inefficient information processing, as suggested, for example, by Bilson (1981).

2.4.1   Foreign exchange market rational bubbles
The presence of rational bubbles may show up as non-zero excess returns even when agents are risk-neutral. A speculative or rational bubble is characterised by an explosive path of the exchange rate which takes it progressively away from the equilibrium level determined by economic fundamentals, causing an increasing divergence of the exchange rate from its equilibrium value. Hence, speculators and investors continue to buy a currency despite the fact that it is already overvalued with respect to the fundamentals, simply because they think that continuation of the bubble will make it profitable to do so. In general, rational bubbles may occur because there are multiple rational expectations equilibria in addition to the market fundamentals solution. For example, consider a typical discrete-time stochastic differential equation that occurs in asset market exchange rate models (see Chapter 4):

$$s_t = \lambda E_t s_{t+1} + v_t. \tag{2.51}$$

Equation (2.51) says that the current value of the exchange rate depends upon the current level of economic fundamentals v_t plus the present value of the expected value of next period's spot rate, discounted using the discount factor λ. Solving this equation forward,

---

[17] A useful approach for comparing the variability of predictable excess returns with the implications of any one model has been provided by Hansen and Jaganathan (1991). They use combinations of excess returns to provide a lower bound on the volatility of the intertemporal marginal rate of substitution in consumption. Analysis of the lower bound is a powerful method since it must hold for any model and is free of parameters.

we obtain:

$$\widetilde{s}_t = \sum_{i=0}^{\infty} \lambda^i E_t v_{t+i}. \tag{2.52}$$

However, (2.52) is only one solution to (2.51) from a potentially infinite class of solutions of the form:

$$s_t = \widetilde{s}_t + B_t, \tag{2.53}$$

where the term B_t satisfies:

$$B_t = \lambda E_t B_{t+1}. \tag{2.54}$$

To see this, lead (2.53) one period and take expectations with respect to information at time t:

$$E_t s_{t+1} = E_t \widetilde{s}_{t+1} + E_t B_{t+1}$$

$$= \sum_{i=0}^{\infty} \lambda^i E_t v_{t+i+1} + E_t B_{t+1}$$

which implies:

$$\lambda E_t s_{t+1} = \sum_{i=0}^{\infty} \lambda^{i+1} E_t v_{t+i+1} + B_t$$

$$= \widetilde{s}_t - v_t + B_t$$

or:

$$s_t = \lambda E_t s_{t+1} + v_t. \tag{2.55}$$

Since (2.55) is identical to (2.51) under the assumption of rational expectations, (2.53) represents a feasible solution to (2.51).

B_t is a rational bubble term, representing the extent of the deviation of the exchange rate from the market equilibrium. Such a rational bubble is important in driving the exchange rate away from the equilibrium suggested by the fundamentals if market agents perceive it to be important. Agents attach a certain probability to the continuation of the bubble next period against the probability of the bubble bursting. The important point is that, given the bubble's asymmetric probability distribution, then the distribution of exchange rate innovations will also be asymmetric. A simple model for a bubble takes the form:

$$B_t = \begin{cases} (\pi \lambda)^{-1} B_{t-1} & \text{with probability } \pi \\ 0 & \text{with probability } 1 - \pi \end{cases} \tag{2.56}$$

which satisfies (2.54). The reader can easily verify that, given a certain process driving the fundamentals, the implied rational expectations forecast errors will have a skewed distribution, even if agents' expectations are formed rationally and therefore, *in general*, conventional inferential procedures may be invalidated.

Turning now to the empirical evidence on bubbles, the literature has pursued three main approaches: the 'variance bounds' (or 'excess volatility') tests, specification tests and runs tests.

Variance bounds tests are based on a very simple idea. Recall once again the forward solution to the asset market model:

$$\widetilde{s}_t = E_t s^*_{t+1} \tag{2.57}$$

where $s^*_t = \sum_{i=0}^{\infty} \lambda^i v_{t+i}$ represents the level at which the exchange rate would settle if agents had 'perfect foresight'. Thus, it follows that:

$$s^*_t = \widetilde{s}_t + n_t \tag{2.58}$$

where $n_t = \sum_{i=0}^{\infty} \lambda^i v_{t+i} - E_t s^*_{t+1}$, i.e. the perfect foresight solution and the fundamentals solution differ from each other by the rational forecast error, n_t. Also, since agents are assumed to form rational expectations, then the fundamentals solution and the forecast errors must satisfy an orthogonality condition, i.e. their covariance equals zero. Thus:

$$var(s^*_t) = var(\widetilde{s}_t) + var(n_t) \tag{2.59}$$

and:

$$var(s^*_t) \geq var(\widetilde{s}_t). \tag{2.60}$$

If B_t equals zero and hence the actual exchange rate equals the solution provided by fundamentals, then (2.60) is expected to hold. If rational bubbles move the actual exchange rate away from the fundamentals solution, however, then (2.60) can no longer be derived:

$$s^*_t = s_t - B_t + n_t,$$

$$var\left(s^*_t\right) = var(s_t) + var(B_t) + var(n_t) - 2cov(s_t, B_t). \tag{2.61}$$

This is the reasoning underlying the variance bounds tests: excess volatility of the actual exchange rate relative to the volatility of the exchange rate based on the fundamentals solution may be considered as evidence suggesting the presence of speculative bubbles. The empirical evidence reported in the literature suggests that excess volatility is indeed present in major exchange rates (Huang, 1981; MacDonald and Taylor, 1993), which may be due to the presence of rational bubbles. Nevertheless, the reliability of the excess volatility tests is questionable, given that they are conditional on a particular exchange rate model and also because the excess volatility of the actual exchange rates relative to the fundamentals solution of the exchange rates may be caused by factors other than rational bubbles (see Flood and Garber, 1980; Leroy, 1984; Flood and Hodrick, 1990).

Another approach undertaken by researchers in testing for the presence of speculative bubbles in exchange rates is originally due to Meese (1986) and is based on the Hausman (1978) specification test. The underlying idea is to compare two estimates of λ from different empirical formulations of a forward-looking asset market exchange rate model, only one of which yields consistent parameter estimates if bubbles are present. Consider equation (2.51) plus an error term:

$$s_t = \lambda E_t s_{t+1} + v_t + \omega_t \tag{2.62}$$

where ω_t is a white-noise error capturing movements in the exchange rate not captured by the model. The parameter λ can be estimated directly, replacing $E_t s_{t+1}$ with s_{t+1}, and employing the McCallum instrumental variables estimator (McCallum, 1976), which yields consistent estimates of λ. This estimator is valid whether or not bubbles are present. The alternative estimate of λ is derived from the fundamentals model as expressed in equation (2.52) which, adding an error term, becomes:

$$\widetilde{s}_t = \sum_{i=0}^{\infty} \lambda^i E_t v_{t+i} + \omega_t. \tag{2.63}$$

To obtain a closed form solution, we need to make some assumptions about the fundamentals v_t. For expositional purposes, assume a simple AR(1) process for v_t:

$$v_t = \kappa v_{t-1} + u_t \qquad |\kappa| < 1, \tag{2.64}$$

where u_t is white noise. Taking conditional expectations of (2.64) and using it in (2.63) gives:

$$\widetilde{s}_t = (1 - \kappa\lambda)^{-1} v_t + u_t. \tag{2.65}$$

In the absence of bubbles, (2.64) and (2.65) may be jointly estimated to generate an estimate of λ which is consistent only under the null hypothesis of no bubbles. Then, the Hausman specification test can be used to discriminate between the two estimates of λ, which will be insignificantly different from one another only if the no-bubbles hypothesis is correct.

Using this approach, Meese (1986) rejects the no-bubbles hypothesis for the dollar–yen, dollar–mark and dollar–sterling exchange rates from 1973 to 1982. Similarly to the excess volatility tests, the specification tests are conditional on the assumed model of exchange rate determination. In particular, Flood and Garber (1980) argue that since the monetary model in general predicts poorly, then an omitted variable problem may potentially bias bubble tests towards rejection of the null hypothesis of no bubbles.

Evans (1986) tests for speculative bubbles in the dollar–sterling exchange rate over the period 1981 to 1984 by testing for a non-zero median in excess returns using a non-parametric test. By rejecting the null hypothesis of a zero median, Evans concludes that speculative bubbles were present in the dollar–sterling exchange rate over the sample period examined. One problem with this approach is that bubbles, perhaps, should not be expected to be present over a four-year period when they are considered a short-run deviation from fundamentals by definition. Also, Evans' findings may be explained not only by the presence of rational bubbles, but also by peso problems and by non-rational expectations which would also produce a skew in forecast errors and hence a non-zero median in excess returns. Flood and Hodrick (1990) argue that a very serious observational equivalence problem exists between expectations of process-switching and bubbles. Given this problem, together with the fact that bubble tests are usually based on a particular model of fundamentals, Flood and Hodrick conclude that the empirical evidence for the existence of rational bubbles in exchange rates is quite thin.

Yet another method of testing for bubbles in foreign exchange markets has been to look for cointegration between the exchange rate and some measure of fundamentals (e.g. MacDonald and Taylor, 1993). The intuition is simple: since bubbles are by definition explosive, they will drive an explosive wedge between the exchange rate and fundamentals. The interpretation of unit-root tests on exchange rate series and cointegration tests on fundamentals-based models of the exchange rate as tests for rational bubbles has, however, been shown to be potentially misleading in the presence of bubbles which collapse from time to time over the sample period, i.e. periodically collapsing bubbles (Evans, 1991).[18] Specifically, Evans (1991) shows that cointegration tests will tend to reject the null hypothesis of no bubbles more often than suggested by the chosen significance level when there are periodically collapsing bubbles. The essence of the problem lies in the fact that periodically collapsing bubbles will tend to generate skewness and excess kurtosis in time series for exchange rates over and above that which may be present in the fundamentals series.[19] Since the maintained hypothesis in standard unit-root and cointegration tests is a linear autoregressive model in which the error term is assumed to be Gaussian, then a test based on the estimated autoregressive coefficients will tend to average out the exploding part of the bubble and its collapse in the estimated coefficients, hence generating bias towards rejection of nonstationarity (Evans, 1991). The bias should be reduced, however, if a test for nonstationarity is used which allows the collapse in the bubble to be attributed largely to a sudden movement in a non-normal error term rather than the estimated coefficients of the autoregressive model. Taylor and Peel (1998) and Sarno and Taylor (1999) employ a test statistic based on the work of Im (1996) which explicitly exploits the skewness and excess kurtosis which bubbles engender in the data and alleviates some of the econometric problems encountered in the presence of periodically collapsing bubbles.[20] More generally, a more powerful approach to testing for the presence of bubbles is to apply robust estimation techniques. It seems likely that robust estimation methods will increasingly be used in the future in the context of testing for rational bubbles in exchange rates.

2.4.2 Rational learning in the foreign exchange market

When agents are learning about their environment they may be unable fully to exploit arbitrage opportunities which are apparent in the data *ex post*. The possibility that learning may be another potential cause of the rejection of the market efficiency hypothesis in the foreign exchange market was first proposed by Lewis (1989a, 1989b, 1995).

As noted earlier, under the rational expectations hypothesis and under the assumption that the underlying distribution of economic disturbances is known to market agents, forecast errors must be orthogonal to the information set used in forming expectations and have mean zero. As with peso problems, which we shall discuss below, learning about the environment can generate forecast errors displaying serial correlation with a non-zero mean.

---

[18] Periodically collapsing bubbles are particularly interesting in analysing the behaviour of exchange rates since they collapse almost surely in finite time. This is an attractive property because bubbles do not seem to be empirically plausible unless they collapse after reaching high levels. Evans (1991) focused on stock prices although the general ideas of that article can be extended directly to exchange rates.

[19] Note, however, that non-normality is a necessary but not sufficient condition for the existence of rational bubbles.

[20] This is clearly demonstrated using Monte Carlo methods by Taylor and Peel (1998), who show that the problem of size distortion is greatly reduced using such a test.

To see why, consider the example examined by Lewis (1989a, 1995). Consider the case that a potential once-and-for-all change in the underlying distribution of the economy exists, such as a shift in monetary policy, which will affect the expected level of the exchange rate:

$$E_t(s_{t+1} \mid M_1) \neq E_t(s_{t+1} \mid M_2), \tag{2.66}$$

where M_1 and M_2 are the old and the new regime respectively (for example, if M_2 represents a tightening of monetary policy, then we might expect $E_t(s_{t+1} \mid M_1) > E_t(s_{t+1} \mid M_2)$). The expected exchange rate at time t is given by:

$$E_t s_{t+1} = (1 - l_t) E_t(s_{t+1} \mid M_2) + l_t E_t(s_{t+1} \mid M_1), \tag{2.67}$$

where l_t denotes the probability at time t of the monetary policy being based on the old regime. Assume agents know that if a regime shift occurred in domestic monetary policy, it was at time $q < t$. Lewis (1989a, 1989b) assumes that market participants use Bayesian forecasting rules to learn about policy changes, and therefore they update their subjective probabilities of the regime being changed according to a rule such as:

$$l_t = \frac{l_{t-1} L(\Delta s_t, \Delta s_{t-1}, \dots, \Delta s_{q+1} \mid M_1)}{(1 - l_{t-1}) L(\Delta s_t, \Delta s_{t-1}, \dots, \Delta s_{q+1} \mid M_2) + l_{t-1} L(\Delta s_t, \Delta s_{t-1}, \dots, \Delta s_{q+1} \mid M_1)} \tag{2.68}$$

where $L(\Delta s_t, \Delta s_{t-1}, \dots, \Delta s_{q+1} \mid M_2)$ and $L(\Delta s_t, \Delta s_{t-1}, \dots, \Delta s_{q+1} \mid M_1)$ represent the likelihood of the observed data given that the new or the old regime is in force respectively. The intuition behind this updating equation is as follows. The quantity l_t, as defined in (2.68) gives the *posterior probability* that there has been no regime shift. It combines the *prior probability* of a regime shift, $(1 - l_{t-1})$, and of no regime shift, l_{t-1}, with the probabilities of observing the data given that a regime shift has or has not occured. This posterior probability is then used as a prior probability in the next updating equation, once more data have become available. If the data seem to be coming from the new regime, for example, then $L(. \mid M_1)$ will tend to shrink as more and more data become available, so that $l_j \to 0$ as j gets larger.

An important feature of (2.68) is that, as long as agents are learning, they will attach non-zero probabilities to both of these regimes being in force, whereas only one of them is actually in force, so that forecast errors, $E_t s_{t+1} - s_{t+1}$, will be serially correlated with a non-zero mean regardless of whether a change in the domestic monetary policy occurs or not.

If the new domestic monetary policy has in fact been put into action at time $q < t$, the probability limit of l_t is zero as agents eventually gather enough data to learn that the regime shift has definitely occurred. After the regime shift has occurred, the forecast errors while the market is learning can be computed as the difference between the observed exchange rate (under the new regime) and the expected exchange rate as given by the weighted average of the rates expected under the old and new regimes:

$$
\begin{aligned}
s_{t+1}^{M_2} - E_t s_{t+1} &= \left[s_{t+1}^{M_2} - E_t(s_{t+1} \mid M_2) \right] - l_t \left[E_t(s_{t+1} \mid M_1) - E_t(s_{t+1} \mid M_2) \right] \\
&= \eta_{t+1} - l_t \nabla s_{t+1}
\end{aligned} \tag{2.69}
$$

where the superscripts M_1 and M_2 indicate that the exchange rates are realised under the old and new monetary regimes respectively; η_{t+1} is the rational expectations forecast error which would occur if agents knew with certainty that the regime shift had occurred; and $\nabla s_{t+1} = [E_t(s_{t+1} \mid M_1) - E_t(s_{t+1} \mid M_2)]$ represents the difference in the expected value of the future exchange rate under the different regimes. Equation (2.69) clearly suggests that as long as a non-zero probability that the old regime is still in action exists, the forecast errors will have a non-zero mean. The effect of this will be to skew the distribution of the composite forecast error defined in (2.69), even though agents are fully rational, with resulting implications for empirical tests of market efficiency.

Lewis (1989a) applies this approach to investigate the behaviour of US dollar–German mark forecast errors during the early 1980s, when markets systematically underpredicted the appreciating trend of the US dollar. The results suggest that forecast errors were on average negative in that period. Again, Lewis (1989b) shows that in the early 1980s, after the tightening of US domestic monetary policy, agents did not learn immediately about the change, and empirical simulations suggest that about half of the US dollar's underprediction of the market as implied by the forward market during that period is consistent with the forecast errors computed using Bayesian learning.

2.4.3   The peso problem

A similar skew in the distribution of forecast errors may occur when agents are fully rational and learn instantly, but they are uncertain about a *future* shift in regime – the so-called 'peso problem'. More specifically, the peso problem refers to the situation where agents attach a small probability to a large change in the economic fundamentals which does not occur in sample. The term was first used to describe the behaviour of the Mexican peso which, although it had been fixed for a decade, traded at a forward discount to the US dollar during the early 1970s, presumably reflecting the market's anticipation of a devaluation although this did not occur until 1976. Rogoff (1979) and Krasker (1980) provide the first theoretical analyses of the peso problem. In estimating the regression of the Mexican peso–US dollar exchange rate on the futures rate, Rogoff (1979) tests the null hypothesis of homogeneity between the two variables, i.e. the hypothesis that the coefficient on the futures rate equals unity. Rogoff argues that the recorded rejection of the null hypothesis may be caused by the market's rational anticipation of a future devaluation in the peso. Krasker (1980) develops a model under conditions of hyperinflation in which it is possible to measure the size of the distortions in the conventional tests for foreign exchange market efficiency when a peso problem exists. Lizondo (1983) also provides a theoretical model of the Mexican peso futures market in which the anticipation of the devaluation is accounted for by rational agents.

The essence of the peso problem can be seen easily by an analysis similar to that used in the previous sub-section. In particular, suppose that agents attach a probability ℓ_t to there being a shift in regime *next* period, represented by shifting from M_1 to M_2 as before. The expected exchange rate will be:

$$E_t s_{t+1} = \ell_t E_t(s_{t+1} \mid M_2) + (1 - \ell_t) E_t(s_{t+1} \mid M_1). \tag{2.70}$$

The forecast error, assuming the regime shift does not in fact occur will be:

$$s_{t+1}^{M_1} - E_t s_{t+1} = \left[s_{t+1}^{M_1} - E_t(s_{t+1} \mid M_1) \right]$$

$$- l_t \left[E_t(s_{t+1} \mid M_2) - E_t(s_{t+1} \mid M_1) \right]$$

$$= \eta_{t+1} + \ell_t \nabla s_{t+1} \tag{2.71}$$

where $\nabla s_{t+1} = [E_t(s_{t+1} \mid M_1) - E_t(s_{t+1} \mid M_2)]$ again represents the difference in the expected value of the future exchange rate under the different regimes. Exactly as in the learning case, there will be a skew in the distribution of forecast errors which will confound econometric analyses, since even a small probability of a large regime shift (small ℓ_t but large ∇s_{t+1}) may generate a large skew.

Note that, even if the regime shift does occur, there will still be a forecast error over and above the usual rational expectations forecast error:

$$s_{t+1}^{M_2} - E_t s_{t+1} = \left[s_{t+1}^{M_2} - E_t(s_{t+1} \mid M_2) \right]$$

$$- (1 - l_t)\left[E_t(s_{t+1} \mid M_2) - E_t(s_{t+1} \mid M_1) \right]$$

$$= \eta_{t+1} + (1 - \ell_t)\nabla s_{t+1}. \tag{2.72}$$

If there is instantaneous learning, however, such as when the regime shift is fully public knowledge (e.g. a new political administration is elected or the currency is devalued), the skew in the distribution of forecast errors will disappear for expectations formed from time $t + 1$ onwards. It is in this sense that the peso problem is a small-sample problem.

Borensztein (1987) analyses, in an efficient-market framework, whether peso problems and speculative bubbles could explain the fact that returns from assets denominated in US dollars exceeded by far the returns from securities very similar to those except for the currency of denomination in the 1980–5 period, providing strong evidence that both models are potential sources of this phenomenon. Lewis (1988, 1991) shows how peso problems can potentially generate biased forecasts of exchange rates, even *after* the policy regime shift has occurred. Also, during the peso problem period, exchange rates may experience bubbles and systematically deviate from the levels implied by the observed fundamentals.[21, 22]

Engel and Hamilton (1990) observe that the dollar exchange rate during the 1980s displayed a pattern of persistent appreciating and then depreciating trends. They develop a model of exchange rate dynamics 'as a sequence of stochastic, segmented time trends', which is found to perform better than the random walk model in forecasting. A similar idea is used by Kaminsky (1993), who explains the apparent irrationality of the floating exchange rate regime since 1973 by arguing that exchange rate forecasts are in fact still rational, but

---

[21] Note the similarity between rational bubbles and peso problems: they are both phenomena consistent with rational behaviour by agents in the economy and have similar effects on the forecast errors distribution. Nevertheless, an important difference exists between the two phenomena in that rational bubbles occur as deviations *from* the fundamentals, whereas peso problems arise because of an expected shift *in* the fundamentals.

[22] Many attempts have been made in the literature to introduce peso problems in open-economy models in order to analyse the effects on exchange rates. For example, Penati and Pennacchi (1989) present a representative agent model which accounts for many empirical macroeconomic regularities characterising exchange rate crises. Prior to the crisis, a peso problem exists and the central bank loses reserves in excess of domestic credit creation, while, at the time of the collapse, the exchange rate may depreciate unexpectedly.

biased if the exchange rate has followed a switching regime process. Kaminsky's estimates suggest that about 75 per cent of this bias can be explained using a switching regime model.[23] Motivated by the studies of Engel and Hamilton (1990) and Kaminsky (1993), Evans and Lewis (1995) show that the peso problem generated by an expected exchange rate regime shift can potentially affect inferences of the risk premium by giving the appearance of a permanent disturbance component contained in the risk premium itself, when this is in fact not present. Moreover, the peso problem may explain the bias in spot–forward foreign exchange regressions such as the Fama regressions discussed above.

A problem with admitting peso problems, bubbles or learning into the class of explanations of the forward discount bias is that, as noted above, a very large number of econometric studies – encompassing a very large range of exchange rates and sample periods – have found that the direction of the bias is the same under each scenario, i.e. the estimated uncovered interest rate parity slope parameter, β in (2.9), is generally negative and closer to minus unity than plus unity. For example, Lewis (1989a), in her study of the relationship of the early 1980s dollar appreciation with learning about the US money supply process, notes a persistence in the forward rate errors which, in itself, is *prima facie* evidence against the learning explanation: agents cannot forever be learning about a once-and-for-all regime shift. Similarly, the peso problem is essentially a small-sample phenomenon; it cannot explain the fact that estimates of β are *generally* negative.

2.5   Rethinking efficiency III: inefficiencies in information processing and survey data studies

A problem with much of the empirical literature on the possible rationalisations of the rejection of the simple, risk-neutral efficient markets hypothesis is that in testing one leg of the joint hypothesis, researchers have typically assumed that the other leg is true. For instance, the search for a stable empirical risk premium model has generally been conditioned on the assumption of rational expectations (see e.g. Fama, 1984; Hodrick and Srivastava, 1984; Bilson, 1985). Other studies assume, however, that investors are risk-neutral and hence that the deviation from the unbiasedness hypothesis would suggest rejection of the rational expectations hypothesis (e.g. Bilson, 1981; Longworth, 1981; Cumby and Obstfeld, 1984).

The availability of survey data on exchange rate expectations has allowed researchers to conduct tests of each component of the joint hypothesis. Once exchange rate expectations are available no need exists to impose any assumption regarding the expectations formation mechanism of market agents. Pathbreaking contributions in this area include the work by Frankel and Froot (1987) and Froot and Frankel (1989).[24] Frankel and Froot consider the standard spot–forward regression:

$$s_{t+k} - s_t = \alpha + \beta\left(f_t^{(k)} - s_t\right) + \eta_{t+k} \tag{2.73}$$

where, under the risk-neutral efficient markets hypothesis, $\alpha = 0$, $\beta = 1$ and η_{t+k} is

---

[23] Kaminsky and Peruga (1991) also analyse the fact that from October 1979 to February 1985 the forward rate systematically underpredicted the US dollar exchange rates by identifying two peso problems during the sample period.

[24] See Takagi (1991) for a survey of this literature.

orthogonal to the information set available at the time at which expectations are formed. The coefficient β in (2.9) and (2.73) may be expressed as in (2.27), i.e. as the ratio of the covariance between the expected change in the exchange rate and the forward premium to the variance of the forward premium. Also, β may be rewritten, using simple algebraic transformations, as:

$$\beta = 1 - \beta^{RE} - \beta^{RP} \tag{2.74}$$

where:

$$\beta^{RE} = \frac{cov\left(\eta_{t+k},\ f_t^{(k)} - s_t\right)}{var\left(f_t^{(k)} - s_t\right)} \tag{2.75}$$

and:

$$\beta^{RP} = \frac{var(\rho_t) + cov\left(\Delta s_{t+k}^e,\ \rho_t\right)}{var\left(f_t^{(k)} - s_t\right)}. \tag{2.76}$$

β^{RE} may be considered as a coefficient measuring the failure of the rational expectations hypothesis, since if it is non-zero it implies that the forecast error η_{t+k} is correlated with information available at time t, while β^{RP} (which is the same as the regression coefficient δ in (2.28) or (2.30)) may be interpreted as a coefficient measuring time variation in the risk premium. (Note that some researchers have interpreted this coefficient as measuring the departure from risk neutrality, which is not strictly correct since β^{RP} will be equal to zero if there is a constant risk premium.) Thus, if survey data are available so that we can measure forecast errors, the rational expectations hypothesis and the hypothesis of a time-varying risk premium can be tested individually by estimating regressions of the form:

$$s_{t+k}^e - s_t = \alpha + \beta^{RE}\left(f_t^{(k)} - s_t\right) + \epsilon_{1,t+k} \tag{2.77}$$

$$f_t^{(k)} - s_{t+k} = \gamma + \beta^{RP}\left(f_t^{(k)} - s_t\right) + \epsilon_{2,t+k} \tag{2.78}$$

(where $\epsilon_{1,t+k}$ and $\epsilon_{2,t+k}$ are regression error terms) and testing for zero slope coefficients.

Using survey data taken from the American Express Bank (AMEX) and from *Economist* financial reports, Frankel and Froot (1987) provide strong evidence for the view that the standard rejection of the joint null hypothesis underlying the market efficiency hypothesis is largely due to the failure of the rational expectations assumption, given that they find a strongly statistically significant estimate of β^{RE}. Froot and Frankel (1989, pp. 159–60) – using data from AMEX, the *Economist* and Money Market Services (MMS) – find that, contrary to the assumption made by some studies,

the systematic portion of forward discount prediction errors does not capture a time-varying risk premium ... We cannot reject the hypothesis that all the bias is attributable to these systematic expectation errors ... We reject the claim that the variance of the risk premium is greater than the variance of expected depreciation. The reverse appears to be the case ... the market risk premium we are trying to measure is constant. We do find a substantial average level of the risk premium. But, to repeat, the premium does not vary with the forward discount as conventionally thought.

Dominguez (1987) also uses the MMS survey data and finds, consistent with the studies by Frankel and Froot, a statistically significant estimate of β^{RE}, suggesting that irrational expectations formation is the cause of the rejection of the market efficiency hypothesis.[25] In particular, the slope coefficient is insignificantly different from unity in the regression of the market survey forecast onto the forward premium. Hodrick (1992) notes, however, that the R^2 in this regression is far from perfect, as it should be if the forward premium is the market's expected rate of depreciation and risk factors are insignificant.

Using survey data provided by Godwin's, a UK financial consultancy, Taylor (1988) reports results which contradict the finding of the empirical literature discussed above (which is based on US data), since he finds that the failure of the joint null hypothesis is largely due to the existence of a significant risk premium. Nevertheless, MacDonald and Torrance (1988) – using survey data from MMS (UK) – find results consistent with Frankel and Froot.

A slightly different approach has been taken by Liu and Maddala (1992a), who use cointegration techniques in order to test the market efficiency hypothesis in foreign exchange markets using survey data from MMS on the pound sterling, German mark, Swiss franc and Japanese yen *vis-à-vis* the US dollar. They test for cointegration between the spot exchange rate and the expected spot exchange rate, which are both found to be nonstationary variables. Their results are different at the one-week-ahead and the one-month-ahead forecast horizons. For weekly data their conclusion is that the violation of the market efficiency hypothesis is due to risk premia, whereas both risk premia and expectational errors cause the rejection of the joint null hypothesis when monthly data are used. The results of Liu and Maddala (1992a) contradict therefore the findings of Frankel and Froot (1987) in that short-term forecasts (one week) appear to be consistent with rational expectations (although the sample periods examined in the two studies are different and so is the econometric procedure employed). Again, Liu and Maddala (1992b) use survey data and, since the spot exchange rate, the expected exchange rate and the forward exchange rate are all found to follow a unit-root process, use cointegration methods for testing the efficient markets hypothesis. Their results support the rational expectations hypothesis but do not support the market efficiency hypothesis, indirectly implying that the rejection of the joint null hypothesis is due to the presence of risk premia.

In general, the overall conclusion that emerges from survey data studies appears to be that *both* risk aversion *and* departures from rational expectations are responsible for the rejection of the simple efficient markets hypothesis.[26]

2.6 Summary and concluding remarks

We have provided a selective overview of the enormous theoretical and empirical literature on foreign exchange market efficiency. In particular, we have considered the literature related

---

[25] Similar results are also provided by Ito (1990), who uses the Japan Center for International Finance survey data set.

[26] McCallum (1994) suggests that the negativity of the estimated uncovered interest rate parity slope coefficient is consistent with simultaneity induced by the existence of a government reaction function in which the interest rate differential is set in order to avoid large current exchange rate movements as well as to smooth interest rate movements. This is a special case of the general point made by Fama (1984) that negativity of estimated β requires negative covariation between the risk premium and the expected rate of depreciation.

to both the uncovered interest parity condition and the covered interest parity condition, providing an account of the recent econometric methods employed in testing the foreign exchange market efficiency hypothesis.

Overall, regardless of the increasing sophistication of the econometric techniques employed and of the increasing quality of the data sets utilised, one conclusion uncontroversially emerges from this literature: the simple efficient markets hypothesis is rejected by foreign exchange market data. Attempts to rationalise this by retaining the assumption of rational expectations and attempting to model risk premia have met with limited success, especially for plausible degrees of risk aversion. It is difficult to explain the persistent rejection of the simple efficiency hypothesis, and the finding of negative discount bias, moreover, by recourse to explanations such as learning, peso problems and bubbles, because these are small-sample problems. Work based on survey data of exchange rate expectations tends to suggest, overall, that there are failures of the assumptions both of rational expectations *and* of risk neutrality.[27]

Appendix A.   Mean of a log-normally distributed variable

A standard result in statistical theory is that, if a variable Z has a log-normal distribution, i.e. $z = \log Z \sim N(\mu_z, \sigma_z^2)$, then $E(Z) = E[\exp(z)] = \exp(\mu_z + \frac{1}{2}\sigma_z^2)$. To see this, note that:

$$E(Z) = E[\exp(z)]$$

$$= \int_{-\infty}^{\infty} \phi(z)\exp(z)dz \qquad (2.A1)$$

where $\phi(z)$ is the normal probability density function, so that:

$$E(Z) = \frac{1}{\sigma_z\sqrt{2\pi}} \int_{-\infty}^{\infty} \exp(z)\exp\left(\frac{-1}{2\sigma_z^2}(z - \mu_z)^2\right) dz$$

$$= \frac{1}{\sigma_z\sqrt{2\pi}} \int_{-\infty}^{\infty} \exp(z)\exp\left(\frac{-1}{2\sigma_z^2}(z^2 - 2\mu_z z + \mu_z^2)\right) dz$$

$$= \frac{1}{\sigma_z\sqrt{2\pi}} \int_{-\infty}^{\infty} \exp\left(\frac{-1}{2\sigma_z^2}[z^2 - 2z(\mu_z + \sigma_z^2) + \mu_z^2]\right) dz$$

$$= \exp\left(\mu_z + \frac{1}{2}\sigma_z^2\right) \left\{ \frac{1}{\sigma_z\sqrt{2\pi}} \int_{-\infty}^{\infty} \exp\left(\frac{-1}{2\sigma_z^2}[z - (\mu_z + \sigma_z^2)]^2\right) dz\right\}. \qquad (2.A2)$$

Now the expression in curly braces gives the area under the normal density with mean $\mu_z + \sigma_z^2$ and variance σ_z^2, and this must be equal to unity. Hence:

$$E(Z) = \exp\left(\mu_z + \frac{1}{2}\sigma_z^2\right). \qquad (2.A3)$$

---

[27] Nevertheless, one should not immediately jump to the conclusion that the forward rate contains *no* information useful for predicting the future spot rate, since, while admitting the failure of simple efficiency, the term structure can be utilised to predict the spot rate with surprising accuracy (Clarida and Taylor, 1997; Clarida, Sarno, Taylor and Valente, 2001).

Appendix B. Siegel's paradox

Note that regression relationships involving exchange rates are normally expressed in logarithms in an attempt to circumvent the so-called 'Siegel paradox' (Siegel, 1972): the market expectation of the exchange rate expressed as the domestic price of foreign currency cannot be equal to the reciprocal of the expected value of the exchange rate expressed as the foreign price of domestic currency. This means, for example, that one cannot simultaneously have unbiased expectations of the future value of, say, the euro–dollar exchange rate (euros per dollar) and of dollar–euro exchange rate (dollars per euro). Suppose that, at time t, an agent attaches a range of probabilities to possible values of the exchange rate, expressed as the domestic price of foreign currency, at time $t + k$, S_{t+k}. This is the subjective probability distribution of S_{t+k}. The mean of this distribution is what we normally think of as the market's expected value of S_{t+k} at time t, $E_t(S_{t+k})$. Corresponding to the subjective probability distribution for S_{t+k}, there will be a subjective probability distribution for $1/S_{t+k}$. However:

$$1/E_t(S_{t+k}) \neq E_t(1/S_{t+k}). \qquad (2.B1)$$

This is a special case of a mathematical result applying to nonlinear functions in general, known as Jensen's inequality. Researchers often try to circumvent this problem by expressing the exchange rates in logarithms, since instead of taking reciprocals to change the numéraire currency, we simply multiply by minus unity, which is a linear transformation, so that Jensen's inequality does not apply. Algebraically:

$$E_t[\log_e(1/S_{t+k})] = E_t\left(-\log_e S_{t+k}\right) \qquad (2.B2)$$

or, for $s_{t+k} = \log_e S_{t+k}$:

$$E_t\left(-s_{t+k}\right) = -E_t\left(s_{t+k}\right). \qquad (2.B3)$$

In fact, though, agents must still form expectations of final payoffs S_{t+k} and $1/S_{t+k}$, so that it is not clear that taking logarithms does avoid the problem.

One can gain further insight into the Siegel paradox as follows. We are interested in the forward rate (in levels) as a spot rate predictor:

$$F_t^{(k)} = E_t(S_{t+k}). \qquad (2.B4)$$

Now, suppose that the exchange rate is log-normally conditionally distributed, so that, given information at time t, Ω_t say, $\log_e S_{t+k} = s_{t+k}$ is normally distributed:[28]

$$s_{t+k}|\Omega_t \sim N[E_t(s_{t+k}), var_t(s_{t+k})]. \qquad (2.B5)$$

---

[28] Note that this assumption is compatible with s_t following a unit-root process, since it is the *conditional* distribution we are interested in. Suppose, for example that the log exchange rate followed a second-order autoregressive unit-root process $s_t = \rho s_{t-1} + (1 - \rho)s_{t-2} + \varepsilon_t$, where $\varepsilon_t \sim N(0, \sigma^2)$. Then the distribution of s_{t+1} conditional on information available at time t is $s_{t+1}|\Omega_t \sim N(\rho s_t + (1 - \rho)s_{t-1}, \sigma^2)$.

Then from standard statistical theory we know that $E_t(S_{t+k}) = E_t[\exp(s_{t+k})] = \exp[E_t(s_{t+k}) + \frac{1}{2}var_t(s_{t+k})]$ (see Appendix A) so that, again using lower-case letters to denote natural logarithms, (2.B4) can be written in logarithmic form as:

$$f_t^{(k)} = E_t(s_{t+k}) + \frac{1}{2}var_t(s_{t+k}), \qquad (2.B6)$$

so the 'Siegel's paradox' term is the variance term which results from log-linearising (2.B4).

If we wanted to view the relationship after changing the numéraire currency, we should be interested in testing the relationship:

$$\left(1/F_t^{(k)}\right) = E_t(1/S_{t+k}). \qquad (2.B7)$$

If the conditional distribution of S_{t+k} at time t is log-normal as before, then $E_t(1/S_{t+k}) = E_t[\exp(-s_{t+k})] = \exp[-E_t(s_{t+k}) + \frac{1}{2}var_t(s_{t+k})]$, so that in logarithms, (2.B6) becomes:

$$-f_t^{(k)} = -E_t(s_{t+k}) + \frac{1}{2}var_t(s_{t+k}), \qquad (2.B8)$$

or:

$$f_t^{(k)} = E_t(s_{t+k}) - \frac{1}{2}var_t(s_{t+k}), \qquad (2.B9)$$

so that the log-linearisation term enters with a different sign according to which currency is viewed as the numéraire. The empirical significance of the Siegel paradox depends, then, on the size of the conditional variance of the exchange rate. In particular, subtracting s_t from both sides of (2.B9), as is effectively done in most regression-based tests of efficiency, we have:

$$f_t^{(k)} - s_t = E_t(s_{t+k}) - s_t + \frac{1}{2}var_t(s_{t+k}), \qquad (2.B10)$$

so that what matters is the conditional variance of the log exchange rate relative to the forward premium.

Following Frankel and Razin (1980) and Engel (1984), and using an argument based on real as opposed to nominal returns to speculation, it is possible to derive an efficiency condition which is independent of the choice of numéraire currency, under the additional assumption of continuous purchasing power parity (PPP). If expected *real* returns are zero, then we have:[29]

$$E_t\left[\frac{F_t^{(k)} - S_{t+k}}{P_{t+k}}\right] = 0. \qquad (2.B11)$$

But if PPP holds continuously, then $S_{t+k}P_{t+k}^* = P_{t+k}$. Substituting this into equation

---

[29] Note that this is just the Euler equation derived in our discussion of the Lucas model, with the coefficient of relative risk aversion, ϕ, set to zero.

(2.B11) and multiplying the numerator and denominator by $[-1/(F_t^{(k)} S_{t+k})]$ yields:

$$E_t \left[F_t^{(k)} \left(\frac{\frac{1}{F_t^{(k)}} - \frac{1}{S_{t+k}}}{P_{t+k}^*} \right) \right] = 0 \qquad (2.B12)$$

and since $F_t^{(k)}$ is known at time t and non-zero, this implies:

$$E_t \left[\frac{\frac{1}{F_t^{(k)}} - \frac{1}{S_{t+k}}}{P_{t+k}^*} \right] = 0 \qquad (2.B13)$$

– i.e. expected real returns from open forward speculation are also zero in the alternative numéraire currency. As we shall see in Chapter 3, however, the assumption of continuous PPP is a very strong one indeed, and is usually rejected by the data for major currencies and exchange rates.

Appendix C.   Generalised method-of-moments estimators

Under rational expectations and risk neutrality, an n-period forward exchange rate should act as an optimal predictor of the n-period-ahead spot exchange rate:

$$s_{t+k} = f_t^{(k)} + \eta_{t+k} \qquad (2.C1)$$

where η_{t+k} is the unpredictable error due to unforeseen events, news, occurring between time $t + 1$ and $t + k$. Because any $k - 1$ consecutive forecast errors must have at least one news item in common, there will be serial correlation up to order $k - 1$. In fact, this pattern of serial correlation, which suddenly jumps to zero after $k - 1$, is consistent with the forecast error following a moving average of order $k - 1$:

$$\eta_t = u_t + \sum_{i=1}^{k-1} \theta_i u_{t-i}, \qquad (2.C2)$$

where u_t is white noise. Suppose one wished to test the simple efficient markets hypothesis by estimating the equation:[30]

$$s_{t+k} - s_t = \alpha + \beta \left(f_t^{(k)} - s_t \right) + \eta_{t+k} \qquad (2.C3)$$

and testing the null hypothesis $H_0 : (\alpha, \beta) = (0, 1)$. Because of the serially correlated error term, although the OLS estimates of α and β remain unbiased and consistent, the standard formula for the covariance matrix of the point estimator will be a biased and inconsistent estimator, thus precluding valid statistical inference.

The standard solution in regression models with serial correlation is to apply generalised least squares (GLS). However, as noted by, among others, Flood and Garber (1980), GLS is generally not the appropriate procedure in models involving rational expectations. This

---

[30] We shall discuss methods-of-moments estimation primarily in terms of estimating an equation such as (2.C3). It should be clear, however, that the procedures discussed are quite general.

can be seen as follows. Write η_{t+k} explicitly as a moving average process:

$$\eta_{t+k} = \theta(L) u_{t+k} \tag{2.C4}$$

where $\theta(L)$ is a $(k-1)$-th order scalar polynomial in the lag operator:

$$\theta(L) = 1 + \sum_{i=1}^{k-1} \theta_i L^i. \tag{2.C5}$$

From (2.C4):

$$\theta^{-1}(L)\eta_{t+k} = u_{t+k}. \tag{2.C6}$$

Thus, passing every variable in (2.C3) through the filter $\theta^{-1}(L)$ will yield an equation with a white-noise disturbance:

$$\theta^{-1}(L)(s_{t+k} - s_t) = \alpha\theta^{-1}(1) + \beta\theta^{-1}(L)\big(f_t^{(k)} - s_t\big) + u_{t+k}. \tag{2.C7}$$

Given $\theta(L)$, GLS amounts to estimating (2.C7) by OLS. In practice, of course, the parameters of $\theta(L)$ will not be known, so that some kind of nonlinear estimation procedure will be required. In general, however, equation (2.C7) should satisfy the classical assumptions for OLS to be valid for this kind of GLS procedure to be valid. In particular, the error term must be independent of the regressors. Note, however, that by (2.C6):

$$E\big\{\big[\theta^{-1}(L)\big(f_t^{(k)} - s_t\big)\big]u_{t+k}\big\} = E\big\{\big[\theta^{-1}(L)\big(f_t^{(k)} - s_t\big)\big]\big[\theta^{-1}(L)\eta_{t+k}\big]\big\}. \tag{2.C8}$$

Now, past news, contained in $\theta^{-1}(L)\eta_{t+k}$, will in general not be orthogonal to later values of the forward premium, contained in $\theta^{-1}(L)(f_t^{(k)} - s_t)$ and hence:

$$E\big\{\big[\theta^{-1}(L)\big(f_t^{(k)} - s_t\big)\big]u_{t+k}\big\} \neq 0 \tag{2.C9}$$

– even though u_t is itself serially uncorrelated. Thus, GLS estimation may yield invalid inferences.

Hansen (1982) suggests the following solution to this problem. Write (2.C3) in matrix notation as:

$$S = FB + \eta \tag{2.C10}$$

where:

$$S' = [(s_{k+1} - s_1)\,(s_{k+2} - s_2)\,\ldots\,(s_{k+T} - s_T)]$$

$$F' = \begin{bmatrix} 1 & 1 & \cdots & 1 \\ \big(f_1^{(k)} - s_1\big) & \big(f_2^{(k)} - s_2\big) & \cdots & \big(f_T^{(k)} - s_T\big) \end{bmatrix}$$

$$\eta' = [\eta_{k+1}\,\eta_{k+2}\,\ldots\,\eta_{k+T}]$$

$$B' = [\alpha\,\beta] \tag{2.C11}$$

with T being the number of observations. The OLS estimator of B is:

$$\widehat{B}' = (F'F)^{-1}F'S, \tag{2.C12}$$

which will be unbiased and consistent even though there is serial correlation of the error term, and the standard estimator of its covariance matrix is:

$$\widehat{cov}(\widehat{B}) = s^2(F'F)^{-1} \tag{2.C13}$$

where:

$$s^2 = \widehat{\eta}'\widehat{\eta}/(T-2) \text{ and } \widehat{\eta} = S - F\widehat{B}. \tag{2.C14}$$

Now (2.C13) will only be valid for an estimator of B as given by (2.C12) if the disturbance vector (η in (2.C10)), has a scalar covariance matrix such as:

$$cov(\eta) = \sigma^2 I. \tag{2.C15}$$

If, however, the elements of η follow a moving average process, the covariance matrix will be non-scalar:

$$cov(\eta) = \Omega. \tag{2.C16}$$

If (2.C16) holds, then the true covariance matrix of the OLS estimator is given by:

$$cov(\widehat{B}) = (F'F)^{-1}(F'\Omega F)(F'F)^{-1}. \tag{2.C17}$$

Hansen's (1982) procedure simply amounts to obtaining a consistent estimate of (2.C17) by replacing the unknown matrix Ω in (2.C17) with a consistent estimator. Since the OLS estimator is consistent, the OLS residuals defined by (2.C14) can be used to construct a consistent estimator of Ω.

Suppose that the autocovariances of the moving average process characterising the disturbance term can be assumed to be constant. Then, since each element of η is serially correlated up to order $k - 1$, Ω will be a symmetric band matrix. Let $\gamma(\tau)$ denote the τ-th order error autocovariance:

$$\gamma(\tau) = E(\eta_{t+k}, \eta_{t+k-\tau}). \tag{2.C18}$$

Then the main diagonal of Ω will have $\gamma(0)$ in each element and the τ-th off-diagonal band will have a typical element ω_τ given by:

$$\omega_\tau = \begin{cases} \gamma(\tau) & \tau = 1, \ldots, k-1 \\ 0 & \tau = k, \ldots, T. \end{cases} \tag{2.C19}$$

Hansen (1982) suggests estimating $\gamma(\tau)$ by the sample moments, i.e.:

$$\widehat{\gamma}(\tau) = \sum_{t=\tau+1}^{T} \widehat{\eta}_{t+k}\widehat{\eta}_{t+k-\tau}. \tag{2.C20}$$

Hansen demonstrates that the following method-of-moments covariance matrix estimator is a consistent estimator of (2.C17):

$$cov(\widehat{B}) = (F'F)^{-1}F'\widehat{\Omega}F(F'F)^{-1} \tag{2.C21}$$

where the estimated $\widehat{\Omega}$ is a $(T \times T)$ symmetric band matrix with the estimated $\widehat{\gamma}(0)$ on the main diagonal and the estimated $\widehat{\omega}_t$ on the t-th off-diagonal band:

$$\widehat{\omega}_\tau = \begin{cases} \widehat{\gamma}(\tau) & \tau = 1, \ldots, k - 1 \\ 0 & \tau = k, \ldots, T. \end{cases} \tag{2.C22}$$

This is the procedure adopted by Hansen and Hodrick (1980). Hansen (1982) also outlines a slightly less restrictive procedure which does not require constant autocovariances, for example when the news term displays heteroscedasticity. If this is the case, we may have

$$E(\eta_{t+k} \eta_{t+k-\tau}) \neq E(\eta_{s+k} \eta_{s+k-\tau}) \tag{2.C23}$$

for some s and t, $s \neq t$. In this case, each element in the lower triangular portion of $\widehat{\Omega}$ (a total of $T(T + 1)/2$ elements) must be estimated separately. Again, Hansen shows that, under certain regularity conditions, an appropriate, consistent estimator of the covariance matrix can be obtained using the sample moments. In particular, Hansen suggests estimating the individual autocovariances as follows. Define:

$$\gamma(i, j) = E(\eta_i \eta_j). \tag{2.C24}$$

Then use the method-of-moments estimator:

$$\widehat{\gamma}(i, j) = \begin{cases} \widehat{\eta}_i \widehat{\eta}_j & \text{if } |i - j| < k \\ 0 & \text{if } |i - j| \geq k \end{cases} \tag{2.C25}$$

and:

$$\widehat{\gamma}(i, j) = \widehat{\gamma}(j, i). \tag{2.C26}$$

The method-of-moments estimator of the covariance matrix in (2.C17) is then given by:

$$cov(\widehat{B}) = (F'F)^{-1} F' \widetilde{\Omega} F (F'F)^{-1} \tag{2.C27}$$

where $\widetilde{\Omega}$ is a symmetric band matrix with (i, j)-th element $\widehat{\gamma}(i, j)$.

Thus, a straightforward solution to the problem of estimating (2.C3) and drawing statistical inferences is to estimate the model by OLS and use a method-of-moments correction to the covariance matrix given either by (2.C21) (assuming constant variances and autocovariances) or (2.C27) (allowing for possible temporal variation in the variances and autocovariances).

One problem with these method-of-moments estimators of Ω is that there is no guarantee that they will be positive definite in small samples. Newey and West (1987) suggest a consistent estimator of Ω which, in general terms, amounts to using one of the above method-of-moments procedures but with discount factors applied to the autocovariances. Newey and West suggest, for example, estimating $\gamma(i, j)$ in (2.C27) by:

$$\widehat{\gamma}(i, j) = \begin{cases} \widehat{\eta}_i \widehat{\eta}_j \delta(i, j) & \text{if } |i - j| < k \\ 0 & \text{if } |i - j| \geq k \end{cases} \tag{2.C28}$$

where the weights $\delta(i, j)$ are given by:

$$\delta(i, j) = [|i - j|/(m + 1)] \tag{2.C29}$$

where m is chosen just large enough to guarantee positive definiteness. Newey and West suggest setting $m = k$, while Frankel and Froot (1987) set $m = 2k$.

Cumby and Obstfeld (1984) point out that although OLS will provide a consistent estimator of the parameters in equations such as (2.C3), it will generally be inefficient relative to an appropriate instrumental variables estimator. Since the forecast error η_{t+k} must be orthogonal to *all* elements of the information set at time t, an instrumental variables estimator can exploit this additional information. Moreover, if (2.C3) omits a stochastic, time-varying risk premium, then the forward premium may be serially correlated with the error term, thereby requiring an instrumental variables estimator. Appropriate instrumental variables estimators in this context have been developed by Hansen (1982) and Cumby, Huizinga and Obstfeld (1983).

Again consider the model in matrix notation, equation (2.C10), and suppose we have a matrix of observations on a set of instruments, Z, correlated with F but orthogonal to η. Hansen (1982) shows that the best estimator of B based on Z is given by:

$$\widetilde{B} = (F'ZM^{-1}Z'F)^{-1}F'ZM^{-1}Z'S \tag{2.C30}$$

where:

$$M = \plim_{T \to \infty}[T^{-1}E(Z'\eta\eta'Z)]. \tag{2.C31}$$

The asymptotic distribution of $\widetilde{B}$ is given by:

$$\sqrt{T}(\widetilde{B} - B) \sim N(0, \Sigma) \tag{2.C32}$$

where:

$$\Sigma = \plim_{T \to \infty} T^2[F'ZM^{-1}Z'F]^{-1}. \tag{2.C33}$$

A consistent estimator of the covariance matrix of $\widetilde{B}$ may then be obtained, for example, by estimating M by:

$$\widetilde{M} = T^{-1}Z'\widetilde{\Omega}Z \tag{2.C34}$$

where $\widetilde{\Omega}$ is as defined in (2.C28) but where it is understood that the estimated residual is obtained from a standard generalised instrumental variables estimation. It should also be noted that this estimator is really a more general form of the method-of-moments estimators discussed above – to see this, simply replace Z with F in equations (2.C30)–(2.C34). For examples of applications of this kind of estimator, see e.g. Cumby and Obstfeld (1984).

Appendix D.   Cointegration and the Granger representation theorem

Cointegration analysis, as originally developed by Engle and Granger (1987), tells us that any two nonstationary series processes, which are found to be integrated of the same order, are cointegrated if a linear combination of the two exists which is itself stationary.[31, 32] If this is the case, then the nonstationarity of one series exactly offsets the nonstationarity of the other and a long-run relationship is established between the two variables. Generally, if two series x_t and y_t both have a stationary, invertible, non-deterministic ARMA representation after differencing d times, i.e. they are both integrated of order d, denoted $I(d)$. An alternative way of expressing this is to say that the series have d unit roots. If x_t and y_t are in fact both $I(d)$, then the linear combination:

$$x_t + \alpha y_t = z_t \tag{2.D1}$$

will in general be found to be $I(d)$ as well. If, exceptionally, a parameter α exists such that z_t in (2.D1) is integrated of order $I(d - c)$, $c > 0$, then the two variables are said to be cointegrated of order d, c, or $CI(d, c)$. If this is the case, then over long periods of time they will tend to move according to (2.D1), since deviations from this linear combination – i.e. z_t – are stationary.

In order to test for cointegration, a widely used methodology is the two-step procedure of Engle and Granger (1987). The preliminary step before proceeding to investigate cointegration is to test for nonstationarity of the series considered (see e.g. Spanos, 1976). Fuller (1976) and Dickey and Fuller (1979, 1981) suggest testing for a unit root on a time series x_t by estimating the auxiliary regression:

$$\Delta x_t = \beta x_{t-1} + \sum_{i=1}^{n} \gamma_i \Delta x_{t-i} + \gamma_0 + u_t \tag{2.D2}$$

where the number of lags n is chosen such that u_t is approximately white noise. For stationarity we require $\beta < 0$, while if x_t is a realisation of a (single) unit-root process, we would find $\beta = 0$. In order to understand the reasoning behind this unit-root test statistic, consider the following $(n + 1)$-th order representation of x_t:

$$x_t = \lambda_0 + \lambda_1 x_{t-1} + \lambda_2 x_{t-2} + \cdots + \lambda_{n+1} x_{t-n-1} + u_t. \tag{2.D3}$$

Now reparameterise (2.D3) as:

$$\Delta x_t = \lambda_0 + \left(\sum_{i=1}^{n+1} \lambda_i - 1 \right) x_{t-1} - \left(\sum_{i=2}^{n+1} \lambda_i \right) \Delta x_{t-1}$$
$$- \left(\sum_{i=3}^{n+1} \lambda_i \right) \Delta x_{t-2} - \cdots - \lambda_{n+1} \Delta x_{t-n} + u_t \tag{2.D4}$$

which is of the form (2.D2). The condition we require for stationarity is that the sum of the autoregressive parameters λ_i is less than one, whilst the sum is equal to unity if the series x_t has a unit root. Therefore, we require the coefficient of x_{t-1} in (2.D2) to be significantly negative for a unit root to be precluded.

The test statistic is the standard 't-ratio' for the estimate of β and the rejection region consists of large negative values. Unfortunately, this 't-ratio' does not follow the standard Student's t-distribution under the null hypothesis, because of the theoretically infinite

---

[31] Strictly speaking, a time series is a particular realisation of a time series process, although as the treatment here is informal, we shall use the terms 'time series' and 'process' interchangeably.

[32] Here, stationarity is understood in terms of *covariance stationarity*: a time series is covariance stationary if it has a constant mean, a finite variance and if the covariance between any two observations is a function only of their distance apart in time.

variance of x_t. Empirical critical values computed using Monte Carlo methods have to be considered. They are given by Fuller (1976) for the Dickey–Fuller statistic (where no lags are included in (2.D2)) and for the augmented Dickey–Fuller (ADF, so termed if lags are included in (2.D2)). Mackinnon (1991) has tabulated response surface estimates of the critical values for the DF and ADF, allowing them to be derived for a variety of sample sizes and number of variables.

If the null hypothesis of nonstationarity of the individual series is rejected, then we cannot go any further. By contrast, if the null hypothesis is not rejected, then it is correct and advisable to test for a unit root on the first difference of the series in question in order to exactly specify the order of integration.[33] Only at this stage might the possibility of cointegration arise. If a linear combination between two or more series is defined which reduces the order of integration, the variables in the estimated regression are said to be cointegrated. Typically, we are dealing with $I(1)$ series and $I(0)$ linear combinations. A straightforward way of estimating the linear combination is by OLS applied to the cointegrating regression:

$$x_t = \delta + \alpha y_t + v_t \qquad (2.D5)$$

where v_t is the fitted residual. Indeed, if cointegration characterises the estimated regression, the OLS estimator of the cointegrating parameter α converges to the true α, as the number of observations increases, more rapidly than it usually does for the OLS estimator under classical assumptions. This is the so-called property of 'super consistency'. More formally, estimates of α are highly efficient with variances $0(T^{-2})$ compared to more usual situations where the variances are $0(T^{-1})$, T being the sample size (Stock, 1987). Offsetting the result of super consistency, however, there is another feature of cointegration analysis: small-sample bias is present in the OLS estimator of the cointegrating parameter and its limiting distribution is non-normal with a non-zero mean. Moreover, Banerjee, Dolado, Hendry and Smith (1986) show that a high R^2 can provide an index of the value of the estimate.[34]

Nevertheless, if the no-cointegration hypothesis cannot be rejected, then the estimated regression is 'spurious' and has no economic meaning, as first discussed by Granger and Newbold (1974). Granger and Newbold also point out that the least squares estimator is not even consistent in this case and customary tests of statistical inference break down. They suggest using the Durbin–Watson statistic, DW, which would tend to a low value since the residuals would be nonstationary. A simple general rule suggested is that $R^2 > DW$ represents a serious indication that the estimated regression is spurious (Granger and Newbold, 1974).

So, if we cannot reject the hypothesis that both x_t and y_t are $I(1)$, then the second step of the procedure is to test the hypothesis of no cointegration:

$$H_0 : v_t \sim I(1) \qquad (2.D6)$$

---

[33] Dickey and Pantula (1988) suggest an extension of the basic procedure if more than one unit root is suspected. The methodology simply consists of performing (augmented) Dickey–Fuller tests on successive differences of the series in question, starting from higher-order unit roots and testing down.

[34] Note, however, that in multivariate models a high R^2 does not imply that each element in the cointegrating vector is estimated with neglegible bias. Therefore, the use of R^2 as a rough index of the small-sample bias is limited to simple bivariate models (Banerjee, Dolado, Hendry and Smith, 1986).

and in practice we test for a unit root in the residual from the cointegrating regression (2.D5) in the same way as outlined for testing for a unit root on any time series. The critical values tabulated by Fuller (1976) cannot be used, however, when testing for nonstationarity in the cointegrating residuals. It is clear intuitively that, since OLS chooses the estimator which minimises the residual variance, we might expect to reject the hypothesis of nonstationarity too often. Appropriate critical values, computed by Engle and Granger (1987) by using Monte Carlo simulations, have to be used to test for a unit root on the cointegrating residuals.[35]

An important implication of cointegration is given by the Granger representation theorem (Engle and Granger, 1987) which shows that if two or more $I(1)$ variables are cointegrated, then there must exist an error correction representation governing their dynamic evolution. This is easy to illustrate for the two-variable case. Suppose that $x_t \sim I(1)$ and $y_t \sim I(1)$ but they are cointegrated such that $z_t \equiv (x_t - \beta y_t) \sim I(0)$. Then z_t must have a stationary autoregressive moving average (ARMA) representation. For simplicity, suppose that this is simply an AR(2) and that y_t is known to follow a simple random walk:

$$(x_t - \beta y_t) = \rho_1(x_{t-1} - \beta y_{t-1}) + \rho_2(x_{t-2} - \beta y_{t-2}) + v_t \qquad (2.D7)$$

$$\Delta y_t = \varepsilon_t \qquad (2.D8)$$

where v_t and ε_t are white-noise disturbances. Manipulating (2.D7) and (2.D8), it is easy to derive the error correction representation:

$$\Delta x_t = \theta_1 \Delta x_{t-1} + \theta_1 \Delta y_{t-1} + \lambda(x_{t-1} - \beta y_{t-1}) + \eta_t \qquad (2.D9)$$

where $\theta_1 = -\rho_2$, $\theta_2 = \rho_2\beta$, $\lambda = (\rho_1 + \rho_2 - 1)$ and $\eta_t = (v_t + \beta\varepsilon_t)$. Since $z_t \sim I(0)$, we must have $(\rho_1 + \rho_2) < 1$, so that $\lambda < 0$. Hence, the error correction form (2.D9) implies that if x is above or below its equilibrium value in relation to y in the previous period, it will tend to adjust towards the equilibrium value in the current period. Note that this simple example is for illustrative purposes only and, in particular, we have assumed there is no feedback from the error correction term $(x_t - \beta y_{t-1})$ onto Δy_t. In general the Granger representation theorem would imply that there must be feedback of this kind onto either Δx_t or Δy_t, or both. The theorem also implies the converse: if an error correction representation between two or more $I(1)$ variables exists, then they must be cointegrated.

References and further readings

Adler, M. and B. Dumas (1983), 'International Portfolio Choice and Corporation Finance: A Synthesis', *Journal of Finance*, 38, pp. 925–84.

Aliber, R.Z. (1973), 'The Interest Rate Parity Theorem: A Reinterpretation', *Journal of Political Economy*, 81, pp. 1451–9.

Baillie, R.T., R.E. Lippens and P.C. McMahon (1983), 'Testing Rational Expectations and Efficiency in the Foreign Exchange Market', *Econometrica*, 51, pp. 553–63.

Balke, N.S. and M.E. Wohar (1998), 'Nonlinear Dynamics and Covered Interest Rate Parity', *Empirical Economics*, 23, pp. 535–59.

[35] See also the response surface estimates of MacKinnon (1991).

Banerjee, A., J.J. Dolado, D.F. Hendry and G.W. Smith (1986), 'Exploring Equilibrium Relationships in Econometrics through Static Models: Some Monte Carlo Evidence', *Oxford Bulletin of Economics and Statistics*, 3, pp. 253–78.

Bekaert, G. (1994), 'The Time Variation of Risk and Return in Foreign Exchange Markets: A General Equilibrium Perspective', *Review of Financial Studies*, 9, pp. 427–70.

Bekaert, G. and R.J. Hodrick (1992), 'Characterizing Predictable Components in Excess Returns on Equity and Foreign Exchange Markets', *Journal of Finance*, 47, pp. 467–509.

(1993), 'On Biases in the Measurement of Foreign Exchange Risk Premiums', *Journal of International Money and Finance*, 12, pp. 115–38.

Beveridge, S. and C.R. Nelson (1981), 'A New Approach to Decomposition of Economic Time Series into Permanent and Transitory Components with Particular Attention to Measurement of the "Business Cycle" ', *Journal of Monetary Economics*, 7, pp. 151–74.

Bilson, J.F. (1981), 'The "Speculative Efficiency" Hypothesis', *Journal of Business*, 54, pp. 435–51.

Borensztein, E.R. (1987), 'Alternative Hypotheses about the Excess Return on Dollar Assets, 1980–84', *International Monetary Fund Staff Papers*, 34, pp. 29–59.

Branson, W.H. (1969), 'The Minimum Covered Interest Needed for International Arbitrage Activity', *Journal of Political Economy*, 77, pp. 1028–35.

Campbell, J.Y. and R.J. Shiller (1987), 'Cointegration and Tests of Present Value Models', *Journal of Political Economy*, 95, pp. 1062–88.

Cheung, Y.-W. and K.S. Lai (1993), 'Finite-Sample Sizes of Johansen's Likelihood Ratio Tests for Cointegration', *Oxford Bulletin of Economics and Statistics*, 55, pp. 313–28.

Clarida, R.H., L. Sarno, M.P. Taylor and G. Valente (2001), 'The Out-of-Sample Success of Term Structure Models as Exchange Rate Predictors: A Step Beyond', *Journal of International Economics*, forthcoming.

Clarida, R.H. and M.P. Taylor (1997), 'The Term Structure of Forward Exchange Premiums and the Forecastability of Spot Exchange Rates: Correcting the Errors', *Review of Economics and Statistics*, 79, pp. 353–61.

Clinton, K. (1988), 'Transactions Costs and Covered Interest Arbitrage: Theory and Evidence', *Journal of Political Economy*, 96, pp. 358–70.

Cumby, R.E., J. Huizinga and M. Obstfeld (1983), 'Two-Step Two-Stage Least Squares Estimation in Models with Rational Expectations', *Journal of Econometrics*, 21, pp. 333–55.

Cumby, R.E. and M. Obstfeld (1981), 'A Note on Exchange-Rate Expectations and Nominal Interest Differentials: A Test of the Fisher Hypothesis', *Journal of Finance*, 36, pp. 697–703.

(1984), 'International Interest Rate and Price Level Linkages under Flexible Exchange Rates: A Review of Recent Evidence', in J.F.O. Bilson and R.C. Marston (eds.), *Exchange Rate Theory and Practice*, National Bureau of Economic Research Conference Report, Chicago: University of Chicago Press, pp. 121–51.

Davidson, J., D.F. Hendry, F. Srba and S. Yeo (1978), 'Econometric Modelling of the Aggregate Time Series Relationships Between Consumers Expenditure and Income in the United Kingdom', *Economic Journal*, 88, pp. 661–92.

Dickey, D. and W.A. Fuller (1979), 'Distribution of the Estimators for Autoregressive Time Series with a Unit Root', *Journal of the American Statistical Association*, 74, pp. 427–31.

(1981), 'Likelihood Ratio Statistics for Autoregressive Time Series with a Unit Root', *Econometrica*, 49, pp. 1057–72.

Dickey, D. and S.G. Pantula (1988), 'Determining the Order of Differencing in Autoregressive Processes', *Journal of Business and Economic Statistics*, 5, pp. 455–61.

Dominguez, K.M. (1987), 'Exchange Rate Efficiency and the Behaviour of International Asset Markets', unpublished Ph.D. thesis, Yale University.

Domowitz, I. and C.S. Hakkio (1985), 'Conditional Variance and the Risk Premium in the Foreign Exchange Market', *Journal of International Economics*, 19, pp. 47–66.

Dooley, M.P. and P. Isard (1980), 'Capital Controls, Political Risk, and Deviations from Interest-Rate Parity', *Journal of Political Economy*, 88, pp. 370–84.

Dooley, M.P. and J.R. Shafer (1984), 'Analysis of Short-Run Exchange Rate Behaviour: March 1973 to November 1981', in D. Bigman and T. Taya (eds.), *Floating Exchange Rates and the State of World Trade Payments*, Cambridge, Mass.: Harper and Row, Ballinger, pp. 43–69.

Einzig, P. (1937), *The Theory of Forward Exchange*, London: Macmillan.

(1962), *The History of Foreign Exchange*, London: Macmillan.

Engel, C. (1984), 'Testing for the Absence of Expected Real Profits from Forward Market Speculation', *Journal of International Economics*, 17, pp. 299–308.

(1992), 'On the Foreign Exchange Risk Premium in a General Equilibrium Model', *Journal of International Economics*, 32, pp. 305–19.

Engel, C. and J. Hamilton (1990), 'Long Swings in the Dollar: Are They in the Data and Do Markets Know It?', *American Economic Review*, 80, pp. 689–713.

Engel, C. and A.P. Rodrigues (1989), 'Tests of International CAPM with Time-Varying Covariances', *Journal of Applied Econometrics*, 4, pp. 119–38.

Engle, R.F. and C.W.J. Granger (1987), 'Co-integration and Error Correction: Representation, Estimation, and Testing', *Econometrica*, 55, pp. 251–76.

Evans, G.W. (1986), 'A Test for Speculative Bubbles in the Sterling Dollar Exchange Rate: 1981–84', *American Economic Review*, 76, pp. 621–36.

(1991), 'Pitfalls in Testing for Explosive Bubbles in Asset Prices', *American Economic Review*, 81, pp. 922–30.

Evans, M.D.D. and K.K. Lewis (1995), 'Do Long-Term Swings in the Dollar Affect Estimates of the Risk Premia?', *Review of Financial Studies*, 8, pp. 709–42.

Fama, E.F. (1970), 'Efficient Capital Markets: A Review of Theory and Empirical Work', *Journal of Finance*, 25, 383–423.

(1976), 'Forward Rates as Predictors of Future Spot Rates', *Journal of Financial Economics*, 3, pp. 361–77.

(1984), 'Forward and Spot Exchange Rates', *Journal of Monetary Economics*, 14, pp. 319–38.

Flood, R.P. and P.M. Garber (1980), 'Market Fundamentals versus Price-Level Bubbles: The First Tests', *Journal of Political Economy*, 88, pp. 745–70.

Flood, R.P. and R.J. Hodrick (1990), 'On Testing for Speculative Bubbles', *Journal of Economic Perspectives*, 4, pp. 85–101.

Frankel, J.A. (1982), 'A Test of Perfect Substitutability in the Foreign Exchange Market', *Southern Economic Journal*, 49, pp. 406–16.

(1988), 'Recent Estimates of Time-Variation in the Conditional Variance and in the Exchange Risk Premium', *Journal of International Money and Finance*, 7, pp. 115–25.

Frankel, J.A. and K.A. Froot (1987), 'Using Survey Data to Test Standard Propositions Regarding Exchange Rate Expectations', *American Economic Review*, 77, pp. 133–53.

Frankel, J.A. and A.T. MacArthur (1988), 'Political vs. Currency Premia in International Real Interest Rate Differentials: A Study of Forward Rates for 24 Countries', *European Economic Review*, 32, pp. 1083–114.

Frenkel, J.A. (1976), 'A Monetary Approach to the Exchange Rate: Doctrinal Aspects and Empirical Evidence', *Scandinavian Journal of Economics*, 78, pp. 200–24.

Frenkel, J.A. and R.M. Levich (1975), 'Covered Interest Arbitrage: Unexploited Profits?', *Journal of Political Economy*, 83, pp. 325–38.

(1977), 'Transaction Costs and Interest Arbitrage: Tranquil versus Turbulent Periods', *Journal of Political Economy*, 85, pp. 1209–26.

Froot, K.A. and J.A. Frankel (1989), 'Forward Discount Bias: Is It an Exchange Risk Premium?', *Quarterly Journal of Economics*, 104, pp. 139–61.

Froot, K.A. and R.H. Thaler (1990), 'Foreign Exchange', *Journal of Economic Perspectives*, 4, pp. 179–92.

Fuller, W.A. (1976), *Introduction to Statistical Time Series*, New York: Wiley and Sons.

Geweke, J.F. and E.L. Feige (1979), 'Some Joint Tests of the Efficiency of Markets for Forward Foreign Exchange', *Review of Economics and Statistics*, 61, pp. 334–41.

Giddy, I.H. and G. Dufey (1975), 'The Random Behaviour of the Flexible Exchange Rates: Implications for Forecasting', *Journal of International Business Studies*, 6, pp. 1–32.

Giovannini, A. and P. Jorion (1987), 'Interest Rates and Risk Premia in the Stock Market and in the Foreign Exchange Market', *Journal of International Money and Finance*, 6, pp. 107–23.

    (1989), 'The Time Variation of Risk and Return in the Foreign Exchange and Stock Markets', *Journal of Finance*, 44, pp. 307–25.

Granger, C.W. and P. Newbold (1974), 'Spurious Regressions in Econometrics', *Journal of Econometrics*, 2, pp. 111–20.

Gregory, A.W. and M.R. Veall (1987), 'Formulating Wald Tests of the Restrictions Implied by the Rational Expectations Hypothesis', *Journal of Applied Econometrics*, 2, pp. 61–8.

Hakkio, C.S. (1981), 'Expectations and the Forward Exchange Rate', *International Economic Review*, 22, pp. 663–78.

Hansen, L.P. (1982), 'Large Sample Properties of Generalised Method of Moments Estimators', *Econometrica*, 50, pp. 1029–54.

Hansen, L.P. and R.J. Hodrick (1980), 'Forward Exchange Rates as Optimal Predictors of Future Spot Rates: An Econometric Analysis', *Journal of Political Economy*, 88, pp. 829–53.

Hansen, L.P. and R. Jagannathan (1991), 'Implications of Security Market Data for Models of Dynamic Economies', *Journal of Political Economy*, 99, pp. 225–62.

Hausman, J.A. (1978), 'Specification Tests in Econometrics', *Econometrica*, 46, pp. 1251–71.

Hawtrey, R.G. (1932), *The Art of Central Banking*, London: Longmans.

Hayashi, F. and C.A. Sims (1983), 'Nearly Efficient Estimation of Time Series Models with Predetermined, but Not Exogenous, Instruments', *Econometrica*, 51, pp. 783–98.

Hendry, D.F., A.R. Pagan and J.D. Sargan (1984), 'Dynamic Specification', in Z. Griliches and M.D. Intriligator (eds.), *Handbook of Econometrics*, vol. I, Amsterdam: North-Holland.

Hodrick, R.J. (1987), *The Empirical Evidence on the Efficiency of Forward and Futures Foreign Exchange Markets*, London: Harwood.

    (1992), 'An Interpretation of Foreign Exchange Market Efficiency Test', Kellogg Graduate School of Management, Northwestern University, mimeo.

Hodrick, R.J. and S. Srivastava (1984), 'An Investigation of Risk and Return in Forward Foreign Exchange', *Journal of International Money and Finance*, 3, pp. 5–29.

    (1986), 'The Covariation of Risk Premiums and Expected Future Spot Exchange Rates', *Journal of International Money and Finance*, 5, Supplement, pp. 5–21.

Huang, R.D. (1981), 'The Monetary Approach to Exchange Rate in an Efficient Foreign Exchange Market: Tests Based on Volatility', *Journal of Finance*, 36, pp. 31–41.

Ito, T. (1990), 'Foreign Exchange Rate Expectations: Micro Survey Data', *American Economic Review*, 80, pp. 434–49.

Johansen, S. (1988), 'Statistical Analysis of Cointegrating Vectors', *Journal of Economic Dynamics and Control*, 12, pp. 231–54.

    (1991), 'Estimation and Hypothesis Testing of Cointegrating Vectors in Gaussian Vector Autoregressive Models', *Econometrica*, 59, pp. 1551–80.

    (1995), *Likelihood-Based Inference in Cointegrated VAR Models*, Oxford: Oxford University Press.

Kaminsky, G.L. (1993), 'Is There a Peso Problem? Evidence from the Dollar/Pound Exchange Rate, 1976–1987', *American Economic Review*, 83, pp. 450–72.

Kaminsky, G.L. and R. Peruga (1991), 'Credibility Crises: The Dollar in the Early 1980s', *Journal of International Money and Finance*, 10, pp. 170–92.

Keynes, J.M. (1923), *A Tract on Monetary Reform*, London: Macmillan.

Kohlhagen, S.W. (1978), 'A Model of Optimal Foreign Exchange Hedging without Exchange Rate Projections', *Journal of International Business Studies*, 9, pp. 9–19.

Krasker, W.S. (1980), 'The "Peso Problem" in Testing the Efficiency of Forward Exchange Markets', *Journal of Monetary Economics*, 6, pp. 269–76.

LeRoy, S.F. (1984), 'Efficiency and the Variability of Asset Prices', *American Economic Review*, 74, pp. 183–7.

Levich, R.M. (1985), 'Empirical Studies of Exchange Rates: Price Behavior, Rate Determination, and Market Efficiency', in R.W. Jones and P.B. Kenen (eds.), *Handbook of International Economics*, vol. II, Amsterdam: North-Holland, pp. 979–1040.

Levich, R.M. and L.R. Thomas (1993), 'The Significance of Technical Trading-Rule Profits in the Foreign Exchange Market: A Bootstrap Approach', *Journal of International Money and Finance*, 12, pp. 451–74.

Levy, E. and A.R. Nobay (1986), 'The Speculative Efficiency Hypothesis: A Bivariate Analysis', *Economic Journal*, 96, Supplement, pp. 109–21.

Lewis, K.K. (1988), 'The Persistence of the "Peso Problem" When Policy Is Noisy', *Journal of International Money and Finance*, 7, pp. 5–21.

(1989a), 'Can Learning Affect Exchange-Rate Behaviour? The Case of the Dollar in the Early 1980s', *Journal of Monetary Economics*, 23, pp. 79–100.

(1989b), 'Changing Beliefs and Systematic Rational Forecast Errors with Evidence from Foreign Exchange', *American Economic Review*, 79, pp. 621–36.

(1991), 'Was There a "Peso Problem" in the U.S. Term Structure of Interest Rates: 1979–1982?', *International Economic Review*, 32, pp. 159–73.

(1995), 'Puzzles in International Financial Markets', in G.M. Grossman and K. Rogoff (eds.), *Handbook of International Economics*, vol. III, Amsterdam: North-Holland, pp. 1913–71.

Liu, P.C. and G.S. Maddala (1992a), 'Using Survey Data to Test Market Efficiency in the Foreign Exchange Markets', *Empirical Economics*, 17, pp. 303–14.

(1992b), 'Rationality of Survey Data and Tests for Market Efficiency in the Foreign Exchange Markets', *Journal of International Money and Finance*, 11, pp. 366–81.

Lizondo, J.S. (1983), 'Foreign Exchange Futures Prices under Fixed Exchange Rates', *Journal of International Economics*, 14, pp. 69–84.

Longworth, D. (1981), 'Testing the Efficiency of the Canadian–U.S. Exchange Market under the Assumption of No Risk Premium', *Journal of Finance*, 36, pp. 43–9.

Lucas, R.E., Jr (1982), 'Interest Rates and Currency Prices in a Two-Country World', *Journal of Monetary Economics*, 10, pp. 335–59.

MacDonald, R. and M.P. Taylor (1991), 'Risk, Efficiency and Speculation in the 1920s Foreign Exchange Market: An Overlapping Data Analysis', *Weltwirtschaftliches Archiv*, 127, pp. 500–23.

(1993), 'The Monetary Approach to the Exchange Rate: Rational Expectations, Long-Run Equilibrium, and Forecasting', *International Monetary Fund Staff Papers*, 40, pp. 89–107.

MacDonald, R. and T. Torrance (1988), 'On Risk, Rationality and Excessive Speculation in the Deutschmark–U.S. Dollar Exchange Market: Some Evidence Using Survey Data', *Oxford Bulletin of Economics and Statistics*, 50, pp. 107–23.

MacKinnon, J.G. (1991), 'Critical Values for Cointegration Tests', in R.F. Engle and C.W.J. Granger (eds.), *Long-Run Economic Relationships: Readings in Cointegration*, Oxford: Oxford University Press, pp. 267–76.

Mark, N.C. (1985), 'On Time Varying Risk Premia in the Foreign Exchange Market: An Econometric Analysis', *Journal of Monetary Economics*, 16, pp. 3–18.

McCallum, B.T. (1976), 'Rational Expectations and the Estimation of Econometric Models: An Alternative Procedure', *International Economic Review*, 17, pp. 484–90.

(1994), 'A Reconsideration of the Uncovered Interest Parity Relationship', *Journal of Monetary Economics*, 33, pp. 105–32.

McCormick, F. (1979), 'Covered Interest Arbitrage: Unexploited Profits? Comment', *Journal of Political Economy*, 87, pp. 411–17.

McCulloch, J.H. (1975), 'Operational Aspects of the Siegel Paradox: Comment', *Quarterly Journal of Economics*, 89, pp. 170–2.

McFarland, J.W., P.C. McMahon and Y. Ngama (1994), 'Forward Exchange Rates and Expectations during the 1920s: A Re-examination of the Evidence', *Journal of International Money and Finance*, 13, pp. 627–36.

Meese, R.A. (1986), 'Testing for Bubbles in Exchange Markets: A Case of Sparkling Rates?', *Journal of Political Economy*, 94, pp. 345–73.

Mussa, M. (1984), 'The Theory of Exchange Rate Determination', in J.F.O. Bilson and R.C. Marston (eds.), *Exchange Rate Theory and Practice*, National Bureau of Economic Research Conference Report, Chicago: University of Chicago Press, pp. 13–58.

Newey, W.K. and K.D. West (1987), 'A Simple, Positive Semi-Definite, Heteroskedasticity and Autocorrelation Consistent Covariance Matrix', *Econometrica*, 55, pp. 703–8.

Peel, D.A. and M.P. Taylor (2002), 'Covered Interest Arbitrage in the Inter-War Period and the Keynes-Einzig Conjecture', *Journal of Money, Credit and Banking*, forthcoming.

Penati, A. and G.G. Pennacchi (1989), 'Optimal Portfolio Choice and the Collapse of a Fixed-Exchange Rate Regime', *Journal of International Economics*, 27, pp. 1–24.

Phillips, P.C.B. and B.E. Hansen (1990), 'Statistical Inference in Instrumental Variables Regression with I(1) Processes', *Review of Economic Studies*, 57, pp. 99–125.

Phillips, P.C.B., J.W. McFarland and P.C. McMahon (1996), 'Robust Tests of Forward Exchange Market Efficiency with Empirical Evidence from the 1920s', *Journal of Applied Econometrics*, 11, pp. 1–22.

Poole, W. (1967), 'Speculative Prices as Random Walks: An Analysis of Ten Time Series of Flexible Exchange Rates', *Southern Economic Journal*, 33, pp. 468–78.

Rogoff, K. (1979), 'Expectations and Exchange Rate Volatility', unpublished Ph.D. thesis, Massachusetts Institute of Technology.

Samuelson, P. (1965), 'Proof that Properly Anticipated Prices Fluctuate Randomly', *Industrial Management Review*, 6, pp. 41–9.

Sarno, L. and M.P. Taylor (1999), 'Moral Hazard, Asset Price Bubbles, Capital Flows, and the East Asian Crisis: The First Tests', *Journal of International Money and Finance*, 18, pp. 637–57.

Shiller, R.J. (1979), 'The Volatility of Long-Term Interest Rates and Expectations Models of the Term Structure', *Journal of Political Economy*, 87, pp. 1190–219.

Sibert, A. (1996), 'Unconventional Preferences: Do They Explain Foreign Exchange Risk Premia?', *Journal of International Money and Finance,* 15, pp. 149–65.

Siegel, J.J. (1972), 'Risk, Interest, and Forward Exchange', *Quarterly Journal of Economics*, 86, pp. 303–9.

Stock, J.H. (1987), 'Asymptotic Properties of Least Squares Estimators of Cointegrating Vectors', *Econometrica*, 55, pp. 1035–56.

Stock, J.H. and M.W. Watson (1987), 'Testing for Common Trends', *Journal of the American Statistical Association*, 83, pp. 1097–107.

Takagi, S. (1991), 'Exchange Rate Expectations: A Survey of Survey Studies', *International Monetary Fund Staff Papers*, 38, pp. 156–83.

Taylor, M.P. (1987), 'Covered Interest Parity: A High-Frequency, High-Quality Data Study', *Economica*, 54, pp. 429–38.

(1988), 'What Do Investment Managers Know? An Empirical Study of Practitioners' Predictions', *Economica*, 55, pp. 185–202.

(1989), 'Covered Interest Arbitrage and Market Turbulence', *Economic Journal*, 99, pp. 376–91.

Taylor, M.P. and D.A. Peel (1998), 'Periodically Collapsing Stock Price Bubbles: A Robust Test', *Economics Letters*, 61, pp. 221–8.

3   Purchasing power parity and the real exchange rate

The purchasing power parity (PPP) exchange rate is the exchange rate between two currencies which would equate the two relevant national price levels if expressed in a common currency at that rate, so that the purchasing power of a unit of one currency would be the same in both economies. This concept of PPP is often termed 'absolute PPP'. 'Relative PPP' is said to hold when the rate of depreciation of one currency relative to another matches the difference in aggregate price inflation between the two countries concerned. If the nominal exchange rate is defined simply as the price of one currency in terms of another, then the real exchange rate is the nominal exchange rate adjusted for relative national price level differences. When PPP holds, the real exchange rate is a constant so that movements in the real exchange rate represent deviations from PPP. Hence, a discussion of the real exchange rate is tantamount to a discussion of PPP.

Although the term 'purchasing power parity' was coined as recently as eighty years ago (Cassel, 1918), it has a very much longer history in economics.[1] While very few contemporary economists would hold that PPP holds continuously in the real world, 'most instinctively believe in some variant of purchasing power parity as an anchor for long-run real exchange rates' (Rogoff, 1996), and indeed the implication or assumption of much reasoning in international macroeconomics is that some form of PPP holds at least as a long-run relationship.[2] Moreover, estimates of PPP exchange rates are important for practical purposes such as determining the degree of misalignment of the nominal exchange rate and the appropriate policy response, the setting of exchange rate parities, and the international comparison of national income levels. It is not surprising, therefore, that a large literature on PPP, both academic and policy-related, has evolved.

[1] The origins of the concept of purchasing power parity have been traced to the writings of scholars from the University of Salamanca in the fifteenth and sixteenth centuries (se e.g. Officer, 1982). Interestingly, the rise in interest in the concept at this time appears to be linked to the prohibition of usury by the Catholic Church. By lending in foreign currency, lenders could justify interest payments by reference to movements in PPP. Thus, Domingo de Bañez could write in 1594: 'one party may lawfully agree to repay a large sum to another, corresponding to the amount required to buy the same parcel of goods that the latter might have bought if he had not delivered his money in exchange'.

[2] This is true both of traditional international macroeconomic analysis (e.g. Dornbusch, 1980) and 'new' open economy models based on an intertemporal optimising framework (Obstfeld and Rogoff, 1995, 1996; Lane, 2001; Sarno, 2001).

In this chapter we review the literature on PPP, providing an extensive discussion of the underlying theory and of the variants of the PPP hypothesis formulated and tested in the literature. We start with a discussion of the basic building-block of PPP, the law of one price (LOOP), which relates to the common-currency prices of similar goods at a disaggregated level, as well as the relationship between the LOOP and PPP at the aggregate level through the use of price indices.[3]

3.1   PPP, the law of one price and price indices

The law of one price is the fundamental building-block of the PPP condition. Formally, the LOOP in its *absolute* version may be written as:

$$P_{i,t} = S_t P_{i,t}^* \qquad i = 1, 2, \ldots, N \tag{3.1}$$

where $P_{i,t}$ denotes the price of good i in terms of the domestic currency at time t, $P_{i,t}^*$ is the price of good i in terms of the foreign currency at time t, and S_t is the nominal exchange rate expressed as the domestic price of the foreign currency at time t. According to equation (3.1), the absolute version of the LOOP essentially postulates that the same good should have the same price across countries if prices are expressed in terms of the same currency of denomination. The basic argument why the LOOP should hold is generally based on the idea of frictionless goods arbitrage.

In its *relative* version, the LOOP postulates the relatively weaker condition:

$$\frac{P_{i,t+1}^* S_{t+1}}{P_{i,t+1}} = \frac{P_{i,t}^* S_t}{P_{i,t}} \qquad i = 1, 2, \ldots, N. \tag{3.2}$$

Obviously, the absolute LOOP implies the relative LOOP, but not vice versa.

Clearly, the LOOP can be adequately tested only if goods produced internationally are perfect substitutes. If this is the case, then the condition of no profitable arbitrage should ensure equality of prices in highly integrated goods markets. Nevertheless, the presence of any sort of tariffs, transport costs and other non-tariff barriers and duties would induce a violation of the no-arbitrage condition and, inevitably, of the LOOP. Also, the assumption of perfect substitutability between goods across different countries is crucial for verifying the LOOP. In general, however, product differentiation across countries creates a wedge between domestic and foreign prices of a product which is proportional to the freedom with which the good itself can be traded.[4]

Formally, by summing all the traded goods in each country, the *absolute* version of the PPP hypothesis requires:

$$\sum_{i=1}^{N} \alpha_i P_{i,t} = S_t \sum_{i=1}^{N} \alpha_i P_{i,t}^*, \tag{3.3}$$

---

[3] For previous surveys of the PPP literature, see, among others, Breuer (1994), Bleaney and Mizen (1995), Froot and Rogoff (1995), Rogoff (1996) and, in the context of a more general survey, Taylor (1995).

[4] An example often used in the literature is the product differentiation of McDonald's hamburgers across countries. Examples of goods for which the LOOP may be expected to hold are gold and other internationally traded commodities (see Rogoff, 1996).

where the weights in the summation satisfy $\sum_{i=1}^{N} \alpha_i = 1$. Alternatively, if the price indices are constructed using a geometric index, then we must form the weighted sum after taking logarithms:

$$\sum_{i=1}^{N} \gamma_i p_{i,t} = s_t + \sum_{i=1}^{N} \gamma_i p_{i,t}^*, \tag{3.4}$$

where the geometric weights in the summation satisfy $\sum_{i=1}^{N} \gamma_i = 1$ and lower-case letters denote logarithms. The weights α_i or γ_i are based on a national price index; in particular, according to the seminal, Cassellian formulation of PPP, the consumer price index (CPI). If the national price levels are P_t and P_t^* or, in logarithms, p_t and p_t^*, then (according to whether the arithmetic or geometric index is used), we can use (3.3) or (3.4) to derive the (absolute) PPP condition:

$$s_t = p_t - p_t^*. \tag{3.5}$$

From equation (3.5) it is easily seen that the real exchange rate, defined here in logarithmic form:

$$q_t \equiv s_t - p_t + p_t^*, \tag{3.6}$$

may be viewed as a measure of the deviation from PPP.

Clearly, deriving PPP from the LOOP introduces a range of index number problems. For example, equations (3.3) and (3.4) implicitly assume that the same weights are relevant in each country, whereas price index weights will typically differ across different countries (perhaps even being zero in one country and non-zero in another for some goods and services) and will also tend to shift through time. In practice, researchers often assume that PPP should hold approximately using the price indices of each country. In the geometric index case, for example, we can rearrange (3.4) to yield:

$$\sum_{i=1}^{N} \gamma_i p_{i,t} = s_t + \sum_{i=1}^{N} \gamma_i^* p_{i,t}^* + \sum_{i=1}^{N} (\gamma_i - \gamma_i^*) p_{i,t}^* \tag{3.7}$$

or:

$$\sum_{i=1}^{N} \gamma_i p_{i,t} = s_t + \sum_{i=1}^{N} \gamma_i^* p_{i,t}^* + u_t, \tag{3.8}$$

where the γ_i^* denote the weights in the foreign price index. Clearly, the greater the disparity between the relevant national price indices, the greater the apparent disparity – represented by u_t – from aggregate PPP, even when the LOOP holds for individual goods. Note, however, that because the geometric price indices are homogeneous of degree one (i.e. an equipro-portionate increase in all prices will raise the overall price level by the same proportion) then differences in weights across countries will matter less where price impulses affect all goods and services more or less homogeneously. An x per cent increase in all prices in the foreign country will lead, for example, to an x per cent increase in the foreign price level and the right-hand side of (3.8) will be augmented by x and the change in the u_t term will be zero. Thus, assuming domestic prices are constant, an x per cent appreciation of the domestic currency is required in order to restore equilibrium.

A similar analysis may be applied when some goods and services are non-traded. Suppose that the LOOP applies only among traded goods. An x per cent increase in all foreign traded goods prices implies, other things equal, an x per cent appreciation of the domestic currency. But if there is also an x per cent rise in all foreign *non-traded* goods prices, the PPP condition based on individual national price indices will also imply an x per cent exchange rate movement.

In practice, it is more common for national statistical bureaux to use arithmetic rather than geometric price indices, although deviations from measured PPP arising from this source are not likely to be large. Considerable differences may arise, however, where price impulses impinge heterogeneously across the various goods and services in an economy and, in particular, where price inflation differs between the traded and non-traded goods sectors. A particular example of this – the Harrod–Balassa–Samuelson effect – is discussed below.

The choice of the appropriate price index to be used in implementing absolute PPP has been the subject of a long debate in the literature, going back at least as far as Keynes (1923). All commonly used price measures include some proportion of non-traded goods, which may induce rejection of PPP or at least of the conditions of homogeneity and proportionality (discussed below) required by PPP. Thus, many attempts exist in the literature to construct appropriate price measures for testing PPP. The most influential work in this context has been carried out by Summers and Heston (1991), who developed the International Comparison Programme (ICP) data set, which reports estimates of absolute PPP for a long sample period and a number of countries, using a common basket of goods across countries. The ICP is not, however, of great practical help in empirical work since it is constructed at large time intervals and, for certain time periods, data are available only for a few countries. Moreover, since extensive use of extrapolation has been made in order to solve this problem, the data presented in the ICP become partially artificial, somehow losing reliability. Overall, therefore, price indices made available by official sources still remain the basis commonly used for implementing absolute PPP, despite the limitations which have been discussed.

In general, however, the difficulty in finding evidence strongly supportive of PPP and the difficulties encountered in moving from the LOOP to PPP have provided a strong motivation for researchers to investigate the LOOP empirically.

3.2   Empirical evidence on the law of one price

Recent econometric tests of the LOOP have often been motivated as a reaction to the rejection of PPP during the recent floating exchange rate regime, which we discuss further below. In general, econometric studies suggest rejection of the LOOP for a very broad range of goods and provide strong empirical evidence both that deviations from the LOOP are highly volatile and that the volatility of relative prices is considerably lower than the volatility of nominal exchange rates. This is suggested, for example, by two influential studies executed in the 1970s. First, Isard (1977) uses disaggregated data for a number of traded goods (chemical products, paper and glass products among others) and for a number of countries, providing strong empirical evidence that the deviations from the LOOP are large and persistent and appear to be highly correlated with exchange rate movements. Second, Richardson (1978) finds very similar results to Isard's, by using data for 4- and 7-digit standard industrial classification (SIC) categories.

Giovannini (1988) uses a partial equilibrium model of the determination of domestic and export prices by a monopolistic competitive firm and argues that the stochastic properties of deviations from the LOOP are strongly affected by the currency of denomination of export prices. In particular, Giovannini uses data on domestic and dollar export prices of Japanese goods and provides evidence that deviations from the LOOP – found to be large not only for sophisticated manufacturing goods but also for commodities such as screws, nuts and bolts – are mainly due to exchange rate movements, consistent with the earlier relevant literature (see also Benninga and Protopapadakis, 1988; Bui and Pippinger, 1990; Goodwin, Grennes and Wohlgenant, 1990; Fraser, Taylor and Webster, 1991; Goodwin, 1992).

Some of the most influential and convincing work in testing for the LOOP is provided by Knetter (1989, 1993). Knetter uses high-quality disaggregated data (7-digit) and provides evidence that large and persistent price differentials exist for traded goods exported to multiple destinations (e.g. for German beer exported to the UK as compared to the US).[5] Another interesting study in this context is due to Engel (1993), who uncovers a strong empirical regularity: the consumer price of a good relative to a different good within a country tends to be much less variable than the price of that good relative to a similar good in another country. This fact holds for all goods except very simple, homogeneous products. Engel suggests that models of real exchange rates are likely to have predictions regarding this relation, so this fact may provide a useful gauge for discriminating among models.

Parsley and Wei (1996) look for convergence towards the LOOP in the absence of trade barriers or nominal exchange rate fluctuations by analysing a panel of fifty-one prices from forty-eight cities in the United States. They find convergence rates substantially higher than typically found in cross-country data, that convergence occurs faster for larger price differences and that rates of convergence are slower for cities further apart. Extending this line of research, Engel and Rogers (1996) use CPI data for both US and Canadian cities and for fourteen categories of consumer prices in order to analyse the stochastic properties of deviations from the LOOP. The authors provide evidence that the distance between cities can explain a considerable amount of the price differential of similar goods in different cities of the same country. Nevertheless, the price differentials are considerably larger for two cities in different countries than for two equidistant cities in the same country. The estimates of Engel and Rogers suggest that crossing the national border – the so-called 'border effect' – increases the volatility of price differentials by the same order of magnitude as would be generated by the addition of between 2,500 to 23,000 extra miles to the distance between the cities considered. Rogers and Jenkins (1995) find similar results to Engel and Rogers, providing evidence that the 'border effect' increases not only the volatility of price differentials but also their persistence.

---

[5] Herguera (1994) investigates the implications of product differentiation for the price adjustment mechanism in international trade using an imperfect competition model. In particular, Herguera finds that market structure, product differentiation and strategic behaviour can explain the persistent price differential of perfectly substitutable goods across countries (see also Chen and Knez, 1995; Dumas, Jennergren and Naslund, 1995).

Among the possible explanations for the violation of the LOOP suggested by the literature, transport costs, tariffs and non-tariff barriers are dominant. An estimate of the wedge driven by the cost of transport is given, for example, by the International Monetary Fund (IMF, 1994): the difference between the value of world exports computed 'free on board' (FOB) and the value of world imports charged in full, or 'cost, insurance and freight' (CIF) is estimated at about 10 per cent and is found to be highly variable across countries. Moreover, the presence of significant non-traded components in the price indices used by the empirical literature may induce apparent violations of the LOOP. Even if the wholesale price index (WPI) includes a smaller non-traded component relative to the consumer price index, that non-traded component may still be significant (e.g. the cost of labour employed and insurance). Moreover, even if tariffs have been considerably reduced over time across major industrialised countries, non-tariff barriers are still very significant. Governments of many countries often intervene in trade across borders using non-tariff barriers in a way that they do not use within their borders (for example, in the form of strict inspection requirements; see Knetter, 1994; Feenstra, 1995; Rogoff, 1996; Feenstra and Kendall, 1997).

Frictions in international arbitrage have important implications and, in particular, imply potential nonlinearities in the deviations from the LOOP. The idea that there may be nonlinearities in goods arbitrage dates at least from Heckscher (1916), who suggested that there may be significant deviations from the LOOP due to international transactions costs between spatially separated markets. A similar viewpoint can be discerned in the writings of Cassel (e.g. Cassel, 1922) and, to a greater or lesser extent, in other earlier writers (Officer, 1982). More recently, a number of authors have developed theoretical models of nonlinear real exchange rate adjustment arising from transactions costs in international arbitrage (e.g. Benninga and Protopapadakis, 1988; Williams and Wright, 1991; Dumas, 1992; Sercu, Uppal and Van Hulle, 1995; O'Connell, 1997; Ohanian and Stockman, 1997). In most of these models, proportional or 'iceberg' transport costs ('iceberg' because a fraction of goods are presumed to 'melt' when shipped) create a band for deviations from the LOOP within which the marginal cost of arbitrage exceeds the marginal benefit. Assuming instantaneous goods arbitrage at the edges of the band then typically implies that the thresholds become reflecting barriers.

Drawing on recent work on the theory of investment under uncertainty, some of these studies show that the thresholds should be interpreted more broadly than simply as reflecting shipping costs and trade barriers *per se*; rather they should be seen as also resulting from the sunk costs of international arbitrage and the resulting tendency for traders to wait for sufficiently large arbitrage opportunities to open up before entering the market (see, in particular, Dumas, 1992; also Dixit, 1989; Krugman, 1989). O'Connell and Wei (1997) extend the iceberg model to allow for fixed as well as proportional costs of arbitrage. This results in a two-threshold model where the real exchange rate is reset by arbitrage to an upper or lower inner threshold whenever it hits the corresponding outer threshold.[6] Intuitively, arbitrage will be heavy once it is profitable enough to outweigh the initial fixed cost, but will stop short of returning the real rate to the PPP level because of the proportional arbitrage costs.

---

[6] In these stylised models, because there is only a single traded good, deviations from PPP are identical to deviations from the LOOP as well as equivalent to movements in the real exchange rate.

Coleman (1995) suggests that the assumption of instantaneous trade should be replaced with the presumption that it takes time to ship goods. In this model, transport costs again create a band of no arbitrage for the real exchange rate, but the exchange rate can stray beyond the thresholds. Once beyond the upper or lower threshold, the real rate becomes increasingly mean-reverting with the distance from the threshold. Within the transactions costs band, when no trade takes place, the process is divergent so that the exchange rate spends most of the time away from parity.

Some empirical evidence of the effect of transactions costs in this context is provided by Davutyan and Pippenger (1990). More recently, Obstfeld and Taylor (1997) have investigated the nonlinear nature of the adjustment process in terms of a threshold autoregressive (TAR) model (Tong, 1990). The TAR model allows for a transactions costs band within which no adjustment in deviations from the LOOP takes place – so that deviations may exhibit unit-root behaviour – while outside of the band, as goods arbitrage becomes profitable and its effects are felt, the process switches abruptly to become stationary autoregressive. Obstfeld and Taylor provide evidence that TAR models work well when applied to disaggregated data, and yield estimates in which the thresholds correspond to popular rough estimates of the order of magnitude of actual transport costs.

A different story for rationalising the rejection of the LOOP comes from the 'pricing to market' (PTM) theory of Krugman (1987) and Dornbusch (1987). Following the developments of theories of imperfect competition and trade, the main feature of this theory is that the same good can be given a different price in different countries when oligopolistic firms are supplying it. This is feasible because there are many industries which can supply separate licences for the sale of their goods at home and abroad.[7] At the empirical level, Knetter (1989, 1993) finds that PTM is much more important for German and Japanese firms than for US companies and that it is a strategy used for a very broad range of goods.[8]

Kasa (1992) argues, however, that the rationale underlying PTM is not price discrimination, as proposed by Krugman and Dornbusch. Kasa argues that PTM is better rationalised by an adjustment cost framework, that is a model in which firms face some sort of menu costs or a model in which consumers face fixed costs when switching between different products (see also Froot and Klemperer, 1989).

In an interesting study, Ghosh and Wolf (1994) examine the statistical properties and the determinants of changes in the cover price of the *Economist* periodical across twelve countries during the recent float. They show that standard tests of PTM may fail to discriminate between the alternative hypothesis of menu costs. Their findings suggest a strong violation of the LOOP and are consistent with menu-cost-driven pricing behaviour.

A final issue worth noting is the possibility that the failure of the LOOP may be explained by institutional factors typical of the twentieth century which have increased the persistence of deviations from the LOOP. Nevertheless, Froot, Kim and Rogoff (1995), using data on

---

[7] Froot and Rogoff (1995) note how the PTM theory not only can explain the long-run deviations from the LOOP, but also has important implications for the transmission mechanism of disturbances from the money market in the presence of nominal rigidities (see also Marston, 1990).

[8] A potential explanation of this finding is provided by Rangan and Lawrence (1993) who argue that, since US firms sell a large part of their exports through subsidiaries, the PTM by US firms may occur at subsidiary level. In this case, the comparisons executed by Knetter may lead to underestimation of the importance of PTM by US firms.

prices for grains and other dairy goods in England and Holland for a series of data from the fourteenth to the twentieth century, provide empirical evidence suggesting that the volatility of the LOOP is quite stable during the whole period, regardless of the many regime shifts during the sample.

3.3   Mean-reversion in real exchange rates

The empirical evidence on PPP is extremely large and the sophistication of the testing procedures employed has developed *pari passu* with advances in econometric techniques. Hence, it is useful to separate the enormous empirical evidence on PPP into six different stages: the early empirical literature on PPP; tests of the random walk hypothesis for the real exchange rate; cointegration studies[9]; long-span studies; panel data studies; and, finally, studies employing nonlinear econometric techniques.

3.3.1   The early empirical literature on purchasing power parity

Absolute PPP implies that the nominal exchange rate is equal to the ratio of the two relevant national price levels. Relative PPP posits that changes in the exchange rate are equal to changes in relative national prices. The early empirical literature, until the late 1970s, on testing PPP is based on estimates of equations of the form:

$$s_t = \alpha + \beta p_t + \beta^* p_t^* + \omega_t, \tag{3.9}$$

where ω_t is a disturbance term. A test of the restrictions $\beta = 1$, $\beta^* = -1$ would be interpreted as a test of absolute PPP, whilst a test of the same restrictions applied to the equation with the variables in first differences would be interpreted as a test of relative PPP. In particular, a distinction is often made between the test that β and β^* are equal and of opposite sign – the symmetry condition – and the test that they are equal to unity and minus unity respectively – the proportionality condition.

In the earlier relevant literature, researchers did not introduce dynamics in the estimated equation in such a way as to distinguish between short-run and long-run effects, even if it was recognised that PPP is only expected to hold in the long run. Nevertheless, the empirical literature based on estimation of equations of the form (3.9) generally suggests rejection of the PPP hypothesis. In an influential study, however, Frenkel (1978) obtains estimates of β and β^* very close to plus and minus unity on data for high inflation countries, suggesting that PPP represents an important benchmark in long-run exchange rate modelling. However, several drawbacks affect this approach. First, Frenkel does not investigate the stochastic properties of the residuals and in particular does not test for stationarity. If the residuals are not stationary, part of the shocks impinging upon the real exchange rate will be permanent, i.e. PPP is violated. Second, apart from hyperinflationary economies, PPP tends to be strongly rejected on the basis of estimates of equations such as (3.9). Frenkel argues, however, that the rejection of PPP may be due only to temporary real shocks and price

[9] See Chapter 2, Appendix D for a brief introduction to unit roots and cointegration.

stickiness in the goods market, and that convergence to PPP is expected to occur in the long run.

Another problem in testing PPP on the basis of estimates of equation (3.9) is the endogeneity of both nominal exchange rates and price levels; indeed, the choice of the variable to be put on the left-hand side of (3.9) is arbitrary. Krugman (1978) constructs a flexible-price exchange rate model in which the domestic monetary authorities intervene against real shocks using expansionary monetary policies, thereby inducing inflation. The model is estimated by instrumental variables (IV) and ordinary least squares (OLS). The IV estimates of β and β^* are closer to unity in absolute value than the OLS estimates, but PPP is still rejected (see also Frenkel, 1981).

The crucial problem, however, is that this early literature does not investigate the stationarity of the residuals in the estimated equation. If both nominal exchange rates and relative prices are nonstationary variables (and are not cointegrated), then (3.9) is a spurious regression and conventional OLS-based statistical inference is invalid (Granger and Newbold, 1974). If the error term in (3.9) is stationary, however, then a strong long-run linear relationship exists between exchange rates and relative prices, but conventional statistical inference is still invalid because of the bias present in the estimated standard errors (Banerjee, Dolado, Hendry and Smith, 1986; Engle and Granger, 1987).[10]

The next stage in the development of this literature was explicitly to address the issue of nonstationarity of the variables under consideration, starting with an analysis of whether the real exchange rate itself is stationary – implying evidence of long-run PPP – or whether it tends to follow a unit-root process – implying absence of any tendency to converge on a long-run equilibrium level.

3.3.2 Tests for a unit root in the real exchange rate

Recall that the real exchange rate in its logarithmic form may be written as:

$$q_t \equiv s_t + p_t^* - p_t. \tag{3.10}$$

The approach taken by the second stage of tests of PPP represented in the empirical literature is based on testing for the nonstationarity of the real exchange rate. Early studies taking this approach include, among others, Roll (1979), Adler and Lehmann (1983), Hakkio (1984), Edison (1985), Frenkel (1986), Huizinga (1987) and Meese and Rogoff (1988). From the mid to late 1980s onwards, a standard approach has been to employ a variant of the augmented Dickey–Fuller (ADF) test for a unit root in the process driving the real rate.[11] This is generally based on an auxiliary regression of the general form:

$$\Delta q_t = \gamma_0 + \gamma_1 t + \gamma_2 q_{t-1} + \Xi(L)\Delta q_{t-1} + e_t, \tag{3.11}$$

where $\Xi(L)$ denotes a p-th order polynomial in the lag operator L, and e_t is a white-noise process. Testing the null hypothesis that $\gamma_2 = 0$, using an ADF test, is tantamount to testing for a single unit root in the data-generating process for q_t and would imply no long-run

---

[10] Cointegration among the variables may also reduce the problem of endogeneity of the right-hand-side variables because of the superconsistency property of OLS in cointegrating regressions; see Engle and Granger (1987).

[11] See Chapter 2, Appendix D for an introduction to unit-root tests.

equilibrium level for q_t. The alternative hypothesis, that PPP holds, requires that $\gamma_1 < 0$.[12] A variant of this approach is to use a modified version of this test to allow for non-Gaussian disturbances (Phillips, 1986; Phillips and Perron, 1988).

A second approach to testing for nonstationarity of the real exchange rate involves variance ratio tests. In this case the persistence of the real exchange rate is measured using a simple nonparametric test, due originally to Cochrane (1988), $z(k)$:

$$z(k) = \frac{1}{k} \frac{var(q_t - q_{t-k})}{var(q_t - q_{t-1})}, \tag{3.12}$$

where k is a positive integer and var stands for variance. If the real exchange rate follows a random walk, then the ratio in (3.12) should equal unity, since the variance of a k-period change should be k times the variance of a one-period change. By contrast, if the real exchange rate exhibits mean-reversion, the ratio $z(k)$ should be in the range between zero and unity.

A third approach employs the techniques developed by the literature on fractional integration, since these techniques allow the researcher to consider a broader range of stationary processes under the alternative hypothesis than do conventional unit-root tests. Formally, the real exchange rate process may be represented as:

$$\Phi(L)(1 - L)^d q_t = \zeta(L)w_t, \tag{3.13}$$

where $\Phi(L)$ and $\zeta(L)$ are both polynomials in L with roots lying outside the unit circle, and w_t is a white-noise process. Under this approach the parameter d is allowed to lie in the continuous interval between zero and unity. Fractionally integrated processes are more persistent than pure autoregressive moving-average (ARMA) processes, but are still stationary. If $d = 0$, then the real exchange rate simply follows an ARMA process. On the other hand, if d, $\Phi(L)$ and $\zeta(L)$ all equal unity, the real exchange rate follows a random walk (see Diebold, Husted and Rush, 1991; Cheung and Lai, 1993a).

Empirical studies employing tests of the type described in this sub-section for testing PPP during the recent float generally cannot reject the random walk hypothesis for the real exchange rates of the currencies of all the major industrialised countries against one another, therefore suggesting that deviations from PPP are permanent (see e.g. Enders, 1988; Taylor, 1988; Mark, 1990; Edison and Pauls, 1993). Two exceptions are Huizinga (1987), who uses variance ratio tests and data for dollar exchange rates against a number of currencies for sample periods shorter than two years, and Chowdhury and Sdogati (1993), who analyse the European Monetary System (EMS) period 1979–90 and find support for PPP for real exchange rates when expressed relative to the German mark, but not when expressed relative to the US dollar.[13]

---

[12] Meese and Rogoff (1988), for example, take this approach; their results provide strong evidence supporting the nonstationarity of the real exchange rate during the floating period.

[13] Another result supportive of PPP is due to Whitt (1992). Whitt uses a Bayesian unit-root test due to Sims (1988), and is able to reject the null hypothesis that the real exchange rate follows a random walk for a number of countries and for both the pre- and the post-Bretton Woods periods.

3.3.3 Cointegration studies of PPP

Cointegration, as originally developed by Engle and Granger (1987), seems to be an ideal approach to testing for PPP.[14] While allowing q_t, the 'equilibrium error' (Granger, 1986), to vary in the short run, a necessary condition for PPP to hold is that q_t is stationary over time. If this is not the case, then the nominal exchange rate and the relative price will permanently tend to diverge. Cointegration analysis tells us that any two nonstationary series which are found to be integrated of the same order are cointegrated if a linear combination of the two exists which is itself stationary. If this is the case, then the nonstationarity of one series exactly offsets the nonstationarity of the other and a long-run relationship is established between the two variables. In our context, if both the nominal exchange rate s_t and the relative price π_t ($\equiv p_t - p_t^*$) have stationary, invertible, non-deterministic ARMA representations after differencing d times, i.e. they are both integrated of order d or $I(d)$, then the linear combination:

$$s_t + \kappa \pi_t = z_t \qquad (3.14)$$

will in general also be found to be $I(d)$, if the real exchange rate has a random walk component. Nevertheless, if a cointegrating parameter α exists such that q_t is integrated of order $I(d - c), c > 0$, then the nominal exchange rate and the relative price are cointegrated of order d, c, or $CI(d, c)$. In the context of PPP testing we want $d = c = 1$, that is s_t and π_t should both be $I(1)$ variables, but z_t should be mean-reverting. In this case, one may feel confident that a strong long-run relationship exists between the two variables considered, since they share a common stochastic trend (Stock and Watson, 1988) and 'cointegration of a pair of variables is at least a necessary condition for them to have a stable long-run (linear) relationship' (Taylor 1988; Taylor and McMahon, 1988).

However, if the no-cointegration hypothesis cannot be rejected, then the estimated regression is just a 'spurious' one and has no economic meaning: the analysis is subject to the same drawbacks as discussed above. Given that no bounded combination of the levels exists, then the error term in the regression must be nonstationary under the null hypothesis.

The main difference between using cointegration in testing for PPP and testing for the nonstationarity of the real exchange rate is that the symmetry and proportionality conditions ($\kappa = -1$ in (3.14)) are not imposed and cannot be tested easily given the bias in the estimated standard errors. Rationales for the rejection of the symmetry and proportionality conditions, based on considerations of measurement errors (in particular systematic differences between actual measured price indices and those theoretically relevant for PPP calculations) and barriers to trade, are provided by, among others, Taylor (1988), Fisher and Park (1991) and Cheung and Lai (1993a, 1993b).

The Johansen (1988, 1991) maximum likelihood estimator circumvents these problems and enables us to test for the presence of multiple cointegrating vectors. Johansen shows how to test for linear restrictions on the parameters of the cointegrating vectors and this

---

[14] See Chapter 2, Appendix D for a brief introduction to cointegration.

is of great interest because it makes it possible to test the symmetry and proportionality conditions exactly.[15]

Earlier cointegration studies generally reported the absence of significant mean-reversion of the exchange rate towards PPP for the recent floating rate experience (Taylor, 1988; Mark, 1990), but were supportive of reversion towards PPP for the inter-war float (Taylor and McMahon, 1988), for the 1950s US–Canadian float (McNown and Wallace, 1989), and for the exchange rates of high-inflation countries (Choudhry, McNown and Wallace, 1991). More recent applied work on long-run PPP among the major industrialised economies has, however, been more favourable towards the long-run PPP hypothesis for the recent float (e.g. Corbae and Ouliaris, 1988; Kim, 1990; Cheung and Lai, 1993a, 1993b).

Overall, cointegration studies highlight some important features of the data. The null hypothesis of no-cointegration is more easily rejected when, in the sample period considered, the exchange rates are fixed rather than floating. Interestingly, stronger evidence supporting PPP is found when the WPI, rather than the CPI, is used, and, even more so, than when the GDP deflator is used. This is easy to explain since the WPI contains a relatively smaller non-tradables component and represents, therefore, a better approximation to the ideal price index required by the PPP hypothesis than either the CPI or the GDP deflator.[16]

Another feature of the data suggested by the cointegration literature is that in bivariate systems cointegration is established more frequently than in trivariate systems and in Engle–Granger two-step procedures. The disappointing finding, however, is that the symmetry and proportionality conditions are very often rejected and the parameters estimated in PPP regressions are often far from the theoretical values. While this result may simply be caused by small-sample bias in the case of two-step cointegration procedures, it is difficult to explain rejections occurring in large samples and in estimates obtained using the Johansen procedure. Thus, the problem may simply be that longer data sets are needed to detect PPP and mean-reversion in the real exchange rate. In general, rejection of PPP may be due to the lack of power of conventional econometric tests. Some notable attempts to overcome this problem are discussed in the following sub-sections.

3.3.4 The power problem

Following an early warning from Frankel (1986, 1990), a number of authors have noted that the tests typically employed during the 1980s to examine the long-run stability of the real exchange rate may have very low power to reject a null hypothesis of real exchange rate in-stability when applied to data for the recent floating rate period alone (e.g. Froot and Rogoff, 1995; Lothian and Taylor, 1996, 1997). The argument is that if the real exchange rate is stable in the sense that it tends to revert towards its mean over long periods of time, then examination of just one real exchange rate over a period of twenty-five years or so may not yield enough information to be able to detect slow mean-reversion towards purchasing power parity.

---

[15] It is also possible to circumvent the problem by simply estimating the regression of the nominal exchange rate on the relative price by fully modified OLS (FM OLS), due to Phillips and Hansen (1990), instead of OLS, since a correction is made for the problem of the bias in the standard errors.

[16] The argument that PPP should hold better with the WPI than with the CPI goes back to Keynes (1932) and McKinnon (1971).

Table 3.1. *Empirical power function for the Dickey–Fuller test*

					T				
ρ	15	20	25	50	75	100	150	200	250
0.950	4.79	5.70	6.02	7.41	9.81	12.54	21.17	32.81	47.31
0.887	6.33	6.99	7.95	15.13	26.03	41.26	75.13	93.80	99.31
0.825	7.44	9.26	11.41	28.07	53.55	78.08	98.21	99.95	100.00

Notes: T is the sample size; ρ is the first-order autocorrelation coefficient.

A straightforward way of illustrating this point is through a simple Monte Carlo experiment. As discussed in the next sub-section, Lothian and Taylor (1996) estimate an AR(1) process for the sterling–dollar and sterling–franc real exchange rates using two centuries of annual data. For sterling–dollar, they report the following AR(1) model:

$$q_t = 0.179 + 0.887\ q_{t-1} + \widehat{\varepsilon}_t,$$
$$(0.049)\quad (0.031)$$
(3.15)

where $\widehat{\varepsilon}_t$ is the fitted residual, which has an estimated standard error of 7.1 per cent and figures in parentheses are estimated standard errors. As discussed below, the estimated first-order autocorrelation coefficient implies a speed of mean-reversion – about 11 per cent per annum – which is quite typical in the literature employing panel data or long spans of data. Indeed, the 95 per cent confidence interval, which ranges from about 0.825 to about 0.95, would certainly encompass the range of reported point estimates (see Rogoff, 1996). Thus, we can use this estimated model as a basis for our Monte Carlo experiments. Accordingly, we simulated data using an artificial data-generating process calibrated on this model for various sample sizes and with the autoregressive coefficient taking the values 0.825, 0.887 and 0.95. In each case, we generated 10,000 artificial data sets of length $T + 100$, where T is the particular sample size, starting with an initial value of $q_0 = 0$. For each artificial data set we then calculated the simple Dickey–Fuller statistic (after discarding the first 100 data points) and compared this to the 5 per cent critical value obtained using the response surface estimates of McKinnon (1991). The proportion of times we were able to reject the null hypothesis of a unit root out of 10,000 cases then gives us the empirical power for that particular sample size and autoregressive coefficient. The resulting empirical power function is tabulated in Table 3.1.[17]

Much of the early work on unit roots and cointegration for real exchange rates was published in the late 1980s and was therefore based on data spanning the fifteen years or so since the start of generalised floating in 1973. As Table 3.1 shows, however, for the speeds of mean-reversion typically recorded in the literature (Froot and Rogoff, 1995; Rogoff, 1996), the probability of rejecting the null hypothesis of a random walk real exchange rate when in fact the real rate is mean-reverting would only be between about 5 and 7.5 per cent. Given that

[17] These results are consistent with those reported in Lothian and Taylor (1997), although the present tabulation is more comprehensive, is based on 10,000 rather than 5,000 simulations, and uses the exact 5 per cent critical values calculated using McKinnon's (1991) response surface estimates.

we have, of course, only one data set on real exchange rates available, an alternative way of viewing this is to note that if real exchange rates are in fact mean-reverting in this fashion, the probability of *never* being able to reject the null hypothesis of a unit root given the available data is in excess of 92 per cent when we have only fifteen years of data available. Even with the benefit of the additional ten years or so of data which is now available, the power of the test increases only slightly, to a maximum of around 11 per cent on the most optimistic view of the speed of mean-reversion. Taking the point estimate obtained by Lothian and Taylor (1996) of 0.887, we confirm their finding that 'even with a century of data on the sterling–dollar real exchange rate, we would have less than an even chance of rejecting the unit root hypothesis' (Lothian and Taylor, 1996, pp. 950–1). Moreover, even if we consider the extreme lower end of the 95 per cent confidence interval of 0.825 for the first-order autocorrelation coefficient, we should still need something like seventy-five years of data in order to be able to reject the null hypothesis with more than 50 per cent probability.[18]

The Monte Carlo evidence of Shiller and Perron (1985) demonstrates, moreover, that researchers cannot circumvent this problem by increasing the frequency of observation – say, from annual to quarterly or monthly – thereby increasing the number of data points available. Given that, in a spectral analysis sense, we are examining the low frequency components of real exchange rate behaviour, we require a long *span* of data in order to improve the power of the test.[19]

This realisation led some researchers to do exactly that, i.e. examine the behaviour of real exchange rates using very long data sets. An alternative means of increasing test power is to keep the same length of data set (say, since 1973) but to test for unit roots jointly using a panel of real exchange rates for a number of countries. This literature is discussed below.

3.3.5 Long-span studies
The first approach considered in the literature to circumventing the low power problem of conventional unit-root tests was to employ long-span data sets.[20] For example, using annual data from 1869 to 1984 for the dollar–sterling real exchange rate, Frankel (1986) estimates an AR(1) process for the real rate with an autoregressive parameter of 0.86 and is able to reject the random walk hypothesis. Long-run PPP for the dollar–sterling exchange rate is also examined by Edison (1987) over the period 1890–1978, using an error-correction mechanism (ECM) of the form:

$$\Delta s_t = \delta_0 + \delta_1 \Delta(p_t - p_t^*) + \delta_2(s_{t-1} - p_{t-1} + p_{t-1}^*) + u_t, \tag{3.16}$$

which has a long-run constant equilibrium level of the real exchange rate. Edison's results provide evidence that PPP holds, but shocks impinging upon the real exchange rate are very

---

[18] Engel (2000), using artificial data calibrated on nominal exchange rates and disaggregated data on prices also shows that standard unit-root and cointegration tests applied to real exchange rate data may have significant size biases and also demonstrates that tests of stationarity may have very low power.

[19] Similar remarks would apply to variance ratio tests and tests for non-cointegration.

[20] As discussed above, alternative unit-root tests may also be sufficiently powerful to detect mean-reversion in real exchange rates. For example, Diebold, Husted and Rush (1991) and Cheung and Lai (1993a) apply fractional integration techniques and find evidence supporting long-run PPP. See also Taylor (2000a).

persistent and the half-life is about 7.3 years. Glen (1992) also finds mean-reversion of the real exchange rates for nine countries and a half-life of 3.3 years over the sample period 1900–1987 (see also Cheung and Lai, 1994).

Lothian and Taylor (1996) use two centuries of data on dollar–sterling and franc–sterling real exchange rates and provide indirect evidence supporting PPP in the recent floating period. They cannot find any significant evidence of a structural break between the pre- and post-Bretton Woods periods using a Chow test and show that the widespread failure to detect mean-reversion in real exchange rates during the recent float may simply be due to the shortness of the sample.

Long-span studies have, however, been subject to some criticism in the literature. One criticism relates to the fact that, because of the very long data spans involved, various exchange rate regimes are typically spanned. Also, real shocks may have generated structural breaks or shifts in the equilibrium real exchange rate (see e.g. Hegwood and Papell, 1999).[21] This is, of course, a 'necessary evil' with long-span studies, of which researchers are generally aware.[22] Moreover, researchers using long-span data are generally at pains to test for structural breaks (see e.g. Lothian and Taylor, 1996).

Nevertheless, in order to provide a convincing test of real exchange rate stability during the post-Bretton Woods period, it is necessary to devise a test using data for that period alone. This provides the impetus for panel data studies of PPP.

3.3.6 Panel data studies

A different approach found in the literature on testing for PPP in order to circumvent the problem of low power displayed by conventional unit-root tests is to increase the number of exchange rates under consideration.

The first attempt is due to Hakkio (1984), who employs generalised least squares (GLS) and tests the null hypothesis of nonstationarity using data for a system of four exchange rates. Hakkio cannot reject, however, the null hypothesis that all real exchange rates under examination follow a random walk.

---

[21] A somewhat less powerful criticism of long-span studies which is occasionally made is that the basket of goods and services considered when forming the relevant national price indices may have altered over time and this in some way invalidates the analysis. To see that this is incorrect, consider the following simple counter-example. Imagine a two-country, two-period world where the LOOP holds continuously. Suppose, moreover, that tastes switch between periods 1 and 2 such that a completely different set of goods is produced in each period. Since the LOOP holds in each period, aggregate PPP will also hold in each period (abstracting from any Harrod–Balassa–Samuelson effects, etc.) despite the fact that the baskets have changed completely.

[22] Lothian and Taylor (1996, pp. 492–4) note, for example:

Confrontation with data spanning several nominal exchange rate regimes is the inevitable cost of increasing the length of the data sample size, but at the same time, it provides the basis for a more stringent test of mean reversion in the real exchange rate than would be possible with shorter though still lengthy samples. A number of studies have documented the increased short-term volatility of real exchange rates during floating-rate regimes. In this paper, however, we are concerned with the longer-run properties of real exchange rates. Although we believe it is quite likely that the time-series properties of real exchange rates will have altered in some respects between regimes, we are in effect examining whether there are significant similarities that carry over. It also seems likely that, over a period of 200 years, there will have been important real shocks to the real exchange rate, some of which may have had permanent components. Our aim is to examine whether the hypothesis of a stationary real exchange rate is a good first approximation that describes the salient characteristics of real exchange rate behavior over such a diverse period as the last two centuries.

Abuaf and Jorion (1990) employ a similar approach in that they examine a system of ten AR(1) regressions for real dollar exchange rates where the first-order autocorrelation coefficient is constrained to be equal across rates, taking account of contemporaneous correlations among the disturbances. The estimation is executed employing Zellner's (1962) 'seemingly unrelated' (SUR) estimator, which is basically multivariate GLS using an estimate of the contemporaneous covariance matrix of the disturbances obtained from individual OLS estimation. Thus, Abuaf and Jorion test the null hypothesis that the real exchange rates are jointly nonstationary for all ten series over the sample period 1973–1987. Their results indicate a marginal rejection of the null hypothesis of joint nonstationarity at conventional nominal levels of significance and are interpreted as evidence in favour of PPP. The study of Abuaf and Jorion (1990) has stimulated a strand of literature which employs multivariate generalisations of unit-root tests in order to increase the test power (e.g. Flood and Taylor, 1996; Frankel and Rose, 1996; Wu, 1996; Coakley and Fuertes, 1997; Lothian, 1997; O'Connell, 1998; Papell, 1998). A number of these studies provide evidence supporting long-run PPP, even only on post-Bretton Woods data, provided a sufficiently broad range of countries is considered.[23]

Taylor and Sarno (1998) and Sarno and Taylor (1998) argue, however, that the conclusions suggested by some of these studies may be misleading because of an incorrect interpretation of the null hypothesis of the multivariate unit-root tests employed by Abuaf and Jorion and the subsequent literature. The null hypothesis in those studies is *joint* nonstationarity of the real exchange rates considered and, hence, rejection of the null hypothesis may occur even if *only one* of the series considered is stationary. Therefore, if rejection occurs when a group of real exchange rates is examined, then it may not be very informative and certainly it cannot be concluded that this rejection implies evidence supporting PPP for all of them. On the basis of a large number of Monte Carlo experiments calibrated on dollar real exchange rates among the G5 countries, for example, Taylor and Sarno (1998) find that, for a sample size corresponding to the span of the recent float, the presence of a single stationary process together with three unit-root processes led to rejection at the 5 per cent level of the joint null hypothesis of non-stationarity in about 65 per cent of simulations when the root of the stationary process was as large as 0.95, and on more than 95 per cent of occasions when the root of the single stationary process was 0.9 or less.[24, 25]

Taylor and Sarno (1998) employ two multivariate tests for unit roots which are shown, using Monte Carlo methods, to be relatively more powerful than traditional univariate tests using data for the G5 over the post-Bretton Woods period. The first test is based on a generalisation of the augmented Dickey–Fuller test where, unlike in Abuaf and Jorion (1990), the autocorrelation coefficients are not constrained to be equal across countries and

---

[23] Flood and Taylor (1996) find strong support for mean-reversion towards long-run PPP using data on twenty-one industrialised countries over the floating rate period and regressing five-, ten- and twenty-year average exchange rate movements on average inflation differentials against the United States.

[24] Note that the artificial data-generating process is calibrated on quarterly data, so that roots of this magnitude are plausible; see Taylor and Sarno (1998) for further details.

[25] O'Connell (1998) points out an additional problem with panel unit-root tests, namely that they typically fail to control for cross-sectional dependence in the data, and shows that this may lead to considerable size distortion, raising the significance level of tests with a nominal size of 5 per cent to as much as 50 per cent.

a more general AR(4) regression for each real exchange rate is considered. Although the null hypothesis is rejected, the test does not allow the authors to identify for how many and for which currencies PPP holds. The second test is based on an extension of the Johansen cointegration procedure, employed by the authors as a multivariate unit-root test. Given that among a system of N $I(1)$ series, there can be at most $N - 1$ cointegrating vectors, rejection of the hypothesis that there are less than N cointegrating vectors among N series is equivalent to rejecting the hypothesis of nonstationarity of *all* of the series. Put another way, the only way there can be N distinct cointegrating vectors among N series is if each of the series is $I(0)$ and thus itself a cointegrating relationship.[26] Therefore, the null hypothesis under the Johansen procedure as applied by Taylor and Sarno is that there are $N - 1$ or fewer cointegrating vectors among the N series concerned in the panel, which implies that at least one of them is nonstationary; rejection of the null hypothesis in this case implies that *all* of the series in the panel are mean-reverting. By rejecting this null hypothesis at the 1 per cent nominal level of significance, Taylor and Sarno provide evidence that real exchange rates for the G5 constructed using the CPI price level are mean-reverting during the recent floating period.

3.3.7　*The purchasing power parity puzzle*

In the previous two sub-sections we have discussed the way in which researchers have sought to address the power problem in testing for mean-reversion in the real exchange rate, either through long-span studies or through panel unit-root studies. As we made clear in our discussion, however, whether or not the long-span or panel-data studies do in fact answer the question whether PPP holds in the long run remains contentious. As far as the long-span studies are concerned, as noted in particular by Frankel and Rose (1996), the long samples required to generate a reasonable level of statistical power with standard univariate unit-root tests may be unavailable for many currencies (perhaps thereby generating a 'survivorship bias' in tests on the available data; see Froot and Rogoff, 1995) and, in any case, may potentially be inappropriate because of differences in real exchange rate behaviour both across different historical periods and across different nominal exchange rate regimes (e.g. Baxter and Stockman, 1989; Hegwood and Papell, 1999). As for panel-data studies, the potential problem with panel unit-root tests, highlighted by the Monte Carlo evidence of Taylor and Sarno (1998), is that the null hypothesis in such tests is generally that *all* of the series are generated by unit-root processes, so that the probability of rejection of the null hypothesis may be quite high when as few as just one of the series under consideration is a realisation of a stationary process.

Even if, however, we were to take the results of the long-span or panel-data studies as having solved the first PPP puzzle, a second PPP puzzle then arises. Among the long-span and panel-data studies which do report significant mean-reversion of the real exchange rate, there appears to be a consensus that the half-life of deviations from PPP is about three to five years (Rogoff, 1996). If we take as given that real shocks cannot account for the major part of the short-run volatility of real exchange rates (since it seems incredible that shocks to real

---

[26] This assumes that the underlying process must be either $I(0)$ or $I(1)$.

factors such as tastes and technology could be so volatile) and that nominal shocks can only have strong effects over a time frame in which nominal wages and prices are sticky, then a second PPP puzzle is the apparently high degree of persistence in the real exchange rate (Rogoff, 1996). Rogoff (1996) summarises this issue as follows: 'The purchasing power parity puzzle then is this: How can one reconcile the enormous short-term volatility of real exchange rates with the extremely slow rate at which shocks appear to damp out?'.

Since Rogoff first noted the PPP puzzle in 1996, researchers have sought to address this as an additional issue in research on real exchange rates. Allowing for underlying shifts in the equilibrium dollar–sterling real exchange rate (Harrod–Balassa–Samuelson effects) over the past two hundred years through the use of nonlinear time trends, for example, Lothian and Taylor (2000) suggest that the half-life of deviations from PPP for this exchange rate may be as low as two-and-a-half years.

Recently, Taylor (2000b) has shown that empirical estimates of the half-life of shocks to the real exchange rate may be biased upwards because of two empirical pitfalls. The first pitfall identified by Taylor relates to temporal aggregation in the data. Using a model in which the real exchange rate follows an AR(1) process at a higher frequency than that at which the data is sampled, Taylor shows analytically that the degree of upward bias in the estimated half-life rises as the degree of temporal aggregation increases, i.e. as the length of time between observed data points increases. The second pitfall concerns the possibility of nonlinear adjustment of real exchange rates. On the basis of Monte Carlo experiments with a nonlinear artificial data-generating process, Taylor shows that there can also be substantial upward bias in the estimated half-life of adjustment from assuming linear adjustment when in fact the true adjustment process is nonlinear. The time aggregation problem is a difficult issue for researchers to deal with since, as discussed above, long spans of data are required in order to have a reasonable level of power when tests of nonstationarity of the real exchange rate are applied, and long spans of high-frequency data do not exist.[27] On the other hand, Taylor also shows that the problem becomes particularly acute when the degree of temporal aggregation exceeds the length of the actual half-life, so that this source of bias may be mitigated somewhat if the researcher believes that the true half-life is substantially greater than the frequency of observation. In any case, the literature to date has only begun to explore the issue of nonlinearities in real exchange rate adjustment.

3.3.8 *Nonlinear real exchange rate dynamics*
The models discussed above in the context of determining the stochastic process of the deviation from the LOOP also imply nonlinearity in the real exchange rate. In fact, they suggest that the exchange rate will become increasingly mean-reverting with the size of the deviation from the equilibrium level. In some models the jump to mean-reverting behaviour is sudden, whilst in others it is smooth, and Dumas (1994) suggests that even in the former case, time aggregation will tend to smooth the transition between regimes. Moreover, if the

---

[27] A possible solution to this would be to use panels of high-frequency data in order to increase test power, although care must in this case be taken to avoid the panel unit-root problem highlighted by Taylor and Sarno (1998).

real exchange rate is measured using price indices made up of goods prices each with a different level of international arbitrage costs, one would expect adjustment of the overall real exchange rate to be smooth rather than discontinuous.

Michael, Nobay and Peel (1997) and Taylor, Peel and Sarno (2001) propose an econometric modelling framework for the empirical analysis of PPP which allows for the fact that commodity trade is not frictionless and for aggregation across goods with different thresholds. To state the issues clearly, recall that equilibrium models of exchange rate determination in the presence of transactions costs have been proposed by Benninga and Protopapadakis (1988), Dumas (1992) and Sercu, Uppal and van Hulle (1995). As a result of the costs of trading goods, persistent deviations from PPP are implied as an equilibrium feature of these models (deviations are left uncorrected as long as they are small relative to the costs of trading). A significant insight into the nature of PPP deviations is provided by Dumas (1992), who analyses the dynamic process of the real exchange rate in spatially separated markets under proportional transactions costs. Deviations from PPP are shown to follow a nonlinear process which is mean-reverting. The speed of adjustment towards equilibrium varies directly with the extent of the deviation from PPP. Within the transaction band, when no trade takes place, the process is divergent so that the exchange rate spends most of the time away from parity. This implies that deviations from PPP last for a very long time (Dumas, 1992, p. 154), although they certainly do not follow a random walk.[28]

Kilian and Taylor (2001) provide an alternative or complementary analysis of why real exchange rates may exhibit nonlinearities in adjustment, based upon a model in which there are heterogeneous agents exerting influence in the foreign exchange market, namely economic fundamentalists, technical analysts and noise traders. It is assumed that traders take the advice of fundamentalists who themselves may differ in opinion as to what the true equilibrium level of the exchange rate is, and therefore in their forecasts. When there is strong disagreement among the fundamentalists, traders will tend to rely at least partly on the advice of technical analysts who use trend-following forecasts which impart a unit root into the exchange rate.[29] Thus, the nominal – and hence the real – exchange rate will tend to move away from the equilibrium level so long as fundamentalists disagree about the level of that equilibrium. As the exchange rate moves further away from equilibrium, however, there is an increasingly greater degree of agreement among the fundamentalists that the exchange rate is above or below its equilibrium, and hence an increasingly strong tendency of the exchange rate to revert back towards the equilibrium level as traders are swayed by an emerging consensus concerning the likely future direction of real and nominal exchange rate movements.[30]

In the procedures conventionally applied to test for long-run PPP, the null hypothesis is usually that the process generating the real exchange rate series has a unit root, while the alternative hypothesis is that all of the roots of the process lie within the unit circle. Thus,

[28] Dumas (1992) conjectures that the Roll (1979) '*ex ante* PPP' hypothesis holds as a limiting case of his model as the degree of risk aversion tends to zero, although see Section 3.4 below.

[29] See Allen and Taylor (1990), Taylor and Allen (1992) and Sarno and Taylor (2001a), for a discussion of the importance of the influence of technical analysis in the foreign exchange market.

[30] Taylor (2001) also provides some evidence that official foreign exchange intervention may impart nonlinearity into real exchange rate movements.

the maintained hypothesis in the conventional framework assumes a linear autoregressive process for the real exchange rate, which means that adjustment is both continuous and of constant speed, regardless of the size of the deviation from PPP. As noted above, however, the presence of transactions costs may imply a nonlinear process which has important implications for the conventional unit-root tests of long-run PPP. Some empirical evidence of the effect of transactions costs on tests of PPP is provided by Davutyan and Pippenger (1990). More recently, Obstfeld and Taylor (1997) have investigated the nonlinear nature of the adjustment process in terms of a threshold autoregressive (TAR) model (Tong, 1990) that allows for a transactions costs band within which no adjustment takes place while outside of the band the process switches abruptly to become stationary autoregressive. While discrete switching of this kind may be appropriate when considering the effects of arbitrage on disaggregated goods prices (Obstfeld and Taylor, 1997), discrete adjustment of the aggregate real exchange rate would clearly be most appropriate only when firms and traded goods are identical. Moreover, many of the theoretical studies discussed above suggest that smooth rather than discrete adjustment may be more appropriate in the presence of proportional transactions costs and, as suggested by Teräsvirta (1994), Dumas (1994) and Bertola and Caballero (1990), time aggregation and nonsynchronous adjustment by heterogeneous agents is likely to result in smooth aggregate regime-switching.

An alternative characterisation of nonlinear adjustment, which allows for smooth rather than discrete adjustment is in terms of a smooth transition autoregressive (STAR) model (Granger and Teräsvirta, 1993). This is the model employed by Michael, Nobay and Peel (1997) and Taylor, Peel and Sarno (2001). In the STAR model, adjustment takes place in every period, but the speed of adjustment varies with the extent of the deviation from parity. A STAR model may be written:

$$[q_t - \mu] = \sum_{j=1}^{p} \beta_j [q_{t-j} - \mu] + \left[\sum_{j=1}^{p} \beta_j^* [q_{t-j} - \mu] \right] \Phi[\theta; q_{t-d} - \mu] + \varepsilon_t \quad (3.17)$$

where $\{q_t\}$ is a stationary and ergodic process, $\varepsilon_t \sim iid(0, \sigma^2)$ and $(\theta \, \mu) \in \{\Re^+ \times \Re\}$, where $\Re$ denotes the real line $(-\infty, \infty)$ and $\Re^+$ the positive real line $(0, \infty)$; the integer $d > 0$ is a delay parameter. The transition function $\Phi[\theta; q_{t-d} - \mu]$ determines the degree of mean-reversion and is itself governed by the parameter θ, which effectively determines the speed of mean-reversion, and the parameter μ which is the equilibrium level of $\{q_t\}$. A simple transition function, suggested by Granger and Teräsvirta (1993), is the exponential function:

$$\Phi[\theta; q_{t-d} - \mu] = 1 - \exp\left[-\theta^2 [q_{t-d} - \mu]^2\right], \quad (3.18)$$

in which case (3.17) would be termed an exponential STAR, or ESTAR, model. The exponential transition function is bounded between zero and unity, $\Phi : \Re \to [0, 1]$, has the properties $\Phi[0] = 0$ and $\lim_{x \to \pm\infty} \Phi[x] = 1$, and is symmetrically inverse-bell shaped around zero. These properties of the ESTAR model are attractive in the present modelling context because they allow a smooth transition between regimes and symmetric adjustment of the real exchange rate for deviations above and below the equilibrium level. The transition parameter θ determines the speed of transition between the two extreme regimes, with lower absolute values of θ implying slower transition. The inner regime corresponds to $q_{t-d} = \mu$, when $\Phi = 0$ and (3.17) becomes a linear $\text{AR}(p)$ model:

$$[q_t - \mu] = \sum_{j=1}^{p} \beta_j [q_{t-j} - \mu] + \varepsilon_t. \tag{3.19}$$

The outer regime corresponds, for a given θ, to $\lim_{[q_{t-d}-\mu] \to \pm\infty} \Phi[\theta; q_{t-d} - \mu]$, where (3.17) becomes a different $\text{AR}(p)$ model:

$$[q_t - \mu] = \sum_{j=1}^{p} (\beta_j + \beta_j^*)[q_{t-j} - \mu] + \varepsilon_t \tag{3.20}$$

with a correspondingly different speed of mean-reversion so long as $\beta_j^* \neq 0$ for at least one value of j.

It is also instructive to reparameterise the STAR model (3.17) as:

$$\Delta q_t = \alpha + \rho q_{t-1} + \sum_{j=1}^{p-1} \phi_j \Delta q_{t-j}$$

$$+ \left\{ \alpha^* + \rho^* q_{t-1} + \sum_{j=1}^{p-1} \phi_j^* \Delta q_{t-j} \right\} \Phi[\theta; q_{t-d}] + \varepsilon_t, \tag{3.21}$$

where $\Delta q_{t-j} \equiv q_{t-j} - q_{t-j-1}$. In this form, the crucial parameters are ρ and ρ^*. Our discussion of the effect of transactions costs above suggests that the larger the deviation from PPP the stronger will be the tendency to move back to equilibrium. This implies that while $\rho \geq 0$ is admissible, we must have $\rho^* < 0$ and $(\rho + \rho^*) < 0$. That is, for small deviations q_t may be characterised by unit root or even explosive behaviour, but for large deviations the process is mean-reverting. This analysis has implications for the conventional test for a unit root in the real exchange rate process, which is based on a linear $\text{AR}(p)$ model, written as an augmented Dickey–Fuller regression:

$$\Delta q_t = \alpha' + \rho' q_{t-1} + \sum_{j=1}^{p-1} \phi_j' \Delta q_{t-j} + \varepsilon_t. \tag{3.22}$$

Assuming that the true process for q_t is given by the nonlinear model (3.21), estimates of the parameter ρ' in (3.22) will tend to lie between ρ and $(\rho + \rho^*)$, depending upon the distribution of observed deviations from the equilibrium level μ. Hence, the null hypothesis H_0: $\rho' = 0$ (a single unit root) may not be rejected against the stationary linear alternative hypothesis H_1: $\rho' < 0$, even though the true nonlinear process is globally stable with $(\rho + \rho^*) < 0$. Thus, failure to reject the unit-root hypothesis on the basis of a linear model does not necessarily invalidate long-run PPP.[31]

---

[31] In empirical applications, Granger and Teräsvirta (1993) and Teräsvirta (1994) suggest choosing the order of the autoregression, p, through inspection of the partial autocorrelation function (PACF); the PACF is to be preferred to the use of an information criterion since it is well known that the latter may bias the chosen order of the autoregression towards low values, and any remaining serial correlation may affect the power of subsequent linearity tests. Granger and Teräsvirta (1993) and Teräsvirta (1994) then suggest applying a sequence of linearity tests to specifically designed artificial regressions for various values of d (see also Luukkonen, Saikkonen and Teräsvirta, 1988). These can be interpreted as second- or third-order Taylor series expansions of the STAR model. This allows detection of general nonlinearity through the significance of the higher-order terms, with the value of d selected as that giving the strongest rejection of the linearity hypothesis.

Michael, Nobay and Peel (1997) apply this model to monthly inter-war data for the French franc–US dollar, French franc–UK sterling and UK sterling–US dollar rates as well as to the Lothian and Taylor (1996) long-span data set. Their results clearly reject the linear framework in favour of an ESTAR process. The systematic pattern in the estimates of the nonlinear models provides strong evidence of mean-reverting behaviour for PPP deviations, and helps explain the mixed results of previous studies. However, the periods examined by Michael, Nobay and Peel are ones over which the relevance of long-run PPP is uncontentious (Taylor and McMahon, 1988; Lothian and Taylor, 1996).

Using data for the recent float, however, Taylor, Peel and Sarno (2001) record empirical results that provide strong confirmation that four major real bilateral dollar exchange rates are well characterised by nonlinearly mean-reverting processes over the floating rate period since 1973. Their estimated models imply an equilibrium level of the real exchange rate in the neighbourhood of which the behaviour of the log-level of the real exchange rate is close to a random walk, becoming increasingly mean-reverting with the absolute size of the deviation from equilibrium, which is consistent with the recent theoretical literature on the nature of real exchange rate dynamics in the presence of international arbitrage costs. Taylor, Peel and Sarno (2001) also estimate the impulse response functions corresponding to their estimated nonlinear real exchange rate models by Monte Carlo integration.[32] By taking account of statistically significant nonlinearities, Taylor, Peel and Sarno find the speed of real exchange rate adjustment to be typically much faster than the very slow speeds of real exchange rate adjustment hitherto recorded in the literature. These results therefore seem to shed some light on Rogoff's PPP puzzle (Rogoff, 1996). In particular, it is only for small shocks occurring when the real exchange rate is near its equilibrium that the nonlinear models consistently yield half-lives in the range of three to five years, which Rogoff (1996) terms 'glacial'. For dollar–mark and dollar–sterling in particular, even small shocks of 1 to 5 per cent have a half-life under three years. For larger shocks, the speed of mean-reversion is even faster.[33, 34]

In a number of Monte Carlo studies calibrated on the estimated nonlinear models, Taylor, Peel and Sarno (2001) also demonstrate the very low power of standard univariate unit-root tests to reject a false null hypothesis of unit-root behaviour when the true model is nonlinearly mean-reverting, thereby suggesting an explanation for the difficulty researchers have encountered in rejecting the linear unit-root hypothesis at conventional significance levels for major real exchange rates over the recent floating rate period. Panel unit-root tests, however, displayed much higher power in their rejection of the false null hypothesis against an alternative of nonlinear mean-reversion, in keeping with the recent literature.

---

[32] Note that, because of the nonlinearity, the half-lives of shocks to the real exchange rates vary both with the size of the shock and with the initial conditions.

[33] Half-lives estimated using ESTAR models fitted to mark-based European real exchange rate series (Taylor and Sarno, 1999) were generally slightly lower than those for dollar-based real exchange rates. This is unsurprising, given the proximity of the European markets involved and the fact that they are operating within a customs union, and accords with previous evidence on the mean-reverting properties of European real exchange rates (e.g. Cheung and Lai, 1998; Canzoneri, Cumby and Diba, 1999).

[34] In a complementary study, Taylor and Peel (2000) fit ESTAR models to deviations of the nominal exchange rate from the level suggested by 'monetary fundamentals', and find that the model performs well for dollar–mark and dollar–sterling over the recent float.

The results of Taylor, Peel and Sarno therefore encompass previous empirical work in this area.[35]

3.4 Efficient markets and purchasing power parity: a cautionary note[36]

There exists a strand of the literature, due originally to Roll (1979) and Adler and Lehmann (1983), which maintains that if international financial markets are efficient, then deviations from PPP – i.e. the real exchange rate – must follow a random walk (or more precisely a martingale) process. This is sometimes termed 'ex ante PPP' or 'efficient markets PPP' (EMPPP).

3.4.1 The Adler–Lehmann formulation

The line of reasoning leading to the EMPPP hypothesis, as set out by Adler and Lehmann (1983), is as follows. Recall that the real exchange rate (the deviation from PPP), q_t, may be expressed in logarithmic form as:

$$q_t \equiv s_t - p_t + p_t^*, \tag{3.23}$$

where s_t is the logarithm of the nominal exchange rate (domestic price of foreign currency), and p_t and p_t^* denote the logarithms of the domestic and foreign price levels respectively.

The concept of foreign exchange market efficiency can be encapsulated in the assumption that uncovered interest rate parity holds and that agents' expectations are rational:[37]

$$E_t(\Delta s_{t+1}) = i_t - i_t^*, \tag{3.24}$$

where E_t denotes the mathematical expectation operator conditional on information at time t; Δ is the first-difference operator such that $\Delta x_{t+1} \equiv x_{t+1} - x_t \; \forall x$; i_t and i_t^* are the one-period nominal interest rates available on similar domestic and foreign securities respectively. Now, using the standard Fisher decomposition of the interest rate, the nominal interest rate differential can be written as the sum of the expected real interest rate differential, $E_t(r_{t+1}) - E_t(r_{t+1}^*)$ and the expected inflation rate differential, $E_t(\Delta p_{t+1}) - E_t(\Delta p_{t+1}^*)$:[38]

$$i_t - i_t^* = [E_t(r_{t+1}) - E_t(r_{t+1}^*)] + [E_t(\Delta p_{t+1}) - E_t(\Delta p_{t+1}^*)]. \tag{3.25}$$

---

[35] In their fitted ESTAR models, the real exchange rate will be closer to a unit-root process the closer it is to its long-run equilibrium. Somewhat paradoxically, therefore, failure to reject a unit root may indicate that the real exchange rate has on average been relatively close to equilibrium, rather than implying that no such long-run equilibrium exists.

[36] This section draws heavily on Taylor and Sarno (2001).

[37] In particular, we are assuming a zero foreign exchange risk premium, in line with the simple efficient markets hypothesis (see Chapter 2). However, admitting a constant risk premium would not alter the conclusions of the analysis at all, while admitting a stationary risk premium would only change the results to the extent that the EMPPP result would be modified to the real exchange rate following a more general unit-root process rather than a simple random walk.

[38] Note that i_t denotes the nominal cost of borrowing from the beginning of period t to the very end of period t, while r_{t+1} denotes the real cost of borrowing over the same period. While i_t is known at the beginning of period t, however, r_{t+1} can only be known at the beginning of period $t + 1$, since the rate of inflation during the period is unknown *ex ante*. Hence, we have adopted the convention of ascribing subscripts to real and nominal interest rates according to the period in which they are known. This allows us to use, without ambiguity, a simple subscript on the expectations operator to denote the dating of the information set upon which expectations are conditioned. Similarly, Δp_{t+1} represents the change in the logarithm of prices between the beginning of period t and the beginning of period $t + 1$.

Hence, subtracting the expected inflation differential from either side of (3.24) implies:

$$E_t(\Delta s_{t+1}) - E_t(\Delta p_{t+1}) + E_t(\Delta p^*_{t+1}) = [i_t - E_t(\Delta p_{t+1})] - [i^*_t - E_t(\Delta p^*_{t+1})],$$

(3.26)

or equivalently, using (3.25):

$$E_t(\Delta q_{t+1}) = E_t(r_{t+1}) - E_t(r^*_{t+1}).$$

(3.27)

Equation (3.27) may be rewritten:

$$\Delta q_{t+1} = E_t(r_{t+1}) - E_t(r^*_{t+1}) + \eta_{t+1},$$

(3.28)

where η_{t+1} is a rational expectations forecast error such that $E_t(\eta_{t+1}) = 0$. The next step is to assume that the expected real interest rate differential is a constant (Adler and Lehmann, 1983):

$$E_t(r_{t+1}) - E_t(r^*_{t+1}) = \gamma.$$

(3.29)

From (3.28) and (3.29) we then immediately derive the martingale relation:

$$q_{t+1} = q_t + \gamma + \eta_{t+1}.$$

(3.30)

According to (3.30), the real exchange rate is a first-order unit-root process, so that there is no tendency to settle down at long-run PPP with a constant level of the real exchange rate. This is the central result in this literature: that long-run PPP is incompatible with efficient international financial markets.

3.4.2   The Roll formulation

Roll (1979) derives a similar result to that of Adler and Lehmann (1983) through an argument based on efficient speculation in real commodities. In particular, suppose that agents resident in the domestic economy buy foreign goods and hold them for one period. The expected nominal return from such a strategy, expressed in foreign currency, must be equal to the expected foreign inflation rate, $E_t(\Delta p^*_{t+1})$. Expressing this expected payoff in real domestic currency terms involves, however, adjusting for expected movements in the nominal exchange rate and in domestic prices, so that the total expected real return to domestic residents speculating in foreign goods must be $E_t(\Delta p^*_{t+1}) + E_t(\Delta s_{t+1}) - E_t(\Delta p_{t+1})$. By a converse argument, this is also the expected real return to foreign residents of speculating in domestic commodities, multiplied by minus one. Roll argues that this expected return must be zero in an efficient market:

$$E_t(\Delta p^*_{t+1}) + E_t(\Delta s_{t+1}) - E_t(\Delta p_{t+1}) = 0.$$

(3.31)

From the definition of the real exchange rate (3.23) this then implies:

$$E_t(\Delta q_{t+1}) = 0,$$

(3.32)

which in turn implies the martingale relation:

$$q_{t+1} = q_t + \eta_{t+1},$$

(3.33)

where η_{t+1} is again a rational expectations forecast error such that $E_t(\eta_{t+1}) = 0$. On closer examination, however, it should be clear that Roll is implicitly making a constant expected real interest rate differential assumption similar to that made by Adler and Lehmann (1983). To see this, note that, in order to purchase the foreign commodities at time t, domestic residents must borrow money at the nominal domestic interest rate i_t (or, equivalently, forego this return on their investment), so that the expected real cost of the funds is $i_t - E_t(\Delta p_{t+1}) = E_t(r_{t+1})$. Moreover, once they have acquired the foreign goods, domestic residents can presumably hire them out for one period. Let the expected nominal rental return from hiring out the foreign goods from the beginning of period t to the beginning of period $t + 1$, net of expected nominal depreciation in the market value of the goods due to hiring them out, be $E_t(h_{t+1}^*)$ or, in real terms, $E_t(h_{t+1}^*) - E_t(\Delta p_{t+1}^*)$.[39] By an arbitrage argument, this must be equal to the expected foreign real interest rate over the same period:

$$E_t(h_t^*) - E_t(\Delta p_{t+1}^*) = E_t(r_{t+1}^*), \tag{3.34}$$

since $E_t(h_{t+1}^*) - E_t(\Delta p_{t+1}^*) > E_t(r_{t+1}^*)$ or $E_t(h_{t+1}^*) - E_t(\Delta p_{t+1}^*) < E_t(r_{t+1}^*)$ would imply profitable arbitrage opportunities available to foreign residents. This means that the net real cost to domestic residents of speculating in foreign goods is just the real interest rate differential, $E_t(r_{t+1}) - E_t(r_{t+1}^*)$. Thus, the condition for the expected real return to foreign goods speculation to be zero, equation (3.31), must be modified to:

$$[E_t\Delta s_{t+1} - E_t(\Delta p_{t+1}) + E_t(\Delta p_{t+1}^*)] - [E_t(r_{t+1}) - E_t(r_{t+1}^*)] = 0, \tag{3.35}$$

or equivalently, using the definition of the real exchange rate:

$$\Delta q_{t+1} = E_t(r_{t+1}) - E_t(r_{t+1}^*) + \eta_{t+1}. \tag{3.36}$$

Equation (3.36) is indeed identical to equation (3.28) above. Then, the martingale relation can again be obtained by setting the expected real interest rate differential to a constant, $E_t(r_{t+1}) - E_t(r_{t+1}^*) = \gamma$, so that (3.36) becomes:

$$q_{t+1} = q_t + \gamma + \eta_{t+1}, \tag{3.37}$$

where $E_t(\eta_{t+1}) = 0$. In fact, Roll explicitly assumes that the expected real interest rate differential is equal to zero, so that (3.37) becomes:[40]

$$q_{t+1} = q_t + \eta_{t+1}. \tag{3.38}$$

---

[39] Note that h_{t+1}^* may alternatively be interpreted as the nominal cost of storage of the commodity from the beginning of period t to the beginning of period $t + 1$, adjusted for any nominal increase in value of the commodity over the period. Clearly, goods would only be bought and stored if the real, inflation-adjusted, increase in value were expected to be greater than the real storage costs, so that $E_t(h_{t+1}^*) - E_t(\Delta p_{t+1}^*) > 0$. Otherwise it would be better simply to purchase the commodity at time $t + 1$.

[40] As Roll (1979, p. 139) puts it: 'we shall see that the expected value of [the real return from foreign intertemporal speculation, i.e. the change in the real exchange rate] can equal a nonzero constant . . . if real interest rates differ in countries A and B'. Clearly, therefore, Roll assumes that real interest parity holds with $\gamma = 0$ in his analysis.

3.4.3 Resolving the conundrum

We are now in a position to resolve the conundrum by analysing the full cointegrating system between the exchange rate and domestic and foreign prices which must exist if the real exchange rate is stationary, whilst allowing for a stationary real interest rate differential.

We have shown that a key assumption in the efficient markets PPP formulation, as derived by both Roll (1979) and Adler and Lehmann (1983), is that the expected real interest rate differential is a constant. Many international financial economists would now probably demur at such an assumption, even under the presumption that international financial markets were operating perfectly efficiently. As Marston (1995, p. 153) notes: 'since there is no single borrower (or investor) who compares these two real interest rates, there is no direct arbitrage that ensures that [real interest rate parity] holds'.

In fact, if the nominal exchange rate is integrated of order one,[41] $I(1)$ – as appears to be a stylised fact for major exchange rates[42] – then the uncovered interest rate parity condition (3.24) would imply that the nominal interest rate differential is stationary.[43] If we assume that inflation is a stationary process – or, equivalently, that prices are $I(1)$ – then the stationarity of the real interest rate differential follows by definition.

Empirically, the evidence appears both to reject real interest rate parity among major industrialised economies and to support the stationarity of real interest rate differentials. In a recent monograph covering these issues, for example, Marston (1995, p. 177) concludes: 'real interest parity is soundly rejected despite the fact that *on average* real interest differentials are close to zero'.[44, 45]

In both the Adler–Lehmann and the Roll formulations of EMPPP, a key equation is derived linking the expected change in the real exchange rate to the expected real interest rate differential, equations (3.28) and (3.36). This may be written in the equivalent form:

$$\Delta q_{t+1} = (i_t - i_t^*) - E_t(\Delta p_{t+1}) + E_t(\Delta p_{t+1}^*) + \eta_{t+1}, \qquad (3.39)$$

where, as throughout, $E_t(\eta_{t+1}) = 0$. Now suppose that the real exchange rate *is* stationary, i.e. $q_t \sim I(0)$. Since $q_t \equiv s_t - (p_t - p_t^*)$, this implies that the vector $X_t = (s_t, p_t, p_t^*)'$ must be cointegrated, assuming that s_t, p_t and p_t^* are each $I(1)$ processes, with known cointegrating vector $f = (1, -1, 1)'$, such that $f'X_t \equiv q_t \sim I(0)$. By the Granger representation theorem (Engle and Granger, 1987), this implies that there exists a vector equilibrium

---

[41] A time series process is said to be integrated of order d, denoted $I(d)$, if it must be first differenced d times in order to induce covariance stationarity. Thus a simple random walk process is integrated of order one, $I(1)$, as are more general processes with a single unit root. A stationary process is, of course, integrated of order zero, $I(0)$.

[42] See e.g. Mussa (1979), Taylor (1995), and the references therein.

[43] This is true even if we allow for deviations from the simple efficient markets hypothesis and admit, in particular, risk premia and deviations from rational expectations – so long as the resulting deviations from uncovered interest parity are themselves stationary (see Clarida and Taylor, 1997).

[44] Emphasis in the original.

[45] For other empirical studies on real interest rate differentials, see, for example, the work of Mishkin (1984) and Mark (1985a, 1985b).

correction (VECM) representation linking s_t, p_t and p_t^* of the form:[46]

$$\Delta X_t = \alpha q_{t-1} + \sum_{i=1}^{k} \Lambda_i \Delta X_{t-i} + \epsilon_t, \qquad (3.40)$$

where $\alpha = (\alpha_1, \alpha_2, \alpha_3)'$ is a 3×1 vector of equilibrium parameters, the Λ_i are 3×3 co-efficient matrices, and ϵ_t is a 3×1 vector of disturbance terms. Let $g = (0, 1, -1)'$, then using the vector equilibrium correction representation (3.40), we have:

$$E_t(\Delta p_{t+1} - \Delta p_{t+1}^*) = g' E_t(\Delta X_{t+1})$$

$$= g' \alpha q_t + \sum_{i=1}^{k} g' \Lambda_i \Delta X_{t-i+1}. \qquad (3.41)$$

Hence, using the Fisher decomposition, as in (3.25), in (3.41), the expected real interest rate differential may be written:

$$E_t(r_{t+1}) - E_t(r_{t+1}^*) = (i_t - i_t^*) - g' \alpha q_t - \sum_{i=1}^{k} g' \Lambda i \Delta X_{t-i+1}. \qquad (3.42)$$

Using (3.42) in (3.28) or in (3.36) we then have:

$$\Delta q_{t+1} = (i_t - i_t^*) - g' \alpha q_t - \sum_{i=1}^{k} g' \Lambda_i \Delta X_{t-i+1} + \eta_{t+1} \qquad (3.43)$$

or:

$$q_{t+1} = (i_t - i_t^*) + (1 - g' \alpha) q_t - \sum_{i=1}^{k} g' \Lambda_i \Delta X_{t-i+1} + \eta_{t+1}. \qquad (3.44)$$

Now since s_t is $I(1)$ by assumption, then from the uncovered interest rate parity condition (3.24), $(i_t - i_t^*)$ is $I(0)$. Also, all of the ΔX_{t-i+1} on the right-hand side of (3.43) and (3.44) are $I(0)$. Hence, the unit root in q_t is precluded so long as $1 > g' \alpha = \alpha_2 - \alpha_3 > 0$. Indeed, this condition is sufficient to preclude the unit root in q_t so long as the right-hand side of (3.42) is not equal to a constant, i.e. so long as the expected real interest rate differential is *not* identically equal to a constant value.[47] But this condition only implies that there is feedback from the lagged level of the real exchange rate onto either domestic or foreign prices, or both, and that this feedback is stabilising on the real exchange rate in its net effect. It will clearly be

---

[46] Recall that Taylor, Peel and Sarno (2001), in an empirical study of a number of major real exchange rates, provide evidence to support the hypothesis that the real exchange rate mean-reverts nonlinearly towards its equilibrium value, such that larger deviations from PPP tend to mean-revert much faster. This empirical evidence is also consistent with a theoretical literature showing that transactions costs in international arbitrage will in general induce nonlinearities of this kind (see Taylor, Peel and Sarno, 2001, for references to this literature). In the present context, this would imply that the vector equilibrium correction system (3.41) would in fact be nonlinear. All of the main results of this chapter would be essentially qualitatively unchanged in the presence of such nonlinearities, however. Indeed, the VECM system (3.41) may be interpreted as a linear approximation to a nonlinear vector equilibrium correction system.

[47] In this case, any effect of the real exchange rate on relative expected inflation would be passed on one-for-one to movements in the nominal interest rate differential, leaving the expected real interest rate differential unchanged.

satisfied if at least one of $\alpha_2 > 0$ and $\alpha_3 < 0$ is true, and if $1 > \alpha_2 - \alpha_3 > 0$ is also true. For $\alpha_2 > 0$, for example, a fall in the level of q_t, i.e. a real appreciation of the domestic currency, will have a negative impact on Δp_{t+1} through the equilibrium correction term $\alpha_2 q_t$. In economic terms, however, this is entirely intuitive: it simply means that a real appreciation of the external value of the currency – i.e. a loss in competitiveness – has a net *long-run* deflationary impact on the economy. In relative terms, given the way in which we have defined the real exchange rate, and given $g'\alpha > 0$, equation (3.41) shows that this implies a positive correlation between the domestic–foreign inflation differential and the level of the real exchange rate. This in turn implies a negative correlation between the real interest rate differential and the level of the real exchange rate; see equation (3.42). Given that uncovered interest parity and the Fisher decomposition together imply that the expected real exchange rate change must be equal to the real interest rate differential (equation (3.27)), this further implies negative correlation between the level of the real exchange rate and its rate of change, which implies mean-reversion of the real exchange rate towards a long-run equilibrium level.[48]

The stationarity of the real exchange rate was of course assumed *ex hypothesi* from the outset, but what we have shown is that stationarity of q_t is *not incompatible* with the uncovered interest rate parity condition and the Fisher decomposition, as the EMPPP strand of the literature seems to imply.[49] Indeed, our economic intuition, as set out in the preceding paragraph, implies that they are highly compatible.

Note that it appears that examination of the full equilibrium correction system is necessary in order to see formally this implication of assuming a stationary real interest rate differential. In equations (3.28) and (3.36), for example, it would seem that stationarity of the real interest rate differential would in fact only imply that the real exchange rate is $I(1)$, which would again preclude long-run PPP. To draw this conclusion, however, would be to overlook the fact that the cointegrated equilibrium correction system implies that the real interest rate differential, since it involves movements in relative inflation, will be negatively correlated with the level of the real exchange rate itself, as equations (3.41)–(3.44) show clearly.

Overall, there were two steps in the resolution of this conundrum. First, we relaxed the assumption, made by both Roll (1979) and Adler and Lehmann (1983), that the expected real interest rate differential is a constant, i.e. that real interest rate parity holds between the two economies concerned. Second, we examined the full dynamic equilibrium correction system linking prices and exchange rates which must exist if the real exchange rate is stationary and the nominal exchange rate and domestic and foreign prices are cointegrated. From this we were able to show that market efficiency is not in fact incompatible with long-run purchasing power parity.

Intuitively, although uncovered interest rate parity and the Fisher decomposition do jointly imply that the expected rate of change of the real exchange rate must be equal to the expected

---

[48] Strictly speaking, we require negative correlation between the level of the real exchange rate and its rate of change, with a correlation coefficient strictly less than unity. This is satisfied formally by the restriction $1 > g'\alpha$ and intuitively by the requirement that the feedback from the real exchange rate to inflation be stabilising.

[49] Note that this is not a circular argument. Admittedly, we started by assuming stationarity of the real exchange rate, but if this were inconsistent with efficient markets then combining it with the uncovered interest rate parity condition would have produced a logical contradiction. Since it did not, long-run PPP and stationarity of the real exchange rate are compatible with an efficient foreign exchange market.

real interest rate differential, that differential itself must in general be negatively correlated with the level of the real exchange rate if a loss in international competitiveness has a net deflationary impact on the economy. This in turn implies mean-reversion of the real exchange rate since it implies that changes in the real exchange rate are negatively correlated with the level of the real exchange rate.

It should be emphasised that the seminal writers on EMPPP – notably Roll (1979) and Adler and Lehmann (1983) – could not have been aware of the implications of cointegration and the Granger representation theorem for their analysis, since these concepts only became widely known after the publication of Engle and Granger's subsequent seminal paper on cointegrated processes (Engle and Granger, 1987). This is, therefore, a clear example of how advances in econometric theory can sometimes lead to advances in our economic and financial understanding.

3.5 Modelling long-run PPP deviations

Modifications and extensions of the simple PPP hypothesis exist which try to rationalise the existence of long-run deviations from PPP. The most popular of these is the Harrod–Balassa–Samuelson model (Harrod, 1933; Balassa, 1964; Samuelson, 1964).[50]

The underlying argument of the Harrod–Balassa–Samuelson model is as follows. Suppose, for the sake of argument, that the law of one price (LOOP) holds among traded goods. In the fast-growing economy, productivity growth will tend to be concentrated in the traded goods sector. This will lead to wage rises in the traded goods sector without the necessity for price rises. Hence traded goods prices can remain constant and the LOOP continues to hold with an unchanged nominal exchange rate. But workers in the non-traded goods sector will also demand comparable pay rises, and this will lead to an overall rise in the CPI. Since the LOOP holds among traded goods and, by assumption, the nominal exchange rate has remained constant, this means that the upward movement in the domestic CPI will not be matched by a movement in the nominal exchange rate so that, if PPP initially held, the domestic currency must now appear overvalued on the basis of comparison made using CPIs expressed in a common currency at the prevailing exchange rate. The crucial assumption is that productivity growth is much higher in the traded goods sector.[51] Note also that the relative price of non-tradables may rise even in the case of balanced growth of the two sectors of the economy, as long as the non-traded goods sector is more labour intensive relative to the traded goods sector.

We can analyse this issue more formally using a simple small open economy model due to Froot and Rogoff (1995).[52] Consider the following production functions for the two sectors of the economy:

$$Y^I = A^I (L^I)^{\theta^I} (K^I)^{1-\theta^I} \qquad I = T, N \qquad (3.45)$$

---

[50] Some researchers suggest that government spending may also generate long-run deviations from PPP because it tends to raise the relative price of services and non-tradables.

[51] This is an argument first advanced and empirically tested by Baumol and Bowen (1966).

[52] Rogoff (1992) extends this model, adding more interesting dynamics, and also provides a more comprehensive treatment of the Harrod–Balassa–Samuelson effect; see also Obstfeld and Rogoff (1996, ch. 4).

where Y^I, K^I, L^I and A^I denote domestic output, capital, labour and productivity in the sector of the economy considered; the superscripts T and N denote the traded and non-traded sectors respectively; time subscripts are omitted for simplicity. The model also assumes perfect factor mobility and perfect competition in both traded and non-traded sectors. Thus, the equations for the world (and domestic) interest rate and wages may be derived as the marginal products of capital and labour in the two sectors as follows:

$$R = (1 - \theta^T)A^T(K^T/L^T)^{-\theta^T} \tag{3.46}$$

$$R = P^N(1 - \theta^N)A^N(K^N/L^N)^{-\theta^N} \tag{3.47}$$

$$W = \theta^T A^T(K^T/L^T)^{1-\theta^T} \tag{3.48}$$

$$W = P^N\theta^N A^N(K^N/L^N)^{1-\theta^N} \tag{3.49}$$

where R denotes the world cost of capital, W is the wage rate measured in tradables and P^N is the relative price of the non-tradable goods. The model (3.45)–(3.49) provides a solution for the four endogenous variables, that is the capital-labour ratios for the two sectors of the economy, the wage rate and the relative price level. Taking logs and totally differentiating (3.45)–(3.49), the model can be rewritten as follows:

$$\underline{a}^T - \theta^T(\underline{k}^T - \underline{l}^T) = 0 \tag{3.50}$$

$$\underline{p}^N + \underline{a}^N - \theta^N(\underline{k}^N - \underline{l}^N) = 0 \tag{3.51}$$

$$\underline{w} = \underline{a}^T + (1 - \theta^T)(\underline{k}^T - \underline{l}^T) \tag{3.52}$$

$$\underline{w} = \underline{p}^N + \underline{a}^N + (1 - \theta^N)(\underline{k}^N - \underline{l}^N) \tag{3.53}$$

where the variables in lower case are in logarithms and the variables underlined are total differentials of the variables in question. Finally, the solutions for the endogenous variables of the model, obtained using (3.50)–(3.53), are:

$$(\underline{k}^N - \underline{l}^N) = (\underline{k}^T - \underline{l}^T) = \underline{w} = \underline{a}^T/\theta^T \tag{3.54}$$

$$\underline{p}^N = (\theta^N/\theta^T)\underline{a}^T - \underline{a}^N. \tag{3.55}$$

According to equation (3.54), the model predicts that the percentage changes in the capital–labour ratio are the same in the traded and non-traded goods sectors and they are also equal to the wage rate change. Equation (3.55) incorporates the Harrod–Balassa–Samuelson condition: the percentage change in the relative price of non-tradables is determined only by the production side of the economy, while demand factors do not affect the real exchange rate in the long run. If the degree of labour and capital intensity is the same in the traded and non-traded sectors, i.e. $\theta^T = \theta^N$, then the percentage change in relative prices is exactly equal to the productivity differential between the two sectors. Nevertheless, if the non-traded sector is more labour intensive than the traded sector, i.e. $\theta^N > \theta^T$, then even in a situation of balanced productivity growth in the two sectors, the relative price of non-tradables will rise. With one component of the CPI constant and the other one increasing, the overall price level must increase.[53, 54]

Japan is often referred to as a good example of the Harrod–Balassa–Samuelson effect in operation, since it has been on average the fastest-growing economy for much of the post-World War II period. In the case of Japan, the effect appears to be significant regardless of the price index used even if, in general, one would expect the Harrod–Balassa–Samuelson effect to be relatively stronger when the CPI is used rather than the WPI, since the latter includes a higher component of tradables (see Rogoff, 1996).[55]

Apart from a few exceptions, however, the empirical evidence provides mixed results on the Harrod–Balassa–Samuelson effect. For example, Rogoff (1992) provides an alternative explanation of the fact that the real exchange rate displays near random walk behaviour that does not require near random walk behaviour in the underlying fundamentals. He builds a neoclassical open-economy model with traded and non-traded goods, where agents are able to smooth their consumption of tradables over time through the international capital markets in the face of productivity shocks in the traded goods sector. In this model, agents cannot, however, smooth productivity shocks in the non-traded goods sector, but these shocks are assumed not to be very significant, as suggested by some theory and empirical evidence (Baumol and Bowen, 1966). The implications and the empirical estimates of the model are in sharp contrast to the predictions of the Harrod–Balassa–Samuelson model, even though the exchange rate considered is the Japanese yen–US dollar rate during the recent float.

Asea and Mendoza (1994) build a neoclassical general equilibrium model which has similar implications to the Harrod–Balassa–Samuelson model. First, productivity differentials determine international differences in relative prices of non-tradable goods. Second, deviations from PPP reflect differences in non-tradable prices. The results from estimating the model on a panel of OECD countries provide empirical evidence that productivity differentials can explain low-frequency differences in relative prices. Nevertheless, predicted relative prices of non-tradable goods cannot explain long-run deviations from PPP.

Some other recent empirical evidence exists, however, in favour of the Harrod–Balassa–Samuelson hypothesis. Heston, Nuxoll and Summers (1994) examine the tradable–non-tradable price differential across countries on the basis of the International Comparison Program (ICP) data set and find, using a variety of regressions, that the difference between tradable and non-tradable price parities moves with income, consistent with the views of Harrod, Balassa and Samuelson.

A number of authors have also suggested that demand factors – notably real government consumption – may generate deviations from PPP if there is a bias towards the service sector, since this will tend to raise the relative price of non-tradables. De Gregorio, Giovannini and

---

[53] An alternative underlying theory which also leads to the Harrod–Balassa–Samuelson hypothesis is due to Kravis and Lipsey (1983) and Bhagwati (1984), who build an imperfect capital mobility model and hence use the assumption that capital–labour ratios are higher in fast-growing countries than in slow-growing ones.

[54] For a comprehensive overview of the theoretical contributions and the empirical evidence on the Harrod–Balassa–Samuelson effect, see Asea and Corden (1994).

[55] Also, Marston (1987) and Edison and Klovland (1987) provide strong empirical evidence for the existence of a Harrod–Balassa–Samuelson effect for the Japanese yen–US dollar and the UK pound–Norwegian krone exchange rates respectively. Similar findings are provided for both Germany and Japan by Hsieh (1982) and Obstfeld (1993).

Wolf (1994) estimate, using panel data methods, regressions of the form:

$$(p^N - p^T)_{i,t} = \phi_i + \varphi_1[(\theta^N/\theta^T)a^T - a^N]_{i,t} + \varphi_2 g_{i,t} + \varphi_3 y_{i,t}, \qquad (3.56)$$

where g denotes the ratio of real government spending (excluding government investment) to real GDP, y is real income per capita, and i is a country subscript. Their empirical
results for a panel of fourteen OECD countries suggest that productivity, government spending and income are all important variables in explaining the tradable–non-tradable price
differential and the parameters φ_1, φ_2 and φ_3 are all statistically significant at conventional
nominal levels of significance and correctly signed.[56] In order to investigate the long-run
significance of the demand factors (g and y), De Gregorio, Giovannini and Wolf also estimate the same regression on average data for the same panel of countries; their results
suggest that demand factors become less important over the long run.[57] De Gregorio and
Wolf (1994) decompose the component of real exchange rate movements determined by
the Harrod–Balassa–Samuelson effect and the component caused by changes in the relative
prices of traded goods, that is changes in the terms of trade. They find that the latter appears
to be more important than the Harrod–Balassa–Samuelson effect in explaining short-term
real exchange rate movements. On the other hand, Chinn (2000), in an analysis of a set
of Asia-Pacific economies, finds that neither government spending nor the terms of trade
appear to be important factors.

Overall, the empirical evidence on the Harrod–Balassa–Samuelson effect is quite mixed.
Even if some evidence exists that the productivity differential is an important factor in
explaining the tradable–non-tradable price differential and the real exchange rate, increasingly strong evidence supporting long-run convergence to PPP is provided by the recent
literature, perhaps simply because technological progress is mobile across borders in the
very long run.[58]

3.6   The source of shocks to real and nominal exchange rates

A related strand of the empirical literature on real exchange rate behaviour has investigated
the source of disturbances (shocks) to real and nominal exchange rates. Much of this evidence comes from employing vector autoregression analysis inspired by the methodology

---

[56] Data for productivity are often computed in this literature using Solow residuals.

[57] Alesina and Perotti (1995) argue that fiscal policy may also have long-run real effects if distortionary taxes are
used in order to finance government spending programmes.

[58] Some researchers also argue that a strong long-run relationship exists between persistent deficits in the current
account balance and the depreciation of the real exchange rate. In fact, a close correlation is often found between
these two variables. For example, Obstfeld and Rogoff (1995) find a large correlation coefficient between trade-
weighted real exchange rate changes and changes in net foreign asset positions for fifteen countries during the
1980s. Correlation between these two endogenous variables does not necessarily imply, however, that there is
causation. For example, Bayoumi, Clark, Symansky and Taylor (1994) use the International Monetary Fund's
MULTIMOD and provide evidence that the correlation between current account deficits and the real exchange
rate is in fact very sensitive to whether the driving factor is fiscal or monetary policy. More generally, current
account deficits may be rationalised on the basis of many different driving factors.

originally developed by Blanchard and Quah (1989).[59] In this section we provide a brief review of this literature.

Lastrapes (1992) applies the Blanchard and Quah (1989) decomposition to real and nominal US dollar exchange rates of five industrialised countries (Germany, UK, Japan, Italy and Canada) over the sample period from 1973 to 1989. Lastrapes finds that real shocks cause a permanent real and nominal appreciation, while nominal shocks are found to cause a permanent nominal depreciation. Evans and Lothian (1993) also examine real dollar exchange rates of four major industrial countries under the recent float and report that transitory shocks play a relatively small role in explaining real exchange rate movements. Their findings, however, also suggest that there are instances when temporary shocks make a more substantial contribution, so that the role of temporary and permanent shocks in driving exchange rate movements may be varying over time. Enders and Lee (1997) discover similar findings in an investigation of the sources of real and nominal exchange rate fluctuations for several major industrialised countries over the post-Bretton Woods period. In a highly cited study, Clarida and Gali (1994) estimate the relative contribution of three types of shocks to four major real US dollar exchange rates during the post-Bretton Woods era. Clarida and Gali assume that one type of shock affects both the real exchange rate and output in the long run. They interpret this shock as a supply shock. Clarida and Gali further assume that another shock affects the real exchange rate in the long run but not output, and they label this as a demand shock. Finally, all shocks that influence neither the long-run real exchange rate nor output are denoted as monetary shocks. Clarida and Gali find that monetary shocks account for 41 per cent of the unconditional variance of changes in the real German mark rate and 35 percent of the unconditional variance of changes in the real Japanese yen rate. They also estimate that monetary shocks account for no more than 3 per cent of the unconditional variance of real exchange rate changes over all horizons for the UK pound and Canadian dollar. Rogers (1999), however, employing a structural vector autoregression on a long-term data set provides evidence that monetary shocks account for almost one-half of the forecast error variance of the real dollar–sterling exchange rate over short horizons. In an earlier study, Eichenbaum and Evans (1995) also investigate the effects of shocks to US monetary policy on exchange rates. Specifically, they consider three measures of these shocks: orthogonalised shocks to the federal funds rate; orthogonalised shocks to the ratio of non-borrowed to total reserves; and changes in the Romer and Romer index of monetary policy. In contrast to a large literature, Eichenbaum and Evans find substantial evidence of a link between monetary policy and exchange rates.[60]

---

[59] Blanchard and Quah (1989) provide an econometric technique which allows researchers to decompose a time series into its temporary and permanent components in the context of a vector autoregression. In their study, they decompose real output into its transitory and permanent components. They motivate their empirical analysis using a stylised macroeconomic model where real output is affected both by demand- and supply-side disturbances, but only supply-side shocks, which they identify as productivity shocks, have permanent effects on output.

[60] In particular, their results suggest that a contractionary shock to US monetary policy leads to (a) persistent, significant appreciations in US nominal and real exchange rates and (b) persistent, significant deviations from uncovered interest rate parity in favour of US interest rates.

One problem with this literature is that identification restrictions are required in the vector autoregression model in order to identify uniquely the model and to generate impulse response functions and variance decompositions. Cushman and Zha (1997) argue that many empirical studies on the effects of monetary policy shocks in small open economies have generated puzzling dynamic responses in various macroeconomic variables due to an identification of monetary policy that is inappropriate for such economies. To remedy this, Cushman and Zha propose that a structural model be estimated to account explicitly for the features of the small open economy. Such a model is applied to Canada and is shown to generate dynamic responses to the identified monetary policy shock that are consistent with standard theory and highlight the exchange rate as a transmission mechanism.[61] More recently, Kim and Roubini (2000) have again emphasised how past empirical research on the effects of monetary policy in closed and open economies has found evidence of several anomalies, including the 'exchange rate' puzzles. Kim and Roubini develop an approach that provides a solution to some of these empirical anomalies in an open-economy setup. They use a structural vector autoregression with non-recursive contemporaneous restrictions and identify monetary policy shocks by modelling the reaction function of the monetary authorities and the structure of the economy. Their empirical findings are that effects of non-US G7 monetary policy shocks on exchange rates and other macroeconomic variables are consistent with the predictions of a broad set of theoretical models. The evidence is consistent with significant, but transitory, real effects of monetary shocks. They also find that initially the exchange rate appreciates in response to a monetary contraction; but after a few months, the exchange rate depreciates over time in accordance with the uncovered interest parity condition. In a related study, Faust and Rogers (1999) start from stating that much empirical work addressing the role of monetary policy shocks in exchange rate behaviour has led to conclusions that have been clouded by the lack of plausible identifying assumptions. Faust and Rogers apply a statistical procedure that allows them to relax identifying assumptions which they view as dubious. Their work overturns some earlier results and strengthens others: (i) contrary to some earlier findings of 'delayed overshooting' of the exchange rate, the peak exchange rate effect of policy shocks may come almost immediately after the shock; (ii) monetary policy shocks lead to large uncovered interest rate parity deviations; (iii) monetary policy shocks may account for a smaller portion of the variance of exchange rates than found in earlier studies. Faust and Rogers conclude that, while (i) is consistent with overshooting, (ii) implies that the overshooting phenomenon cannot be driven by Dornbusch's (1976) mechanism, and (iii) gives reason to doubt whether monetary policy shocks are the main source of exchange rate volatility. Another interesting extension of this literature is the study by Kim (2001), who develops a structural vector autoregression to analyse jointly the effects of foreign exchange policy (setting exchange reserves) and conventional monetary policy (setting money supply and the interest rate) on the exchange rate, two types of policy reactions to the exchange rate, and interactions between the two types of policies. Kim finds several interactions among the two types of policies and the exchange rate, confirming the need for a joint analysis. He also finds that foreign exchange policy has

[61] See also Prasad (1999), who develops an empirical framework for analysing the dynamics of the trade balance in response to different types of macroeconomic shocks.

significant stabilising effects on the exchange rate, suggesting that it may be important to model foreign exchange policy explicitly when modelling exchange rate behaviour.

Although the majority of studies in this literature focus on major industrialised countries, there are a few studies investigating developing and newly developed economies. The evidence provided by this literature is clear: movements in real exchange rates of these economies are largely driven by real shocks. For example, Chen and Wu (1997) focus on real exchange rate movements of four Pacific Rim countries, providing evidence of the key role played by permanent shocks in explaining the variability of the real exchange rates examined. Chen and Wu also find that real innovations account for more than 90 per cent of variations in the real Korean won at all time horizons. More recently, Hoffmaister and Roldos (2001) analyse the real Korean and Brazilian exchange rates *vis-à-vis* the US dollar and illustrate that temporary shocks can hardly explain any real exchange rate movements.

Overall, the literature on identifying the source of shocks driving real and nominal exchange rates has provided mixed results. While this literature suggests that both nominal (e.g. monetary) and real shocks explain both nominal and real exchange rate movements, the relative importance of nominal and real shocks varies across studies when the exchange rates examined involve major industralised countries. With regard to developing and newly developed economies, however, although there have been relatively fewer studies, there seems to be a consensus that real exchange rates are largely driven by real shocks.

Note that, despite the mixed findings of this literature, at least for real exchange rates among developed countries, the implicit assumption underlying Rogoff's (1996) 'PPP puzzle' is that real exchange rates must be largely driven by nominal shocks, at least in the short run, in order to account for their high volatility. This is an area which would clearly repay further research.[62]

3.7 Summary and concluding remarks

Within the vast literature on PPP and real exchange rates, professional opinion concerning the validity of PPP between the currencies of the major industrialised countries, in both the short and long run, appears to have shifted several times in the post-war period.

While most empirical studies in the period before the breakdown of the Bretton Woods system tended to support the existence of a fairly stable real exchange rate over the long run (e.g. Friedman and Schwartz, 1963), the prevailing orthodoxy at the outset of the more recent floating rate period in the early 1970s seemed to favour the much stronger proposition of *continuous* PPP, a view apparently associated with the monetary approach to the exchange rate (e.g. Frenkel, 1976). The observed high volatility in real exchange rates during the 1970s rapidly led, however, to the view that PPP had 'collapsed' (see e.g. Frenkel, 1981). Subsequently, largely as a result of studies published mostly in the 1980s which could not reject the hypothesis of random walk or martingale behaviour in real exchange rates (Roll, 1979; Adler and Lehmann, 1983) and later cointegration studies which similarly found no evidence of long-run PPP (Taylor, 1988; Mark, 1990), the professional consensus shifted

---

[62] Note also that many of these studies implicitly assume a unit root in the real exchange rate. Extending this research under the mantained hypothesis of a stationary real exchange rate would be a worthwhile avenue for future research.

yet again to a position opposite to the strongly held belief in continuous PPP which had dominated barely a decade before, i.e. towards a view that PPP was of virtually no use empirically over any time horizon (e.g. Stockman, 1987).[63]

More recently, following an early warning from Frankel (1986), a number of authors noted that the tests typically employed during the 1980s to test for long-run stability of the real exchange rate may have very low power to reject a null hypothesis of real exchange rate instability when applied to data for the recent floating rate period alone (e.g. Froot and Rogoff, 1995; Lothian and Taylor, 1996, 1997). The argument is that if the real exchange rate is in fact stable in the sense that it tends to revert towards its mean over long periods of time, then examination of just one real exchange rate over a period of twenty-five years or so may not yield enough information to be able to detect slow mean-reversion towards purchasing power parity. This led to two developments in research, both aimed at circumventing the problem of low power displayed by conventional unit-root tests applied to the real exchange rate.

One potential solution advanced by a number of researchers involves increasing the power of unit-root tests by increasing the length of the sample period under consideration (e.g. Diebold, Husted and Rush, 1991; Cheung and Lai, 1993a; Lothian and Taylor, 1996). These studies have in fact been able to find significant evidence of real exchange rate mean-reversion.

Other researchers have sought to increase test power by using panel unit-root tests applied jointly to a number of real exchange rate series over the recent float and, in many of these studies, the unit-root hypothesis is also rejected for groups of real exchange rates (e.g. Flood and Taylor, 1996; Frankel and Rose, 1996; Wu, 1996; Papell, 1998; Sarno and Taylor, 1998; Taylor and Sarno, 1998)[64].

In our view, however, whether or not the long-span or panel-data studies do provide convincing evidence in favour of PPP remains contentious. As far as the long-span studies are concerned, as noted in particular by Frankel and Rose (1996), the long samples required to generate a reasonable level of statistical power with standard univariate unit-root tests may be unavailable for many currencies (perhaps thereby generating a 'survivorship bias' in tests on the available data; Froot and Rogoff, 1996) and, in any case, may potentially be inappropriate because of differences in real exchange rate behaviour both across different historical periods and across different nominal exchange rate regimes (e.g. Baxter and Stockman, 1989; Hegwood and Papell, 1998). As for panel-data studies, a very serious problem with panel unit-root tests, highlighted by the Monte Carlo evidence of Taylor and Sarno (1998), is that the null hypothesis in such tests is generally that *all* of the series are generated by unit-root processes, so that the probability of rejection of the null hypothesis may be quite high when as few as just one of the series under consideration is a realisation of a stationary process.

Moreover, even if we take the results of the long-span or panel-data studies as having established the validity of long-run PPP, another puzzle then arises as follows. Among the long-span and panel-data studies which do report significant mean-reversion of the real

---

[63] A notable exception to this general view was Officer (1982).

[64] A third method for increasing the power of unit-root tests, by employing univariate tests based on generalised or weighted least squares estimators, has recently been proposed by Cheung and Lai (1998).

exchange rate, there appears to be a consensus that the size of the half-life of deviations from PPP is about three to five years. If we take as given that real shocks cannot account for the major part of the short-run volatility of real exchange rates (since it seems incredible that shocks to real factors such as tastes and technology could be so volatile) and that nominal shocks can only have strong effects over a time frame in which nominal wages and prices are sticky, then a second PPP puzzle is the apparently high degree of persistence in the real exchange rate (Rogoff, 1996).

A promising strand of research which goes some way towards resolving both fundamental puzzles in this literature – namely whether PPP holds and whether one can reconcile estimated half-lives of shocks to the real exchange rates with their observed high volatility – has investigated the role of nonlinearities in real exchange rate adjustment towards long-run equilibrium. Taylor, Peel and Sarno (2001) provide evidence of nonlinear mean-reversion in a number of major real exchange rates during the post-Bretton Woods period such that real exchange rates behave more like unit-root processes the closer they are to long-run equilibrium and, conversely, become more mean-reverting the further they are from equilibrium. Moreover, while small shocks to the real exchange rate around equilibrium will be highly persistent, larger shocks mean-revert much faster than the 'glacial rates' previously reported for linear models (Rogoff, 1996). Further, Taylor, Peel and Sarno reconcile these results with the huge literature on unit roots in real exchange rates through Monte Carlo studies and, in particular, demonstrate that when the true data-generating process implies nonlinear mean-reversion of the real exchange rate, standard univariate unit-root tests will have very low power, while multivariate unit-root tests will have much higher power to reject a false null hypothesis of unit-root behaviour.

The main conclusion emerging from the recent literature on testing the validity of the PPP hypothesis appears to be that PPP might be viewed as a valid long-run international parity condition when applied to bilateral exchange rates obtaining among major industrialised countries and that mean-reversion in real exchange rates displays significant nonlinearities. Further exploration of the importance of nonlinearities in real exchange rate adjustment therefore seems warranted.

In particular, further work on real exchange rates might usefully be addressed to unravelling the relative contribution of prices and nominal exchange rates to movements in real exchange rates. This might be done, for example, in the context of nonlinear vector error correction models of the nominal exchange rate and domestic and foreign prices and other variables.[65] Such a framework might also be extended to allow the relative impact of monetary and fiscal policy on real exchange rate movements to be isolated and to investigate whether stronger evidence might be adduced for the Harrod–Balassa–Samuelson effect. Finally, the implications of nonlinearities in real exchange rate movements for exchange rate forecasting and, in turn, the influence of official exchange rate intervention in generating exchange rate nonlinearites, have yet to be fully examined.[66]

---

[65] See Sarno (2000), Sarno, Taylor and Peel (2000), and Peel and Taylor (2002) for examples of nonlinear vector error correction modelling.

[66] See Kilian and Taylor (2001); Clarida, Sarno, Taylor and Valente (2001); Sarno and Taylor (2001b); and Taylor (2001).

References and further readings

Abuaf, N. and P. Jorion (1990), 'Purchasing Power Parity in the Long Run', *Journal of Finance*, 45, pp. 157–74.

Adler, M. and B. Lehmann (1983), 'Deviations from Purchasing Power Parity in the Long Run', *Journal of Finance*, 38, pp. 1471–87.

Alesina, A. and R. Perotti (1995), 'Taxation and Redistribution in an Open Economy', *European Economic Review*, 39, pp. 961–79.

Allen, H. and M.P. Taylor (1990), 'Charts, Noise and Fundamentals in the Foreign Exchange Market', *Economic Journal*, 100, pp. 49–59.

Asea, P.K. and W.M. Corden (1994), 'The Balassa–Samuelson Model: An Overview', *Review of International Economics*, 2, pp. 191–200.

Asea, P.K. and E.G. Mendoza (1994), 'The Balassa-Samuelson Model: A General-Equilibrium Appraisal', *Review of International Economics*, 2, pp. 244–67.

Balassa, B. (1964), 'The Purchasing Power Parity Doctrine: A Reappraisal', *Journal of Political Economy*, 72(August), pp. 584–96.

Banerjee, A., J.J. Dolado, D.F. Hendry and G.W. Smith (1986), 'Exploring Equilibrium Relationships in Econometrics through Static Models: Some Monte Carlo Evidence', *Oxford Bulletin of Economics and Statistics*, 3, pp. 253–78.

Baumol, W.J. and W.G. Bowen (1966), *Performing Arts: The Economic Dilemma*, New York: The Twentieth Century Fund.

Baxter, M. and A.C. Stockman (1989), 'Business Cycles and the Exchange Rate System', *Journal of Monetary Economics*, 23, pp. 377–400.

Bayoumi, T., P. Clark, S. Symansky and M.P. Taylor (1994), 'The Robustness of Equilibrium Exchange Rate Calculations to Alternative Assumptions and Methodology', in J. Williamson (ed.), *Estimating Equilibrium Exchange Rates*, Washington D.C.: Institute for International Economics, pp. 19–59

Benninga, S. and A.A. Protopapadakis (1988), 'The Equilibrium Pricing of Exchange Rates and Assets When Trade Takes Time', *Journal of International Economics*, 7, pp. 129–49.

Bertola, G. and R.J. Caballero (1990), 'Kinked Adjustment Costs and Aggregate Dynamics', in O.J. Blanchard and S. Fischer (eds.), *NBER Macroeconomics Annual*, Cambridge, Mass: MIT Press, pp. 237–88.

Bhagwati, J.N. (1984), 'Why Are Services Cheaper in the Poor Countries?', *Economic Journal*, 94, pp. 279–86.

Blanchard, O.J. and D. Quah (1989), 'The Dynamic Effects of Aggregate Demand and Supply Disturbances', *American Economic Review*, 79, pp. 655–73.

Bleaney, M. and P. Mizen (1995), 'Empirical Tests of Mean Reversion in Real Exchange Rates: A Survey', *Bulletin of Economic Research*, 47, pp. 171–95.

Breuer, J.B. (1994), 'An Assessment of the Evidence on Purchasing Power Parity', in J. Williamson (ed.), *Estimating Equilibrium Exchange Rates*, Washington, D.C.: Institute for International Economics, pp. 245–77.

Bui, N. and J. Pippenger (1990), 'Commodity Prices, Exchange Rates and Their Relative Volatility', *Journal of International Money and Finance*, 9, pp. 3–20.

Canzoneri, M.B., R.E. Cumby and B. Diba (1999), 'Relative Labor Productivity and the Real Exchange Rate in the Long Run: Evidence for a Panel of OECD Countries', *Journal of International Economics*, 47, pp. 245–66.

Cassel, G. (1918), 'Abnormal Deviations in International Exchanges', *Economic Journal*, 28, pp. 413–15.

(1922), *Money and Foreign Exchange After 1914*, London: Constable.

Chen, Z. and P.J. Knez (1995), 'Measurement of Market Integration and Arbitrage', *Review of Financial Studies*, 8, pp. 287–325.

Cheung, Y.-W. and K.S. Lai (1993a), 'A Fractional Cointegration Analysis of Purchasing Power Parity', *Journal of Business and Economic Statistics*, 11, pp. 103–12.

(1993b), 'Long-Run Purchasing Power Parity during the Recent Float', *Journal of International Economics*, 34, pp. 181–192.

(1994), 'Mean Reversion in Real Exchange Rates', *Economics Letters*, 46, pp. 251–256.

(1998), 'Parity Reversion in Real Exchange Rates During the Post-Bretton Woods Period', *Journal of International Money and Finance* 17, pp. 597–614.

Chinn, M.(2000), 'The Usual Suspects? Productivity and Demand Shocks and Asia-Pacific Real Exchange Rates', *Review of International Economics,* 8, pp. 20–43.

Choudhry, T., R. McNown and M. Wallace (1991), 'Purchasing Power Parity and the Canadian Float in the 1950s', *Review of Economics and Statistics*, 73, pp. 558–63.

Chowdhury, A.R. and F. Sdogati (1993), 'Purchasing Power Parity in the Major EMS Countries: The Role of Price and Exchange Rate Adjustment', *Journal of Macroeconomics*, 15, pp. 25–45.

Clarida, R.H. and J. Gali (1994), 'Sources of Real Exchange-Rate Fluctuations: How Important Are Nominal Shocks?', *Carnegie–Rochester Conference Series on Public Policy*, 41, pp. 1–56.

Clarida, R.H., L. Sarno, M.P. Taylor and G. Valente (2001), 'The Out-of-Sample Success of Term Structure Models as Exchange Rate Predictors: A Step Beyond', *Journal of International Economics*, forthcoming.

Clarida, R.H. and M.P. Taylor (1997), 'The Term Structure of Forward Exchange Premiums and the Forecastability of Spot Exchange Rates: Correcting the Errors', *Review of Economics and Statistics*, 79, pp. 353–61.

Coakley, J. and A.M. Fuertes, (1997), 'New Panel Unit Root Tests of PPP', *Economics Letters*, 57, pp. 17–22

Cochrane, J.H. (1988), 'How Big Is the Random Walk in GNP?', *Journal of Political Economy*, 96, pp. 893–920.

Coleman, A.M.G. (1995), 'Arbitrage, Storage and the Law of One Price: New Theory for the Time Series Analysis of an Old Problem', Discussion Paper, Department of Economics, Princeton University.

Corbae, D. and S. Ouliaris (1988), 'Cointegration and Tests of Purchasing Power Parity', *Review of Economics and Statistics*, 70, pp. 508–11.

Cushman, D.O. and T. Zha (1997), 'Identifying Monetary Policy in a Small Open Economy under Flexible Exchange Rates', *Journal of Monetary Economics*, 39, pp. 433–48.

Davutyan, N. and J. Pippenger (1990), 'Testing Purchasing Power Parity: Some Evidence of the Effects of Transactions Costs', *Econometric Reviews*, 9, pp. 211–40.

De Grauwe, P. (1990), *International Money: Post-War Trends and Theories*, Oxford: Clarendon Press.

De Gregorio, J., A. Giovannini and H.C. Wolf (1994), 'International Evidence on Tradables and Nontradables Inflation', *European Economic Review*, 38, pp. 1225–44.

De Gregorio, J. and H.C. Wolf (1994), 'Terms of Trade, Productivity, and the Real Exchange Rate', Working Paper No. 4807, National Bureau of Economic Research.

Diebold, F.X., S. Husted and M. Rush (1991), 'Real Exchange Rates under the Gold Standard', *Journal of Political Economy,* 99, pp. 1252–71.

Dixit, A.K. (1989), 'Hysteresis, Import Penetration and Exchange Rate Pass-Through', *Quarterly Journal of Economics*, 104, pp. 205–28.

Dornbusch, R. (1987), 'Purchasing Power Parity', in J. Eatwell, M. Milgate and P. Newman (eds.), *The New Palgrave: A Dictionary of Economics*, London: Macmillan, pp. 1075–85.

Dumas, B. (1992), 'Dynamic Equilibrium and the Real Exchange Rate in Spatially Separated World', *Review of Financial Studies*, 5, pp. 153–80.

(1994), 'Partial Equilibrium Versus General Equilibrium Models of the International Capital Market', in F. van der Ploeg (ed.), *The Handbook of International Macroeconomics*, Oxford: Blackwell, ch. 10.

Dumas, B., L.P. Jennergren and B. Naslund (1995), 'Siegel's Paradox and the Pricing of Currency Options', *Journal of International Money and Finance*, 14, pp. 213–23.

Edison, H.J. (1985), 'Purchasing Power Parity: A Quantitative Reassessment of the 1920s Experience', *Journal of International Money and Finance*, 4, pp. 361–72.

(1987), 'Purchasing Power Parity in the Long Run', *Journal of Money, Credit and Banking*, 19, pp. 376–87.

Edison, H.J. and J.T. Klovland (1987), 'A Quantitative Reassessment of the Purchasing Power Parity Hypothesis: Evidence from Norway and the United Kingdom', *Journal of Applied Econometrics*, 2, pp. 309–33.

Enders, W. (1988), 'ARIMA and Cointegration Tests of PPP under Fixed and Flexible Exchange Rate Regimes', *Review of Economics and Statistics*, 70, pp. 504–8.

Engel, C. (1993), 'Real Exchange Rates and Relative Prices: An Empirical Investigation', *Journal of Monetary Economics*, 32, pp. 35–50.

(1999), 'Accounting for U.S. Real Exchange Rate Changes', *Journal of Political Economy*, 107, pp. 507–38.

(2000), 'Long-Run PPP May Not Hold after All', *Journal of International Economics*, 51, pp. 243–73.

Engel, C. and J.H. Rogers (1996), 'How Wide Is the Border?', *American Economic Review*, 86, pp. 1112–25.

Engle, R.F. and C.W.J. Granger (1987), 'Co-integration and Error Correction: Representation, Estimation, and Testing', *Econometrica*, 55, pp. 251–76.

Evans, M.D.D. and J.R. Lothian (1993), 'The Response of Exchange Rates to Permanent and Transitory Shocks under Floating Exchange Rates', *Journal of International Money and Finance*, 12, pp. 563–86.

Faruqee, H. (1995), 'Long-Run Determinants of the Real Exchange Rate: A Stock-Flow Perspective', *International Monetary Fund Staff Papers*, 42, pp. 80–107.

Feenstra, R.C. (1995), 'Exact Hedonic Price Indexes', *Review of Economics and Statistics*, 77, pp. 634–53.

Feenstra, R.C. and J.D. Kendall (1997), 'Pass-Through of Exchange Rates and Purchasing Power Parity', *Journal of International Economics*, 43, pp. 237–61.

Fisher, E.O.N. and J.Y. Park (1991), 'Testing Purchasing Power Parity under the Null Hypothesis of Co-integration', *Economic Journal*, 101, pp. 1476–84.

Flood, R.P. and M.P. Taylor (1996), 'Exchange Rate Economics: What's Wrong with the Conventional Macro Approach?', in J.A. Frankel, G. Galli and A. Giovannini (eds.), *The Microstructure of Foreign Exchange Markets*, Chicago: Chicago University Press, pp. 261–94.

Frankel, J.A. (1986), 'International Capital Mobility and Crowding Out in the US Economy: Imperfect Integration of Financial Markets or Goods Markets?', in R.W. Hafer (ed.), *How Open is the US Economy?*, Lexington: Lexington Books, pp. 33–67.

(1990), 'Zen and the Art of Modern Macroeconomics: The Search for Perfect Nothingness', in W. Haraf and T. Willett (eds.), *Monetary Policy for a Volatile Global Economy*, Washington, D.C.: American Enterprise Institute, pp. 117–23.

Frankel, J.A. and A.K. Rose (1996), 'A Panel Project on Purchasing Power Parity: Mean Reversion Within and Between Countries', *Journal of International Economics*, 40, pp. 209–24.

Fraser, P., M.P. Taylor and A. Webster (1991), 'An Empirical Examination of Long-Run Purchasing Power Parity as Theory of International Commodity Arbitrage', *Applied Economics*, 23, pp. 1749–59.

Frenkel, J.A. (1976), 'A Monetary Approach to the Exchange Rate: Doctrinal Aspects and Empirical Evidence', *Scandinavian Journal of Economics*, 78, pp. 200–24.

(1978), 'Purchasing Power Parity: Doctrinal Perspective and Evidence from the 1920s', *Journal of International Economics*, 8, pp. 169–91.

(1981), 'The Collapse of Purchasing Power Parities during the 1970s', *European Economic Review*, 16, pp. 145–65.

Frenkel, J.A. and H.G. Johnson (1978), *The Economics of Exchange Rates*, Reading, Mass.: Addison-Wesley.

Frenkel, J.A. and M.L. Mussa (1985), 'Asset Markets, Exchange Rates, and the Balance of Payments', in R.W. Jones and P.B. Kenen (eds.), *Handbook of International Economics*, vol. II, Amsterdam: North-Holland, ch. 14.

Friedman, M. and A.J. Schwartz (1963), *A Monetary History of the United States: 1867–1960*, Princeton, N.J.: Princeton University Press for the National Bureau of Economic Research.

Froot, K.A., M. Kim and K. Rogoff (1995), 'The Law of One Price Over 700 Years', Working Paper No. 5132, National Bureau of Economic Research.

Froot, K.A. and P.D. Klemperer (1989), 'Exchange Rate Pass-Through When Market Share Matters', *American Economic Review*, 79, pp. 637–54.

Froot, K.A. and K. Rogoff (1995), 'Perspectives on PPP and Long-Run Real Exchange Rates', in G.M. Grossman and K. Rogoff (eds.), *Handbook of International Economics*, vol.III, Amsterdam: North-Holland, pp. 1647–88.

Gaillot, H.J. (1970), 'Purchasing Power Parity as an Explanation of Long-Term Changes in Exchange Rates', *Journal of Money, Credit, and Banking*, 2, pp. 348–57.

Ghosh, A.R. and H.C. Wolf (1994), 'Pricing in International Markets: Lessons from the Economist', Working Paper No. 4806, National Bureau of Economic Research.

Giovannini, A. (1988), 'Exchange Rates and Traded Goods Prices', *Journal of International Economics*, 24, pp. 45–68.

Glen, J.D. (1992), 'Real Exchange Rates in the Short, Medium, and Long Run', *Journal of International Economics*, 33, pp. 147–66.

Goldstein, M. and M.S. Khan (1985), 'Income and Price Effects in Foreign Trade', in R.W. Jones and P.B. Kenen (eds.), *Handbook of International Economics*, vol. II, Amsterdam: North-Holland, ch. 20.

Goodwin, B.K. (1992), 'Multivariate Cointegration Tests and the Law of One Price in International Wheat Markets', *Review of Agricultural Economics*, 14, pp. 117–24.

Goodwin, B.K., T. Grennes and M.K. Wohlgenant (1990), 'Testing the Law of One Price When Trade Takes Time', *Journal of International Money and Finance*, 9, pp. 21–40.

Granger, C.W.J. (1986), 'Developments in the Study of Cointegrated Variables', *Oxford Bulletin of Economics and Statistics*, 48, pp. 213–28.

Granger, C.W.J. and M.J. Morris (1976), 'Time Series Modelling and Interpretation', *Journal of the Royal Statistical Society*, Series A, 139, pp. 246–57.

Granger, C.W.J. and P. Newbold (1974), 'Spurious Regressions in Econometrics', *Journal of Econometrics*, 2, pp. 111–20.

Granger, C.W.J. and T. Teräsvirta (1993), *Modelling Nonlinear Economic Relationships*, Oxford: Oxford University Press.

Haggan, V. and T. Ozaki (1981), 'Modelling Nonlinear Random Vibrations Using an Amplitude-Dependent Autoregressive Time Series Model', *Biometrika*, 68, pp. 189–96.

Hakkio, C.S. (1984), 'A Re-examination of Purchasing Power Parity: A Multi-Country and Multi-Period Study', *Journal of International Economics*, 17, pp. 265–77.

Hakkio, C.S. and M. Rush (1991), 'Cointegration: How Short Is the Long Run?', *Journal of International Money and Finance*, 10, pp. 571–81.

Harrod, R. (1933), *International Economics*, London: James Nisbet.

Harvey, A.C. (1981), *Time Series Models*, Hemel Hempstead: Philip Allan.

Heckscher, E.F. (1916), 'Vaxeal Kursens Grundval vid Pappersmyntfot', *Ekonomisk Tidskrift*, 18(2), pp. 309–12.

Hegwood, N.D. and D.H. Papell (1998), 'Quasi Purchasing Power Parity', *International Journal of Finance and Economics*, 3, pp. 279–89.

Herguera, I. (1994), 'Exchange Rate Uncertainty, Market Structure and the Pass-Through Relationship', *Economic Notes*, 23, pp. 292–307.

Heston, A., D.A. Nuxoll and R. Summers (1994), 'The Differential-Productivity Hypothesis and Purchasing-Power Parities: Some New Evidence', *Review of International Economics*, 2, pp. 227–43.

Hsieh, D.A. (1982), 'The Determination of the Real Exchange Rate: The Productivity Approach', *Journal of International Economics*, 12, pp. 355–62.

Huizinga, J. (1987), 'An Empirical Investigation of the Long-Run Behaviour of Real Exchange Rates', *Carnegie–Rochester Conference Series on Public Policy*, 27, pp. 149–214.

Isard, P. (1977), 'How Far Can We Push the "Law of One Price"?', *American Economic Review*, 67, pp. 942–8.

Johansen, S. (1988), 'Statistical Analysis of Cointegrating Vectors', *Journal of Economic Dynamics and Control*, 12, pp. 231–54.

(1991), 'Estimation and Hypothesis Testing of Cointegrating Vectors in Gaussian Vector Autoregressive Models', *Econometrica*, 59, pp. 1551–80.

Kasa, K. (1992), 'Adjustment Costs and Pricing-to-Market: Theory and Evidence', *Journal of International Economics*, 32, pp. 1–30.

Keynes, J.M. (1932), *Essays in Persuasion*, New York: Harcourt Brace.

Kilian, L. and M.P. Taylor (2001), 'Why is it so Difficult to Beat the Random Walk Forecast of Exchange Rates?', *Journal of International Economics*, forthcoming.

Kim, S. (2001), 'Monetary Policy, Foreign Exchange Policy, and the Exchange Rate in a Unifying Framework', University of Illinois, Urbana-Champaign, mimeo.

Kim, S. and N. Roubini (2000), 'Exchange Rate Anomalies in the Industrial Countries: A Solution with a Structural VAR Approach', *Journal of Monetary Economics*, 45, pp. 561–86.

Kim, Y. (1990), 'Purchasing Power Parity in the Long Run: A Cointegration Approach', *Journal of Money, Credit, and Banking*, 22, pp. 491–503.

Kindleberger, C.P. (1973), *The World in Depression, 1929–1939*, University of California Press.

Knetter, M.M. (1989), 'Price Discrimination by U.S. and German Exporters', *American Economic Review*, 79, pp. 198–210.

(1993), 'International Comparisons of Price-to-Market Behaviour', *American Economic Review*, 83, pp. 473–86.

(1994), 'Did the Strong Dollar Increase Competition in U.S. Product Markets?', *Review of Economics and Statistics*, 76, pp. 192–5.

Kravis, I.B. and R.E. Lipsey (1983), *Toward an Explanation of National Price Levels*, Princeton Studies in International Finance No. 52, Princeton, N.J.: International Finance Section, Department of Economics, Princeton University.

Krugman, P.R. (1978), 'Purchasing Power Parity and Exchange Rates: Another Look at the Evidence', *Journal of International Economics*, 8, pp. 397–407.

(1987), 'Pricing to Market When the Exchange Rate Changes', in S.W. Arndt and J.D. Richardson (eds.), *Real–financial Linkages Among Open Economies*, Cambridge, Mass.: MIT Press, pp. 49–70.

(1989), *Exchange Rate Instability*, Cambridge, Mass.: MIT Press.

Lane, P.R. (2001), 'The New Open Economy Macroeconomics: A Survey', Discussion Paper No. 2115, Centre for Economic Policy Research (forthcoming *in Journal of International Economics*).

Lastrapes, W.D. (1992), 'Sources of Fluctuations in Real and Nominal Exchange Rates', *Review of Economics and Statistics*, 74, pp. 530–9.

Lothian, J.R. (1997), 'Multi-Country Evidence on the Behavior of Purchasing Power Parity under the Current Float', *Journal of International Money and Finance*, 16, pp. 19–35.

Lothian, J.R. and M.P. Taylor (1996), 'Real Exchange Rate Behaviour: The Recent Float from the Perspective of the Past Two Centuries', *Journal of Political Economy*, 104, pp. 488–510.

(1997), 'Real Exchange Rate Behaviour: The Problem of Power and Sample Size', *Journal of International Money and Finance*, 16, pp. 945–54.

(2000), 'Purchasing Power Parity Over Two Centuries: Strengthening the Case for Real Exchange Rate Stability', *Journal of International Money and Finance*, 19, pp. 759–64

Luukkonen, R., P. Saikkonen and T. Teräsvirta (1988), 'Testing Linearity Against Smooth Transition Autoregressive Models', *Biometrika*, 75, pp. 491–9.

Mark, N.C. (1985a), 'A Note on International Real Interest Rate Differentials', *Review of Economics and Statistics*, 67, pp. 681–4.

(1985b), 'Some Evidence on the International Inequality of Real Interest Rates', *Journal of International Money and Finance*, 4, pp. 18–208.

(1990) 'Real and Nominal Exchange Rates in the Long Run: An Empirical Investigation', *Journal of International Economics,* 28, pp. 115–36.

(2001), *International Macroeconomics and Finance: Theory and Empirical Methods*, London: Blackwell Publishers.

Marston, R.C. (1987), 'Real Exchange Rates and Productivity Growth in the United States and Japan', in S.W. Arndt and J.D. Richardson (eds.), *Real–Financial Linkages Among Open Economies*, Cambridge, Mass.: MIT Press, pp. 71–96.

(1990), 'Pricing to Market in Japanese Manufacturing', *Journal of International Economics*, 29, pp. 217–36.

(1995), *International Financial Integration: A Study of Interest Rate Differentials Between the Major Industrial Countries*, Cambridge: Cambridge University Press.

McKinnon, R.I. (1971), *Monetary Theory and Controlled Flexibility in the Foreign Exchanges*, Princeton, N.J.: International Finance Section, Department of Economics, Princeton University.

McNown, R. and M. Wallace (1989), 'National Price Levels, Purchasing Power Parity, and Cointegration: A Test of Four High Inflation Economies', *Journal of International Money and Finance*, 8, pp. 533–45.

Meese, R.A. and K. Rogoff (1988), 'Was It Real? The Exchange Rate–Interest Differential Relation over the Modern Floating-Rate Period', *Journal of Finance*, 43, pp. 933–48.

Michael, P., A.R. Nobay and D.A. Peel (1997), 'Transactions Costs and Non-Linear Adjustment in Real Exchange Rates: An Empirical Investigation', *Journal of Political Economy*, 105, pp. 862–79.

Mishkin, F. S. (1984), 'Are Real Interest Rates Equal across Countries? An Empirical Investigation of International Parity Conditions', *Journal of Finance*, 39, pp. 1345–57.

Mussa, M.L. (1979), 'Empirical Regularities in the Behavior of Exchange Rates and Theories of the Foreign Exchange Market', *Carnegie–Rochester Conference Series on Public Policy*, 11, pp. 9–57.

(1984), 'The Theory of Exchange Rate Determination', in J.F.O. Bilson and R.C. Marston (eds.), *Exchange Rate Theory and Practice*, National Bureau of Economic Research Conference Report, Chicago: University of Chicago Press, pp. 13–58.

Obstfeld, M. (1993), 'Model Trending Real Exchange Rates', Working Paper No. C93-011, Center for International and Development Economics Research, University of California at Berkeley.

Obstfeld, M. and K. Rogoff (1995), 'Exchange Rate Dynamics Redux', *Journal of Political Economy*, 103, pp. 624–60.

(1996), *Foundations of International Macroeconomics*, Cambridge, Mass.: MIT Press.

Obstfeld, M. and A.M. Taylor (1997), 'Nonlinear Aspects of Goods-Market Arbitrage and Adjustment: Heckscher's Commodity Points Revisited', *Journal of the Japanese and International Economies*, 11, pp. 441–79.

O'Connell, P. and S.-J. Wei (1997), 'The Bigger They Are, The Harder They Fall: How Price Differences Between US Cities are Arbitraged', Working Paper No. 6089, National Bureau of Economic Research.

O'Connell, P.G.J. (1997), 'Perspectives on Purchasing Power Parity', unpublished Ph.D. thesis, Harvard University.

(1998), 'The Overvaluation of Purchasing Power Parity', *Journal of International Economics*, 44, pp. 1–19.

Officer, L.H. (1976), 'The Purchasing-Power-Parity Theory of Exchange Rates: A Review Article', *International Monetary Fund Staff Papers*, 23, pp. 1–60.

(1982), *Purchasing Power Parity and Exchange Rates: Theory, Evidence and Relevance*, Greenwich, Conn.: JAI Press.

Ohanian, L.E. and A.C. Stockman (1997), 'Arbitrage Costs and Exchange Rates', Discussion Paper, Department of Economics, University of Rochester, (paper presented at the CEPR–PIES Conference on *Market Integration and Real Exchange Rates'*, Georgetown University, Washington, D.C., 2–3 May 1997).

Papell, D.H. (1998), 'Searching for Stationarity: Purchasing Power Parity Under the Current Float', *Journal of International Economics*, 43, pp. 313–32.

Parsley, D.C. and S.J. Wei (1996), 'Convergence to the Law of One Price without Trade Barriers or Currency Fluctuations,' *Quarterly Journal of Economics*, 111, pp. 1211–36.

Peel, D.A. and M.P. Taylor (2002), 'Covered Interest Rate Arbitrage in the Inter-War Period and the Keynes–Einzig Conjecture', *Journal of Money, Credit, and Banking*, forthcoming.

Perron, P. (1989), 'The Great Crash, the Oil Price Shock, and the Unit Root Hypothesis', *Econometrica*, 57, pp. 1361–401.

Phillips, P.C.B. (1986), 'Understanding Spurious Regressions in Econometrics', *Journal of Econometrics*, 33, pp. 311–40.

Phillips, P.C.B. and P. Perron (1988), 'Testing for a Unit Root in Time Series Regressions', *Biometrika*, 75, pp. 335–46.

Prasad, E. (1999), 'International Trade and the Business Cycle', *Economic Journal*, 109, pp. 588–606.

Rangan, S. and R.Z. Lawrence (1993), 'The Responses of U.S. Firms to Exchange Rate Fluctuations: Piercing the Corporate Veil', *Brookings Papers on Economic Activity*.

Richardson, J.D. (1978), 'Some Empirical Evidence on Commodity Arbitrage and the Law of One Price', *Journal of International Economics*, 8, pp. 341–51.

Rogers, J.H. (1999), 'Monetary Shocks and Real Exchange Rates', *Journal of International Economics*, 49, pp. 269–88.

Rogers, J.H. and M. Jenkins (1995), 'Haircuts or Hysteresis? Sources of Movements in Real Exchange Rates', *Journal of International Economics*, 38, pp. 339–60.

Rogoff, R. (1992), 'Traded Goods Consumption Smoothing and the Random Walk Behaviour of the Real Exchange Rate', *Monetary and Economic Studies*, 10, pp. 1–29.

(1996), 'The Purchasing Power Parity Puzzle', *Journal of Economic Literature*, 34, pp. 647–68.

Roll, R. (1979), 'Violations of Purchasing Power Parity and their Implications for Efficient International Commodity Markets', in M. Sarnat and G.P. Szego (eds.), *International Finance and Trade*, vol. I, Cambridge, Mass.: Ballinger, pp. 133–76.

Samuelson, P.A. (1964), 'Theoretical Notes on Trade Problems', *Review of Economics and Statistics*, 46 (May), pp. 145–54.

Sarno, L. (2000), 'Real Exchange Rate Behaviour in the Middle East: A Re-examination', *Economics Letters*, 66, pp. 127–36.

(2001), 'Towards a New Paradigm in Open Economy Modeling: Where Do We Stand?', *Federal Reserve Bank of St. Louis Review*, 83(3), pp. 21–36.

Sarno, L. and M.P. Taylor (1998), 'Real Exchange Rates Under the Recent Float: Unequivocal Evidence of Mean Reversion', *Economics Letters*, 60, pp. 131–7.

(2001a), *The Microstructure of the Foreign Exchange Market*, Princeton Special Papers in International Finance.

(2001b), 'Official Intervention in the Foreign Exchange Market: Is it Effective and, if so, How Does it Work?', *Journal of Economic Literature*, 39, pp. 839–68.

Sarno, L., M.P. Taylor and D.A. Peel (2000), 'Nonlinear Equilibrium Correction in US Real Money Balances, 1869–1997', *Journal of Money, Credit and Banking*, forthcoming.

Sercu, P., R. Uppal and C. van Hulle (1995), 'The Exchange Rate in the Presence of Transactions Costs: Implications for Tests of Purchasing Power Parity', *Journal of Finance*, 50, pp. 1309–19.

Shiller, R.J. and P. Perron (1985), 'Testing the Random Walk Hypothesis: Power Versus Frequency of Observation', *Economics Letters*, 18, pp. 381–6.

Sims, C.A. (1988), 'Bayesian Skepticism on Unit Root Econometrics', *Journal of Economic Dynamics and Control*, 12, pp. 463–74.

Stock, J.H. and M.W. Watson (1988), 'Testing for Common Trends', *Journal of the American Statistical Association*, 83, pp. 1097–107.

Summers, R. and A. Heston (1991), 'The Penn World Table (Mark 5): An Expanded Set of International Comparisons, 1950–1988', *Quarterly Journal of Economics*, 106, pp. 327–68.

Taylor, A.M. (2000a), 'A Century of Purchasing Power Parity', University of California at Davis, mimeo (forthcoming in *Review of Economics and Statistics*).

(2000b), 'Potential Pitfalls for the Purchasing Power Parity Puzzle? Sampling and Specification Biases in Mean Reversion Tests of the Law of One Price', Working Paper No. 7577, National Bureau of Economic Research (forthcoming in *Econometrica*).

Taylor, M.P. (1988), 'An Empirical Examination of Long-Run Purchasing Power Parity Using Cointegration Techniques', *Applied Economics*, 20, pp. 1369–81.

(1995), 'The Economics of Exchange Rates', *Journal of Economic Literature*, 33, pp. 13–47.

Taylor, M.P. and H. Allen (1992), 'The Use of Technical Analysis in the Foreign Exchange Market', *Journal of International Money and Finance*, 11, pp. 304–14.

Taylor, M.P. (2001), 'Is Official Exchange Rate Intervention Effective?' University of Warwick, mimeo.

Taylor, M.P. and P.C. McMahon (1988), 'Long-Run Purchasing Power Parity in the 1920s', *European Economic Review*, 32, pp. 179–97.

Taylor, M.P. and D.A. Peel (2000) 'Nonlinear Adjustment, Long-Run Equilibrium and Exchange Rate Fundamentals', *Journal of International Money and Finance*, 19, pp. 33–53.

Taylor, M.P., D.A. Peel and L. Sarno (2001), 'Nonlinear Mean-Reversion in Real Exchange Rates: Towards a Solution to the Purchasing Power Parity Puzzles', *International Economic Review*, 42, pp. 1015–42.

Taylor, M.P. and L. Sarno (1998), 'The Behaviour of Real Exchange Rates During the Post-Bretton Woods Period', *Journal of International Economics*, 46, pp. 281–312.

(1999), 'Nonlinearities in European Real Exchange Rate Adjustment', Department of Economics, University of Oxford, mimeo.

(2001), 'Efficient Markets, Purchasing Power Parity and the Behaviour of the Real Exchange Rate: Resolving the Conundrum', University of Warwick, mimeo.

Teräsvirta, T. (1994), 'Specification, Estimation and Evaluation of Smooth Transition Autoregressive Models', *Journal of the American Statistical Association*, 89, pp. 208–18.

Tong, H. (1990), *Nonlinear Time Series: A Dynamical System Approach*, Oxford: Clarendon Press.

Whitt, J.A., Jr (1992), 'The Long-Run Behaviour of the Real Exchange Rate: A Reconsideration', *Journal of Money, Credit, and Banking*, 24, pp. 72–82.

Williams, J.C. and B.D. Wright (1991), *Storage and Commodity Markets*, Cambridge: Cambridge University Press.

Wu, Y. (1996), 'Are Real Exchange Rates Non-Stationary?: Evidence from a Panel-Data Test', *Journal of Money, Credit, and Banking*, 28, pp. 54–63.

Zellner, A. (1962), 'An Efficient Method of Estimating Seemingly Unrelated Regressions and Tests for Aggregation Bias', *Journal of the American Statistical Association*, 57, pp. 348–68.

4 Exchange rate determination: theories and evidence

The very early Keynesian approach to exchange rate determination and exchange rate movements was developed initially by Lerner (1936), Metzler (1942a, 1942b), Harberger (1950), Laursen and Metzler (1950) and Alexander (1952). To a large extent, these studies focus on the importance of the elasticities of demand for and supply of exports and imports as well as the demand for and supply of foreign currency, and on the investigation of the conditions under which a devaluation may be effective in improving the balance of trade. In particular, the contributions to the elasticity approach by Marshall (1923), Lerner (1936) and Harberger (1950) are often celebrated for formalising the sufficient condition for a devaluation of the exchange rate to improve the balance of trade – that the sum of the demand elasticities of imports and exports be greater than unity in absolute value.[1] During the 1950s and 1960s, the subsequent literature on open-economy macroeconomics was based on the underlying theory that the elasticities approach captures the short-run movements in the exchange rate, whereas the multiplier approach is the relevant exchange rate determination model in the medium term.[2]

Notable work in the World War II and immediate post-war periods includes studies by Nurkse (1944) and Friedman (1953). The former warns against the dangers of 'bandwagon effects', thereby providing a case for fixed exchange rates. However, Friedman (1953) argues strongly in favour of floating exchange rates on the grounds that speculation may produce stabilising effects in the foreign exchange market. During the same period, Meade (1951) produced his important contribution to this literature by opening up the Keynesian income–expenditure model.

---

[1] This result is often termed the Marshall–Lerner–Harberger condition, or sometimes just the Marshall–Lerner condition. Its derivation is straightforward. If domestic and foreign prices and income are held fixed, then imports, M, and exports, X, are assumed to be a function only of the nominal exchange rate, S, the domestic price of foreign currency. Hence, the balance of trade in domestic currency terms is: $B(S) = X(S) - SM(S)$. Differentiating with respect to S, the condition for a devaluation (increase in S) to improve the balance of trade, $(\partial B/\partial S) > 0$, is $(\partial X/\partial S) - M - S(\partial M/\partial S) > 0$. Rearranging this expression after dividing by M and assuming initial balance so that $X = SM$, we obtain: $(S/X)(\partial X/\partial S) - (S/M)(\partial M/\partial S) > 1$, which is the condition that the sum of the price elasticities of demand for imports and exports must be unity. (Since $(\partial M/\partial S) < 0$, the price elasticity of demand for imports is $-(S/M)(\partial M/\partial S)$.)

[2] See Taylor (1990, ch. 1) for a history of thought on the economics of the balance of payments and exchange rate movements since the seventeenth century.

The major advance in exchange rate modelling in the post-war period was, however, made in the early 1960s, primarily by Mundell (1961, 1962, 1963). Mundell and, subsequently, Fleming (1962) extended the Keynesian income–expenditure model by introducing capital flows into the analysis. Mundell's contribution in this respect is difficult to overstate. As Dornbusch (1980, pp. 4–5) notes:

[Mundell] created models and concepts that rapidly became the Volkswagens of the field – easy to drive, reliable, and sleek. Mundell drew on the Canadian experience to point out the striking implications of capital mobility for the conduct of stabilisation policy. He pursued that question in several directions – the proper assignment of instruments, policy under fixed and flexible exchange rates, and the role of exchange-rate margins. But his innovation went beyond posing important new questions in that he created simple, forceful models to serve as organizing frameworks for thought and policy and as springboards for posing new problems.

Although it is capable of allowing for flexible or sticky but adjustable prices in various ways, Mundell's framework initially adopted a fix-price assumption. At the outset of the recent period of floating exchange rates among the major industrialised nations, in the early 1970s, the extreme opposite assumption, of perfectly flexible prices and continuous purchasing power parity, was made in the monetary approach to the exchange rate. Although this was the dominant exchange rate model at the outset of the recent float, its poor empirical performance during the 1970s led to the development of the sticky-price, or overshooting exchange rate, model of Dornbusch (1976). At the same time, other researchers explored the avenue of analysing exchange rate movements within a general portfolio balance framework. Another strand of the theoretical literature has looked at exchange rate behaviour within an optimising general equilibrium framework, often in a two-country setting. While we discuss some of the early contributions to this literature in the present chapter, there has recently been a recrudescence of work on optimising open-economy general equilibrium models, spurred by the highly influential work of Obstfeld and Rogoff (e.g. 1995), and so the literature on the 'new open-economy macroeconomics' is given full chapter-length treatment in the next chapter.

We also examine in the present chapter the empirical evidence on exchange rate determination. Research in this area has looked at a number of issues – the in-sample fit of empirical models derived from the various theoretical models, the out-of-sample forecasting performance of exchange rate models, empirical tests of theoretical restrictions, and so forth.

Over the last fifty years, exchange rate arrangements among the major industrialised countries have been subject to several regime shifts that in each case have stimulated research in exchange rate economics. The Bretton Woods system of pegged exchange rates was in force until the early 1970s; after its breakdown, exchange rates have been governed, by and large, by a floating system. Nevertheless, during the recent floating period, various exchange rate agreements were at various times in force between the authorities of some of the major industrialised countries in order to let their exchange rates float within specified bounds. The most important example of this kind of arrangement was the European Monetary System (EMS), while more informal exchange rate arrangements were established for a while under the Louvre Accord adopted by the G7 countries in 1987. On 1 January 1999, the exchange rates between the currencies of the eleven European countries participating in European Economic and Monetary Union (EMU) were irrevocably fixed as these countries began the final transition to a single European currency, the euro. These exchange rate regime shifts have influenced the focus of researchers on the behaviour of exchange rates. The monetary and the portfolio balance models of exchange rates, developed during the earlier phase of the recent float, for example, may be considered as following the research agenda in open-economy macroeconomics of the Bretton Woods era which focused largely on freely floating exchange rates. The increasing interest in target zone models, official intervention in foreign exchange markets and in the theory of optimum currency areas represents a direct response to the establishment of pegged exchange rate systems, in particular the EMS, and then currency unions, in particular EMU. In this chapter, we shall be concerned with the theory and evidence relating to exchange rate determination under a largely freely floating exchange rate regime. The theory and evidence relating to currency unions, pegged exchange rate regimes, target zones and intervention are discussed later in the book.

4.1 Theories of exchange rate determination

In this section we describe the main features of the theory of exchange rate determination as it has developed since the 1960s. The earliest model we discuss – albeit in a modern formulation – is the Mundell–Fleming model. As we noted above, however, the dominant model in the early 1970s, at the outset of the recent float, was the flexible-price monetary model, which subsequently gave way to the sticky-price, or overshooting, model. Work on the portfolio balance model ran broadly parallel to this work, and work on general equilibrium models was somewhat later. Despite this chronology, as will subsequently become apparent, it is logically more appealing to discuss the sticky-price model after the Mundell–Fleming model and before the flexible-price monetary model, and this is what is done below. We then go on to discuss equilibrium models and liquidity models of exchange rate determination – which may be viewed in some ways as generalisations of the monetary model – and the portfolio balance model, before turning to an examination of the empirical evidence on the various theories.

4.1.1 The Mundell–Fleming model

The Mundell–Fleming model has had a tremendous impact on research on the theory of exchange rate determination. The original Mundell–Fleming model assumed static expectations, although the generalisation to regressive expectations or to perfect foresight or rational expectations is relatively straightforward. In this sub-section, we describe the Mundell–Fleming model under the assumption of perfect foresight. As we noted above, the original Mundell-Fleming model assumed fixed prices. While price fixity or stickiness of some kind is a characteristic feature of the model, we relax this assumption very slightly in the version presented here to allow for movements in the exchange rate to have a feedback effect on the domestic consumer price level. This allows slightly more generality, which we can then adjust to the stricter fix-price assumption.

The three basic equations in this version of the Mundell–Fleming model may be written:

$$\dot{s} = i - i^*, \tag{4.1}$$

$$m = \sigma s + \kappa y - \theta i \tag{4.2}$$

and:

$$\dot{y} = \chi(\alpha + \mu s - \psi i - y). \tag{4.3}$$

All variables except interest rates are in logarithms; s is the domestic price of foreign currency, i and i^* are the domestic and foreign interest rates, m is the level of the money supply, y is domestic income, and a dot over a variable denotes a time derivative. The uncovered interest parity (UIP) condition (4.1) is expressed in continuous time and assuming perfect foresight. Because the model is log-linear, assuming perfect foresight is effectively equivalent to assuming rational expectations (the certainty equivalence result). Equation (4.2) is a domestic money market equilibrium condition, where we have effectively assumed that the consumer price level, p^c say, is a geometric weighted average of the domestic currency prices of foreign and domestic goods, $p^c = \sigma(s + p^*) + (1 - \sigma)p$, where σ is the weight attached to foreign prices in the consumer price index. Since we assume that domestic and foreign prices are fixed, we can normalise p and p^* to zero, so that only σs appears in (4.2). Equation (4.3) relates movements in aggregate output to excess demand in the goods market. This embodies the underlying Keynesian nature of the model in that output is ultimately demand-determined, although in the short run there may be discrepancies between aggregate demand and supply as output adjusts in response to movements in demand. Aggregate demand is assumed to be a function of an autonomous component, α, and a component depending upon international competitiveness which can be thought of as net export demand, and an interest-rate-sensitive component such as investment or private consumption.[3] Note that, as in standard Keynesian analysis, aggregate demand may also be a function of output and this is also consistent with (4.3) so long as the marginal propensity to consume out of income is less than unity.[4]

Assuming that the money supply is exogenously set by the monetary authorities, using equations (4.1) and (4.2) yields:

$$\dot{s} = \frac{\sigma}{\theta}s + \frac{\kappa}{\theta}y - \frac{1}{\theta}m - i^*. \tag{4.4}$$

Substituting for i in (4.2) and using (4.3) yields:

$$\dot{y} = \chi\left[\alpha + \left(\mu - \frac{\sigma\psi}{\theta}\right)s - \left(1 + \frac{\psi\kappa}{\theta}\right)y + \frac{\psi}{\theta}m\right]. \tag{4.5}$$

---

[3] Since domestic and foreign prices are held constant, net export demand is effectively a function of the nominal exchange rate.

[4] Suppose aggregate demand is given by $\alpha' + \mu's + \nu y$ where $0 < \nu < 1$, and $\dot{y}$ is again a function of excess aggregate demand: $\dot{y} = \chi'[\alpha' + \mu's + \nu y - y]$. This is equivalent to $\dot{y} = \chi[\alpha + \mu s - y]$, where $\alpha = \alpha'/(1 - \nu)$, $\mu = \mu'/(1 - \nu)$ and $\chi = \chi'(1 - \nu)$.

The perfect-foresight Mundell–Fleming model may thus be written in the form of the two differential equations (4.3) and (4.5), rewritten in matrix form:

$$\begin{bmatrix} \dot{s} \\ \dot{y} \end{bmatrix} = \begin{bmatrix} \sigma/\theta & \kappa/\theta \\ \chi(\mu - \sigma\psi/\theta) & -\chi(1 + \psi\kappa/\theta) \end{bmatrix} \begin{bmatrix} s \\ y \end{bmatrix} + \begin{bmatrix} -\frac{1}{\theta}m - i^* \\ \chi(\alpha + \frac{\psi}{\theta}m) \end{bmatrix}. \tag{4.6}$$

Saddlepath stability of this system is guaranteed if $\chi(\mu - \sigma\psi/\theta) > 0$ (so that the determinant of the coefficient matrix is negative; see Blanchard and Kahn, 1980) which in turn implies that $\mu/\psi > \sigma/\theta$. Intuitively, this means that exchange rate movements must have a much bigger effect on aggregate demand than interest rates do, where 'much bigger' is judged with respect to the relative sensitivities of the money market to the exchange rate and the interest rate. This is to avoid potentially unstable feedback between the two markets. This condition is probably uncontentious, however, for two reasons. First, if we set $\sigma = 0$ as in Mundell's original treatment, the condition is automatically satisfied. Second, there is empirical evidence to suggest that both private consumption and investment expenditure are extremely insensitive to interest rate movements (see Taylor, 1999, for a recent survey), so that ψ is likely to be very small. Assuming, therefore, that this condition is satisfied, the coefficient matrix in (4.6) has a negative determinant and hence the system has a unique convergent saddlepath. In fact, since, on the basis of the empirical evidence, it seems safe to assume that ψ is very small, we shall, for simplicity, set it to zero, so that the system becomes:

$$\begin{bmatrix} \dot{s} \\ \dot{y} \end{bmatrix} = \begin{bmatrix} \sigma/\theta & \kappa/\theta \\ \chi\mu & -\chi \end{bmatrix} \begin{bmatrix} s \\ y \end{bmatrix} + \begin{bmatrix} -\frac{1}{\theta}m - i^* \\ \chi\alpha \end{bmatrix} \tag{4.7}$$

where the second row is in fact just equation (4.3) with ψ set to zero. Setting $\dot{s} = 0$ in the first row of (4.7) gives the locus of points at which there is equilibrium in the money market and which, following the standard terminology of Hicks (1937), we might term the *LM* curve. Similarly, setting $\dot{y} = 0$ in the second row gives the locus of points at which there is goods market equilibrium, or the *IS* curve in Hicksian terminology.[5]

The qualitative solution to (4.7) is shown in Figure 4.1, where the saddlepath slopes down from left to right in (y, s)-space. Under the assumption that agents are not willing to participate in an unstable economy (see Shiller, 1978), the economy is always on the saddlepath and – given the assumption that output adjusts sluggishly – the exchange rate has to jump in response to shocks which shift the saddlepath, and then converge towards the equilibrium along the new saddlepath.

Consider, for example, the effect of an increase in the money supply, which induces a shift in the *LM* curve to the right (*LM'*). The long-run exchange rate will depreciate proportionately (i.e. s will be higher). The stable saddlepath, which originally went through point A, must now go through the new long-run equilibrium C (Figure 4.2). Because output takes time to adjust, however, the economy cannot jump directly from A to C. Instead, the

---

[5] Note that this neat identification of $\dot{s} = 0$ and $\dot{y} = 0$ with the traditional *LM* and *IS* curves would not be possible if $\psi \neq 0$.

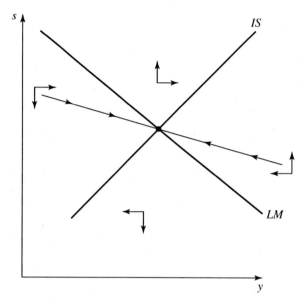

Figure 4.1. The qualitative saddlepath solution to the perfect-foresight Mundell–Fleming model.

exchange rate initially jumps above its long-run equilibrium in order to get on to the new saddlepath, and output then adjusts slowly and the economy moves along the saddlepath from B to the new long-run equilibrium C. Therefore, the net effect of the money supply increase is a long-run depreciation of the exchange rate, with initial overshooting, and a long-run increase in output.

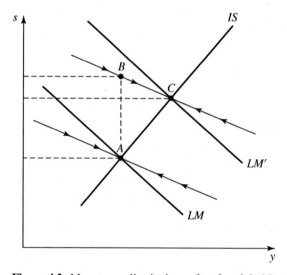

Figure 4.2. Monetary policy in the perfect-foresight Mundell–Fleming model.

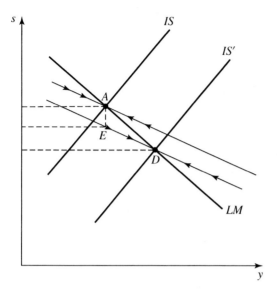

Figure 4.3. Fiscal policy in the perfect-foresight Mundell–Fleming model.

Now consider the effect of an expansionary fiscal policy, which induces a shift of the *IS* curve to the right (*IS'*). This can be thought of for simplicity as an increase in the autonomous component of aggregate demand. The long-run exchange rate will appreciate proportionately (i.e. *s* will be lower). The stable saddle-path, which originally went through point *A* must now go through the new long-run equilibrium *D* (Figure 4.3). However, because output takes time to adjust to the higher level of aggregate demand, the economy cannot jump directly from *A* to *D*. Instead, the exchange rate initially jumps below its long-run equilibrium in order to get on to the new saddlepath, and output then adjusts slowly and the economy moves along the saddlepath from *E* to the new long-run equilibrium *D*. Therefore, the net effect of the expansionary fiscal policy is a long-run appreciation of the exchange rate, with initial undershooting, and a long-run increase in output.

Note, however, that if the feedback from the exchange rate onto domestic prices is very small, i.e. σ is small, then the *LM* curve (or $\dot{s} = 0$ locus) will be very steep in (y, s)-space – indeed, a vertical line in the limiting case of $\sigma = 0$. In this case, fiscal policy will be completely ineffective in its effects on real output. This is obvious diagrammatically (simply redraw Figure 4.3 with a vertical *LM* curve). Intuitively, the increase in the autonomous component of aggregate demand is completely offset by an immediate appreciation of the domestic currency which chokes off net exports. From the UIP condition, we know that domestic and foreign interest rates must be equalised in equilibrium. For money market equilibrium, this implies a given level of the velocity of circulation $(m - y)$ which cannot be affected by fiscal policy so long as $\sigma = 0$. Hence, for a given level of the money supply, fiscal policy has no effect on real output. This is often thought of as the standard case in the Mundell–Fleming model, although – as the above discussion makes clear – it should be seen as a limiting case of the model.

The above treatment of the Mundell–Fleming model may seem unusual to readers who have previously met it largely in comparative-static diagrammatic form. But this is only because Mundell and Fleming were writing in the early 1960s, before many of the techniques and assumptions used above – notably perfect foresight or rational expectations and saddlepath analysis – became standard. In fact, the Mundell–Fleming model may be seen as an early prototype for many of the exchange rate models discussed in this chapter. Replacing the assumption of price fixity with price stickiness, for example, yields the Dornbusch (1976) exchange rate overshooting model, which we turn to next.

4.1.2   The sticky-price monetary model

The sticky-price monetary model (SPMM), due originally to Dornbusch (1976), allows short-term overshooting of the nominal and real exchange rates above their long-run equilibrium levels. In the SPMM, it is assumed that there are 'jump variables' in the system – exchange rates and interest rates – compensating for stickiness in other variables – notably goods prices. Consider the effects of a cut in the nominal domestic money supply. Since goods prices are sticky in the short run, this implies an initial fall in the real money supply and a consequent rise in interest rates in order to clear the money market. The rise in domestic interest rates then leads to a capital inflow and an appreciation of the nominal exchange rate (a rise in the value of domestic currency in terms of foreign currency). Investors are aware that they are artificially forcing up the value of the domestic currency and that they may therefore suffer a foreign exchange loss when the proceeds of their investment are used to repay liabilities in foreign currency. Nevertheless, as long as the *expected* foreign exchange loss – the expected rate of depreciation of the domestic currency – is less than the *known* capital market gain – the interest rate differential – risk-neutral investors will continue to borrow abroad in order to buy domestic assets. A short-run equilibrium is achieved when the expected rate of depreciation is just equal to the interest rate differential, i.e. when uncovered interest rate parity holds. Since the expected rate of depreciation must be non-zero for a non-zero interest rate differential, the exchange rate must have overshot its long-run, purchasing-power-parity equilibrium. In the medium run, however, domestic prices begin to fall in response to the fall in the money supply. This alleviates pressure in the money market (the real money supply rises) and domestic interest rates start to decline. The exchange rate then depreciates slowly towards long-run purchasing power parity. Thus, this model can explain the apparent paradox that the exchange rates of currencies for countries with relatively higher interest rates tend to be expected to depreciate: the initial interest rate rise induces a sharp exchange rate appreciation, followed by a slow depreciation as prices adjust, which continues until long-run purchasing power parity is satisfied.

The essential characteristics of the SPMM model can be seen in a three-equation structural model in continuous time, holding foreign variables and domestic income constant:[6]

$$\dot{s} = i - i^* \tag{4.8}$$

$$m = p + \kappa \overline{y} - \theta i \tag{4.9}$$

$$\dot{p} = \gamma \left[\alpha + \mu \left(s - p \right) - \overline{y} \right]. \tag{4.10}$$

---

[6] These are simplifying rather than necessary assumptions.

This system is similar to that analysed above in our discussion of the Mundell–Fleming model, with a number of important differences. A bar denotes a variable in long-run equilibrium; thus output is assumed to be fixed for simplicity since it is always at its long-run equilibrium. Equation (4.8) again represents the uncovered interest parity condition expressed in continuous time and using certainty equivalence because of the log-linearity of the model. Equation (4.9) is a domestic money-market equilibrium condition except domestic prices cannot now be normalised to zero. Movements in the nominal exchange rate can still have an effect on the domestic price level, except that now we can think of this as part of the effect on prices coming through equation (4.10). This equation replaces the equation for movements in aggregate output which we used above and is a fairly standard Phillips curve relationship, relating domestic price movements to excess aggregate demand. Aggregate demand is assumed to be a function of an autonomous component, α, and a component depending upon international competitiveness which can be thought of as net export demand.[7] We could also add in an interest-sensitive component of aggregate demand here, although, as it will have no qualitative effect at all on the model, it is suppressed for simplicity.

Unlike in the Mundell–Fleming model, output is no longer demand determined: excess aggregate demand simply leads to inflation rather than an increase in output. While Dornbusch (1976, 1980) does extend his model to allow for short-run deviations of output around the equilibrium level, the qualitative results of the model are left unchanged, and so we keep y fixed here for simplicity. This is a key difference in the two models, effectively resulting from substituting a price adjustment equation for an output adjustment equation. This is enough to generate monetary neutrality in the model. Indeed, one might even say that money neutrality is effectively assumed in the Dornbusch model since, if output must be at the 'natural' level in the long run, and interest rates must be at the level of foreign interest rates, the monetary equilibrium equation, (4.9), shows us that prices must be proportional to money in the long run. By similar reasoning, long-run goods market equilibrium (set $\dot{p} = 0$ in (4.10)) implies that the nominal exchange rate must also be proportional to prices in the long run. Thus, a form of long-run PPP may be said to hold in the Dornbusch model, but this is strictly as a result of its money neutrality. Because of the neutrality of money in this model, it is often termed the sticky-price monetary model.

Given that output must be at the natural rate $\bar{y}$ in long-run equilibrium, it is convenient to solve the model by considering deviations of s and y around their long-run levels. In long-run, non-inflationary equilibrium, the rate of depreciation is zero (and so is the nominal interest rate differential in equation (4.8)) and the price level is at its long-run value. We assume, again for simplicity, that the money supply is set exogenously by the authorities so that we regard the current level of m as the long-run equilibrium level.[8] Hence, the long-run money-market equilibrium condition is:

$$m - \bar{p} = \kappa \bar{y} - \theta i^*. \tag{4.11}$$

---

[7] Foreign prices are again held constant and normalised so that their logarithm is zero.
[8] This assumption may appear to sit uneasily with the assumption of perfect foresight. The key issue is, however, that the money supply is exogenous to the model.

Subtracting (4.9) from (4.11) yields:

$$p - \bar{p} = \theta(i - i^*) \tag{4.12}$$

or, using (4.8):

$$\dot{s} = (1/\theta)(p - \bar{p}). \tag{4.13}$$

Note also that, in the goods market, in non-inflationary, long-run equilibrium, the Phillips curve equation, (4.10), becomes:

$$0 = \gamma[\alpha + \mu(\bar{s} - \bar{p}) - \bar{y}]. \tag{4.14}$$

Subtracting (4.14) from (4.10) yields:

$$\dot{p} = \gamma\mu(s - \bar{s}) - \gamma\mu(p - \bar{p}). \tag{4.15}$$

Finally, the differential equations (4.13) and (4.15) may be written in matrix form as:

$$\begin{bmatrix} \dot{s} \\ \dot{p} \end{bmatrix} = \begin{bmatrix} 0 & 1/\theta \\ \gamma\mu & -\gamma\mu \end{bmatrix} \begin{bmatrix} s - \bar{s} \\ p - \bar{p} \end{bmatrix}. \tag{4.16}$$

The coefficient matrix in (4.16) has a negative determinant $(-\gamma\mu/\theta)$ and hence the system has a unique convergent saddlepath (Blanchard and Kahn, 1980). The qualitative solution to (4.16) is shown in Figure 4.4, where the saddlepath slopes down from left to right in (p, s)-space.

If λ is the negative, stable root of the system, then the equation of the law of motion governing s must satisfy:

$$\dot{s} = -\lambda(s - \bar{s}). \tag{4.17}$$

Finally, using (4.17) in (4.13) yields the equation of the saddlepath:

$$s = \bar{s} - (1/\theta\lambda)(p - \bar{p}). \tag{4.18}$$

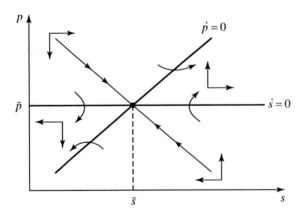

Figure 4.4. The qualitative solution to the sticky-price monetary model.

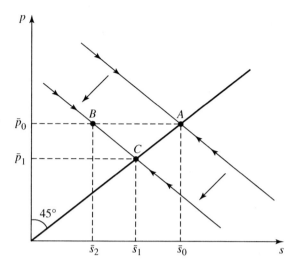

Figure 4.5. Overshooting following a monetary contraction.

Consider again, for example, the effects of a cut in the money supply. In the long run, the price level will be lower, at $\bar{p}_1$ instead of the initial level $\bar{p}_0$ in Figure 4.5, because of the neutrality of money in this model. Because long-run purchasing power parity holds in the model, holding foreign prices constant, the long-run exchange rate will appreciate proportionately (i.e. s will be lower), moving from $\bar{s}_0$ to $\bar{s}_1$ along the 45° ray. The stable saddlepath, which originally went through point A must now go through the new long-run equilibrium C. Because prices take time to adjust, however, the economy cannot jump directly from A to C. Instead, prices remain fixed instantaneously and the exchange rate jumps to $\bar{s}_2$ in order to get on to the new saddlepath. Prices then adjust slowly and the economy moves along the saddlepath from B to the new long-run equilibrium C. Therefore, the net effect of the money supply cut is a long-run appreciation of $\bar{s}_0 - \bar{s}_1$, with an initial overshoot of $\bar{s}_2 - \bar{s}_1$.

As noted above, the sticky-price model may also be extended in order to allow for short-run effects on output (see Dornbusch, 1976, 1980). Moreover, Buiter and Miller (1981) extend the model in order to allow for a non-zero core rate of inflation – that is, the inflation differential is non-zero even when net aggregate demand is zero. In this setting, Buiter and Miller investigate the impact of the discovery of a natural resource – say oil or gas – on the exchange rate and conclude that, since the income increase induced by the discovery causes an increase in the demand for non-oil output, then – given that long-run output is fixed – the exchange rate has to appreciate in the long run in order to worsen the terms of trade and reduce long-run demand; this is the so-called 'Dutch disease' (see also Forsyth and Kay, 1989).[9]

---

[9] Calvo and Rodriguez (1977) and Girton and Roper (1981) modify the SPMM by relaxing the assumption of non-substitutability of monies.

4.1.3   The flexible-price monetary model

The monetary approach to the exchange rate emerged as the dominant exchange rate model at the start of the recent float in the early 1970s (see Frenkel, 1976; Mussa, 1976, 1979; Frenkel and Johnson, 1978). We can start by analysing it within the same continuous time framework already used to analyse the Mundell–Fleming and Dornbusch models, in order to demonstrate their relationship to one another. In particular, consider again the three structural equations of the sticky-price model:

$$\dot{s} = i - i^* \tag{4.19}$$

$$m = p + \kappa \bar{y} - \theta i \tag{4.20}$$

$$\dot{p} = \gamma [\alpha + \mu (s - p) - \bar{y}]. \tag{4.21}$$

We again assume that output is at its natural level. Now, however, we assume that prices are perfectly flexible. This can be captured in this framework by letting γ tend to a very large number in the price adjustment equation (4.21). This implies that movements in the exchange rate must be directly proportional to movements in prices not only in the long run but *continuously*; in other words, continuous (relative) purchasing power parity must hold. Thus, s must be equal to p up to a constant ($v = (\bar{y} - \alpha)/\mu$) at any point in time:

$$s = p + v. \tag{4.22}$$

Substituting for p from (4.20) in (4.22), we can then solve for the exchange rate:

$$s = m - \kappa \bar{y} + \theta(i - i^*) + v', \tag{4.23}$$

where $v' = v + \theta i^*$. Given that we are adopting the 'small country' assumption whereby we can assume that all foreign variables are held constant, equation (4.23) may be thought of as the basic equation of the monetary approach to the exchange rate. The essential differences between the three models may thus be encapsulated as follows. In the Mundell–Fleming model, output is demand determined and prices are fixed. In the Dornbusch model, output is at its natural level, at least in the long run, and prices adjust sluggishly to excess demand. In the flexible-price monetary model (FPMM), output is again at its natural level, but prices are flexible and adjust instantly in response to excess demand.

It is more usual, however, to develop the monetary model in discrete time and to treat the foreign country symmetrically with the domestic country, as follows.

The monetary approach starts from the definition of the exchange rate as the relative price of two monies and attempts to model that relative price in terms of the relative supply of and demand for those monies. In discrete time, using time subscripts for emphasis, and asterisks to denote foreign variables and parameters, monetary equilibria in the domestic and foreign country respectively are given by:

$$m_t = p_t + \kappa y_t - \theta i_t \tag{4.24}$$

$$m_t^* = p_t^* + \kappa^* y_t^* - \theta^* i_t^*. \tag{4.25}$$

In the FPMM, the domestic interest rate is exogenous in the long run and determined in world markets, because of the implicit assumption of perfect capital mobility.

Also, purchasing power parity is assumed to hold in the model. In the continuous time framework discussed above, we showed that it is natural to assume continuous relative purchasing power parity. In fact, early proponents of the monetary approach generally assumed the even stronger proposition that absolute purchasing power parity holds continuously:

$$s_t = p_t - p_t^*. \tag{4.26}$$

The domestic money supply determines the domestic price level and hence the exchange rate is determined by relative money supplies. Equating (4.24) and (4.25) and using (4.26), the solution for the nominal exchange rate is:

$$s_t = (m_t - m_t^*) - (\kappa y_t - \kappa^* y_t^*) + (\theta i_t - \theta^* i_t^*), \tag{4.27}$$

– the fundamental equation of the FPMM. The model is often simplified by assuming that the income elasticities and interest rate semi-elasticities of money demand are the same for the domestic and foreign country ($\kappa = \kappa^*$ and $\theta = \theta^*$) so that the equation reduces to:

$$s_t = (m_t - m_t^*) - \kappa(y_t - y_t^*) + \theta(i_t - i_t^*) \tag{4.28}$$

– which is analogous to our continuous-time formulation (4.23) if foreign variables are held constant.

According to equation (4.28), an increase in the domestic money supply relative to the foreign money stock, for example, induces a depreciation of the domestic currency in terms of the foreign currency, that is a rise in the nominal exchange rate s_t expressed as the domestic price of foreign currency. A rise in domestic real income, *ceteris paribus*, creates an excess demand for the domestic money stock. In an attempt to increase their real money balances, domestic residents reduce expenditure and prices fall until money-market equilibrium is achieved. Via purchasing power parity, the fall in domestic prices (with foreign prices constant) implies an appreciation of the domestic currency in terms of the foreign currency.

By invoking the uncovered interest parity condition the expected rate of depreciation of the domestic currency, Δs_{t+1}^e, can also be substituted for the nominal interest rate differential $(i_t - i_t^*)$, in the resulting equation to yield:

$$s_t = (m_t - m_t^*) - \kappa(y_t - y_t^*) + \theta \Delta s_{t+1}^e. \tag{4.29}$$

Equation (4.29) may in turn be reparameterised as:

$$s_t = (1 + \theta)^{-1}(m_t - m_t^*) - \kappa(1 + \theta)^{-1}(y_t - y_t^*) + \theta(1 + \theta)^{-1} s_{t+1}^e. \tag{4.30}$$

By iterating forward in (4.30), the rational expectations solution to (4.29) may be written:

$$s_t = (1 + \theta)^{-1} \sum_{i=0}^{\infty} \left(\frac{\theta}{1 + \theta} \right)^i E_t[(m_{t+i} - m_{t+i}^*) - \kappa(y_{t+i} - y_{t+i}^*)], \tag{4.31}$$

where $E_t[\cdot]$ denotes the mathematical expectation conditional on the information set available at time t. It is well known from the rational expectations literature, however, that equation (4.31) represents only one solution to (4.29) from a potentially infinite set. In general, given the exchange rate determined according to equation (4.31), say $\widetilde{s}_t$, (4.29) has multiple rational expectations solutions according to:

$$s_t = \widetilde{s}_t + B_t \tag{4.32}$$

where the rational bubble term B_t satisfies

$$E_t(B_{t+1}) = \theta^{-1}(1 + \theta)B_t. \tag{4.33}$$

Therefore, $\widetilde{s}_t$ simply represents the rational expectations solution to the FPMM in the absence of rational bubbles (see also our discussion of rational bubbles in Chapter 2). Rational bubbles represent significant departures from the fundamentals of the model which would not be detected in a specification such as (4.28). Thus, testing for the presence of bubbles can be interpreted as an important specification test of the model (see Meese, 1986).

Overall, although the simplicity of the FPMM is very attractive, a large number of assumptions are needed in order to achieve this simplicity. Open-economy macroeconomics is essentially about six aggregate markets: goods, labour, money, foreign exchange, domestic bonds (i.e. non-money assets) and foreign bonds. The FPMM concentrates, however, directly on equilibrium conditions in only one of these markets – the money market. This is implicitly achieved in the following fashion. By assuming perfect substitutability of domestic and foreign assets, the domestic and foreign bond markets essentially become a single market. Assuming that the exchange rate adjusts freely to equilibrate supply and demand in the foreign exchange market and also assuming equilibrium in the goods market (through perfectly flexible prices) and in the labour market (through perfectly flexible wages) then implies equilibrium in three of the five remaining markets. Recalling Walras' law, according to which equilibrium in $n - 1$ markets of an n-market system implies equilibrium in the n-th market, equilibrium of the full system in the model is then determined by equilibrium conditions for the money market. The flexible-price monetary model is thus, implicitly, a market-clearing general equilibrium model in which continuous purchasing power parity among national price levels is assumed (see Taylor, 1995).

The very high volatility of real exchange rates during the 1970s float, casting serious doubts on the assumption of continuous purchasing power parity, led, however, to the development of two further classes of models: sticky-price monetary models and equilibrium models. Having discussed the SPMM in the previous sub-section, we now turn to equilibrium models.

4.1.4 Equilibrium models and liquidity models

Equilibrium exchange rate models of the type developed originally by Stockman (1980) and Lucas (1982) analyse the general equilibrium of a two-country model by maximising the expected present value of a representative agent's utility, subject to budget constraints and cash-in-advance constraints (by convention, agents are required to hold local currency, the accepted medium of exchange, to purchase goods).[10] In an important sense, equilibrium models are an extension or generalisation of the flexible-price monetary model that allows for multiple traded goods and real shocks across countries. A simple equilibrium model can be sketched as follows.[11] Consider a one-period, two-country, two-good world in which prices are flexible and markets are in equilibrium, as in the flexible-price monetary model, but in which, in contrast to the monetary model, agents distinguish between domestic and foreign goods, x and y respectively, in terms of well-defined preferences.[12] Further, for simplicity, assume that all agents, domestic or foreign, have identical homothetic preferences.[13] Also, assume that households in the two countries are equally wealthy and hold exactly the same fractions of their wealth in the stock of any firm. The nominal money supplies in the domestic and foreign countries, M^s and M^{*s} respectively, are exogenous, fixed by the governments (or central banks) of the two countries, whereas the demand for domestic and foreign money, M^d and M^{*d} respectively, is equal to:

$$M^d / P_x = \Xi \tag{4.34}$$

$$M^{d*} / P_y^* = \Xi^*, \tag{4.35}$$

where P_x (P_y^*) is the nominal price of good x (y) in terms of the domestic (foreign) currency, and Ξ (Ξ^*) is the real demand for the domestic (foreign) currency measured in terms of the good x (y). In equilibrium, money demand equals money supply and a solution for nominal export prices (i.e. the GDP deflators), P_x and P_y^*, is given by:

$$P_x = M^s / \Xi \tag{4.36}$$

$$P_y^* = M^{*s} / \Xi^*. \tag{4.37}$$

The nominal exchange rate enters the model because the real exchange rate, that is the relative price of the good y in terms of the good x, is:

$$\Pi = S P_y^* / P_x \tag{4.38}$$

where S is the nominal exchange rate. In particular, given domestic and foreign output of x and y respectively, the equilibrium relative price of foreign output, Π, must be the slope of a representative agent's indifference curve at the point $(y/n, x/n)$ in foreign–domestic output per capita space (where $n/2$ is the number of individuals in each economy), as in Figure 4.6.

Using (4.36) and (4.37) in (4.38) and solving for the nominal exchange rate yields:

$$S = \frac{M^s \Xi^*}{M^{*s} \Xi} \Pi \tag{4.39}$$

---

[10] See Stockman (1987) for a more extensive, largely non-technical exposition. This literature may also be seen as an offshoot of the real business cycle literature.

[11] See also our discussion of a version of the Lucas model in the context of spot and forward rates in Chapter 2.

[12] For simpliciy, no borrowing or lending is assumed to take place.

[13] For non-homothetic preferences, many disturbances create transfer-problem-like conditions with unpredictable effects on terms of trade.

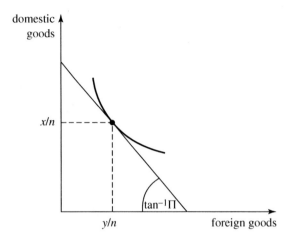

Figure 4.6. Determination of the real exchange rate in the equilibrium model.

or, adding a time subscript and expressing all variables in natural logarithms:

$$s_t = m_t - m_t^* - \xi_t + \xi_t^* + \pi_t. \tag{4.40}$$

Equation (4.40) is, in this very simple formulation, the key equation determining the nominal exchange rate in the equilibrium model, and brings out very clearly the fact that the equilibrium model can be viewed as a generalisation of the monetary model.[14] Indeed, relative monetary expansion leads to a depreciation of the domestic currency (one-for-one in this simple formulation) as in the simple monetary model. Also, an increase in ξ_t lowers domestic nominal prices and the nominal exchange rate, that is induces an appreciation of the domestic currency. Nevertheless, some of the implications of the equilibrium model are either qualitatively or quantitatively different from the implications of the flexible-price monetary model or else incapable of analysis within a purely monetary framework. As an example of the latter, consider an exogenous shift in preferences away from foreign goods towards domestic goods, represented as a flattening of indifference curves as in Figure 4.7 (from I_1 to I_2). With per capita outputs fixed, this implies a fall in the relative price of foreign output (or conversely a rise in the relative price of domestic output) – Π falls (from Π_1 to Π_2 in Figure 4.7). Assuming unchanged monetary policies, this movement in the real exchange rate will, however, be brought about entirely (and swiftly) by a movement in the nominal exchange rate without any movement in national price levels. Thus, demand shifts are capable of explaining the observed volatility of nominal exchange rates in excess of volatility in relative prices in equilibrium models. The fall in S, in this case matching the fall in Π, will be observed as a decline in domestic competitiveness. It would be a mistake, however, to infer that this rise in the relative price of domestic goods was caused by the appreciation of the domestic currency: both are the result of the underlying demand shift.

---

[14] Because of the strict cash-in-advance constraint, the assumed preferences and the fixed output levels, intertemporal considerations are absent from this very simple formulation.

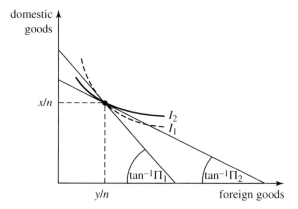

Figure 4.7. The effect on the real exchange rate of a preference shift towards foreign goods.

In this simple equilibrium model, an increase in domestic productivity (output per capita) has two analytically separate effects. The first effect – the 'relative price effect' – involves a reduction in the relative price of domestic output and so an increase in Π which, through (4.40), will tend to raise S (depreciate the domestic currency). The second effect – the 'money demand effect' – will tend to appreciate the domestic currency as the transactions demand for money rises, exactly as in the monetary model. Whether the exchange rate rises or falls depends upon the relative size of these effects which, in turn, depends upon the degree of substitutability between domestic and foreign goods; the higher the degree of substitutability, the smaller the relative price effect will be. Thus, supply disturbances will only generate volatility of nominal exchange rates in excess of the volatility of relative prices if the degree of substitutability between domestic and foreign goods is relatively small (Obstfeld and Stockman, 1985).

In the simple equilibrium model sketched here, we have implicitly made a number of simplifying assumptions. A particularly important assumption is that individuals in either economy hold exactly the same fractions of their wealth in any firm, domestic or foreign. If this assumption is violated, then supply and demand shifts will alter the relative distribution of wealth between domestic and foreign residents as, for example, one country becomes relatively more productive. This, in turn, will affect the equilibrium level of the exchange rate (Stockman, 1987).

In the more recent literature on liquidity models of the exchange rate, some authors have extended the equilibrium model framework by incorporating an extra cash-in-advance constraint on agents. In these models, agents are required to hold cash not only to purchase goods but also to purchase assets (as originally suggested in a closed-economy context by Lucas, 1990). In the two-country model of Grilli and Roubini (1992), for instance, the money supply and bond issue of each country are linked through the government budget constraint, and agents must decide on how much domestic and foreign currency to hold in order to purchase domestic and foreign goods and assets. Once this decision is made, subsequent shocks to bond and money supplies will affect nominal interest rates (in order to clear bond markets) and also, since the expected rate of monetary *growth* (as opposed to the *level* of the money supply) and hence expected inflation is unaffected, will affect real interest rates. This in turn affects the nominal and real exchange rates.

Beaudry and Devereux (1995) construct a dynamic general equilibrium model designed to explore the relationship between money shocks and the real exchange rate. A crucial feature of this model is the presence of increasing returns to scale in technology. This allows for an equilibrium in monopolistic competitive price-setting in which prices are endogenously sticky. Hence, the combination of increasing returns to scale and short-term price stickiness leads to significant money non-neutrality. Under a floating exchange rate system, a monetary shock induces an immediate and persistent nominal and real depreciation as well as persistent positive effects on output, consumption and investment.

It is interesting to contrast liquidity models with the sticky-price monetary model, since the latter assumes sticky goods prices and instantaneous portfolio adjustment, while liquidity models essentially assume slow portfolio adjustment and perfectly flexible goods prices. Many of the implications of the two models are similar. In particular, the two models are observationally equivalent with respect to the impact of monetary shocks: a positive shock to the money supply leads to a decline in real and nominal interest rates in both models, the domestic currency appreciates against the foreign currency in both real and nominal terms, and output rises (in response to lower real interest rates) until prices and portfolios are again in equilibrium. The most striking difference between equilibrium and disequilibrium models of exchange rate determination involves the policy implications of the two classes of models. In particular, in equilibrium models, the government cannot affect the real exchange rate by changing the nominal exchange rate, for example through foreign exchange market intervention, target zones or similar means. Further, equilibrium models of the exchange rate imply that changes in the exchange rate do not induce changes in inflation: the exchange rate is an endogenous variable. Hence, exchange rate changes are not helpful, for example, in formulating monetary policies designed to keep inflation low. This also implies that the choice of the exchange rate regime to be employed is not very important for the real exchange rate or the trade balance. Consequently, in an equilibrium model framework, undervalued or overvalued currencies are not an important issue and governments should not use, in principle, protectionist policies as a reaction to changes in the exchange rate. Overall, the main implication of the equilibrium theory of the exchange rate is that exchange rate behaviour is consistent with the notion that markets work properly if they are permitted to do so (Stockman, 1987).

More recent work on equilibrium models has fallen within the general area of the 'new open-economy macroeconomics', which explores open-economy issues including exchange rate determination in the context of dynamic general equilibrium models with explicit microfoundations, nominal rigidities and imperfect competition (e.g. Obstfeld and Rogoff, 1995). Because of the importance of this new strand of the literature, however, it is given full chapter-length treatment in this book (Chapter 5).

4.1.5   The portfolio balance model

A distinguishing feature of the portfolio balance model (PBM) among exchange rate models is the assumption of imperfect substitutability between domestic and foreign assets.[15] More precisely, the assumptions, present both in the flexible-price and the sticky-price monetary models, that domestic and foreign assets are perfect substitutes and that the wealth effects of current account imbalances are negligible are relaxed in the portfolio balance model (see Dornbusch and Fischer, 1980; Isard, 1980; Branson, 1983, 1984). In common with the class of monetary models, however, the level of the exchange rate is determined by supply of and demand for financial assets, at least in the short run. Nevertheless, the exchange rate is the main determinant of the current account balance; that is to say, a surplus (deficit) in the current account balance is associated with a rise (fall) in net domestic holdings of foreign assets, which influences the level of wealth, and in turn the level of the demand for assets, which ultimately affects the exchange rate. The PBM is, therefore, a dynamic model of exchange rate determination based on the interaction of asset markets, current account balance, prices and the rate of asset accumulation. It allows us to distinguish between short-run, or flow equilibrium and the dynamic adjustment to the long-run, stock equilibrium (a static level of wealth and no tendency of the system to move away from equilibrium).

In this sub-section, we use a basic model in order to give a flavour of the class of portfolio balance models. We begin by analysing the short-run determination of the exchange rate and then focus on the dynamic adjustment to long-run equilibrium.

4.1.5.1   Short-run exchange rate determination and monetary policy in the portfolio balance model
Consider a model in which the net financial wealth of the private sector (W) is divided into three components: money (M), domestically issued bonds (B) and foreign bonds denominated in foreign currency and held by domestic residents (B^*). B can be thought of as government debt held by the domestic private sector; B^* is the level of net claims on foreigners held by the private sector. Since, under a free float, a current account surplus must be exactly matched by a capital account deficit – i.e. capital outflow, and hence an increase in net foreign indebtedness to the domestic economy – the current account must determine the rate of accumulation of B^* over time. With foreign and domestic interest rates given by i and i^*, we can express our definition of wealth and domestic demand functions or its components as follows:[16]

$$W \equiv M + B + SB^* \tag{4.41}$$

$$M = M(i, \; i^* + \widehat{S^e})W \qquad M_1 < 0, \; M_2 < 0 \tag{4.42}$$

$$B = B(i, \; i^* + \widehat{S^e})W \qquad B_1 > 0, \; B_2 < 0 \tag{4.43}$$

$$SB^* = B^*(i, \; i^* + \widehat{S^e})W \qquad B_1^* < 0, \; B_2^* > 0 \tag{4.44}$$

$$\dot{B}^* = T(S/P) + i^* B^* \qquad T_1 > 0 \tag{4.45}$$

---

[15] A comprehensive treatment of the portfolio balance model is given in Branson and Henderson (1985).

[16] X_k denotes the partial derivative of $X(\cdot)$ with respect to the k-th argument, for $X = M, B, B^*, T$. The change to upper-case letters here indicates that variables are in levels rather than logarithms. As throughout, interest rates are in decimal terms (e.g. 0.05 is 5 per cent).

where $\widehat{S}^e$ denotes the expected rate of depreciation of the domestic currency. Equation (4.41) is an identity defining wealth and (4.42), (4.43) and (4.44) are standard asset demand functions. Note that, in line with most expositions of the portfolio balance model, the scale variable is the level of wealth, W, and the demand functions are homogeneous in wealth; this allows them to be written in nominal terms (assuming homogeneity in prices and real wealth, prices cancel out; see Tobin, 1969). Note, however, that goods prices are indeterminate in this model (in what follows we assume long-run neutrality). Equation (4.45) gives the rate of change of B^*, the capital account, as equal to the current account, which is in turn equal to the sum of the trade balance, $T(\cdot)$ and net debt service receipts, i^*B^*. The trade balance depends positively on the level of the real exchange rate (a devaluation improves the trade balance).

For simplicity, assume initially static expectations, i.e. the expected rate of depreciation is set to zero in the model. Figure 4.8 shows the short-run determination in the PBM in (S, i)-space. The BE line is the locus of equilibrium points in the domestic asset market, whereas the FE line is the locus of points where demand for foreign assets is equal to the supply of foreign assets, which is fixed in the short run. Finally, along the ME schedule the money market is in equilibrium. In order to justify the slope of these schedules, consider that a depreciation of the exchange rate (increase in S) is associated with an increase in the value of foreign assets B^* measured in terms of the domestic currency and hence an increase in wealth W. The increase in wealth leads also to an increase in both M and B. Interest rates must rise for the equilibrium in the money market to be maintained, which implies that the ME schedule is upward-sloping in (S, i)-space. Nevertheless, the domestic interest rate must fall in order to maintain equilibrium in the domestic bond market, which implies that the BE line is downward-sloping. Also, as the domestic interest rate rises, agents adjust their portfolios by substituting domestic for foreign bonds; hence the domestic demand for foreign bonds falls and the foreign currency proceeds from selling foreign assets are

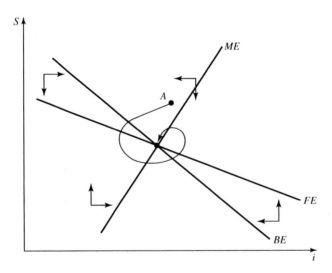

Figure 4.8. Global stability of a short-run equilibrium.

converted into domestic currency, inducing a fall in S. Thus, the FE schedule is downward-sloping in (S, i)-space, but flatter than the BE schedule under the assumption that a change in the domestic interest rate has a greater effect on domestic bond demand than on foreign bond demand.

The short-run equilibrium levels of the interest rate and the exchange rate are, therefore, determined by the intersection of the ME, BE and FE schedules. Also, given the adding-up constraint implied by (4.41), equilibrium in two of the three markets considered implies equilibrium in the remaining market, by Walras' law, and therefore, in practice, the analysis of the PBM may be conducted examining any two of the three schedules in Figure 4.8.

The global stability of the short-run equilibrium may be established as follows. Any point which is away from the BE schedule will induce a change in the interest rate – for a given level of the nominal exchange rate – such that a domestic bond market equilibrium is reached along the BE line. Similarly, given a certain interest rate, any point away from the FE line will induce a change in the exchange rate such that equilibrium in the foreign asset market is achieved along the FE line. Following this line of reasoning, starting from any point away from the intersection of the BE and FE schedules the economy tends towards equilibrium, the system being therefore globally stable.

The comparative-static effects of increases in money, M, domestic bonds, B, and foreign bonds, B^*, is straightforward. An increase in M induces, *ceteris paribus*, agents to adjust their portfolios by buying both domestic and foreign bonds: the FE schedule shifts upwards, while the BE schedule shifts downwards and a new equilibrium is established at a lower level of the interest rate and a higher level of the nominal exchange rate. Nevertheless, an increase in B^* generates excess supply of foreign currency as agents try to adjust their portfolios. Both the BE and the FE schedules shift to the left and intersect at a point where equilibrium is established at the initial interest rate but at a lower nominal exchange rate, i.e. at a point vertically below the initial equilibrium. Finally, an increase in B causes interest rates to rise as the excess supply of domestic bonds tends to depress their market price – the BE schedule shifts upwards. Consequently, the FE schedule shifts upwards because the demand for foreign assets increases, given the increase in wealth. If B and B^* are close substitutes, however, the wealth effect may be expected to be swamped by the substitution effect of increased holdings of domestic bonds, and net sales of foreign bonds follow, ultimately inducing a fall of the nominal exchange rate (appreciation of the domestic currency). Conversely, if B and B^* are not close substitutes in portfolios, then the wealth effect dominates the substitution effect, leading to a rise (depreciation) of the nominal exchange rate, as agents increase their holdings of foreign bonds.

Now consider an open-market purchase of domestic bonds by the authorities, paid for by printing money of the amount ΔM. Assume initially that domestic bond holdings fall by an amount ΔB such that $\Delta M + \Delta B = 0$. Since this operation affects directly the money and domestic bond market, it is convenient to carry out the analysis using the ME and BE schedule in this case. In order to induce the private sector to increase its money-holding and the wealth-holders to part willingly with domestic assets, a reduction in the interest rate, given a certain exchange rate and the price of domestic bonds, is needed. Hence, the ME and BE schedules both shift to the left. Also, since the new equilibrium must be at the intersection of the *ME*, *BE* and *FE* schedules and the *FE* schedule (unchanged in this case) is assumed to be downward-sloping and flatter than the *BE* line, the interest rate falls and the exchange rate depreciates as an effect of the initial increase in money entirely used to purchase domestic bonds.

Next consider the effect of open-market operations in foreign assets, assuming that $\Delta M + S \Delta B^* = 0$. The interest rate falls as a consequence of the excess money supply – the *ME* line shifts to the left – and the purchase of foreign assets in foreign currency by the government induces a depreciation of the exchange rate – the *FE* schedule shifts to the right. Given that the equilibrium must also lie on the *BE* schedule (unchanged), the new equilibrium is at a lower interest rate and higher exchange rate.

The qualitative effects of the open-market operations are, therefore, the same regardless of whether the government uses the printed money for buying domestic or foreign assets. Nevertheless, quantitatively the effects are different. Since the *FE* schedule is flatter than the *BE* schedule, in fact, it is clear that the change in the exchange rate caused by open-market operations involving domestic assets is smaller relatively to open-market operations involving foreign assets, while the effect on the domestic interest rate is greater. This is what one would expect intuitively, since the direct effect of the purchase of domestic assets is on the domestic interest rate, whereas the purchase of foreign assets affects the exchange rate more directly. Overall, therefore, the impact of open-market operations on the exchange rate and interest rate may strongly depend on the combination of domestic and foreign assets purchased by the government in its open-market operations.[17]

So far, however, we have only analysed short-run equilibrium in the PBM. As discussed in the following section, this kind of equilibrium cannot be the long-run equilibrium, because the stocks of assets held will typically be changing in some respect. Since flows are simply changes in stocks, we call this short-run equilibrium, *flow* equilibrium. In order to characterise long-run, or *stock* equilibrium, we need to make sure that there is no tendency for changes in the levels of the stocks of the various assets held by domestic residents.

4.1.5.2 Dynamic adjustment and long-run equilibrium in the portfolio balance model The preceding analysis did not investigate the impact of monetary policy on exchange rates through changes in prices in the PBM, nor on the dynamic stock–flow interaction of changes in the exchange rate, the current account and the level of wealth. In fact, an increase in the money supply is expected to lead to a price increase, which will affect net exports and hence influence the current account balance. In turn, this will affect the level of wealth which feeds back into the asset market, affecting the exchange rate during the adjustment to long-run equilibrium. Assuming that the foreign price level is constant, the current account of the balance of payments, CA, expressed in foreign currency, is:

$$CA = T(S/P) + i^* B^* \tag{4.46}$$

where the trade balance, $T(\cdot)$, is a function of competitiveness, i.e. it improves if the exchange rate rises or the domestic price level falls. Note that, if the economy considered is a capital exporter and $i^* B^*$ is positive, then a balance on the current account requires a deficit on the

---

[17] A comprehensive discussion of the effects of official intervention in the foreign exchange market through the portfolio balance channel is given later in the book.

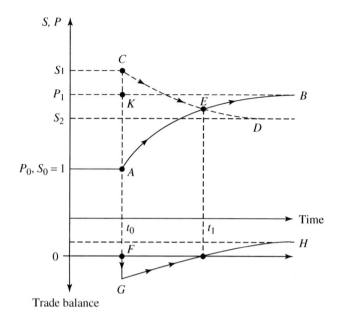

Figure 4.9. The dynamics of an open-market purchase of domestic bonds in the portfolio balance model.

trade balance. Also, since a non-zero current account induces changes in B^* and hence in wealth, a trade deficit may be required in long-run equilibrium.

Now consider again the case analysed previously of an open-market operation by which the government purchases domestic bonds by printing money. Recall that, in order to induce agents to hold more money and fewer bonds, the domestic interest rate falls (the price of domestic bonds rises) and, as agents attempt to compensate for the reduction in their portfolios of the level of domestic interest-bearing assets by buying foreign bonds, the exchange rate will depreciate, driving up the domestic currency value of foreign bonds. The net impact effect is a lower domestic interest rate and a depreciated currency.

Suppose that the economy was initially in equilibrium with a trade balance of zero and net foreign assets of zero (and hence a current account of zero). This is depicted in Figure 4.9 at the point corresponding to time t_0. The figure is drawn so that the initial (t_0) values of the price level and the exchange rate are normalised to unity. Assuming that the Marshall–Lerner–Harberger condition holds, the improvement in competitiveness will improve the trade balance from zero to a positive amount (FG) (ignoring any 'J-curve effects').[18] This means that the current account goes into surplus and domestic residents begin to acquire net foreign assets. Residents will then attempt to sell some of their foreign assets in order to rebalance their portfolios, and the domestic currency will begin to appreciate – in

[18] The 'J-curve effect' refers to the case where a devaluation initially worsens the trade balance before improving it. The reasoning is that the change in relative prices brought about by the devaluation initially reduces the domestic currency amount received from foreigners for domestic exports, and increases the domestic currency amount paid to foreigners for domestic imports, hence initially worsening the trade balance before the relative price changes begin to affect the demand for imports and for exports. The term presumably refers to the shape of a supposed graph of the time profile of the trade balance following a devaluation.

the diagram from point C along CD. This erosion of competitiveness will lead to a deterioration of the trade balance along GH. Meanwhile, the increase in the money supply will have begun to increase prices along the path AB towards the new long-run equilibrium price level P_1; this adds to the deterioration of competitiveness and hence the trade balance. At point E (time t_1), the exchange rate and the price level are equal in value and hence their ratio is unity – the same as the initial ratio at time t_0. Since we have implicitly held foreign prices constant, this means that the real exchange rate is back to its original level and so the trade balance must also be back to its original level, i.e. zero. This is no longer enough to restore long-run stock equilibrium, however. Domestic residents have now acquired a positive level of net foreign assets and will be receiving a stream of interest income i^*B^* from abroad. Thus, they are still acquiring foreign assets and the domestic currency is still appreciating as agents attempt to rebalance their portfolios and sell these foreign assets. In order for the current account balance to be zero, the trade balance must actually go into deficit. This requires a further fall of the exchange rate to its long-run equilibrium level S_2, by which time the price level has reached its long-run equilibrium level P_1 and the current account just balances $(-T(S_2/P_1) = i^*B^*)$ so that there is no further net accumulation of foreign assets. Therefore, the overall effect of the open-market purchase on the exchange rate is a long-run depreciation from S_0 to S_2, with an initial overshoot of $(S_1 - S_2)$. Essentially, the PBM generates the overshooting result suggested by the SPMM: the nominal exchange rate jumps above its long-run level and then adjusts slowly. Unlike in the SPMM, however, in the PBM the exchange rate overshooting is not due just to price stickiness. Even if prices fully adjust immediately to an increase in the money supply, as long as the new short-run equilibrium exchange rate S_1 exceeds P_1, the trade balance will have increased because of the rise in the real exchange rate and hence a slow appreciation towards the long-run exchange rate level will follow. Thus, there may be overshooting in the PBM even in the absence of sticky prices.

4.1.5.3   Rational expectations in the portfolio balance model   Our exposition of the portfolio balance model above assumed that exchange rate expectations are static, so that the expected rate of depreciation is zero. However, most of the properties of the model still remain intact when rational expectations are introduced, except that impact effects become much more pronounced and a key distinction must now be drawn between anticipated disturbances (the effect of which will already be discounted into the current exchange rate level) and unanticipated disturbances (which require an initial jump in the exchange rate and then a slow adjustment to the new equilibrium).[19] We now analyse the PBM (4.41)–(4.45) assuming that agents form rational expectations.

The rational expectations portfolio balance model (REPBM), (4.41)–(4.45), can be solved qualitatively by using a phase diagram in (B^*,S)-space. A dynamic equation for B^* is already given by (4.45), while a dynamic equation for S may be derived in the following way. Dividing (4.42) and (4.44) by W and totally differentiating – holding the foreign

---

[19] An even more general model would also allow for the interaction between production, consumption, saving and the level of wealth (see Branson and Henderson, 1985).

interest rate constant, yields:

$$\begin{bmatrix} d(SB^*/W) \\ d(M/W) \end{bmatrix} = \begin{bmatrix} B_1^* & B_2^* \\ M_1 & M_2 \end{bmatrix} \begin{bmatrix} di \\ d\widehat{S}^e \end{bmatrix} \tag{4.47}$$

which implies:

$$\begin{bmatrix} di \\ d\widehat{S}^e \end{bmatrix} = \frac{1}{(B_1^* M_2 - M_1 B_2^*)} \begin{bmatrix} M_2 & -B_2^* \\ -M_1 & B_1^* \end{bmatrix} \begin{bmatrix} d(SB^*/W) \\ d(M/W) \end{bmatrix} \tag{4.48}$$

so that an equation for $d\widehat{S}^e$ can be derived:

$$d\widehat{S}^e = (B_1^* M_2 - M_1 B_2^*)^{-1}[-M_1 d(SB^*/W) + B_1^* d(M/W)]. \tag{4.49}$$

Interpreting the coefficients of SB^*/W and M/W in equation (4.49) as the partial derivatives of an adjustment function for the expected rate of depreciation, we can write:

$$\widehat{S}^e = \varrho[(SB^*/W), (M/W)] \qquad \varrho_1 > 0, \, \varrho_2 < 0 \tag{4.50}$$

where the signs of the derivatives in (4.50) are inferred from (4.49).

Now assume for a moment that the expected rate of depreciation is zero, which implies that the differential of the exchange rate is also zero. Given that S and B^* enter $\varrho(\cdot)$ multiplicatively (in SB^* and W), changes in S and B^* which keep SB^* constant will also maintain the expected rate of depreciation constant. Thus, the locus of points for which both the expected rate of depreciation and the differential of the exchange rate equal zero must be a rectangular hyperbola of the form:

$$SB^* = \varsigma \tag{4.51}$$

for constant ς. This is shown in Figure 4.10 under the implicit assumption that B^* is positive. Note that, according to equations (4.50)–(4.51), an increase in S or B^* from a point on the rectangular hyperbola leads to a depreciation of the exchange rate S, $S > 0$.

On the basis of equation (4.45), a locus of points along which the differential of B^* equals zero slopes downwards in (B^*, S)-space in such a way that positive changes in S or B^* tend to increase B^*, $B^* > 0$ (Figure 4.10). This figure also shows that a necessary condition for the existence of a saddle-path equilibrium is that the schedule along which the differential of B^* is zero is flatter than the rectangular hyperbola along which the differential of the nominal exchange rate is zero in the neighbourhood of the intersection.[20] In fact, from (4.51):

$$\left.\frac{dS}{dB^*}\right|_{\dot{S}=0} = -\frac{S}{B^*}, \tag{4.52}$$

whereas from (4.45):[21]

$$\left.\frac{dS}{dB^*}\right|_{\dot{B}^*=0} = -\frac{i^*}{T_S} \tag{4.53}$$

---

[20] To verify this, redraw Figure 4.10 with the $\dot{B}^* = 0$ locus steeper than the $\dot{S} = 0$ locus in the neighbourhood of the intersection, and then draw in the arrows of motion.

[21] For transparency we are using the notation $T_s \equiv T_1$.

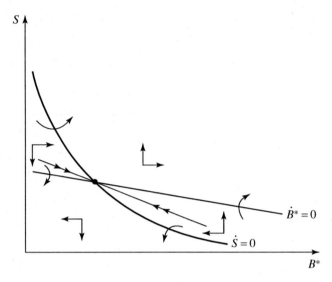

Figure 4.10. The saddlepath equilibrium for the rational expectations portfolio balance model.

where $T_S > 0$. Thus, the condition required for a saddle-path equilibrium may be expressed as:

$$-\frac{S}{B^*} < -\frac{i^*}{T_S} \tag{4.54}$$

or, since in equilibrium the differential of B^* is zero, so that, from (4.45), $T + i^* B^* = 0$

$$\left|\frac{ST_S}{T}\right| > 1 \tag{4.55}$$

which is equivalent to the traditional Marshall–Lerner–Harberger condition.

It is interesting to compare the impacts on the exchange rate of a real shock and of a monetary shock. Consider first the effect of a positive real shock to the current account. Given (4.45), the locus of points for which the differential of B^* is zero is now consistent with lower values of both S and B^*, i.e. it shifts downwards. From initial equilibrium, therefore, the positive real current account shock must cause the exchange rate to jump downwards and the domestic currency to appreciate. However, the exchange rate then moves slowly along the saddlepath, as the stock of foreign assets rises and the domestic currency depreciates further, until full stock equilibrium is reached. Clearly, the exchange rate initially undershoots and then appreciates towards the new long-run equilibrium. Hence positive real current account disturbances induce immediate partial adjustment of the exchange rate to long-run equilibrium in the REPBM – i.e. undershooting.

By contrast, if a monetary shock occurs, only the rectangular hyperbola along which the differential of S is zero is affected, shifting upwards. In this case, the domestic currency immediately depreciates and overshoots and then appreciates towards the long-run equilibrium. Moreover, given that the rectangular hyperbola is downward-sloping, a monetary expansion induces a long-run appreciation of the domestic currency in the REPBM. This is because the initial large overshooting (depreciation) generates a current account surplus and hence an accumulation of foreign assets. Hence, the subsequent rise in B^* leads to the appreciation of currency towards the new long-run equilibrium as agents attempt to rebalance their portfolios.

4.2   Empirical exchange rate modelling

So far, we have dealt only with the theory of exchange rate determination, which must form the basis of our understanding of exchange rate behaviour. However, a theory is, in an important operational sense, meaningless unless it is capable of being developed and refined into an empirical model with testable implications.[22] In this section we therefore outline the empirical work that has been done on exchange rate modelling over the last quarter of a century or so.

4.2.1   The empirical evidence on the monetary class of models

In a much cited paper, Frenkel (1976) finds strong evidence in support of the flexible-price monetary model (FPMM) for the German mark–US dollar exchange rate during the German hyperinflation of the 1920s. He estimates a version of the FPMM where he replaces the expected change in the nominal exchange rate with the forward premium by invoking the uncovered interest parity condition. In addition, because he is dealing with the German hyperinflation, Frenkel ignores relative income movements since they are swamped in magnitude by movements in the German money supply. For the same reason, he ignores movements in the US money supply. Thus, he simply regresses the logarithm of the nominal exchange rate onto the logarithm of the German money supply and the logarithm of the forward premium. He obtains an estimated coefficient on the money demand variable close to unity (0.975) and a positive estimated coefficient on the forward premium, and therefore takes this as strongly supportive of the FPMM. In retrospect, of course, it is clear that allowance should have been made for the nonstationarity of the time series under conditions of hyperinflation, although Frenkel's estimated equation might be reinterpreted as a cointegrating relationship.[23]

The subsequent accumulation of data during the 1970s allowed estimation of the model using data for major exchange rates during the recent float and these early studies were also broadly supportive of the flexible-price monetary model. Bilson (1978), for example, tests the FPMM for the German mark–UK pound exchange rate (with the forward premium substituted for the expected rate of exchange rate depreciation and with no restrictions on the coefficients on domestic and foreign money) over the sample period from January 1972

---

[22] We are here paraphrasing Samuelson (1948, p. 7): 'The usefulness of our theory emerges from the fact that by our analysis we are often able to determine the nature of changes in our unknown variables resulting from a designated change in one or more parameters. In fact, our theory is meaningless in the operational sense unless it does imply some restrictions upon empirically observable quantities, by which it could conceivably be refuted.'

[23] Frenkel reports a Durbin–Watson statistic of 1.91, which suggests that the residuals may, in fact, be stationary.

to April 1976. Accounting for multicollinearity using the Theil–Goldberger mixed estimation procedure, Bilson derives an equilibrium exchange rate equation which is strongly
supportive of the FPMM.[24] Hodrick (1978) also tests the FPMM for the US dollar–German
mark and the UK pound–US dollar rates over the period July 1972 to June 1975, reporting
results which are highly supportive of the FPMM. Putnam and Woodbury (1980) estimate
the FPMM for the sterling–dollar exchange rate over the period 1972 to 1974: all of the
coefficients are significant at the 5 per cent nominal level of significance and are correctly
signed; the money supply term is, however, significantly different from unity. In his study of
the German mark–US dollar rate, Dornbusch (1984) attempts to improve the specification
of the monetary approach equation by assuming that the dependent variable, $(s - m + m^*)_t$,
follows a simple partial adjustment mechanism and enriches the specification of the money
demand function by introducing the long-term interest rate as an additional opportunity
cost variable. Overall, the estimates reported by Dornbusch are supportive of the model; in
particular, the lagged adjustment term and the long-term interest rate differential term are
found to be strongly significant, while the relative income and the short-term interest rate
differential term are insignificant.

Beyond the late 1970s, however, the FPMM (or its real interest rate differential variant;
see Frankel, 1979[25]) ceases to provide a good explanation of variations in exchange rate
data: the estimated equations break down, providing poor fits, exhibiting incorrectly signed
coefficients and failing to pass conventional diagnostic tests (Taylor, 1995). In particular,
estimates of equations for the dollar–mark rate often produce coefficients which imply
that increases in Germany's money supply during the recent float caused its currency to
appreciate.[26] Some authors sought to explain this breakdown on the ground of econometric
misspecification, while others argued that large current account deficits or surpluses during
the period examined generated important wealth effects which are not adequately captured
by the simple monetary model (see, for example, Frankel, 1982a).

Nevertheless, the evidence for the sticky-price monetary model is also weak when the
data period is extended beyond the late 1970s. For example, while Driskell (1981) reports
single-equation estimation results largely favourable to the SPMM for the Swiss franc–
US dollar rate over the sample period 1973–7, Backus (1984) finds little support using
US–Canadian data for the period 1971–80.

Meese (1986) tests for rational bubbles in the monetary model framework; he estimates
both a version of equation (4.28), which produces consistent estimates even in the presence
of bubbles, and a closed-form solution of (4.31), whose estimates are consistent only if
there are no rational bubbles, using dollar–mark and dollar–sterling data for the period

---

[24] Note that a general problem affecting estimates of the equation representative of the various empirical formulations of the monetary approach is the potential simultaneity bias, arising, for example, because of
unsterilised intervention. In principle, therefore, two-stage least squares is more appropriate than ordinary
least squares estimation (see, for example, Artus, 1976; Frenkel and Johnson, 1976; Frankel, 1979; Mussa,
1981).

[25] Frankel (1979) argues that a shortcoming of the sticky-price monetary model is that it does not allow a role
for secular differences between inflation rates. His model is a variant of the FPMM based on real interest rate
differentials where the long-term interest rate differential is used as a proxy for the long-term inflation rate
differential.

[26] Frankel (1982a) called this the 'mystery of the multiplying marks'.

1973–82. Meese finds that the two sets of parameters estimates are significantly different and hence rejects the no-bubbles hypothesis, although he notes that this is conditional upon having a correct formulation of the underlying model. Hence he actually rejects a joint null hypothesis of no bubbles and that the FPMM is correct.

An extended version of the SPMM due to Buiter and Miller (1981) has also been tested empirically by Barr (1989) and Smith and Wickens (1986, 1990) using data for major US dollar exchange rates: both studies provide evidence in favour of the model. Smith and Wickens (1986) also simulate the model and find that a 21 percent over-shooting of the exchange rate occurs in response to a 5 per cent change in the money supply.

The implication of the SPMM that there is a proportional variation between the real exchange rate and the real interest rate differential has also attracted the attention of a large literature. Nevertheless, a number of studies have failed to find strong evidence for this relationship; notably, Meese and Rogoff (1988) could not find cointegration between real exchange rates and real interest rate differentials.[27] Recent work suggests, however, that this may be due to omitted variables which are important determinants of the equilibrium real exchange rate or the risk premium (e.g. Throop, 1993). Baxter (1994) uses band-spectral regression techniques and finds that there may be a significant positive correlation between real interest rate differentials and real exchange rates at 'business-cycle' (six to thirty-two quarters) and 'trend' (more than thirty-two quarters) frequencies.

More recently, MacDonald and Taylor (1993, 1994) apply multivariate cointegration analysis and dynamic modelling techniques to a number of exchange rates and find some evidence supporting the monetary model as a long-run equilibrium towards which the exchange rate converges, while allowing for complex short-run dynamics. Van den Berg and Jayanetti (1993) also employ the Johansen procedure in order to test for cointegration in a monetary model setting using long-span black-market exchange rate series, and find strong support for the monetary approach to the exchange rate. They also interpret their results as evidence that the rejection of the monetary model on exchange rate data for the floating period may simply be due to the lack of power of conventional cointegration tests with insufficiently large sample periods or number of observations. McNown and Wallace (1994) test for cointegration in a FPMM-based regression using data for three high-inflation countries, namely Argentina, Chile and Israel (currencies expressed *vis-à-vis* the US dollar), providing further evidence in support of the monetary approach. Since all of the monetary models collapse to an equilibrium condition of the form (4.28) in the long run, however, these tests have no power to discriminate between the alternative varieties. The usefulness of the cointegration approach suggested by these studies should, moreover, be taken as at most tentative: their robustness across different data periods and exchange rates has yet to be demonstrated.

Flood and Rose (1995) construct a general test of excess volatility in the context of the monetary model. The underlying idea is to compare the volatility of the 'traditional fundamentals', say TF_t, and the volatility of the 'virtual fundamentals', VF_t. Flood and

---

[27] See also McNown and Wallace (1989) and Edison and Pauls (1993).

Rose measure the virtual fundamentals as:

$$VF_t = s_t - \vartheta(i - i^*)_t \qquad (4.56)$$

whereas the traditional fundamentals are described by an equation like:

$$TF_t = (m - m^*)_t - \psi(y - y^*)_t. \qquad (4.57)$$

Observing the increased volatility of exchange rates under floating as opposed to fixed exchange rate regimes, Flood and Rose argue that any tentatively adequate exchange rate model should have fundamentals which are also much more volatile during floating rate regimes. In fact, they find little change in the volatility of economic fundamentals suggested by flexible-price or sticky-price monetary models across different nominal exchange rate regimes for a number of OECD exchange rates. Similar evidence is reported by Baxter and Stockman (1989), who examine the time series behaviour of a number of key macroeconomic aggregates for forty-nine countries over the post-war period. Although they detect evidence of higher real exchange rate variability under flexible exchange rates than under pegged nominal exchange rate regimes, Baxter and Stockman find no systematic differences in the behaviour of the macroeconomic aggregates under alternative exchange rate arrangements. Again, this suggests that there are speculative forces at work in the foreign exchange market which are not reflected in the usual menu of macroeconomic fundamentals.[28]

Meese and Rose (1991) argue that there may be nonlinearity in the demand for money functions and therefore the simple log-linear forms of the monetary model may be misspecified. First, nonlinearity may arise because of 'time deformation', which occurs if the appropriate time scale for foreign exchange markets 'accelerates' in terms of calendar time in periods when there is a very large amount of new information available. Second, nonlinearities may simply be detected due to misspecification of the functional form itself in the empirical model. Third, the data generation process may be genuinely nonlinear. However, Meese and Rose (1991) do not find, using both parametric and nonparametric econometric techniques, any empirical evidence of nonlinearities, and hence conclude that accounting for nonlinearities may not be a valid way for improving the statistical performance of the monetary model.

A novel approach towards testing the monetary class of models has recently been suggested by Taylor and Peel (2000). They, in line with Meese and Rose (1991), also argue that the breakdown in the empirical performance of asset markets models of exchange rate determination may be due to the fact that the adjustment towards long-run equilibrium is nonlinear, which standard econometric procedures may not be able detect. Using data on dollar–mark rates and associated monetary model fundamentals for the US and Germany during the recent float, Taylor and Peel find evidence of cointegration in a static regression that is consistent with the monetary class of models but also report evidence of nonlinearity in the estimated cointegrating residuals which are well approximated by an exponential smooth transition autoregressive model (ESTAR) of the type described in Chapter 3. Hence Taylor and Peel model the deviations from the monetary model as an ESTAR. Interestingly,

---

[28] See also Dornbusch and Frankel (1988) and Marston (1989).

the estimated model proposed by them implies random walk behaviour for small deviations of the nominal exchange rate from the monetary fundamentals, but very fast adjustment for large deviations. Their results are thus consistent with the evidence on nonlinear real exchange rate adjustment which we discussed in Chapter 3.

4.2.1.1 Tests of the rational expectations monetary model Some researchers have empirically examined the rational expectations solution to the monetary model; this requires, however, additional assumptions in order to arrive at a closed-form solution. This approach involves directly modelling the future expected exchange rate in the rational expectations solution to the monetary model, equation (4.31), which we write here as:

$$s_t = (1 + \theta)^{-1} \sum_{i=0}^{\infty} \left(\frac{\theta}{1 + \theta} \right)^i E(v_{t+i} \mid \Omega_t) \tag{4.58}$$

where:

$$v_t = [(m - m^*)_t - \kappa(y - y^*)_t] \tag{4.59}$$

and where we have now made clear that we are conditioning on the information set Ω_t at time t, i.e. $E_t(\cdot) = E(\cdot \mid \Omega_t)$. An important early study in this area is due to Hoffman and Schlagenhauf (1983), who estimate (4.58) directly. Using data for the US dollar–German mark, US dollar–UK pound and US dollar–French franc exchange rates, Hoffman and Schlagenhauf find evidence supporting the rational expectations monetary model.[29]

Although some authors find that the rational expectations monetary model works satisfactorily for the 1980s, more recent studies strongly reject the rational expectations restrictions in the monetary model. MacDonald and Taylor (1993), for example, apply the methodology proposed by Campbell and Shiller (1987) for testing rational expectations present-value models to the foreign exchange market. The underlying idea is that, given the forward solution to the monetary model (4.58), the exchange rate should be cointegrated with the forcing variables contained in v_t. In fact, subtracting v_t from both sides of (4.58) yields, after a little manipulation:

$$s_t - v_t = \sum_{i=1}^{\infty} \left(\frac{\theta}{1 + \theta} \right)^i E\left(\Delta v_{t+i} \mid \Omega_t \right). \tag{4.60}$$

Assuming that the fundamentals are $I(1)$ processes, the right-hand side of (4.60) is stationary; hence the left-hand side must also be stationary and, if the nominal exchange rate is $I(1)$, this implies cointegration between the exchange rate and the fundamentals with certain restrictions on the parameters:

$$C_t = s_t - m_t + m_t^* + \kappa y_t - \kappa^* y_t^* \sim I(0). \tag{4.61}$$

Note that Hoffman and Schlagenhauf (1983), writing before the literature on unit roots and cointegration became generally known, use a first-difference transformation of all

---

[29] Hoffman and Schlagenhauf's empirical approach is based on the assumption that the fundamentals v_t are generated by an ARIMA (1,1,0) process. Baillie and McMahon (1989) note that the assumed ARIMA (1,1,0) may be seen as a model of extrapolative expectations rather than rational expectations. See also Woo (1985) for further extended versions of the monetary model.

the variables. Engle and Granger (1987) show, however, that an empirical model in first-differences is misspecified if the variables in question are cointegrated, because the error correction term is omitted.[30] Thus, an appropriate procedure for testing the rational expectations monetary model is testing for cointegration in (4.61) and, if cointegration is established, imposing more stringent restrictions. In practice, if cointegration is established in (4.61) (C_t and Δv_t are both stationary, $I(0)$ processes), there is a Wold representation that may be approximated by a p-th order vector autoregression. If we define the vector $z_t = [\Delta v_t, \dots, \Delta v_{t-p+1}, \dots, C_t, \dots, C_{t-p+1}]'$, then this vector autoregression or VAR may be expressed in companion form as follows:

$$
\begin{bmatrix} \Delta v_t \\ \Delta v_{t-1} \\ \vdots \\ \Delta v_{t-p+1} \\ C_t \\ C_{t-1} \\ \vdots \\ C_{t-p+1} \end{bmatrix} = \begin{bmatrix} \zeta_1 & \zeta_2 & \cdots & \zeta_p & \gamma_1 & \gamma_2 & \cdots & \gamma_p \\ \cdots & \cdots & \cdots & \cdots & \cdots & \cdots & \cdots & \cdots \\ I_{p-1} & & O_{p-1} & & O_{p-1} & & O_{p-1} & \\ \cdots & \cdots & \cdots & \cdots & \cdots & \cdots & \cdots & \cdots \\ \theta_1 & \theta_2 & \cdots & \theta_p & \mu_1 & \mu_2 & \cdots & \mu_p \\ \cdots & \cdots & \cdots & \cdots & \cdots & \cdots & \cdots & \cdots \\ O_{p-1} & & O_{p-1} & & I_{p-1} & & O_{p-1} & \end{bmatrix} \begin{bmatrix} \Delta v_{t-1} \\ \Delta v_{t-2} \\ \vdots \\ \Delta v_{t-p} \\ C_{t-1} \\ C_{t-2} \\ \vdots \\ C_{t-p} \end{bmatrix} + \begin{bmatrix} e_{1t} \\ \cdots \\ 0_{p-1} \\ \cdots \\ e_{2t} \\ \cdots \\ 0_{p-1} \end{bmatrix}
$$

$$(4.62)$$

where I_{p-1} and O_{p-1} are, respectively, identity and null square matrices of order $(p-1)$ and 0_{p-1} is a column vector of order $(p-1)$. In a more compact form this may be written:

$$z_t = A z_{t-1} + e_t. \qquad (4.63)$$

Define g' and h' as two selection row vectors of order $2p$ containing unity in the $(p+1)$-th and first elements respectively and zeros elsewhere. Then:

$$C_t = g' z_t \qquad (4.64)$$

$$\Delta v_t = h' z_t. \qquad (4.65)$$

Now, consider the mathematical expectation of z, k periods ahead, formed as:

$$E(z_{t+k} \mid H_t) = A^k z_t, \qquad (4.66)$$

where H_t is the information set including only current and lagged values of C_t and Δv_t.

We are now in a position to test the forward-looking FPMM formulation, as set out in (4.60), as a set of cross-equation restrictions on the parameters of this VAR. The left-hand side of (4.60), in terms of the VAR, is given by (4.64) above, since $C_t = s_t - v_t$. The

---

[30] See Appendix D to Chapter 2 for a brief introduction to unit roots and cointegration.

right-hand side of (4.60), in terms of the VAR, may be deduced as follows. Projecting (4.60) onto H_t and applying the law of iterated expectations[31] yields:

$$\sum_{i=1}^{\infty} \left(\frac{\theta}{1+\theta}\right)^i E(\Delta v_{t+i} \mid H_t) = \sum_{i=1}^{\infty} \left(\frac{\theta}{1+\theta}\right)^i h' A^i z_t$$

$$= h' \left(\frac{\theta}{1+\theta}\right) A \left[I_{2p} - \left(\frac{\theta}{1+\theta}\right) A\right]^{-1}$$

$$= C_t^*, \text{say} \tag{4.67}$$

where C_t^* represents the 'theoretical spread' and we have used standard matrix algebra analogous to summing an infinite geometric progression.[32] If the forward-looking FPMM (4.60) is correct, then $C_t^* = C_t$, so that, from (4.64) and (4.67), we can deduce $2p$ linear cross-equation restrictions on the parameters of the p-th order VAR for $(C_t, \Delta v_t)'$:

$$g' - h' \left(\frac{\theta}{1+\theta}\right) A \left[I_{2p} - \left(\frac{\theta}{1+\theta}\right) A\right]^{-1} = 0 \tag{4.68}$$

or:

$$g' \left[I_{2p} - \left(\frac{\theta}{1+\theta}\right) A\right] - h' \left(\frac{\theta}{1+\theta}\right) A = 0, \tag{4.69}$$

where I_{2p} is an identity matrix of order $2p$. These restrictions may be tested by means of a Wald test on the estimated VAR.[33] In general, however, deviations from the null hypothesis, although they may show up as significant rejections of these restrictions, may not be *economically* important, since they may be caused, for example, by data measurement errors. An alternative or complementary procedure may simply be to compare the time series properties of the actual and theoretical spreads, C_t and C_t^*, to see if they are in any way similar to one another. Note also that testing for cointegration in this context is *tantamount* to testing for the presence of bubbles in the monetary model, since this would preclude cointegration (although see our discussion of bubbles and cointegration in Chapter 2). Using the testing procedure outlined above, MacDonald and Taylor (1993) strongly reject the restrictions imposed on the data by the forward-looking rational expectations monetary model using data for the German mark–US dollar exchange rate over the sample period from January 1976 to December 1990. Furthermore, they graph the actual and theoretical spread series and show that they are vastly different from one another. Despite these formal and informal rejections of the rational expectations version of the FPMM, the monetary model *is* validated, however, as a long-run equilibrium relationship, in the sense that MacDonald and Taylor find a unique cointegrating vector among the fundamentals and the exchange

---

[31] Since $H_t \subseteq \Omega_t$, projecting an expectation conditional on Ω_t onto H_t results in an expectation conditional on H_t – this is the law of iterated expectations.

[32] This sum will exist if the VAR is stable, as it must be because of the assumption we have made about cointegration of the variables in question.

[33] See MacDonald and Taylor (1993) for a discussion of the econometric issues related to this technique.

rate which appears to satisfy monetary restrictions such as homogeneity of relative money. They also show that the imposition of the long-run monetary model restrictions in a dynamic error-correction model produces superior exchange rate forecasts to those provided by a random walk model of the exchange rate.

4.2.2 Testing equilibrium and liquidity models

In order to specify and solve an equilibrium model it is necessary to make a set of assumptions, such as uniform preferences or a specific utility function, which no one would seriously expect to hold exactly in the real world, even though the qualitative predictions of the model may be valid. Thus, these models are not amenable to direct econometric testing. Rather, researchers have sought to test the broad, rather than specific, implications of this class of models for exchange rate behaviour.

Stylised facts of the recent float include the high volatility of real exchange rates, the very high correlation of changes in real and nominal exchange rates and the absence of strongly mean-reverting properties in either series. As discussed above, equilibrium models are capable of explaining the variability of nominal exchange rates in excess of relative price variability (and hence the variability of real exchange rates), but so is the sticky-price monetary model. Some authors have argued, however, that the difficulty researchers have experienced in rejecting the hypothesis of nonstationarity in the real exchange rate is evidence against the sticky-price model and in favour of equilibrium models. Explaining the persistence in both real and nominal exchange rates over the recent float within the framework of the sticky-price model, it is argued, involves assuming either implausibly sluggish price adjustment or else that movements in nominal exchange rates are due largely to permanent real disturbances (Stockman, 1987). Equilibrium models, on the other hand, are not contradicted by persistence in real and nominal exchange rate movements. In the simple equilibrium model sketched above, for example, permanent shocks to technology permanently affect the equilibrium real exchange rate. Moreover, a permanent shift in preferences could lead, in this model, to a permanent shift in nominal and real exchange rates with domestic price levels unchanged – showing how equilibrium models are consistent with persistent, correlated movements in real and nominal exchange rates.

There are two basic responses to this line of argument. First, as Frankel (1990) argues forcibly, non-contradiction is not the same as confirmation: simply being consistent with the facts is not enough to demonstrate the empirical validity of a theory. Second, as discussed in Chapter 3, there is now emerging evidence that real exchange rates may, in fact, be mean-reverting.[34]

One testable implication of the simplest equilibrium models is the neutrality of the exchange rate with respect to the exchange rate regime: since the real exchange rate is determined by real variables such as tastes and technology, its behaviour ought to be independent of whether the nominal exchange rate is pegged or allowed to float freely. Although the

---

[34] Note, however, that mean-reversion in the real exchange is not inconsistent with the broad class of equilibrium models, since it is possible that real shocks themselves are mean-reverting, e.g. because of technology diffusion.

major real exchange rates have been demonstrably more volatile during the recent floating period, this may be due to the greater variability of underlying real shocks during this
period. Stockman's (1983) study of thirty-eight countries over a variety of time periods
(including, for example, countries whose currencies remained pegged to the dollar after
1973) does conclude, however, that real exchange rates are significantly more volatile
under floating nominal rate regimes.[35] This evidence does, indeed, constitute a rejection
of the simplest equilibrium models, although it is possible that the evidence is to some
extent confounded by the endogeneity of the choice of exchange rate regime, i.e. countries experiencing greater real disturbances are more likely to choose flexible exchange
rate systems. Moreover, Stockman (1983) also shows that the assumptions necessary for
regime-neutrality are in fact quite restrictive in a fully specified equilibrium model, and
include Ricardian equivalence, no wealth-distribution effects of nominal price changes, no
real effects of inflation, no real effects of changes in the level of the money supply, complete
asset markets, completely flexible prices and identical sets of government policies under
different exchange rate systems. Since it is unlikely that all of these conditions will be met
in practice, Stockman argues that only the simplest class of equilibrium models should
be rejected, and that equilibrium models should be developed which relax some or all of
these assumptions. In a subsequent paper, Stockman (1988) notes that countries with fixed
exchange rates are more likely to introduce controls on trade or capital flows in order to
control losses of international reserves. Thus, a disturbance that would tend to raise the
relative price of foreign goods (e.g. a preference shift towards foreign goods) will raise the
probability that the domestic country will, at some future point, impose capital or trade
restrictions that will raise the future relative world price of domestic goods. With intertemporal substitution, this induces a higher world demand for domestic goods now, serving to
offset partly the direct effect of the disturbance, which was to raise the relative price of the
foreign good, and hence to reduce the resulting movement in the real exchange rate. Thus,
countries with pegged exchange rates will experience lower volatility in the real exchange
rate than countries with flexible exchange rates.

Empirical studies of the implications of liquidity models include Clarida and Gali (1994),
Eichenbaum and Evans (1995) (for the US), Grilli and Roubini (1993) (for the other G7
countries) and Nana, Hall and Philpott (1995) (for New Zealand and Australia). These
researchers provide evidence that unanticipated monetary contractions lead to increases in
the level of domestic interest rates and an appreciation of the domestic currency in both real
and nominal terms, which is inconsistent with most equilibrium models in which nominal
shocks should not affect real variables, but is consistent with liquidity models with asset-
market cash-in-advance constraints. As already discussed earlier, however, sticky-price
monetary models and liquidity models are observationally equivalent in this respect.

Overall, therefore, although the empirical evidence rejects the very simplest equilibrium
models, it is not possible at this stage to draw any firm conclusions concerning the empirical
validity of the whole class of equilibrium or liquidity models.

---

[35] See also Mussa (1986) and Baxter and Stockman (1989).

4.2.3   Testing the portfolio balance model

The portfolio balance model of exchange rates has not attracted a large empirical literature relative to the monetary class of models, perhaps because many problems are encountered in mapping the theoretical framework of the PBM into real-world financial data. In particular, the choice of non-monetary assets to be considered is difficult and data are not always available on a bilateral basis.

Recalling that the crucial features of the PBM are that imperfect substitution of domestic and foreign bonds is assumed and that wealth enters asset demand equations as a scale variable, the asset sector of a basic portfolio model for the domestic country may be written as:

$$m_t - p_t = \alpha_0 y_t + \alpha_1 i_t + \alpha_2 i_t^* + \alpha_3 w_t \qquad \alpha_0, \alpha_3 > 0, \; \alpha_1, \alpha_2 < 0 \quad (4.70)$$

$$b_t - p_t = \beta_0 y_t + \beta_1 i_t + \beta_2 i_t^* + \beta_3 w_t \qquad \beta_0, \beta_1, \beta_3 > 0, \; \beta_2 < 0 \quad (4.71)$$

$$fb_t + s_t - p_t = \gamma_0 y_t + \gamma_1 i_t + \gamma_2 i_t^* + \gamma_3 w_t \qquad \gamma_0, \gamma_1, \gamma_3 > 0, \; \gamma_2 < 0 \quad (4.72)$$

where b denotes domestic, non-traded bonds, fb denotes foreign, traded bonds, w is real wealth, money demand and bonds demand are set equal to their respective supplies and the conventional interest parity condition is used for defining the relationship between domestic and foreign interest rates. Thus, the exchange rate in the PBM (4.70)–(4.72) is determined by money- and bond-market conditions.

Two types of test have been conducted in the relevant empirical literature. The first type is based on the reduced-form solution of the short-run PBM in order to measure its explanatory power, under the assumption that expectations are static. The second type of test – the so-called inverted asset demand approach, as opposed to the direct demand approach – of the PBM concentrates on solving the PBM for the risk premium and tests for the perfect substitution of bonds denominated in different currencies. Thus, the reduced-form exchange rate equation derived from the system (4.70)–(4.72) (and assuming a similar set of equations for the foreign country) is of the form:

$$s_t = g(m, m^*, b, b^*, fb, fb^*)_t. \qquad (4.73)$$

Log-linear versions of reduced-form portfolio balance exchange rate equations, using cumulated current accounts for the stock of foreign assets, have been estimated for many of the major exchange rates for the 1970s float, with poor results: estimated coefficients are often insignificant and there is a persistent problem of residual autocorrelation (e.g. Branson, Halttunen and Masson, 1977; Bisignano and Hoover, 1982; Dooley and Isard, 1982).[36]

Lewis (1988) estimates foreign bond demand equations from the PBM for five countries: the US, the UK, Germany, Japan and Canada. While other studies limit the portfolio choice to domestic assets relative to a composite foreign asset, Lewis' approach is interesting because it considers a decomposition of the foreign asset by currency. Further, Lewis exploits the cross-equation correlation that arises from this decomposition in order to obtain more efficient estimates of the parameters, and provides some empirical support for the PBM.

---

[36] In practice, b and b^* are not included in the estimated regression in a number of studies (e.g. Branson, Halttunen and Masson, 1977).

The imperfect substitutability of domestic and foreign assets which is assumed in the PBM is equivalent to assuming that there is a risk premium separating expected depreciation and the domestic–foreign interest differential, and in the PBM this risk premium will be a function of relative domestic and foreign debt outstanding. An alternative, indirect method of testing the PBM, called the inverted demand approach, is to test for empirical relationships of this kind; however, these have usually reported statistically insignificant relationships (Frankel, 1982b, c; Rogoff, 1984).

In a recent study of the effectiveness of exchange rate intervention for the US dollar–German mark and US dollar–Swiss franc bilateral exchange rates during the 1980s, Dominguez and Frankel (1993) measure the risk premium using survey data and show that the resulting measure can in fact be explained by an empirical model which is consistent with the portfolio balance model with the additional assumption of mean-variance optimisation on the part of investors.[37] In some ways, the relative success of the Dominguez and Frankel (1993) study is consistent with the recent empirical literature on foreign exchange market efficiency, discussed in Chapter 2, which suggests the existence of significant foreign exchange risk premia and non-rational expectations.[38]

4.2.3.1   The hybrid monetary-portfolio balance exchange rate model   Some researchers have attempted to improve the performance of both the monetary approach and the portfolio balance approach to exchange rate determination by considering empirical models which incorporate features of both approaches. In particular, omitting risk in the monetary model, where no allowance is made for imperfect substitutability of non-monetary assets, may be an important source of misspecification. Nevertheless, a general drawback of empirical studies on the PBM is that expectations are not given an important role, since the assumption of static expectations is conventionally adopted. In fact, since the exchange rate determined in the PBM is expected to balance the current account, agents forming rational expectations will revise their expected exchange rate when news on the future path of the current account become available; hence, these news items should in principle be considered as explanatory variables of the exchange rate in the PBM. The hybrid monetary-portfolio balance model (HMPBM) represents a synthesis of the features of the monetary model and the PBM in which allowance is made for a risk premium and news about the current account.

Hooper and Morton (1982), for example, assume that the risk premium depends upon the cumulated current account surplus net of the cumulation of foreign exchange market intervention. Their results, obtained using data for the dollar effective exchange rate in the 1970s, are mixed: the monetary model variables are statistically significant at conventional nominal levels of significance and correctly signed, but among the portfolio balance variables only the news term is statistically significant while the risk premium is statistically insignificant and wrongly signed. Nevertheless, Hooper and Morton interpret their results as an important improvement relative to monetary models and to the PBM.

---

[37] Results supportive of the PBM are also provided by Karfakis and Kim (1995) using Australian data for the period July 1985 to December 1992.

[38] The study of Dominguez and Frankel is discussed later in the book.

Hacche and Townend (1981) test a variant of the HMPBM, distinguished by the inclusion of the price of oil, using data for the UK pound effective exchange rate. Their model, however, performs poorly, presumably because they do not use instrumental variable estimation, thus obtaining biased and inconsistent estimates. Notably, Frankel (1984) estimates the HMPBM not including the news term and solving the model for the risk premium. Using data for five currencies *vis-à-vis* the US dollar, Frankel finds the risk premium to be statistically significant at conventional nominal levels of significance, while the monetary terms are often found to be not statistically significantly different from zero.

4.3   The out-of-sample forecasting performance of asset approach exchange rate models

Another way of examining the empirical content of exchange rate models is to examine their out-of-sample forecasting performance. In a landmark paper, Meese and Rogoff (1983) compare the out-of-sample forecasts produced by various exchange rate models with forecasts produced by a random walk model, by the forward exchange rate, by a univariate regression of the spot rate and by a vector autoregression. They use rolling regressions to generate a succession of out-of-sample forecasts for each model and for various time horizons. The conclusion which emerges from this study is that, on a comparison of root mean square errors, none of the asset market exchange rate models outperforms the simple random walk, even though actual future values of the right-hand-side variables are allowed in the dynamic forecasts (thereby giving the models a very large informational advantage). In particular, Meese and Rogoff compare random walk forecasts with those produced by the flexible-price monetary model, Frankel's (1979) real interest rate differential variant of the monetary model and the synthesis of the monetary and portfolio balance models suggested by Hooper and Morton (1982).

The study by Meese and Rogoff (1983) also suggests that the estimated models may have been affected by simultaneity bias. Imposing coefficient constraints taken from the empirical literature on money demand, Meese and Rogoff find that although the coefficient-constrained asset-reduced forms still fail to outperform the random walk model for most horizons up to a year, combinations of parameter constraints can be found such that the models do outperform the random walk model for horizons beyond a year. Even at these longer horizons, however, the models are unstable in the sense that the minimum root mean square error models have different coefficient values at different horizons.

Woo (1985) and Finn (1986) go further in that they estimate versions of the rational expectations form of the FPMM adding a partial adjustment term in money demand and hence perform a forecasting exercise of the type of Meese and Rogoff. Woo finds that his formulation outperforms the random walk model in terms of both the mean absolute errors and the root mean square errors for the German mark–US dollar exchange rate. Finn's results are slightly weaker in that the model forecasts do not beat, but do as well as, the random walk model.

A different modification of the Meese and Rogoff approach is to employ a time-varying parameter model. In fact, the poor forecasting performance noted by Meese and Rogoff may be due to the fact that the parameters in the estimated equations are unstable. This instability may be rationalised on a number of grounds: in response to policy regime changes as an example of a Lucas critique problem (Lucas, 1976); or because of implicit instability in the money demand or purchasing power parity equations; or because of agents' heterogeneity leading to different responses to macroeconomic developments over time. Notably, Schinasi and Swamy (1989) use a Kalman-filter maximum likelihood estimation technique to estimate time-varying parameter models which are found to outperform the random walk model of the exchange rate for certain time periods and currencies.

The forecasting performance of the PBM is assessed by Boughton (1984) who estimates a version of the PBM using fixed-coefficients methods, comparing it with the alternative of a random walk model. Using quarterly data for a number of currencies, Boughton finds that the forecasting performance of the PBM is slightly better than the random walk model.

A general finding in this literature is that one key to improving forecast performance based on economic fundamentals lies in the introduction of equation dynamics. This has been done in various ways: by using dynamic forecasting equations for the forcing variables in the forward-looking, rational expectations version of the flexible-price monetary model, by incorporating dynamic partial adjustment terms into the estimating equation, by using time-varying parameter estimation techniques, and, most recently, by using dynamic error-correction forms (e.g. Koedijk and Schotman, 1990; MacDonald and Taylor, 1993, 1994; Throop, 1993).

Nevertheless, it remains true that most studies which claim to have beaten the random walk in out-of-sample forecasting turn out to be fragile in the sense that it is generally hard to replicate the superior forecasting performance for alternative periods and alternative currencies.

A related approach, originally due in the context of foreign exchange market analysis to Mark (1995), considers long-horizon predictability through analysis of equations of the form:

$$\Delta_k s_{t+k} = \alpha + \beta_k (z_t - s_t) + u_{t+k} \tag{4.74}$$

where z_t is an exchange rate fundamental, for example that suggested by the monetary class of models, $z_t \equiv [(m_t - m_t^*) - \kappa(y_t - y_t^*)]$, and u_{t+k} is a disturbance term.[39] If the fundamental in question helps forecast the exchange rate, then we should find $\beta_k < 0$ and significantly different from zero. In a series of forecasting tests over very long horizons for a number of quarterly dollar exchange rates, Mark finds that equation (4.74) may be able to predict the nominal exchange rate only at long horizons, such as the four-year horizon. Moreover, both the goodness of in-sample fit and the estimated absolute value of β_k rise as the horizon k extends. Mark interprets this as evidence that, while quarter-to-quarter exchange rate movements may be noisy, systematic movements related to the fundamentals become apparent in long-horizon changes. In a follow-up study, Mark and Choi (1997) examine monthly real exchange rates between the US and the UK, Canada, Germany and

---

[39] Mark chooses *a priori* values for κ equal to 1.0 and 0.3.

Japan from 1961 to 1993 (hence using data pre- and post-Bretton Woods), and find that the deviation of the log real exchange rate from its time-varying, long-run equilibrium value contains a statistically significant predictable component at the four-year horizon over a forecast period extending from 1985 to 1993. Interestingly, while fixed-effects regressions employing differentials in productivity, real interest rates and per capita income display some predictive power, fundamentals based on simple monetary models are generally more accurate and significant.

In general, long-horizon regressions have been used extensively in the literature, but with mixed success (see Kilian, 1999; Kilian and Taylor, 2001). One reason may be that previous research has focused on linear models. In fact, in a linear world, it can be argued that there is no rationale for conducting long-horizon forecast tests. The problem is that under linearity, k-step-ahead forecasts are obtained by linear extrapolation from one-step-ahead forecasts. Thus, by construction, there cannot be any gain in power at higher horizons (see Berben and van Dijk, 1998; Kilian, 1999; Berkowitz and Giorgianni, 2001). However, the evidence of nonlinear mean-reversion in the exchange rate, provided, for example, by Taylor and Peel (2000) and Taylor, Peel and Sarno (2001), offers a new rationale for the use of long-horizon regression tests. Following this line of reasoning, Kilian and Taylor (2001), using several major US dollar exchange rates during the recent float, find strong evidence of long-horizon predictability of the nominal exchange rate using a simple purchasing power parity measure of fundamentals (i.e. they set z_t equal to the logarithm of relative prices) when allowance is made for underlying nonlinearity in the data-generating process. They demonstrate, however, using Monte Carlo techniques, that the improvement over a simple random walk model may be slight even when we know the form of the true nonlinear exchange rate model, because of the low power of existing recursive forecasting tests.

4.4   Summary and concluding remarks

In this chapter we have presented an overview of the underlying theoretical framework of conventional models of exchange rate determination over the past forty years or so, beginning with the seminal Mundell–Fleming model, and going on to the sticky-price monetary model, the flexible-price monetary model, equilibrium models of exchange rate and liquidity models, and the portfolio balance model. The detailed explanation of the theoretical foundations of these theories was then followed by a presentation of the testing procedures that may be undertaken for estimating and testing exchange rate models in various different formulations and a survey of the evidence from the empirical literature. Finally, we also discussed the evidence on the out-of-sample forecasting performance of exchange rate models.

Overall, the conclusion emerges that, although the theory of exchange rate determination has produced a number of plausible models, empirical work on exchange rates has still not produced models that are sufficiently statistically satisfactory to be considered reliable and robust, either in-sample or in out-of-sample forecasting, or which help us discriminate between the various theories on offer. In particular, although empirical exchange rate models occasionally generate apparently satisfactory explanatory power in-sample, they generally fail badly in out-of-sample forecasting tests in the sense that they fail to outperform a random walk. Where results are reported that a model has performed much better than a simple random walk out of sample, the results tend to be fragile in that they are hard to replicate for alternative currencies and sample periods (Taylor, 1995).[40] 'Thus, from the early 1980s onward, exchange rate forecasting in general became increasingly to be seen as a hazardous occupation, and this remains largely the case' (Clarida, Sarno, Taylor and Valente, 2001).

One finding which does, however, seem to have some validity, is that the monetary model does resurface in a number of empirical studies as a *long-run* equilibrium condition, especially where cointegration techniques have been applied. That is to say, there appears to be some long-run correlation between the exchange rate and the relative velocity of circulation. This finding itself is not, of course, completely robust, but it occurs with sufficient regularity in the empirical literature as to suggest that we may be observing the emergence of a stylised fact. Since a very large class of models are, in fact, consistent with the monetary model as a long-run equilibrium condition, this does not help us discriminate very much between the various alternatives, but it does at least have strong theoretical underpinning from a number of directions.

Moreover, very recent work has suggested that there may be important nonlinearities in the foreign exchange market – a result which has surfaced in previous chapters. In particular, in Chapter 3 we suggested that, in very broad terms, there may be evidence of long-run purchasing power parity (PPP) holding, but that deviations from PPP may be inherently nonlinear in the way they move back towards equilibrium. We would suggest that many economists would find uncontentious the proposition that the national price level is proportional *in the long run* to the velocity of circulation or even to the money supply itself. But if this is the case, then nonlinear adjustment of the nominal exchange rate towards long-run monetary fundamentals is tantamount to nonlinear adjustment of the real exchange rate towards long-run PPP, so that the empirical evidence on nonlinear adjustment of real and nominal exchange rates, such as it is at present, is at least consistent. This is clearly an important area for future research.

Our discussion of the theory of exchange rate determination has been largely traditional in this chapter, in the sense that we have discussed a set of models whose underlying structure follows traditional macroeconomics in being rather *ad hoc*. We did, however, touch upon equilibrium and liquidity models, which attempt to model the exchange rate within a fully optimising framework based upon the 'deep structure' of the economy. Recently, spurred on by the seminal work of Obstfeld and Rogoff, this fully optimising approach has seen a recrudescence in the form of the 'new open-economy macroeconomics', which examines exchange rate behaviour within an optimising general equilibrium framework, often in a two-country setting and often with imperfect competition. This is the subject matter of the next chapter.

---

[40] The stylised fact that a model that forecasts well for one exchange rate and time period will tend to perform badly when applied to another exchange rate and/or time period, emphasised by Taylor (1995), might be termed 'Taylor's law'.

References and further readings

Alexander, S.S. (1952), 'Effects of a Devaluation on a Trade Balance', *International Monetary Fund Staff Papers*, 2, pp. 263–78.

Artus, J.R. (1976), 'Exchange Rate Stability and Managed Floating: The Experience of the Federal Republic of Germany', *International Monetary Fund Staff Papers*, 23, pp. 312–33.

Backus, D. (1984), 'Empirical Models of the Exchange Rate: Separating the Wheat from the Chaff', *Canadian Journal of Economics*, 17, pp. 824–46.

Baillie, R.T. and P.C. McMahon (1989), *The Foreign Exchange Market: Theory and Econometric Evidence*, Cambridge: Cambridge University Press.

Barr, D.G. (1989), 'Exchange Rate Dynamics: An Empirical Analysis', in R. MacDonald and M.P. Taylor (eds.), *Exchange Rates and Open Economy Macroeconomics*, Oxford: Blackwell, pp. 109–29.

Barro, R.J. (1977), 'Long-Term Contracting, Sticky Prices, and Monetary Policy', *Journal of Monetary Economics*, 3, pp. 305–16.

Baxter, M. (1994), 'Real Exchange Rates and Real Interest Differentials: Have We Missed the Business-Cycle Relationship?', *Journal of Monetary Economics*, 33, pp. 5–37.

Baxter, M. and A.C. Stockman (1989), 'Business Cycles and the Exchange-Rate Regime: Some International Evidence', *Journal of Monetary Economics*, 23, pp. 377–400.

Beaudry, P. and M.B. Devereux (1995), 'Money and the Real Exchange Rate with Sticky Prices and Increasing Returns', *Carnegie–Rochester Conference Series on Public Policy*, 43, pp. 55–101.

Beck, S.E. (1993), 'The Ricardian Equivalence Proposition: Evidence from Foreign Exchange Markets', *Journal of International Money and Finance*, 12, pp. 154–69.

Berben, R.-P. and D. van Dijk (1998), 'Does the Absence of Cointegration Explain the Typical Findings in Long-Horizon Regressions?', Tinbergen Institute, Erasmus University, Rotterdam, mimeo.

Berkowitz, J. and L. Giorgianni (2001), 'Long-Horizon Exchange Rate Predictability?', *Review of Economics and Statistics*, 83, pp. 81–91.

Bilson, J.F.O. (1978), 'The Monetary Approach to the Exchange Rate: Some Empirical Evidence', *International Monetary Fund Staff Papers*, 25, pp. 48–75.

Bisignano, J. and K. Hoover (1982), 'Some Suggested Improvements to a Simple Portfolio Balance Model of Exchange Rate Determination with Special Reference to the U.S. Dollar/Canadian Dollar Rate', *Weltwirtschaftliches Archiv*, 118, pp. 19–38.

Blanchard, O. and C.M. Kahn (1980), 'The Solution of Linear Difference Models Under Rational Expectations', *Econometrica*, 48, pp. 1305–11.

Boughton, J.M. (1984), 'Exchange Rate Movements and Adjustment in Financial Markets: Quarterly Estimates for Major Currencies', *International Monetary Fund Staff Papers*, 31, pp. 445–68.

Branson, W.H. (1983), 'Macroeconomic Determinants of Real Exchange Risk', in R.J. Herring (ed.), *Managing Foreign Exchange Risk*, Cambridge: Cambridge University Press.

—— (1984), 'A Model of Exchange Rate Determination with Policy Reaction: Evidence from Monthly Data', in P. Malgrange and P.A. Muet (eds.), *Contemporary Macroeconomic Modelling*, Oxford: Basil Blackwell.

Branson, W.H., H. Halttunen and P. Masson (1977), 'Exchange Rates in the Short Run: The Dollar–Deutschemark Rate', *European Economic Review*, 10, pp. 303–24.

Branson, W.H. and D.W. Henderson (1985), 'The Specification and Influence of Asset Markets', in R.W. Jones and P.B. Kenen (eds.), *Handbook of International Economics*, vol. II, Amsterdam: North-Holland, pp. 749–805.

Buiter, W.H. and M. Miller (1981), 'Monetary Policy and International Competitiveness: The Problems of Adjustment', *Oxford Economic Papers*, 33, Supplement, pp. 143–75.

Calvo, G.A. and C.A. Rodriguez (1977), 'A Model of Exchange Rate Determination under Currency Substitution and Rational Expectations', *Journal of Political Economy*, 85, pp. 617–25.

Campbell, J.Y. and R.J. Shiller (1987), 'Cointegration and Tests of Present Value Models', *Journal of Political Economy*, 95, pp. 1062–88.

Clarida, R.H. and J. Gali (1994), 'Sources of Real Exchange-Rate Fluctuations: How Important Are Nominal Shocks?', *Carnegie–Rochester Conference Series on Public Policy*, 41, pp. 1–56.

Clarida, R.H., L. Sarno, M.P. Taylor and G. Valente (2001), 'The Out-of-Sample Success of Term Structure Models as Exchange Rate Predictors: A Step Beyond', *Journal of International Economics*, forthcoming.

Copeland, L.S. (1984), 'The Pound Sterling/US Dollar Exchange Rate and the "News" ', *Economics Letters*, 15, pp. 16, 123–7.

Cornell, B. (1983), 'Money Supply Announcements and Interest Rates: Another View', *Journal of Business*, 56, pp. 1–23.

Dominguez, K.M. and J.A. Frankel (1993), *Does Foreign Exchange Intervention Work?*, Washington, D.C.: Institute for International Economics.

Dooley, M. and P. Isard (1982), 'A Portfolio-Balance Rational-Expectations Model of the Dollar–Mark Exchange Rate', *Journal of International Economics*, 12, pp. 257–76.

Dornbusch, R. (1976), 'Expectations and Exchange Rate Dynamics', *Journal of Political Economy*, 84, pp. 1161–76.

  (1980), 'Exchange Rate Economics: Where Do We Stand?', *Brookings Papers on Economic Activity*, 1, pp. 143–85.

  (1984), 'Monetary Policy under Exchange Rate Flexibility', in D. Bigman and T. Taya (eds.), *Floating Exchange Rates and the State of World Trade Payments*, Cambridge, Mass.: Harper & Row, Ballinger, pp. 3–31.

Dornbusch, R. and S. Fischer (1980), 'Exchange Rates and the Current Account', *American Economic Review*, 70, pp. 960–71.

Dornbusch, R. and J.A. Frankel (1988), 'The Flexible Exchange Rate System: Experience and Alternatives', in S. Borner (ed.), *International Finance and Trade in a Polycentric World* (Proceedings of a conference held in Basel, Switzerland, by the International Economic Association), New York: St Martin's Press in association with the International Economic Association, pp. 151–97.

Driskell, R.A. (1981), 'Exchange Rate Dynamics: An Empirical Investigation', *Journal of Political Economy*, 89, pp. 357–71.

Edison, H.J. and B.D. Pauls (1993), 'A Re-assessment of the Relationship between Real Exchange Rates and Real Interest Rates: 1974–1990', *Journal of Monetary Economics*, 31, pp. 165–87.

Edwards, S. (1982), 'Exchange Rates and "News": A Multi-Currency Approach', *Journal of International Money and Finance*, 1, pp. 211–24.

  (1983), 'Floating Exchange Rates, Expectations and New Information', *Journal of Monetary Economics*, 11, pp. 321–36.

Eichenbaum, M. and C.L. Evans (1995), 'Some Empirical Evidence on the Effects of Shocks to Monetary Policy on Exchange Rates', *Quarterly Journal of Economics*, 110, pp. 975–1009.

Engel, C. and J. Frankel (1984), 'The Secular Inflation Term in Open-Economy Phillips Curves', *European Economic Review*, 24, pp. 161–4.

Engle, R.F. and C.W.J. Granger (1987), 'Co-integration and Error Correction: Representation, Estimation, and Testing', *Econometrica*, 55, pp. 251–76.

Finn, M.G. (1986), 'Forecasting the Exchange Rate: A Monetary or Random Walk Phenomenon?', *Journal of International Money and Finance*, 5, pp. 181–93.

Fleming, J.M. (1962), 'Domestic Financial Policies Under Fixed and Under Floating Exchange Rates', *International Monetary Fund Staff Papers*, 12, pp. 369–80.

Flood, R.P. and A.K. Rose (1995), 'Fixing Exchange Rates: A Virtual Quest for Fundamentals', *Journal of Monetary Economics*, 36, pp. 3–37.

Forsyth, P. and J. Kay (1989), 'The Economic Implications of North Sea Oil Revenues', in D. Helm, J. Kay and D. Thompson (eds.), *The Market for Energy*, Oxford: Oxford University Press, pp. 349–76.

Frankel, J.A. (1979), 'On the Mark: A Theory of Floating Exchange Rates Based on Real Interest Differentials', *American Economic Review*, 69, pp. 610–22.

(1982a), 'The Mystery of the Multiplying Marks: A Modification of the Monetary Model', *Review of Economics and Statistics*, 64, pp. 515–19.

(1982b), 'A Test of Perfect Substitutability in the Foreign Exchange Market', *Southern Economic Journal*, 49, pp. 406–16.

(1982c), 'In Search of the Exchange Risk Premium: A Six-Currency Test Assuming Mean-Variance Optimization', *Journal of International Money and Finance*, 1, pp. 255–74.

(1984), 'Tests of Monetary and Portfolio Balance Models of Exchange Rate Determination', in J.F.O. Bilson and R.C. Marston (eds.), *Exchange Rate Theory and Practice*, National Bureau of Economic Research Conference Report, Chicago: University of Chicago Press, pp. 239–60.

(1990), 'Zen and the Art of Modern Macroeconomics: A Commentary', in W.S. Haraf and T.D. Willett (eds.), *Monetary Policy for a Volatile Global Economy*, Washington, D.C.: American Enterprise Institute, pp. 117–23.

Frankel, J.A. and G.A. Hardouvelis (1985), 'Commodity Prices, Money Surprises and Fed Credibility', *Journal of Money, Credit, and Banking*, 17, pp. 425–38.

Frankel, J.A. and A.K. Rose (1995), 'Empirical Research on Nominal Exchange Rates', in G. Grossman and K. Rogoff (eds.), *Handbook of International Economics*, vol. III, Amsterdam: Elsevier Science, pp. 1689–729.

Frenkel, J.A. (1976), 'A Monetary Approach to the Exchange Rate: Doctrinal Aspects and Empirical Evidence', *Scandinavian Journal of Economics*, 78, pp. 200–24.

Frenkel, J.A. (1981), 'Flexible Exchange Rates, Prices, and the Role of "News": Lessons from the 1970s', *Journal of Political Economy*, 89, pp. 665–705.

Frenkel, J.A. and H.A. Johnson (1976), *The Monetary Approach to the Balance of Payments*, Toronto: University of Toronto Press.

(eds.) (1978), *The Economics of Exchange Rates: Selected Studies*, Reading, Mass.: Addison-Wesley.

Friedman, M. (1953), 'The Case for Flexible Exchange Rates', in M. Friedman, *Essays in Positive Economics*, Chicago: University of Chicago Press, pp. 157–203.

Girton, L. and D.E. Roper (1981), 'Theory and Implications of Currency Substitution', *Journal of Money, Credit, and Banking*, 13, pp. 12–30.

Grilli, V. and N. Roubini (1992), 'Liquidity and Exchange Rates', *Journal of International Economics*, 32, pp. 339–52.

(1993), 'Liquidity, Capital Controls, and Exchange Rates', *Journal of International Money and Finance*, 12, pp. 139–53.

Hacche, G. and J.C. Townend (1981), 'Monetary Models of Exchange Rates and Exchange Market Pressure: Some General Limitations and an Application to Sterling's Effective Rate', *Weltwirtschaftliches Archiv*, 117, pp. 622–37.

Harberger, A.C. (1950), 'Currency Depreciation, Income and the Balance of Trade', *Journal of Political Economy*, 58, pp. 47–60.

Hardouvelis, G.A. (1988), 'Economic News, Exchange Rates and Interest Rates', *Journal of International Money and Finance*, 7, pp. 23–35.

Hicks, J. (1937), 'Mr Keynes and the Classics', *Econometrica*, 5, pp. 142–59.

Hodrick, R.J. (1978), 'An Empirical Analysis of the Monetary Approach to the Determination of the Exchange Rate,' in J.A. Frankel, and H.A. Johnson (eds.), *The Economics of Exchange Rates: Selected Studies*, Reading, Mass.: Addison-Wesley, pp. 97–116.

Hoffman, D.L. and D.E. Schlagenhauf (1983), 'Rational Expectations and Monetary Models of Exchange Rate Determination: An Empirical Examination', *Journal of Monetary Economics*, 11, pp. 247–60.

Hogan, W.P. and I.G. Sharpe (1984), 'Regulation, Risk and the Pricing of Australian Bank Shares, 1957–1976', *Economic Record*, 60, pp. 34–44.

Hooper, P. and J. Morton (1982), 'Fluctuations in the Dollar: A Model of Nominal and Real Exchange Rate Determination', *Journal of International Money and Finance*, 1, pp. 39–56.

Isard, P. (1980), 'Lessons from an Empirical Model of Exchange Rates', *International Monetary Fund Staff Papers*, 34, pp. 1–28.

Johnson, H.G. (1961), 'Towards a General Theory of the Balance of Payments', in H.G. Johnson, *International Trade and Economic Growth: Studies in Pure Theory*, Cambridge, Mass.: Harvard University Press, pp. 153–68.

Karfakis, C. and S.J. Kim (1995), 'Exchange Rates, Interest Rates and Current Account News: Some Evidence from Australia', *Journal of International Money and Finance*, 14, pp. 575–95.

Keynes, J.M. (1936), *The General Theory of Employment, Interest and Money*, New York: Harcourt, Brace & Co.

Kilian, L. (1999), 'Exchange Rates and Monetary Fundamentals: Evidence on Long-Horizon Predictability', *Journal of Applied Econometrics*, 14, pp. 491–510.

Kilian, L. and M.P. Taylor (2001), 'Why Is It So Difficult to Beat the Random Walk Forecast of Exchange Rates?', *Journal of International Economics*, forthcoming.

Koedijk, K.G. and P. Schotman (1990), 'How to Beat the Random Walk: An Empirical Model of Real Exchange Rates', *Journal of International Economics*, 29, pp. 311–32.

Laursen, S. and L.A. Metzler (1950), 'Flexible Exchange Rates and the Theory of Employment', *Review of Economics and Statistics*, 32, pp. 281–99.

Lerner, A.P. (1936), 'The Symmetry Between Export and Import Taxes', *Economica*, 3, pp. 306–13.

Lewis, K.K. (1988), 'Testing the Portfolio Balance Model: A Multi-lateral Approach', *Journal of International Economics*, 24, pp. 109–27.

Lucas, R.E., Jr (1976), 'Econometric Policy Evaluation: A Critique', *Journal of Monetary Economics*, 1, Supplementary Series, pp. 19–46.

(1982), 'Interest Rates and Currency Prices in a Two-Country World', *Journal of Monetary Economics*, 10, pp. 335–59.

(1990), 'Liquidity and Interest Rates', *Journal of Economic Theory*, 50, pp. 237–64.

MacDonald, R. and M.P. Taylor (1993), 'The Monetary Approach to the Exchange Rate: Rational Expectations, Long-Run Equilibrium, and Forecasting', *International Monetary Fund Staff Papers*, 40, pp. 89–107.

(1994), 'The Monetary Model of the Exchange Rate: Long-Run Relationships, Short-Run Dynamics and How to Beat a Random Walk', *Journal of International Money and Finance*, 13, pp. 276–90.

Mark, N.C. (1995), 'Exchange Rates and Fundamentals: Evidence on Long-Horizon Predictability', *American Economic Review*, 85, pp. 201–18.

Mark, N.C. and D.Y. Choi (1995), 'Real Exchange-Rate Prediction over Long Horizons', *Journal of International Economics*, 43, pp. 29–60.

Marshall, A. (1923), *Money, Credit and Commerce*, London: Macmillan.

Marston, R.C. (1989), 'Real and Nominal Exchange Rate Variability', *Empirica*, 16, pp. 147–60.

McNown, R. and M. Wallace (1989), 'Co-integration Tests for Long Run Equilibrium in the Monetary Exchange Rate Model', *Economics Letters*, 31, pp. 263–7.

(1994), 'Cointegration Tests of the Monetary Exchange Rate Model for Three High-Inflation Economies', *Journal of Money, Credit, and Banking*, 26, pp. 396–411.

Meade, J.E. (1951), *The Theory of International Economic Policy, vol. I: The Balance of Payments*, London: Oxford University Press.

Meese, R.A. (1986), 'Testing for Bubbles in Exchange Markets: A Case of Sparkling Rates?', *Journal of Political Economy*, 94, pp. 345–73.

Meese, R.A. and K. Rogoff (1983), 'Empirical Exchange Rate Models of the Seventies: Do They Fit Out of Sample?', *Journal of International Economics*, 14, pp. 3–24.

(1988), 'Was It Real? The Exchange Rate–Interest Differential Relation over the Modern Floating-Rate Period', *Journal of Finance*, 43, pp. 933–48.

Meese, R.A. and A.K. Rose (1991), 'An Empirical Assessment of Non-Linearities in Models of Exchange Rate Determination', *Review of Economic Studies*, 58, pp. 603–19.

Metzler, L.A. (1942a), 'Underemployment Equilibrium in International Trade', *Econometrica*, 10, pp. 97–112.

(1942b), 'The Transfer Problem Reconsidered', *Journal of Political Economy*, 50, pp. 397–414.

Mundell, R.A. (1961), 'A Theory of Optimum Currency Areas', *American Economic Review*, 51, pp. 657–65.

(1962), 'The Appropriate Use of Monetary and Fiscal Policy for Internal and External Stability', *International Monetary Fund Staff Papers*, 12, pp. 70–9.

(1963), 'Capital Mobility and Stabilization Policy Under Fixed and Flexible Exhange Rates', *Canadian Journal of Economics and Political Science*, 29, pp. 475–85.

Mussa, M. (1976), 'The Exchange Rate, the Balance of Payments and Monetary and Fiscal Policy under a Regime of Controlled Floating', *Scandinavian Journal of Economics*, 78, pp. 229–48.

(1979), 'Empirical Regularities in the Behaviour of Exchange Rates and Theories of the Foreign Exchange Market', *Carnegie-Rochester Conference Series on Public Policy*, 11, pp. 9–57.

(1981), 'The Role of Official Intervention', *Group of Thirty Occasional Papers*, no. 6.

(1986), 'Nominal Exchange Rate Regimes and the Behavior of Real Exchange Rates: Evidence and Implications', *Carnegie-Rochester Conference Series on Public Policy*, 25, pp. 117–213.

Nana, G., V.B. Hall and B.P. Philpott (1995), 'Trans-Tasman CGE Modelling: Some Illustrative Results from the Joani Model', *Economic Modelling*, 12, pp. 377–89.

Nurkse, R. (1944), *International Currency Experience: Lessons of the Interwar Period*, Geneva: League of Nations.

Obstfeld, M. and A.C. Stockman (1985), 'Exchange-Rate Dynamics', in R. Jones and P.B. Kenen (eds.), *Handbook of International Economics*, vol. II, Amsterdam: North-Holland, pp. 917–77.

Pagan, A. (1984), 'Econometric Issues in the Analysis of Regressions with Generated Regressors', *International Economic Review*, 25, pp. 221–47.

Putnam, B.H. and J.R. Woodbury (1980), 'Exchange Rate Stability and Monetary Policy', *Review of Business and Economic Research*, 15, pp. 1–10.

Rogoff, K. (1984), 'On the Effects of Sterilized Intervention: An Analysis of Weekly Data', *Journal of Monetary Economics*, 14, pp. 133–50.

Samuelson, P. (1948), *Foundations of Economic Analysis*, Cambridge, Mass.: Harvard University Press.

Schinasi, G.J. and P.A.V.B. Swamy (1989), 'The Out-of-Sample Forecasting Performance of Exchange Rate Models When Coefficients Are Allowed to Change', *Journal of International Money and Finance*, 8, pp. 375–90.

Shiller, R. (1978), 'Rational Expectations and the Dynamic Structure of Macroeconomic Models: A Critical Review', *Journal of Monetary Economics*, 4, pp. 1–44.

Smith, P.N. and M.R. Wickens (1986), 'An Empirical Investigation into the Causes of Failure of the Monetary Model of the Exchange Rate', *Journal of Applied Econometrics*, 1, pp. 143–62.

(1990), 'Assessing the Effects of Monetary Shocks on Exchange Rate Variability with a Stylised Econometric Model of the UK', in A.S. Courakis and M.P. Taylor (eds.), *Private Behaviour and Government Policy in Interdependent Economies*, Oxford: Oxford University Press, pp. 53–72.

Stockman, A.C. (1980), 'A Theory of Exchange Rate Determination', *Journal of Political Economy*, 88, pp. 673–98.

(1983), 'Real Exchange Rates under Alternative Nominal Exchange-Rate Systems', *Journal of International Money and Finance*, 2, pp. 147–66.

(1987), 'The Equilibrium Approach to Exchange Rates', *Federal Reserve Bank of Richmond Economic Review*, 73, March–April, pp. 12–30.

(1988), 'Real Exchange-Rate Variability under Pegged and Floating Nominal Exchange-Rate Systems: An Equilibrium Theory', *Carnegie–Rochester Conference Series on Public Policy*, 29, pp. 259–94.

Taylor, M.P. (1990), *The Balance of Payments*, Cheltenham: Edward Elgar Publishing Ltd.

(1995), 'The Economics of Exchange Rates', *Journal of Economic Literature*, 33, pp. 13–47.

(1999), 'Real Interest Rates and Macroeconomic Activity', *Oxford Review of Economic Policy*, 15, pp. 95–113.

Taylor, M.P. and D.A. Peel (2000), 'Nonlinear Adjustment, Long-Run Equilibrium and Exchange Rate Fundamentals', *Journal of International Money and Finance*, 19, pp. 33–53.

Throop, A.W. (1993), 'A Generalized Uncovered Interest Parity Model of Exchange Rates', *Federal Reserve Bank of San Francisco Economic Review*.

Tobin, J. (1969), 'A General Equilibrium Approach to Monetary Theory', *Journal of Money, Credit, and Banking*, 1, pp. 15–29.

Turnovsky, S.J. and K.M. Ball (1983), 'Covered Interest Parity and Speculative Efficiency: Some Empirical Evidence for Australia', *Economic Record*, 59, pp. 271–80.

Urich, T.J. (1982), 'The Information Content of Weekly Money Supply Announcements', *Journal of Monetary Economics*, 10, pp. 73–88.

Urich, T.J. and P. Wachtel (1984), 'The Structure of Expectations of the Weekly Money Supply Announcement', *Journal of Monetary Economics*, 13, pp. 183–94.

van den Berg, H. and S.C. Jayanetti (1993), 'A Novel Test of the Monetary Approach Using Black Market Exchange Rates and the Johansen–Juselius Cointegration Method', *Economics Letters*, 41, pp. 413–18.

Woo, W.T. (1985), 'The Monetary Approach to Exchange Rate Determination under Rational Expectations: The Dollar–Deutschmark Rate', *Journal of International Economics*, 18, pp. 1–16.

5 New open-economy macroeconomics

This chapter surveys the recent literature on 'new' open-economy macroeconomics. This literature, stimulated primarily by the seminal work of Obstfeld and Rogoff (1995, 1996), reflects the attempt by researchers to formalise exchange rate determination in the context of dynamic general equilibrium models with explicit microfoundations, nominal rigidities and imperfect competition.

The main objective of this research programme is to develop a new workhorse model for open-economy macroeconomic analysis. Relative to most of the more traditional models of exchange rate determination which we discussed in the last chapter, notably the Mundell–Fleming model, the sticky-price and flexible-price monetary models and the portfolio balance model, the new open-economy models seek to offer a more rigorous analytical foundation based on fully specified microfoundations. On the other hand, however, the main virtue of the more traditional models is their simpler analytical structure, which makes them easier to discuss and use in applied policy analysis. Moreover, because the predictions of new open-economy models are often quite sensitive to the particular specification of the microfoundations, policy evaluation and welfare analysis are usually dependent on the particular specification of preferences and nominal rigidities. In turn, this generates a need for the profession to agree on the 'correct', or at least 'preferable', specification of the microfoundations. The counter-argument would be that the traditional models achieve their analytical simplicity by making a number of implicit assumptions which are simply made more specific in new open-economy models, thereby allowing economists to scrutinise them more carefully.

This chapter reviews the key contributions in the new open-economy macroeconomics which have been made since the seminal 'redux' paper by Obstfeld and Rogoff (1995) (although we also note some important precursors of this work) and discusses some of the most controversial issues currently being debated in this literature.

5.1 The redux model

5.1.1 The baseline model

Obstfeld and Rogoff (1995) is the study often considered as having initiated the literature on the new open-economy macroeconomics (see, for example, Lane, 2001; Corsetti and

Pesenti, 2001; Sarno, 2001) and in many ways it is a path-breaking contribution; it is certainly the seminal paper of this literature. However, a precursor of the Obstfeld and Rogoff model that deserves to be noted here is the model proposed by Svensson and Wijnbergen (1989). They present a stochastic, two-country, neoclassical, rational expectations model with sticky prices that are set by monopolistically competitive firms, where possible excess capacity is allowed in order to facilitate examination of the international spillover effects of monetary disturbances on output. In contrast to the standard prediction of the Mundel–Fleming–Dornbusch framework that a monetary expansion at home leads to a recession abroad (see e.g. Dornbusch, 1976; Obstfeld and Rogoff, 1996), the paper suggests that the spillover effects of monetary policy are in fact ambiguous and depend upon the relative size of the intertemporal and intratemporal elasticities of substitution in consumption. It is also fair to say that the need for rigorous microfoundations in open-economy models is not novel in new open-economy macroeconomics and was emphasised by a number of researchers prior to Obstfeld and Rogoff (1995); notable examples are Stockman (1980, 1987), Lucas (1982) and Backus, Kehoe and Kydland (1992, 1994, 1995), among others.

The baseline model proposed by Obstfeld and Rogoff (1995) is a two-country, dynamic general equilibrium model with microfoundations that allows for nominal price rigidities, imperfect competition and a continuum of agents who both produce and consume. Each agent produces a single differentiated good. All agents have identical preferences, characterised by an intertemporal utility function that depends positively on consumption and real money balances but negatively on work effort. Effort is positively related to output. The exchange rate is defined as the domestic price of foreign currency. The domestic and foreign countries are designated Home and Foreign, respectively.

Formally, consider a two-country world inhabited by a continuum of producer-consumers, indexed by $z \in [0, 1]$, with $[0, n]$ in the Home country and $(n, 1]$ in the Foreign country. Each of the producer-consumers produces a single differentiated good, also indexed by z, and has the same preferences as all other producer-consumers. The intertemporal utility function of a typical Home agent z, say U_t, depends positively on consumption, C, positively on real money balances, M/P, and negatively on work effort, which is positively related to output, y (so that utility is decreasing in y):

$$ U_t = \sum_{s=t}^{\infty} \beta^{(s-t)} \left[\frac{\sigma}{\sigma - 1} C_s^{\frac{\sigma-1}{\sigma}} + \frac{\chi}{1 - \varepsilon} \left(\frac{M_s}{P_s} \right)^{1-\varepsilon} - \frac{\kappa}{\mu} y_s(z)^\mu \right], \tag{5.1} $$

where C is a constant-elasticity-of-substitution (CES) index of consumption; β is the subjective discount factor and $\sigma, \chi, \varepsilon, \kappa$ and μ are parameters, $\sigma, \chi, \varepsilon, \kappa > 0; \mu > 1; 0 < \beta < 1$. Denoting by $c(z)$ the Home individual consumption of good z and by $\theta(>1)$ the elasticity of demand with respect to relative price faced by each monopolist, then (dropping time subscripts for clarity) C is given by the expression:

$$ C = \left[\int_0^1 c(z)^{\frac{\theta-1}{\theta}} dz \right]^{\frac{\theta}{\theta-1}}. \tag{5.2} $$

Thus, the demand of the Home individual and the total demand for good z are given by:

$$c(z) = C \left(\frac{p(z)}{P} \right)^{-\theta} \tag{5.3}$$

and:

$$y^d(z) = \left(\frac{p(z)}{P} \right)^{-\theta} C^w, \tag{5.4}$$

where P is the cost of living index (or consumption-based money price index) in the Home country; $p(z)$ is the domestic price of z; aggregate global consumption $C^w \equiv Q + nG + (1-n)G^*$, with G denoting per capita real home government consumption (and asterisks denoting Foreign variables), and $Q \equiv [nC + (1-n)C^*]$ denoting total private world consumption. Equation (5.3) is obtained by maximising $C = [\int_0^1 c(j)^{\frac{\theta-1}{\theta}} dz]^{\frac{\theta}{\theta-1}}$ subject to the nominal budget constraint $\int_0^1 p(z)c(z)dz = Z$, where Z is any fixed total nominal expenditure on goods. Equation (5.4) is obtained by aggregating globally.

Because there are no impediments or costs to trade between countries in this model, the law of one price (LOOP) holds for each individual good, so that:

$$p(z) = Sp^*(z), \tag{5.5}$$

where S denotes the nominal exchange rate. Also, the cost of living index (defined as the minimum expenditure of domestic money needed to purchase one unit of C) is given by:

$$P = \left[\int_0^1 p(z)^{1-\theta} dz \right]^{\frac{1}{1-\theta}}$$

$$= \left[\int_0^n p(z)^{1-\theta} dz + \int_n^1 Sp^*(z)^{1-\theta} dz \right]^{\frac{1}{1-\theta}}, \tag{5.6}$$

and, because preferences are identical across countries, purchasing power parity (PPP) holds:

$$P = SP^*. \tag{5.7}$$

Obstfeld and Rogoff also assume that there is an integrated world capital market in which both countries can borrow and lend. The only internationally traded asset is a riskless real bond B, denominated in the composite consumption good. Then, the dynamic budget constraint may be written in real terms as follows:

$$B_{s+1} + \frac{M_s}{P_s} = (1+r)B_s + \frac{M_{s-1}}{P_s} + \frac{p_s(z)}{P_s} y_s(z) - C_s - T_s, \tag{5.8}$$

where r is the real interest rate and taxes T are related to government spending according to the relationship:

$$G_s = T_s + \frac{M_s - M_{s-1}}{P_s}. \tag{5.9}$$

Agents maximise lifetime utility subject to the budget constraint (identical for domestic and foreign agents):

$$\Lambda_s = \sum_{s=t}^{\infty} \beta^{(s-t)} \left[\frac{\sigma}{\sigma-1} \ln C_s^{\frac{\sigma-1}{\sigma}} + \frac{\chi}{1-\varepsilon} \ln \left(\frac{M_s}{P_s} \right)^{1-\varepsilon} - \frac{\kappa}{\mu} y_s(z)^{\mu} \right]$$

$$- \sum_{s=t}^{\infty} \lambda_s \left[B_{s+1} + \frac{M_s}{P_s} - (1+r)B_s - \frac{M_{s-1}}{P_s} - \frac{p_s(z)}{P_s} y_s(z) + C_s + T_s \right]. \quad (5.10)$$

Assuming that the real interest rate, r, is linked to the nominal interest rate, i, through real interest parity according to $1 + i_s = (P_{s+1}/P_s)(1+r_s)$, maximisation of Λ_t implies first-order conditions that yield:

$$C_{s+1} = \beta^s (1+r_s)^{\sigma} C_s \quad (5.11)$$

$$\frac{\chi (M_s/P_s)^{-\varepsilon}}{C_s^{-1/\sigma}} = \frac{i_t}{1+i_t} \quad (5.12)$$

$$y_s(z)^{\mu-1+(1/\theta)} = \left(\frac{\theta-1}{\theta\kappa} \right) C_s^{-1/\sigma} [Q_s + nG_s + (1-n)G_s^*]^{1/\theta}, \quad (5.13)$$

and analogous conditions for the Foreign individual. Utility maximisation, then, implies three clearly interpretable conditions. The first, equation (5.11), is the standard Euler equation, which implies a flat consumption path over time for a constant real interest rate. The second condition, equation (5.12), is the money-market equilibrium condition that equates the marginal rate of substitution of consumption for the services of real money balances to the consumption opportunity cost of holding real money balances (the nominal interest rate). The representative agent directly benefits from holding money in the utility function but loses the interest rate on the riskless bond as well as the opportunity to eliminate the cost of inflation. (Note that money demand depends on consumption rather than income in this model.) The third condition, equation (5.13), requires that the marginal utility of the higher revenue earned from producing one extra unit of output equals the marginal disutility of the needed effort, and so can be interpreted as a labour–leisure trade-off equation.

The steady state (denoted by an upper bar) implied by the above first-order conditions can then be calculated. At the zero-inflation steady state, with $\overline{G} = \overline{T}$ and $\overline{G}^* = \overline{T}^*$, the Euler equation implies the following steady state for the real interest rate:

$$\overline{r} = \frac{1-\beta}{\beta}. \quad (5.14)$$

Denoting foreign assets as F and using the identity that net foreign assets must be zero $(nF + (1-n)F^* = 0)$, the consumption steady state is:

$$\overline{C} = \overline{r}\overline{F} + \frac{\overline{py}}{\overline{P}} - \overline{G} \quad (5.15)$$

or:

$$\overline{C} = -\overline{r} \left(\frac{n}{1-n} \right) \overline{F} + \frac{\overline{p}^* \overline{y}^*}{\overline{P}^*} - \overline{G}^*. \quad (5.16)$$

Then, in the special case when net foreign assets are zero and government spending levels are equal, a closed-form solution (denoted with a zero subscript) for income and real money balances is obtained:

$$y_0 = y_0^* = \left(\frac{\theta - 1}{\theta \kappa}\right)^{\frac{\sigma}{\sigma(\mu - 1) + 1}} \tag{5.17}$$

$$\frac{M_0}{P_0} = \frac{M_0^*}{P_0^*} = \left(\frac{1 - \beta}{\chi}\right)^{\frac{1}{\varepsilon}} y_0^{-\frac{1}{\sigma \varepsilon}}. \tag{5.18}$$

Because this framework is based on a market structure which allows for imperfect competition where each agent has some degree of market power arising from product differentiation, steady-state output is sub-optimally low. As $\theta \to \infty$, the elasticity of demand increases and the various goods become closer substitutes and, consequently, monopoly power decreases. According to equation (5.17), then, as $\theta \to \infty$, output approaches the level corresponding to a perfectly competitive market.[1]

A main focus of Obstfeld and Rogoff (1995) is the impact of a monetary shock on real money balances and output. Under perfectly flexible prices, a permanent shock produces no dynamics and the world economy remains in steady state (prices increase by the same proportion as the money supply). That is, an increase in the money supply has no real effects and cannot remedy the sub-optimal output level. Money is neutral.[2]

With prices displaying stickiness in the short run, however, monetary policy may have real effects. If the money supply increases, because prices are fixed, the nominal interest rate falls and hence the exchange rate depreciates. This is because, on account of arbitrage in the foreign exchange market, uncovered interest parity holds. Foreign goods become more expensive relative to domestic goods, generating a temporary increase in the demand for domestic goods and inducing an increase in output. Consequently, monetary shocks generate real effects on the economy. But how can one ensure that producers are willing to increase output? If prices are fixed, output is determined by demand. Because a monopolist always prices above marginal cost, it is profitable to meet unexpected demand at the fixed price. Noting that in this model the exchange rate rises less than the money supply, currency depreciation shifts world demand towards domestic goods, which causes a short-run rise in domestic income. Home residents consume some of the extra income but, because they want to smooth consumption over time, they also save part of it. Therefore, while in the long run the current account is balanced, in the short run Home runs a current account surplus. With higher long-run wealth, Home agents shift at the margin from work to leisure, thereby reducing Home output. Nevertheless, because Home agents' real income and consumption rise in the long run, the exchange rate does not necessarily depreciate.

---

[1] From equation (5.17), it follows that $(\frac{\theta - 1}{\kappa \theta}) \to (\frac{1}{\kappa})$ and $(\frac{1 + \theta}{\theta}) \to 1$.

[2] Note that in the redux model and in a number of subsequent papers, monetary shocks are discussed without a formalisation of the reaction functions of the monetary authorities. However, some recent studies have investigated formally reaction functions in new open-economy macroeconomic models; see, for example, Ghironi and Rebucci (2000) and the references therein.

Unlike the scenario in a sticky-price overshooting model of the kind originally suggested by Dornbusch (1976) and discussed in Chapter 4, the redux model does not yield exchange rate overshooting in response to monetary shocks. The exchange rate effect is smaller the larger the elasticity of substitution, θ; as θ approaches infinity Home and Foreign goods become closer substitutes, producing larger shifts in demand with the exchange rate changing only slightly.

Finally, it can be demonstrated that a monetary expansion leads to a first-order welfare improvement. Because the price exceeds the marginal cost in a monopolistic equilibrium, global output is inefficiently low. An unanticipated money shock raises aggregate demand, stimulating production and mitigating the distortion.

Summing up, in the redux model, monetary shocks can generate persistent real effects, affecting consumption and output levels and the exchange rate, although both the LOOP and PPP hold. Welfare rises by equal amounts at home and abroad after a positive monetary shock, and production is moved closer to its efficient (perfectly competitive market) level. Adjustment to the steady state occurs within one period, but money supply shocks can have real effects lasting beyond the time frame of the nominal rigidities because of the induced short-run wealth accumulation via the current account. Money is not neutral, even in the long run.

5.1.2 A small open-economy version of the baseline model

The baseline redux model and most of the subsequent literature on the new open-economy macroeconomics are based on a two-country framework, which allows an explicit analysis of international transmission channels and the endogenous determination of interest rates and asset prices. Nevertheless, similar but simpler models may be constructed under the assumption of a small open-economy, rather than a two-country, framework. In the small open-economy version it is also easier to allow a distinction between tradable and non-tradable goods in the analysis. Obstfeld and Rogoff (1995) provide such an example in their appendix. In this model, monopolistic competition characterises the non-tradable goods sector. The tradable goods sector is characterised by a single homogeneous tradable good that sells for the same price all over the world in a perfectly competitive market with flexible prices. The representative agent in the small open economy, Home, has an endowment of the tradable good in constant quantity in each period and monopoly power over the production of one of the non-tradable goods.

In this situation, a permanent monetary shock does not generate a current account imbalance. Because output of tradable goods is fixed, current account behaviour is determined by the time path for tradables consumption, which, under log-separable preferences and a discount rate equal to the world interest rate, implies a perfectly flat optimal time path for consumption. Hence, the current account remains in balance. Unlike the scenario in the baseline redux model, however, exchange rate overshooting may occur in this model. Since the monetary shock does not produce a current account imbalance, money is neutral in the long run and the nominal exchange rate rises proportionately to the money stock. Because the consumption elasticity of money demand is less than unity (by assumption), the nominal exchange rate overshoots its long-run level.

Lane (1997) uses this small open-economy model to examine discretionary monetary policy and the impact of openness (measured by the relative size of the tradables sector) on the equilibrium inflation rate. A more open economy (with a large tradables sector) gains less from 'surprise' inflation because the output gain from a monetary expansion is exclusively obtained in the non-tradables sector and is relatively low. Since the equilibrium inflation rate under discretion is positively related to the gains from 'surprise' inflation (Barro and Gordon, 1983), the model predicts that more open economies have lower equilibrium inflation rates (see also Kollman, 1997; Velasco, 1997).

Lane (2000) further extends this model by considering an alternative specification of the utility function under which monetary shocks generate current account imbalances. The sign of the current account response is ambiguous, however. In fact, it depends upon the interplay between the intertemporal elasticity of substitution, σ, and the intratemporal elasticity of substitution, θ. σ governs the willingness to substitute consumption across periods, while θ governs the degree of substitutability between traded and non-traded consumption. If $\sigma < \theta$, a positive monetary shock generates a current account surplus; however, a current account deficit occurs if $\sigma > \theta$, while the current account remains in balance if $\sigma = \theta$. Hence, this model clearly illustrates how the results stemming from this class of models are sensitive to the specification of the microfoundations.

The implications of small open-economy models of this class seem plausible. While the relevant literature (and consequently the rest of this chapter) largely uses a two-country global economy framework, we think it might also be worthwhile to pursue research based on the small open-economy assumption. Indeed, this assumption seems a plausible approximation for most advanced industrialised countries, except the United States. Further, testing the empirical implications of the small open-economy models discussed in this section represents a new line of research for applied economists.

5.2   Rethinking the redux model

5.2.1   Nominal rigidities

As mentioned earlier, subsequent work has modified many of the assumptions of the redux model. In this sub-section, we discuss modifications based on the specification of nominal rigidities. The new open-economy literature discussed here provides some novel insights in this context and is capable of generating predictions which may be evaluated empirically as a basis for choosing among alternative specifications of stickiness in macroeconomic models. Whether the extension from closed- to open-economy models does help to achieve consensus on the specification of nominal rigidities remains to be seen (see, for example, the arguments presented by Obstfeld and Rogoff, 2000a, discussed below).

With respect to nominal rigidities, the redux model assumes that prices are set one period in advance, which implies that adjustment to equilibrium is complete after one period. As Corsetti and Pesenti (2001) emphasise, however, if price stickiness is motivated by fixed menu costs, firms have an incentive to adjust prices immediately after a shock if the shock is large enough to violate their participation cost by raising the marginal cost above the price. Hence, the redux analysis may be seen as plausible only within the relevant range of shocks.

Hau (2000) generalises the redux model in three ways to investigate the role of wage rigidities and non-tradables for the international transmission mechanism. First, following Blanchard and Kiyotaki (1987), the model allows for factor markets and for nominal rigidities originating from sticky wages. Second, Hau assumes flexible price-setting in local currency and does not assume international goods arbitrage. While the law of one price (LOOP) still holds because of optimal monopolistic price-setting, non-tradables in the consumer price index produce deviations from purchasing power parity. Third, unlike the scenario in the redux analysis, Hau also allows for non-tradable goods. The main result of the paper is that wage rigidities have similar implications to rigid domestic producer prices. In some sense, the results of the redux analysis are confirmed in the context of a market structure with wage rigidities. However, non-tradables modify the transmission mechanism in important ways. A larger non-tradables share implies that exchange rate movements are magnified, since the money-market equilibrium relies on a short-run price adjustment carried out by fewer tradables. This effect is interesting since it may help explain the observed high volatility of the nominal exchange rate relative to price volatility.

Within the framework of price level rigidities, however, a more sophisticated way of capturing price stickiness is through staggered price-setting that allows smooth, rather than discrete, aggregate price level adjustment. Staggering price models of the type developed by, among others, Taylor (1980) and Calvo (1983) are classic examples. Kollman (1997) calibrates a dynamic open-economy model with both sticky prices and sticky wages and then explores the behaviour of exchange rates and prices in response to monetary shocks with predetermined price- and wage-setting and Calvo-type nominal rigidities. His results suggest that Calvo-type nominal rigidities match very well the observed high correlation between nominal and real exchange rates and the smooth adjustment in the price level, but they match less well correlations between output and several other macroeconomic variables.

Chari, Kehoe and McGrattan (1998, 2000) link sticky price models to the behaviour of the real exchange rate in the context of a new open-economy macroeconomic model. They start by noting that the data for advanced countries show large and persistent deviations of real exchange rates from purchasing power parity that appear to be driven primarily by deviations from the LOOP for tradable goods. That is, real and nominal exchange rates are about six times more volatile than relative price levels and both are highly persistent, with first-order serial correlation coefficients of the order of about 0.83 and 0.85, respectively, at annual frequency.[3] Chari, Kehoe and McGrattan then develop a sticky-price model with price-discriminating monopolists that produces deviations from the LOOP for tradable goods. However, their benchmark model, which has prices set for one quarter at a time and a unit consumption elasticity of money demand, does not come close to reproducing

---

[3] This corresponds to the three- to five-year half-life of real exchange rates discussed in Chapter 3.

the serial correlation properties of real and nominal exchange rates noted above. A model in which producers set prices for six quarters at a time and with a consumption elasticity of money demand of 0.27 does much better in generating persistent and volatile real and nominal exchange rates. The first-order serial correlation coefficients of real and nominal exchange rates are 0.65 and 0.66, respectively, and exchange rates are about three times more volatile than relative price levels.

In a closely related paper, Jeanne (1998) attempts to assess whether money can generate persistent economic fluctuations in a dynamic general equilibrium model of the business cycle. Jeanne shows that a small nominal friction in the goods market can make the response of output to monetary shocks large and persistent if it is amplified by real-wage rigidity in the labour market. He also argues that, for plausible levels of real-wage rigidity, a small degree of nominal stickiness may be sufficient for money to produce economic fluctuations as persistent as those observed in the data.[4]

Obstfeld and Rogoff (2000a), which we discuss further below, develop a stochastic new open-economy model based on sticky nominal wages, monopolistic competition, and exporter-currency pricing. Solving explicitly the wage-setting problem under uncertainty allows analysis of the welfare implications of alternative monetary regimes and their impact on expected output and terms of trade. To motivate their model, Obstfeld and Rogoff show that observed correlations between terms of trade and exchange rates appear to be more consistent with their assumptions about nominal rigidities than with the alternative specification based on local-currency pricing.

We now turn to a discussion of various reformulations of the redux model based upon the introduction of pricing to market.

5.2.2   *Pricing to market*

While the redux model assumes that the LOOP holds for all tradable goods, a number of researchers have questioned the model on the grounds that deviations from the LOOP across international borders appear to be larger than can be explained by geographical distance or transport costs (see, for example, Engel, 1993; Engel and Rogers, 1996). Some authors have therefore extended the redux model by combining international segmentation with imperfectly competitive firms and local-currency pricing (essentially, pricing to market, or PTM). As discussed in Chapter 3, Krugman (1987) used the term PTM to characterise price discrimination for certain types of goods (such as automobiles and many types of electronics) where international arbitrage is difficult or perhaps impossible. This may be due, for example, to differing national standards (for example, 100-volt light-bulbs are not used in Europe, and left-hand-drive cars are not popular in the United Kingdom, Australia or Japan). Further, monopolistic firms may be able to limit or prevent international goods arbitrage by refusing to provide warranty service in one country for goods purchased in another. To the extent that prices cannot be arbitraged, producers can discriminate among different international markets.

---

[4] See also Andersen (1998), Benigno (1999), and Bergin and Feenstra (2000a,b).

Studies allowing for PTM typically find that it may play a central role in exchange rate determination and in international macroeconomic fluctuations. This happens because PTM acts to limit the pass-through from exchange rate movements to prices, reducing the 'expenditure-switching' role of exchange rate changes and potentially generating greater exchange rate variability than would be obtained in models without PTM. Also, nominal price stickiness, in conjunction with PTM, magnifies the response of the exchange rate to macroeconomic fundamentals shocks. Further, by generating deviations from purchasing power parity, PTM models also tend to reduce the co-movement in consumption across countries while increasing the co-movement of output, in keeping with some well-known empirical regularities (see Backus, Kehoe and Kydland, 1992). Finally, the introduction of PTM has important welfare implications for the international transmission of monetary policy shocks, as discussed below.

Betts and Devereux (2000), for example,[5] characterise PTM by assuming that prices of many goods are set in the local currency of the buyer and do not adjust at high frequency. Consequently, real exchange rates move with nominal exchange rates at high frequency. These assumptions also imply that price/cost markups fluctuate endogenously in response to exchange rate movements rather than nominal prices (see also Knetter, 1993, on this point). In the Betts–Devereux framework, traded goods are characterised by a significant degree of national market segmentation and trade is carried out only by firms. Households cannot arbitrage away price differences across countries, and firms engage in short-term nominal price-setting. Therefore, prices are sticky in terms of the local currency.

The Betts–Devereux model is based on an economy with differentiated products and assumes that firms can price-discriminate among countries. With a high degree of PTM (that is, when a large fraction of firms engage in PTM), a depreciation of the exchange rate has little effect on the relative price of imported goods faced by domestic consumers. This weakens the allocative effects of exchange rate changes relative to a situation where prices are set in the seller's currency; in the latter case, pass-through of exchange rates to prices is immediate. Hence, PTM reduces the expenditure-switching effects of exchange rate depreciation, which generally implies a shift of world demand towards the exports of the country whose currency is depreciating. Because domestic prices show little response to exchange rate depreciation under PTM, the response of the equilibrium exchange rate may be substantially magnified and, consistent with well-known observed empirical regularities, exchange rates may vary more than relative prices.

PTM also has implications for the international transmission of macroeconomic shocks. In the absence of PTM, for example, monetary disturbances tend to generate large positive co-movements of consumption across countries but large negative co-movements of output. However, PTM reverses the ordering: the deviations from purchasing power parity induced by PTM make consumption co-movements fall. At the same time, the elimination of expenditure-switching effects of the exchange rate enhances co-movements of output across countries.

---

[5] The model of Betts and Devereux (2000) is used as a representative of this class of PTM models in this sub-section. Other examples of models adopting PTM are Betts and Devereux (1996, 1997, 1999a,b), Chari, Kehoe and McGrattan (1998, 2000) and Bergin and Feenstra (2000a,b).

In terms of welfare, recall that the framework based on the LOOP and purchasing power parity generally suggests that an unanticipated monetary expansion increases the welfare of all agents at home and abroad. With PTM, however, a domestic monetary expansion increases home welfare but reduces foreign welfare, and monetary policy is a 'beggar-thy-neighbour' instrument. Therefore, the PTM framework, unlike the framework based on the LOOP and purchasing power parity, provides a case for international monetary policy co-ordination.

Overall, the PTM framework suggests that goods market segmentation might help explain international quantity and price fluctuations and may have important implications for the international transmission of economic shocks, policy and welfare.

5.2.3   The indeterminacy of the steady state

In the framework proposed by Obstfeld and Rogoff (1995), the current account plays a crucial role in the transmission of shocks. However, the steady state is indeterminate and both the consumption differential between countries and an economy's net foreign assets are nonstationary. After a monetary shock, the economy will move to a different steady state until a new shock occurs. When the model is log-linearised to obtain closed-form solutions of the endogenous variables, one is approximating the dynamics of the model around a moving steady state. Some researchers have argued that this makes the conclusions implied by the model questionable, and, in particular, that the reliability of the log-linear approximations is low because variables wander away from the initial steady state.

Many subsequent variants of the redux model de-emphasise the role of net foreign assets accumulation as a channel of macroeconomic interdependence between countries. This is done by assuming that (a) the elasticity of substitution between domestic and foreign goods is unity or (b) financial markets are complete. Both of these assumptions imply that the current account does not react to shocks (see, for example, Corsetti and Pesenti, 2001; and Obstfeld and Rogoff, 2000a).[6] While this framework achieves the desired result of determinacy of the steady state, it requires strong assumptions – (a) or (b) above – to shut off the current account, which are unrealistic. In a sense these solutions circumvent the problem of indeterminacy, but they do not solve it.

Ghironi (2000a) provides an extensive discussion of the indeterminacy and nonstationarity problems in the redux model. Ghironi also provides a tractable two-country model of macroeconomic interdependence that does not rely on either of the above assumptions in that the elasticity of substitution between domestic and foreign goods can be different from unity and that financial markets are incomplete, consistent with reality. Using an overlapping generations structure, Ghironi shows how there exists a steady state, endogenously determined, to which the world economy reverts following temporary shocks. Accumulation of net foreign assets plays a role in the transmission of shocks to productivity. Finally, Ghironi also shows that shutting off the current account may lead to

---

[6] This is a problem often encountered in the international real business cycles literature. Note, however, that the role of current account dynamics in generating persistent effects of transitory shocks has often been found to be quantitatively unimportant in this literature. See the discussion on this point by Baxter and Crucini (1995) and Kollmann (1996).

large errors in welfare comparisons, which calls for rethinking of several results in this literature.

The issue of indeterminacy of the steady state in new open-economy models is an area of current debate and clearly warrants further attention from researchers in this area.

5.2.4 Preferences

While the explicit treatment of microfoundations is a key advantage of new open-economy macroeconomic models over the Mundell–Fleming–Dornbusch model, the implications of such models depend on the specification of preferences. One convenient assumption in the redux model is the symmetry with which home and foreign goods enter preferences in the constant-elasticity-of-substitution utility function. Corsetti and Pesenti (2001) extend the redux model to investigate the effects of a limited degree of substitution between home and foreign goods. In their baseline model, the LOOP still holds and technology is described by a Cobb–Douglas production function, with a unit elasticity of substitution between home and foreign goods and constant income shares for home and foreign agents. The model illustrates that the welfare effects of expansionary monetary and fiscal policies are related to internal and external sources of economic distortion, namely, monopolistic supply in production and monopoly power of a country. For example, an unanticipated exchange rate depreciation can be 'beggar-thyself' rather than 'beggar-thy-neighbour', since gains in domestic output are offset by losses in consumers' purchasing power and a deterioration in terms of trade. Also, openness is not inconsequential: smaller and more open economies are more prone to inflationary consequences. Fiscal shocks, however, are generally 'beggar-thy-neighbour' in the long run, but they raise domestic demand in the short run for given terms of trade. These results provide a role for international policy co-ordination, which is not the case in the redux model.[7]

An important assumption in the redux model is that consumption and leisure are separable. This assumption is not compatible, however, with a balanced growth path if trend technical progress is confined to the market sector. As a country becomes richer, labour supply gradually declines, converging to a situation in which labour supply is zero, unless the intertemporal elasticity of substitution is unity. Chari, Kehoe and McGrattan (1998), for example, employ a preference specification with nonseparable consumption and leisure (which is fairly standard, for example, in the real business cycles literature). This preference specification is compatible with a balanced growth path and is also consistent with the high real exchange rate volatility that is observed in the data. A more elastic labour supply and a greater intertemporal elasticity of substitution in consumption generates more volatile real exchange rates. Hence, this preference specification provides more plausible implications for the short-run dynamics of several macroeconomic variables than the redux model and better matches some observed regularities.[8]

---

[7] Benigno (2000), Betts and Devereux(1999b), Devereux (1999), Doyle (2000) and Tille (1998a,b), among others, represent attempts to model explicitly international policy co-ordination in variants of the Corsetti–Pesenti model. See also Obstfeld and Rogoff (2000b).

[8] A further modification of the redux model considered by researchers involves the introduction of non-tradables in the analysis, which typically implies an increase in the size of the initial exchange rate response to a monetary shock; see, for example, Ghironi (2000b), Hau (2000) and Warnock (1999).

While the discussion in this sub-section has focused on only two issues with regard to the specification of preferences (the degree of substitutability of home and foreign goods in consumption and the separability of consumption and leisure in utility) the results of models with explicit microfoundations may depend crucially on the specification of the utility function in other ways. Relaxing the symmetry assumption in the utility function and allowing for nonseparable consumption and leisure, for example, would yield more plausible and more general utility functions. Of course, there are other important related issues and, in this respect, the closed-economy literature can lend ideas on how to proceed.

5.2.5   Financial markets structure

The redux model assumes that there is international trade only in a riskless real bond and hence financial markets are not complete. Deviations from this financial markets structure have been examined in several papers. Chari, Kehoe and McGrattan (1998) compare, in the context of their PTM model, the effects of monetary shocks under complete markets and under a setting where trade occurs only in one noncontingent nominal bond denominated in the domestic currency. Their results show that the redux model is rather robust in this case. In fact, incompleteness of financial markets appears to imply small and probably insignificant differences for the persistence of monetary shocks.

A related study by Sutherland (1996) analyses trading frictions (which essentially allow for a differential between domestic and foreign interest rates) in the context of an intertemporal general equilibrium model where financial markets are incomplete and the purchase of bonds involves convex adjustment costs. Goods markets are perfectly competitive and goods prices are subject to Calvo-type sluggish adjustment. Sutherland shows that barriers to financial integration have a larger impact on output the greater the degree of price inertia. With substantial price inertia, output adjusts slowly and more agents smooth their consumption pattern via international financial markets. Sutherland's simulations suggest that financial market integration increases the volatility of a number of variables when shocks originate from the money market but decreases the volatility of most variables when shocks originate from real demand or supply; these results also hold in the generalisation of Sutherland's model by Senay (1998). For example, a positive domestic monetary shock induces a domestic interest rate decline and, therefore, a negative interest rate differential with the foreign country. In turn, the negative interest rate differential produces a smaller exchange rate depreciation and a larger jump in relative domestic consumption. This implies that domestic output rises by less in this model than in the baseline redux model.

Obstfeld and Rogoff (1995) defend their assumptions regarding the financial markets structure of the redux model, stating that it would seem incoherent to analyse imperfections or rigidities in goods markets, while at the same time assuming that international capital markets are complete. Indeed, one may argue that if there were complete international risk-sharing, it is unclear how price or wage rigidities could exist. Nevertheless, the assumption of full international capital integration is very controversial. While many economists would agree that the degree of financial integration has increased over time (at least across major industrialised countries), it is perhaps fair to say that there are still important frictions in financial markets (see Obstfeld, 1995). Given the controversies over what may constitute a realistic financial markets structure, the analysis of the impact of barriers to financial integration remains an avenue of research in its own right.

5.2.6 The role of capital

The literature has largely neglected the role of capital in new open-economy models. For example, competitive models with capital can deliver effects of supply shocks similar to those typically found in monopolistically competitive models with endogenous utilisation of capital (see, for example, Finn, 2000). Chari, Kehoe and McGrattan (1998, 2000) also argue that capital (omitted in the redux model and most subsequent variants of it) may play an important role because monetary shocks can cause investment booms by reducing the short-term interest rate and hence generate a current account deficit (rather than a surplus, as in the redux model). Explicitly allowing for capital in new open-economy models is an important immediate avenue for future research.

5.3 Stochastic general equilibrium open-economy models

Recently, the certainty equivalence assumption that characterises much of the literature discussed above (including the redux model) has been relaxed. While certainty equivalence allows researchers to approximate exact equilibrium relationships, it 'precludes a serious welfare analysis of changes that affect the variance of output' (Kimball, 1995, p. 1243). Following this line of reasoning, Obstfeld and Rogoff (1998) first extend the redux model and the work by Corsetti and Pesenti (2001) to a stochastic environment. More precisely, the innovation in Obstfeld and Rogoff (1998) involves moving away from the analysis of only unanticipated shocks.

5.3.1 Risk and exchange rates

The Obstfeld and Rogoff (1998) model may be interpreted as a sticky-price monetary model in which risk has an impact on asset prices, short-term interest rates, the price-setting decisions of individual producers, expected output and international trade flows. This approach allows Obstfeld and Rogoff to quantify the welfare trade-off between alternative exchange rate regimes and to relate this trade-off to a country's size. Another important finding of this model is that exchange rate risk affects the level of the exchange rate. Not surprisingly, as discussed below, the model has important implications for the behaviour of the forward premium and for the forward discount bias.

The structure of the Obstfeld and Rogoff (1998) model adds uncertainty to the redux model. Most results are standard and qualitatively identical to those of the redux model. However, one of the most original results of this approach is the equation describing the equilibrium exchange rate. To obtain the equilibrium exchange rate, Obstfeld and Rogoff (1998) assume that Home and Foreign have equal trend inflation rates (equal to the long-run nominal interest rates through the Fisher equation) and use conventional log-linearisations (in addition to the assumption that purchasing power parity holds) to obtain an equation of nominal exchange rate determination. This equation may be interpreted as a monetary-model-type equation where conventional macroeconomic fundamentals determine the exchange rate. Also, this exchange rate equation is the same as in the redux model, except for a time-varying risk premium term. Under the assumption of no bubbles, the solution of the model suggests that a level risk premium enters the exchange rate equation. In some sense, this model may explain the failure of conventional monetary models of exchange rate determination in terms of an omitted variable in the exchange rate equation, namely, exchange rate risk (a similar result was obtained by Hodrick, 1989, in the context of a cash-in-advance flexible-price exchange rate model). For example, lower relative risk of investments in the Home currency induces a fall in the domestic nominal interest rate and an appreciation of the domestic currency, capturing the idea of a 'safe haven' effect on the Home currency.

For reasonable interest rates, a rise in Home monetary variability induces both a fall in the level of the exchange rate risk premium and a fall in the forward premium (the latter fall is shown to be much larger in magnitude). This result contradicts the conventional wisdom that financial markets attach a positive risk premium to the currency with higher monetary volatility. The intuition is explained by Obstfeld and Rogoff (1998, p. 24) as follows:

[A] rise in Home monetary volatility may lead to a fall in the forward premium, even holding expected exchange rate changes constant. Why? If positive domestic monetary shocks lead to increases in global consumption, then domestic money can be a hedge, in real terms, against shocks to consumption. (The real value of Home money will tend to be unexpectedly high in states of nature where the marginal utility of consumption is high.) Furthermore – and this effect also operates in a flexible-price model – higher monetary variability raises the expectation of the future real value of money, other things equal.

This result provides a novel theoretical explanation of the forward premium puzzle which we discussed in Chapter 2 – namely that the forward premium or interest rate differential appears to be negatively rather than positively correlated with subsequent exchange rate movements, contradicting uncovered interest rate parity. According to the Obstfeld and Rogoff (1998) analysis, not only should high interest rates not necessarily be associated with expected depreciation, but the opposite may also be true, especially for countries with similar trend inflation rates. This is clearly an area which would repay further theoretical and empirical research.

Nevertheless, the results produced by this model may well depend critically on the specification of the microfoundations and are, therefore, subject to the same caveats raised by the literature questioning the appropriateness of the redux specification. Thus, it is legitimate to wonder how adopting alternative specifications of utility, different nominal rigidities, etc., as discussed above, would affect the results of the Obstfeld and Rogoff (1998) stochastic model. The next sub-section discusses, for example, the changes induced by the introduction of PTM in this model.

5.3.2   Related studies

The Obstfeld and Rogoff (1998) analysis described above is based on the following assumptions: (a) that producers set prices in their own currency, (b) that the price paid by foreigners for domestic goods (and the price paid by domestic residents for foreign goods) varies instantaneously when the exchange rate changes, and (c) that the LOOP holds. Devereux and Engel (1998) extend Obstfeld and Rogoff's analysis by assuming PTM and that producers set a price in the domestic currency for domestic residents and in the foreign currency for foreign residents. Hence, when the exchange rate fluctuates, the LOOP does not hold. The risk premium depends on the type of price-setting behaviour of producers. Devereux and Engel compare the agent's welfare in fixed and flexible exchange rate arrangements and find that exchange rate systems matter not only for the variances of consumption, real balances and leisure, but also for their mean values once risk premia are incorporated into pricing decisions. Since PTM insulates consumption from exchange rate fluctuations, floating exchange rates are less costly under PTM than under producer currency pricing. Consequently, a flexible regime generally dominates a pegged regime in terms of welfare.

Engel (1999) makes four points in summarising the evidence on the foreign exchange risk premium in this class of general equilibrium models. First, while the existence of a risk premium in flexible-price general equilibrium models depends on the correlation of exogenous monetary shocks and aggregate supply shocks, the risk premium arises endogenously in sticky-price models. Second, the distribution of aggregate supply shocks does not affect the foreign exchange risk premium in sticky-price models. Third, given that the risk premium depends on the prices faced by consumers, when the LOOP does not hold there is no unique foreign exchange risk premium since producers set prices in consumers' currencies. Fourth, standard stochastic dynamic general equilibrium models do not usually imply large risk premia.

The common feature in these models is that the exchange rate risk premium is an important determinant of the equilibrium level of the exchange rate. It remains an open question whether one could build a sticky-price model capable of convincingly explaining the forward premium puzzle. Nevertheless, this seems a promising avenue for future research.

5.4   New directions

5.4.1   The source of nominal rigidities and the choice between local- and foreign-currency pricing

Obstfeld and Rogoff (2000a) may have again set new directions for stochastic open-economy models of the class discussed in this chapter. They begin by noting that the possibilities for modelling nominal rigidities are more numerous in a multicurrency international economy than in a single-money closed-economy setting and that, in an international setting, it is natural to consider the possibility of segmentation between national markets. Obstfeld and Rogoff then address the empirical issue of whether local-currency pricing or foreign-currency pricing is closer to reality. They argue that, if imports are invoiced in the importing country's currency, unexpected currency depreciations should be associated with improvements (rather than deteriorations) in the terms of trade. They then show that this implication is inconsistent with the data. Indeed, their evidence suggests that aggregate data may favour a traditional framework in which exporters largely invoice in home currency and nominal exchange rate changes have significant short-run effects on international competitiveness and trade.

The main reservations of Obstfeld and Rogoff about the PTM-local currency pricing framework employed by several papers in this literature are captured by the following observations. First, a large fraction of measured deviations from the LOOP result from non-tradable components incorporated in consumer price indices for supposedly traded goods (for example, rents, distribution services, advertising, etc.); it is not clear whether the extreme market segmentation and pass-through assumptions of the PTM-local currency pricing approach are necessary in order to explain the close association between deviations from the LOOP and exchange rates. Second, price stickiness induced by wage stickiness is likely to be more important in determining persistent macroeconomic fluctuations since trade invoicing cannot generate sufficiently high persistence (invoicing largely applies to contracts of ninety days or less). Third, the direct evidence on invoicing is largely inconsistent with the view that exporters set prices mainly in importers' currencies; the United States is, however, an exception. Fourth, international evidence on markups is consistent with the view that invoicing in exporters' currencies is the predominant practice (see, for example, Goldberg and Knetter, 1997).

Obstfeld and Rogoff (2000a) build a stochastic dynamic open-economy model with nominal rigidities in the labour market (rationalised on the basis of the first two observations above) and foreign-currency pricing (rationalised on the basis of the last two observations above). They consider a standard two-country global economy where Home and Foreign produce an array of differentiated tradable goods (Home and Foreign are of equal size). In addition, each country produces an array of differentiated non-traded goods. Workers set next period's domestic-currency nominal wages and then meet labour demand in the light of realised economic shocks. Prices of all goods are completely flexible.

Obstfeld and Rogoff provide equilibrium equations for preset wages and a closed-form solution for each endogenous variable in the model as well as solutions for variances and for utility. In particular, the solution for the exchange rate indicates that a relative Home-money supply increase that occurs after nominal wages are set would cause an overshooting depreciation in the exchange rate. A fully anticipated change, however, causes a precisely equal movement in the wage differential and in the exchange rate.

With this structure, Obstfeld and Rogoff derive welfare results on two fronts. First, they show that constrained-efficient monetary policy rules replicate the flexible-price equilibrium and feature a procyclical response to productivity shocks.[9] For example, a positive productivity shock that would elicit greater labour supply and output under flexible wages optimally induces an expansionary Home monetary response when wages are set in advance. The same shock elicits a contractionary Foreign monetary response, but the net global monetary

---

[9] These monetary policy rules are (a) constrained since they are derived by maximising an average of Home and Foreign expected utilities subject to the optimal wage-setting behaviour of workers and price-setting behaviour of firms described in the model, and (b) efficient since the market allocation cannot be altered without making one country worse off, given the constraints.

response is always positive. Also, optimal monetary policy allows the exchange rate to fluctuate in response to cross-country differences in productivity shocks. This conclusion is similar to the result obtained by King and Wolman (1996) in a rational expectations model where monetary policy has real effects because imperfectly competitive firms are constrained to adjust prices only infrequently and to satisfy all demand at posted prices. In the King–Wolman sticky-price model, it is optimal to set monetary policy so that the nominal interest rate is close to zero (that is, neutralising the effect of the sticky prices), replicating in an imperfectly competitive model the result that Friedman found under perfect competition. Under a perfect inflation target, the monetary authority makes the money supply evolve so that a model with sticky prices behaves much like one with flexible prices.

Second, Obstfeld and Rogoff calculate the expected utility for each of three alternative monetary regimes, namely, an optimal floating rate regime, world monetarism (under which two countries fix the exchange rate while also fixing an exchange-rate-weighted average of the two national money supplies), and an optimal fixed rate regime. The outcome is that the expected utility under an optimal floating rate regime is highest. This result is intuitively obvious given that optimal monetary policy in this model involves allowing the exchange rate to fluctuate in response to cross-country differences in productivity shocks. Fixed rate regimes would only be worthwhile if productivity shocks at home and abroad were perfectly correlated.[10]

The Obstfeld and Rogoff (2000a) model addresses several theoretical and policy questions, including welfare analysis under alternative nominal regimes. The assumption that nominal exchange rate movements shift world demand between countries in the short run, which plays a crucial role in the traditional Mundell–Fleming–Dornbusch framework, is shown to be consistent with the facts and can reasonably be used as a building block in stochastic open-economy models. Needless to say, this approach warrants further generalisations and refinements. In particular, note that the current account is shut off in Obstfeld and Rogoff (2000a) in order to avoid the indeterminacy problem discussed earlier. However, shutting off the current account makes the model less plausible from an empirical point of view since it distorts the dynamics of the economy being modelled.

5.4.2 Non-zero international trade costs

The new open macroeconomics literature to date has (implicitly or explicitly) assumed that there are no costs of international trade. Nevertheless, the introduction of some sort of international trade costs – including, *inter alia*, transport costs, tariffs and non-tariff barriers – may be key to understanding how to improve empirical exchange rate models and explaining several unresolved puzzles in international macroeconomics and finance. While the allowance of trade costs in open-economy modelling is not a new idea and goes back at least to Samuelson (1954) or even to Heckscher (1916), Obstfeld and Rogoff (2000c) have recently stressed the role of trade costs as a key factor in elucidating what the profession may be missing in explaining six puzzling empirical findings.

---

[10] Indeed, the results suggest that the difference between the expected utility under an optimal floating rate regime and the expected utility under an optimal fixed rate regime may not be too large if the variance of productivity shocks is very small or the elasticity of utility with respect to effort is very large.

The largely illustrative nature of the broad-ranging paper of Obstfeld and Rogoff (2000c) is such that in the analysis of most of the puzzles they consider they do not present a formal new open macroeconomic model incorporating imperfect competition and do not allow for price or wage stickiness. Nevertheless, their simple model shows how the addition of trade costs may help explain the trade home-bias puzzle, the saving–investment correlation puzzle, the equity home-bias puzzle and the consumption correlation puzzle.

The first four puzzles considered by Obstfeld and Rogoff are as follows. The trade home-bias puzzle, highlighted by McCallum (1995) is concerned with the fact that people seem to have a strong preference for consumption of domestic goods. The saving–investment correlation puzzle, noted by Feldstein and Horioka (1980), has to do with the small imbalances experienced by most major industrialised countries relative to saving and investment over protracted periods of time, suggesting a low degree of international capital mobility. The equity home-bias puzzle, first highlighted by French and Poterba (1991) is concerned with the fact that investors seem to have a strong preference for domestic equity in managing their portfolios, despite the rapid growth of international capital markets towards the end of the last century and a much expanded world market for equities. The consumption correlation puzzle, first stressed by Backus, Kehoe and Kydland (1992), is concerned with the observed low correlation of consumption across major industrialised countries.

With regard to the trade home-bias puzzle, Obstfeld and Rogoff show the existence of a theoretical relationship between trade costs and home bias in trade and derive the following nonlinear relationship:

$$\frac{d \log(C_H / p C_F)}{d \log \tau} = \frac{\tau}{1 - \tau}(\theta - 1) = \text{EHB}, \qquad (5.19)$$

where C_H and C_F denote home consumption of the home-produced good and the foreign-produced good, respectively; $p \equiv P_F / P_H$ with P_F and P_H denoting the home prices of the foreign good and the home good respectively; τ denotes 'iceberg' shipping costs ('iceberg' because a fraction of goods are presumed to 'melt' when shipped); θ is the elasticity of import demand with respect to price; $\frac{\tau}{1-\tau}(\theta - 1)$ is the elasticity of home bias (EHB). According to equation (5.19), in the absence of trade costs ($\tau = 0$), there is no trade home bias ($C_H / p C_F = 1$). However, the higher are trade costs (the closer τ is to unity), the greater the impact of a 1 per cent reduction in trade costs on home bias. For example, if $\tau = 0.25$ and $\theta = 6$ (regarded by Obstfeld and Rogoff as empirically plausible values), the elasticity of home bias with respect to trade costs equals 1.67. A relatively high elasticity of substitution could then explain a large fraction of the observed home bias in trade.[11]

Having established plausible trade costs as essential elements of their analysis, Obstfeld and Rogoff (2000c) then examine the Feldstein–Horioka saving–investment puzzle and show that trade costs can create a wedge between the effective real interest rates faced by borrowers and lenders, again with a highly nonlinear effect in that it manifests itself strongly only when current account imbalances become very large. Obstfeld and Rogoff argue that such incipient real interest rate effects keep observed current account imbalances within a relatively modest range and show that, empirically, countries with current account

[11] Obviously, $\lim_{\tau \to \infty} \text{EHB} = 1$.

deficits (surpluses) typically have higher (lower) real interest rates, as predicted by their theoretical argument. Using similar arguments, Obstfeld and Rogoff then provide similar nonlinear relationships that may also largely explain the equity home-bias puzzle and the consumption correlation puzzle.

In the context of more sophisticated models in the spirit of the new open macroeconomics, Obstfeld and Rogoff (2000c) claim that international trade costs should be essential in shedding light on two further puzzles in international finance, namely the purchasing power parity puzzle and the exchange rate disconnect puzzle, again through the introduction of some important nonlinearities.

The purchasing power parity (PPP) puzzle (Rogoff, 1996) was discussed at length in Chapter 3, and may be recapitulated here as follows. Among the studies which do report significant mean-reversion of the real exchange rate, there appears to be a consensus that the size of the half-life of deviations from PPP is about three to five years. If we take as given that real shocks cannot account for the major part of the short-run volatility of real exchange rates (since it seems incredible that shocks to real factors such as tastes and technology could be so volatile) and that nominal shocks can only have strong effects over a time frame in which nominal wages and prices are sticky, then the PPP puzzle is concerned with the apparently inexplicable high degree of persistence in the real exchange rate (Rogoff, 1996). Nevertheless, this PPP puzzle may be seen as just one example of the broader exchange rate disconnect puzzle, namely the fact that the exchange rate seems to be only weakly (except in the long run) related to virtually any macroeconomic aggregates (see Chapter 4). Notably, the work of Meese and Rogoff (1983) showed that conventional exchange rate determination models do not forecast satisfactorily the exchange rate and cannot beat even a naive random walk model; the literature following the Meese–Rogoff study has recorded only occasional success in providing good exchange rate models for forecasting purposes. Also, the study of Baxter and Stockman (1989) found that the transition to a freely floating exchange rate regime only led to a substantial upward shift in both nominal and real exchange rate variability but virtually no change in the distributions of conventional macroeconomic fundamentals.

With regard to the PPP puzzle and real exchange rate behaviour, the importance of transactions costs in generating important nonlinearities in real exchange rate adjustment were discussed at length in Chapter 3, so we can summarise that discussion here. Building on early suggestions of the importance of transactions costs in this context by, among others, Heckscher (1916), Cassel (1922) and, to a greater or lesser extent, other earlier writers (see Officer, 1982), a number of authors have developed theoretical models of nonlinear real exchange rate adjustment arising from transactions costs in international arbitrage (e.g. Dumas, 1992; Sercu, Uppal and Van Hulle, 1995; Sercu and Uppal, 2000).[12] In most of these models, proportional or iceberg transport costs create a band for the real exchange rate within which the marginal cost of arbitrage exceeds the marginal benefit. Assuming instantaneous goods arbitrage at the edges of the band then typically implies that the thresholds become reflecting barriers. Drawing on recent work on the theory of

---

[12] See Chapter 3 for further references.

investment under uncertainty, some of these studies show that the thresholds should be interpreted more broadly than as simply reflecting shipping costs and trade barriers *per se*; rather they should also be seen as resulting from the sunk costs of international arbitrage and the consequent tendency for traders to wait for sufficiently large arbitrage opportunities to open up before entering the market (see, in particular, Dumas, 1992). Overall, these models suggest that the exchange rate will become increasingly mean-reverting with the size of the deviation from the equilibrium level. In some models the jump to mean-reverting behaviour is sudden, whilst in others it is smooth, and Dumas (1994) suggests that even in the former case, time aggregation will tend to smooth the transition between regimes. Moreover, if the real exchange rate is measured using price indices made up of goods prices each with a different level of international arbitrage costs, one would expect adjustment of the overall real exchange rate to be smooth rather than discontinuous.

Clearly, in the presence of nonlinearities in the unknown true data-generating process of the real exchange rate, the half-lives recorded by the (linear) literature, forming the body of evidence which generated the PPP puzzle, may have been substantially exaggerated. An emerging empirical literature is, however, starting to use nonlinear models that can capture some of the implications of the theoretical literature on real exchange rate deter-mination under transactions costs (see Chapter 3). For example, Taylor, Peel and Sarno (2001) provide strong confirmation that the four major real bilateral dollar exchange rates among the G5 countries are well characterised by nonlinearly mean-reverting processes over the floating rate period since 1973. The estimated nonlinear models imply an equilib-rium level of the real exchange rate in the neighbourhood of which the behaviour of the log-level of the real exchange rate is close to a random walk, but which becomes increas-ingly mean-reverting with the absolute size of the deviation from equilibrium, consistent with the theoretical contributions on the nature of real exchange rate dynamics in the pre-sence of international arbitrage costs discussed earlier. Their estimated impulse response functions suggest that, because of the intrinsic nonlinearity of the models, the half-lives of shocks to the real exchange rates vary both with the size of the shock and with the initial conditions, implying that the speed of real exchange rate adjustment is much faster than the apparently 'glacial' (Rogoff, 1996) speeds of real exchange rate adjustment recorded hitherto.

The reasoning applied to the PPP puzzle may also be applied to the much broader range of puzzles related to the weak short-term feedback links between the exchange rate and conventional macroeconomic fundamentals, namely the exchange rate disconnect puzzle. As discussed in the previous chapter, for example, Kilian and Taylor (2001) suggest that nonlinearities in exchange rate movements induced by transactions costs may shed some light on why it is so hard to beat the random walk forecast of exchange rates.

Overall, the 'unified theory' of Obstfeld and Rogoff (2000c) helps elucidate what the profession may be missing when trying to explain several puzzling empirical findings using trade costs as the fundamental modelling feature, with sticky prices playing a distinctly secondary role. It is to be hoped that future research in new open macroeconomics will follow the suggestion of Obstfeld and Rogoff in making explicit allowance for non-zero international trade costs.

5.5 Summary and concluding remarks

In this chapter, we have selectively reviewed the recent literature on the new open-economy macroeconomics, which has been growing exponentially since the appearance of Obstfeld and Rogoff's seminal 'redux' paper in 1995. The increasing sophistication of stochastic open-economy models allows rigorous welfare analysis and provides new explanations of several puzzles in international macroeconomics and finance. Whether this approach will become the new workhorse model for open-economy macroeconomics, whether a preferred specification within this class of models will be reached, and whether this approach will provide insights on the development of better-fitting empirical exchange rate models are open questions.

Although theory in the spirit of the new open macroeconomics is developing very rapidly, there seems to be little effort at present to test the predictions of new open-economy models, and this is an area where further research might be done. If a consensus in the profession on a particular model specification is to develop, this theoretical apparatus has to produce clear estimatable equations.[13]

Agreeing on a particular new open-economy model is hardly possible at this stage. This is the case not least because it requires agreeing on assumptions which are often difficult to test directly (such as the specification of the utility function) or because they concern issues about which many economists have strong beliefs on which they have not often been willing to compromise (such as whether nominal rigidities originate from the goods market or the labour market or whether nominal rigidities exist at all). Achieving a new paradigm for open-economy modelling is, however, a major challenge which lies ahead for the profession. While the profession shows some convergence towards a *consensus approach* in macroeconomic modelling (where the need for microfoundations, for example, seems widely accepted), it seems very unlikely that a *consensus model* will emerge in the foreseeable future.

At present, because of the extreme care needed in their handling and their fragility in some directions, new open-economy models are perhaps more analogous to finely tuned, thoroughbred racehorses than workhorses. While highly valuable in themselves, further research is necessary to see if the breed can be made more robust.

References and further readings

Andersen, T.M. (1998), 'Persistency in Sticky Price Models', *European Economic Review*, 42, pp. 593–603.

Backus, D.K., P.J. Kehoe and F.E. Kydland (1992), 'International Real Business Cycles', *Journal of Political Economy*, 100, pp. 745–75.

(1994), 'Dynamics of the Trade Balance and the Terms of Trade: The J-Curve?', *American Economic Review*, 84, pp. 84–103.

(1995), 'International Business Cycles: Theory and Evidence', in T.F. Cooley (ed.), *Frontiers of Business Cycle Research*, Princeton, N.J.: Princeton University Press, pp. 331–56.

---

[13] Steps toward new open-economy macroeconometrics have recently been made, for example by Ghironi (2000c) and Bergin (2001).

Barro, R.J. and D.B. Gordon (1983), 'Rules, Discretion and Reputation in a Model of Monetary Policy', *Journal of Monetary Economics*, 12, pp. 101–21.

Baxter, M. and M. Crucini (1995), 'Business Cycles and the Asset Structure of Foreign Trade', *International Economic Review*, 36, pp. 821–54.

Baxter, M. and A.C. Stockman (1989), 'Business Cycles and the Exchange-Rate Regime: Some International Evidences', *Journal of Monetary Economics*, 23, pp. 377–400.

Benigno, G. (1999), 'Real Exchange Rate Persistence with Endogenous Monetary Policy', University of California, Berkeley, mimeo.

Benigno, P. (2000), 'Optimal Monetary Policy in a Currency Area', New York University, mimeo.

Bergin, P.R. (2001), 'Putting the "New Open Economy Macroeconomics" to a Test', University of California, Davis, mimeo.

Bergin, P.R. and R.C. Feenstra (2000a), 'Pricing to Market, Staggered Contracts and Real Exchange Rate Persistence', University of California, Davis, mimeo.

(2000b), 'Staggered Pricing, Translog Preferences, and Endogenous Persistence', *Journal of Monetary Economics*, 45, pp. 657–80.

Betts, C. and M.B. Devereux (1996), 'The Exchange Rate in a Model of Pricing-to-Market', *European Economic Review*, 40, pp. 1007–21.

(1997), 'The International Monetary Transmission Mechanism: A Model of Real Exchange Rate Adjustment under Pricing-to-Market', University of British Columbia, mimeo.

(1999a), 'The International Effects of Monetary and Fiscal Policy in a Two-Country Model', University of British Columbia, mimeo.

(1999b), 'International Monetary Policy Coordination and Competitive Depreciation: A Re-Evaluation', University of British Columbia, mimeo.

(2000), 'Exchange Rate Dynamics in a Model of Pricing-to-Market', *Journal of International Economics*, 50, pp. 215–44.

Blanchard, O.J. and K. Nobuhiro (1987), 'Monopolistic Competition and the Effects of Aggregate Demand', *American Economic Review*, 77, pp. 647–66.

Calvo, G.A. (1983), 'Staggered Prices in a Utility-Maximizing Framework', *Journal of Monetary Economics*, 12, pp. 383–98.

Cassel, G. (1922), *Money and Foreign Exchange After 1914*, London: Constable.

Chari, V. V., P.J. Kehoe and E.R. McGrattan (1998), 'Monetary Shocks and Real Exchange Rates in Sticky Price Models of International Business Cycles', Federal Reserve Bank of Minneapolis, mimeo.

(2000), 'Sticky Price Models of the Business Cycles: Can the Contract Multiplier Solve the Persistence Problem?', *Econometrica*, 68, pp. 1151–79.

Corsetti, G. and P. Pesenti (2001), 'Welfare and Macroeconomic Interdependence', *Quarterly Journal of Economics*, 116, pp. 421–45.

Devereux, M.B. (1999), 'Do Fixed Exchange Rates Inhibit Macroeconomic Adjustment?', University of British Columbia, mimeo.

Devereux, M.B. and C. Engel (1998), 'Fixed vs. Floating Exchange Rates: How Price Setting Affects the Optimal Choice of Exchange-Rate Regime', Working Paper No. 6867, National Bureau of Economic Research.

Dixon, H. and N. Rankin (1994), 'Imperfect Competition and Macroeconomics: A Survey', *Oxford Economic Papers*, 46, pp. 171–99.

Dornbusch, R. (1976), 'Expectations and Exchange Rate Dynamics', *Journal of Political Economy*, 84, pp. 1161–76.

Doyle, B.M. (2000), 'Reputation and Currency Crises (or "Countries of a Feather Devalue Together")', Board of Governors of the Federal Reserve System, Washington, D.C., mimeo.

Dumas, B. (1992), 'Dynamic Equilibrium and the Real Exchange Rate in Spatially Separated World', Review of Financial Studies, 5, pp. 153–80.

(1994), 'Partial Equilibrium Versus General Equilibrium Models of the International Capital Market', in F. Vander Ploeg (ed.), *The Handbook of International Macroeconomics*, Oxford: Blackwell, ch.10.

Engel, C. (1993), 'Real Exchange Rates and Relative Prices: An Empirical Investigation', *Journal of Monetary Economics*, 32, pp. 35–50.

(1999), 'Accounting for U. S. Real Exchange Rate Changes', *Journal of Political Economy*, 107, pp. 507–38.

Engel, C. and J.H. Rogers (1996), 'How Wide Is the Border?', *American Economic Review*, 86, pp. 1112–25.

Feldstein, M. and C. Horioka (1980), 'Domestic Saving and International Capital Movements', *Economic Journal*, 90 (June), pp. 314–29.

Finn, M.G. (2000), 'Perfect Competition and the Effects of Energy Price Increases on Economic Activity', *Journal of Money, Credit, and Banking*, 32, pp. 400–16.

Fleming, J.M. (1962), 'Domestic Financial Policies Under Fixed and Under Floating Exchange Rates', *International Monetary Fund Staff Papers*, 9, pp. 369–80.

French, K.R. and J.M. Poterba (1991), 'Investor Diversification and International Equity Market', *American Economic Review*, 81(2), pp. 222–6.

Ghironi, F. (2000a), 'Macroeconomic Interdependence Under Incomplete Markets', Federal Reserve Bank of New York, mimeo.

(2000b), 'U.S.–Europe Economic Interdependence and Policy Transmission', Federal Reserve Bank of New York, mimeo.

(2000c), 'Towards New Open Economy Macroeconometrics', Federal Reserve Bank of New York, mimeo.

Ghironi, F. and A. Rebucci (2000), 'Monetary Rules for Emerging Market Economies', Federal Reserve Bank of New York and International Monetary Fund, mimeo.

Goldberg, P.K. and M.M. Knetter (1997), 'Goods Prices and Exchange Rates: What Have We Learned?', *Journal of Economic Literature*, 35, pp. 1243–72.

Hau, H. (2000), 'Exchange Rate Determination: The Role of Factor Price Rigidities and Nontradables', *Journal of International Economics*, 50, pp. 421–47.

Heckscher, E.F. (1916), 'Vaxelkursens Grundval vid Pappersmyntfot', *Ekonomisk Tidskrift*, 18(2), pp. 309–12.

Hodrick, R.J. (1989), 'Risk, Uncertainty, and Exchange Rates', *Journal of Monetary Economics*, 23, pp. 433–59.

Jeanne, O. (1998), 'Generating Real Persistent Effects of Monetary Shocks: How Much Nominal Rigidity Do We Really Need?', *European Economic Review*, 42, pp. 1009–32.

Kilian, L. and M.P. Taylor (2001), 'Why Is It so Difficult to Beat the Random Walk Forecast of Exchange Rates?', University of Michigan and University of Warwick, mimeo.

Kimball, M.S. (1995), 'The Quantitative Analytics of the Basic Neomonetarist Model', *Journal of Money, Credit, and Banking*, 27, pp. 1241–77.

King, R.G. and A.L. Wolman (1996), 'Inflation Targeting in a St Louis Model of the 21st Century', *Federal Reserve Bank of St Louis Review*, 78, pp. 83–107.

Knetter, M.M. (1993), 'International Comparisons of Price-to-Market Behavior', *American Economic Review*, 83, pp. 473–86.

Kollman, R. (1996), 'Incomplete Asset Markets and the Cross-Country Consumption Correlation Puzzle', *Journal of Economic Dynamics and Control*, 20, pp. 945–61.

(1997), 'The Exchange Rate in a Dynamic-Optimizing Current Account Model with Nominal Rigidities: A Quantitative Investigation', Working Paper WP/97/07, International Monetary Fund.

Krugman, P.R. (1987), 'Pricing to Market When the Exchange Rate Changes', in S.W. Arndt and J.D. Richardson, *Real–Financial Linkages Among Open Economies*, Cambridge, Mass. MIT Press, pp. 49–70.

Lane, P.R. (1997), 'Inflation in Open Economies', *Journal of International Economics*, 42, pp. 327–47.
(2000), 'Money Shocks and the Current Account', in G. Calvo, R. Dorbusch and M. Obstfeld (eds.), *Money, Factor Mobility and Trade: Essays in Honor of Robert Mundell*, Cambridge, Mass.: MIT Press.
(2001), 'The New Open Economy Macroeconomics: A Survey', *Journal of International Economics*, 54, pp. 235–66.
Lucas, R.E., Jr. (1982), 'Interest Rates and Currency Prices in a Two-Country World', *Journal of Monetary Economics*, 10, pp. 335–59.
McCallum, J. (1995), 'National Borders Matter: Canada–U.S. Regional Trade Patterns', *American Economic Review*, 85(3), pp. 615–23.
Meese, R.A. and K. Rogoff (1983), 'Empirical Exchange Rate Models of the Seventies: Do They Fit Out of Sample?', *Journal of International Economics*, 14, pp. 3–24.
Mundell, R.A. (1962), 'The Appropriate Use of Monetary and Fiscal Policy for Internal and External Stability', *International Monetary Fund Staff Papers*, 9, pp. 70–9.
(1963), 'Capital Mobility and Stabilization Policy Under Fixed and Flexible Exchange Rates', *Canadian Journal of Economics and Political Science*, 29, pp. 475–85.
Obstfeld, M. (1995), 'International Capital Mobility in the 1990s', in P.B. Kenen (ed.), *Understanding Interdependence: The Macroeconomics of the Open Economy*, Princeton, N.J.: Princeton University Press, pp. 201–61.
Obstfeld, M. and K. Rogoff (1995), 'Exchange Rate Dynamics Redux', *Journal of Political Economy*, 103, pp. 624–60.
(1996), *Foundations of International Macroeconomics*, Cambridge, Mass.: MIT Press.
(1998), 'Risk and Exchange Rates', Working Paper No. 6694, National Bureau of Economic Research.
(2000a), 'New Directions for Stochastic Open Economy Models', *Journal of International Economics*, 50, pp. 117–53.
(2000b), 'Do We Really Need a New International Monetary Compact?', Working Paper No. 7864, National Bureau of Economic Research.
(2000c), 'The Six Major Puzzles in International Macroeconomics: Is There a Common Cause?', Working Paper No. 7777, National Bureau of Economic Research (forthcoming in B. Bernanke and K. Rogoff (eds.), *National Bureau of Economic Research Macroeconomics Annual 2000*, Cambridge, Mass: National Bureau of Economic Research and MIT Press.
Rogoff, R. (1996), 'The Purchasing Power Parity Puzzle', *Journal of Economic Literature*, 34, pp. 647–68.
Samuelson, P. (1954), 'The Transfer Problem and Transport Costs: An Analysis of Effects of Trade Impediments', *Economic Journal*, 64, pp. 264–89.
Sarno, L. (2001), 'Toward a New Paradigm in Open Economy Modelling: Where Do We Stand?', *Federal Reserve Bank of St. Louis Review*, 83, pp. 21–36.
Senay, O. (1998), 'The Effects of Goods and Financial Market Integration on Macroeconomic Volatility', *Manchester School*, Supplement, 66, pp. 39–61.
Sercu, P. and R. Uppal (2000), *Exchange Rate Volatility, Trade, and Capital Flows under Alternative Exchange Rate Regimes*, Cambridge: Cambridge University Press.
Sercu, P., R. Uppal and C. van Hulle (1995), 'The Exchange Rate in the Presence of Transactions Costs: Implications for Tests of Purchasing Power Parity', *Journal of Finance*, 50, pp. 1309–19.
Stockman, A.C. (1980), 'A Theory of Exchange Rate Determination', *Journal of Political Economy*, 88, pp. 673–98.
(1987), 'The Equilibrium Approach to Exchange Rates', *Federal Reserve Bank of Richmond Economic Review*, 73, pp. 12–30.
Sutherland, A. (1996), 'Financial Market Integration and Macroeconomic Volatility', *Scandinavian Journal of Economics*, 98, pp. 521–39.

Svensson, L.E.O. and S. van Wijnbergen (1989), 'Excess Capacity, Monopolistic Competition, and International Transmission of Monetary Disturbances', *Economic Journal*, 99, pp. 784–805.

Taylor, J.B. (1980), 'Aggregate Dynamics and Staggered Contracts', *Journal of Political Economy*, 88, pp. 1–23.

Taylor, M.P., D.A. Peel and L. Sarno (2001), 'Nonlinear Mean-Reversion in Real Exchange Rates: Towards a Solution to the Purchasing Power Parity Puzzles', *International Economic Review*, 42, pp. 1015–42.

Tille, Cédric (1998a), 'Substitutability and Welfare', Federal Reserve Bank of New York, mimeo.

(1998b), 'The Welfare Effects of Monetary Shocks under Pricing to Market: A General Framework', Federal Reserve Bank of New York, mimeo.

Velasco, A. (1997), 'Multiplicity and Cycles in a Real Model of the Open Economy', New York University, mimeo.

Walsh, C.E. (1998), *Monetary Theory and Policy*, Cambridge, Mass.: MIT Press.

Warnock, F.E. (1999), 'Idiosyncratic Tastes in a Two-Country Optimizing Model: Implications of a Standard Presumption', International Finance Discussion Paper No. 631, Board of Governors of Federal Reserve System.

6   Currency unions, pegged exchange rates and target zone models

In this chapter we discuss the operation of exchange rate regimes which contrast with the paradigm of a free float. In particular, we discuss research which has been done on exchange rate target zones, in which the authorities undertake to maintain the exchange rate within a pre-agreed target range or zone. Even further along the line from a free float, we also consider the case where countries effectively irrevocably fix the nominal exchange rate between themselves by choosing to use the same currency and entering into a currency union.

While the literature on target zones is relatively recent, dating from Williamson (1985), Williamson and Miller (1987) and Krugman (1991), that on currency unions has a much longer history, dating back to the seminal work of Mundell (1961), McKinnon (1963) and Kenen (1969). However, the general debate as to the desirability of fixed rather than flexible exchange rates has an even longer pedigree, dating back at least to Nurkse (1944) and Friedman (1953) and extending right up to the present day, and we provide a brief discussion of this in the next section, before turning our attention to currency unions and then target zones in the ensuing two sections.

6.1   Fixed versus floating exchange rates

The establishment of the International Monetary Fund at the Bretton Woods Conference of 1944 ushered in the post-war period of fixed exchange rates under what subsequently became known as the Bretton Woods system. That fixed exchange rates were chosen by the architects of the new international financial system reflects the prevalent view at that time in both academic and policy-making circles favouring such a system. Nurkse (1944), for example, argued that a system of floating exchange rates would be destabilising because of market psychology which generates periods of overreaction and bandwagon effects. Barely a decade later, however, Friedman (1953) produced his now celebrated apologia of flexible exchange rates by arguing – far from the case of irrational herding effects foreseen by Nurkse – that speculation would have stabilising effects in the foreign exchange market because agents who base their trading on anything other than sound analysis of economic fundamentals would quickly be driven out of business by the 'smart speculators' who do base their views on fundamentals. Effectively, therefore, Friedman argued in favour of flexible exchange rates by assuming a form of market efficiency.

170

In a highly influential paper, Poole (1970), focused on the criteria to be considered in making the choice between a monetary policy of interest rate targeting and a monetary policy of money supply targeting, thereby sparking a large literature (see, for example, Turnovsky, 1976; Boyer, 1978; Parkin, 1978; Genberg, 1989; Garber and Svensson, 1995). Poole shows – in the context of a Hicksian *IS-LM* framework – that the choice depends on the type of shocks – real or monetary – impinging upon the open economy. In general, the literature exploring the problem of choosing the optimal monetary and exchange rate regime is based on policy rules contingent upon the available, incomplete information on the underlying, unobservable *IS* and *LM* shocks to minimise a weighted sum of the variances of output and inflation. The conclusion advanced by this literature is that if the variance of the *LM* (*IS*) shock is significantly larger than the variance of the *IS* (*LM*) shock, then a fixed (floating) exchange rate regime is to be preferred. If there is no significant difference between the variances of the two shocks, however, a managed floating regime is the optimal choice.[1]

The problem of choosing the optimal exchange rate regime and the optimal macro-economic policy was tackled using a different approach by another large strand of literature which emerged during the 1980s, stemming from the original work by Kydland and Prescott (1977). This literature initially aimed at solving the problem of choosing an optimal and time-consistent monetary policy in a closed economy and then extended the analysis to the choice of the best exchange rate regime in the context of an open economy (see Persson and Tabellini, 1999). In general, the firmest conclusion of this literature is that government policy should be as predictable and credible as possible (see Barro and Gordon, 1983; Backus and Driffill, 1985; Rogoff, 1985). Rogoff (1985) argues that the optimal choice may be to appoint an independent, conservative central banker who does not share the societal utility function, but rather places a very large (virtually infinite) weight on inflation-rate stabilisation relative to employment-rate stabilisation – a conclusion that is entirely intuitive in a world with a long-run vertical supply curve or Phillips curve, so that expansionary monetary policy can have no long-run real effects. Alternatively, a central bank may enhance its reputation by pegging the exchange rate to the currency of a country with an independent, disciplined, conservative central banker and establishing a fixed exchange rate regime – thereby importing credibility (see Giavazzi and Pagano, 1988; Currie, 1992). Also, in these reputational models, a fixed multilateral exchange rate arrangement with other countries is expected to induce more discipline than a unilateral system because of the loss of reputation which would be incurred if the abandonment of the arrangement occurs.

6.2   Currency unions

6.2.1   *The theory of optimum currency areas*
Widening the domain of operation of a certain currency may yield similar benefits to those obtained in moving from barter to monetary exchange, particularly through the further

---

[1] The results are unchanged even when a vertical aggregate supply line and wage indexation are allowed for in the model.

elimination of transactions costs. Nevertheless, the relevant literature suggests that the global economy is not an optimal currency area.

The analysis that follows is based on what is called the 'theory of optimum currency areas'. This theory is due primarily to the seminal work of Mundell (1961), McKinnon (1963) and Kenen (1969), who especially focused on the cost side of the cost-benefit analysis of monetary integration. Mundell pointed out the circumstances that should be present for a currency union to be successful. He argued that (a) wage/price flexibility or (b) factor (labour and/or capital) mobility may represent adequate mechanisms capable of inducing automatic adjustments to idiosyncratic shocks to aggregate demand. If at least one of these two factors is present in an economy, no need to change the exchange rate arises for the authorities and the cost of relinquishing the exchange rate instrument by joining a monetary union (MU) is nil or at least very low. If neither (a) nor (b) is satisfied, however, and hence wages and prices are 'sticky' and factor mobility is not high enough, then shifts in demand facing one region relative to another will lead to unemployment and inflation differentials, unless nominal exchange rate flexibility is guaranteed. In this case, the loss of the chance of changing the exchange rate in order to offset the effect of demand shifts represents a significant cost for the countries joining an MU.

Nevertheless, this is not the only cost of forming an MU. Different preferences of countries towards inflation and unemployment make the establishment of a common currency costly (De Grauwe, 1975; Backus and Driffill, 1985). These differences, however, cannot be a serious obstacle to entering into an MU, if one accepts that countries cannot really choose an optimal point on their short-run Phillips curve – or at least cannot sustain such a position in the long run. That is to say, if advanced economies are characterised by a long-run vertical Phillips curve (LVPC), the output–inflation trade-off is illusory.

Also, differences in labour market institutions may induce a cost in an MU. This is because, with each supply shock, wages and prices may be affected differently, making it difficult to offset these differentials if nominal exchange rate flexibility is not permitted (Bruno and Sachs, 1985; Calmfors and Driffill, 1988).[2]

Another potential problem in MUs stems from the fact that differences in growth rates across countries may lead to trade balance problems for the fast-growing countries, whose imports tend to grow faster than their exports (under the assumption of equality of income elasticity of imports in all countries). In order to avoid this problem, there are two possibilities. Either a depreciation of the currency is operated by the fastest-growth country (not possible in an MU) or a deflationary policy must occur. In the latter case the growth process will obviously be constrained.

At least one other cost should be considered in the analysis: the loss of seigniorage. Differences in fiscal systems across countries induce governments to choose different combinations of debt and monetary financing of the government budget deficit. In particular, countries with an underdeveloped fiscal system find it easier to increase revenues by inflation

---

[2] This work suggests that strong nonlinearity exists between the degree of centralisation of the wage bargaining and the macroeconomic performance of a country. De Grauwe (1990) also provides empirical support for this idea.

(the so-called 'inflation tax') than by increasing taxes.[3] Effectively, the purchasing power of the seigniorage which the authorities enjoy is, through inflation, obtained through a tax on real money balances held by the private sector. This policy option is clearly precluded in an MU where control of the national money supply has been relinquished.

Some light can be shed on the issues just discussed by looking at the empirical evidence on the presence in the European Union (EU) of the traditional conditions required for an optimal currency area. As far as labour mobility is concerned, a particularly relevant study is due to Eichengreen (1990). He argues that both labour mobility and migration in the United States are much higher than within the EU. Theoretically, however, capital mobility is capable of substituting for labour mobility in absorbing idiosyncratic shocks. Mobility of financial capital is generally supposed to be very high between industrialised countries without exchange controls, as has been the case in Europe since July 1990.[4] However, what really matters is not just financial capital mobility, but also the mobility of physical capital. This is because, for shock absorption to occur within the European Monetary Union (EMU), it is not only necessary for capital mobility to offset differences between national savings and investments; private sector investment must also occur. Mobility of physical capital is generally higher within than between countries, because of the absence of exchange rate risk, similarity of regulations, common national features, etc. Feldstein and Horioka (1980) argue and produce empirical evidence to show that the correlation between domestic savings and domestic investment in industrialised countries is quite high, which can be interpreted as a sign of low international capital mobility. However, little correlation between the same variables is found within Britain, which implies perfect capital mobility (Bayoumi and Rose, 1994), and, very interestingly, savings–investment correlations in countries which were members of the European Monetary System (EMS) are found to be much lower than those of non-EMS countries (Bhandari and Mayer, 1990; Sarno and Taylor, 1998; Bayoumi, Sarno and Taylor, 1999). The latter result suggests that exchange rate stability may itself be effective in increasing capital mobility.

Nevertheless, physical capital mobility can only be expected to play the role of labour mobility in the long run, in the sense that it may be successful in reducing regional disparities across countries over time, rather than accommodating temporary shocks. This is because long periods of time are needed for the installation of plant and equipment and, therefore, even within the same country, flows of physical capital are often insufficient to induce (fast) recovery of less developed areas. Clear examples are the persistence of low income per capita in the south of Italy, the north of England, West Virginia in the United States and the maritime provinces of Canada. This makes it doubtful whether a

---

[3] There is also evidence, for example, that the southern European countries – Portugal, Spain, Italy and Greece – suffer this cost in a very acute form in the present European economic and monetary union (e.g. Dornbusch, 1988; Giavazzi, 1989; Grilli, 1989).

[4] The abolition of the remaining capital controls (July 1990) was the first stage towards EMU as envisaged by the Delors Report. The second stage (January 1994) concerned the creation of the European Monetary Institute (EMI), which in some sense represented the precursor of the European Central Bank (ECB). The third stage, which occurred on 1 January 1999, required the irrevocable fixing of exchange rates and the operationalisation of the ECB.

single currency union induces mobility of physical capital sufficient to offset (temporary and/or persistent) asymmetric shocks and to eliminate regional disparities.

Turning to the evaluation of the other condition required by the theory of optimal currency areas – i.e. wage/price flexibility – it must be said that it is now fairly common to assume that in advanced industrialised economies, wages and prices are somewhat 'sticky' in the short run and flexible in the long run.[5] This short-run stickiness may differ, however, across countries and in some cases it may be low enough to limit the importance of the use of the exchange rate as an instrument of adjustment.[6]

Overall, therefore, the literature is quite pessimistic concerning the desirability and sustainability of a European currency union, at least under the traditional criteria defined by the early literature on optimum currency areas. Nevertheless, some criticisms of the theory of optimum currency areas are worth considering and also the benefits of monetary integration have to be taken into account before giving a final judgement on the desirability of a monetary union.

First, demand shifts tend to be symmetric across countries and even more symmetric in an MU. The empirical evidence on the nature of the shocks hitting the Exchange Rate Mechanism (ERM) countries suggests that from 1982[7] onwards the ERM was effective in making the responses of member countries to shocks more similar. Indeed, since the 1970s, shocks hitting the ERM countries became more symmetric than shocks outside the ERM. The significant effectiveness of the ERM in making the responses of member countries to shocks more similar and elongated is consistent with the thesis that the reduction of real exchange rate variation has induced strong policy co-ordination among members (Bayoumi and Taylor, 1995).

A second criticism of Mundell's theory regards the implication that fast-growing countries may face trade balance problems. This is due to the fact that fast-growing countries typically experience fast-growing levels of imports. If these countries are not allowed to depreciate in order to make exports increase at the same rate as imports, then they may have to constrain their growth. However, the empirical evidence is generally against this view (European Commission, 1990): there seems to be no relation between economic growth and real depreciation. A feasible interpretation of this result, due to Krugman (1989), is that fast-growing countries have income elasticities of exports which are higher than those of slow-growing countries. Also, for fast-growing countries income elasticities of exports are typically higher than income elasticities of their imports. According to this analysis, fast-growing countries increase their exports at a rate compatible with their imports, with no need for exchange rate changes or for growth constraints. A second argument, which can be used to explain the lack of correlation between economic growth and real depreciation, is that the productivity of capital is generally higher for fast-growing countries. Therefore, given

---

[5] Implicit in the early literature on the theory of optimum currency areas was the assumption of fixity of prices and domestic output, at least in the short run.

[6] Bruno and Sachs (1985) provide evidence which suggests that Europe is quite close (and closer than the USA) to real wage rigidity, while the reverse is true for nominal wage rigidity.

[7] In fact, 1982 is generally considered by the literature as the year when realignment became less frequent and the start of a more credible, 'new EMS' (Giavazzi and Spaventa, 1990) occurred.

no exchange rate uncertainty, large capital flows coming from the slow-growing countries can offset the current account deficits of fast-growing countries, re-establishing equilibrium in the trade balance (De Grauwe, 1997). In conclusion, if this analysis is correct, no cost of joining an MU arises for fast-growing countries.

Another criticism of the theory of optimum currency areas stems from the idea that the exchange rate may not be effective in correcting for asymmetric demand shifts or that alternative policies may be used in place of changes in the exchange rate. De Grauwe (1997) shows this criticism to be invalid. Indeed, even if an alternative policy can be designed which produces the same final effect as an exchange rate change, the dynamics of the macroeconomic variables following exchange rate changes is quite peculiar and perhaps faster. Therefore there is little doubt that the loss of the exchange rate tool represents a significant cost for a country joining an MU.

A more important criticism stems from the literature on time consistency and credibility (Kydland and Prescott, 1977; Barro and Gordon, 1983). The crucial point emphasised by this literature concerns whether the exchange rate tool should be used in a discretionary way. For example, a devaluation does not turn out to be a flexible instrument which can be used frequently. This is because, when used once, a devaluation affects the expectations of economic agents in such a way that it is more difficult to use it successfully in the future. Also, nominal exchange rate changes can only lead to temporary real exchange rate changes (which also depend on the openness of the economy). Moreover, the empirical evidence suggests that the initial favourable effect of a devaluation disappears over time. By contrast, a devaluation can be very effective when it is perceived as an extraordinary event (for instance the Belgian and Danish devaluations in 1982). This suggests that, overall, in relinquishing the exchange rate instrument by joining an MU, a country suffers a cost, but this cost is probably lower than is assumed in the traditional analysis of optimum currency areas.

Also, the effectiveness of exchange rate flexibility is a function of the openness of the economy considered. For relatively open countries the cost of relinquishing the exchange rate instrument is lower (McKinnon, 1963). Alternative instruments (for example, fiscal policies) able to restore equilibrium in the balance of payments in response to shocks are less costly for a relatively open economy than for a relatively closed one. Therefore, the cost of the loss of flexibility of the exchange rate is a decreasing function of the openness of the country concerned (Krugman, 1990). Given the objective of price stability, very open economies are good candidates for participating in an MU. Masson and Taylor (1993) provide evidence that all of the European Union countries have a high degree of openness, while the European Union as a whole is a relatively closed economy. This suggests that European Union countries constitute an optimal currency area, under this criterion.

Extending now the analysis to the benefits of monetary integration, these are found mainly at a micro level, unlike the costs. They are primarily the elimination of transactions costs and of the risk due to exchange rate uncertainty. While the welfare gains from the elimination of transactions costs are quite obvious, the welfare gains from the reduction of risk due to exchange rate uncertainty are not. Uncertainty of exchange rate movements means uncertainty of future revenues of the firms, which represents a welfare loss for risk-averse managers and shareholders. Also the informational role of the price system is improved as long as exchange rate uncertainty is reduced. However, it must be noted that empirically there turns out to be no strong link between exchange rate uncertainty and economic growth (De Grauwe, 1997).

The benefits from an MU also increase with the openness of the economy. The greater is the volume of transactions in the common currency area, the greater is the cost saving, other things being equal. This implies that, as the openness of a country increases, a critical level is reached where the benefits offset the costs of joining an MU. The costs, however, are not the same for different schools of thought. From a Keynesian point of view, costs are higher than from a monetarist point of view. This is because for monetarists the exchange rate instrument is not considered an effective tool for correcting disequilibria between different countries in the long run, and so its loss does not matter too much. Moreover, Keynesians generally assume the presence of more wage and labour market rigidities than monetarists, which makes the exchange rate instrument an even more powerful tool. It follows that the critical level of openness of a country necessary for the benefits to exceed the costs of monetary integration and make desirable the participation in an MU is probably greater for Keynesians than for monetarists.

6.2.2   The credibility problem of exchange rate commitments

The main problem that a currency union faces is one of credibility. In the economic and monetary union, for example, the costs of disinflation are lower if the supranational authority is able to commit itself to price stability in a strong and credible way. If this is the case, a shift towards a more favourable short-run Phillips curve, due to lower expectations of inflation, may occur. The convergence of inflationary expectations and the stability of exchange rates are necessary conditions for success. In the European Monetary System (EMS), which was essentially an incomplete MU, national authorities of the Exchange Rate Mechanism (ERM) member countries had to show a strong commitment to exchange rate fixity and make it credible. However, as long as inflation rates had not fully converged, exchange rate fixity simply implied a continuous change in the real exchange rate.

Credibility of exchange rate fixity is a problem of all pegged exchange rate systems, and it is for obvious reasons linked to the cost-benefit analysis of relinquishing the exchange rate instrument. Economic agents realise that there may be future situations in which a change in the exchange rate would minimise the adjustment costs for an economy and therefore the incentive arises for the authorities to renege on their commitment. The credibility problem can only be solved if the authorities, in playing their game against the other economic agents, are really able to convince speculators that their only objective is the maintenance of fixed exchange rates, regardless of the costs induced by this strategy.

Also, recalling the Barro–Gordon (1983) analysis, differing government reputations (Backus and Driffill, 1985) and the way in which they are interpreted by economic agents may undermine the credibility of exchange rate commitments. This approach implies that, if a high-inflation country pegs its currency to the currency of a low-inflation country, it will have a serious credibility problem and the mere fixing of the exchange rate does not allow it to gain full credibility. This is because the gain from reneging and devaluing its currency – and hence the temptation to do so – may be perceived as very large. Moreover, given the assumption of rational expectations in the Barro–Gordon model, economic agents will adjust their expectations of inflation and prevent disinflation from occurring. The exchange rate commitment collapses. However, this approach seems too pessimistic. In particular, it does not explain why the ERM, despite the existence of credibility problems, survived and effectively paved the way for EMU. Indeed, the main framework of the ERM was such that the credibility problem was, at least partially, circumvented. The relatively large bands of fluctuation in the ERM, especially if compared to the tight bands of ±1 per cent in the Bretton Woods system, made it possible for the authorities of high-inflation countries to change the exchange rate by small amounts, without having to face speculative crises. Although this feature of the system still was not able to solve the credibility problem for countries like Italy in 1992, it contributed significantly to the survival of the ERM itself.

Some recent literature, challenging the conclusions stemming from the traditional approach to credibility given in the Barro–Gordon model, argues that a high-inflation country, when it commits itself to exchange rate fixity, faces different incentives from the case when it announces a reduction in inflation (letting exchange rates float freely).[8] In this line of reasoning, exchange rate fixity will lead to a lower inflation rate than the alternative policy of announcing an exchange rate target, if it can be accepted that the cost of a devaluation is higher than the cost of changing the announced target rate of inflation (see Giavazzi and Giovannini, 1989; Giavazzi and Pagano, 1989). This analysis is indeed able to explain the survival of the ERM and the birth of EMU: exchange rate fixity has imposed discipline on high-inflation countries, who are provided with large gains by credibly pegging their currency to the currency of low-inflation countries. The ERM did not induce significant monetary discipline in the first phase (pre-1982), probably because there was little credibility in the commitment of some countries. Notably, France and Italy devalued frequently until the middle of the 1980s, failing to import inflationary discipline from Germany. From the second half of the 1980s, however, both of these countries became more rigid in sticking to their commitment, even accepting high unemployment rates. At that stage the inflationary discipline of the ERM started to take off and the commitment to exchange rate fixity gained credibility (Giavazzi and Spaventa, 1990).

6.3 Exchange rate behaviour under target zone arrangements: the basic target zone model

Since the collapse of the Bretton Woods system in the early 1970s, most major exchange rates have not been officially pegged, but have been allowed to float more or less freely for the longest period in recent economic history. Many smaller central banks have adopted, however, policies of pegging their exchange rates to the major currencies and the Exchange Rate Mechanism (ERM) of the European Monetary System (EMS) involved member European countries pegging their exchange rates against one another within a pre-agreed range. A 'target zone' is a range within which the authorities are committed to keeping the nominal

---

[8] By contrast, in the Barro–Gordon model it is implicitly assumed that the incentives to renege are the same whether a reduction in inflation is announced or a commitment to exchange rate fixity is made.

exchange rate. The ERM is an example of a multilateral target zone, the theory of which has not yet been fully worked out. The best examples of unilateral target zones, to which much of existing target zone theory applies, were those pursued by the three Nordic countries outside the ERM: Finland, Norway and Sweden. Following some earlier work on exchange rate target zone models by, among others, Williamson (1985), Frenkel and Goldstein (1986), Williamson and Miller (1987), the seminal paper in this literature by Krugman, circulated since 1987, was published in 1991 (Krugman, 1991). Since then a substantial literature on this topic has appeared with remarkable speed.[9]

The basic Krugman model (Krugman, 1991) is expressed in continuous time and requires the application of stochastic calculus in order to derive a closed-form solution for the exchange rate. Consider a flexible-price monetary model of the exchange rate where equilibrium is assumed to be achieved instantaneously in both asset and commodity markets, expressed in continuous time by the following equations:

$$s = f + \lambda E(ds)/dt \tag{6.1}$$

$$df = \mu dt + \sigma dz. \tag{6.2}$$

Equation (6.1) is a simple flexible-price monetary model of the exchange rate of the kind discussed in Chapter 4, except that it is expressed in continuous time and we have grouped together all of the 'economic fundamentals' such as relative money supply and relative income into a catch-all 'fundamentals' term f. In turn, equation (6.2) states that small (infinitesimal) changes in f are equal to a known deterministic component equal to the time increment dt times a drift factor μ, and a purely random component dz, scaled by its own standard deviation σ. In fact, z is a particular form of stochastic process known as a *standard Wiener* or *Brownian motion* process. We can think of this as the continuous-time analogue of a random walk.

Under a free float, the authorities are assumed not to intervene and alter f at the edges of the target zone in order to keep s within the band. We can think of this as unsterilised intervention which directly moves the level of the domestic money supply and hence f. Thus, the expected rate of depreciation must be equal to zero and, from (6.1), the level of the exchange rate is determined simply by the level of the fundamentals and there is direct one-to-one proportionality:

$$s = f. \tag{6.3}$$

Thus, in a plot of the exchange rate s against the fundamentals, f, s would lie on a 45° ray (the 'free-float' line FF in Figure 6.1 below).

In the target zone model, however, the authorities are assumed to intervene and alter f infinitesimally at the edges of the band in order to keep s within the band between its upper

---

[9] Bertola (1994) provides a comprehensive and technical exposition of the target zone literature. Froot and Obstfeld (1991a, 1991b) give a rigorous presentation of the Krugman model, with several extensions and some analysis of regime shifts. Krugman and Miller (1992) also provide a critical assessment of the basic target zone model. Finally, Garber and Svensson (1995) and Svensson (1992) provide a more selective survey of the target zone literature.

and lower limits, $s^{\max}$ and $s^{\min}$ respectively. If the target zone is credible and the market believes that intervention will take place and be successful at the edges of the band, then this will affect crucially the solution to the model, as we shall see. To obtain a closed-form solution for the target zone model, we need to examine the properties of Wiener processes more closely and apply certain results in stochastic calculus and an important theorem known as Itô's lemma. We therefore turn to a brief digression on these issues.

6.3.1 A brief digression on stochastic calculus and Itô's lemma[10]

Consider a *Brownian motion* or *Wiener process* of the form

$$f(t) = \mu t + \sigma z(t) \tag{6.4}$$

where z is a *standard* Wiener process. Effectively, the value of f at time t is equal to a deterministic trend part, μt, which cumulates the drift in the process, and a purely random part, σz. The key properties of a standard Wiener process such as z are that it is continuous, with non-overlapping increments which are independent of one another, and for which increments in the process are normally distributed with a mean of zero and a variance equal to the distance apart in time of the increments:

$$z(t_2) - z(t_1) \sim N[0, (t_2 - t_1)]. \tag{6.5}$$

In fact, from (6.4)–(6.5) we can easily infer the distribution of increments in f:

$$f(t_2) - f(t_1) \sim N[\mu(t_2 - t_1), \sigma^2(t_2 - t_1)]. \tag{6.6}$$

Equation (6.4) is often written in its derivative form:

$$df(t) = \mu dt + \sigma dz(t), \tag{6.7}$$

which is the continuous-time analogue of a random walk with drift. Note that (6.7) implies $E(df) = \mu dt$, since $f(t_2) - f(t_1)$ tends to df as t_2 tends to t_1, and $E(dz) = 0$.

Continuous-time stochastic processes of this sort have a number of important and useful properties. For example, suppose we want to work out the value of $(df)^2$:

$$(df)^2 = \mu^2(dt)^2 + \sigma^2(df)^2 + 2\mu\sigma(dz)(dt). \tag{6.8}$$

Now, because $(dt)^2$ and $(dz)(dt)$ are products of infinitesimals, we can think of them as of 'the second order of smalls' and set them to zero:

$$(dt)^2 = 0, \tag{6.9}$$

$$(dz)(dt) = 0. \tag{6.10}$$

The quantity $(df)^2$, however, cannot be zero because, from (6.6), it has a non-zero expected value: the variance of an increment in z in the time interval dt, which is just the time interval

---

[10] We give only a brief and informal discussion of stochastic calculus here. For a more detailed treatment of these issues, see, for example, Dixit (1993).

itself, in this case dt, and hence:

$$E(df)^2 = \sigma^2 dt. \tag{6.11}$$

This result is due to the stochastic element of this branch of calculus. Even though $(df)^2$ is the product of two infinitesimal values, it has a non-zero expectation because f is a stochastic process and has non-zero second moments.[11] Equations (6.9) and (6.10), in contrast, each involve the product of two infinitesimals at least one of which, dt, is deterministic rather than stochastic.

Probably the most important result in stochastic calculus – the one that has rendered it so useful in economics and finance and very many other fields – is due to Itô (1951), and is known as *Itô's lemma*. Suppose we have a continuous, twice-differentiable function of the Brownian motion f, $g(f)$ say. Then if we take a Taylor series expansion of g around a point f_1, we have:

$$g(f) = g(f_1) + g'(f_1)(f - f_1) + \frac{1}{2}g''(f_1)(f - f_1)^2$$

$$+ \frac{1}{3!}g'''(f_1)(f - f_1)^3 + \text{higher-order terms.} \tag{6.12}$$

Taking the limit as f_1 shrinks towards f, equation (6.12) implies:

$$\lim_{f_1 \to f}[g(f) - g(f_1)] = dg$$

$$= g'df + \frac{1}{2}g''(df)^2 + \frac{1}{3!}g'''(df)^3 + \text{higher-order terms.} \tag{6.13}$$

Now, we have already seen that $(df)^2$ is non-zero because it has a non-zero expectation. Higher-order terms in df, however, can be set to zero since they are the higher-order products of infinitesimals. Moreover, from (6.6) we know that df is normally distributed and the moments of the normal distribution above the second moment are all zero. Hence, (6.13) collapses to:

$$dg = g'df + \frac{1}{2}g''(df)^2. \tag{6.14}$$

Equation (6.14) is Itô's lemma. This apparently innocuous result has far-reaching implications and, in the present context, allows us to obtain a closed-form solution for the basic target zone model, as we shall now immediately see.[12]

6.3.2 *Solving the basic target zone model*

Armed with our new tools, we can now solve the basic model, equations (6.1) and (6.2). Start by assuming that the solution is of the form $s = g(f)$, where g is a well-behaved,

---

[11] Note that the same would be true of dz, since it is also a continuous-time stochastic process, so that $E(dz^2) = dt$, although $(dz)(dt) = 0$.

[12] Itô's lemma is stated here without proof, although, intutitively, it can be seen to be related to a second-order Taylor series expansion, where certain cross-products and higher-order terms disappear because they are of the 'second (or higher) order of smalls'.

twice-differentiable function of f. Then by Itô's lemma:

$$ds = g'df + \frac{1}{2}g''(df)^2. \tag{6.15}$$

Taking expectations and using (6.2) and (6.11):

$$\frac{E(ds)}{dt} = g'\mu + \frac{\sigma^2}{2}g''. \tag{6.16}$$

Substituting (6.16) into (6.1), we then have:

$$s = f + \lambda\left(g'\mu + \frac{\sigma^2}{2}g''\right). \tag{6.17}$$

This is a second-order differential equation in g, which has a general solution of the form:[13]

$$s = f + M\exp(\xi_1 f) + N\exp(\xi_2 f) \tag{6.18}$$

where ξ_1 and ξ_2 are the roots of the quadratic equation in ξ:

$$\xi^2\lambda\frac{\sigma^2}{2} + \xi\lambda\mu - 1 = 0, \tag{6.19}$$

and where M and N are constant terms determined by the boundary conditions of the model.

To solve for M and N and hence for the model, we can apply the so-called 'smooth-pasting conditions', which entail that the permissible exchange rate path – in (f, s)-space – must 'paste' smoothly onto the upper and lower edges of the band. This result is quite intuitive: if the exchange rate path were simply to 'bump into' the edge of the band at an angle, traders would be offered a one-way bet, since they would know that the authorities would intervene at the edge of the band to bring the rate back inside the target zone. Because traders would start taking positions in anticipation of the one-way bet before it occurred, this would tend to work against the influence of the fundamentals as the band is approached; for example, a currency depreciating because of weak fundamentals will be bought near the edge of the band in anticipation of official support. Thus, the exchange rate becomes increasingly less responsive to movements in the fundamentals as the edges of the band are approached and, in the limit, the slope of the TZ line in Figure 6.1, which measures the responsiveness of the exchange rate to the fundamentals, tends to zero. Define f^u and f^l as the levels of fundamentals corresponding to the upper and lower bounds of s in the target zone, i.e. $g(f^u) \equiv s^{\max}$ and $g(f^l) \equiv s^{\min}$, and consider what happens when the authorities intervene, for example, in defence of the upper limit of the target zone. In particular, consider a point f^* in the neighbourhood of f^u where the authorities intervene by reducing the nominal money supply in such a way that f falls by a discrete amount equal to Δf. Hence, whenever the exchange rate gets to $g(f^*)$, the authorities intervene by a discrete amount Δf, resulting in the exchange rate becoming instantly equal to $g(f^* - \Delta f)$. As

---

[13] See e.g. Chiang (1984).

soon as s touches $g(f^*)$, then, traders face a riskless opportunity, since they can sell foreign currency just before the intervention and make a percentage profit equal to the difference between $g(f^*)$ and $g(f^* - \Delta f)$. The arbitrage opportunity is only eliminated if the size of the discrete intervention is known to market agents and the foreign exchange market is efficient, in which case:

$$g(f^*) = g(f^* - \Delta f). \tag{6.20}$$

Now suppose that intervention is not discrete but infinitesimal, that is authorities intervene at f^u so that s does not jump discretely, but moves by an infinitesimal amount which is just enough to keep s inside the band. Formally, we can let the size of the intervention, Δf, tend to zero. Dividing both sides of the arbitrage condition (6.20) by Δf, rearranging and taking its limit yields:

$$\lim_{\Delta f \to 0} \frac{g(f^*) - g(f^* - \Delta f)}{\Delta f} = 0 \tag{6.21}$$

which is the boundary condition on the first derivative of $g(f)$ or, in other words, the smooth-pasting condition:

$$g'(f^u) = 0, \tag{6.22}$$

where we have used the fact that $f^* = f^u$ when intervention is infinitesimal. By a symmetric argument with regard to intervention in support of the lower edge of the band, the other smooth-pasting condition can also be derived:

$$g'(f^l) = 0. \tag{6.23}$$

These two extra conditions then allow us to solve for the closed-form solution of the model completely:

$$s = f + \lambda\mu + A_1 \exp(\xi_1 f) + A_2 \exp(\xi_2 f) \tag{6.24}$$

$$A_1 = \frac{\lambda\sigma^2}{2\omega}[\exp(\xi_2 f^l) - \exp(\xi_2 f^u)]\xi_2 < 0 \tag{6.25}$$

$$A_2 = \frac{\lambda\sigma^2}{2\omega}[\exp(\xi_1 f^u) - \exp(\xi_1 f^l)]\xi_1 > 0 \tag{6.26}$$

$$\omega = \exp(\xi_1 f^u + \xi_2 f^l) - \exp(\xi_1 f^l + \xi_2 f^u) > 0 \tag{6.27}$$

$$\xi_{1,2} = -\frac{\mu}{\sigma^2} \pm \sqrt{\frac{\mu^2}{\sigma^4} + \frac{2}{\lambda\sigma^2}}. \tag{6.28}$$

The model is considerably simplified if we assume zero drift in the underlying fundamentals, i.e. $\mu = 0$, and symmetry of the target zone around a central parity normalised to zero, so that $s^{\min} = -s^{\max}$ and $f^u = -f^l = f^*$ (where we have implicitly normalised the fundamentals

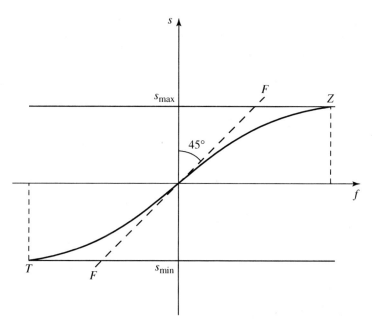

Figure 6.1. The basic target zone model.

so that $g(0) = 0$):

$$s = f + A[\exp(\xi f) - \exp(-\xi f)] \tag{6.29}$$

$$A = \frac{\exp(-\xi f^*) - \exp(\xi f^*)}{\xi[\exp(2\xi f^*) - \exp(-2\xi f^*)]} < 0 \tag{6.30}$$

$$\xi = \sqrt{\frac{2}{\lambda \sigma^2}} > 0. \tag{6.31}$$

Since no additional insight is gained by assuming a drift in the fundamentals or asymmetry of the band, it is more convenient to work with this simplified form of the model for expositional purposes.

We showed above that, in the case of zero intervention by the authorities, i.e. a free float, the relationship between the exchange rate and the fundamentals is simply given by a 45° ray through the origin, line FF in Figure 6.1. Line TZ in Figure 6.1 gives the solution to the target zone model, $s = g(f)$, or equation (6.29) as we have derived it. The smooth-pasting conditions are evident in Figure 6.1 by the fact that TZ pastes smoothly onto the upper and lower bounds of the target zone. As we have drawn the diagram, however, we have assumed that TZ generally is less steep than FF. This is implicitly due to an effect which economists have dubbed the 'honeymoon effect'. Intuitively, if s is near the top of the band (above the central parity) the probability is higher that the exchange rate will touch the edge of the band and trigger intervention by the authorities. Thus, the probability that the exchange rate will fall is higher than the probability that it will rise. Hence, market agents will bid the exchange rate below the level it would be at if there were no probability of intervention – i.e. s must lie below the free-float line. By a symmetric argument, when s is near the lower edge of the band, it must be above the free-float line. Thus, the honeymoon effect implies that a credible target zone is stabilising in the sense that the range of variation in the exchange rate will be smaller, for any given range of variation in the fundamentals, than the range which would obtain under a free float. This means that a target zone arrangement is particularly attractive to policy-makers because they can bring about large changes in the fundamentals – notably the money supply – in order to achieve domestic policy targets and still have a smaller range of fluctuation in the exchange rate than they would have under a free float.[14]

6.4   The empirical failure of the basic target zone model[15]

6.4.1   Testing the implications of the basic target zone model

The basic target zone model presented in the previous section has clear implications for exchange rates and interest rates as well as for their relationship with the fundamentals under target zone arrangements. These implications have been widely tested empirically on data for the European Monetary System, the Nordic countries, the Bretton Woods system and the Gold Standard. In general, these tests have rejected the basic model.

The basic target zone model has a number of strong, observable implications for exchange rates. A particularly important one is that the distribution of exchange rates within the band must display a U-shape, that is the exchange rate must be for most of the time near the target zone boundaries. This result simply follows from the fact that the exchange rate lies along an S-shaped function in (s, f)-space and, as a consequence of the smooth-pasting conditions, the exchange rate is inelastic to the fundamentals near the edges of the band. This implies that the exchange rate moves slowly near the edges of the band, where it should appear often. By contrast, the fundamentals move at a constant speed between the bounds and therefore their distribution is uniform.

The implication of a U-shaped distribution function for the exchange rate is, however, strongly rejected by the empirical evidence which, by contrast, suggests a hump-shaped distribution function for exchange rates operating under target zone arrangements, with most of the probability mass lying in the interior of the band and only a small portion near the edges of the band (see, for example, Flood, Rose and Mathieson, 1991; Bertola and Caballero, 1992; Lindberg and Söderlind, 1994a).[16]

The basic model also implies negative covariation between the deviation of the exchange rate within the band from the central parity, and the domestic–foreign interest rate differential. This follows from the honeymoon effect (s is expected to fall near the top of the band and rise near the bottom of the band) and from uncovered interest rate parity (the

---

[14] The term 'honeymoon effect' probably reflects a degree of cynicism, since for the honeymoon effect to be present the target zone arrangement must be fully credible, and the language suggests that this will only be the case when the arrangement is relatively new.

[15] The material in this section is also well covered in Svensson (1992) and Garber and Svensson (1995).

[16] From the same argument it follows that heteroscedasticity of the exchange rate is expected, with lower variability when the exchange rate is closer to the edges of the band.

expected change in s is equal to the interest rate differential), which is implicitly assumed since the model assumes market efficiency. However, the empirical evidence strongly rejects this prediction of the basic target zone model. According to the sample period considered, the correlation reported by the empirical literature is either not statistically significantly different from zero at conventional nominal levels of significance or, when significant, the correlation is generally positive (see, for example, Flood, Rose and Mathieson, 1991; Svensson, 1991a; Lindberg and Söderlind, 1994a).

A third (and indeed obvious) implication of the basic target zone model is that the exchange rate should display a nonlinear S-shape when plotted against the fundamentals. This has also been investigated in the empirical literature. Plots of the exchange rate against the fundamentals (variously defined), as well as more sophisticated tests, do not reveal anything resembling the predicted S-shape (Meese and Rose, 1990; Flood, Rose and Mathieson, 1991; Lindberg and Söderlind, 1994a).

6.4.2 Testing the assumptions of the basic target zone model

The two crucial assumptions of the basic target zone model, perfect credibility and the characterisation of official interventions as marginal, are testable individually.

Given the history of the European Monetary System and the frequency of realignment which occurred especially in the first phase of its existence, perfect credibility does not seem a reasonable assumption. Moreover, clear empirical evidence exists that many of the realignments were actually anticipated. In fact, the empirical literature stresses that the large interest rate differentials observed immediately before some of the realignments can be interpreted as evidence that investors demanded very high interest rates as a compensation for the anticipated devaluation of the currency (this was the case, for example, before the last devaluation of the French franc).

One way of testing the credibility assumption in a more formal way is to use a procedure proposed by Svensson (1991b), which consists of examining whether forward exchange rates for different maturities fall outside the exchange rate band. If this is the case for some maturity, under the assumption of perfect international capital mobility, the exchange rate target zone cannot be perfectly credible. In fact, if there were perfect credibility, there would be unexploited profit opportunities in the forward exchange market. The assumption of perfect credibility is generally rejected, using various testing approaches, by most of the empirical literature and for most of the exchange rate target zones examined (see Flood, Rose and Mathieson, 1991; Svensson, 1991b).

The other assumption of the basic target zone model, that central banks only use marginal interventions, is also strongly rejected by the empirical literature for countries on which data on intervention operations are available. Most tellingly, marginal interventions appear to represent the exception rather than the rule followed by central banks (see Giavazzi and Giovannini, 1989; Dominguez and Kenen, 1992; Lindberg and Söderlind, 1994a).

Overall, therefore, the basic target zone model is strongly rejected by the empirical evidence on the ground of the underlying assumptions and, not surprisingly, on the basis of its implications. Nevertheless, a rapidly developing and interesting literature, discussed below, has extended the basic target zone model by relaxing some or all of the underlying assumptions and therefore altering or softening in some way the implications of the model.

6.4.3 Direct tests of the basic target zone model

Direct empirical tests of the basic target zone model have also been performed, employing both parametric and nonparametric techniques and considering explicitly selected fundamentals. Pesaran and Samiei (1992a,b), for example, use a rational expectations model where the exchange rate is specified as a controlled price with an upper and a lower target zone boundary. Their model is parametric and estimation is in discrete time, in contrast to all the other contributions to the empirical literature on target zone models. Using monthly data for the French franc–German mark exchange rate and fundamentals of the type included in the monetary model for the sample period from May 1979 to May 1989, Pesaran and Samiei find that their model outperforms linear exchange rate models.

Meese and Rose (1990), however, employ the nonparametric methods of locally weighted regressions (LWR) (see Diebold and Nason, 1990) and use weekly data for the French franc and the German mark against the US dollar for the sample period 1899–1909 and daily data for the French franc and the Danish krone against the German mark for the sample period 14 March 1979 to 1 March 1989 and find results which support the model in-sample, but not out-of-sample.[17]

Other researchers do not specify explicitly the fundamentals in testing the basic target zone model. For example, Flood, Rose and Mathieson (1991) use a nonlinear model assuming a value of λ on the basis of previous studies and reject the basic target zone model using daily data for all the EMS countries and Euro-interest rates during the sample period 30 March 1979 to 16 May 1990.

Smith and Spencer (1992) test the target zone model using data for the German mark–Italian lira exchange rate from 14 January 1987 to 20 September 1989 using a sophisticated estimation method for the parameters of the model, via the method-of-simulated-moments (MSM) estimator. This method involves choosing parameters of the model so that the simulated moments of the model match the empirical moments. Their results provide evidence against the model. De Jong (1994) estimates the parameters of the basic target zone model using maximum likelihood estimation and the MSM estimator on data for a number of currencies. He finds significant nonlinearities for three of the six currencies considered. However, the target zone model in its basic formulation cannot explain the full observed kurtosis and conditional heteroscedasticity of exchange rate returns.

Koedijk, Stork and de Vries (1992) also allow for the presence of generalised autoregressive conditional heteroscedasticity, GARCH(1,1) errors in the MSM estimator, but they still reject the basic target zone model for a number of EMS currencies.

Lindberg and Söderlind (1994a) provide some supportive evidence for the basic target zone model using daily data for the Swedish krona and Euro-interest rates from 4 January 1982 to 15 November 1990, and employing the MSM estimator and the LWR nonparametric

---

[17] Pessach and Razin (1994) use ordinary least squares and instrumental variable estimation and find some support for the target zone model with Israeli data.

method. Even if their results are supportive of the target zone model in-sample, the performance of the model out-of-sample is, however, very unsatisfactory.

In two recent contributions (Iannizzotto and Taylor, 1999; Taylor and Iannizzotto, 2001) Iannizzotto and Taylor estimate a target zone model for several ERM exchange rates during the 1980s and early 1990s, by the MSM, taking account of the continuous-time specification by using daily data and allowing for the interruptions of holidays and weekends. Their work has several interesting implications. In particular, in contrast to much of the earlier empirical evidence on the basic target zone model, they generally obtain empirical estimates of the model's parameters which are statistically significant and plausible in magnitude, and they are unable to reject the model on the basis of specification tests. However, they find a very limited honeymoon effect. This is because the estimated value of λ is in fact very small, so that the *TZ* line is very close to the *FF* line. Assuming that a simple monetary-type model of the exchange rate is underlying the formulation, this parameter is equal to the semi-elasticity of money demand. Iannizzotto and Taylor are therefore able to check whether their estimates of λ are plausible by comparing them with estimates from the empirical money demand literature, as well as with what other researchers on target zones have deemed plausible. Their conclusion is that their estimates are in fact extremely plausible. This finding has at least three implications for the literature. First, the fact that a plausible parameterisation of the target zone model leads to virtually no honeymoon effect is striking, since the honeymoon effect has often been advanced as a rationale for introducing target zone arrangements because it implies that fundamentals may be manipulated to achieve domestic targets with relatively little cost in terms of exchange rate effects. The authors show, in fact, that in order to obtain the familiar S-shaped *TZ* curve of the kind illustrated in Figure 6.1 and displayed in most theoretical papers on the basic target zone model, one would have to assume an interest rate semi-elasticity of money demand some 100 to 200 times greater than those reported in the literature on money demand studies. Second, this work has implications for the empirical literature since, even under a credible target zone arrangement, there will be very little nonlinearity in the relationship between the fundamentals and the exchange rate, so that failure to find evidence of such nonlinearity may not be that surprising. Third, in a range of Monte Carlo experiments calibrated on their estimated models, Iannizzotto and Taylor show that the target zone model is also likely to induce little observable evidence of mean-reversion of the exchange rate towards the central parity, since, except at the very edges of the band, its behaviour is close to that of a freely floating exchange rate. The authors therefore caution against tests for mean-reversion as an indirect test of a target zone model or as an indirect test of the underlying degree of credibility of a target zone arrangement. Overall, this work is among the most favourable evidence in support of the basic target zone model and also explains why other researchers have failed to find supportive evidence. On the other hand, in suggesting that the empirical relevance of the honeymoon effect is slight, Iannizzotto and Taylor challenge an important element of the rationale for introducing target zone arrangements in the first place.

Notwithstanding this evidence, however, the overwhelming conclusion of the previous empirical literature on the basic target zone model was that it had performed badly and that it was therefore in need of modification.

6.5   Modifications to the basic target zone model I: imperfect credibility

Given the empirical rejection of the basic target zone model, a number of authors have sought to rehabilitate the model by modifying its underlying assumptions to allow for imperfect credibility of the arrangement, intramarginal intervention, sticky prices, and so on. If it is assumed that the target zone is not perfectly credible, a number of the empirical findings discussed in the previous section may be rationalised. For example, the target zone model predicts that the level of the exchange rate will be negatively correlated with expected depreciation within the band. If agents perceive a non-zero probability of realignment, however, so that the target zone is not perfectly credible, total expected depreciation will be the sum of expected depreciation within the band plus the expected change in the central parity. There is, however, no reason why the exchange rate should be negatively correlated with the expected movement in the parity – quite the opposite, in fact. Hence, incorporating imperfect credibility may explain the lack of strong negative correlation between exchange rates within a target zone and the interest rate differential. Svensson (1993) estimates confidence intervals for expected depreciation within the band from simple linear regressions of the exchange rate on the lagged exchange rate. He uses these estimates to show that, although the credibility of the EMS grew significantly over its period of operation, it was never perfectly credible in the sense of the realignment risk being insignificant for the majority of member countries' currencies.

In fact, a straightforward way to incorporate imperfect credibility into the basic target zone model is to assume that economic agents do not know for sure whether the central bank is going to defend the target zone. If we allow a finite probability that the target zone is defended, ϕ say, then a weaker version of the honeymoon effect materialises in which stabilising exchange rate expectations enter the exchange rate function (6.1) with probability ϕ and, therefore, the exchange rate equation inside the band becomes a weighted average of the free float and the perfectly credible target zone model. In turn, this implies that the exchange rate will be closer to the band margin for any given value of the fundamentals f than it would be in a situation of perfect credibility.

In order to incorporate imperfect credibility in the basic target zone model, the relevant literature has followed two different approaches. First, some researchers assume exogeneity of the realignment risk (e.g. Bertola and Caballero, 1990, 1992; Svensson, 1991c; Bertola and Svensson, 1993). Second, other authors endogenise the risk of realignment by assuming that this is a function of the position of the exchange rate in the band (e.g. Tristani, 1994; Werner, 1995).

6.5.1   Target zone models with exogenous probability of realignment

The key features of the family of models with exogenous probability of realignment can be seen as follows. Their central insight is that the smooth-pasting conditions (6.22) and (6.23) need not apply. To see this, recall that the smooth-pasting conditions are essentially conditions ruling out riskless arbitrage at the instant the exchange rate hits the edge of the band when the arrangement is fully credible. When the arrangement is less than fully credible, we now have to apply a similar 'no arbitrage' condition where the probability of a realignment is factored in. For concreteness, suppose that the strategy adopted by the central bank consists of successfully defending the central parity with probability ϕ and realigning to a new central parity with probability $(1 - \phi)$. The defence can only take place when the exchange rate hits its upper bound. If the target zone arrangement which prevails the instant after the exchange rate reaches this point – involving either the old parity with probability ϕ or the new parity with probability $(1 - \phi)$ – is perceived as fully credible, then the actual value of the exchange rate as it hits the edge of the band must be equal to its expected value an instant later, which will be a weighted average of target zone solutions of the kind (6.29), centred on the old and new parities and weighted with probabilities ϕ and $(1 - \phi)$ respectively.

One problem with this kind of model, however, is that the history of the ERM suggests that realignments do not occur when exchange rates approach the edges of the band, but rather in the interior of the band; that is, the timing of the realignment does not appear to depend upon the position of the exchange rate inside the band. Therefore, Bertola and Svensson (1993) build a model of time-varying realignment risk where the devaluation risk is introduced as an additional random variable by allowing for jumps of the central parity at the instant a realignment occurs.[18] They assume that the expected rate of realignment equals the difference between the interest rate differential and the expected rate of currency depreciation within the band. This method has been named by the literature the 'drift-adjustment' method to estimated realignment expectations, since the interest rate differential is adjusted by the 'drift' of the exchange rate within the band.[19] Using this approach, Bertola and Svensson (1993), for example, show that the deterministic relationship between the position of the exchange rate within the band and the interest rate differential becomes blurred in an environment of stochastic devaluation risk, therefore eliminating one of the implications of the basic target zone model which is rejected by the empirical evidence. The assumption that the devaluation risk is an exogenous stochastic process represents, however, a rather unsatisfactory modelling hypothesis from a strictly economic point of view and has induced other researchers to model the realignment risk in order to build more realistic target zone models.[20]

6.5.2 Target zone models with endogenous probability of realignment

Tristani (1994) and Werner (1995) present target zone models which endogenise the risk of realignment by stipulating that the realignment probability increases as the fundamentals deviate from the central parity. This assumption can be formalised into a relationship of the form:

$$E(dc) = \eta \frac{p}{w}(f - c)dt, \tag{6.32}$$

where c denotes the central parity (we previously held c fixed and normalised it to zero), w denotes the width of the target zone, η is a positive constant denoting the absolute size

---

[18] See also Svensson (1991c).
[19] The drift-adjustment method is empirically employed by Frankel and Phillips (1992), Lindberg, Söderlind and Svensson (1993), Svensson (1993) and Rose and Svensson (1995).
[20] See also Bartolini and Bodnar (1992).

of the realignment, and p is a positive constant scaling the probability of realignment. If we think of the probability of realignment for a given value of the fundamentals f as $(p/w)|f - c|$, which varies from zero when the exchange rate is at its central parity to $(p/w)|f - c|$ elsewhere in the band, this is consistent with (6.32). Define the deviations of the exchange rate and of the fundamentals from the central parities (in logarithms):

$$\widetilde{s} \equiv s - c \tag{6.33}$$

$$\widetilde{f} \equiv f - c \tag{6.34}$$

respectively. The expected variation of the exchange rate may be expressed as the sum of its expected rate of variation within the band and the expected rate of devaluation (revaluation):

$$\frac{E(ds)}{dt} = \frac{E(d\widetilde{s})}{dt} + \frac{E(dc)}{dt}. \tag{6.35}$$

Substituting (6.35) into the exchange rate equation (6.1) and using the identities (6.33) and (6.34), the following stochastic differential equation is obtained:

$$\widetilde{s} = \widetilde{f}\left(1 + \frac{\lambda\eta p}{w}\right) + \frac{\lambda E(d\widetilde{s})}{dt}. \tag{6.36}$$

Equation (6.36) can be transformed into an ordinary second-order differential equation by assuming that it has a continuous, twice-differentiable solution and thus applying Itô's lemma to calculate the expected change in the log-deviation of the exchange rate from the central parity. The general solution then emerges as:

$$\widetilde{s} = \widetilde{f}\left(1 + \frac{\lambda\eta p}{w}\right) + A[\exp(\xi\widetilde{f}) - \exp(-\xi\widetilde{f})] \tag{6.37}$$

where $\xi = \sqrt{2/\lambda\sigma^2}$. Clearly, equation (6.37) collapses to the solution of the basic target zone model under perfect credibility, i.e. when the parameter p is set to zero. As before, assuming that infinitesimal intervention is expected at the edges of the band, A may be uniquely determined by imposing the smooth-pasting conditions $g'(\widetilde{f}^u) = g'(\widetilde{f}^l) = 0$ for $\widetilde{f}^l = -\widetilde{f}^u$. Similarly to the basic target zone model, a negative value of A is obtained, again implying an S-shaped exchange rate function for the solution $\widetilde{s} = g(\widetilde{f})$. The slope of the curve (and hence the magnitude of the honeymoon effect) can, however, be crucially affected by the potential realignment probability; the curve is, however, always steeper than the solution implied by the basic target zone model. This is true even at the centre of the band, where the probability of realignment is actually zero. To see this, note that the slope of the solution curve in (s, f)-space is given by differentiating (6.37) with respect to $\widetilde{f}$ and setting $\widetilde{s} = \widetilde{f} = 0$:

$$\frac{d\widetilde{s}}{d\widetilde{f}} = \left(1 + \frac{\lambda\eta p}{w}\right) + \xi A[\exp(\xi\widetilde{f}) + \exp(-\xi\widetilde{f})]$$

$$\Rightarrow \frac{d\widetilde{s}}{d\widetilde{f}}\bigg|_{\widetilde{f}=0} = 1 + \frac{\lambda\eta p}{w} + 2\xi A. \tag{6.38}$$

Recalling that $A < 0$, this slope may clearly be greater than, less than or equal to unity because $\lambda \eta p / w \gtreqless |2\alpha A|$. Therefore, a high probability scale parameter p or a large potential size of realignment η can offset totally the honeymoon effect, to the extent that the permissible range of variation of the fundamentals may be lower for any given range of fluctuation in the exchange rate, relative to the range available under a fully credible target zone – or even that available under a free float. Intuitively, policy is in a strait-jacket because of the fear of triggering a realignment.

Another interesting feature of the model concerns its implications for interest rate differentials for different maturities, worked out analytically by Werner (1995). Werner shows that for instantaneous and short-term maturities, the relationship between the interest rate differential and the exchange rate inside the band is, in general, first increasing and then decreasing. However, the relationship may be always decreasing, for certain values of the parameters. For the long-term interest rate differential there should be no significant correlation. Werner also tests empirically some of the implications of the model on data for Italy, France, the Netherlands, Belgium, Denmark and Ireland and interprets his results as evidence supporting the model.

A problem with this family of models, however, is that the relatively steeper S-shaped solution curve implies an even stronger U-shaped empirical distribution of the exchange rate within the band, which is strongly rejected by the data. This problem may be solved by introducing a mean-reverting component into the process of the fundamentals. This may arguably be seen as representing a reasonable modelling assumption and approximating better the behaviour of the monetary authorities, who perhaps prefer to defend the target zone by intramarginal interventions, instead of marginal intervention. As noted by Svensson (1993): 'target zones are better described as being similar to managed floats with intramarginal mean-reverting interventions, with additional marginal interventions defending the target zone in the rare cases when the exchange rate reaches the edge of the band'. Thus, introducing a mean-reverting component in the process of the fundamentals may generate a hump-shaped exchange rate distribution, as suggested by Delgado and Dumas (1992), Lindberg and Söderlind (1994b) and Tristani (1994, pp. 10–11).

6.5.3 Empirical evidence on the devaluation risk

Theoretically, the extensions of the basic target zone model which relax the perfect credibility assumption suggest that exchange rate behaviour cannot be described by just one forcing variable, the fundamentals, but that another stochastic process must be considered, representing realignment or devaluation risk.[21] Hence, the relevant empirical literature tends to evaluate the weight of this second forcing variable by estimating the devaluation risk. As already noted above, the interest rate differential may be decomposed into two components: the expected rate of depreciation inside the band and the devaluation risk, and researchers have generally exploited this decomposition in some way. Overall, the empirical literature provides strong support for the presence of a significant devaluation risk. Some researchers estimate a non-stochastic devaluation risk (see e.g. Svensson, 1991c,

---

[21] A realignment must always involve the devaluation of one currency relative to another at the central parity.

who uses monthly data for the Swedish krona from 1986:2 to 1989:2). Weber (1992) also finds results supporting the existence of a significant time-varying devaluation risk using data on all EMS currencies and Euro-rates. Most studies, however, consider a stochastic devaluation risk, again finding strongly supportive evidence for the significance of the devaluation risk for a number of currencies and sample periods.[22] Overall, given the theoretical and empirical improvements obtained by the introduction of a second stochastic variable in the model, it seems that this may represent a promising avenue for future research.

6.6   Modifications to the basic target zone model II: intramarginal intervention

Another interesting extension of the basic target zone model considered by the literature is concerned with incorporating intramarginal intervention. Intramarginal interventions are empirically documented in Dominguez and Kenen (1991) and Lindberg and Söderlind (1994b). Incorporating intramarginal intervention into target zone models has the pleasing implication that it substantially reduces the impact of the smooth-pasting conditions. This is because, as the exchange rate approaches the edges of the band, the authorities are already known to be intervening. The perceived probability of hitting the edge of the band is, therefore, lower than under the basic target zone model, where intervention is assumed to be always at the very edges of the band, i.e. marginal. The probability of a riskless arbitrage opportunity occurring will therefore be lower and the slope of the curve relating the exchange rate to the fundamentals will be closer to a straight line, with smooth-pasting occurring only when the exchange rate is very close to the band. Thus, the presence of intramarginal intervention may explain why researchers have found little evidence of nonlinearities or the characteristic S-shaped curve (Lindberg and Söderlind, 1994b; Iannizzotto and Taylor, 1999; Taylor and Iannizzotto, 2001). Moreover, the introduction of intramarginal intervention into the basic target zone model also helps explain the fact that empirical distributions of exchange rates within the band are hump-shaped, with most of the observations in the middle of the exchange rate band, rather than U-shaped as predicted by the basic target zone model. In fact, the most reasonable explanation of the hump-shaped distribution of the exchange rate is perhaps exactly the fact that the exchange rate is kept in the middle of the band by intramarginal, 'leaning-against-the wind' interventions occurring in the interior of the target zone (see Garber and Svensson, 1995).

If we again define $\tilde{s}$ as the deviation from the central parity, $\tilde{s} \equiv s - c$, then the standard exchange rate equation (6.1) becomes:

$$s = f + \lambda \frac{E(d\tilde{s})}{dt} + \lambda \frac{E(dc)}{dt}. \tag{6.39}$$

---

[22] These studies include, among others, Chen and Giovannini (1992), Frankel and Phillips (1992), Caramazza (1993), Lindberg, Söderlind and Svensson (1993), Svensson (1993), Lindberg and Söderlind (1994b), Mizrach (1995) and Rose and Svensson (1995). See De Arcangelis (1994) for a detailed survey of this particular strand of the empirical literature on target zone models.

Subtracting the central parity c from both sides of equation (6.39) gives:

$$\tilde{s} = h + \lambda \frac{E(d\tilde{s})}{dt}, \tag{6.40}$$

where the drift is defined as the sum of the deviation of the fundamentals from the central parity, $\tilde{f} \equiv f - c$ and the product of λ and the expected rate of realignment:

$$h \equiv \tilde{f} + \lambda \frac{E(dc)}{dt}. \tag{6.41}$$

Now, we can develop some insight into what a target zone model with intramarginal intervention would look like by first developing a model of managed floating, in which there is no commitment to defend the bands of the target zone, but intervention is assumed to ensure that the expected rate of change (the drift) of the composite fundamentals towards the central parity is proportional to the deviation from the central parity:

$$\frac{E(dh)}{dt} = -\rho h, \qquad \rho > 0 \tag{6.42}$$

where ρ denotes the rate of mean-reversion. The solution to this model is:[23]

$$\tilde{s} = \frac{h}{1 + \lambda\rho}. \tag{6.43}$$

Figure 6.2 illustrates the solution to the managed-float model. As in the basic target zone model, the $45°$ line (FF) corresponds to the free-float exchange rate regime. However, under a managed float where intervention generates mean-reversion of the exchange rate towards the central parity, the model outcome is a straight line consistent with the exchange rate and the fundamentals moving proportionately, denoted MM in Figure 6.2, which is flatter than the free-float line since $(1 + \lambda\rho)^{-1} < 1$. Thus, even in the absence of a strict target zone, a managed-float exchange rate regime implies a honeymoon effect and a reduction in the expected volatility of the exchange rate relative to a pure free-float system. Clearly, the latter result is due to the mean-reversion induced by the central bank's intervention: whenever the exchange rate is above the central parity, for example, the currency is expected to appreciate (s goes down), which by itself leads to the reduction of the exchange rate.

We can now gain some considerable intuition as to what the solution would look like to a target zone model where both marginal and intramarginal interventions are used by the central bank. The solution to such a model is drawn as the TT curve in Figure 6.2: the curve is very close to the managed-float (MM) line, but it has a slight S-shape in order to meet the smooth-pasting conditions when touching the edges of the band, and there is a slight additional honeymoon effect relative to the managed-float regime because of the higher probability of intervention when near the edges of the band. Note, however, that once allowance is made for intramarginal as well as marginal intervention, the probability of the exchange rate actually touching the edge of the band and triggering marginal intervention will be small, albeit non-zero, implying that the additional honeymoon effect

---

[23] To check this, note that it implies that $E(d\tilde{s})/dt = (1 + \lambda\rho)^{-1}E(dh)/dt = -\rho h(1 + \lambda\rho)^{-1}$. Substituting this into (6.40) yields $\tilde{s} = h(1 + \lambda\rho)^{-1}$.

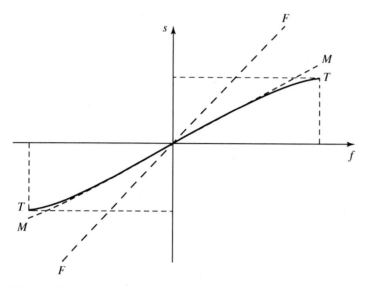

Figure 6.2. Intramarginal interventions.

and the deviation of the *TT* line from the *MM* line is quite small outside of the very close neighbourhood of the edges of the band, where the smooth-pasting conditions must apply (Garber and Svensson, 1995).

Overall, the implications of incorporating intramarginal intervention in the basic target zone model go a long way towards explaining the well-established stylised facts of exchange rate behaviour within target zones, in particular the apparent lack of marked nonlinearity.

6.7   Modifications to the basic target zone model III: price inertia

The extensions of the basic target zone model discussed above are still based on the flexible-price monetary model and thus also on the underlying strong assumption of continuous purchasing power parity (PPP). Given the widely reported rejection of continuous PPP, however (see Chapter 3), a logical, more realistic extension of the basic target zone model is to allow for some sort of price stickiness and short-run deviations from PPP.

The article which first introduces price stickiness in a target zone model is due to Miller and Weller (1991). Their model, which incorporates aspects of the overshooting model of Dornbusch (1976) into a target zone framework, consists of the following equations:

$$m - p = \kappa y - \lambda i \tag{6.44}$$

$$y = -\gamma(i - \pi) + \eta(s - p) \tag{6.45}$$

$$E(ds) = (i - i^*)dt \tag{6.46}$$

$$dp = \phi(y - \bar{y})dt + \sigma dz \tag{6.47}$$

$$\pi = E(dp)/dt. \tag{6.48}$$

Equation (6.44) describes the money-market equilibrium condition or *LM* curve; equation (6.45) is an *IS* curve relating the level of output to the real exchange rate $(s - p)$ and the real interest rate $(i - \pi)$, where π is defined by equation (6.48) as the instantaneous expected rate of inflation; equation (6.46) describes the UIP condition in continuous time; and equation (6.47) is a continuous-time Phillips curve relationship according to which price adjustment is sluggish but responds to deviations of actual output from the level of output consistent with full employment.

The model becomes deterministic if $\sigma = 0$ and displays saddlepath stability. The motion of the stochastic system, however, is more complex relative to the target zone models which we have examined hitherto. Solving equations (6.44)–(6.48) for dp and $E(ds)$ we have:

$$dp = \phi Z^{-1} [\lambda \eta(s - m) - (\gamma + \lambda \eta)(p - m) - (\kappa \gamma + \lambda)\bar{y}] dt + \sigma dz \quad (6.49)$$

$$E(ds) = Z^{-1} [(1 - \kappa \eta - \phi \gamma)(p - m) - \kappa \eta(s - m) + \phi \gamma \kappa \bar{y}] dt - i^* dt \quad (6.50)$$

where $Z = (\kappa \gamma + \lambda - \phi \gamma \lambda)$. Equations (6.49) and (6.50) may be rewritten as a system of two stochastic differential equations:

$$\begin{bmatrix} dp \\ E(ds) \end{bmatrix} = A \begin{bmatrix} (p - m)dt \\ (s - m)dt \end{bmatrix} + B \begin{bmatrix} i^* dt \\ \bar{y} dt \end{bmatrix} + \begin{bmatrix} \sigma dz \\ 0 \end{bmatrix} \quad (6.51)$$

where the coefficient matrices A and B are given by:

$$A = Z^{-1} \begin{bmatrix} -\phi(\gamma + \lambda \eta) & \phi \lambda \eta \\ 1 - \kappa \eta - \phi \gamma & \kappa \eta \end{bmatrix}, \qquad B = Z^{-1} \begin{bmatrix} 0 & -\phi(\kappa \gamma + \lambda) \\ -Z & -\phi \gamma \kappa \end{bmatrix} \quad (6.52)$$

and saddlepath stability requires the condition $\kappa \gamma > \lambda (\phi \gamma - 1)$ or $\kappa/\lambda > \phi - 1/\gamma$. For convenience, the model can be redefined in terms of the deviations of $(p - m)$ and $(s - m)$ from the long-run equilibrium of the deterministic system and hence (6.51) becomes:

$$\begin{bmatrix} dp \\ E(ds) \end{bmatrix} = A \begin{bmatrix} (p - m)dt \\ (s - m)dt \end{bmatrix} + \begin{bmatrix} \sigma dz \\ 0 \end{bmatrix}. \quad (6.53)$$

In order to find a solution to (6.53), Miller and Weller (1991) assume, for m constant, the relationship:

$$s = m + g(p - m) \quad (6.54)$$

and, applying Itô's lemma and the conventional rules of stochastic calculus, obtain:

$$ds = g'(p - m)dp + \frac{\sigma^2}{2} g''(p - m)dt. \quad (6.55)$$

Taking expectations of both sides of equation (6.55) yields:

$$E(ds) = g'(p - m)E(dp) + \frac{\sigma^2}{2} g''(p - m)dt. \quad (6.56)$$

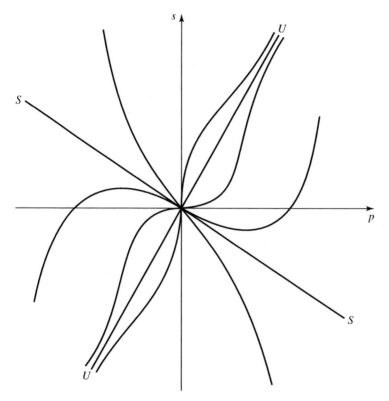

Figure 6.3. Stochastic solutions passing through the origin.

Using (6.53), (6.54) and (6.56) then yields the second-order differential equation:

$$\frac{\sigma^2}{2} g''(p-m) = [a_{21}(p-m) + a_{22}g(p-m)] - [a_{11}(p-m) + a_{12}g(p-m)] g'(p-m)$$

(6.57)

where a_{ij} denotes the element in the i-th row and the j-th column of the coefficient matrix A. The differential equation (6.57) does not have a closed-form solution, but a qualitative analysis of its implications can still be executed. Note that the only linear solutions to (6.57) correspond to the stable and unstable arms of the deterministic saddlepath, i.e. it is equivalent to setting $\sigma = 0$. Clearly, the solution corresponding to the stable arm of the saddlepath is the unique free-float solution, which also guarantees a stationary distribution for the exchange rate (see Miller and Weller, 1991). Simply imposing the condition $g(0) = 0$ gives an infinite family of trajectories passing through the origin, as shown in Figure 6.3, where m is set equal to zero for convenience.

Given that all trajectories are antisymmetric, the analysis may be performed by considering, for example, the two left-hand quadrants. In the region between the unstable saddle-path UU and the vertical axis, a typical path is first concave and then convex, approaching the UU curve asymptotically. The trajectories between the UU schedule and the stable saddlepath SS,

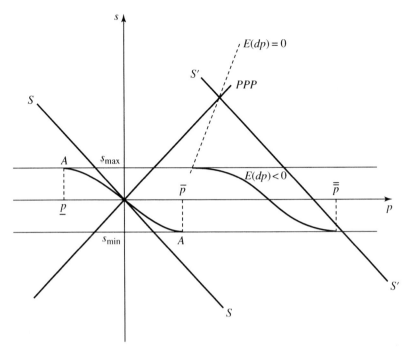

Figure 6.4. Sliding along the band.

however, are first convex and then concave, again converging to the UU line asymptotically. Finally the trajectories between the SS line and the vertical axis are all concave.

Next, it is interesting to identify the relevant set of trajectories when we assume a nominal band for the exchange rate positioned symmetrically about long-run equilibrium.[24] Assume that the exchange rate band – say $[s^{\min}, s^{\max}]$ – is fully credible and consider the model with price inertia (6.44)–(6.48), where infinitesimal monetary intervention is used by the monetary authorities in order to keep the exchange rate inside the band. As usual, the solution to (6.57) is found by imposing two boundary conditions, which obviously are the smooth-pasting conditions. Even if it is not possible to find a closed-form solution for the exchange rate, the main features of the stochastic system may be determined, again using topological analysis.

The dynamic behaviour of the system is depicted in Figure 6.4. From the system of stochastic differential equations (6.53) the $E(ds)/dt = 0$ and $dp/dt = 0$ (UU) schedules may be rewritten as:

$$s = \left(\frac{\kappa\eta + \phi\gamma - 1}{\kappa\eta}\right)p + \left(\frac{1 - \phi\gamma}{\kappa\eta}\right)m \tag{6.58}$$

$$s = -\left(\frac{1 + \gamma}{\lambda\eta}\right)p + \left(\frac{2\lambda\eta + \gamma}{\lambda\eta}\right)m - \left(\frac{Z\sigma}{\phi\lambda\eta}\right)\frac{dz}{dt} \tag{6.59}$$

---

[24] Miller and Weller (1991) also examine the implications of a real exchange rate band. For brevity, however, we only describe the analysis with a nominal exchange rate band here.

with the following slopes:

$$\frac{ds}{dp}\bigg|_{E(ds)/dt=0} = \left(\frac{\kappa\eta + \phi\gamma - 1}{\kappa\eta}\right) \tag{6.60}$$

$$\frac{ds}{dp}\bigg|_{dp/dt=0} = -\left(\frac{1+\gamma}{\lambda\eta}\right). \tag{6.61}$$

The nature of the solutions, obtained by numerical methods, for an overshooting exchange rate is shown in Figure 6.4, where the $E(ds)/dt = 0$ schedule is flatter than the $dp/dt = 0$ schedule. The condition $\kappa\eta + \phi\gamma < 1$ corresponds to the scenario of the Dornbusch (1976) overshooting model in which the $E(ds)/dt = 0$ curve slopes downwards. Points to the left (right) of the $E(ds)/dt = 0$ schedule represent situations in which the domestic interest rate is negative (positive), i.e. an expected appreciation (depreciation) of the domestic currency is necessary for the UIP condition (6.46) to hold. The $dp/dt = 0$ schedule represents situations in which the real exchange rate associated with equilibrium in the goods market is constant and has a positive slope.[25] The free-float saddlepath depicted in Figure 6.4 hits the exchange rate boundaries at an angle, so is not a feasible target zone saddlepath since it does not satisfy smooth-pasting. There is, however, a unique saddlepath that is tangent to the boundaries of the target zone, obviously passing through the origin; this is the AA line. The main implication of the AA line is that, as in the basic target zone model, imposing currency bands induces less volatile exchange rates as an effect of the credible expectation of central bank intervention.[26] Note also that Miller and Weller (1991) show that sustaining a nominal band by infinitesimal intervention is found – in the model (6.44)–(6.48) – to change the shape of the S-shaped curve inside the band.

Also, note that when, for example, the exchange rate hits the lower edge of the band and hence the monetary authorities increase the money supply in order to keep the exchange rate inside the band, the equilibrium point will move up the 45° line and the S-curve will shift to the right. Any reverse shocks to prices move the exchange rate into the interior of the band on the new S-shaped curve. The exchange rate remains on this curve until it again hits the edge of the band.

Sutherland (1994) determines the testable implications of the sticky-price target zone model in order to test whether the assumption of perfect price flexibility explains the apparent empirical failure of target zone models. Sutherland's results are encouraging. First, while the perfectly credible flexible-price target zone model implies a U-shaped distribution function of the exchange rate within the band, the distribution function for the credible sticky-price model is ambiguous since it is determined by two opposing forces.[27] Similarly to the basic target zone model, expectations about marginal central bank intervention induce

---

[25] Points to the left (right) of the dp/dt schedule represent situations of excess demand (supply).

[26] Miller and Weller (1991) also analyse the implications of introducing a non-zero probability of realignment in a sticky-price target zone model of this type.

[27] For a detailed, technical description of the methods for deriving the unconditional probability distribution function of the exchange rates as well as of the fundamentals, see Harrison (1985), Karatzas and Shreve (1988), Dixit (1993) or Bertola (1994).

the distribution function to follow a U-shape but the mean-reversion of the price level generated by disequilibria in the goods market also induces a tendency towards a hump-shaped density function. Therefore, the distribution functions of the exchange rate implied by the target zone model in the sticky-price formulation are relatively more consistent with the distributions suggested by the EMS exchange rate data. Second, the sticky-price target zone model predicts very different behaviour from the flexible-price model for the real exchange rate and the real interest rate, while offering nearly the same predictions for the nominal exchange rates and interest rates as the flexible-price target zone model. Third, the sticky-price model does not predict a deterministic relationship between the interest rate differential and the position of the exchange rate within the band, unlike the flexible-price version of the target zone model. Overall, therefore, Sutherland concludes that the sticky-price version can explain a broader range of empirical features than the flexible-price target zone model and should be preferred by researchers.

Beetsma and van der Ploeg (1994) extend the framework of Miller and Weller (1991) by building a model based on a stochastic version of the Dornbusch (1976) overshooting model with shocks to aggregate supply. They add three realistic features to the basic target zone model. First, they allow for imperfect substitutability in consumption between home and foreign goods, thereby effectively relaxing the assumption of continuous PPP. Second, they also allow for sluggishness in adjustment prices and wages. Third, they consider both marginal and intramarginal interventions in the foreign exchange market.

The rationale behind their model is that, given a unique relationship between the exchange rate and the fundamentals, there are two factors which can explain the hump-shaped exchange rate distribution suggested by the empirical evidence: the shape of the exchange rate solution in terms of the fundamentals (which is, in fact, the basis of the explanation provided by Bertola and Caballero, 1992) and mean-reversion in the fundamentals. Beetsma and Van der Ploeg explain the hump-shaped distribution of the exchange rate on the basis of both these factors. In particular, they allow for central bank intervention within the band in the form of a feedback rule for changes in the price level:

$$m = \overline{m} + \chi p, \qquad (6.62)$$

where $\overline{m}$ denotes a discretionary policy variable which is activated when the exchange rate is at the target zone boundaries and χ measures the degree of intramarginal intervention of the central bank in response to price changes within the band. Note that the Miller and Weller (1991) model is nested in the Beetsma and Van der Ploeg model, in that setting $\chi = 0$ makes the latter model collapse exactly to the Miller and Weller form. According to (6.62), in the case of perfect monetary accommodation ($\chi = 1$) the central bank always responds to price shocks by using monetary policy, thus achieving perfect stabilisation of the real exchange rate (PPP also holds). Nevertheless, in a case of underaccommodation, when $\chi < 1$ (overaccommodation, when $\chi > 1$), a positive price change always induces an underproportionate (overproportionate) adjustment in the nominal money supply, therefore reducing (increasing) real money balances. A negative value of χ also represents a feasible case, and implies, for example, that the central bank reacts to a rise in the price level by reducing the money supply, that is the central bank uses intramarginal intervention for 'leaning against the wind'.[28]

In contrast to the Miller and Weller (1991) model, the model of Beetsma and van der Ploeg (1994) has clearer implications for the implied exchange rate density function. Either a hump-shaped or a U-shaped distribution may be obtained, depending on the degree of marginal intervention, i.e. on the value of χ. In fact, Beetsma and Van der Ploeg (1994) show that the mean-reversion introduced by the sluggish adjustment of prices and wages combined with a certain degree of intramarginal intervention can generate a hump-shaped exchange rate distribution and that the hump shape is more likely to arise 'when the degree of monetary accommodation is close to what is needed to peg the nominal exchange rate' – i.e. when the fundamentals must deviate a great deal from their mean value for the exchange rate to approach the boundaries. The conclusion of Beetsma and Van der Ploeg (1994) is, therefore, that the observed hump-shaped distributions of several EMS exchange rates are likely to be caused by the significant use of intramarginal, not just marginal, intervention.

6.8   Summary and concluding remarks

We began this chapter by briefly analysing the problem of choosing the optimal exchange rate regime. In Section 6.2 we outlined and critically evaluated the traditional cost-benefit analysis of a currency union according to the theory of optimum currency areas. A large part of the chapter was devoted to the description of the literature on target zone models, starting with the seminal paper of Krugman (1991) and the basic target zone model. In Section 6.3 we described the underlying assumptions and the analytical derivation of the basic target zone model, illustrating the main results of the 'honeymoon effect' (credible target zones are inherently stabilising in the sense that they allow a wider range of variation for the fundamentals for any given range of variation of the exchange rate) and 'smooth-pasting' (the exchange rate is highly insensitive to the fundamentals when the exchange rate is close to the edges of the band). In Section 6.4 we also described the empirical implications of the basic target zone model for exchange rate behaviour and for interest rate differentials and surveyed the empirical evidence on the assumptions, implications and direct tests of the basic target zone model.

Given the widespread rejection of the basic target zone model, a theoretical literature has developed more realistic versions of the target zone model. In particular, some studies – described in Section 6.5 – have relaxed the unrealistic assumption of perfect credibility and allowed for a non-zero probability of realignment. Other researchers have allowed for intramarginal exchange rate intervention, in addition to the marginal intervention assumed in the basic target zone model; this literature was dealt with in Section 6.6. Another strand of the theoretical literature, described in Section 6.7, has introduced price stickiness in the basic target zone model, which becomes a stochastic version of the overshooting exchange rate model. All of these extensions of the basic target zone model enable us to improve the realism of the implications of the model for exchange rates, interest rate differentials and

---

[28] Given the assumption of perfect substitutability of foreign and domestic assets, all intramarginal interventions considered are non-sterilised.

the distribution of the exchange rate implied by the model, as well as the realism of the underlying assumptions.

Nevertheless, much work has still to be done in this area. The models are still rather simple and there is certainly scope for more realistic intervention policies, such as explicit exchange rate and interest rate smoothing. Also the theory of multilateral target zones has not yet been worked out (see, however, Jorgenson and Mikkelsen, 1996) and a number of normative issues remain unsolved and controversial, including the identification of the conditions under which a fixed or a pegged exchange rate regime is to be preferred to a floating exchange rate regime, or the optimal width of the band of a target zone.

Moreover, virtually all of the target zone models considered by the literature have the common feature that exchange rates are determined by the path of current fundamentals and the expectations of rational agents. In any case, as our discussion of the empirical evidence of foreign exchange market efficiency in Chapter 2 showed, the simple efficient markets hypothesis is strongly rejected by the data. Yet this is an implicit assumption of virtually all target zone models. In addition, the target zone literature tends to assume either an underlying flexible-price monetary exchange rate model, or else an underlying modified, sticky-price monetary model. But as our discussion of the empirical evidence on exchange rate models in Chapter 4 showed, the flexible-price monetary model is strongly rejected by the data and there is no overwhelming empirical support for a sticky-price monetary model. Indeed, as Krugman and Miller (1993) point out, it is somewhat ironic that assumptions such as these should be made in the target zone literature when in the past policy-makers have been willing to enter into target zone arrangements precisely because of their scepticism concerning the efficiency of the foreign exchange market and the rationality of market participants. A possible fruitful avenue for future research might therefore involve the analysis of target zone arrangements with allowance for heterogeneous agents.[29]

Appendix A.   The method of simulated moments

Direct econometric estimation of the basic target zone model has been attempted with the method of simulated moments (MSM) for both ERM currencies (Smith and Spencer, 1991; De Jong, 1994; Iannizzotto and Taylor, 1999; Taylor and Iannizzotto, 2001) and the Nordic target zone (Lindberg and Söderlind, 1994). The MSM is convenient in that it provides a way of circumventing the problem of a vaguely defined, possibly very complicated fundamentals term. The MSM estimator (Lee and Ingram, 1991; Duffie and Singleton, 1993) is based on the iterated generation of artificial data by a computer procedure, for some given values of the underlying parameters of the model. At each replication, the statistical moments of the artificial data, averaged across a large number of replications, are computed and compared with the statistical moments of the actual data. A loss function, which weighs, in an appropriate metric, the deviations between the simulated and the actual moments, is minimised recursively by changing the parameter values until the algorithm converges and further reductions in the loss function become negligible. The parameter values thus

---

[29] See Krugman and Miller (1993) for a model incorporating the effects of chartist analysis into a target zone framework.

obtained are the MSM estimates. Formally, define:

$$H_Z(k) = \frac{1}{Z} \sum_{z=1}^{Z} h(k_z) \tag{6.A1}$$

$$H_N[y(\beta)] = \frac{1}{N} \sum_{j=1}^{N} h[y_j(\beta)] \tag{6.A2}$$

as $(m \times 1)$ sample moments of, respectively, the observed data $(k_z, z = 1, \ldots, Z)$ for Z observations; and the simulated data, conditional on a $(k \times 1)$ vector of parameters β, $(y_j(\beta), j = 1, \ldots, N)$ for N simulated observations.

Lee and Ingram (1991) show that under weak regularity conditions and given a symmetric weighting matrix W_Z, the MSM estimator is found by minimising the following loss function with respect to the parameter vector β:

$$L = \{H_Z(k) - H_N[y(\beta)]\}' W_Z \{H_Z(k) - H_N[y(\beta)]\}. \tag{6.A3}$$

Hansen (1982) shows that W_Z^*, defined as follows, is an optimal choice for the weighting matrix in the sense that it yields the smallest asymptotic covariance matrix for the estimator:

$$W_Z^* = \left(1 + \frac{1}{n}\right)^{-1} \Omega^{-1}, \tag{6.A4}$$

where $\Omega = \sum_{i=-\infty}^{\infty} R_x(i)$ for $R_x(i)$ defined as the i-th autocovariance matrix of the population moments of the observed process, and $n = N/Z$ is the ratio of the length of the simulated series to the length of the observed series. In practice, Ω may be estimated using a consistent estimator such as that suggested by Newey and West (1987). Given $W_Z = W_Z^*$, the MSM estimator $\widehat{\beta}_{ZN}$ converges in distribution to the normal:

$$\sqrt{Z}(\widehat{\beta}_{ZN} - \beta_0) \xrightarrow{D} N\left(0, \left[B'\left(1 + \frac{1}{n}\right)^{-1}\Omega^{-1}B\right]^{-1}\right) \quad \text{as } Z, N \longrightarrow \infty, \tag{6.A5}$$

where β_0 is the true parameter vector and $B = E\{\partial h[y_j(\beta)]/\partial \beta\}$. From (6.A5) it is clear that setting n large will improve the efficiency of the estimator. On the other hand, increasing n is very costly in terms of computer time since at each iteration or sub-iteration of the minimisation algorithm, n sets of data must be simulated and the moments computed and compared.

In order to test whether the moment restrictions imposed on the model are true, a result proved by Hansen (1982) may be exploited, to the effect that, under the null hypothesis of no errors in specification, the minimised value of the criterion function (6.A3) converges asymptotically to a chi-square distribution with degrees of freedom equal to the difference between the number of moment conditions (m) and the number of parameters being estimated (k):

$$Z\{H_Z(k) - H_N[y(\widehat{\beta})]\}' W_Z^*\{H_Z(k) - H_N[y(\widehat{\beta})]\} \xrightarrow{D} \chi^2(m - k). \tag{6.A6}$$

References and further readings

Abadir, K.M. (1999), 'An Introduction to Hypergeometric Functions for Economists', *Econometric Reviews*, 18, pp. 287–330.

Backus, D. and J. Driffill (1985), 'Inflation and Reputation', *American Economic Review*, 75, pp. 530–8.

Barro, R. and D. Gordon (1983), 'Rules, Discretion and Reputation in a Model of Monetary Policy', *Journal of Monetary Economics*, 12, pp. 101–21.

Bartolini, L. and G.M. Bodnar (1992), 'Target Zones and Forward Rates in a Model with Repeated Realignments', *Journal of Monetary Economics*, 30, pp. 373–408.

Bayoumi, T.A. and A.K. Rose (1993), 'Domestic Savings and Intra-national Capital Flows', *European Economic Review*, 37, pp. 1197–202.

Bayoumi, T.A., L. Sarno and M.P. Taylor (1999), 'European Capital Flows and Regional Risk', *Manchester School*, 67, pp. 21–38.

Bayoumi, T.A. and M.P. Taylor (1999), 'Macroeconomic Shocks, the ERM, and Tri-polarity', *Review of Economics and Statistics*, 77, pp. 321–31.

Beetsma, R.M.W.J. and F. van der Ploeg (1994), 'Intramarginal Interventions, Bands and the Pattern of EMS Exchange Rate Distributions', *International Economic Review*, 35, pp. 583–602.

Bertola, G. (1994), 'Continuous-Time Models of Exchange Rates and Intervention', in F. van der Ploeg (ed.), *Handbook of International Economics*, Oxford: Blackwell, pp. 251–98.

Bertola, G. and R.J. Caballero (1992), 'Target Zones and Realignments', *American Economic Review*, 82, pp. 520–36.

Bertola, G. and L.E.O. Svensson (1993), 'Stochastic Devaluation Risk and the Empirical Fit of Target-Zone Models', *Review of Economic Studies*, 60, pp. 689–712.

Bhandari, J. and T. Mayer (1990), 'A Note on Saving–Investment Correlations in the EMS', Working Paper No. WP/90/97, International Monetary Fund.

Boyer, R.S. (1978), 'Financial Policies in an Open Economy', *Economica*, 45, pp. 39–57.

Bruno, M. and J. Sachs (1985), *Economics of Worldwide Stagflation*, Oxford: Blackwell.

Calmfors, L. and J. Driffill (1988), 'Bargaining Structure, Corporatism and Macroeconomic Performance', *Economic Policy*, 6, pp. 13–61.

Caramazza, F. (1993), 'French–German Interest Rate Differentials and Time-Varying Realignment Risk', *International Monetary Fund Staff Papers*, 40, pp. 567–83.

Chen, Z. and A. Giovannini (1992), 'Target Zones and the Distribution of Exchange Rates: An Estimation Method', *Economics Letters*, 40, pp. 83–9.

Chiang, A.C. (1984), *Fundamental Methods of Mathematical Economics*, Singapore: McGraw-Hill.

Currie, D. (1992), 'European Monetary Union: Institutional Structure and Economic Performance', *Economic Journal*, 102, pp. 248–64.

De Arcangelis, G. (1994), 'Exchange Rate Target Zone Modelling: Recent Theoretical and Empirical Contributions', *Economic Notes*, 23, pp. 74–115.

De Grauwe, P. (1975), 'Conditions for Monetary Integration: A Geometric Interpretation', *Weltwirtschaftliches Archiv*, 111, pp. 634–46.

(1990), 'The Cost of Disinflation and the European Monetary System', *Open Economies Review*, 1, pp. 147–73.

(1997), *The Economics of Monetary Integration*, Oxford: Oxford University Press.

de Jong, F. (1994), 'A Univariate Analysis of EMS Exchange Rates Using a Target Zone Model', *Journal of Applied Econometrics*, 9, pp. 31–45.

Delgado, F. and B. Dumas (1992), 'Target Zones, Broad and Narrow', in P.R. Krugman and M.H. Miller (eds.), *Exchange Rate Targets and Currency Bands*, Cambridge: Cambridge University Press, pp. 35–56.

Diebold, F.X. and J.A. Nason (1990), 'Nonparametric Exchange Rate Prediction?', *Journal of International Economics*, 28, pp. 315–32.

Dixit, A. (1992), 'Investment and Hysteresis', *Journal of Economic Perspectives*, 6, pp. 107–32.
(1993), *The Art of Smooth Pasting*, Chur: Harwood Academic.
Dominguez, K.M. and P.B. Kenen (1991), 'On the Need to Allow for the Possibility that Governments Mean What They Say: Interpreting the Target-Zone Model of Exchange-Rate Behaviour in the Light of EMS Experience', Working Paper No. 3670, National Bureau of Economic Research.
(1992), 'Intramarginal Intervention in the EMS and the Target-Zone Model of Exchange-Rate Behaviour', *European Economic Review*, 36, pp. 1523–32.
Dornbusch, R. (1976), 'Expectations and Exchange Rate Dynamics', *Journal of Political Economy*, 84, pp. 1161–76.
(1988), 'The European Monetary System, the Dollar and the Yen', in F. Giavazzi, S. Micossi and M. Miller (eds.), *The European Monetary System*, Cambridge: Cambridge University Press, pp. 23–36.
Dumas, B. (1992), 'Speculative Attacks on Target Zones: Discussion', in P.R. Krugman and M.H. Miller (eds.), *Exchange Rate Targets and Currency Bands*, Cambridge: Cambridge University Press, pp. 133–139.
Eichengreen, B. (1990), 'One Money for Europe? Lessons from the US Currency Union', *Economic Policy*, 10, pp. 117–87.
European Commission (1990), 'One Market, One Money: An Evaluation of the Potential Benefits and Costs of Forming an Economic and Monetary Union', *European Economy*, no. 44, Commission of the European Communities, Brussels.
Feldstein, M. and C. Horioka (1980), 'Domestic Saving and International Capital Flows', *Economic Journal*, 90, pp. 314–29.
Flood, R.P. and P.M. Garber (1991), 'The Linkage between Speculative Attack and Target Zone Models of Exchange Rates', *Quarterly Journal of Economics*, 106, pp. 1367–72.
Flood, R.P., A.K. Rose and D.J. Mathieson (1991), 'An Empirical Exploration of Exchange-Rate Target-Zones', *Carnegie–Rochester Conference Series on Public Policy*, 35, pp. 7–66.
Frankel, J.A. and K.A. Froot (1987), 'Using Survey Data to Test Standard Propositions Regarding Exchange Rate Expectations', *American Economic Review*, 77, pp. 133–53.
(1990), 'Chartists, Fundamentalists, and Trading in the Foreign Exchange Market', *American Economic Review*, 80, pp. 181–5.
Frankel, J. and S. Phillips (1992), 'The European Monetary System: Credible at Last?', *Oxford Economic Papers*, 44, pp. 791–816.
Frenkel, J.A. and M. Goldstein (1986), 'A Guide to Target Zones', *International Monetary Fund Staff Papers*, 33, pp. 633–73.
Friedman, M. (1953), 'The Case for Flexible Exchange Rates', in M. Friedman, *Essays in Positive Economics*, Chicago: University of Chicago Press, pp. 157–203.
Froot, K.A. and M. Obstfeld (1991a), 'Stochastic Process Switching: Some Simple Solutions', *Econometrica*, 59, pp. 241–50.
(1991b), 'Exchange-Rate Dynamics under Stochastic Regime Shifts: A Unified Approach', *Journal of International Economics*, 31, pp. 203–29.
Garber, P.M. and L.E.O. Svensson (1995), 'The Operation and Collapse of Fixed Exchange Rate Regimes', in G. Grossman and K. Rogoff (eds.), *Handbook of International Economics*, vol. III, Amsterdam: North-Holland, ch. 36.
Genberg, H. (1989), 'Exchange Rate Management and Macroeconomic Policy: A National Perspective', *Scandinavian Journal of Economics*, 91, pp. 439–69.
Giavazzi, F. (1989), 'The European Monetary System: Lessons from Europe and Perspectives in Europe', *Economic and Social Review*, 20, pp. 73–90.
Giavazzi, F. and A. Giovannini (1989), 'Monetary Policy Interactions under Managed Exchange Rates', *Economica*, 56, pp. 199–213.
Giavazzi, F. and M. Pagano (1988), 'The Advantage of Tying One's Hands: EMS Discipline and Central Bank Credibility', *European Economic Review*, 32, pp. 1055–75.

(1989), 'Confidence Crises and Public Debt Management', Discussion Paper No. 318, Centre for Economic Policy Research.

Giavazzi, F. and L. Spaventa (1990), 'The "New" EMS', in P. de Grauwe and L. Papademos (eds.), *The European Monetary System in the 1990s*, London: Longman, pp. 65–85.

Grilli, V. (1989), 'Seigniorage in Europe', in M. de Cecco and A. Giovannini (eds.), *A European Central Bank? Perspectives on Monetary Unification after Ten Years of the EMS*, Cambridge: Cambridge University Press, pp. 53–79.

Hansen, L.P. (1982), 'Large Sample Properties of Generalized Method of Moments Estimators', *Econometrica*, 50, pp. 1029–54.

Harrison, M. (1985), *Brownian Motion and Stochastic Flow System*, New York: Wiley.

Iannizzotto, M. and M.P. Taylor (1999), 'The Target Zone Model, Non-Linearity and Mean Reversion: Is the Honeymoon Really Over?', *Economic Journal*, 109, pp. C96–C110.

Itô, K. (1951), 'On Stochastic Differential Equations', *Memoirs of the American Mathematical Society*, 4 (1), pp. 1–51.

Jorgensen, B.N. and H.O. Mikkelsen (1996), 'An Arbitrage Free Trilateral Target Zone Model', *Journal of International Money and Finance*, 15, pp. 117–34.

Karatzas, I. and S.E. Shreve (1988), *Brownian Motion and Stochastic Calculus*, New York: Springer-Verlag.

Kenen, P. (1969), 'The Theory of Optimum Currency Areas: An Eclectic View', in R.A. Mundell and A. Swoboda (eds.), *Monetary Problems in the International Economy*, Chicago: University of Chicago Press, pp. 41–60.

Koedijk, K.G., P.A. Stork and C.G. de Vries (1992), 'Differences between Foreign Exchange Rate Regimes: The View from the Tails', *Journal of International Money and Finance*, 11, pp. 462–73.

Krugman, P.R. (1989), 'Differences in Income Elasticities and Trends in Real Exchange Rates', *European Economic Review*, 33, pp. 1031–47.

(1990), 'Policy Problems of a Monetary Union', in P. de Grauwe and L. Papademos (eds.), *The European Monetary System in the 1990s*, London: Longman, pp. 48–64.

(1991), 'Target Zones and Exchange Rate Dynamics', *Quarterly Journal of Economics*, 106, pp. 669–82.

Krugman, P.R. and M.H. Miller (eds.) (1992), *Exchange Rate Targets and Currency Bands*, Cambridge: Cambridge University Press.

Krugman, P.R. and M.H. Miller (1993), 'Why Have a Target Zone?', *Carnegie–Rochester Conference Series on Public Policy*, 38, pp. 279–314.

Kydland, F. and E. Prescott (1977), 'Rules Rather than Discretion: The Inconsistency of Optimal Plans', *Journal of Political Economy*, 85, pp. 473–91.

Lee, B.-S. and B.F. Ingram (1991), 'Simulation Estimation of Time-Series Models', *Journal of Econometrics*, 47, pp. 197–205.

Lindberg, H. and P. Söderlind (1994a), 'Testing the Basic Target Zone Model on Swedish Data 1982–1990', *European Economic Review*, 38, pp. 1441–69.

(1994b), 'Intervention Policy and Mean Reversion in Exchange Rate Target Zones: The Swedish Case', *Scandinavian Journal of Economics*, 96, pp. 499–513.

Lindberg, H., P. Söderlind and L.E.O. Svensson (1994), 'Devaluation Expectations: The Swedish Krona 1985–92', *Economic Journal*, 103, pp. 1170–9.

Masson, P.R. and M.P. Taylor (1993), 'Currency Unions: A Survey of the Issues', in P.R. Masson and M.P. Taylor (eds.), *Policy Issues in the Operation of Currency Unions*, Cambridge: Cambridge University Press, pp. 1–40.

McFadden, D. (1989), 'A Method of Simulated Moments for Estimation of Discrete Response Models without Numerical Integration', *Econometrica*, 57, pp. 995–1026.

McKinnon, R.I. (1963), 'Optimum Currency Areas', *American Economic Review*, 53, pp. 717–25.

Meese, R.A. and A.K. Rose (1990), 'Nonlinear, Nonparametric, Nonessential Exchange Rate Estimation', *American Economic Review*, 80, pp. 192–6.

Miller, M.H. and P. Weller (1991), 'Exchange Rate Bands with Price Inertia', *Economic Journal*, 101, pp. 1380–99.

Mizrach, B. (1995), 'Target Zone Models with Stochastic Realignments: An Econometric Evaluation', *Journal of International Money and Finance*, 14, pp. 641–57.

Mundell, R.A. (1961), 'A Theory of Optimum Currency Areas', *American Economic Review*, 51, pp. 657–65.

Newey, W. and K. West (1987), 'A Simple, Positive Semi-Definite, Heteroscedasticity and Autocorrelation Consistent Covariance Matrix', *Econometrica*, 55, pp. 703–8.

Nurkse, R. (1944), *International Currency Experience: Lessons of the Interwar Period*, Geneva: League of Nations.

Parkin, M. (1978), 'A Comparison of Alternative Techniques of Monetary Control under Rational Expectations', *Manchester School*, 46, pp. 252–87.

Persson, T. and Tabellini, G. (1999), 'Political Economics and Macroeconomic Policy', in J.B. Taylor and M. Woodford (eds.), *Handbook of Macroeconomics*, vol. 1C, Amsterdam: Elsevier, pp. 1397–482.

Pesaran, M.H. and H. Samiei (1992a), 'An Analysis of the Determination of the Deutsche Mark/French Franc Exchange Rate in a Discrete-Time Target-Zone Model', *Economic Journal*, 102, pp. 388–401.

(1992b), 'Estimating Limited-Dependent Rational Expectations Models with an Application to Exchange Rate Determination in a Target Zone', *Journal of Econometrics*, 53, pp. 141–63.

Pessach, S. and A. Razin (1994), 'Targeting the Exchange Rate under Inflation', *Review of International Economics*, 2, pp. 40–9.

Poole, W. (1970), 'Optimal Choice of Monetary Policy Instruments in a Simple Stochastic Macro Model', *Quarterly Journal of Economics*, 85, pp. 197–216.

Rogoff, K. (1985), 'Can Exchange Rate Predictability Be Achieved Without Monetary Convergence?', *European Economic Review*, 28, pp. 93–115.

Rose, A.K. and L.E.O. Svensson (1995), 'Expected and Predicted Realignments: The FF/DM Exchange Rate during the EMS, 1979–93', *Scandinavian Journal of Economics*, 97, pp. 173–200.

Sarno, L. and M.P. Taylor (1998), 'Savings–Investment Correlations: Transitory versus Permanent', *Manchester School*, 66, pp. 17–38.

Smith, G.W. and M.G. Spencer (1992), 'Estimation and Testing in Models of Exchange Rate Target Zones and Process Switching', in P.R. Krugman and M.H. Miller (eds.), *Exchange Rate Targets and Currency Bands*, Cambridge: Cambridge University Press, pp. 211–39.

Sutherland, A. (1994), 'Target Zone Models with Price Inertia: Solutions and Testable Implications', *Economic Journal*, 104, pp. 96–112.

Svensson, L.E.O. (1991a), 'The Simplest Test of Target Zone Credibility', *International Monetary Fund Staff Papers*, 38, pp. 655–65.

(1991b), 'Target Zones and Interest Rate Variability', *Journal of International Economics*, 31, pp. 27–54.

(1991c), 'The Term Structure of Interest Rate Differentials in a Target Zone: Theory and Swedish Data', *Journal of Monetary Economics*, 28, pp. 87–116.

(1992), 'An Interpretation of Recent Research on Exchange Rate Target Zones', *Journal of Economic Perspectives*, 6, pp. 119–44.

(1993), 'Assessing Target Zone Credibility: Mean Reversion and Devaluation Expectations in the ERM, 1979–1992', *European Economic Review*, 37, pp. 763–93.

Taylor, M.P. and H. Allen (1992), 'The Use of Technical Analysis in the Foreign Exchange Market', *Journal of International Money and Finance*, 11, pp. 304–14.

Taylor, M.P. and M. Iannizzotto (2001), 'On the Mean-Reverting Properties of Target Zone Exchange Rates: A Cautionary Note', *Economics Letters*, 71, pp. 117–29.

Tristani, O. (1994), 'Variable Probability of Realignment in a Target Zone', *Scandinavian Journal of Economics*, 96, pp. 1–14.

Turnovsky, S.J. (1976), 'The Relative Stability of Alternative Exchange Rate Systems in the Presence of Random Disturbances', *Journal of Money, Credit, and Banking*, 8, pp. 29–50.

Weber, A.A. (1992), 'Time-Varying Devaluation Risk, Interest Rate Differentials and Exchange Rates in Target Zones: Evidence from the EMS', Discussion Paper No. 611, Centre for Economic Policy Research.

Werner, A.M. (1995), 'Exchange Rate Target Zones, Realignments and the Interest Rate Differential: Theory and Evidence', *Journal of International Economics*, 39, pp. 353–67.

Williamson, J. (1985), *The Exchange Rate System* (rev. edn), Policy Analyses in International Economics series, no. 5, Washington, D.C.: Institute for International Economics.

Williamson, J. and M.H. Miller (1987), *Targets and Indicators: A Blueprint for the International Coordination of Economic Policy*, Policy Analyses in International Economics series, no. 22, Washington, D.C.: Institute for International Economics.

7   Official intervention in the foreign exchange market

Official intervention in the foreign exchange market occurs when the authorities buy or sell foreign exchange, normally against their own currency, in order to affect the exchange rate.[1] Whether, by what means, by how much and for how long the authorities can affect the exchange rate through intervening in the market are questions of crucial policy importance and a vast academic and policy-related literature has grown up in order to address them.[2]

Given its policy importance, it is perhaps not surprising that this literature has been the venue for a substantial and ongoing economic controversy. In so far as a consensus is discernible among economists and policy-makers concerning the effectiveness and desirability of exchange rate intervention, it appears to have shifted several times over the past quarter of a century. At the time of the collapse of the Bretton Woods adjustable peg exchange rate system in the early 1970s, when the impotence of the authorities to hold the parities in the face of massive speculative attack had apparently been demonstrated only too well,[3] the profession appeared strongly to favour a pure float, involving zero intervention. The 1970s experience with floating exchange rates among the major industrialised countries, and the ensuing volatility of both nominal and real exchange rates, however, led to a shift in this consensus so that, by the late 1970s, both economists and policy-makers – particularly of countries which had suffered a substantial loss in competitiveness – frequently criticised the US authorities for not intervening in support of the dollar.

---

[1] For surveys in book form related to official intervention, see Kenen (1988), Pilbeam (1991), Dominguez and Frankel (1993a), Edison (1993) and Almekinders (1995). See also the contributions in Canzoneri, Ethier and Grilli (1996), which cover a number of issues related to 'The New Transatlantic Economy', ranging from transatlantic policy co-ordination with sticky labour markets to co-ordinated exchange rate intervention following the Plaza and Louvre agreements in comparison with the experience of the European Monetary System prior to the 1992 crisis, *inter alia*. For a treatment of exchange rate intervention and related issues in the Pacific Basin, see Glick (1998), while for a collection of key articles on official intervention, see Eijffinger (1998).

[2] In this chapter we largely confine ourselves to surveying the literature which has been published during the last twenty-five years or so, since the breakdown of the Bretton Woods system. Important earlier contributions would include Keynes (1923) and Kenen (1960, 1965).

[3] Williamson (1977, p. 50) notes: 'By the time that the adjustable peg was abandoned, capital mobility had developed to the point where the Bundesbank could take in well over $1 billion in an hour when the market had come to expect that another parity change was impending.'

Nevertheless, partly as a result of the realisation of the speed and ease with which capital could move between developed countries, the prevailing consensus among economists, policy-makers and foreign exchange market practitioners during the early 1980s appeared to be that intervention – and in particular sterilized intervention, where the effects of intervention on the domestic money supply are neutralised – was not effective in anything but the very short run. Not only was this view prevalent among academic economists, it also appeared to be the consensus view of policy-makers, symbolised by the conclusions of the Jurgensen Report (1983) on exchange rate intervention, which had been commissioned by the 1982 G7 Economic Summit of Heads of Government at Versailles.[4, 5]

Following the strong and chronic overvaluation of the US dollar during the early to mid 1980s, and a communiqué issued by the leaders of the G5 industrialised countries at the Plaza Hotel in New York in September 1985 to the effect that concerted intervention would be undertaken to bring down the high dollar, however, the consensus appeared to have shifted once more.[6] Following the decline of the US dollar during the late 1980s, a subsequent meeting of the leaders of the G7 industrialised nations, held at the Louvre in Paris in February 1987, led to the agreement that co-ordinated exchange rate intervention should be undertaken to stabilise the US dollar within informal 'reference ranges', although precise target zone bands were not established.[7]

Following the Plaza and Louvre meetings, official intervention in the markets for the major exchange rates has been regular and at times heavy (Obstfeld, 1990). In addition, exchange rate intervention, together with macro policy co-ordination, has also played an important role in the Exchange Rate Mechanism (ERM) of the European Monetary System (EMS) of target zones between European exchange rates.[8]

---

[4] See Dominguez and Frankel (1993a) for an historical account.

[5] The Jurgensen Report did not provide very explicit conclusions. The official press release of the finance ministries and central bank governors of the G7 stated, however, that the main results of the Jurgensen Report might be summarised as follows: sterilised intervention affects long-run exchange rates much less than non-sterilised intervention; sterilised intervention can influence exchange rates only in the short run; co-ordinated intervention can be much more powerful relative to official intervention by a single country's authorities.

[6] Some authors argue that this embodiment of a new intervention regime started at the beginning of 1985, since the dollar had its peak in February 1985 and was already depreciating at the time of the Plaza Agreement. In fact, large sales of dollars were operated by some European central banks (especially the Bundesbank) in February and March of that year (see Dominguez and Frankel, 1993a). For a descriptive overview of the events during the period from the Plaza Agreement to the Louvre Accord, see also Funabashi (1988).

[7] The agreement is clearly embodied in the following quotation from the official press release of the Louvre Accord: 'The Ministers and Governors agreed that the substantial exchange rate intervention since the Plaza Agreement will increasingly contribute to reducing external imbalances and have now brought their currencies within ranges broadly consistent with underlying economic fundamentals . . . Further substantial exchange rate shifts among their currencies could damage growth and adjustment prospects in their countries.'

[8] Following the ERM crisis of 1992–3 and a number of other currency crises during the 1990s, there have been calls from various quarters for measures to be put in place to safeguard against speculative attacks when they are apparently unrelated to the underlying economic fundamentals. In 1994, for example, the Bretton Woods Commission, headed by the former chairman of the Federal Reserve, Paul Volcker, recommended that the International Monetary Fund set up an intervention fund to help countries stave off attacks on their currencies (see, e.g., *Economist*, 1995). In a related literature, economists have debated the desirability and feasibility of imposing capital controls or taxes on foreign exchange transactions as a means of 'throwing sand in the wheels of finance' (Tobin, 1969; Eichengreen and Wyplosz, 1993; Eichengreen, Tobin and Wyplosz, 1995; Garber and Taylor, 1995).

7.1   The mechanics of official exchange rate intervention

7.1.1   The case for official exchange rate intervention

A central argument used in the literature in order to promote a case for exchange rate intervention is the so-called 'wrong-rate' argument: under a floating exchange rate system, an inefficient foreign exchange market may tend to generate the wrong rate (which implies *ex ante* abnormal returns) rather than the 'correct rate' (the exchange rate which fully reflects the economic fundamentals) which would arise if agents in the foreign exchange market used all available relevant information. Hence, official intervention may be a useful instrument to induce a 'more appropriate rate', that is to say to move the exchange rate towards what the authorities believe to be the correct rate.

Clear examples of inefficiencies of this type may be situations in which speculation is destabilising, such as, for instance, in the presence of excessive risk aversion or 'band-wagon effects'.[9] When speculation is destabilising, exchange rate theory recommends a policy of 'leaning against the wind', according to which the authorities should intervene by selling the currency while it is appreciating and buying it back at a lower rate when it starts to depreciate. The wrong-rate argument implicitly assumes, therefore, that foreign exchange market inefficiency and destabilising speculation provide scope for central bank intervention, which may be effective in 'correcting' the wrong rate as well as allowing profits from leaning against the wind.[10] In addition, the wrong-rate argument also assumes that investors do not use all available information and that official intervention is, on balance, stabilising, which implicitly requires the assumption that the authorities use information more efficiently than speculators (see Friedman, 1953).

Additional sources of instability in the foreign exchange market are phenomena such as the peso problems originally suggested by Rogoff (1979), where agents attach a small probability to a large movement in the exchange rate (e.g. following a particular political election result), and speculative bubbles, where, for example, speculators are willing to hold an overvalued currency because they believe that the probability of a further appreciation is higher than the probability of a significant depreciation. These phenomena may prolong a currency overvaluation and eventually lead to a crash with large macroeconomic costs, as would happen, for example, at the sudden arrival of information which diverts a large number of speculators from 'feeding' the bubble (Dornbusch, 1983).

[9] Excessive risk aversion may occur when the market attaches too high a probability to the occurrence of a devaluation of a weak currency (or to the occurrence of an appreciation of a strong currency) in a way which is not consistent with the economic fundamentals. This situation would make a strong currency overvalued and a weak currency undervalued. In these cases, official intervention may reduce the distortion caused by excessive risk aversion of investors. Also, while risk aversion is consistent *per se* with efficiency of the foreign exchange market, excessive risk aversion is not, since part of the risk premium required by investors is not justified by the fundamentals. Similarly, a wrong exchange rate may be generated in the presence of bandwagon effects arising, for example, in a situation of self-generating speculation not justified by the fundamentals.

[10] Note that destabilising speculation does not necessarily imply that speculation pushes the exchange rate away from the correct rate; generally, speculation is destabilising also if the exchange rate overreacts or underreacts to news. Hence, speculation would still be destabilising if an exchange rate moves in the right direction in response to news and adjusts towards the correct rate implied by the fundamentals, but at too slow a pace. In other words, the adjustment process will be faster the more stabilising (less destabilising) speculation is.

In addition, many professional exchange rate traders do not generally base their forecasts on fundamentals-based models, and often use simple extrapolative techniques and more or less subjective pattern recognition methods such as 'technical' or 'chartist' analysis (see Allen and Taylor, 1990; Taylor and Allen, 1992).

Overall, therefore, there are a number of reasons why the actual exchange rate may be driven away from the rate implied by the fundamentals and, even under the rational expectations hypothesis, speculative bubbles and peso problems may arise and grow in a situation in which – contrary to Friedman's (1953) analysis – destabilising speculators are not driven out of the market but, rather, may be responsible for the persistence of a wrong exchange rate path over a protracted period of time.

Nevertheless, another argument supportive of a case for exchange rate management is that some information available to and used by market agents may be inaccurate or misleading, in comparison to the authorities' information set.[11] The superiority of the information set of the central bank may be justified on the grounds that the authorities should at least know more about future policy actions which may affect the exchange rate, and, therefore, the effects of those actions can be fully anticipated by the central bank. In this sense, foreign exchange intervention may be viewed as a commitment by the authorities to undertake a certain course of action: official intervention increases authorities' credibility by persuading private agents that macroeconomic objectives announced will be supported by the authorities' intervention and fulfilled.

Another argument advanced by the literature in order to justify exchange rate intervention draws on conventional theories of exchange rate determination (see Chapter 4). Exchange rate overshooting and cross-country policy interdependence, for example, may justify exchange rate intervention since temporary monetary disturbances may be offset by appropriately using official intervention, which may ultimately reduce exchange rate volatility. Clearly, in a perfect world with no frictions of any sort, where market clearing occurs instantaneously in every market, information is perfect and agents form rational expectations, exchange rate overshooting and cross-country policy interdependence do not necessarily provide a case for official intervention in the foreign exchange market. In a 'second best' world, however, with rigidities and imperfections of various sorts in both labour and goods markets, the textbook model may be misleading if taken too seriously and it is a well-known result of the theory of the second best that the introduction of a further distortion in the presence of existing distortions does *not necessarily* lower welfare (Pilbeam, 1991).

A similar argument in favour of exchange rate intervention is the so-called 'adjustment argument'. Finance theory suggests that official intervention is important in smoothing the adjustment process of exchange rates from their short-run values towards their long-run equilibrium. This adjustment process may be very painful and cause large costs if purely determined by market forces. Notably, Corden's (1981, 1982) work on balance of payments management shows how, using a typical 'vicious circle' example, a case for official

---

[11] This raises the question of why the central bank does not make its information set available to the other market participants since this would eliminate the informational asymmetry, helping speculators to act in a stabilising manner. This issue is discussed specifically below.

intervention arises. Hence, exchange rate intervention may allow the monetary authorities to smooth the adjustment of exchange rates towards their long-run equilibrium value and permit the adjustment to occur at the optimal pace determined by the authorities on the basis of the minimisation of some sort of adjustment cost function.

Nevertheless, although the above discussion provides a number of potential reasons why exchange rate intervention may be effective, it is not at all clear that official intervention will always be beneficial. In particular, the authorities may not be capable of identifying correctly the exchange rate implied by the fundamentals or, more simply, even if they are able to do so, the costs of exchange rate intervention may be too high relative to its benefits since, in practice, official intervention may have some perverse effects. This is because official intervention in foreign exchange markets induces speculators to revise their expectations and, if this revision occurs in a perverse direction – say because of a lack of credibility of the authorities' intentions – international capital flows may be generated which can in part, totally, or more than completely offset the initial direct effect of the authorities' intervention. On the other hand, if private market participants correctly understand, believe and approve the authorities' intervention policies, their actions may reinforce the effects of exchange rate intervention, in which case the size of official intervention required may be reduced. In other words, the extent of official intervention which is needed to move the exchange rate towards a certain target also depends crucially on the reaction of the private sector.[12]

A further difficulty in designing exchange rate intervention is concerned with the fact that the authorities may not easily understand when a certain observed disturbance is temporary or permanent and, therefore, whether it requires a specific response in the foreign exchange market or not. Feldstein (1986), for example, observes: 'Exchange rate market intervention aimed at smoothing a transitory disturbance may in fact be a counterproductive or futile attempt to prevent a basic shift in the equilibrium exchange rate.' In other words, in most cases the need for official intervention can be stated with certainty only *ex post*. In addition, depending on the specific circumstances, different types of intervention are needed (e.g. leaning against or with the wind) and it proves extremely difficult to theorists to specify a set of specific conditions under which certain actions should be undertaken.[13]

[12] Fellner (1982) shows that a fundamental condition for exchange rate intervention to be effective and beneficial is that it is supported, reinforced and complemented by appropriate domestic policies, since an appropriate combination of intervention and domestic policies increases the likelihood of intervention being stabilising rather than destabilising. Fellner also stresses that, in designing exchange rate intervention, the authorities should take into account not only the reaction of other market participants, but also the reaction of foreign authorities – primarily major trading partners – who may be affected by official intervention, as the ultimate effect of the domestic official intervention depends upon the intervention operations adopted by all countries whose actions have a significant impact on the domestic economy. This argument also provides a simple rationale to explain why co-ordinated intervention may be much more effective than unilateral intervention, as some empirical evidence seems to indicate (e.g. the Jurgensen Report, 1983).

[13] Note the distinction between the intentions of the monetary authorities in the different cases of a leaning-against-the-wind policy and a leaning-with-the-wind policy. The former intervention operation reflects an attempt by the monetary authorities to move the exchange rate in the opposite direction from its current trend and therefore the authorities' intervention is motivated by the intention to calm disorders in the foreign exchange market, characterised by, for example, unusually large bid–ask spreads or excessively volatile price movements. In contrast, leaning-with-the-wind intervention involves operations motivated by the authorities' willingness to support the recent trend of the exchange rate (e.g. the intervention sanctioned by the 1985 Plaza agreement).

Table 7.1. *Monetary authorities' stylised balance sheet*

Assets	Liabilities
Net foreign assets (NFA)	*Monetary base (M)*
Gold	Total currency in circulation
Foreign currency	Reserve liabilities to commercial banks
Net domestic assets (NDA)	*Net worth (NW)*
Government securities	Spending surpluses
Loans on commercial banks	Net interests and capital gains from assets
Other	

7.1.2 Non-sterilised and sterilised intervention

Official intervention is said to be sterilised when the authorities – simultaneously or with a very short lag – take action to offset or 'sterilise' the effects of a change in official foreign asset holdings on the domestic monetary base. On the other hand, non-sterilised intervention occurs when authorities buy or sell foreign exchange, normally against their own currency, without such offsetting actions. Clearly non-sterilised intervention will affect directly the domestic money supply and therefore its effect on the exchange rate is contentious only in so far as the effects of changes in the money supply on the exchange rate are contentious – a debate which perhaps belongs more to the area of exchange rate determination (see Chapter 4). In general, a strong consensus exists in the profession that non-sterilised intervention can influence the exchange rate in a similar way to monetary policy by inducing changes in the stock of the monetary base which, in turn, induces changes in broader monetary aggregates, interest rates, market expectations and, ultimately, the exchange rate. Nevertheless, the effectiveness of sterilised intervention is very controversial and, accordingly, the core of the debate on the effectiveness of official intervention in the foreign exchange market largely relates to sterilised intervention.[14]

Consider Table 7.1, which gives a stylised representation of the balance sheet of a country's monetary authorities (that is, the central bank and exchange-stabilisation authorities combined). The monetary base comprises currency and deposit liabilities to banks. Net worth of the financial authorities includes accrued spending surpluses, accumulated net interest receipts and capital gains on their holdings of net domestic and foreign assets. From Table 7.1, it follows that:

$$M \equiv NFA + (NDA - NW) \equiv NFA + DC \qquad (7.1)$$

where DC, defined as net domestic assets less net worth ($DC \equiv NDA - NW$), represents the stock of domestic credit made available by the monetary authorities.

Foreign exchange market intervention by the monetary authorities involves a purchase or sale of foreign assets. When official intervention is non-sterilised, the purchase (sale) of

---

[14] For an early elegant description of the mechanics of exchange rate intervention, see Adams and Henderson (1983).

foreign currency by the authorities leads to an increase (decrease) in NFA and an equivalent increase (decrease) in M. Therefore, non-sterilised intervention has the same impact on monetary liabilities as an open-market operation, and the only difference between the two is that by a non-sterilised intervention operation the monetary authorities alter M through a change in foreign asset holdings rather than through a change in domestic asset holdings.

On the other hand, if intervention is fully sterilised then domestic credit is altered so that:

$$\Delta DC = -\Delta NFA \tag{7.2}$$

also implying:

$$\Delta M = \Delta NFA + \Delta DC = 0 \tag{7.3}$$

where Δ denotes the change in the relevant stock. Normally, intervention would be sterilised by sales or purchases of domestic-currency bills or bonds by the monetary authorities so that the effects on the monetary base of changes in the holdings of net foreign assets are in fact offset one-for-one by the effects of changes in net domestic asset holdings:

$$\Delta NDA = -\Delta NFA \tag{7.4}$$

Hence, in the case of sterilised intervention, the effect on the exchange rate is expected to occur because of a change in the composition of assets through two possible channels: by changing the relative supplies of assets (the portfolio balance channel) or by signalling policy intentions (the expectations, or signalling, channel).

According to the portfolio balance channel (Isard, 1980; Branson, 1983, 1984), by altering the relative supplies of domestic and foreign bonds there will be little or perhaps no movement in domestic interest rates since the monetary base is held constant and, therefore, the spot exchange rate must shift in order to affect the domestic value of foreign bonds and the expected return from holding them. For example, an increase in the supply of euro-denominated assets in the hands of the public relative to the supply of dollar-denominated assets necessitates a fall in the relative price of euro-denominated assets. If domestic and foreign assets are regarded by agents as perfect substitutes, however, sterilised intervention may have no significant effect – through the portfolio balance channel – on the exchange rate. This follows because agents will be indifferent as to the relative amounts of domestic and foreign assets they are holding – they will care only about the total amount and hence no change in market-clearing prices or quantities is required.[15]

Even if perfect substitutability holds, however, in theory sterilised intervention can still be effective through the expectations, or signalling, channel (Mussa, 1981): in response to sterilised intervention, agents may revise their expectations of the future exchange rate, altering the expected rate of depreciation and hence the return to foreign bond holdings. In the limiting case of perfect substitutability, the current exchange rate jumps to the new

[15] Also, in a Ricardian world where private agents offset expected future tax payments (which will be required to service extra government debt) against current holdings of domestic bonds, imperfect substitutability would no longer be a sufficient condition for sterilised intervention to influence the current exchange rate (Frankel, 1979; Obstfeld, 1982; Backus and Kehoe, 1989).

expected future level in order to set the expected rate of depreciation to zero (assuming no change in domestic interest rates occurs).

Notice that, since unsuccessful intervention is costly, if official intervention is expected to be effective through the signalling channel, there is an incentive for the authorities to manifest clearly their policy intentions. As Kenen (1988, p. 52) puts it: 'The rules for exchange rate management should be as transparent as possible. That is to maintain credibility, not by studied ambiguity, which breeds disagreement and distrust.' At any time, however, a government will be pursuing many macroeconomic policy goals and the trade-offs amongst these will be highly complex, hence complicating significantly the judgement of other market agents about the time-consistency of a certain announced exchange rate policy.

Stein (1989) presents a model in which market agents have incomplete information about the authorities' utility trade-off between the exchange rate target and a domestic policy target. Stein first shows that, for a policy to be time-consistent, the authorities must announce a *range* for the future exchange rate since the announcement of any *precise* target may not be credible. More generally, the monetary authorities of many major industrialised countries tend to adopt exchange rate policies which are consistent with the fulfilment of preannounced targets for the growth rate of monetary aggregates.

Following Gardner (1983) and Almekinders (1995), the trade-off between the attainment of a target level of money stock (m_t^T) and a target level of the exchange rate (s_t^T) may be formalised in a simple fashion using a quadratic loss function for the monetary authorities of the form:

$$\pounds_t = \left(m_t - m_t^T\right)^2 + \omega\left(s_t - s_t^T\right)^2 \qquad \omega \geq 0 \qquad (7.5)$$

where $\pounds_t$, m_t and s_t denote the loss to the monetary authorities, the domestic monetary base and the nominal exchange rate (domestic price of foreign currency) at time t respectively, while ω is the relative weight attached to the monetary and exchange rate targets by the monetary authorities. If the authorities only care about the attainment of the preannounced monetary target – say in order to build their reputation and hence benefit by relatively lower inflation expectations and wages claims from trade unions – then $\omega = 0$ in equation (7.5). However, if $\omega = 0$ and no official intervention policy is undertaken by the monetary authorities, then the exchange rate has to bear entirely the burden of adjustment: any expected appreciation of the domestic currency will induce speculators to buy the currency, hence generating the actual appreciation of the currency itself. Alternatively, the monetary authorities may use sterilised intervention which can effectively induce the independence of exchange rates and monetary targets ($\Delta NDA = -\Delta NFA$), ultimately generating only a change in the composition of the private sector's portfolio.[16]

Later in the chapter, we provide a more detailed discussion of the two channels of influence for official intervention and of the relevant empirical evidence. We now turn to the discussion of a number of highly debated preliminary issues in the context of official intervention in the foreign exchange market.

---

[16] See also Artis and Karakitsos (1985) and Kenen (1988).

7.1.3   Other issues in official intervention

7.1.3.1   Public versus secret intervention   Most actual interventions in the foreign exchange market have been, at least partially, secret, not publicly announced by the monetary authorities. In addition, given the anonymity of most exchange rate transactions, it is generally very difficult to identify the counterparts of a foreign exchange transaction, which makes it a formidable task to detect and measure the extent of intervention operations.

Nevertheless, secrecy of official intervention is difficult to explain, given the mechanics sketched earlier which suggests that the signalling channel is expected to work by altering the expectations of other market agents through exchange policy announcements by the authorities.

A number of explanations have been proposed in an attempt to justify the widespread practice of secrecy of official intervention. In their monograph, Dominguez and Frankel (1993a) distinguish among three types of arguments in favour of secrecy of official intervention: arguments based on the central bank's desire to minimise the effects of an unwanted intervention operation; arguments based on perceived risk and volatility in the foreign exchange market; and portfolio adjustment arguments.

The first argument is based on the idea that intervention may not be judged appropriate by the central bank, as may happen when the decision to intervene in the foreign exchange market is taken outside the central bank. In the United States, for example, the decision to intervene in the foreign exchange market may be taken by the Treasury Department although it is (in fact, it must be) executed by the Federal Reserve Bank, even when the Federal Reserve Bank has objections to the decision. In such circumstances, therefore, secrecy of official exchange rate intervention is used with the aim of minimising the impact of the operation. Another example of secrecy of official intervention belonging to the first class of arguments may be a situation in which the intervention operation is considered inconsistent with other macroeconomic policies which are being pursued or have been announced and, therefore, for reputational reasons, secrecy of official intervention by the central bank may be the optimal choice, even if it sacrifices the effect of the operation through the signalling channel. This, however, invites the question as to why the authorities should be pursuing a set of mutually inconsistent policies.

The second argument in support of secret exchange rate intervention is based on the idea that, in a situation of high uncertainty and volatility of foreign exchange markets, it may be particularly risky for a central bank to announce publicly the intention of intervening, especially if its reputation is not sufficiently strong and the announcement may not be believed by a large number of investors (Cukierman and Meltzer, 1986).

The final argument for secrecy of intervention is a portfolio adjustment argument: the central bank may simply want to adjust its own foreign exchange portfolio in order to have sufficient reserves in currencies expected to be needed to carry out future intervention operations. In this case a public announcement may be misleading for the market in that it may be perceived as an attempt to move the exchange rate in a certain direction rather than an attempt by the central bank to adjust its portfolio.

Given that most intervention operations are not announced publicly by central banks, the above reasoning would imply that most operations are either decided outside the central bank or without the approval of the central bank, or that they occur in a situation of high uncertainty or volatility of exchange rates, or that they are not intended to affect the exchange rate. The first possibility seems, however, quite unlikely given that most central banks in major industrialised countries are relatively independent and authoritative. While the first explanation may have been plausible in some past situations (especially in the UK and the USA), it seems unlikely to be the case for many central banks nowadays. The second argument for the secrecy of official intervention may perhaps be a more reasonable explanation in the light of the high volatility of many currencies' exchange rates. The third argument, based on portfolio adjustment, is certainly less interesting and is not adequate to explain why there are so many secret official interventions: if intervention in the foreign exchange market is in fact largely induced by portfolio adjustment intentions, then the authorities would continuously be planning future interventions to be greater than current interventions, which seems absurd.

Overall, since the second argument, which we consider the most plausible, seems unlikely to explain all of the secret intervention operations occurring in foreign exchange markets, further analysis is required to provide better explanations of the widespread practice of secret official intervention in the foreign exchange market.

7.1.3.2 International co-ordination of official intervention   Co-ordinated (or concerted) official intervention in the foreign exchange market occurs when two or more central banks intervene simultaneously in the market in support of the same currency, according to an explicit or implicit international agreement of co-operation.[17] In practice, however, concerted official intervention in the foreign exchange market has largely consisted of information-sharing and discussions, with small modifications of the individual intervention operations.

The rationale for international co-ordination of official intervention is the existence of significant spillover effects of domestic policies to other countries. For example, under a floating exchange rate system, official intervention in one country may be expected to change the value of the domestic currency with respect to other currencies, thereby affecting trading partners' economies. Standard economic theory suggests that, in an interdependent world economy, a Pareto-optimal outcome may be achieved by taking into account the spillover effects of macroeconomic policies and by forming policies which exploit the existence of these cross-country interdependencies for the mutual benefit of the participants in the co-ordinated intervention (Bryant, 1995). Moreover, the empirical evidence to date indicates that internationally co-ordinated intervention may be more effective than unilateral official intervention operations (Kenen, 1995). Obstfeld (1990) argues, for example, that sterilised intervention in itself has not played an important role in promoting exchange rate realignment since the 1985 Plaza Accord, and realignments have occurred largely as a result of appropriate macro-policy co-ordination.

The literature investigating the implications of policy co-ordination among interdependent economies typically adopts a game-theoretic modelling approach which is commonly

---

[17] Some researchers use a more restrictive definition of concerted intervention which does not include operations which would have been undertaken by the individual central banks even in the absence of any co-ordination (e.g. Wallich, 1984; Rogoff, 1985).

referred to as the 'policy-optimisation' analysis. In a typical game, the rational agents are national governments, whose preferences are formalised using a loss function biased towards domestic welfare. Co-operative and nonco-operative games can then be analysed and the outcomes from the two types of games can be compared in order to infer the optimal strategy for governments. In choosing its loss-minimising strategy, each national government also takes into account the preferences and the reactions of the other governments (e.g. Buiter and Eaton, 1985; Cooper, 1985). However, although the policy-optimisation approach has generated some valuable insights, its underlying strong rational-choice assumptions have often been questioned and the approach seems to have become increasingly less popular over time.[18]

With regard to non-sterilised intervention, the benefits from co-ordination of non-sterilised operations are identical to the benefits from monetary policy co-ordination. Nevertheless, the advantage of co-ordination of non-sterilised official intervention over monetary policy co-ordination is that the former, unlike the latter, creates an explicit incentive to co-ordinate monetary policies consistent with exchange rate targets for the countries involved (see Dominguez and Frankel, 1993a).

However, the advantages of co-ordination for sterilised exchange rate intervention are less straightforward. In fact, the effectiveness of sterilised intervention through the portfolio balance channel is totally independent of monetary policy effectiveness and, therefore, countries can design concerted official intervention without relinquishing sovereignty over domestic monetary policy. If sterilised intervention works through the signalling channel though, there may be gains from co-ordinating official intervention. This is because the co-ordination of multiple signals is more likely to convince speculators that the signalled policy is credible than an individual signal, implying that sterilised official intervention co-ordination may help central banks with relatively low reputation or credibility (Kenen, 1988, ch. 6; Dominguez and Frankel, 1993a).[19]

Nevertheless, another recent formal treatment of these issues by Flandreau (1998) has gone one step further in demonstrating the gains from co-ordination of official intervention in the foreign exchange market. Flandreau constructs a model where several target zones coexist and parities are defended by manipulating money supplies in participating countries. As a result, interventions aimed at one given exchange rate also affect other exchange rates, implying that shocks on each fundamental affect the whole range of exchange rates involved, intramarginal interventions arise endogenously and the stationary distributions of exchange rates and fundamentals are influenced by the 'rules of the game' regarding currencies used in intervention and sterilisation procedures. The model ultimately predicts large gains from international co-ordination for all participating countries since 'intramarginal targets' are

[18] Two alternative, but less commonly adopted approaches to the analysis of international co-ordinated macroeconomic policy are the so-called 'rule' analysis, which focuses on international co-operation through presumptive rules or guidelines, and 'institutional' analysis, a more general approach which attempts to nest both the policy-optimisation approach and the rule analysis (see Bryant, 1995). See also the papers in Wihlborg, Fratianni and Willett (1991).

[19] A number of episodes in economic history suggest that, in general, co-ordinated macroeconomic policies across countries may be much more effective than unilaterally designed policies. See Isard (1995, ch. 12) for an interesting historical overview of international policy co-operation.

generated to which exchange rates tend to return and their location is shown to depend on the intervention–sterilisation mix adopted by monetary authorities.

Overall, therefore, the existence of significant gains from international co-ordination of official intervention relative to individual intervention appears to be an accepted theoretical result as well as a stylised fact.

7.1.3.3 The profitability of intervention

According to Friedman's (1953) view on official intervention, a central bank which is successful in stabilising the exchange rate should, in principle, make a profit at the expense of speculators, which implies that if official intervention is not profitable it is not effective. This is the rationale for measuring the profitability of intervention as a means of evaluating the effectiveness of official intervention.

Empirical studies focusing on the profitability of intervention operations are, however, limited, especially because of the significant difficulties encountered in trying to calculate profits and losses in this context. The econometric procedures employed by researchers vary from study to study, but the conclusion generally suggested by the relevant literature is that central banks tend to earn profits from their intervention operations.

Researchers typically measure central banks' profits from official intervention on the basis of equations of the form:

$$z_t = \sum_{k=1}^{t} \left[f x_k (s_t - s_k) + s_k (i_k^* - i_k) \sum_{j=1}^{k} f x_j \right] \tag{7.6}$$

where z_t denotes profits, $f x_k$ denotes purchases of foreign exchange, s_t and s_k are end-of-period nominal exchange rates (domestic prices of foreign currency) at times t and k respectively, and i_k and i_k^* denote the domestic and foreign interest rates respectively at time k; all variables are expressed in natural logarithms except for the interest rates. In this equation, profits are determined by two factors: (a) the differential between the end-of-period exchange rate at time t and the exchange rate at which the foreign currency was purchased at time k; and (b) the interest rate differential between the two countries whose currencies are involved in the intervention operation.

The empirical evidence provided by researchers on the profitability of intervention in the 1980s, well surveyed by Edison (1993), Sweeney (1997) and Neely (1998), suggests that profits from intervention operations may vary significantly according to the sample period considered but, in general and in the long run, central banks make profits.

A general fundamental drawback, however, of this strand of the literature is concerned with the implicit assumption that the profitability of intervention represents a valid criterion by which to measure the effectiveness of official intervention. As clearly shown by, among others, Edison (1993), it is possible to think about very realistic situations in which stabilising (effective) official intervention may not be profitable and, vice versa, situations in which official intervention may be destabilising but profitable. The argument is that, if the authorities were to purchase foreign exchange when its price was low and sell it when its price was high, then, abstracting from interest-rate considerations, intervention would be profitable even if the purchases and sales had no significant effect on exchange rates. If the central bank can earn profits on intervention that has no effect on exchange rates, then it is difficult to argue that those profits imply that intervention has a stabilising effect on exchange rates. In general, therefore, profitability of intervention is *not* a test of its effectiveness in moving exchange rates.

Nevertheless, central bank intervention losses or profits vary widely, with some studies reporting substantial losses, others substantial profits. In most cases, however, estimated profits are not risk-adjusted, although risk adjustment may have a very significant effect. Also, profit estimates involve time series which are generally found to be integrated of order one (hence nonstationary), implying that test statistics in this context are likely to have non-standard distributions; very few studies take this factor into account. Estimates of risk-adjusted profits for the US and the Swedish central banks, computed allowing for non-standard distributions, suggest that none of these central banks had made losses and may even have made significant profits (see Sweeney, 1997).

A different but related recent literature focuses on the relationship between central bank intervention and trading-rule profits in foreign exchange markets. Studies in this context often examine moving average trading rules, which are utilised in both futures and spot foreign exchange markets to show that substantial profits can be earned for various currencies (Taylor and Allen, 1992). Also, central bank intervention is usually found to be strongly associated with the profitability of trading returns for these major currencies and partially explains returns (Szakmarky and Mathur, 1997). However, this literature largely focuses on investigating whether simple rules used by traders have some predictive value over the future movement of foreign exchange rates in connection with central bank activity, with the main objective of finding out to what extent foreign exchange predictability can be confined to periods of central bank activity in the foreign exchange market. The emerging stylised fact from the relevant literature seems to be that, after removing periods in which the central bank has been particularly active in the foreign exchange market, exchange rate predictability is dramatically reduced (LeBaron, 1996).[20]

We now turn to a brief discussion of data issues in the context of empirical research on official foreign exchange intervention.

7.1.3.4   Data on exchange rate intervention   An important issue in the empirical literature on official intervention is concerned with data availability. Although one might expect that data defined in terms of the monetary authorities' balance sheets would be easily accessible, in practice it has been very difficult until very recently to collect data on official intervention at reasonable frequencies.

Monthly and quarterly data on monetary authorities' international reserves are given in most central banks' statistical publications, while quarterly data are available, for example, from the International Financial Statistics database of the International Monetary Fund. In fact, a number of empirical studies on official intervention have used changes in reserves as a proxy for intervention flows. These data, however, represent a very inaccurate proxy since monetary authorities' international reserves may change for a number of reasons

---

[20] Leahy (1989) analyses the profitability of US official intervention, extending the sample period to part of the 1980s, and reports results consistent with Jacobson's (1983) study using a more general formula for the computation of profits.

other than, and often not related to, official intervention. Reserves increase, for example, with interest receipts on official portfolio holdings, and fluctuate widely with valuation changes on existing reserves. Most tellingly, reserves do not include transactions that are in fact intervention operations, such as the so-called hidden reserves, which may be seen as changes of official deposits of foreign currency with domestic currency and are regularly used by a number of central banks; in particular, they are very frequently adopted by the Bank of Japan (see Dominguez and Frankel, 1993a; Edison, 1993).

Ideally, any study on official intervention which attempts to be informative on both the short- and long-term effectiveness of official intervention should use minute-by-minute data, since this is the time scale on which intervention of the monetary authorities in the foreign exchange market occurs. Nevertheless, daily data may represent a sufficiently good approximation.

The present discussion is obviously closely linked to investigation of the reasons for which secrecy – or omission of a detailed report – on official intervention is maintained also *ex post* by monetary authorities. While arguments exist in favour of the secrecy of official intervention, it is unclear why central banks have not been interested for a long time in releasing data *ex post* to researchers.

A change in this practice has been made, however, by the US authorities, as US daily data for intervention are now available, following the authorisation by the US Treasury to the Board of Governors of the Federal Reserve System to release them in the early 1990s. Germany and Japan have recently followed the example of the United States. The other G7 countries have not yet followed this practice and, therefore, the process of gathering intervention data still requires the reconstruction of the operations of the monetary authorities on the basis of reports in the financial press. These, however, are not expected to report comprehensively every secret operation, especially small ones which may not be identified even by traders in the foreign exchange market.

An alternative strategy, recently proposed by Weymark (1997a,b) would be to construct an index of intervention activity which can be calculated on the basis of observed data. The intervention index proposed by Weymark measures intervention activity as the proportion of exchange market pressure relieved by exchange market intervention. Weymark establishes analytically the properties of the intervention index using a rational expectations model of a small open economy. Weymark also shows how to calculate measures of bilateral and multilateral intervention for Canada over the period 1975–90. Weymark's measure may represent a plausible alternative to measured changes in international reserves.

7.2 The channels of influence of official intervention

In theory, sterilised intervention may influence the exchange rate through two channels: by changing the relative supplies of assets, and by signalling policy intentions.

7.2.1 The channels of influence: the portfolio balance channel

The effects of official intervention through the portfolio balance channel can be analysed within the framework of a portfolio balance model (PBM) of exchange rate determination in which investors balance their portfolio among the assets of various countries on the basis of their relative expected returns.

In order to illustrate the mechanics of the portfolio balance channel, suppose, for example, that the authorities purchase foreign exchange and carry out an open-market sale of domestic bonds in order to sterilise the effect of a rise in official reserves on the money supply. If domestic and foreign bonds are perfect substitutes in private agents' portfolios (so that the PBM essentially collapses to a monetary model) and agents' portfolios were initially in stock equilibrium, then investors will sell foreign bonds one for one with the increase in domestic bonds. Thus, the private sector will sell the same amount of foreign currency that the authorities bought, and there will be a zero net effect on the level of the exchange rate.

Also, note that, in a Ricardian world where private agents offset expected future tax payments (which will be required to service extra government debt) against currency holdings of domestic bonds (Barro, 1974), imperfect substitutability would no longer be a sufficient condition for sterilised intervention to influence the current exchange rate. If Ricardian equivalence does not hold, however, and domestic and foreign bonds are less than perfectly substitutable, official intervention will have a net effect on the level of the exchange rate.

In the PBM, the assumptions – underlying both the flexible-price and the sticky-price monetary models – that domestic and foreign assets are perfect substitutes and that the wealth effects of a current account imbalance are negligible are relaxed (see Isard, 1980; Branson, 1983, 1984). In common with the class of monetary models, however, the level of the exchange rate is determined in the PBM by supply and demand for domestic and foreign financial assets. Nevertheless, the exchange rate's main determinant is the current account balance; a surplus (deficit) in the current account balance is associated with a rise (fall) in net domestic holdings of foreign assets, which influences the level of wealth and, in turn, the level of the demand for assets, and ultimately affects the exchange rate. The PBM may be seen, therefore, as a dynamic model of exchange rate determination based on the interaction of asset markets, current account balance, prices and the rate of asset accumulation, which allows one to distinguish between the short-run (flow) equilibrium and the long-run (stock) equilibrium.

In order to analyse the effectiveness of (sterilised) official intervention, a large number of studies focus on the traditional formulation of the PBM under the assumption that the Ricardian equivalence theorem does not hold. In that framework, investors allocate their wealth among different assets in proportions that are assumed to be increasing functions of the expected return on each asset. Moreover, under the assumption that investors are risk-averse and that rates of return are uncertain, investors maximise expected profits by diversifying their portfolios.

The PBM has not attracted a large empirical literature relative to other models of exchange rate determination and in particular relative to monetary models, perhaps because many problems are encountered in mapping the theoretical framework of the PBM into real-world financial data. In particular, the choice of non-monetary assets to be considered in the empirical model is difficult and data are not always available on a bilateral basis. In general, however, two types of tests have been conducted by the relevant empirical literature. The first type is based on estimating a reduced-form solution of the PBM in order to measure its explanatory power; this approach is often called the direct demand approach. The second type focuses on solving the PBM for the risk premium and testing for perfect substitutability of bonds denominated in different currencies: the inverted demand approach.[21]

The assumption of imperfect substitutability of domestic and foreign assets in the PBM is equivalent to assuming that there is a risk premium separating expected depreciation and the domestic–foreign interest differential; also, in the PBM this risk premium turns out to be a function of relative domestic and foreign debt outstanding. In estimating the portfolio balance model using the inverted asset demand approach, researchers typically estimate an equation where the risk premium (say ρ) is a function of domestic and foreign bond holdings (B and B^*) (and, in more complex formulations, of income and wealth):

$$\rho_t = \rho_1 B_t + \rho_2 B_t^* \tag{7.7}$$

where, for simplicity, we have assumed a linear static specification. Typically, the risk premium is measured by deviations from uncovered interest parity, either assuming rational expectations or employing survey data (see Chapter 2). Under the null hypothesis that assets are perfectly substitutable at home and abroad, the coefficients on the bond holdings variable should all be zero. On the other hand, if the portfolio balance channel hypothesis holds, then the coefficients on bond holdings should be statistically significant.

In general, the empirical literature on testing the PBM suggests that sterilised intervention is effective at most in the very short term (e.g. Frankel, 1982a; Rogoff, 1984; Lewis, 1988; Edison, 1993), while the joint hypothesis of rational expectations and perfect substitutability of domestic and foreign assets is regularly rejected. Also, much of this literature suggests that the exchange rate effects of intervention through the portfolio balance channel are very small in size (e.g. see Frankel, 1982a; Obstfeld, 1983; Rogoff, 1984; Danker, Haas, Henderson, Symansky and Tryon, 1987; Lewis, 1988).

An early study in this context is due to Loopesko (1984), who uses a measure of cumulated daily data on official intervention for the G7 countries instead of a measure of outstanding asset stocks to estimate the PBM using the inverted demand approach. The joint hypothesis of rational expectations and perfect substitutability is tested by estimating an equation for the risk premium where the explanatory variables considered are lags of the dependent variable, lagged exchange rates and the cumulated intervention proxy variable. The coefficient on the lagged cumulated intervention variable is found to be statistically significantly different from zero at conventional nominal levels of significance for various sample periods considered. Loopesko concludes that the results provide evidence that sterilised intervention is short-term effective through the portfolio balance channel.

As a part of the 1983 G7 Working Group project, Danker, Haas, Henderson, Symansky and Tryon (1987) estimate the PBM using both the direct demand approach and the inverted demand approach with quarterly data for the United States, Germany, Japan and Canada.

---

[21] Log-linear versions of reduced-form portfolio balance exchange rate equations, using cumulated current accounts for the stock of foreign assets, have been estimated for various major exchange rates for the 1970s float, with poor results (e.g. Branson, Halttunen and Masson, 1977; Dooley and Isard, 1982). More recently, Lewis (1988) estimates foreign bond demand equations derived from the PBM of exchange rate determination for five countries. While other studies limit the portfolio choice to domestic assets relative to a composite foreign asset, Lewis' approach is interesting because it considers a decomposition of the foreign asset by currency. Further, Lewis exploits the cross-equation correlation that arises from this decomposition in order to obtain more efficient estimates of the parameters, providing some empirical evidence in support of the PBM.

In general, they find that the coefficients on the risk premium variable are correctly signed, albeit not always statistically significantly different from zero. Some of the coefficients on the other explanatory variables are, however, wrongly signed, and the joint hypothesis of rational expectations and perfect substitution is strongly rejected. The study is, overall, inconclusive with respect to the effectiveness of sterilised intervention.

Further evidence on the effectiveness of sterilisation policy through the portfolio balance channel comes from estimation of fully specified macroeconomic models which incorporate portfolio balance equations. At least two studies should be noted in this context. Obstfeld (1983) investigates the effectiveness of sterilised intervention operated by the Bundesbank during the period 1975–81. The policy dilemma faced by West Germany during that period was the conflict between internal and external equilibrium, that is the conflict between the attainment of domestic policy targets and the attainment of external policy targets. Obstfeld estimates a postulated reaction function for the Bundesbank during the sample period considered and provides strong evidence that sterilised intervention played a very important role since only a very small proportion of the changes in reserves affected the monetary base. In order to assess the effectiveness of German official intervention, Obstfeld also estimates a structural portfolio balance macroeconomic model for Germany, under the assumption of perfect foresight. Obstfeld concludes, however, that official intervention in Germany was not effective and the Bundesbank could only influence the exchange rate by altering current or expected future money-market conditions since the time span over which sterilised intervention proved to be effective was about one month.

A similar approach is taken by Blundell-Wignall and Masson (1985), who consider a sticky-price portfolio balance model which may be viewed as a variant of Dornbusch's (1976) overshooting model, allowing for asset supplies through a risk premium variable, in order to analyse the dynamic effects of a postulated intervention rule of the monetary authorities. Estimating the model for Germany during the 1973–82 period, Blundell-Wignall and Masson find that the risk premium parameter is statistically significant at standard nominal levels of significance, albeit small in magnitude. The estimation results also indicate that the main concern of the Bundesbank's policy was with real exchange rate stabilisation during the sample. While no strong support is found for nominal exchange rate overshooting in the short run, the authors suggest that real exchange rates depreciated substantially as prices took a longer time to adjust. Overall, the results are not particularly supportive of the effectiveness of sterilised intervention, since the effect of intervention is statistically significant but small in magnitude and short-lived.[22]

Another strand of the literature has investigated the effectiveness of sterilised official intervention using variants of the PBM which incorporate mean-variance optimisation, following the seminal paper by Frankel (1982b). Frankel's insight is to exploit the fact that the coefficients of inverted portfolio balance equations are found to be related to the variance-covariance matrix. Frankel incorporates mean-variance optimisation in the portfolio balance framework, yielding a multicurrency asset-demand equation in which investors maximise some function of the mean and the variance of their end-of-period wealth. Frankel (1982b)

---

[22] Similar findings are also provided by Tryon (1983).

then estimates a PBM with mean-variance optimisation and tests the null hypothesis that the parameter representing the coefficient of risk aversion is equal to zero – which would imply that countries' assets are perfect substitutes and there are no risk premia – against the alternative hypothesis that rates of return are related to asset supplies in the PBM. His empirical results suggest that the null hypothesis cannot be rejected for the portfolio of six major industrialised countries. However, Frankel and Engel (1984) are able to reject the joint null hypothesis of rational expectations and perfect substitutability using an inverted demand PBM, although, within a PBM with mean-variance optimisation with the same currencies as in Frankel (1982b) and allowing for stochastic rates of inflation, they reject the mean-variance constraints. Overall, the disappointing but important finding in both Frankel's (1982b) study and Frankel and Engel's (1984) study is that no statistical link appears to exist between asset supplies and the risk premium, implying that sterilised intervention cannot influence the risk premium or the exchange rate and is, therefore, ineffective.[23]

Some support for significant portfolio balance effects is provided by Ghosh (1992). Ghosh's approach is to use a forward-looking monetary model of the exchange rate in order to capture signalling effects. Since the monetary model implies that the exchange rate is a function of expected future monetary fundamentals, the monetary policy signalling effects must be captured. This then allows Ghosh to test for the effects of sterilised intervention through channels other than the signalling channel. Using monthly data for the US dollar–German mark rate over the period 1980–8, Ghosh provides evidence for a weak, but statistically significant, portfolio influence on the exchange rate. His model also performs well in forecasting, displaying a very high correlation between the actual and fitted values of the exchange rate and outperforming an alternative random walk model in out-of-sample forecasting. In a sense, as Ghosh notes (1992, p. 217), his approach is mildly 'schizophrenic', in that a significant portfolio balance effect implies rejection of the monetary model. Ghosh argues, however, that other indicators of the monetary model's performance, such as in-sample fit and predictive performance, indicate that 'the model provides a reasonable filter for removing the influence of agents' expectations of future policies' (ibid.).

Karfakis and Kim (1995) investigate the relationship between exchange rates, interest rates and current account news using Australian data for the period from July 1985 to December 1992. They provide evidence that the Australian dollar depreciated over the sample examined and interest rates rose as a result of an announcement of a larger than expected current account deficit. Karfakis and Kim interpret their results as consistent with the view that market participants expected a foreign exchange market intervention sale of the Australian dollar by the Reserve Bank of Australia and that they used a portfolio balance model when responding to news.

The conventional wisdom that official intervention is ineffective has been strongly challenged by Dominguez and Frankel (1993b). Using survey data on US dollar–German mark and US dollar–Swiss franc exchange rate expectations to construct measures of the risk premium as the deviation from uncovered interest rate parity, Dominguez and Frankel

---

[23] This finding is replicated by subsequent studies which extend Frankel's framework by allowing for inflation risk and disturbances in the asset market (Lewis, 1988) or by allowing for autoregressive conditional heteroscedasticity in the variance of the expected return (Engel and Rodrigues, 1989).

(1993b) find that intervention variables have statistically significant explanatory power for the risk premium. In particular, effectiveness of sterilised intervention is established both through the portfolio balance channel (with mean-variance optimisation) and the signalling channel. We provide a longer discussion of this study below.

We now turn to a discussion of the other potential channel through which official exchange rate intervention may operate, the signalling, or expectations, channel.

7.2.2   The channels of influence: the signalling channel

The signalling, or expectations, channel (Mussa, 1981) assumes that intervention affects exchange rates by providing the market with new relevant information, under the implicit assumption that the authorities have superior information to other market participants and that they are willing to reveal this information through their actions in the foreign exchange market. More precisely, the effect of sterilised intervention through the signalling channel occurs because private agents change their exchange rate expectations either because they change their view of the likely future actions of the monetary authorities or because they change their view of the *impact* of certain actions of the monetary authorities. Even in a simple flexible-price monetary model, for example, sterilised intervention could affect the exchange rate through the signalling channel by altering agents' expectations about future movements in relative money or income, which then feeds back into the current exchange rate. Sterilised intervention may be effective through the signalling channel even if domestic and foreign assets are perfectly substitutable.[24]

The empirical literature investigating the significance of the signalling channel is relatively recent but growing, and draws especially on the release of daily data on intervention by the US authorities in the early 1990s.

Dominguez (1987) investigates the ability of monetary authorities to signal monetary policy intentions and affect market expectations of the future exchange rate, using weekly US data for the February 1977–February 1981 period. Dominguez estimates regressions of the intervention variable on money surprises, defined on the basis of publicly available pre-announced money supply forecasts. The results suggest that money supply surprises display positive correlation with intervention during periods of high reputation and credibility of the monetary authorities. Dominguez (1987) also estimates a simple regression of exchange rate changes on intervention as a test of the signalling channel hypothesis and finds that in periods of high reputation and heavy sterilised official intervention, the monetary authorities are able to influence exchange rate changes, which are found to be positively related to intervention.

---

[24] The theory of the signalling channel of official intervention has attracted some renewed interest in recent years. Reeves (1997), for example, constructs a two-country model to examine the theoretical implication of the signalling channel of foreign exchange market interventions that sterilised interventions represent signals of future monetary policy and hence affect exchange rate expectations. Within a game-theoretic framework which allows for partial credibility and non-rational expectations, both nonco-operative and co-operative policies of exchange rate management are derived. Reeves model predicts that, in order to maintain credibility in the future, sterilised interventions must be accommodated by corresponding subsequent changes in the money supply, implying that official intervention does not represent an instrument independent of general monetary policy. Reeves also illustrates that the implied trade-off between internal and external policy objectives makes the co-ordination of official intervention operations advantageous, even in the case of conflicting exchange rate targets. See also Reeves (1998).

Overall, Dominguez interprets her results as evidence supportive of the signalling hypothesis. Obstfeld (1990) examines the effectiveness of foreign exchange intervention after the 1985 Plaza Hotel announcement by the G5 countries, when a substantial realignment of exchange rates occurred and, at the same time, foreign exchange market intervention – mainly concerted and sterilised – was undertaken on a scale not seen since the early 1970s. Obstfeld concludes, however, that sterilised intervention has played a relatively minor role in promoting exchange rate realignment. Instead, he argues that clear shifts in the patterns of monetary and fiscal policy were the main policy factors determining currency values during the late 1980s.

Another interesting contribution to this literature is due to Humpage (1989), who tests the hypothesis that sterilised intervention operates through the signalling channel through a regression of the form:

$$s_t = \beta_0 + \beta_1 s_{t-2} + \sum_{i=1}^{p} \beta_{2i} INT_{t-i} + \sum_{j=1}^{q} \beta_{3j}(i_{t-j} - i^*_{t-j}) + \varepsilon_t, \tag{7.8}$$

where INT_t denotes the intervention variable and ε_t is a white-noise error; the twice-lagged nominal exchange rate is a proxy for the expected exchange rate and the interest rate differential is expected to capture the effect of monetary policy changes. Humpage tests the null hypothesis that sterilised intervention operates through the signalling channel, H_0: $\beta_1 = 1$ and $\beta_{2i} > 0$ in (7.8), using daily data for the Japanese yen–US dollar and the German mark–US dollar exchange rates from 3 August 1984 to 30 October 1987, dividing the sample into five sub-periods. His empirical results are, however, disappointing in that the null hypothesis that sterilised intervention operates through the signalling channel is rejected and the intervention variable is generally not found to be statistically significantly different from zero at conventional nominal levels of significance. Also, no statistically significant difference is found between co-ordinated and unilateral intervention.[25]

Eijffinger and Gruijters (1991a,b) investigate the effectiveness of sterilised intervention through the signalling channel, using a very similar approach to Humpage (1989), for the daily German mark–US dollar exchange rate from February 1985 to September 1988. Their results are consistent with Humpage (1989) and Humpage and Osterberg (1990) in that the effect of sterilised intervention on the exchange rate is found to be very small.

A different approach is taken by Dominguez (1990), who estimates an inverted portfolio balance equation with the risk premium as the dependent variable, under the assumption of rational expectations. Nevertheless, Dominguez argues that her estimation procedure provides information on the effectiveness of sterilised intervention through the signalling channel rather than the portfolio balance channel because the explanatory variable used in the estimated regression is actual intervention rather than cumulated intervention, the variable more commonly used in the literature. Dominguez estimates a regression of the form:

$$\rho_t = \gamma_0 + \gamma_1 INT^C_{t-1} + \gamma_2 INT^{NC}_{t-1} + \omega_t, \tag{7.9}$$

---

[25] See also Humpage and Osterberg (1990), who use a similar approach to Humpage (1989) and find similar results, although they also allow for generalised autoregressive conditional heteroscedasticity in the error term.

where ρ_t is the risk premium, INT_t^C and INT_t^{NC} are defined as co-ordinated and nonco-ordinated actual intervention, and ω_t is a white-noise error. Using daily data for the same currencies as Humpage (1989) and for a very similar sample period (January 1985 to December 1987), Dominguez produces results for five sub-periods. For the first two sub-periods, the estimation produces significant and correctly signed coefficients on the intervention variables, while in the remaining sub-periods the coefficients are either significant but wrongly signed or correctly signed but not statistically significantly different from zero at the 5 per cent significance level. Also, in contrast to Humpage (1989) and Humpage and Osterberg (1990), different effects are found for co-ordinated and nonco-ordinated intervention for various sub-periods and, in general, the coefficient on co-ordinated intervention is found to be more strongly statistically significant.

More recently, Dominguez and Frankel (1993a) employ an alternative estimation procedure, different from all previous studies, as they test both channels of influence without assuming rational expectations of exchange rates; in fact, the expected future US dollar–German mark exchange rates used in the estimation are weekly and biweekly survey data on market forecasts. Dominguez and Frankel estimate a two-equation system where one of the equations defines the expectations formation mechanism and the other is an inverted portfolio balance equation which allows for mean-variance optimisation.[26] Moreover, Dominguez and Frankel consider all the fundamentals usually considered in traditional exchange rate determination models as explanatory variables, thereby providing a more carefully specified reduced-form regression for the exchange rate relative to previous studies. Intervention is defined in three different ways: one-day intervention (occurring at the end of the day before the survey), one-week or two-week intervention (i.e. cumulated between survey forecasts) and cumulated intervention (cumulated from the beginning of the sample period). The authors also distinguish, in some of the many regressions estimated in their study, between public and secret intervention. Overall, Dominguez and Frankel provide strong statistical evidence that sterilised intervention is effective through both the portfolio balance channel and the signalling channel. They also show that, for certain parameter values and under the two assumptions that interest rates are constant and that expectations are neither adaptive nor extrapolative, the quantitative effects of sterilised intervention may be substantial. The results are probably the most supportive of the effectiveness of official intervention in the whole literature. The use of survey data, the bilateral (rather than multilateral) basis of the estimated regression, the sample period considered (only data for the 1980s) and the constraint of mean-variance optimisation imposed in the inverted portfolio balance equation are all factors that may have generated the findings of Dominguez and Frankel (1993a). The authors conclude their monograph with a certain degree of optimism:

Our results suggest that intervention can be effective, especially if it is publicly announced and concerted. It may be that sterilized intervention can only have effects in the short term. But if 'short-term

[26] More precisely, the expectations formation mechanism is described by an equation where the investor's forecast of the expected future exchange rate is the dependent variable and the explanatory variables are the difference between the contemporaneous and the lagged exchange rate and three different dummies for information on intervention reported in newspapers, actual intervention operated by the Bundesbank and actual intervention by the Federal Reserve Bank, when reported in the newspapers.

effects' include the bursting of a nine-month bubble earlier than it would otherwise have burst, then such an effect may be all that is needed . . . Our specific recommendations are quite modest: that the authorities make their interventions public, that an interagency process regularly consider exchange rate developments in light of developments in the fundamentals, and the G7 discussions on macroeconomic policy and exchange rates be integrated. (pp. 139–40)

In a further study, Dominguez and Frankel (1993c), using survey data on dollar–mark exchange rate expectations, provide evidence that official announcements of exchange rate policy and reported intervention significantly affect exchange rate expectations and that, overall, the effectiveness of intervention, in terms of significantly affecting both weekly and daily exchange rate changes, is very much enhanced if it is publicly announced.

While each of the last two studies by Dominguez and Frankel cited above employs daily data obtained from the US and German authorities, Catte, Galli and Rebecchini (1994) also employ daily data on the intervention of Japanese authorities and analyse co-ordinated G3 intervention over the 1985–91 period. Some seventeen episodes of co-ordinated intervention identified over this period are examined, and the authors claim that all were successful in the sense of reversing the trend in the dollar and, in the case of the Plaza episode (late 1985), making the dollar resume its fall. Of ten major turning points in the dollar–mark exchange rate over the period examined, the authors identify nine as coinciding exactly with periods of concerted intervention. Note that Catte, Galli and Rebecchini make no attempt to disentangle sterilised from non-sterilised intervention; neither do they attempt to disentangle the portfolio balance and signalling channel effects. In interpreting their results, however, Catte, Galli and Rebecchini do seem to favour the signalling channel hypothesis.

An interesting recent contribution in this area is due to Lewis (1995), who uses publicly available data on US foreign exchange rate intervention for the period from 1985 through 1990 and examines the relationship between foreign exchange market intervention and monetary policy, testing the hypothesis that official intervention signals changes in future monetary policy as well as the hypothesis that changes in monetary policy may induce leaning-against-the-wind interventions. Lewis' study provides persuasive supportive evidence for both hypotheses, suggesting that official intervention may predict monetary policy variables and vice versa. In her study, Lewis also examines the response of exchange rates to shocks in various monetary policy variables and finds that positive innovations in non-borrowed reserves are related more to depreciation in the dollar exchange rate than to M1.

More recently, Kaminsky and Lewis (1996) examine the prediction of signalling channel theory that central banks signal a more contractionary monetary policy in the future by buying domestic currency today and, therefore, that expectations of future tighter monetary policy make the domestic currency appreciate, even though the current monetary effects of the intervention are typically offset by sterilisation. Kaminsky and Lewis then argue that this expectation presumes that central banks in fact back up interventions with subsequent changes in monetary policy, and also provide evidence in favour of this presumption.

Another interesting contribution, due to Bonser-Neal, Roley and Sellon (1998), re-examines the relationship between the Federal Reserve monetary policy actions, US interventions in currency markets and exchange rates using an alternative measure of monetary policy actions – the Federal Reserve's federal funds interest rate target. The authors find that the exchange rate generally responds immediately to US monetary policy actions and that this response is usually consistent with the overshooting hypothesis. The authors also find evidence of signalling and leaning against the wind in US intervention policies over the sample period.

Another closely related strand of the literature has recently addressed the question of whether there is a link between central bank intervention and the volatility of foreign exchange rates. Bonser-Neal and Tanner (1996), for example, test the effects of central bank intervention on the *ex ante* volatility of the US dollar–German mark and the US dollar–Japanese yen rates between 1985 and 1991, estimating *ex ante* volatility using the implied volatilities of currency option prices and also controlling for the effects of other macroeconomic announcements. Bonser-Neal and Tanner find little support for the hypothesis that central bank intervention is associated with a positive change in *ex ante* exchange rate volatility or with no change.

A rigorous theoretical model explaining the rationale of a link between intervention and exchange rate volatility is provided by Baillie and Osterberg (1997), who construct a two-country intertemporal asset-pricing model which implies that central bank foreign exchange intervention affects the forward exchange risk premium. Baillie and Osterberg estimate their model using daily foreign exchange intervention data for the US, German and Japanese central banks, and provide considerable empirical support of the model's prediction that intervention influences the risk premium in the forward market. Purchases of dollars by the Federal Reserve are found to be associated with excess dollar-denominated returns, and there is persuasive evidence that intervention has increased rather than reduced exchange rate volatility.

Chang and Taylor (1998) go one step ahead in that they examine the effects of intervention by the Bank of Japan using intraday data from 1 October 1992 to 30 September 1993 and news related to the Bank of Japan intervention in the yen–dollar market retrieved from Reuters' reports. They find that yen-dollar volatility varies significantly differently across periods from one before to one after Reuters' intervention reports. Using autoregressive conditional heteroscedasticity models (Engle, 1982), Chang and Taylor find that their intervention proxy has the largest effect on high-frequency volatility thirty to forty-five minutes prior to Reuters' reports of intervention.

Overall, the evidence on the effectiveness of official intervention, through either the portfolio balance channel or the signalling channel, is still mixed, although the recent literature does suggest a significant effect of official intervention on both the level and the change of exchange rates. Given the increasing availability of daily data on intervention, however, further empirical research on the effectiveness of intervention is likely.

7.3   Central bank reaction functions

7.3.1   A positive approach to foreign exchange intervention

Although the evidence discussed above concerning the effectiveness of official intervention is quite mixed, most central banks regularly conduct foreign exchange operations. This section provides a positive approach to official intervention, describing the relationship between the objectives and the constraints faced by the monetary authorities when designing and implementing exchange rate policies, in an attempt to shed light on the behaviour of central banks in foreign-currency markets and on their reaction functions.

The theoretical literature on optimal exchange rate management is enormous (e.g. see, among others, Boyer, 1978; Artis and Currie, 1981; Batchelor and Wood, 1982; Artis and Karakitsos, 1985; Bhandari, 1985; Canzoneri and Underwood, 1985; Flood and Hodrick, 1987; Turnovsky, 1987; Kenen, 1988; Glick and Hutchison, 1989). The conventional theoretical analysis mainly focuses on designing an exchange rate policy which minimises the variance of output around its natural rate.[27] Also, the traditional approach taken by this literature is based on a flow model of the exchange rate which accounts for three types of currency flows: flows generated by current account transactions (CA), net flow demand for domestic currency through the capital account of the balance of payments (ΔK) and currency flows arising directly from central bank intervention in the market (INT) (see Black, 1985; Neumann, 1985). The market-clearing condition involving those three currency flows may be written:

$$INT_t = CA_t + \Delta K_t, \tag{7.10}$$

where the left-hand side and the right-hand side of the equation describe the net supply of, and the net demand for, domestic currency, respectively. The current account flow is assumed to be some function of the lagged real exchange rate, i.e. $CA = CA(q_{t-1}, q_{t-2}, \ldots)$ where q_t denotes the real exchange rate in the domestic economy, while a function for the net flow demand for domestic currency through the capital account of the balance of payments may be derived, for example, using the framework of speculative dynamics models developed by Stein (1987) and De Long, Shleifer, Summers and Waldmann (1990).

According to these models, the investor's optimum position in domestic-currency-denominated assets, say K^*, depends on three factors:

$$K_t^* = (\overset{+}{\rho_t}, \overset{-}{\gamma}, \overline{var}_t s_{t+1}), \tag{7.11}$$

where ρ_t and γ denote the risk premium and the risk aversion coefficient respectively, $var_t s_{t+1}$ is the conditional variance of the next-period spot rate, and the positive (negative) sign over a variable indicates that the variable in question is positively (negatively) related to K^*. According to (7.11), investors invest more in assets denominated in the domestic currency the higher the deviation from uncovered interest parity (equal to the risk premium), the lower their aversion to risk and the lower the conditional variance of the next-period spot rate (see Almekinders, 1995).[28]

The theoretical literature in this context essentially models official intervention by assuming a particular central bank loss function from which, given a particular process governing

---

[27] This implicitly assumes, however, that the main concern of the monetary authorities is to choose the optimal degree of non-sterilised intervention in response to idiosyncratic shocks, and therefore, in some sense, this approach neglects the fact that the monetary authorities widely use sterilised intervention.

[28] For simplicity, it is assumed that the conditional variance of the future spot rate is constant, i.e. $var_{t-1}s_t = var_t s_{t+1} = var_{t+1} s_{t+2}$, and, incidentally, that the exchange rate is stationary, which may well not be the case.

exchange rate movements,[29] estimatable central bank reaction functions can be derived. Several authors assume, for example, that the central bank has a single-period, quadratic, symmetric loss function of the deviation of the current exchange rate from its target level, and that there are costs of intervening in the foreign exchange market (e.g. see Almekinders, 1995).[30]

While this class of models provides useful insights on the strategic behaviour of the monetary authorities and allows researchers to derive reaction functions which can be easily estimated, they do suffer, however, from some drawbacks. In particular, these models treat the central bank on the same terms as the other market participants, who, therefore, do not have any informational gain from monitoring the actions of the central bank. It may be more appropriate to withdraw this assumption in future studies: even if, in general, the volume of intervention that a central bank can generate is not strongly significant in highly integrated foreign exchange markets, central banks should have a larger information set, not least because they know more about their own future actions than do other market participants.[31, 32]

A move in this direction is due to Bhattacharya and Weller (1997), who build an asymmetric information model of sterilised intervention where the equilibrium is characterised by a situation in which the central bank has inside information about its exchange rate target whereas risk-averse speculators have inside information about future spot rates. In that framework, circumstances may arise in which 'perverse' responses to intervention may occur, and ultimately the model provides a rationale for secrecy with regard not only to the scale, but also to the target, of official intervention.[33]

Game-theoretic approaches have also been undertaken by researchers (e.g. Alogoskoufis, 1994). Typically, these models analyse the interaction between the central bank and private rational speculators in the foreign exchange market: in the event of a shock, observed by both parties, the central bank wishes to counterbalance the effect of the shock and

---

[29] Assuming, for example, that the exchange rate follows a random walk process $s_t = \alpha_0 + s_{t-1} + \epsilon_t$, where α_0 denotes the constant rate of exchange rate depreciation and ϵ_t is a white-noise error, and allowing for official sterilised intervention in the exchange rate equation yields $\Delta s_t = \alpha_0 + \alpha_1 INT_t + \epsilon_t$, with $\alpha_1 > 0$.

[30] These costs may be, for example, bureaucratic costs incurred during the decision-making process for designing the optimal intervention strategy or financial losses caused by a purchase (sale) of foreign currency which is not followed by future appreciation (depreciation) of the domestic currency. While in the absence of intervention costs the central bank counteracts to every single idiosyncratic shock, in the presence of positive costs of intervention, the decision to respond to a shock with sterilised intervention is based on a cost-benefit analysis of foreign exchange intervention (see Almekinders, 1995).

[31] On the one hand, if official intervention is to work through the signalling channel, then ideally every intervention operation of the central bank in the foreign exchange market should be announced publicly since the announcement will increase the chance of the operation being successful. On the other hand, however, some theoretical models (e.g. Cukierman and Meltzer, 1986; Balke and Haslag, 1992) show that a necessary condition for official intervention to be effective is the maintenance of the informational advantage. In this sense, public announcements of future official intervention by central banks may heavily undermine the effectiveness of the intervention operation.

[32] A recent paper which conflicts with this presumption is due to Humpage (1997), who investigates the forecast value of US interventions in the foreign exchange market. The rationale is that evidence of superior forecasting skill would imply that the US monetary authorities act with better information than the market and that intervention could alter foreign exchange traders' expectations about exchange rates. The analysis presented by Humpage (1997) shows, however, that this was not the case for US official intervention during the period 1990–7, and official transactions by US monetary authorities do not seem to improve the efficiency with which the foreign exchange market obtains information.

[33] See also Cukierman and Meltzer (1986) and Balke and Haslag (1992).

stabilise the exchange rate. Given the fact that the scale of official intervention is not very significant relative to the daily turnover in the market, the central bank has an incentive to use secret intervention in order to surprise private speculators and increase the effectiveness of the intervention operation. Rational agents will expect, however, a higher volume of intervention and, therefore, the ultimate result of the game between the central bank and the private speculators is the generation of some sort of 'intervention bias'. Clearly, the preferences of the central bank and the shape of its loss function, in addition to the degree of central bank independence, are crucial in determining the final outcome of the game between the central bank and the rational speculators in the market in these models (see Rogoff, 1985; Cukierman, 1992; Debelle, 1993; and Eijffinger and Schaling, 1993).

7.3.2   The empirics of central bank reaction functions

The empirical literature on central bank reaction functions has typically reported very simple estimated functions in order to shed light on the behaviour of central banks in the foreign exchange market and test the theoretical predictions discussed earlier.[34] While the dependent variable in these reaction functions is always some measure of official intervention, the explanatory variables considered vary across studies. In most cases, however, exchange rate changes and deviations of the actual exchange rate from its target level are included. A typical reaction function takes the following form:

$$INT_t = \beta_0 + \beta_1\left(s_t - s_t^T\right) + \beta_2\Delta s_t + \zeta\mathbf{X}_t + v_t, \qquad \beta_1 < 0 \qquad (7.12)$$

where $\mathbf{X}_t$ is a vector of economic factors which may influence official intervention (e.g. lagged intervention or the country's trade balance position) and v_t is a white-noise error.[35] The sign of β_1 is expected to be negative if the volume of intervention is inversely related to the deviations of the actual exchange rate from its target level, whereas β_2 is unconstrained and an estimated negative (positive) sign indicates that the central bank sells (buys) foreign exchange (domestic currency) when the currency has depreciated (appreciated), implying that the central bank pursues a policy of leaning against (with) the wind.[36]

Notably, Neumann (1984) estimates a simple reaction function for the Bundesbank of this form and provides evidence suggesting that the objective of the Bundesbank's intervention is smoothing changes in the real exchange rate. Hutchison (1984) investigates the behaviour of the Bank of Japan by estimating a conventional reaction function and provides strong evidence that the Bank of Japan pursues a strategy of leaning against the wind. This result has received further support in a number of empirical studies, discussed below. Gartner

---

[34] There is by now a very large and growing body of empirical literature on the reaction functions of central banks and governments. The literature especially focuses on monetary policy reaction functions; see, for example, Tullio and Ronci (1997) and Clarida, Gali and Gertler (1998) and the references therein. The focus of this section is, however, exclusively on reaction functions specifically designed to shed light on exchange rate management.

[35] Although some researchers estimate equations like (7.12) by ordinary least squares, instrumental variable estimation is strongly advised, given the endogeneity of the variables in (7.12).

[36] Early studies on reaction functions considered regressions of the change in reserves on the change of the exchange rate and generally found a statistically significant leaning-against-the-wind term (see e.g. Artus, 1976; Hacche and Townend, 1981).

(1987) investigates the behaviour of the Swiss central bank, estimating a simple reaction function of the type (7.12). His results suggest that a policy of leaning against the wind was followed by the Swiss central bank and the deviations of the actual exchange rate from its target level are the main factors which induce the central bank to intervene (both β_1 and β_2 statistically significant and correctly signed).[37] The only study on UK data is due to Kearney and MacDonald (1986) who estimate a small macroeconomic model based on Obstfeld (1983). They also investigate when and why the central bank intervened in the foreign exchange market, providing evidence that the Bank of England intervened during the 1980s mainly for smoothing exchange rate movements, but did not target the level of the exchange rate.

Gaiotti, Giucca and Micossi (1989) estimate a reaction function of the type (7.12) using quarterly data for Germany and Japan from 1973 to 1987. They provide strong evidence suggesting that both countries' central banks pursued a leaning-against-the-wind policy during the sample period considered and that the Bank of Japan responded more strongly to exchange rate changes. Interestingly, the empirical results also suggest that the response to exchange rate changes is asymmetric for both central banks, but in different directions. While the Bank of Japan was reacting more against the yen's appreciations, the Bundesbank reacted relatively more strongly against the depreciation of the mark. Also, the estimate of β_1 was found to be statistically significant for both central banks' reaction functions, suggesting a significant response of central banks against deviations of the actual exchange rate from the target level of the exchange rate.[38]

More recently, Takagi (1990) estimates a simple reaction function for Japanese official intervention in which the only explanatory variable considered is exchange rate changes. Takagi's results are consistent with Gaiotti, Giucca and Micossi (1989) in that the coefficient on the exchange rate change is statistically significantly different from zero and negative. Moreover, the response to shocks appears to be asymmetric, but in the opposite direction suggested by Gaiotti, Giucca and Micossi, implying that the Bank of Japan intervenes more often when the yen depreciates than when it appreciates.

Note that this strand of the empirical literature assumes that central banks tend to sterilise their interventions in the foreign exchange market. However, the question whether central banks fully sterilise their intervention operations is also addressed explicitly by some researchers. The standard approach followed is to estimate a regression with domestic credit or the monetary base as dependent variable and changes in net foreign reserves, contemporaneous output gap and inflation as explanatory variables.[39] The following two forms of

---

[37] The traditional approach to the estimation of sterilisation equations has often been criticised on various grounds. In particular, Roubini (1988) attacks the *ad hoc* specification of the reaction function of the monetary authorities typical of this literature. Roubini proposes an alternative analytical model where the sterilisation equations are derived from an explicit maximisation problem solved by the monetary authority. In such a model, the optimal intervention and sterilisation policies of the monetary authority are shown to be a function of the different disturbances hitting the economy and the preferences of the monetary authority.

[38] Eijffinger and Gruijters (1991a, b) also investigate the behaviour of the Bundesbank and find, using daily data for intervention from February 1985 to September 1988, that smoothing exchange rate fluctuations by leaning against the wind was the policy followed by the Bundesbank over the sample period.

[39] Again, given the endogeneity among those variables, instrumental variables estimation is required.

reaction functions have been considered and estimated by some studies in this literature:

$$\Delta DC_t = \mu_1 \Delta NFA_t + \mu_2(y - y^*)_t + \mu_3 \pi_t + \omega_{1t} \tag{7.13}$$

$$\Delta MB_t = \nu_1 \Delta NFA_t + \nu_2(y - y^*)_t + \nu_3 \pi_t + \omega_{2t} \tag{7.14}$$

where DC_t denotes domestic credit, NFA_t denotes net foreign assets, $(y - y^*)_t$ is the gap between current output and its natural level, π_t denotes inflation, MB_t represents the domestic monetary base, Δ represents a change in a stock, and ω_{1t} and ω_{2t} are error terms. Information with regard to the degree of sterilisation used by central banks is provided by estimates of the coefficients μ_1 and ν_1. In particular, the estimated μ_1 coefficient is expected to be negative; if it is not statistically significantly different from -1, sterilisation is full, while if it is greater than -1 and less than zero, sterilisation is only partial. The interpretation of ν_1 is different in the sense that full sterilisation is consistent with an estimated value for ν_1 which is not significantly different from zero.

The relevant empirical literature suggests that there is a tendency to sterilise fully all intervention operations. For example, Obstfeld (1983) examines the Bundesbank's tendency to sterilise during the sample period 1975–81 and finds that the German central bank sterilised completely during the sample period and attempted to attain domestic objectives using domestic credit policies while using sterilised intervention to stabilise the exchange rate. By contrast, Neumann (1984), Gaiotti, Giucca and Micossi (1989) and von Hagen (1989) provide evidence that the Bundesbank's sterilisation is generally not complete, but rather that the degree of sterilisation varies over time (Neumann's sample period overlaps with the one in Obstfeld's study, while Gaiotti, Giucca and Micossi use data for the period 1973–87). Von Hagen (1989) and Neumann and von Hagen (1991) distinguish between the behaviour of the Bundesbank in the short and long runs and conclude that sterilisation is full in the short run but only partial in the long run, i.e. that the Bundesbank does not sterilise intervention permanently.

Also, using Japanese data, some researchers provide evidence suggesting that the Bank of Japan fully sterilises its intervention. While this result is very strong in Gaiotti, Giucca and Micossi's (1989) study, Takagi (1991) could detect some variation in the degree of sterilisation of the Bank of Japan and found, in particular, that the degree of sterilisation used by the Bank of Japan seems to have decreased over time during the post-Bretton Woods period.[40]

More recently, Almekinders and Eijffinger (1996) have proposed a novel approach to deriving a central bank intervention reaction function. In particular, a generalised autoregressive conditional heteroscedasticity model for exchange rates is amended to allow intervention to have an effect on both the mean and the variance of exchange rate returns. An intervention reaction function is obtained by combining the model with a loss function for the central bank. Their estimation results suggest that both the Bundesbank and the Federal Reserve largely adopt a leaning-against-the-wind policy and have often reacted to increases in the conditional variance of daily German mark–US dollar returns.

---

[40] See also Mastropasqua, Micossi and Rinaldi (1988).

Evidence on the reaction functions of central banks in developing countries and transition economies is still very sparse, perhaps because the economic and political environment has been much more unstable in these countries and, most importantly, because data are less reliable or often not available. Two studies are, however, worth noting. Ronci and Tullio (1996) find a very stable reaction function for the Central Bank of Brazil during the high inflation period from 1980 to 1993. More recently, Tullio and Natarov (1999) estimate a daily reaction function for the Central Bank of Russia using daily data for the period from 1 October 1996 to 1 October 1997. The authors find a systematic and significant reaction of the bank to changes in market yields, to deviations of the market exchange rate from the central rate of the narrow rouble–US dollar corridor, to changes in the regulations concerning repatriation of foreign capital and to changes in the differential between yields on taxable and non-taxable Treasury bills.

Overall, therefore, both the literature on the effectiveness of exchange rate intervention and the empirical literature on central bank reaction functions provide mixed results and certainly represent avenues for future research, especially in the light of the greater data availability in recent years.

7.4 Summary and concluding remarks

In this chapter we have surveyed the recent theoretical and empirical literature on foreign exchange market intervention. We examined the rationale for exchange rate management, and discussed a number of relevant specific issues such as the secrecy of intervention, the role of international co-ordination, the profitability of intervention operations and the data on official intervention. We then described the mechanics of official intervention through the portfolio balance channel and the signalling, or expectations, channel, also providing a review of the empirical literature on the effectiveness of official intervention. We briefly presented the simple positive theory of exchange rate intervention used by the literature to derive estimatable reaction functions and discussed the empirical evidence on central bank reaction functions.

Overall, the evidence on the effectiveness of official intervention, through either the portfolio balance channel or the signalling channel, is still mixed, although the more recent literature does suggest a significant effect of official intervention on both the level and the change of exchange rates. Nevertheless, it is perhaps fair to say that the studies of the 1990s, which are largely supportive of the effectiveness of intervention, should perhaps be given more weight than the studies of the 1980s, which largely rejected the effectiveness of intervention. This is because of the removal of the two major handicaps characterising the empirical studies of the 1980s, namely the lack of data on intervention and the lack of survey data on exchange rate expectations. Thus, the evidence provided by Dominguez and Frankel (1993a,b,c) and subsequent studies using these high-quality data seems to us to be sufficiently strong and econometrically sound to allow us to conclude cautiously that official intervention can be effective, especially if the intervention is publicly announced and concerted and provided that it is consistent with the underlying stance of monetary and fiscal policy. Nevertheless, further empirical work in this area is clearly warranted, especially given the increasing availability of high-quality daily data on intervention.

Of the two traditional channels of influence, it is tempting to conjecture that the portfolio balance channel will diminish in importance over time – at least in the major industrialised countries – as international capital markets become increasingly integrated and the degree of substitutability between financial assets denominated in the major currencies increases. This suggests that, if intervention in the major currencies is effective at all through either of the traditional channels of influence, it will in future be effective primarily through the signalling channel, particularly if it is internationally concerted.[41] Another argument for the lesser importance of the portfolio balance channel is that the typical size of intervention operations is a very tiny fraction of total foreign exchange market turnover.[42] On the other hand, it is perhaps misleading to compare the scale of official intervention to market turnover, since turnover relates to *gross* market activity, whereas it may be more relevant to compare the actual or desired *net* change in traders' end-of-day stock positions. This would certainly be much smaller than overall turnover but, unfortunately, we have no measure of it.

If, however, the signalling channel is taken seriously, then an important 'secrecy puzzle' emerges: many actual intervention operations in the foreign exchange market are secret. Given that the signalling channel is expected to work through altering the expectations of other market agents through policy announcements by monetary authorities, this is something of a puzzle which has not yet been adequately resolved in the literature. We conjecture that further analysis of second-generation currency crisis models may ultimately shed some light on this puzzle, in that secrecy may reflect an attempt by the authorities to affect the exchange rate through the portfolio balance channel without triggering a self-fulfilling attack on the currency. Given our conclusion that the portfolio balance channel is likely to be of less importance than the signalling channel and is likely to further diminish in importance in the future, however, this raises the issue of whether or not major monetary authorities are in fact using the intervention tool optimally. Further work on this issue is clearly required.

Finally, it is perhaps worth mentioning a third possible channel of influence for intervention which has, to date, received very little attention in the literature. This is through its role in remedying a co-ordination failure in the foreign exchange market. One way to think about this is as follows. First, the foreign exchange market may be subject to irrational speculative bubbles brought about by important non-economic factors such as chartist or technical analysis which are known to have a significant effect on the market and which may impart swift movements of the exchange rate away from the level consistent with the underlying

---

[41] The view that intervention is most effective through the signalling channel and when it is internationally concerted also appears to be widely held by policy-makers and influential policy advisors. For example, at a press conference on 19 September 2000, held at the annual meetings of the IMF and World Bank, Michael Mussa said the following of official intervention: 'It does tend to be significantly more effective when that intervention is co-ordinated among the major countries and when those countries, in effect, send the signal that it is their joint judgement that markets have taken exchange rates substantially away from fundamentals and that some correction is warranted. I think it also tends to be significantly more effective when there is some signal that monetary policy in one or more of the major areas is likely to be supportive of the intervention.'

[42] Writing in the early 1990s, Dominguez and Frankel (1993a, pp. 88–9) argue that, at $200 million per day, the typical intervention operation is dwarfed by the worldwide volume of trading of some $1,000 billion.

economic fundamentals (Frankel and Froot, 1990; Taylor and Allen, 1992). Once the exchange rate has moved a long way from the fundamental equilibrium, it may be very hard for individual market agents to act to bring about a reversion of the exchange rate, even though they may strongly believe it to be misaligned, because of a co-ordination failure. If all of the 'smart money' traders were to act simultaneously so as to sell the currency which is overvalued according to the economic fundamentals, then the bubble would be pricked. In practice, once the exchange rate gets stuck into a trend – perhaps because of the widespread use of trend-following trading rules (Taylor and Allen, 1992) – it takes a great deal of courage for an individual trader to attempt to buck the market. Publicly announced intervention operations can here be seen as fulfilling a co-ordinating role in that they may organise the 'smart money' to enter the market at the same time. This route for the effectiveness of intervention might be termed the 'co-ordination channel'. The mid-1980s dollar overvaluation provides a good case study of the co-ordination channel: contemporary commentaries reveal a clear consensus on the dollar overvaluation yet it apparently took the publicly announced Plaza Agreement of the G5 countries to successfully puncture the bubble.

The co-ordination channel is implicit in Dominguez and Frankel's (1993a) discussion of intervention, and belief in its importance appears to form an important part of policymakers' views on intervention (see e.g. Wadhwani, 2000; Cecchetti, Genberg, Lipsky and Wadhwani, 2000). Nevertheless, it has received scant attention in the academic literature to date. In our view, further theoretical and empirical work on the co-ordination channel is likely to be a very important avenue for future research in this area.[43]

References and further readings

Adams, D. and D. Henderson (1983), 'Definition and Measurement of Exchange Rate Intervention', Staff Studies 126, Washington, D.C., Board of Governors of the Federal Reserve System.

Allen, H.L. and M.P. Taylor (1990), 'Charts, Noise and Fundamentals in the Foreign Exchange Market', Economic Journal, 100, pp. 49–59.

Almekinders, G.J. (1995), Foreign Exchange Intervention, Cheltenham: Edward Elgar Publishing Ltd.

Almekinders, G.J. and S.C.W. Eijffinger (1996), 'A Friction Model of Daily Bundesbank and Federal Reserve Intervention', Journal of Banking and Finance, 20, pp. 1365–80.

Alogoskoufis, G.S. (1994), 'On Inflation, Employment and the Optimal Exchange Rate Regime', in F. van der Ploeg, F. (ed.), Handbook of International Economics, Oxford: Blackwell, pp. 192–223.

Artis, M.J. and D.A. Currie (1981), 'Monetary Targets and the Exchange Rate: A Case for Conditional Targeting', in W.A. Eltis and P.J.N. Sinclair (eds.), The Money Supply and the Exchange Rate, Oxford: Clarendon Press, pp. 176–200.

Artis, M.J. and E. Karakitsos (1985), 'Monetary and Exchange Rate Targets in an Optimal Control Setting', in J.S. Bhandari (ed.), Exchange Management Under Uncertainty, Cambridge, Mass.: MIT Press, pp. 212–46.

---

[43] The recent paper by Popper and Montgomery (2001) is a first attempt to formalise an idea that is very close to the co-ordination channel. Popper and Montgomery develop a model where some agents can gain by sharing among themselves private information about transitory exchange rate disturbances and the central bank can affect the exchange rate by aggregating and disseminating agents' information through official intervention in the foreign exchange market.

Artus, J.R. (1976), 'Exchange Rate Stability and Managed Floating: The Experience of the Federal Republic of Germany', *International Monetary Fund Staff Papers*, 23, 312–33.

Backus, D.K. and P.J. Kehoe (1989), 'On the Denomination of Government Debt: A Critique of the Portfolio Balance Approach', *Journal of Monetary Economics*, 23, 359–76.

Baillie, R.T. and W.P. Osterberg (1997), 'Central Bank Intervention and Risk in the Forward Market', *Journal of International Economics*, 43, pp. 483–97.

Balke, N.S. and J.H. Haslag (1992), 'A Theory of FED Watching in a Macroeconomic Policy Game', *International Economic Review*, 33, pp. 619–28.

Barro, R.J. (1974), 'Are Government Bonds Net Wealth?', *Journal of Political Economy*, 82, pp. 1095–117.

Batchelor, R.A. and G.E. Wood (1982), 'Floating Exchange Rates: The Lessons of Experience', in R.A. Batchelor and G.E. Wood (eds.), *Exchange Rate Policy*, London: Macmillan.

Bhandari, J.S. (ed.) (1985), *Exchange Rate Management Under Uncertainty*, Cambridge, Mass.: MIT Press.

Bhattacharya, U. and P. Weller (1997), 'The Advantage of Hiding One's Hand: Speculation and Central Bank Intervention in the Foreign Exchange Market', *Journal of Monetary Economics*, 39, pp. 251–77.

Black, S.W. (1985), 'The Effect of Alternative Intervention Policies on the Variability of Exchange Rates: The Harrod Effect', in J.S. Bhandari (ed.), *Exchange Rate Management Under Uncertainty*, Cambridge, Mass.: MIT Press, pp. 72–82.

Blundell-Wignall, A. and P.R. Masson (1985), 'Exchange Rate Dynamics and Intervention Rules', *International Monetary Fund Staff Papers*, 32, pp. 132–59.

Bonser-Neal, C., V.V. Roley and G.H. Sellon Jr (1998), 'Monetary Policy Actions, Intervention, and Exchange Rates: A Reexamination of the Empirical Relationships Using Federal Funds Rate Target Data', *Journal of Business*, 71, pp. 147–77.

Bonser-Neal, C. and G. Tanner (1996), 'Central Bank Intervention and the Volatility of Foreign Exchange Rates: Evidence from the Options Market', *Journal of International Money and Finance*, 15, pp. 853–78.

Boyer, R.S. (1978), 'Optimal Foreign Exchange Market Intervention', *Journal of Political Economy*, 86, pp. 1045–55.

Branson, W.H. (1983), 'Macroeconomic Determinants of Real Exchange Risk', in R.J. Herring (ed.), *Managing Foreign Exchange Risk*, Cambridge: Cambridge University Press, pp. 33–74.

(1984), 'A Model of Exchange Rate Determination with Policy Reaction: Evidence from Monthly Data', in P. Malgrange and P.A. Muet (eds.), *Contemporary Macroeconomic Modelling*, Oxford: Blackwell, pp. 128–50.

Branson, W.H., H. Halttunen and P. Masson (1977), 'Exchange Rates in the Short Run: The Dollar–Deutsche Mark Rate', *European Economic Review*, 10, 395–402.

Branson, W.H. and D.W. Henderson (1985), 'The Specification and Influence of Asset Markets', in R.W. Jones and P.B. Kenen (eds.), *Handbook of International Economics*, vol. II, Amsterdam: North-Holland, pp. 749–805.

Bryant, R.C. (1995), 'International Cooperation in the Making of National Macroeconomic Policies: Where Do We Stand?', in P.B. Kenen (ed.), *Understanding Interdependence: The Macroeconomics of the Open Economy*, Princeton, N.J. Princeton University Press, pp. 391–447.

Buiter, W.H. and J. Eaton (1985), 'Policy Decentralization and Exchange Rate Management in Interdependent Economies', in J.S. Bhandari (ed.), *Exchange Rate Management Under Uncertainty*, Cambridge, Mass.: MIT Press, pp. 31–54.

Canzoneri, M.B., W.J. Ethier and V. Grilli (eds.) (1996), *The New Transatlantic Economy*, Cambridge: Cambridge University Press.

Canzoneri, M.B. and J.M. Underwood (1985), 'Wage Contracting, Exchange Rate Volatility, and Exchange Intervention Policy', in J.S. Bhandari (ed.) *Exchange Rate Management Under Uncertainty*, Cambridge, Mass.: MIT Press, pp. 247–71.

Catte, P., G. Galli and S. Rebecchini (1994), 'Concerted Interventions and the Dollar: An Analysis of Daily Data', in P.B. Kenen, F. Papadia and F. Saccomanni (eds.), *The International Monetary System*, Cambridge: Cambridge University Press, pp. 201–39.

Cecchetti, S.G., H. Genberg, J. Lipsky and S. Wadhwani (2000), 'Asset Prices and Central Bank Policy. The Geneva Report on the World Economy No. 2', Centre for Economic Policy Research and International Centre for Monetary and Banking Studies.

Chang, Y. and S.J. Taylor (1998), 'Intraday Effects of Foreign Exchange Intervention by the Bank of Japan', *Journal of International Money and Finance*, 17, pp. 191–210.

Clarida, R.H., J. Gali and M. Gertler (1998), 'Monetary Policy Rules in Practice: Some International Evidence', *European Economic Review*, 42, pp. 1033–67.

Cooper, R.N. (1985), 'Economic Interdependence and Coordination of Economic Policies', in R.W. Jones and P.B. Kenen (eds.), *Handbook of International Economics*, vol. II, Amsterdam: North-Holland, pp. 1195–234

Corden, W.M. (1981), *Inflation, Exchange Rates and the World Economy*, Oxford: Clarendon.

(1982), 'Exchange Rate Protection', in R.N. Cooper, P.B. Kenen, J.B. Macedo and J.V. Ypersele (eds.), *The International Monetary System Under Flexible Exchange Rates*, Cambridge, Mass.: Ballinger, pp. 17–33.

Cukierman, A. (1992), *Central Bank Strategy, Credibility and Independence*, Cambridge, Mass.: MIT Press.

Cukierman, A. and A.H. Meltzer (1986), 'A Theory of Ambiguity, Credibility and Inflation under Discretion and Asymmetric Information', *Econometrica*, 54, pp. 1099–128.

Danker, D.J., R.A. Haas, D.W. Henderson, S.A. Symansky and R.W. Tryon (1987), 'Small Empirical Models of Exchange Market Intervention: Applications to Germany, Japan and Canada', *Journal of Policy Modelling*, 9, pp. 143–73.

De Long, J.B., A. Shleifer, L.H. Summers and R.J. Waldmann (1990), 'Positive Feedback Investment Strategies and Destabilizing Rational Speculation', *Journal of Finance*, 45, pp. 379–95.

Debelle, G. (1993), 'Central Bank Independence: A Free Lunch?', Working Paper, MIT.

Dominguez, K.M. (1987), 'Exchange Rate Efficiency and the Behavior of International Asset Markets', unpublished Ph.D. thesis, Yale University.

(1990), 'Market Responses to Coordinated Central Bank Intervention', *Carnegie–Rochester Conference Series in Public Policy*, 32, pp. 121–63.

Dominguez, K.M. and J.A. Frankel (1993a), *Does Foreign Exchange Intervention Work?*, Washington, D.C.: Institute for International Economics.

(1993b), 'Does Foreign Exchange Intervention Matter? The Portfolio Effect', *American Economic Review*, 83, pp. 1356–69.

(1993c), 'Foreign Exchange Intervention: An Empirical Assessment', in J.A. Frankel (ed.), *On Exchange Rates*, Cambridge, Mass.: MIT Press, pp. 327–45.

Dooley, M. and P. Isard (1982), 'A Portfolio-Balance Rational-Expectations Model of the Dollar–Mark Rate', *Journal of International Economics*, 12, pp. 257–76.

Dornbusch, R. (1976), 'Expectations and Exchange Rate Dynamics', *Journal of Political Economy*, 84, pp. 1161–76.

(1983), 'Exchange Risk and the Macroeconomics of Exchange Rate Determination', in R. Hawkins, R. Levich and C. Wihlborg (eds.), *The Internationalization of Financial Markets and National Economic Policy*, Greenwich, Conn.: JAI Press.

Economist (1995), 'A Survey of the World Economy: Who's in the Driving Seat? – Not-So-Divine Intervention', 7 October.

Edison, H.J. (1993), *The Effectiveness of Central-Bank Intervention: A Survey of the Literature After 1982*, Special Papers in International Economics, 18, Princeton University.

Eichengreen, B., J. Tobin and C. Wyplosz (1995), 'Two Cases for Sand in the Wheels of International Finance', *Economic Journal*, 105, pp. 162–72.

Eichengreen, B. and C. Wyplosz (1993), 'The Unstable EMS', *Brookings Papers in Economic Activity*, 1, pp. 51–143.

Eijffinger, S.C.W. (ed.) (1998), *Foreign Exchange Intervention: Objectives and Effectiveness*, Cheltenham: Edward Elgar Publishing Ltd.

Eijffinger, S.C.W. and N.P.D. Gruijters (1991a), 'On the Short Term Objectives of Daily Intervention by the Deutsche Bundesbank and the Federal Reserve System in the US Dollar/Deutsche Mark Exchange Market', *Kredit und Capital*, 24, pp. 50–72.

(1991b), 'On the Effectiveness of Daily Interventions by the Deutsche Bundesbank and the Federal Reserve System in US Dollar/Deutsche Mark Exchange Market', in E. Baltensperger and H.W. Sinn (eds.), *Exchange Regimes and Currency Union*, London: Macmillan, pp. 131–56.

Eijffinger, S.C.W. and E. Schaling (1993), 'Central Bank Independence in Twelve Industrial Countries', *Banca Nazionale del Lavoro Quarterly Review*, 184, pp. 1–41.

Engel, C.M. and A.P. Rodrigues (1989), 'Tests of International CAPM with Time-Varying Covariances', *Journal of Applied Econometrics*, 4, pp. 119–38.

Engle, R.F. (1982), 'Autoregressive Conditional Heteroscedasticity with Estimates of the Variance of United Kingdom Inflation', *Econometrica*, 50(4), pp. 987–1007.

Feldstein, M. (1986), 'New Evidence on the Effects of Exchange Rate Intervention', Working Paper No. 2052, National Bureau of Economic Research.

Fellner, W. (1982), 'The Valid Core of Rational Expectations Theory and the Problems of Exchange Rate Relations', in R.N. Cooper, P.B. Kenen, J.B. Macedo and J.V. Ypersele (eds.), *The International Monetary System Under Flexible Exchange Rates*, Cambridge, Mass.: Ballinger.

Flandreau, M. (1998), 'The Burden of Intervention: Externalities in Multilateral Exchange Rates Arrangements', *Journal of International Economics*, 45, pp. 137–71.

Frankel, J.A. (1979), 'The Diversifiability of Exchange Risk', *Journal of International Economics*, 9, pp. 379–93; reprinted in J.A. Frankel (ed.), *On Exchange Rates*, Cambridge, Mass.: MIT Press (1993).

(1982a), 'A Test of Perfect Substitutability in the Foreign Exchange Market', *Southern Economic Journal*, 49, pp. 406–16.

(1982b), 'In Search of the Exchange Rate Premium: A Six-Currency Test Assuming Mean-Variance Optimization', *Journal of International Money and Finance*, 1, pp. 255–73.

Frankel, J.A. and C.M. Engel (1984), 'Do Asset Demand Functions Optimize Over the Mean and Variance of Real Returns? A Six-Currency Test', *Journal of International Economics*, 17, pp. 309–23.

Friedman, M. (1953), 'The Case for Flexible Exchange Rates', in M. Friedman, *Essays in Positive Economics*, Chicago: University of Chicago Press, pp. 157–203.

Funabashi, Y. (1988), *Managing the Dollar: From the Plaza to the Louvre*, Washington, D.C.: Institute for International Economics.

Gaiotti, E., P. Giucca and S. Micossi (1989), 'Cooperation in Managing the Dollar (1985–1987): Interventions in Foreign Exchange Markets and Interest Rates', *Temi di Discussione del Servizio Studi* No. 119, Banca d'Italia.

Garber, P. and M.P. Taylor (1995), 'Sand in the Wheels of Foreign Exchange Markets: A Sceptical Note', *Economic Journal*, 105, pp. 173–80.

Gardner, G.W. (1983), 'The Choice of Monetary Policy Instruments in an Open Economy', *Journal of International Money and Finance*, 2, pp. 347–54.

Gartner, M. (1987), 'Intervention Policy Under Floating Exchange Rates: An Analysis of the Swiss Case', *Economica*, 54, pp. 439–53.

Ghosh, A.R. (1992), 'Is It Signalling? Exchange Intervention and the Dollar–Deutschemark Rate', *Journal of International Economics*, 32, pp. 201–20.

Glick, R. (ed.) (1998), *Managing Capital Flows and Exchange Rates: Perspectives from the Pacific Basin*, Cambridge: Cambridge University Press.

Glick, R. and M.M. Hutchison (1989), 'Exchange Rates and Monetary Policy', *Federal Reserve Bank of San Francisco Economic Review*.

Hacche, G. and J. Townend (1981), 'Exchange Rates and Monetary Policy: Modelling Sterling's Effective Exchange Rate 1972–1980', in W.A. Eltis and P.J.N. Sinclair (eds.), *The Money Supply and the Exchange Rate*, Oxford: Clarendon Press, pp. 201–47.

Humpage, O.F. (1989), 'On the Effectiveness of Exchange-Market Intervention', Federal Reserve Bank of Cleveland, mimeo.

(1997), 'Recent U.S. Intervention: Is Less More?', *Federal Reserve Bank of Cleveland Economic Review*, 33, pp. 2–10.

Humpage, O.F. and W.P. Osterberg (1990), 'Intervention and the Foreign Exchange Risk Premium: An Empirical Investigation of Daily Effects', *Global Finance Journal*, 3, pp. 23–50.

Hutchinson, M.M. (1984), 'Official Japanse Intervention in Foreign Exchange Markets: Leaning Against the Wind?', *Economics Letters*, 15, pp. 115–20.

Isard, P. (1980), 'Lessons from an Empirical Model of Exchange Rates', *International Monetary Fund Staff Papers*, 34, pp. 1–28.

(1995), *Exchange Rate Economics*, Cambridge: Cambridge University Press.

Jacobson, L.R. (1983), *Calculations of Profitability for US Dollar–Deutsche Mark Intervention*, Staff Studies 131, Board of Governors of the Federal Reserve System, Washington, D.C.

Jurgensen, P. (1983), 'Report of the Working Group on Exchange Market Intervention' [Jurgensen Report], Treasury Department, Washington, D.C.

Karfakis, C. and S.-J. Kim (1995), 'Exchange Rates, Interest Rates and Current Account News: Some Evidence from Australia', *Journal of International Money and Finance*, 14, pp. 575–95.

Kaminsky, G.L. and K.K. Lewis (1996), 'Does Foreign Exchange Intervention Signal Future Monetary Policy?', *Journal of Monetary Economics*, 37, pp. 285–312.

Kearney, C. and R. MacDonald (1986), 'Intervention and Sterilisation Under Floating Exchange Rates: the UK 1973–1983', *European Economic Review*, 30, pp. 345–64.

Kenen, P.B. (1960), *British Monetary Policy and the Balance of Payments, 1951–1957*, Cambridge, Mass.: Harvard University Press.

(1965), 'Trade, Speculation and the Forward Exchange Rate', in R.E. Baldwin *et al.* (eds.), *Trade, Growth and the Balance of Payments*, Chicago: Rand McNally, pp. 143–69. Reprinted in P.B. Kenen, *Essays in International Economics*, Princeton: Princeton University Press.

(1980), *Essays in International Economics*, Princeton: Princeton University Press.

(1982), 'Effects of Intervention and Sterilization in the Short Run and in the Long Run', in R.N. Cooper, P.B. Kenen, J.B. Macedo and J.V. Ypersele (eds.), *The International Monetary System Under Flexible Exchange Rates*, Cambridge, Mass.: Ballinger, pp. 51–68.

(1988), *Managing Exchange Rates*, Chatham House Papers, London: Routledge.

(ed.) (1995), *Understanding Interdependence: The Macroeconomics of the Open Economy*, Princeton: Princeton University Press.

Keynes, J.M. (1923), *A Tract on Monetary Reform*, London: Macmillan.

Leahy, M.P. (1989), 'The Profitability of US Intervention', International Finance Discussion Papers No. 343, Board of Governors of the Federal Reserve System, Washington, D.C.

LeBaron, B. (1996), 'Technical Trading Rule Profitability and Foreign Exchange Intervention', Working Paper No. 5505, National Bureau of Economic Research.

Lewis, K.K. (1988), 'Testing the Portfolio Balance Model: A Multi-lateral Approach', *Journal of International Economics*, 24, pp. 109–27.

(1995), 'Are Foreign Exchange Intervention and Monetary Policy Related and Does It Really Matter?', *Journal of Business*, 68, pp. 185–214.

Loopesko, B.E. (1984), 'Relationships Among Exchange Rates, Intervention, and Interest Rates: An Empirical Investigation', *Journal of International Money and Finance*, 3, pp. 257–77.

Mastropasqua, C., S. Micossi and R. Rinaldi (1986), 'Intervention, Sterilisation and Monetary Policy in European Monetary System Countries, 1979–1987', in F. Giavazzi, S. Micossi and M. Miller (eds.), *The European Monetary System: Proceedings of a Conference Organised by the Banca d'Italia, STEP, and CEPR*, Cambridge: Cambridge University Press, pp. 252–87.

Mussa, M. (1981), *The Role of Official Intervention*, New York: Group of Thirty.

Neumann, M. (1984), 'Intervention in the Mark/Dollar Market: the Authorities' Reaction Function', *Journal of International Money and Finance*, 3, pp. 223–39.

Neumann, M. and J. von Hagen (1991), 'Monetary Policy in Germany', in M. Fratianni and D. Salvatore (eds.), *Handbook of Monetary Policy*, Westport, Conn.: Greenwood Press.

Obstfeld, M. (1982), 'Can We Sterilize? Theory and Evidence', *American Economic Review Papers and Proceedings*, 72 (2), pp. 45–50.

(1983), 'Exchange Rates, Inflation and the Sterilization Problem. Germany 1975–81', *European Economic Review*, 21, pp. 161–89.

(1990), 'The Effectiveness of Foreign-Exchange Intervention: Recent Experience: 1985–1988', in W.H. Branson, J.A. Frenkel and M. Goldstein (eds.), *International Policy Coordination and Exchange Rate Fluctuations*, Chicago: University of Chicago Press, pp. 197–237.

Obstfeld, M. and K. Rogoff (1995), 'Exchange Rate Dynamics Redux', *Journal of Political Economy*, 103, pp. 624–60.

(1996), *Foundations of International Macroeconomics*, Cambridge, Mass: MIT Press.

Pilbeam, K. (1991), *Exchange Rate Management*, London: Macmillan.

Popper, H. and J.D. Montgomery (2001), 'Information Sharing and Central Bank Intervention in the Foreign Exchange Market', *Journal of International Economics*, 55, pp. 295–316.

Reeves, S.F. (1997), 'Exchange Rate Management When Sterilized Interventions Represent Signals of Monetary Policy', *International Review of Economics and Finance*, 6, pp. 339–60.

(1998), 'Partial Credibility, Information Selection and the Signalling Channel of Sterilized Interventions', *Journal of Economic Integration*, 13, pp. 108–30.

Rogoff, K. (1979), 'Expectations and Exchange Rate Volatility', unpublished Ph.D. thesis, Massachusetts Institute of Technology.

(1984), 'On the Effects of Sterilized Intervention: An Analysis of Weekly Data', *Journal of Monetary Economics*, 14, pp. 133–50.

(1985), 'The Optimal Degree of Commitment to an Intermediate Monetary Target', *Quarterly Journal of Economics*, 100, pp. 1169–89.

Ronci, M. and G. Tullio (1996), 'Brasilian Inflation from 1980 to 1993: Causes, Consequences and Dynamics', *Journal of Latin American Studies*, 28, pp. 635–65.

Roubini, N. (1988), 'Offset and Sterilization Under Fixed Exchange Rates with an Optimizing Central Bank', Working Paper No. 2777, National Bureau of Economic Research.

Sarno, L. and M.P. Taylor (2001), 'Official Intervention in the Foreign Exchange Market: Is It Effective and, If So, How Does It Work?', *Journal of Economic Literature*, 39, pp. 839–68.

Stein, J.C. (1987), 'Informational Externalities and Welfare-Reducing Speculation', *Journal of Political Economy*, 95, pp. 1234–45.

(1989), 'Cheap Talk and the Fed: A Theory of Imprecise Policy Announcements', *American Economic Review*, 79(1), pp. 32–42.

Sweeney, R.J. (1997), 'Do Central Banks Lose on Foreign-Exchange Intervention? A Review Article', *Journal of Banking and Finance*, 21, pp. 1667–84.

Szakmarky, A.C. and I. Mathur (1997), 'Central Bank Intervention and Trading Rule Profits in Foreign Exchange Markets', *Journal of International Money and Finance*, 16, pp. 513–35.

Takagi, S. (1990), 'Foreign Exchange Market Intervention and Domestic Monetary Control in Japan, 1973–89', University of Osaka, mimeo.

(1991), 'Foreign Exchange Market Intervention and Domestic Monetary Control in Japan, 1973–1989', *Japan and the World Economy*, 3, pp. 147–80.

Taylor, D. (1982), 'Official Intervention in the Foreign Exchange Market, or, Bet Against the Central Bank', *Journal of Political Economy*, 90, pp. 356–68.

Taylor, M.P. (1995), 'The Economics of Exchange Rates', *Journal of Economic Literature*, 83, pp. 13–47.

Taylor, M.P. and H.L. Allen (1992), 'The Use of Technical Analysis in the Foreign Exchange Market', *Journal of International Money and Finance*, 11, pp. 304–14.

Tobin, J. (1969), 'A General Equilibrium Approach to Monetary Theory', *Journal of Money, Credit, and Banking*, 1, pp. 15–29.

Tryon, R.W. (1983), *Small Empirical Models of Exchange Market Intervention: A Review of the Literature*, Staff Studies 134, Board of Governors of the Federal Reserve System, Washington, D.C.

Tullio, G. and V. Natarov (1999), 'Daily Interventions by the Central Bank of Russia in the Treasury Bill Market', *International Journal of Finance and Economics*, 4, pp. 229–42.

Tullio, G. and M. Ronci (1997), 'Central Bank Autonomy, the Exchange Rate Constraint and Inflation: The Case of Italy', *Open Economies Review*, 1, pp. 31–49.

Turnovsky, S.J. (1987), 'Optimal Monetary Policy and Wage Indexation Under Alternative Disturbances and Information Structures', *Journal of Money, Credit, and Banking*, 19, pp. 157–80.

von Hagen, J. (1989), 'Monetary Targeting with Exchange Rate Constraints: The Bundesbank in the 1980s', *Federal Reserve Bank of St Louis Review*, 71, pp. 53–69.

Wadhwani, S. (2000), 'The Exchange Rate and the Monetary Policy Committee: What Can We Do?', Speech to the Senior Business Forum at the Centre for Economic Performance, 31 May.

Wallich, H. (1984), 'Institutional Cooperation in the World Economy', in J. Frenkel and M. Mussa (eds.), *The World Economic System: Performance and Prospects*, Dover N.H.: Auburn House, pp. 85–99.

Weymark, D.N. (1997a), 'Measuring the Degree of Exchange Market Intervention in a Small Open Economy', *Journal of International Money and Finance*, 16, pp. 55–79.

(1997b), 'Measuring Exchange Market Pressure and Intervention in Interdependent Economies: A Two-Country Model', *Review of International Economics*, 5, pp. 72–82.

Wihlborg, C., M. Fratianni and T.D. Willett (eds.) (1991), *Financial Regulation and Monetary Arrangements After 1992*. Contributions to Economic Analysis, vol. 204, Amsterdam: North-Holland.

Williamson, J. (1977), *The Failure of World Monetary Reform 1971–74*, London: Nelson.

8 Models of currency crisis and speculative attack

The last decade of the twentieth century witnessed a number of currency crises affecting the international financial markets. The economies of the various countries which suffered financial crises and attacks on their currencies from international speculators were, moreover, quite diverse. They ranged from a number of Latin American economies, where economists were quick to point out apparent inconsistencies between the stance of domestic macroeconomic policy and a commitment to a fixed exchange rate; to advanced European economies where there appeared to be no such inconsistencies but instead a perceived *temptation* of the authorities to pursue more of an expansionary domestic policy; to the 'tiger economies' of East Asia, where, prior to the crisis, the economic fundamentals appeared very strong and macroeconomic policy appeared entirely consistent with the fixed exchange rate rule.

Accordingly, a literature has sprung up in recent years in order to explain these phenomena. In this chapter we briefly review this work. There are three main strands of this literature, broadly corresponding to the three cases discussed above, and we shall tackle them in turn.

8.1   First-generation currency crisis models

The first strand of the literature – often referred to as the first-generation currency crisis approach – starts with the seminal article by Krugman (1979), itself largely drawing on previous related work by Salant and Henderson (1978).[1] Krugman (1979) builds a model of a small open economy and shows that, under a fixed exchange rate regime, excess creation of domestic credit relative to money demand growth may generate the conditions for a sudden speculative attack against the domestic currency, ultimately leading to the abandonment of the fixed exchange rate peg and the switch to a flexible exchange rate.

To illustrate the main features of the model, assume that domestic money demand is given by:

$$m^d - p = -\lambda i, \tag{8.1}$$

[1]   Salant and Henderson (1978) build a model in which the government uses a stockpile of an exhaustible resource in order to stabilise its price and show how this policy ultimately induces a speculative attack in which private agents purchase the entire remaining stock. Nevertheless, a crucial difference between Krugman's (1979) model and that of Salant and Henderson (1978) is that in the foreign exchange market there is always the possibility of external borrowing to supplement the reserves of the central bank, unlike in resource markets (see Salant, 1983).

where m^d, p and i denote domestic money demand, the domestic price level and the domestic nominal interest rate respectively; all variables except for the interest rate are in logarithms; and $\lambda > 0$. For simplicity, we exclude domestic income from the money demand function (this is equivalent to holding income constant and normalising its logarithm to zero). In turn, the money supply is made up of domestic credit and international reserves, say d and r respectively in logarithmic terms, implying the accounting identity:[2]

$$m^s \equiv d + r. \tag{8.2}$$

Also assume that the money market clears:

$$m^d = m^s = m, \tag{8.3}$$

and that both uncovered interest parity (in its continuous-time, perfect-foresight form) and purchasing power parity hold:

$$\dot{s} = i - i^* \tag{8.4}$$

$$s = p - p^*, \tag{8.5}$$

where s is the nominal exchange rate (domestic price of the foreign currency), an asterisk denotes foreign variables, and a dot the time derivative of the variable in question.

If the domestic authorities are running an expansionary fiscal policy, they will have to finance this by issuing government debt. This will tend to raise the money supply (identity (8.2)) and hence, since domestic and foreign interest rates must be equal for $\dot{s} = 0$ (equation (8.4)), domestic prices begin to rise (equation (8.1)), bringing about an incipient depreciation of the currency (i.e. rise in s – equation (8.4)). To arrest this and maintain the exchange rate at $\bar{s}$, the authorities intervene and purchase the domestic currency. This leads to a fall in reserves, r. The intervention will, for the time being, be successful when the rate of fall of the stock of foreign reserves is just equal to the rate of expansion of domestic credit, so that the money market is balanced. Eventually, however, the stock of foreign reserves will be exhausted and the authorities will no longer be able to defend the fixed rate. Knowing this, speculators will attack the exchange rate.

If we set s equal to its fixed rate $\bar{s}$, set $\dot{s} = 0$ and substitute from (8.2)–(8.5) into (8.1), we have:

$$\bar{s} = d + r - p^* + \lambda i^*. \tag{8.6}$$

The policy problem is that d is rising while p^* and i^* are fixed exogenously. Thus, according to (8.6), the exchange rate can only be maintained at $\bar{s}$ so long as r is falling to offset the rise in d, and this cannot be maintained indefinitely. Thus the simple message conveyed is that intervention cannot be successful in the long run if the stance of domestic macroeconomic policy is fundamentally inconsistent with a fixed exchange rate.

In Krugman's (1979) continuous-time, perfect-foresight model an explicit solution for the timing of the collapse of the fixed exchange rate system was not given, because the nonlinearity of the model led to nontractable mathematical expressions. Nevertheless, Flood and Garber (1984) use an elegant log-linear generalisation of Krugman's model which

---

[2] Clearly, this identity should be linear in levels rather than logarithms, so that it is really an approximation as expressed.

allows the explicit derivation of the time of occurrence of the crisis, under the assumption that the post-collapse regime is a free-float system (see also Flood and Garber, 1991; Agénor, Bhandari and Flood, 1992; Garber and Svensson, 1995).

Note that once the stock of reserves is exhausted, two things must happen: the exchange rate will be forced off the peg and allowed to float, and the money supply will begin to rise at the same rate as the level of domestic credit. Hence, following the exhaustion of reserves, the exchange rate will have to be at a level consistent with uncovered interest rate parity in which the rate of depreciation is equal to the domestic–foreign interest rate differential, and with a level of the domestic interest rate consistent with domestic money-market equilibrium; call this the 'shadow exchange rate', $\widetilde{s}$. Then, from (8.1)–(8.5), the shadow rate must be consistent with:

$$\widetilde{s} = d - p^* + \lambda i^* + \lambda \dot{\widetilde{s}}. \tag{8.7}$$

Let the instantaneous rate of depreciation of the exchange rate immediately after a successful attack be γ, i.e. $\dot{\widetilde{s}} = \gamma$ Substituting this in (8.7) we have:

$$\widetilde{s} = d - p^* + \lambda i^* + \lambda \gamma. \tag{8.8}$$

Differentiating (8.8) with respect to time, we have, since everything on the right-hand side except d is constant:

$$\dot{\widetilde{s}} = \dot{d}. \tag{8.9}$$

Thus, γ must be equal to the rate of expansion of domestic credit, $\dot{\widetilde{s}} = \dot{d} = \gamma$. Equation (8.8) therefore gives an expression for the level of the exchange rate the instant after a successful attack on the currency, i.e. the 'shadow rate'.

Speculators are free at any point to launch an attack on the currency and exhaust the stock of reserves. If the shadow rate is different from the level of the exchange rate peg, then either a speculative attack would be unprofitable (the shadow value of the domestic currency is higher than the actual value at the fixed rate), or else an attack would be profitable (the shadow value of the currency is lower than the value at the fixed exchange rate). If we start from a position where a speculative attack would be unprofitable – the fixed rate is greater than the shadow rate, where the exchange rate is defined as the domestic-currency price of foreign currency – then the shadow rate must approach the fixed rate and eventually exceed it. This follows because the domestic credit component of the monetary base is growing on account of the fiscal deficit, but is being offset by the fall in reserves. Since the equilibrium level of the exchange rate will be determined by the level of the monetary base (assuming an underlying monetary exchange rate model), a higher domestic component must imply a more depreciated currency once the reserves component of the monetary base is zero. Once the shadow rate exceeds the fixed exchange rate, a speculative attack will be immediately launched. In fact, by speculative competition, the attack will be launched as soon as the shadow rate and the fixed rate coincide, ruling out any jump in the exchange rate in the transition from a fixed to a floating exchange rate.

We are now in a position to work out the timing of the attack. Note that, when the attack is launched there will be a discrete drop in reserves (to a level of zero) as the authorities vainly try to defend the peg. Let this be Δr. Given the money supply identity (8.2), this means that there will be also be a discrete fall in the money supply of:

$$\Delta m^s = \Delta r. \tag{8.10}$$

Moreover, since the rate of depreciation of the currency is γ immediately after the successful attack, by uncovered interest rate parity, (8.4), the domestic interest rate must jump from i^* to $i^* + \gamma$. Hence, from the money demand equation (8.1), there will be a discrete *fall* in money demand of $-\lambda\gamma$:

$$\Delta m^d = -\lambda\gamma. \tag{8.11}$$

For the money market to clear at an interest rate consistent with uncovered interest parity, the fall in money supply due to the fall in reserves must be exactly equal to the fall in demand due to the jump in the interest rate, i.e. $\Delta m^s = \Delta m^d$ which, from (8.10) and (8.11), implies:

$$\Delta r = -\lambda\gamma. \tag{8.12}$$

Now recall that, before the attack, domestic credit was rising at the rate γ, and reserves were *falling* at an exactly equal rate. Thus, if the stock of reserves at some initial period, time 0, say, were r_0, and if the time from the base period until the instant of the attack is T, then the level of reserves at the instant before the attack is launched is $r_0 - \gamma T$. But this level must be just enough to be completely exhausted by the attack, so that:

$$r_0 - \gamma T = -\Delta r \tag{8.13}$$

or, using (8.12) to substitute for Δr and solving for T:

$$T = (r_0 - \lambda\gamma)/\gamma. \tag{8.14}$$

Equation (8.14) thus gives the unique timing of the attack. It is, moreover, entirely intuitive in its implications: the higher the stock of initial reserves and/or the lower the rate of expansion of domestic credit, the greater the time before the attack is launched.

In these first-generation speculative attack models, intervention is doomed to ultimate failure. But this is really by assumption, for the following reasons. First, as we noted in Chapter 7, a major argument in favour of intervention is that the market may otherwise set the exchange rate at the wrong level according to the economic fundamentals – we termed this the 'wrong rate' argument. In contrast, the first-generation speculative attack models assume that the authorities are attempting to defend the wrong rate, since the presumption is that the fixed rate which the authorities are attempting to defend is incompatible with the underlying stance of monetary and fiscal policy. Second, the effects of intervention through the portfolio balance channel are precluded by assuming a simple underlying monetary model of the exchange rate, which assumes perfect substitutability between domestic and foreign assets – also reflected in the fact that only non-sterilised intervention is considered (since sterilised intervention is completely ineffective under these conditions). Third, the signalling effects of intervention are ruled out because agents know that the authorities' monetary policy is ultimately unsustainable.

The implicit assumption of perfect substitutability between domestic and foreign assets has been relaxed in the modified first-generation models of Flood, Garber and Kramer (1996) and Flood, Hodrick, Isard and Kramer (1996). These models allow a role for sterilised intervention by introducing a risk premium – itself a function of domestic and foreign bond holdings – into the uncovered interest rate parity condition. A speculative attack now affects these relative holdings through the effects of sterilisation of intervention, and by speculative competition as above, the attack will again be timed so that there is no jump in the exchange rate when the reserves are exhausted, the difference now being that the driving variable is the relative stock of domestic and foreign assets via the risk premium.[3] Flood and Marion (2000) have introduced uncertainty into this modified first-generation framework with full sterilisation of intervention by allowing the risk-adjusted uncovered interest rate parity condition to take the following form:

$$i_t = i_t^* + E_t \widetilde{s}_{t+1} - \widetilde{s}_t + \beta_t (b_t - b_t^* - \widetilde{s}_t), \tag{8.15}$$

where $\widetilde{s}_t$ denotes the shadow exchange rate, b_t denotes domestic bond holdings and an asterisk denotes a foreign variable (all variables except interest rates are in logarithms). Flood and Marion derive this condition through a standard mean-variance analysis of wealth optimisation, and show that the time-varying parameter β_t is a function of a taste parameter z and the one-step-ahead conditional variance of the shadow exchange rate: $\beta_t = z \cdot var(\widetilde{s}_{t+1})$. This model now contains an important nonlinearity which allows multiple solutions. For example, if agents expect more exchange rate variability following the collapse of the peg, then the risk premium will be higher and so, by equation (8.15), will be the domestic interest rate. This then affects the domestic demand for money, affecting the expected shadow exchange rate and hence increasing its conditional variance, in a self-fulfilling fashion.

  The empirical literature on testing first-generation models is rather sparse, and empirical implementations have focused mainly on developing countries. Also, researchers have typically modified the assumption regarding the post-attack regime depending upon the historical experience of the particular country examined, hence slightly changing the basic framework to adapt it to the specific case analysed. A notable example is the study of Blanco and Garber (1986), who adapt the basic model of speculative attack assuming a regime of recurring discontinuous devaluations to investigate the exchange rate dynamics of the Mexican peso using quarterly data for the sample period 1973–82. Interestingly, their empirical results suggest that the estimated probabilities of devaluations jumped to peak values of 20 per cent just before the two major devaluations of the Mexican peso in 1976 and 1982 respectively and then fell again to low values after the devaluations had occurred.[4]

[3] As Flood and Marion (1999) note, however, 'the introduction of a risk premium into a perfect foresight model is an anomaly, to say the least'.

[4] Goldberg (1994) also uses a speculative attack model to estimate *ex ante* probabilities of currency crises and sizes of expected devaluations month by month for Mexico during the period 1980–6. Precisely, Goldberg studies the effects of fiscal and monetary shocks on attacks on the Mexican peso in both the fixed exchange rate regime and the ensuing crawling peg regime. The forces contributing to speculative attacks on the Mexican peso include both fiscal and monetary shocks, external credit shocks and shocks in price differentials. The empirical results indicate that a reduction of domestic credit growth, an increase in the uncertainty about domestic credit growth, and a reduction of the size and an increase in the frequency of currency realignments might have greatly reduced the amount of speculation against the Mexican peso during the sample period examined. See also Connolly and Taylor (1984).

Cumby and van Wijnbergen (1989) also use a first-generation model to examine the Argentinian experiment with a crawling peg between December 1978 and February 1981, providing plausible estimates of the one-month-ahead probability of the collapse of the crawling peg (about 80 per cent). Their empirical results also indicate that the viability of an exchange rate regime depends strongly on the domestic credit policy followed by the authorities, in the sense that if this policy is not consistent with their exchange rate policy, their credibility and therefore the confidence of agents in the crawling peg system is undermined.

Grilli (1990) investigates the effectiveness of the borrowing policies of the monetary authorities in resolving exchange rate crises. Grilli shows why obtaining credit in foreign currency may avoid or at least delay the devaluation in a fixed exchange rate system, therefore creating the problem of choosing the optimal size of the loan or the line of credit for financing a government deficit. Grilli especially focuses on the attacks on the US gold standard from 1894 to 1896 and provides evidence suggesting that the borrowing policy followed by the US Treasury in those years was effective in that the amount of the borrowing undertaken by the Treasury may have been optimal. The main contribution of Grilli's study is that, while the previous literature on speculative attacks considers the minimum level of the central bank's foreign reserves as an exogenous variable, in fact it is crucial to endogenise this variable in the model and take more seriously the degree of government commitment to a fixed exchange rate system.

Overall, however, the results of the empirical literature, although limited in scope, are quite encouraging in that estimates of the probability of devaluation are usually plausible and generally quite high before actual devaluations occur, while very low in tranquil times.

8.2   Second-generation currency crisis models

An important characteristic of first-generation speculative attack or currency crisis models is that the stance of domestic macroeconomic policy is fundamentally at odds with the exchange rate peg, leading to the continuous depletion of a finite stock of reserves. The essential characteristic of second-generation currency crisis models is that a speculative attack may be successful even when the stance of monetary and fiscal policy is consistent with the level of the exchange rate which the authorities are pegging, in the sense that there may be no initial loss of reserves arising from a policy of simultaneously pursuing internal targets and pegging the exchange rate at a certain level. There must, however, be a *temptation* for the authorities to devalue the currency or even to abandon the peg altogether in order to pursue a more expansionary domestic policy. Even when there are high political costs to devaluing, the fact that speculators know that the authorities are tempted to do so may in fact be enough to bring about the devaluation. These models thus show how speculative attacks can be self-fulfilling. Formally, this shows up in the model having multiple solutions so that very small disturbances can lead to a discrete jump from an initial equilibrium with a fixed exchange rate to another equilibrium with a devalued exchange rate or even to a floating rate with zero commitment of the authorities to the peg.

The first-generation speculative attack models combine linearity in behaviour – a log-linear money demand function – with perfect foresight, to produce a unique timing of the speculative attack when the stance of domestic monetary and fiscal policy is inconsistent with the exchange rate peg. In second-generation models (Obstfeld, 1994, 1996), however, the emphasis is generally on policy rule nonlinearities, such as a shift in domestic monetary policy conditional on whether or not there is a speculative attack.[5] If the timing and intensity of the attack depend upon whether or not there is a shift in monetary policy and vice versa, then the possibility of multiple equilibria (i.e. the non-uniqueness of the timing of the attack), together with the possibility that the attack may be self-fulfilling by leading to a shift in policy, becomes intuitively clear. The possibility of multiple equilibria in such circumstances may be viewed in some ways as a co-ordination problem: if there were one large trader able to undertake massive speculation and lead the attack[6] then the multiple equilibria may collapse to a unique equilibrium. If speculators are dispersed, with heterogeneous expectations and liquidity constraints, however, then the possibility of multiple equilibria seems greater.

Consider the following version of the model analysed by Obstfeld (1996). We assume that the government conducts its exchange rate policy according to a loss function of the form:

$$L = \theta(\dot{p})^2 + (y - \widetilde{y})^2, \tag{8.16}$$

where θ is the relative weight given to inflation, $\dot{p}$, in the loss function, and $\widetilde{y}$ is the target level of real output, y. Real output, in turn, is assumed to be determined according to a 'surprise supply curve' relationship of the form:

$$y = \overline{y} + (\dot{p} - \dot{p}^e) - v, \tag{8.17}$$

where $\overline{y}$ denotes the natural level of output, $\dot{p}^e$ denotes expected inflation, and v represents a stochastic output shock. We have defined v so that it represents a negative output shock – the higher v is, the lower is output. Note the target level of output, $\widetilde{y}$, will in general differ from the natural rate of output, $\overline{y}$, by an amount k:

$$\widetilde{y} - \overline{y} = k > 0. \tag{8.18}$$

We shall term this quantity, k, the level of output target bias. A positive amount of output target bias is a characteristic which second-generation models borrow from earlier models of monetary policy credibility (see e.g. Persson and Tabellini, 1999, and the references therein). It can be rationalised by various arguments; for example, that the natural or equilibrium level of unemployment is higher than the socially optimal level because of labour market rigidities of various kinds, or perhaps because wage negotiators only care about the welfare of employed workers ('insiders') and do not take into account the effects of their

---

[5] The Flood and Marion (2000) analysis, discussed above, shows how introducing nonlinearity into the model and relaxing the perfect-foresight assumption generates multiple solutions and opens up the possibility of self-fulfilling speculative attacks. These features are, in fact, key characteristics of second-generation speculative attack models, so that the Flood–Marion (2000) model may be seen in some respects as bridging the 'generation gap'.

[6] As the financier George Soros supposedly did against sterling in the Exchange Rate Mechanism crisis of 1992–3.

negotiations on the unemployed (whom they regard as 'outsiders'). In any case, the effect is to impart a *temptation* towards inflationary policy on the part of the authorities, which in turn is the source of the authorities' temptation to 'cheat' by surprising people with a devaluation and resulting inflation which, through the supply curve (8.17), raises output. Because the markets know that the authorities have this weakness, they know the authorities can be tempted to succumb to a speculative attack, abandon the peg and devalue the currency.

For simplicity, we assume also that purchasing power parity holds,

$$s = p - p^*, \tag{8.19}$$

and that the foreign price level is held exogenously constant, so that $\dot{p} = \dot{s}$, and $\dot{p}^e = \dot{s}^e$. Thus, the loss function (8.16) may be rewritten in the form:

$$L = \theta(\dot{s})^2 + (\dot{s} - \dot{s}^e - v - k)^2. \tag{8.20}$$

A second important feature that second-generation speculative attack models share with monetary policy credibility models is the sequencing of policy decisions. We assume that the private sector has to choose or set $\dot{s}^e$ before observing the output shock, v, and, obviously, before observing the actual rate of depreciation, $\dot{s}$. The authorities, on the other hand, can choose $\dot{s}$ after observing both $\dot{s}^e$ and v. Suppose the authorities allow $\dot{s} > 0$, i.e. they devalue the exchange rate. Then, differentiating (8.20) with respect to $\dot{s}$, setting the resulting first-order condition to zero and solving for $\dot{s}$, we can see that, given $\dot{s}^e$ and v, the authorities will choose a devaluation of:

$$\dot{s} = \frac{\dot{s}^e + v + k}{1 + \theta}; \tag{8.21}$$

this is effectively the authorities' reaction function. This formula is entirely intuitive. Because the rate of depreciation is equal to the rate of inflation, the authorities can increase output through a surprise devaluation. The actual devaluation involved in this surprise policy will clearly be an increasing function of the expected devaluation, negative output shocks and the level of output target bias. On the other hand, because devaluation leads to inflation, the optimal devaluation will be a decreasing function of the weight given to inflation in the loss function, i.e. θ. Although this model is essentially a 'one-shot game', we can think of this reaction function as applying in the case of zero commitment to a fixed exchange rate, since it implies that the authorities will allow or indeed engineer a devaluation even when the expected devaluation, $\dot{s}^e$, or the output shock, v, are small. The rational expectation of devaluation when there is zero commitment to a fixed rate[7] is:

$$E(\dot{s}) = \frac{k}{1 + \theta} + \frac{\dot{s}^e}{1 + \theta} \tag{8.22}$$

since $E(v) = 0$. Further, in equilibrium, agents' expectations must be rational i.e. consistent

---

[7] We prefer to think of this as the line corresponding to zero commitment of the authorities to a fixed rate rather than as the line corresponding to a free float. This is because the line allows 'engineered' devaluation by the authorities, while a free float, strictly speaking, entails zero intervention. It might alternatively be labelled as a managed float.

with the model ($\dot{s}^e = E(\dot{s})$), so that a solution under zero commitment to the exchange rate is an expected devaluation of

$$E(\dot{s}) = \frac{k}{\theta}. \tag{8.23}$$

We now begin to see the importance of the target output bias in the model: even under zero commitment to a fixed exchange rate, it is this fundamental weakness in policy design that generates devaluation.

Substituting (8.20) in (8.21), we can derive the value of the loss function with a *discretionary* movement in the exchange rate, L^D say:

$$L^D = \frac{\theta}{(1+\theta)}(\dot{s}^e + v + k)^2. \tag{8.24}$$

If, on the other hand, the authorities simply stick to the fixed exchange rate *rule*, so that $\dot{s} = 0$, the value of the loss function, L^R say, is simply:

$$L^R = (\dot{s}^e + v + k)^2. \tag{8.25}$$

For a given expected devaluation $\dot{s}^e$, therefore, it is clear that, as the model is set up at present, discretion is preferable to rules in the sense that:

$$L^D < L^R, \tag{8.26}$$

so that the authorities will clearly be tempted to renege on the fixed exchange rate rule and follow a discretionary policy of devaluation.

The foregoing analysis assumes, however, that there are no costs to the authorities of the devaluation. The devaluation will generally be justified by the authorities invoking an 'escape clause' whereby it is claimed that the devaluation has been brought about because of other overriding considerations, such as the need to raise output and reduce unemployment. Generally, however, we can think of such escape clauses as being costly for a government to invoke. For example, there may be an international loss in the prestige of the country from dropping out of a pegged exchange rate system; or inflation may rise, which may damage the prestige of the government. Also, we must remember that we are dealing with a model which is essentially a one-shot game which does not take into account the effects of loss of credibility of the authorities. We can introduce the costs of the authorities' loss of credibility or prestige into the analysis in a simple fashion by adding an extra term, $C(\dot{s})$, into the loss function to reflect the costs of either devaluing or revaluing:

$$L = \frac{\theta}{2}(\dot{p})^2 + \frac{1}{2}(y - \tilde{y})^2 + C(\dot{s}). \tag{8.27}$$

This extra term, the cost of invoking the escape clause, is defined as:

$$C(\dot{s}) = 0 \qquad \text{if} \quad \dot{s} = 0,$$
$$C(\dot{s}) = \overline{C} > 0 \qquad \text{if} \quad \dot{s} > 0, \tag{8.28}$$
$$C(\dot{s}) = \underline{C} > 0 \qquad \text{if} \quad \dot{s} < 0.$$

A devaluation or revaluation will thus occur when the loss under a devaluation, including the costs of invoking the escape clause, are less than the costs of keeping the exchange rate fixed at the existing rate, i.e. when:

$$L^D + C(\dot{s}) < L^R, \tag{8.29}$$

or:

$$L^R - L^D > C(\dot{s}). \tag{8.30}$$

Using the expressions for L^D and L^R in (8.24) and (8.25), this condition becomes:

$$\frac{(\dot{s}^e + v + k)^2}{(1+\theta)} > C(\dot{s}). \tag{8.31}$$

Now, the only stochastic element in the model is the negative output shock v. Hence, we can think of a devaluation being triggered when a sufficiently large output shock arrives. Thus, we can solve (8.31) for a critical value of the output shock, so that devaluation occurs when the output shock exceeds this value, i.e. when:

$$v > \sqrt{\overline{C}(1+\theta)} - k - \dot{s}^e. \tag{8.32}$$

For concreteness, assume that the output shock is uniformly distributed in the interval[8] $(-V, V)$, $v \sim U(-V, V)$. Clearly, it does not make sense to have a devaluation trigger greater than the greatest possible value of v (i.e. V) or less than its smallest possible value (i.e. $-V$). Hence, define the devaluation trigger, the level above which values of v will trigger a devaluation, as:

$$\overline{v} \equiv \max \left\{ \min \left\{ \left[\sqrt{\overline{C}(1+\theta)} - k - \dot{s}^e \right], V \right\}, -V \right\}. \tag{8.33}$$

This expression has an appealing interpretation. Apart from the boundary conditions, the devaluation trigger is decreasing in k and $\dot{s}^e$: a devaluation is more likely to occur if agents *expect* a large depreciation, and/or if the amount of output target bias is large and the authorities are constantly tempted to inflate. It is, on the other hand, increasing in $\overline{C}$ and θ: the higher the costs of invoking the escape clause and the higher the weight attached to beating inflation, the less likely the authorities are to succumb to a devaluation.

Note, however, that (8.32) represents only one solution for the trigger, since we need also to consider the negative square root. Intuitively, this corresponds to the case where negative output shocks are low enough to trigger a revaluation (negative devaluation), i.e. when:

$$v < -\sqrt{\underline{C}(1+\theta)} - k - \dot{s}^e. \tag{8.34}$$

Again, however, it does not make sense for the revaluation trigger to be less than the lower bound on v (i.e. $-V$) or greater than the upper bound (i.e. V). Hence, we can define it as:

$$\underline{v} \equiv \min \left\{ \max \left\{ \left[-\sqrt{\underline{C}(1+\theta)} - k - \dot{s}^e \right], -V \right\}, V \right\}. \tag{8.35}$$

Note that it follows immediately from the definitions given in (8.33) and (8.35) that $\underline{v} \leq \overline{v}$.

---

[8] This assumption does not affect the central insights of the model in that qualitatively similar results could be derived so long as v is symmetrically distributed.

Since we are implicitly assuming market efficiency, there will also be a lower bound to the expected depreciation, $\dot{s}^e$. Assuming uncovered interest parity, we have $\dot{s}^e = i - i^*$, where i and i^* denote the domestic and foreign nominal interest rates. If we assume that the domestic nominal interest rate cannot be less than zero, this gives a lower bound of $\dot{s}^e = -i^*$. We assume that at this level of expected devaluation (in fact, since $\dot{s}^e < 0$, it is an expected revaluation) the parameters $\underline{C}$, $\overline{C}$, θ, k and V are such that $\underline{v} > -V$ and $\overline{v} < V$.

The rational, or model-consistent, expected devaluation, $E(\dot{s})$, will be a weighted average of the devaluation which is expected to occur if $v > \overline{v}$ (i.e. $E(\dot{s} \mid v > \overline{v})$) and the revaluation which is expected to occur if $v \leq \underline{v}$ (i.e. $E(\dot{s} \mid v \leq \underline{v})$), with the weights given by the probability of each event occurring:

$$E(\dot{s}) = \Pr\{v > \overline{v}\}E(\dot{s} \mid v > \overline{v}) + \Pr\{v \leq \underline{v}\}E(\dot{s} \mid v \leq \underline{v}). \tag{8.36}$$

Since the output shock is uniformly distributed, $v \sim U(-V, V)$, the probability that v exceeds the upper critical value is:

$$\Pr\{v > \overline{v}\} = \frac{V - \overline{v}}{2V}. \tag{8.37}$$

Similarly:

$$\Pr\{v \leq \underline{v}\} = \frac{\underline{v} - (-V)}{2V}$$
$$= \frac{\underline{v} + V}{2V}. \tag{8.38}$$

Also, from the expression (8.21), we can write:

$$E(\dot{s} \mid v > \overline{v}) = \frac{E(v \mid v > \overline{v}) + (\dot{s}^e + k)}{1 + \theta}$$
$$= \frac{(V + \overline{v})/2 + (\dot{s}^e + k)}{1 + \theta} \tag{8.39}$$

and:

$$E(\dot{s} \mid v \leq \underline{v}) = \frac{E(v \mid v \leq \underline{v}) + (\dot{s}^e + k)}{1 + \theta}$$
$$= \frac{(-V + \underline{v})/2 + (\dot{s}^e + k)}{1 + \theta}. \tag{8.40}$$

Hence, (8.36) becomes:

$$E(\dot{s}) = \left\{\frac{\underline{v} + V}{2V}\right\}\left\{\frac{(-V + \underline{v})/2 + (\dot{s}^e + k)}{1 + \theta}\right\}$$
$$+ \left\{\frac{V - \overline{v}}{2V}\right\}\left\{\frac{(V + \overline{v})/2 + (\dot{s}^e + k)}{1 + \theta}\right\}, \tag{8.41}$$

which simplifies to:

$$E(\dot{s}) = \left\{ \frac{1}{1+\theta} \right\} \left\{ \left[1 - \frac{(\bar{v} - \underline{v})}{2V} \right] (\dot{s}^e + k) - \frac{(\bar{v}^2 - \underline{v}^2)}{4V} \right\}. \tag{8.42}$$

Equation (8.42) shows the relationship between $E(\dot{s})$ and $\dot{s}^e$ in the model. In equilibrium, expectations must be consistent with the model, i.e. rational, so that $\dot{s}^e = E(\dot{s})$. Hence, if we draw this curve in $[\dot{s}^e, E(\dot{s})]$-space, the points where it intersects a 45° ray through the origin will give us the solutions. But what will this curve look like? This is a non-trivial question since, from (8.33) and (8.35), both $\bar{v}$ and $\underline{v}$ depend upon the expected depreciation $\dot{s}^e$.

Consider first small values of $\dot{s}^e$. By our foregoing assumption, even when $\dot{s}^e$ is at its minimum value of $-i^*$, both $\underline{v}$ and $\bar{v}$ are within the permissible range of values of v, i.e. $-V < \underline{v} \le \bar{v} < V$. Hence, from the definitions (8.33) and (8.35), we have $\underline{v} = [-\sqrt{C(1 + \theta)} - k - \dot{s}^e]$ and $\bar{v} = [\sqrt{C(1 + \theta)} - k - \dot{s}^e]$. Thus, $(\partial \underline{v}/\partial \dot{s}^e) = (\partial \bar{v}/\partial \dot{s}^e) = -1$. Intuitively, these partial derivatives imply that both the devaluation and revaluation triggers shrink as $\dot{s}^e$ rises and the probability of a devaluation increases. Differentiating (8.42) with respect to $\dot{s}^e$ using these partial derivatives yields:

$$\frac{\partial E(\dot{s})}{\partial \dot{s}^e} = \frac{1}{1+\theta}, \tag{8.43}$$

so that (8.42) must represent a straight line with slope $(1 + \theta)^{-1} < 1$. In fact, this line has the same slope as (8.22), the equation which holds under zero commitment to the peg.

Now consider intermediate values of $\dot{s}^e$ such that $\underline{v} = -V$ but $-V < \bar{v} = [\sqrt{C(1 + \theta)} - k - \dot{s}^e] < V$. We have $(\partial \bar{v}/\partial \dot{s}^e) = -1$ as before, but now $(\partial \underline{v}/\partial \dot{s}^e) = 0$ as $\underline{v}$ cannot shrink any further. The derivative of (8.42) with respect to $\dot{s}^e$ is seen to be:

$$\frac{\partial E(\dot{s})}{\partial \dot{s}^e} = \frac{1}{2(1 + \theta)} \left[1 + \frac{(\dot{s}^e + k)}{V} \right]. \tag{8.44}$$

Hence, in this region of the curve, the slope is increasing in $\dot{s}^e$.

Finally, consider larger values of $\dot{s}^e$. In particular, suppose that $\dot{s}^e$ is so large that $[\sqrt{C(1 + \theta)} - k - \dot{s}^e] < -V$. Then, from (8.33), we have $\bar{v} = -V$. However, we know that $\underline{v} \le \bar{v}$ and, indeed, from the definition of $\underline{v}$ given in (8.35), this would imply $\underline{v} = \bar{v} = -V$. Since the distribution of v is such that $v \ge -V$, a revaluation is in fact precluded with certainty. On the other hand, this means that the probability of the trigger for a devaluation being exceeded is unity. Setting $\underline{v} = \bar{v}$ in (8.42), we have:

$$E(\dot{s}) = \frac{k}{1+\theta} + \frac{\dot{s}^e}{1+\theta}, \tag{8.45}$$

i.e. a straight line with slope $(1 + \theta)^{-1} < 1$ and intercept $k(1 + \theta)^{-1}$. Note that (8.45) is identical to the equation linking $E(\dot{s})$ and $\dot{s}^e$ which we derived assuming zero commitment to the fixed exchange rate, i.e. equation (8.22). This is again intuitive: if there is to be a revaluation with certainty, this is essentially the same as saying that the authorities have zero commitment to the exchange rate peg.

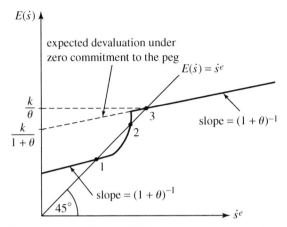

Figure 8.1. Multiple equilibria in the second-generation model.

We are now in a position to gather this information together and infer what the curve (8.42) looks like in $[\dot{s}^e, E(\dot{s})]$-space. The three cases discussed above are as follows:

$$\frac{\partial E(\dot{s})}{\partial \dot{s}^e} = \begin{cases} \frac{1}{1+\theta} & \text{for} & -V < \underline{v} < \overline{v} < V & -\text{small } \dot{s}^e \\ \frac{1}{2(1+\theta)}\left[1 + \frac{(\dot{s}^e+k)}{V}\right] & \text{for} & \underline{v} = -V; -V < \overline{v} < V & -\text{intermediate } \dot{s}^e \\ \frac{1}{1+\theta} & \text{for} & \underline{v} = \overline{v} = -V & -\text{large } \dot{s}^e \end{cases}$$
$$(8.46)$$

In Figure 8.1 we have drawn a curve which has a shape consistent with (8.46) in $[\dot{s}^e, E(s)]$-space. The third section of the curve, which holds for the largest values of $\dot{s}^e$, is identical to the curve which obtains under zero commitment to the peg, (8.21), which has intercept $k(1 + \theta)^{-1}$. The first section is also linear and is parallel to this section. The first linear section must, however, have a smaller intercept than $k(1 + \theta)^{-1}$, since the intermediate, nonlinear section, has a slope increasing in $\dot{s}^e$. We have also drawn a 45° ray through the origin in the diagram, so that the points where this ray intersects the curve represent solutions to the model. We know from (8.23) that if there is an intersection with the third section, this is at the point $\dot{s}^e = E(\dot{s}) = k/\theta$.

The important point to note, however, is that since the slope of the straight-line segments of the curve is less than unity (the slope of the 45° ray through the origin), there may be up to three solutions to the model (labelled 1, 2 and 3 in Figure 8.1). This potential multiple equilibrium feature of the model is central to understanding second-generation speculative attack models. In particular, Obstfeld (1994, 1996) argues that it may be sudden shifts in expectations, from one equilibrium to another, which show up as sudden speculative attacks following from a sudden and self-fulfilling upward shift in the expected devaluation of the currency.

Note that *some* devaluation in the model – at least as the model is depicted in Figure 8.1 – is inevitable. However, it may be that the devaluation at equilibrium 1 is consistent with an agreed band of fluctuation of the exchange rate, such as the fluctuation bands of the former Exchange Rate Mechanism (ERM) of the European Monetary System. Nevertheless, although they might prefer this smaller devaluation, the authorities are unable to stop the

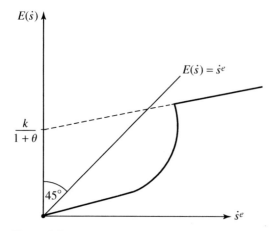

Figure 8.2. Reducing k or increasing θ may generate a unique, zero-devaluation equilibrium.

economy jumping to equilibrium 2, outside of the agreed band, or even to equilibrium 3, the solution consistent with zero commitment to the peg.

Note also that the probability of a successful speculative attack occurring is not independent either of the underlying economic fundamentals or of the policy behaviour of the authorities. To see this, consider the following. Since the first section is parallel to the third section and the third section, if it were extended to join the vertical axis, would have intercept $k(1 + \theta)^{-1}$, the whole curve – all three sections – must shift down as k falls and/or as θ rises. But shifting this curve down could lead, for example, to the multiple equilibria of Figure 8.1 collapsing into a single equilibrium with zero expected devaluation, as in Figure 8.2.[9] This could be brought about by reducing k – either by reducing the target rate of output towards the natural rate (reducing the inconsistency of the inflation and output targets) or by increasing the natural rate (improving the fundamentals) – and/or by increasing θ, the weight on inflation in the social loss function, i.e. adopting a more conservative policy stance towards inflation.

Second-generation models have not been extensively tested empirically to date, although they seem particularly appealing for explaining the crises faced by some ERM countries in the 1990s. In particular, the attack on the French franc during the 1992–3 ERM crisis is often cited as an example of a situation where the underlying pre-attack economic fundamentals did not suggest any major inconsistency between domestic and external policy objectives; this observation supports the relevance of a self-fulfilling attack explanation. Moreover, the relatively high level of French unemployment at this time suggests that the authorities were tempted to devalue, even though there was no initial inconsistency between the exchange rate peg and the stance of domestic macroeconomic policy.

A notable empirical paper in this context is due to Jeanne (1997), who studies the respective roles of the fundamentals and self-fulfilling speculation in currency crises. Jeanne first presents a model of a fixed exchange rate system in which self-fulfilling speculation

---

[9] This example is only illustrative – it is possible that forcing the first linear segment of the curve to pass through the origin would still admit equilibria such as 2 and 3 in Figure 8.1.

can arise following a bifurcation in the fundamentals. He then estimates the model in the case of the 1992–3 crisis of the French franc and, as might be expected, finds evidence that self-fulfilling speculation was at work.

Some authors (e.g. Morris and Shin, 1998) have argued that a serious shortcoming of the second-generation models is the lack of a proper rationale as to why there may be sudden shifts in expectations. Indeed, as Obstfeld (1994) notes in the concluding section of his seminal paper, 'If speculative currency crises are a manifestation of possible multiple equilibria, an obvious barrier to understanding them is the lack of any convincing account of how and when market expectations coordinate on a particular set of expectations.' Morris and Shin (1998) demonstrate that, even though self-fulfilling currency attacks lead to multiple equilibria when fundamentals are common knowledge, there is a unique equilibrium when speculators face a small amount of noise in their signals about the fundamentals. This unique equilibrium depends not only on the fundamentals but also on financial variables, such as the quantity of hot money in circulation and the costs of speculative trading.

8.3   Third-generation currency crisis models

A large and growing literature on currency and financial crises has developed recently in the wake of the 1997–8 East Asian financial and currency crisis. Apparently, these models were developed primarily because the East Asian crisis appeared not to be characterised by the fiscal deficits which typically trigger a crisis in first-generation currency crisis models, and nor did there appear to be any strong temptation for the authorities to abandon a fixed exchange rate system in order to pursue a more expansionary monetary policy, as one might expect in a second-generation model. In fact, these 'third-generation' models are really models of financial sector crisis rather than of speculative attack or currency crisis *per se*.

Third-generation models, while varying widely, have as a consistent central feature a 'moral hazard' view of the underlying causes of the financial crisis (e.g. McKinnon and Pill, 1996; Bhattacharya, Claessens, Ghosh, Hernandez and Alba, 1998; Corsetti, Pesenti and Roubini, 1998; Edison, Luangaram and Miller, 1998; Krugman, 1998). According to this view, a crucial role in the generation of currency crisis is played by financial intermediaries whose liabilities are perceived as having an implicit government guarantee, but which may be essentially unregulated. This may create what is generally defined as a moral hazard problem, in which financial intermediaries are able to raise money at safe interest rates and then lend it at much higher rates to finance risky investments. This generates domestic asset price bubbles, sustained by a circular process in which the proliferation of risky lending drives up the prices of risky assets, making the financial condition of these institutions appear to be sounder than it actually is. At some point, however, the bubble bursts and the mechanics of the crisis are then described by the same circular process in reverse: asset prices begin to fall, making the insolvency of financial intermediaries highly visible, forcing them to cease operations and generating increasingly fast asset price deflation, and leading to actual or incipient capital flight as asset prices collapse. The massive capital flight then generates a collapse in the external value of the currency, which cannot be defended by the authorities.

While casual empiricism suggests that this class of models appear to match the features of the East Asian crisis, Sarno and Taylor (1999) provide the first empirical tests of these models through an examination both of stock market behaviour and of the nature of various categories of capital flows to East Asian economies. In particular, Sarno and Taylor test for and provide evidence in favour of the presence of asset price bubbles in a set of East Asian economies (as well as Australia and Japan) in the period leading up to the crisis, and also show that capital flows to these countries were highly reversible, as predicted by the moral hazard view, hence concluding that third-generation models may be vital for understanding the 1997–8 East Asian crisis.

8.4   Summary and concluding remarks

Clearly, the three strands of the literature on speculative attacks and currency crises offer rather different – albeit related – fundamental views of the mechanics of a currency crisis. Each has interesting policy implications.

The simple policy lesson of the first-generation models is that the authorities should ensure the consistency of internal and external targets; to do otherwise is to live on borrowed time.

The second-generation models have more subtle policy implications, however. Here, it is not so much the blatant inconsistency of policy that is at issue as the perceived *temptation* of the authorities to pursue a domestic policy that is more expansionary than is consistent with a fixed exchange rate, even though they are not pursuing such a policy before the attack is launched. Here, the policy implications are perhaps a little more difficult to deal with at a practical level but, in principle at least, are still reasonably straightforward. If, for example, the socially optimal or desired level of output is above the level consistent with stable prices (i.e. the natural level), then the authorities should try and raise the natural rate, for example by pursuing supply-side policies such as reforming the labour market, encouraging investment in capital and infrastructure and so on. In addition or alternatively, they can try and persuade the electorate to accept more realistic targets for output and employment.[10] They can also reduce their actual and perceived ability to act on temptation by handing over the conduct of monetary policy to a conservative central banker (Rogoff, 1985), through central bank independence and by repeated and subsequently justified affirmations of fiscal prudence and general policy toughness towards inflation.[11]

The third-generation models imply different policy prescriptions for what is essentially a different set of problems. Here what is at issue is the *transparency* of the risks and rewards associated with investment opportunities. The moral hazard in these models arises because foreign investors are unaware of the true risks they are running and perhaps because they also

---

[10] The ambitious post-war commitment of successive British governments to full employment, following the publication of the Beveridge Report in 1942, combined with a largely unreformed labour market and strong labour union power, provides an interesting 'second-generation' rationale for the wave of attacks on sterling during the Bretton Woods period, culminating in the 1967 devaluation.

[11] Substantial central bank independence, through policy announcements on inflation and supply-side policies, appears to characterise much of the economic policy of the British Labour government since taking office in 1997.

mistakenly perceive government guarantees on their investments that do not in fact exist. As in all moral hazard problems, there is an informational asymmetry. Hence, reducing the informational asymmetry will reduce the problem. Improving transparency through, for example, government investment agencies offering relevant local information services might be a step in the right direction. In practice, however, when international investors are investing in countries where not only the language but also the political, legal and corporate governance systems are fundamentally different from those prevailing in their home countries, this may be easier said than done.

References and further readings

Agénor, P.-R., J.S. Bhandari and R.P. Flood (1992), 'Speculative Attacks and Models of Balance of Payments Crises', Working Paper No. 3919, National Bureau of Economic Research. Condensed version published in *International Monetary Fund Staff Papers*, 39, pp. 357–94 (1992).

Bhattacharya, A., S. Claessens, S. Ghosh, L. Hernandez and P. Alba (1998), 'Volatility and Contagion in a Financially-Integrated World: Lessons from East Asia's Recent Experience', paper presented at the CEPR–World Bank conference on *Financial Crises: Contagion and Market Volatility*, London, May.

Blanco, H. and P.M. Garber (1986), 'Recurrent Devaluation and Speculative Attacks on the Mexican Peso', *Journal of Political Economy*, 94, pp. 148–66.

Canzoneri, M.B., W.J. Ethier and V. Grilli (eds.) (1996), *The New Transatlantic Economy*, Cambridge: Cambridge University Press.

Connolly, M.B. and D. Taylor (1984), 'The Exact Timing of the Collapse of an Exchange Rate Regime and Its Impact on the Relative Price of Traded Goods', *Journal of Money, Credit and Banking*, 16, pp. 194–207.

Corsetti, G., P. Pesenti and N. Roubini (1998), 'What Caused the East Asian Currency and Financial Crisis?', paper presented at the CEPR–World Bank conference on *Financial Crises: Contagion and Market Volatility*, London, May.

Cukierman, A. (1992), *Central Bank Strategy, Credibility and Independence*, Cambridge, Mass.: MIT Press.

Cukierman, A. and A.H. Meltzer (1986), 'A Theory of Ambiguity, Credibility and Inflation under Discretion and Asymmetric Information', *Econometrica*, 54, pp. 1099–128.

Cumby, R.E. and S. van Wijnbergen (1989), 'Financial Policy and Speculative Runs in a Crawling Peg: Argentina, 1979–1981', *Journal of International Economics*, 27, pp. 111–27.

Dornbusch, R. (1983), 'Exchange Risk and the Macroeconomics of Exchange Rate Determination', in R. Hawkins, R. Levich, C. Wihlborg (eds.), *The Internationalization of Financial Markets and National Economic Policy*, Greenwich, Conn.: JAI Press.

Edison, H., P. Luangaram and M. Miller (1998), 'Asset Bubbles, Domino Effects and "Lifeboats": Elements of the East Asian Crisis', paper presented at the CEPR–World Bank conference on *Financial Crises: Contagion and Market Volatility*, London, May.

Eichengreen, B., J. Tobin and C. Wyplosz (1995), 'Two Cases for Sand in the Wheels of International Finance', *Economic Journal*, 105, pp. 162–72.

Flood, R.P. and P.M. Garber (1984), 'Collapsing Exchange Rate Regimes: Some Linear Examples', *Journal of International Economics*, 16, pp. 1–13.

——— (1991), 'The Linkage between Speculative Attack and Target Zone Models of Exchange Rates', *Quarterly Journal of Economics*, 106, pp. 1367–72.

Flood, R.P., P.M. Garber and C. Kramer (1996), 'Collapsing Exchange Rate Regimes: Another Linear Example', *Journal of International Economics*, 41, pp. 223–34.

Flood, R.P., R.J. Hodrick, P. Isard and C. Kramer (1996), 'Economic Models of Speculative Attacks and the Drachma Crisis of May 1994', *Open Economies Review*, 7, pp. 583–92.

Flood, R.P. and N.P. Marion (1997a), 'The Size and Timing of Devaluations in Capital-Controlled Countries', *Journal of Development Economics*, 54, pp. 123–47.

(1997b), 'Policy Implication of "Second-Generation" Crisis Models', *International Monetary Fund Staff Papers*, 44, pp. 383–90.

(1999), 'Perspectives on the Recent Currency Crisis Literature', *International Journal of Finance and Economics*, 4, pp. 1–26.

(2000), 'Risk Predictions: An Application to Speculative Attacks', *Journal of International Economics*, 50, pp. 245–68.

Garber, P.M. and L.E.O. Svensson (1995), 'The Operation and Collapse of Fixed Exchange Rate Regimes', in G.M. Grossman and K. Rogoff (eds.), *Handbook of International Economics*, vol. III, Amsterdam: North-Holland, pp. 1865–911.

Garber, P. and M.P. Taylor (1995), 'Sand in the Wheels of Foreign Exchange Markets: A Sceptical Note', *Economic Journal*, 105, pp. 173–80.

Gardner, G.W. (1983), 'The Choice of Monetary Policy Instruments in an Open Economy', *Journal of International Money and Finance*, 2, pp. 347–54.

Glick, R. (ed.) (1998), *Managing Capital Flows and Exchange Rates: Perspectives from the Pacific Basin*, Cambridge: Cambridge University Press.

Glick, R. and M.M. Hutchison (1989), 'Exchange Rates and Monetary Policy', *Federal Reserve Bank of San Francisco Economic Review*.

Goldberg, L.S. (1994), 'Predicting Exchange Rate Crises: Mexico Revisited', *Journal of International Economics*, 36, pp. 413–30.

Grilli, V. (1990), 'Managing Exchange Rate Crises: Evidence from the 1890s', *Journal of International Money and Finance*, 9, pp. 258–75.

Jeanne, O. (1996), 'Les Modèles de crise de change: un essai de synthèse en relation avec la crise du franc de 1992–1993' (with English summary), *Economie et Prévision*.

(1997), 'Are Currency Crises Self-Fulfilling? A Test', *Journal of International Economics*, 43, pp. 263–86.

Kenen, P.B. (ed.) (1995), *Understanding Interdependence: The Macroeconomics of the Open Economy*, Princeton: Princeton University Press.

Krugman, P. (1979), 'A Model of Balance of Payments Crises', *Journal of Money, Credit, and Banking*, 11, pp. 311–25.

(1998), 'What Happened to Asia?', Department of Economics, Massachusetts Institute of Technology, mimeo.

McKinnon, R. and H. Pill (1996), 'Credible Liberalizations and International Capital Flows: The Overborrowing Syndrome', in T. Ito and A.O. Krueger (eds.), *Financial Deregulation and Integration in East Asia*, Chicago: Chicago University Press, pp. 7–42.

Morris, S. and H.S. Shin (1998), 'Unique Equilibrium in a Model of Self-Fulfilling Currency Attacks', *American Economic Review*, 88 (3), pp. 587–97.

Obstfeld, M. (1994), 'The Logic of Currency Crises', *Cahiers Economiques et Monetaires*, 43, pp. 189–213.

(1996), 'Models of Currency Crisis with Self-Fulfilling Features', *European Economic Review*, 40, pp. 1037–48.

Obstfeld, M. and K. Rogoff (1995), 'Exchange Rate Dynamics Redux', *Journal of Political Economy*, 103, pp. 624–60.

(1996), *Foundations of International Macroeconomics*, Cambridge, Mass: MIT Press.

Persson, T. and G. Tabellini (1999), 'Political Economics and Macroeconomic Policy', in J.B. Taylor and M. Woodford (eds.), *Handbook of Macroeconomics*, Vol. 1C, part 7, ch. 22.

Rogoff, K. (1985), 'The Optimal Degree of Commitment to an Intermediate Monetary Target', *Quarterly Journal of Economics*, 100, pp. 1169–89.

Salant, S. (1983), 'The Vulnerability of Price Stabilization Schemes to Speculative Attacks', *Journal of Political Economy*, 31, pp. 1–38.

Salant, S. and D. Henderson (1978), 'Market Anticipation of Government Policy and the Price of Gold', *Journal of Political Economy*, 86, pp. 627–48.

Sarno, L. and M.P. Taylor (1999), 'Moral Hazard, Asset Price Bubbles, Capital Flows, and the East Asian Crisis: The First Tests', *Journal of International Money and Finance*, 18, pp. 637–57.

(2001), 'Official Intervention in the Foreign Exchange Market: Is It Effective and, If So, How Does It Work?', *Journal of Economic Literature*, 39, pp. 839–68.

Taylor, M.P. (1995), 'The Economics of Exchange Rates', *Journal of Economic Literature*, 83, pp. 13–47.

Wihlborg, C., M. Fratianni and T.D. Willett (eds.) (1991), *Financial Regulation and Monetary Arrangements After 1992*. Contributions to Economic Analysis, vol. 204, Amsterdam North-Holland.

9 Foreign exchange market microstructure

A stylised fact, now routinely recorded in the empirical literature on exchange rate determination, is that, while macroeconomic fundamentals – variables such as relative money supply or relative velocity of circulation, for example – appear to be important determinants of exchange rate movements over relatively long horizons and in economies experiencing pathologically large movements in such fundamentals (such as during a hyperinflation), there seem to be substantial and often persistent movements in exchange rates which are largely unexplained by macroeconomic fundamentals (Frankel and Rose, 1995; Taylor, 1995; Flood and Taylor, 1996). The recent and emerging literature on foreign exchange market microstructure therefore reflects, in some measure, an attempt by researchers in international finance to understand the mechanisms generating these deviations from macroeconomic fundamentals which appear to characterise exchange rate movements (Taylor, 1995; Flood and Taylor, 1996; Lyons, 1999).[1] At the same time, the microstructure literature is also concerned with other issues which are seen to be of interest in their own right by international financial economists, such as the transmission of information between market participants, the behaviour of market agents, the relationship between information flows, the importance of order flow, the heterogeneity of agents' expectations and the implications of such heterogeneity for trading volume and exchange rate volatility.

The approach followed by the microstructure literature is often quite different from the conventional macroeconomic approach to exchange rate modelling in both its assumptions and its methodology. With regard to its assumptions, for example, the foreign exchange microstructure approach, unlike the conventional macroeconomic one, typically does not assume that only public information is relevant to exchange rates, that foreign exchange market agents are homogeneous, or that the mechanism used for trading is inconsequential (Lyons, 1999); indeed, these issues are often the very subject of investigation themselves. With respect to methodology, instead of starting with a set of macroeconomic relationships

---

[1] One way in which a speculative movement of the exchange rate away from the level consistent with the macroeconomic fundamentals could begin, for example, is if some agents have destabilising expectations. This may be the case, for example, if a 5 per cent appreciation leads agents to expect a 10 per cent appreciation, which leads them to buy the appreciating currency, causing it to appreciate faster, in a self-fulfilling fashion. 'Bandwagon' effects of this kind have been examined by Frankel and Froot (1987a), Allen and Taylor (1990) and others using survey data on expectations. The evidence to date tentatively suggests that expectations may be more destabilising over relatively short horizons.

such as money demand and purchasing power parity or demand functions for aggregate asset markets such as domestic bonds, foreign bonds and money, which are then used to solve for the exchange rate, the microstructure literature typically takes an essentially *microeconomic* approach by analysing the behaviour of and interaction between individual decision-making units in the foreign exchange market.[2] Simply put, the microstructure literature is concerned with the details and importance of the mechanics of foreign exchange trading, whereas the traditional macro approach typically takes these for granted and, by and large, implicitly dismisses them as unimportant.

This view of the provenance and approach of the foreign exchange market microstructure literature is well encapsulated in the following two quotations:

This 'market microstructure' approach represents a radical departure from the traditional modelling strategy of treating foreign exchange rates as a macroeconomic relative price. (Frankel and Rose, 1995)

It is apparent that there are important influences, not on the list of standard macro fundamentals, that affect short-run exchange rate behaviour . . . and it is in this context that new work on the microstructure of the foreign exchange market seems both warranted and promising. (Flood and Taylor, 1996)

However, its seems plausible to believe that future research on foreign exchange markets will increasingly tend to merge macroeconomic and microstructural issues and approaches, so that 'the uneasy dichotomy between macro and micro approaches is destined to fade' (Lyons, 1999).

For this process to continue there needs to be a wider awareness and understanding of the microstructure literature. That is one reason for including the present chapter, which surveys this literature, in this volume.[3]

9.1   The foreign exchange market

9.1.1   Institutional features of the foreign exchange market

A large proportion of the early microstructure literature focuses on the analysis of the institutional features of the foreign exchange market and their implications for the performance of the market itself. The two main distinguishing features of the foreign exchange market relative to other financial markets are that the foreign exchange market is a *largely* decentralised market and that trading volume is very large and mainly carried out between

---

[2] The microstructure approach is also to be distinguished from the dynamic optimising approach of the 'new open-economy macroeconomics' (e.g. Obstfeld and Rogoff, 1995, 1996; Lane, 2001) in that, while the new open-economy macro literature does explicitly take an optimising approach (usually of representative agents in two economies) rather than relying on 'off the peg' macroeconomic behavioural relationships, it is generally concerned with the interaction between whole economies rather than with the functioning of the foreign exchange market *per se*.

[3] To some extent researchers have occasionally employed methods of analysis which effectively synthesise macro and micro approaches. For example, Taylor's (1987, 1989) studies of covered interest parity may be viewed as early microstructural analysis, using high-frequency data and microstructure tools, of an issue hitherto debated at the macroeonomic level using data at lower frequency.

market-makers.[4] A decentralised market is a market where participants – market-makers, brokers and customers[5] – are generally physically separated from each other and their transactions occur through telephone, telex or computer network contact. Hence, while in a centralised market trade is carried out at a publicly announced price and all traders in the market face the same trading opportunities, in a decentralised system prices are quoted and transactions executed in private meetings (where it is understood that such meetings may take place through some form of electronic medium; see Schwartz, 1988; Wolinsky, 1990). For example, while the New York Stock Exchange (NYSE) and the London Stock Exchange (LSE) are centralised markets, the direct foreign exchange market may be better classified as decentralised and the brokered market may be classified as quasi-centralised, since each foreign exchange broker accumulates a sub-set of market-makers' limit orders, where a limit order is simply understood to be an offer by a bank to buy or sell (but not both) a certain amount of currency against another currency at a specified rate of exchange.

The empirical evidence from the microstructure literature to date strongly suggests that differences in the degree of centralisation across markets may be very important in explaining differences in the performance of markets. A widely held view is that, by tending to centralise trading and price information, the brokered market uses time more efficiently, eliminates significant arbitrage opportunities rapidly and assures dealers that orders are executed according to price priority (see Garbade, 1978; Garbade, Pomrenze and Silber, 1979; Glosten and Milgrom, 1985).[6]

Flood (1994) investigates the intraday operational efficiency of the US foreign exchange market by executing simulation experiments calibrated on a particular market structure for market-makers, brokers and customers. His results suggest that the traditional view that centralisation is a key factor for achieving operational efficiency is correct. In particular, his simulation results indicate that significant operational inefficiencies may be explained by temporary inventory imbalances inherent in a decentralised market. The results also suggest that this inefficiency could be largely alleviated by centralising price information.

Interesting work on the implications of decentralisation in this context is due to Perraudin and Vitale (1996), who construct an elegant theoretical framework for a decentralised dealer

---

[4] Another institutional feature of the foreign exchange market often emphasised by the relevant literature, briefly discussed below, is that a large fraction of the trading volume in the market is concerned with the trade of forward contracts (see Flood, 1991; Bank for International Settlements, 1998). Forward positions (mainly outrights and swaps) are taken by traders for a currency whose exchange rate can fluctuate greatly over time, in order to minimise the risk and uncertainty surrounding their business dealings in the immediate future (hence, hedging against adverse exchange rate movements), and by dealers and speculators hoping to earn windfall profits from correctly anticipating exchange rate movements.

[5] Broadly speaking, a market-maker is a firm (typically a bank) attached to the foreign exchange market which is engaged in the buying and selling of currencies and by doing so acts to establish a market for these currencies in the sense of standing ready to buy and sell – i.e. make a 'two-way' price for – particular currencies against one another. Such firms generally make significant profits from the difference between the 'bid' exchange rate price at which they buy a currency and the (higher) 'ask' price at which they sell it. While the market-maker may be seen as the *principal* in the buying and selling of currencies, the broker acts as an *agent* on behalf of customers wishing to sell or buy currencies.

[6] In particular, the sequential-trade model proposed by Glosten and Milgrom (1985), designed to capture how bid and ask prices evolve in a dealership market as orders arrive in sequence, is one of the benchmark models in the relevant literature. For a comprehensive discussion of the Glosten–Milgrom model and its subsequent extensions, see Lyons (1999).

market and focus on the implications for price information transmission mechanisms and efficiency in the foreign exchange market. In their model inter-bank trading is modelled such that market-makers 'sell' each other information about their transactions with outside customers by adjusting the bid and ask prices and the bid–ask spread in their price quotations (e.g. by lowering the bid and the ask price for a particular currency if the bank has been given a large amount of that currency). This modelling assumption in turn implies that market-makers can capture, through inter-dealer trades, the informational rents associated with receiving outside orders and optimally adjust bid–ask spreads to maximise those rents and elicit information. Their model also indicates that bid–ask spreads are wider in decentralised markets since, using wider spreads, dealers can discourage liquidity traders who are very reactive to price changes and, therefore, increase the informativeness of their order flow.[7] Nevertheless, the most important result of Perraudin and Vitale is perhaps that decentralised markets are much less prone to crashes than centralised markets. The intuition behind the latter result is the following: information on order flow is used to update subjective estimates of the underlying value of exchange rates; so, even when a centralised market would collapse because of the excessive number of informed traders, dealers will still have an incentive to preserve some turnover in a decentralised market since they can use the information in the order flow in future trading. Finally, Perraudin and Vitale's model also indicates a difference in exchange rate behaviour between the two types of market system: in a centralised market, bid and ask quotes are martingales with respect to the information available to foreign exchange dealers, whereas in a decentralised market bid–ask spreads shrink as order flow provides new information.

Thus, one important implication of the high degree of decentralisation of the foreign exchange market is that there is, in general, some degree of fragmentation: not all dealer quotes are observable and, therefore, transactions may occur at the same time at different prices. This feature strongly distinguishes the foreign exchange markets from other financial – e.g. equity – markets. Another important implication of decentralisation is that the foreign exchange market has a low degree of transparency compared to other financial markets, where trades must be disclosed within minutes by law. This is due to the fact that foreign exchange markets have no disclosure requirement and, hence, trades are not observable. As a consequence, given that order flow is not fully observable and, hence, cannot communicate information about fundamentals as it may do in other financial markets, trading flows are less informative than they normally are in other financial markets.

Another important feature of the foreign exchange market is that market-makers, who by definition provide two-way bid and ask prices, largely dominate the market at commercial and investment banks, either trading with each other directly – more than half of the spot-market trading volume – or through foreign exchange brokers – about 40 per cent of the trading volume.[8] In the direct market, banks contact each other and the bank receiving a call acts as a market-maker for the currency traded by providing bid and ask prices for the

---

[7] Liquidity traders can be thought of as agents who need to purchase or sell foreign exchange because of international trade in goods and services and who do not speculate or hedge their exposure in any way. Hence, their orders are largely random.

[8] Bank for International Settlements (1998).

bank placing the call. Brokered transactions occur when brokers collect limit orders from market-making banks; the limit orders, specifying the quantity and the price of an offer to buy or sell, remain with the broker until they are withdrawn by the market-making bank.[9] Brokers trade by keeping a 'book' of market-makers' limit orders for buying and selling from which they quote the 'inside spread' (that is, the best bid and ask orders) upon demand. Traditionally, the brokered market has been conducted by telephone on direct lines between brokers and banks although, as we discuss below, an important recent feature of the foreign exchange market has been the development of electronic screen-based broking systems. Only a small fraction of the spot-market volume (about 5 per cent, for example, in the United States) is traded by customers of the market-makers for the purpose of completing transactions in international trade (goods-market transactions). Nevertheless, customers trade only with market-making banks, not with brokers since brokers might not adequately assess the creditworthiness of the customers. Finally, the other participants in the foreign exchange market are central banks who trade mainly for completing their own transactions or in an attempt to influence exchange rate movements through official intervention.[10, 11]

Another classifying distinction is between 'single-auction' and 'double-auction' systems. In the former system, prices are specified either to buy or to sell, not both; in the latter system, market-makers provide two-way prices on both bid and ask. Clearly, in the direct foreign exchange market, market-makers provide double-auction prices, whereas the brokered market is single-auction. The type of auction used in a market is also closely related to the degree of centralisation of the market itself. As noted by Flood (1991), for example, the absence of market-makers in a single-auction market and, therefore, the presence of larger search costs lead to greater centralisation of price information. However, decentralisation of price information leads to a tendency towards double-auction prices in order to facilitate the searching process for the counterpart (see also Goldberg and Tenorio, 1997, and the references therein).

---

[9] The advantages of brokered transactions are well known and include the rapid dissemination of orders to other market-makers, anonymity in quoting and the freedom not to quote to other market-makers on a reciprocal basis, which may be required in direct transactions.

[10] Clearly, while market-makers may trade on their own account, brokers do not do so, but profit by charging a fee for the service of bringing market-makers together.

[11] Another distinction often made in the microstructural finance literature, originally due to Garman (1976) and Schwartz (1988), is between a continuous (asynchronous) market and a call (synchronous) market; this distinction allows categorisation of markets by their degree of temporal consolidation. In a continuous market, such as the foreign exchange market, trade is allowed to occur at its own pace and transactions are processed as they arrive. In a call market, trade only occurs at predetermined times, and transactions orders are detained until the next call before being executed. A basic general drawback of microeconomic models is that they tend to assume *a priori* call markets, where a Walrasian auctioneer calls out a series of prices and stops only when demand equals supply in the market at the called price. The optimal degree of consolidation is not easy to identify theoretically as there is a trade-off between the allocational efficiency of the Walrasian call market and the informational efficiency and immediacy of the continuous market. The main argument against a continuous market and in favour of a call market is that the former may reduce allocational efficiency and the informativeness of prices. This is the case because, in a continuous market, transactions may fully satisfy some consumers and producers at some point and, hence, cause a shift in supply and demand schedules, ultimately affecting the equilibrium price. However, the synchronous market has the disadvantage of imposing waiting costs on agents between calls, leading to situations where, for example, investors may be willing to pay some sort of liquidity premium for trading immediately. Most importantly, in the time between successive calls, an additional source of uncertainty is introduced in the market, which may generate higher volatility.

With regard to the system of communication of prices, a distinction is generally made in the microstructural finance literature between 'open-bid' and 'limit-book' markets. In the former case, offers to buy or sell at a specified price are announced to all agents in the market, whereas, in the latter, offers will only be known to the entity placing the order and perhaps to a disinterested auctioneer. Clearly, the direct market is an open-bid market while the brokered market is a limit-book market. In principle, however, the optimal system of price communication is the one which minimises the cost of searching out a counterparty in the transactions. Given that the foreign exchange market is not fully centralised, it might be argued that the system is not cost-minimising.[12]

One issue which seems not to have been fully examined in this connection is the importance of credit and the role of clearing houses. In a decentralised market, where trade takes place in private meetings between parties, an assessment of credit risk (whether the counterparty will deliver the agreed amount of funds at the agreed time in the agreed location) is presumably made before a deal is struck. In fact, banks will usually have a prudential limit, determined by its senior management, on the credit exposure which it is willing to have with any other particular counterparty at any point in time and will not deal with that counterparty once this is reached until the net exposure is diminished. The existence of such prudential limits may clearly be problematic for a fully centralised system, where prices are public information and the counterparty is only known *after* the deal is struck. In practice, centralised financial exchanges often circumvent this problem by having a clearing-house system. For example, the London Clearing House (LCH) acts as the central counterparty for trades conducted on several of the London financial exchanges, including the London International Financial Futures and Options Exchange (LIFFE). This enables the LCH to 'guarantee' the financial performance of every contract registered with it by its members (the clearing members of the exchanges) up to and including delivery, exercise and/or settlement. Both sides of a trade are entered in an electronic registration system by the exchange members and/or the exchange itself, where they are matched and confirmed. At the end of each business day the trade is registered in the name of the LCH and the original contract between the two agents is cancelled and substituted with two new ones – one between the LCH and the clearing-member seller, the other between the LCH and the clearing-member buyer – known in legal terms as 'novation'. A clearing-house system thus serves two functions in a centralised market. First, it obviates the need to assess the credit rating of the counterparty – or indeed the need to identify the counterparty at all – before a trade is made. Second, since all trades are effectively made with the clearing house, only the *net* position at the end of the day is important for settlement purposes. In a decentralised system, trades may be made with very many counterparties so that, while the net position at the end of the trading day may be close to zero, the trader may have largely filled up a number of credit limits and will still have to carry out all of the trades agreed (with the consequent transactions costs). In the brokered foreign exchange market, although dealers trading on a

---

[12] The distinction between the terms 'open-bid' and 'limit-book' may, however, become obsolete in the future, and readers should be aware that usage of these terms may be shifting; see, for example, the joint usage in Glosten (1994). The distinction is made here as a classificatory device which is useful for our purposes and is at present fairly standard usage.

price quoted by a broker will not know the identity of the counterparty until after the trade has been made, it occasionally happens that trades have to be cancelled once the identities are revealed to both sides of the trade by the broker and one party finds that its credit limit with the counterparty is full. (In practice, where a limit order is placed with a broker by a small or exotic bank, the broker may try to circumvent this problem by quoting the inside spread ignoring this limit order and then adding that a better bid or offer is available for a certain amount from an 'exotic' – allowing dealers to ask the identity of the bank before the trade takes place.) Thus, the need to assess creditworthiness prior to effecting a trade in the absence of a foreign exchange market clearing house may explain why the majority of foreign exchange trading is between dealers (some 63 per cent in April 1998 according to the Bank for International Settlements (1998)). Moreover, in the absence of an international clearing-house system, market-makers in the foreign exchange market may in fact fulfil many of the functions of a clearing house and this may explain why the market allows them to earn significant profits on the bid–ask spread, as noted above. Hence, the issue of credit and creditworthiness may explain many of the observed institutional features of the foreign exchange market, including the predominant system of communication of prices (open-bid and inter-dealer) and the importance of established market-makers. This is clearly an issue that would repay further research.

Another important feature of the foreign exchange market is the development, since 1992, of proprietary screen-based electronic foreign exchange dealing and broking systems such as the Reuters 2000–2 Dealing System and the Electronic Broking System (EBS) Spot Dealing System, which also may be seen to perform many of the functions of a clearing house and which are an important driving force towards the 'virtual centralisation' of the global foreign exchange market. The Reuters 2000–2 and EBS are anonymous interactive broking and dealing systems delivered over proprietary networks and combining standard limit-book broking services with the opportunities for electronic trading. Deals are completed by keystroke or automatic deal-matching within the system. An important feature of these systems is their pre-screened credit facility, so that although the limit-book prices appearing on the dealer's screen appear anonymous, the system has automatically checked that the bank to which the price is being fed has a sufficient open credit limit with the originator of the price, thereby eliminating the potential for failed deals because of counterparty credit issues. Thus, traders know they can deal on the prices they can see. Credit limits are set and maintained by the designated bank staff and can be modified at any time during the trading day. Access to the credit file is password-driven and confidential. Further, an automated electronic interface between the system and a bank's internal banking system applications allows for net rather than gross transaction processing between counterparties and the elimination of duplicate trade entry activity; this is not quite the same as dealing with a clearing house, but does substantially reduce transactions costs. These electronic dealing and broking systems appear to be growing rapidly in use. Reuters currently offer their 2000–2 service in forty countries and EBS is currently subscribed to by 800 banks throughout the world, using some 2,500 workstations to transact average daily volumes in excess of $90 billion (although this is still very small in relation to the total amount of daily foreign exchange transactions).[13] It seems likely that the further development of these services may lead to the centralisation of the foreign exchange market through computer networking – or 'virtual centralisation'.

Overall, the direct foreign exchange market may be classified as decentralised, open-bid and double-auction, while the brokered foreign exchange market may be classified as quasi-centralised, limit-book and single-auction. The growing importance of electronic broking services suggests that the foreign exchange market may become increasingly centralised.

9.1.2 Foreign exchange market activity

Exchange-traded business is regularly collected and well documented by the Bank for International Settlements (BIS) from individual foreign exchange markets. The BIS provides a triennial *Central Bank Survey of Foreign Exchange and Derivatives Market Activity*, which represents the most reliable source of information of foreign exchange market activity, with a geographical coverage of forty-three countries (see BIS, 1998). Below we provide a brief overview of real-world foreign exchange market activity, largely based on the last survey of the BIS in 1998.

The average daily global turnover in traditional foreign exchange market segments (spot transactions, outright forwards and foreign exchange swaps)[14] was about $1.5 trillion in 1998. Forward instruments (outright forwards and foreign exchange swaps) are in a dominant position relative to spot transactions, with a market share of 60 per cent which seems to be still increasing, while the foreign exchange market is dominated by inter-dealer business (about 63 per cent) and cross-border transactions (about 54 per cent). The falling spot-market share is not caused by a reduction in turnover in absolute terms, but by the rapid increase of the turnover of derivatives markets.[15, 16]

With regard to currency composition, the US dollar, as one would expect, is by far the most actively traded currency, being involved in 87 per cent of all transactions worldwide

[13] These figures were taken from the EBS and Reuters websites, from which up-to-date information on these services may be obtained by interested readers at http://www.ebsp.com (for EBS) and http://www.reuters.com/transactions/d22s.htm (for Reuters 2000–2).

[14] Spot transactions are outright transactions involving the exchange of two currencies at a rate agreed on the date of the contract for 'value' or delivery (cash settlement) within two business days. Outright forwards are transactions involving the exchange of two currencies at a rate agreed on the date of the contract for value or delivery at some time in the future (more than two business days later). Foreign exchange swaps are transactions which involve the actual exchange of two currencies (principal amount only) on a specific date at a rate agreed at the time of conclusion of the contract (the short leg), and a reverse exchange of the same two currencies at a date further in the future at a rate (generally different from the rate applied to the short leg) agreed at the time of the contract (the long leg).

[15] Tight arbitrage relationships link the sub-markets of the foreign exchange market and the microstructure is not identical for each sub-market. The foreign exchange microstructure literature to date has focused largely, if not entirely, on the spot market. Extending both the theoretical and empirical foreign exchange microstructure literature to the analysis of derivatives markets is a very important immediate avenue of research.

[16] Our interpretation of volume shares from different instruments is essentially literal. However, one may argue, for example, that swaps do not involve net demand in one direction or the other. Rather, a currency swap can be replicated by buying a bond in one currency and selling a bond in another: the arbitrage does not involve a net foreign exchange transaction. So, currency swaps – with their large notional values – might lead us to underestimate the importance of the spot market in terms of net order flow (i.e. in terms of market-clearing net demand).

due to its predominance in commercial relations and its market liquidity as well as its extensive use as a vehicle currency for cross-trading between other currencies. The German mark is the second most used international currency, with almost a third of all currency trades, although the currency was increasingly used as a proxy for the euro in the period before its launch. The Japanese yen is the third most used international currency with about 21 per cent of all currency trades, while the UK pound is fourth with 11 per cent of trades.

With regard to geographical patterns, one noticeable feature of the foreign exchange market is the increasing concentration of its turnover in a few centres, namely the UK (32 per cent), the USA (18 per cent), Japan (8 per cent) and Singapore (7 per cent). While low or negative growth has characterised some smaller countries during the 1990s (e.g. Finland, Austria and Sweden), a number of other countries have experienced quite spectacular growth rates, especially in the second half of the 1990s (e.g. Greece, Ireland, Portugal, South Africa and the Netherlands).[17]

The run-up to the single European currency has been associated with various strategies, and the beginning of the disappearance of a number of European currencies and their replacement by the euro on 1 January 1999 considerably modified the configuration of markets and related trading strategies as well as the evolution of risk exposure and management over time. Overall, however, foreign exchange market activity is continuing to grow, largely due to the rapid growth of derivatives products, and understanding its future evolution as well as the effects of the emerging euro market poses new challenges to, as well as new opportunities for, both practitioners and academics.

9.2   Exchange rate expectations

9.2.1   Survey data studies
The process by which agents form expectations of future exchange rates is an issue which has attracted the attention of much of the early literature on foreign exchange market microstructure. The simplifying assumption which underlies virtually all the traditional asset-approach-based exchange rate models is that expectations are rational; hence, the expected exchange rate has usually been measured in empirical studies using either the forward discount or the interest rate differential, implicitly assuming uncovered interest rate parity (UIP) or UIP and covered interest rate parity (Taylor, 1995). The approach followed by a large microstructure literature has been to employ direct measures of expectations, that is data on exchange rate expectations from surveys of market participants conducted by financial services companies.[18]

While the various studies utilising these data sets differ in their specific approaches and results, it is possible to discern some general qualitative results from survey data on foreign

---

[17] Although one may think that the advent of the euro may have caused the decline in some European centres, the strong growth rates experienced by Ireland, Portugal and the Netherlands suggest that other factors are operating. In particular, Portugal's growth might be due to the positive effects of the liberalisation of the foreign exchange market which was completed in 1992. Greece experienced large capital inflows after the devaluation in March 1998 and the entry of the drachma into the Exchange Rate Mechanism. The Netherlands saw strong growth in its local market due to institutional investors expanding their international portfolios.

[18] See Takagi (1991) or Frankel and Rose (1995) for an overview of survey data studies.

exchange markets. For example, all survey data sets suggest strong heterogeneity of expectations and an increasing dispersion of expectations (measured by the standard deviation or interquantile range, for example) at longer forecast horizons. Another important feature of foreign exchange survey data sets is that they tend to display a 'twist' in expectations: longer-run expectations tend to reverse the direction of shorter-run expectations or, in other words, while a depreciation tends to be followed by expectations of further depreciations in the short run, it is followed by expectations of a moderate appreciation in the long run.[19]

Surveys have often been used for examining, in spot–forward regressions, the behaviour of foreign exchange market risk premia and for assessing the validity of the rational expectations hypothesis in this context (see Taylor, 1995). The main conclusions of these studies are that survey data generally indicate the presence of a non-zero risk premium, which appears to be stable and uncorrelated with the forward discount, and that tests of the rational expectations hypothesis generally reject both the unbiasedness condition (the condition that the expected spot exchange rate is an unbiased predictor of the future spot exchange rate) and the orthogonality condition (the condition that prediction errors are uncorrelated with any variable in the set of available current information at the time the prediction is made) (see Takagi, 1991; Taylor, 1995).

A rather strong consensus also exists in this literature strongly rejecting the hypothesis that agents' expectations are static (expected change in the exchange rate is zero) and also rejecting the hypothesis that exchange rate expectations exhibit bandwagon effects (expected change in the exchange rate is greater than the most recent change) (see e.g. Dominguez, 1987; Frankel and Froot, 1987a,b, 1990a,b; Allen and Taylor, 1990; Ito, 1990; Taylor and Allen, 1992).

Overall, the empirical microstructure literature focusing on expectations formation mechanisms, while providing clear evidence in favour of the existence of risk premia and against the pure rational expectations hypothesis, also suggests that the true, unknown expectations formation process used by agents operating in the foreign exchange market is likely to be more complex than typically assumed by the conventional literature in exchange rate economics and that heterogeneity of expectations may be crucial (e.g. Taylor and Allen, 1992). In turn, these findings raise important issues for further empirical and theoretical research in both exchange rate economics and microstructural finance. While further empirical work on survey data is needed for establishing the robustness of these findings, theoretical work on expectations formation and the causes and implications of the heterogeneity of expectations seems an immediate avenue for future research.

---

[19] The discrepancy between the short- and the long-run exchange rate expectations formation mechanisms adopted by agents in the foreign exchange market suggests a tendency for *short-run* expectations to respond to lagged exchange rate changes in the same direction (moving *away from* the long-run equilibrium exchange rate), while *long-run* expectations appear to respond to lagged exchange rate changes in the opposite direction (moving *towards* the long-run equilibrium exchange rate). This behavioural discrepancy has been rationalised by Froot and Ito (1989) using the concept of *consistency*, which may be considered a weaker condition than full rationality. Nevertheless, the results of Froot and Ito (1989) indicate that expectations generally do not satisfy the consistency condition: 'In every one of twenty sets of time-series estimates encompassing four surveys, five forecast horizons and five currencies, shorter-term expectations overreact relative to longer-term expectations when the exchange rate changes' (Froot and Ito, 1989, p. 506). See also Pesaran (1989) for an alternative derivation of the consistency condition suggested by Froot and Ito (1989).

9.2.2   Order flow studies

An interesting related literature has shown that time-aggregated order flow variables may have more explanatory power than macro variables in explaining exchange rate behaviour. 'Order flow' in this context is taken to be a variant of the more familiar concept of 'net demand', and measures the net of buyer-initiated orders and seller-initiated orders. As noted by Lyons (1999), it is a variant of, rather than a synonym for, 'net demand' because, in equilibrium, order flow does not necessarily equal zero.

The finding that order flow has more explanatory power than macro variables in explaining exchange rate behaviour, especially in the short run, is interesting and has a clear interpretation in terms of expectations formation mechanisms. The fact that order flow contributes to explaining exchange rate determination does not necessarily imply that order flow is the underlying driver of exchange rates, however. Indeed, it may well be that macroeconomic fundamentals are the underlying driving force, but that conventional measures of the macroeconomic fundamentals are so imprecise that an order-flow 'proxy' performs better in estimation. This interpretation as a proxy is particularly plausible with respect to expectations; that is, even if macro variables fully describe the true model, when implemented empirically these variables may provide a poor measure of *expected* future fundamentals. Thus, it may be that order flow simply provides a more precise proxy for variation in these expectations. In this sense, unlike expectations measured from survey data, order flow represents a willingness to back one's beliefs with real money (see the discussion by Lyons, 1999).

A notable recent paper in this literature is due to Evans and Lyons (1999), who provide a model which sheds light on the role of order flow in determining exchange rates. In their model, order flow is a proximate determinant of price. Using data on signed order flow from the Reuters dealing system, they provide evidence that order flow is a significant determinant of some major bilateral exchange rates, obtaining coefficients of determination significantly larger than the ones usually obtained using standard macroeconomic models of nominal exchange rates. Evans and Lyons also show that their model of daily exchange rate changes produces good out-of-sample forecasts at short horizons, beating the alternative of a random walk model in standard measures of forecast accuracy.

9.3   Chartist analysis

An alternative explanation of the discrepancy between short- and long-run exchange rate expectations is that foreign exchange market participants may use different forecasting techniques for different expectations horizons. So, the predominant technique for shorter-run exchange rate forecasting may be chartist analysis, for example, whereas the technique used for longer-run forecasting may be based on fundamental analysis or conventional exchange rate determination models.

Chartist (or 'technical') analysis involves using charts of financial asset price movements, often with the aid of additional descriptive statistics, to try to infer the likely course of future prices and hence derive forecasts and trading strategies. The trends and patterns that chartists look at are generally arrived at by loose inductive reasoning. Perhaps the most famous example of a chartist technique (indicating a trend reversal) is the 'head and shoulders' (see Allen and Taylor, 1990; Taylor and Allen, 1992). Often, chartists use trends and patterns to identify broad ranges within which exchange rates or asset prices are expected to trade, attempting to 'set the parameters' for price movements. Chartist analysts may also employ one or more mechanical indicators when forming a general view, which may be trend-following (e.g. based on moving averages) or non-trend-following (e.g. rate-of-change indicators or 'oscillators' used under the assumption that there is a tendency for markets to 'correct' when an asset has been 'overbought' or 'oversold'). In practice, chartist analysis tends to be a combination of pattern and trend recognition, along with information from basic statistical indicators.

9.3.1   Chartist analysis in the foreign exchange market

While casual observation suggests that the use of chartist analysis in major financial markets is widespread, evidence on its use has largely been anecdotal (e.g. Malkiel, 1996). However, a questionnaire survey conducted by the Group of Thirty (1985) reported that 97 per cent of banks and 87 per cent of securities houses believed that the use of technical analysis has a significant impact on the foreign exchange market.

Recent applied work on the use of technical analysis includes that of Allen and Taylor (Allen and Taylor, 1990; Taylor and Allen, 1992), who carried out a study of the London foreign exchange market on behalf of the Bank of England. They conducted a questionnaire survey, sent to over 400 chief foreign exchange dealers in the London market in November 1988, which achieved a response rate of over 60 per cent (see Taylor and Allen, 1992). The survey asked dealers questions concerning the particular chartist methods used in practice and the role of chartists within organisations. It also attempted to elicit views (both quantitative and qualitative) on how market participants view the role of chartism. A broad consensus emerged on the weights given to chartist analysis at differing time horizons. At short time horizons (intraday to one week), approximately 90 per cent of respondents reported using some chartist input when forming their exchange rate expectations, with 60 per cent judging charts to be at least as important as fundamentals. At longer forecast horizons, from one month to one year, the weight given to economic fundamentals increased. At the longest forecast horizons, of one year or longer, the skew towards fundamentals was most pronounced with around a third of respondents relying on pure fundamentals and some 85 per cent judging fundamentals to be more important than charts. It appeared, however, that there was a persistent 2 per cent or so of respondents who apparently never used fundamental economic analysis at any horizon. Other findings of the Taylor–Allen study were that dealers perceived chartist analysis and fundamental (economic) analysis to be complementary approaches, and that a significant proportion viewed technical analysis as self-fulfilling.

In addition, Allen and Taylor (1990) analyse the accuracy of a number of individual technical analysts' one-week and four-week-ahead forecasts of three major exchange rates. They find that some individuals were able to outperform a range of alternative forecasting procedures over a ten-month period, including a random walk model, vector autoregressions and univariate autoregressive moving average time series models. Interestingly, however,

Allen and Taylor (1990) also report a significant degree of heterogeneity among chartists' forecasts: not all chartists see the same signals (or interpret them in the same fashion) at the same point in time; given the multiplicity of possible patterns and interpretations of statistical measures, this is perhaps not altogether surprising.

More recently, Curcio and Goodhart (1992, 1993) report the results of a controlled experiment in which university students participated in simulated financial asset-trading either with or without the use of chartist computer software. Although Curcio and Goodhart find no significant difference in the level of notional profitability between subjects using the chartist software and those not using it, the *variance* of the level of notional profits was significantly lower among the group using the chartist software.

A more recent piece of evidence is due to Menkhoff (1998), who examines some of the basic assumptions of the noise trading approach by means of a questionnaire mailed to foreign exchange market participants in Germany. Menkhoff identifies two groups, characterised by their use of different types of information: rational arbitrageurs (who rely primarily on fundamental analysis) and not-fully-rational noise traders (who prefer other forms of analysis to fundamental analysis). The empirical results also suggest the existence of short horizons and sentiments assumed by the noise trading approach, although these cannot be exclusively related to the respective groups. This suggests that rational agents may use non-fundamental analysis to exploit less-rational noise traders.[20]

In a related study, Lui and Mole (1998) report the results of a questionnaire survey conducted in February 1995 on the use by foreign exchange dealers in Hong Kong of fundamental and technical analysis to form their forecasts of exchange rate movements. Lui and Mole find that about 85 per cent of respondents rely on both fundamental analysis and technical analysis for predicting future rate movements at different time horizons. However, they also find that at shorter horizons there exists a skew towards reliance on technical analysis as opposed to fundamental analysis, although the skew becomes steadily reversed as the length of horizon considered is extended. Technical analysis is considered *slightly* more useful in forecasting trends than fundamental analysis, but *significantly* more useful in predicting turning points. News related to interest rates appears to be a relatively important fundamental factor in exchange rate forecasting, while moving average and other trend-following systems are the most useful technical methods.

Recent interesting work is due to Cheung and Wong (1999, 2000), who report findings from a survey of practitioners in the inter-bank foreign exchange markets in Hong Kong, Tokyo and Singapore. The majority of respondents agree that non-fundamental factors have significant effects on short-run exchange rates and that speculation increases volatility while improving liquidity and efficiency. In a further study, due to Cheung and Chinn (1999), findings are presented from a survey of practitioners in the US inter-bank foreign exchange markets. Their findings also suggest that technical trading best characterises 30 per cent of traders, although this proportion has been increasing over the last five years. Incorporation of news about fundamentals into exchange rate expectations occurs very rapidly and news about interest rates appears to be relatively more important. As one would

---

[20] See also Menkhoff (1997).

expect, macroeconomic fundamentals appear to be particularly important for long-run exchange rate expectations.[21] Using UK survey data, similar results are recorded by Cheung, Chinn and Marsh (1999), who confirm that non-fundamental factors are thought to dominate short-horizon movements in exchange rates. Fundamentals, however, are deemed important over much shorter horizons that the mainstream empirical literature would suggest.

At the very least, therefore, the empirical evidence suggests that the attitude of many financial economists towards chartist analysis – that 'technical strategies are usually amusing, often comforting, but of no real value' (Malkiel, 1996, p. 154) – should not be held with one hundred per cent confidence, at least in the foreign exchange market.

9.3.2   The impact of chartist analysis

Analysis of non-fundamental influences in financial markets is a growing area of academic literature, and the ground has been shifting away from widespread academic scepticism of non-fundamentals to active investigation of the many phenomena not captured by traditional economic models. While studies of the stock market have recently begun to analyse the influence of non-fundamental factors in a general fashion (e.g. Shiller, 1984; De Long, Shleifer, Summers and Waldmann, 1989), investigations which specifically consider the role of chartism have so far largely been confined to the foreign exchange market.

Goodhart (1988) presents a discussion of how exchange rate misalignment might occur by considering the possibility that the rate is determined by the balance of chartist and fundamentalist predictions. This is in some ways similar to the simple model of the stock market suggested by Shiller (1984), in which the equilibrium price depends on the balance between fundamentalists ('smart money') and ordinary investors who subscribe to popular models. A similar approach is developed more formally by Frankel and Froot (1990b), who explain the sharp rise in the demand for the US dollar over the 1981–5 period as a shift in the weight of market opinion away from fundamentalists and towards chartists. This shift is modelled as a Bayesian response to the inferior forecasting performance of the economic fundamentalists.

Bilson (1990) emphasises that technical traders employing 'overbought' or 'oversold' indicators ('oscillators') will tend to impart nonlinearity into exchange rate movements since small exchange rate changes which do not trigger the oscillator will tend to be positively correlated because of the effect of trend-following trading programs; on the other hand, larger exchange rate movements, which trigger an oscillator, indicating that a currency has been 'oversold' or 'overbought', will be negatively correlated. Bilson (1990) estimates simple nonlinear exchange rate equations which are consistent with this pattern of serial correlation and records some moderate success in capturing exchange rate changes.[22]

---

[21] Cheung and Chinn (1999) also report evidence that speculation and official intervention, while perceived to increase market volatility, are likely to restore equilibrium by moving exchange rates towards their long-run values. Finally, traders do not value purchasing power parity highly as a long-run equilibrium concept, although they appear to believe that it might be useful for horizons of at least six months.

[22] Hsieh (1988) also detects evidence of nonlinearities in exchange rate movements. See also De Grauwe, Dewachter and Embrechts (1993).

Researchers have also begun to analyse related microstructure issues such as the volume of trade in foreign exchange markets, and address the question why, for example, trade volume is very much higher on a gross basis (among foreign exchange dealers and brokers) than on a net basis (involving non-financial companies).[23] Frankel and Froot (1990b), for example, provide strong evidence that the volume of trade and market volatility is related to the heterogeneity of exchange rate expectations, as reflected in the dispersion in survey expectations (see also Ito, 1990; Hogan and Melvin, 1994).

Other studies in the relevant market microstructure literature have looked at the way information is processed and transmitted through the market, and the relationship of information processing to market volatility and volume. Lyons (1995), for example, reports evidence that volume affects the bid–ask spread through the information signalled by market volume as well as the desire of market-makers to control their inventory of currencies. Bessembinder (1994) reports evidence that bid–ask spreads widen as proxies for inventory-carrying costs increase. Bollerslev and Melvin (1994) provide empirical support for a model in which the bid–ask spread is determined by underlying uncertainty concerning exchange rate movements. In related work on market volatility, several articles have documented regularities in market volatility (e.g. Hsieh, 1988), and the contagion of exchange rate volatility across foreign exchange markets (the so-called 'meteor shower'), which may be interpreted as evidence of information processing (Engle, Ito and Lin, 1990; Hogan and Melvin, 1994).

9.3.3   Modelling expectations of chartists, fundamentalists and portfolio managers

A formal model of expectations of agents in the foreign exchange market, classified as chartists, fundamentalists or portfolio managers, is provided in a highly influential article by Frankel and Froot (1987b), which represents the cornerstone of the subsequent literature on modelling expectations of investors in the foreign exchange market as well as in other financial markets. Their model, designed to explain the demand for the US dollar during the 1980s, is a combination of two different models: 'It is as if there are actually two models of the dollar operating, one at each end of the spectrum, and a blend in between' (Frankel and Froot, 1987b). The two models considered by the authors are a fundamentalist model, for which they assume a Dornbusch overshooting model (long-run), and a chartist model, for which Frankel and Froot use a simple autoregressive integrated moving average (ARIMA) forecasting equation (short-run).

The value of a currency can then be driven by the decisions of portfolio managers who consider a weighted average of the expectations of fundamentalists and chartists of the following form:

$$\Delta s_{t+1}^{m} = \omega_t \Delta s_{t+1}^{f} + (1 - \omega_t)\Delta s_{t+1}^{c}, \tag{9.1}$$

where Δs_{t+1}^{m}, Δs_{t+1}^{f} and Δs_{t+1}^{c} denote the rate of change in the spot rate expected by portfolio managers (the market), fundamentalists and chartists respectively, while ω_t is the

---

[23] Frankel and Froot (1990b), for example, suggest that over 95 per cent of market transactions in major exchange rates occur between foreign exchange market dealers or brokers, while Lyons (1995) suggests that over 80 per cent occurs between market-makers alone.

weight given to the fundamentalist view by portfolio managers. Assuming for simplicity that $\Delta s_{t+1}^c = 0$, equation (9.1) becomes:

$$\Delta s_{t+1}^m = \omega_t \Delta s_{t+1}^f, \tag{9.2}$$

and hence:

$$\omega_t = \Delta s_{t+1}^m / \Delta s_{t+1}^f. \tag{9.3}$$

Consider a general model of exchange rate determination of the form:

$$s_t = c\Delta s_{t+1}^m + z_t, \tag{9.4}$$

where z_t denotes the fundamentals. Clearly, equation (9.4) is a very general exchange rate model which can be interpreted in terms of any of the asset-pricing exchange rate determination models. The Frankel–Froot model incorporates an expectations formation mechanism of the form (9.1) within a general asset-pricing model of the type (9.4).

Frankel and Froot (1987b) analyse the simple case when chartists believe that the exchange rate follows a random walk, $\Delta s_{t+1}^c = 0$, assuming a process governing the evolution of the weight ω_t and using simulation methods rather than computing the closed-form solution of the model. Frankel and Froot also fully specify a mechanism to endogenise the fundamentals in order to incorporate in the model the effects of current account imbalances, allowing the currency to revert to equilibrium and circumventing the drawbacks of an exogenous specification of the economic fundamentals – in particular, the implication that the spot rate may be stuck at a disequilibrium level.[24]

The simulation results suggest that a bubble in the exchange rate is generated as an effect of the attempt by portfolio managers to learn the model. When the bubble takes off, as well as when it collapses, portfolio managers learn more slowly about the model than when they are changing it by revising the weights associated with the fundamentalist and chartist views. When the weight given to the fundamentalist view tends to either of its extreme values (zero and unity), however, then the portfolio managers' exchange rate determination model tends to the correct model. Also, the revisions of the weight become smaller until the approximation of the portfolio managers' model to the correct one is perfect, implying that portfolio managers change the model more slowly than they learn it.

Following Frankel and Froot's seminal article, a number of researchers have constructed models in the context of the foreign exchange market as well as of other financial markets in attempts to illustrate the role of non-fundamentalist traders in generating bubble-type phenomena. All these models have in common that they consider at least two types of traders who differ in their forecasts or beliefs and that the outcome they predict is characterised by complicated nonstationary dynamics, which is typical of many financial markets. Among these, it is worth citing De Long, Shleifer, Summers and Waldmann (1989, 1990a,b), Kirman (1991) and Goldberg and Frydman (1993). These models do present some characteristics which are typical of financial markets. In general, they predict that periods of steady

---

[24] Note also that the model assumes less than fully rational behaviour as none of the three classes of agents condition their forecasts on the full information set of the model.

evolution are interrupted by bubbles and crashes, with noise around the turning point when the switch from one regime to another occurs. Opinions in the market are usually modified endogenously as a result of the interaction between agents. Mistakes are made by agents at turning points when the opinion of the majority is not clear, but these episodes are not long enough for learning or for profitable arbitrage opportunities to be generated (see e.g. Kirman, 1991). De Grauwe and Dewachter (1993) use a model which combines chartists and fundamentalists to show how chaotic behaviour of the exchange rate may be generated; the exchange rate generated by such a process would be essentially unpredictable, regardless of whether the underlying model is deterministic or stochastic (see also Goodhart, 1988). If these models accurately describe the foreign exchange market, then the discrepancy between short- and long-run expectations of the exchange rate may no longer be considered a puzzle for the profession.

9.3.4   Summarising chartist analysis

While it seems certain that economic fundamentals will eventually win through in the longer term, it is likely that short-term price movements may be dominated by 'popular' models and theories, one of which is chartist analysis. Clearly, simple reliance on extrapolation and inductive reasoning, as in chartist analysis, is ultimately unsatisfactory. It may be that chartists (and foreign exchange dealers in general), by working with the minutiae of market price movements, are able to 'get a feel' for local approximations to processes which are too complex, short-term or nonlinear to be captured adequately by the current state of financial economics. In any event, the fact that chartist techniques are subscribed to by large numbers of financial market practitioners implies that chartism should not be lightly dismissed either by other practitioners or by researchers.

In conclusion, therefore, chartist analysis, although clearly unsatisfactory in its subjectivity and its reliance on extrapolation and inductive reasoning, is still widely used by market practitioners. At the same time, standard exchange rate economics has performed rather poorly both as a predictor and as an explainer of exchange rate movements (Frankel and Rose, 1995; Taylor, 1995; Evans and Lyons, 1999). Further research on chartist analysis is clearly warranted.

9.4   Time-varying volatility, market location and trading volume

9.4.1   Time-varying volatility in the foreign exchange market

Before going on to discuss work which has examined time-varying volatility in the context of market microstructure, we first consider this issue in more general terms.

It is a stylised fact that the foreign exchange market is characterised by time-varying volatility (notably see Engle, Ito and Lin, 1990). The modelling of time-varying volatility in the foreign exchange market is the focus of an enormous literature on the microstructure of foreign exchange markets which is largely dominated by models of autoregressive conditional heteroscedasticity (ARCH) and generalised ARCH (GARCH). The basic insight behind ARCH models, first introduced by Engle (1982), is that the second moment of the distribution of exchange rates is serially correlated. ARCH models are nonlinear conditionally Gaussian models where the conditional variance is a function of the lagged error terms.[25] Engle's (1982) ARCH model may be written as follows:

$$y_t \mid \Omega_{t-1} \sim N(x_t \beta, h_t) \tag{9.5}$$

$$h_t = f(\epsilon_{t-1}, \epsilon_{t-2}, \ldots, \epsilon_{t-q}, \ldots, \alpha) \tag{9.6}$$

$$\epsilon_t = y_t - x_t \beta, \tag{9.7}$$

implying that the conditional distribution of y_t, given the information set Ω_{t-1}, is normal with mean and variance equal to $x_t \beta$ (a linear function of, say, k independent variables x_t) and h_t (a function of, say, q lagged error terms and other exogenous variables) respectively. Equation (9.6) may be parameterised as:

$$h_t = \alpha_0 + \sum_{j=1}^{q} \alpha_j \epsilon_{t-j}^2 \qquad \alpha_j \geq 0 \quad \forall j \tag{9.8}$$

for an ARCH(q) model. These models can be estimated by maximum likelihood methods and a simple Lagrange multiplier (LM) test for the presence of ARCH effects may be constructed from an auxiliary regression of the form:

$$\widehat{\epsilon}_t^2 = \alpha_0 + \alpha_1 \widehat{\epsilon}_{t-1}^2 + \cdots + \alpha_q \widehat{\epsilon}_{t-q}^2, \tag{9.9}$$

where $\widehat{\epsilon}_t$ denotes the residual from ordinary least squares estimation of (9.7). Under the null hypothesis that $\alpha_j = 0 \ \forall j$, the LM statistic TR^2 (T being the number of observations and R^2 being the coefficient of determination from (9.9)) is asymptotically distributed as $\chi^2(q)$.

A simple but important extension of the ARCH model is the GARCH model due to Bollerslev (1986). A GARCH(p,q) model may be written as:

$$h_t = \alpha_0 + \sum_{j=1}^{q} \alpha_j \epsilon_{t-j}^2 + \sum_{j=1}^{p} \beta_j h_{t-j}. \tag{9.10}$$

Since ϵ_t^2 has the same properties as an ARMA process, the appropriate orders of a GARCH process may be determined following the criteria typical of the Box–Jenkins approach (Box and Jenkins, 1970) on the autocorrelations and partial autocorrelations of the squares of a set of residuals.[26]

A common finding of the literature using high-frequency financial data is, in general, the strong persistence implied by the estimates of the conditional variance functions of excess returns. This is consistent with the presence of a near-unit-root in the autoregressive polynomial in (9.10), i.e. $\alpha_1 + \cdots + \alpha_q + \beta_1 + \cdots + \beta_p = 1$. This situation is depicted by

---

[25] In a linear model, each observation may be expressed as a linear function of current and lagged error terms and, under the assumption that the error terms are normally distributed, the full set of observations will also have a multivariate normal distribution. In a nonlinear model, however, assuming normality of the conditional distribution of each observation does not necessarily imply that the unconditional distribution of the observations is normal. Nevertheless, the assumption of normality is still widely used and nonlinear models of this kind are identified as conditionally Gaussian.

[26] For comprehensive expositions of ARCH and GARCH models as well as their properties and their extensions – such as ARCH in mean (ARCH-M) and GARCH in mean (GARCH-M), where the basic ARCH and GARCH frameworks are extended in such a way that the mean is also allowed to depend on its own conditional variance – see Engle, Lilien and Robins (1987), and Bollerslev, Chou and Kroner (1992).

Engle and Bollerslev (1986) as an integrated GARCH (IGARCH) model. The strong implication of this class of models is that current information remains important in forecasting the conditional variance for the indefinite future.

Time-varying volatility models of the types described above have been applied to exchange rates by, among others, Domowitz and Hakkio (1985), Engle and Bollerslev (1986), Milhoj (1987), Hsieh (1988), McCurdy and Morgan (1988), and Baillie and Bollerslev (1989) (for a survey see Bollerslev, Chou and Kroner, 1992, pp. 37–46). For example, Hsieh (1988) uses daily data for five exchange rates *vis-à-vis* the US dollar from 1973 to 1983. The main purpose of this paper is to investigate empirically the statistical properties of the data and, in particular, to discriminate between two competing explanations for the observed heavy tails of the distribution of exchange rates: namely, that the data are independently drawn from a heavy tail distribution which remains fixed over time or that the data come from distributions which vary over time. Hsieh's results suggest the rejection of the former hypothesis. An interesting finding is that the rejection can be attributed to changing means and variances in the data and an ARCH(9) model is able to capture most of the nonlinear stochastic dependencies present in the data. Similar results are provided by Milhoj (1987), Diebold (1988) and Diebold and Nerlove (1989). These findings have subsequently been reinforced by studies using GARCH formulations, including those by McCurdy and Morgan (1988), Hsieh (1989a,b), Kugler and Lenz (1990).

Diebold and Nason (1990) argue, however, that it is not clear whether the conditional heteroscedasticity detected in the prediction error of linear exchange rate models is a property of the true data-generating process or whether it is due to some sort of general misspecification associated with linear conditional-mean representations. Diebold and Nason address this issue by estimating nonparametrically the conditional-mean functions of ten nominal dollar spot rates for the sample period 1973–87, used to generate in-sample and out-of-sample nonparametric forecasts. Interestingly, their findings are not supportive of the idea that nonlinearities exist in exchange rates which can be exploited for prediction purposes. The results of Diebold and Nason are also consistent with other similar studies, such as, notably, Meese and Rose (1991).

Another interesting finding, suggested by both Diebold (1988) and Baillie and Bollerslev (1989), is that ARCH effects are strongly statistically significant on daily and weekly exchange rate data, but they tend to weaken and eventually disappear with less frequently sampled data, that is to say ARCH effects 'aggregate out' over time. Also, the assumption of normality appears to be a good approximation for four-week or perhaps two-week frequency data, but not for higher frequencies. Baillie and Bollerslev (1989) also estimate a GARCH(1,1) model and report a value of $\alpha_1 + \beta_1$ very close to unity, suggesting an IGARCH process (see also Diebold, 1988).[27]

---

[27] An interesting theoretical contribution in this context is due to Hodrick (1989), who motivates his study on the basis of the failure of log-linear exchange rate models of the 1970s and the observed variability of the risk premium in the foreign exchange market. Rational, maximising models predict that changes in conditional variances of monetary policy, government spending and income growth affect risk premia, generating conditional volatility of exchange rates. Hodrick examines theoretically how changes in these exogenous conditional variances affect the level of the current exchange rate and quantifies the extent to which this channel explains exchange rate volatility using ARCH models.

Andersen and Bollerslev (1998) have recently raised the level of analysis considerably beyond the standard GARCH approach in this literature. Their paper provides a detailed characterisation of the volatility in the German mark–US dollar foreign exchange market using an annual sample of five-minute returns. Their empirical model captures the intraday activity patterns, the macroeconomic announcements and the volatility persistence (ARCH) known from daily returns. Andersen and Bollerslev quantify the different features and show that they account for a substantial fraction of return variability, both at the intraday and daily level.[28]

ARCH models of the exchange rate also have important implications for foreign exchange market efficiency. The relevant empirical literature systematically finds that the forward rate is not an unbiased predictor of the corresponding future spot rate. Under the rational expectations hypothesis, however, the existence of a risk premium can still reconcile this stylised fact with efficiency in the foreign exchange market (see Hakkio, 1981; Hodrick and Srivastava, 1984; Domowitz and Hakkio, 1985; Baillie, 1989). Several different specifications of the risk premium, in making the risk premium a function of the time-varying conditional variance of the spot exchange rate, have been attempted in the empirical literature. In particular, a number of authors have used ARCH-type models for the risk premium, largely reporting unsatisfactory results. Several researchers argue, however, that the weak results obtained using univariate ARCH-type models to estimate time-varying risk premia may simply be due to the fact that the conditional variances may be poor proxies for risk. Hence, in principle, a risk premium may be modelled more satisfactorily by making it a function of time-varying cross-currency conditional covariances rather than just its own conditional variance. Following this argument, several researchers have estimated multivariate ARCH models as a test of the foreign exchange market efficiency hypothesis (see Lee, 1988; Baillie and Bollerslev, 1990). Tests of the conditional capital asset pricing model (CAPM) which allow for a time-varying conditional covariance matrix have been made, for example, by Mark (1988) and Giovannini and Jorion (1989), and these indicate a much better performance of the model than the traditional CAPM (see also Kaminsky and Peruga, 1990).

Multivariate ARCH models have also been used for investigating various policy issues associated with the foreign exchange market. Examples are Diebold and Pauly (1988) and Bollerslev (1990), who analyse the effect on the short-run volatility of the exchange rate of the introduction of the European Monetary System. These studies conclude that an increase in the conditional variances and covariances among the member countries of the EMS occurred after 1979 and interpret this finding as being a result of increased policy co-ordination.

We now examine the implications of time-varying volatility in the foreign exchange market for work on market microstructure.

9.4.2   *Volatility and market location*
A number of researchers, notably Engle, Ito and Lin (1990), argue that in an efficient foreign exchange market, the ARCH effects characterising high-frequency data may well be

---

[28] See also DeGennaro and Shrieves (1995) and Melvin and Yin (1999).

present, and are caused by the amount of information or the quality of information reaching the market in clusters or else by the time necessary for market agents to fully process the new information. This argument seems consistent with Fama's original observation on volatility clusters: 'large daily price changes tend to be followed by large daily changes. The signs of the successive changes are apparently random, however, which indicates that the phenomenon represents a denial of the random walk model but not of the market efficiency hypothesis. Nevertheless, it is interesting to speculate why the phenomenon might arise' (Fama, 1970, p. 396). Baillie and Bollerslev (1991), for example, use four-hourly exchange rate series for a six-month period in 1986 and develop a seasonal GARCH model to describe the time-dependent volatility of each exchange rate series. Their empirical results suggest that hourly patterns of volatility are remarkably similar across countries and appear to be strongly associated to the opening and closing of the major world markets. Also, the US foreign exchange market is found to display more volatility than the European market.

Pathbreaking work in this literature is due to Engle, Ito and Lin (1990) and Ito, Engle and Lin (1992),[29] who make use of meteorological analogies for stating their intuition:

Using meteorological analogies, we suppose that news follows a process like a heat wave so that a hot day in New York is likely to be followed by another hot day in New York but not typically by a hot day in Tokyo. The alternative analogy is a meteor shower which rains down on the earth as it turns. A meteor shower in New York will almost surely be followed by one in Tokyo. To anticipate our conclusion, volatility appears to be a meteor shower rather than a heat wave.

Engle, Ito and Lin (1990) use intraday data on the Japanese yen–US dollar exchange rate from 3 October 1985 to 26 September 1986, and define four separate market locations: Europe, New York, Pacific and Tokyo. They consider non-overlapping markets within a day with market 1 being open first; volatility generated in a previously open market segment can be considered exogenous and part of the information set for market segment 2 the subsequent day. Engle, Ito and Lin's model is a GARCH-based vector autoregression (VAR) model for per-hour volatility, of the form:

$$\epsilon_{i,t}|\psi_{i,t} \sim N(0, h_{i,t}) \qquad i = 1, 2, \ldots, n$$

$$h_{i,t} = \omega_i + \beta_i h_{i,t-1} + \sum_{j=1}^{i-1} \alpha_{ij}\epsilon_{j,t}^2 + \sum_{j=1}^{n} \alpha_{ij}\epsilon_{j,t-1}^2, \qquad (9.11)$$

where $\epsilon_{j,t}$ is defined as the intraday exchange rate change divided by the square root of business hours in market j on date t; $\psi_{i,t}$ is the information set for the market segment i at time t – which includes past information up until $(t-1)$ and current information from market 1 to market $(i-1)$, i.e. $\psi_{i,t} = \{\epsilon_{i-1,t}, \epsilon_{i-2,t}, \ldots, \epsilon_{1,t}\}$ and is a sub-set of $\psi_{n,t-1}$ with

[29] Similar arguments were present, however, in the theoretical models of foreign exchange market dynamics built by Kyle (1985) and Admati and Pfeiderer (1988). These models have the peculiar feature that prices do not fully incorporate all the information available about the fundamental value until the end of trading, thereby providing an explanation of volatility spillovers. Hence, these models are consistent with semi-strong form efficiency of the foreign exchange market, not with strong form.

$n > i - 1$.[30, 31] The heat wave hypothesis tested by Engle, Ito and Lin against the alternative meteor shower hypothesis amounts to a test of H_0: $\alpha_{ij} = 0$, for $i \neq j$, jointly against the alternative H_1: $\alpha_{ij} \neq 0$ for $i \neq j$.

Another innovation of Engle, Ito and Lin's (1990) study is that they develop a technique for analysing the dynamic interaction generated by country-specific news. The intuition is to assume that the expected future per-hour variance in a market segment is a function of a shock to a different market segment. Hence, using vector notation, equation (9.11) may be rewritten as:

$$h_{t+1} = \kappa + Bh_t + A\epsilon_{t+1} + C\epsilon_t, \tag{9.12}$$

where κ is a vector of constants, $h_t = (h_{1,t}, \ldots, h_{n,t})'$, $\epsilon_t = (\epsilon_{1,t}^2, \ldots, \epsilon_{n,t}^2)'$ and:

$$A = \begin{pmatrix} 0 & 0 & 0 & \ldots & 0 \\ \alpha_{21} & 0 & 0 & \ldots & 0 \\ \vdots & & & & \vdots \\ \alpha_{n1} & \alpha_{n2} & \ldots & \ldots & 0 \end{pmatrix}, \quad B = \begin{pmatrix} \beta_{11} & 0 & 0 & \ldots & 0 \\ 0 & \beta_{22} & 0 & \ldots & 0 \\ \vdots & & & & \vdots \\ 0 & 0 & & \ldots & \beta_{nn} \end{pmatrix},$$

$$C = \begin{pmatrix} \alpha_{11} & \alpha_{12} & \ldots & \alpha_{1n} \\ 0 & \alpha_{22} & \ldots & \alpha_{2n} \\ \vdots & & & \vdots \\ 0 & \ldots & \ldots & \alpha_{nn} \end{pmatrix}. \tag{9.13}$$

Defining $h_{t+s/nt} \equiv E(h_{t+s} \mid \psi_{n,t})$ and taking the iterated expectation of h_{t+s}, Engle, Ito and Lin prove that the vector of conditional heteroscedasticity of all the markets follows a process of the form:

$$(I - A)\, h_{t+s/kt} = \kappa + (B + C)\, h_{t+s-1/kt}. \tag{9.14}$$

Thus, if $R_{ik}(s) \equiv \partial h_{i,t+s/kt}/\partial \epsilon_{k,t}^2$ (for $i, k = 1, \ldots, n$) is the impulse response function of per-hour volatility of market i to the squared innovation of market k, taking the derivative of (9.14) allows us to obtain $R_{ik}(s)$ by solving recursively the equation:

$$(I - A)\, R_k(s) = (B + C)\, R_k(s - 1) \qquad s \geq 2, \tag{9.15}$$

where $R_k(s) = [R_{ik}(s)]_{n \times 1}$. Using simulation methods, EIL could derive per-hour volatility in each market segment in response to per-hour volatility of the other market segments and calculate impulse responses.

Applying their model to Japanese yen–US dollar intraday exchange rate data, Engle, Ito and Lin strongly reject the hypothesis of heat waves and interpret this rejection as being consistent either with market dynamics exhibiting volatility persistence (caused, for

---

[30] Various assumptions underlie the model. In particular, Engle, Ito and Lin (1990) assume market efficiency, which implies that intraday exchange rate changes are distributed with mean zero and that $\epsilon_{i,k}$ and $\epsilon_{i,k}$ are uncorrelated for $i \neq j$.

[31] Engle, Ito and Lin (1990) also derive the likelihood function and a MLE (which is simply an extension of the MLE developed by Engle and Bollerslev, 1986) in order to estimate their model.

example, by private information or heterogeneous beliefs) or with stochastic policy co-ordination or competition. Hence, they investigate the dynamic effect of country-specific innovations on conditional volatility in the subsequent markets. Engle, Ito and Lin's findings suggest that Tokyo news has the largest impact on volatility spillovers of the Japanese yen–US dollar exchange rate. Finally, the impulse response curves are computed to examine the reaction of one market's volatility to news coming from another market. The empirical results suggest a cross-country dynamic effect in the short run which gradually dies out. Overall, therefore, their study finds a case for volatility clustering of the meteor shower type rather than the heat wave type.[32]

9.4.3   Public information or private information?

A common feature of empirical and theoretical studies is the crucial role of information, especially macroeconomic news, in determining price volatility (see e.g. Oldfield and Rogalski, 1980; French and Roll, 1986; Harris, 1986). It is a widely held view (and a common implicit assumption in conventional macroeconomic models of exchange rate determination) that all agents in the foreign exchange market project on the same public information set, which implies that private information is irrelevant. Some recent studies challenge this view, however.

Harvey and Huang (1991) investigate the volatility implications of foreign exchange trading using transaction data on futures contracts from the Chicago Mercantile Exchange (CME) and the London International Financial Futures and Options Exchange (LIFFE). Precisely, they analyse the role of public news announcements in determining volatility patterns. Harvey and Huang compute the hourly variance rates for exchange-trading and non-exchange-trading intervals and compute the ratios of these variance rates as well as the ratios of total variance rates. The rationale underlying the computation of these ratios is the so-called public information hypothesis, which suggests that even if trading outside exchange-trading time is important, the exchange-trading variance rate may exceed the non-exchange-trading variance rate because individual exchange rates are affected by public information available to the countries concerned as well as to other countries. Hence, the availability of this public information released during trading hours in both countries may be expected to play a role in determining the volatility of the exchange rate, implying that volatility may be higher at times when important macroeconomic news is made available.

This view contrasts with that of French and Roll (1986), who suggest that trading based on private information induces higher volatility when the market is open than when the market is closed (see also the theoretical framework of Admati and Pfleiderer, 1988; and Foster and Viswanathan, 1990). The empirical results of Harvey and Huang's study provide strong evidence that the intraday volatility on the international monetary market varies

---

[32] See also the closely related study by Hogan and Melvin (1994), who examine the role that news and hetero-geneous expectations play in meteor shower effects. Their empirical focus is on the US trade balance news, which is shown to have a significant and persistent effect on the exchange rate and its conditional variance. Also, the impact of US trade balance news is not confined to the US foreign exchange market. The degree to which US trade balance news affects other geographical market locations appears to be functionally related to heterogeneous priors.

largely by day of the week and, in particular, the opening on Friday (and, to a lesser extent, Thursday) is characterised by very high volatilities. Harvey and Huang interpret these results as evidence supportive of the public information hypothesis since, in the United States, most of the important public macroeconomic announcements take place on Friday and, to a lesser extent, on Thursday. Overall, US–European and US–Japanese exchange rate volatilities are found to be higher during US trading hours, while European cross-rate volatilities are found to be higher during European trading hours. While the disclosure of private information through trading may in part explain these volatility patterns, macroeconomic announcements appear more likely to be the cause of increases in volatility.

Wasserfallen and Zimmermann (1985) and Goodhart and Giugale (1993) investigate the systematic patterns of intraday volatility of exchange rates and conclude that volatility is lower during intervals when trading volume is known to be smaller (e.g. weekends and lunch hours) and is higher during the first trading hour on Monday for each currency in the domestic country, regardless of the fact that other markets opened earlier. This evidence may be considered supportive of the private information hypothesis, although both the efficient markets hypothesis and the hypothesis that news drives exchange rate volatility are not entirely discarded (see Goodhart and Giugale, 1993, pp. 18–19).

Demos and Goodhart (1996) also note that trading volume declines immediately before the weekend and report a strong correlation of intraday patterns in exchange rate volatility and trading activity; they are high, for example, both at the opening and at the closing of the market, displaying essentially a U-shaped pattern. It is not clear, however, whether large volumes and volatilities are caused by efficient processing of fundamentals or other factors, such as noise trading or bandwagon effects.

A number of studies in the microstructure literature have reported a strong contemporaneous correlation between trading volume and volatility of exchange rates; see, among others, Cornell (1981), Grammatikos and Saunders (1986), Karpoff (1987). The relationship between volume and volatility is important for at least three reasons, noted very clearly by Jorion (1996):

First, it provides insight into the structure of financial markets by relating new information arrival to market prices. Also it has implications for the design of new future contracts; a positive relation suggests that a new futures contract can succeed only when there is 'sufficient' price uncertainty with the underlying asset, which cannot be effectively cross-hedged with other contracts. Finally, the price–volume relation has a direct bearing on the empirical distribution of speculative prices.

Generally, the literature on the relationship between volume and volatility interprets the positive correlation between these two variables as arising from a common driving variable. This theory is the so-called mixture distribution hypothesis (MDH), first proposed by Clark (1973) and Epps and Epps (1976): price variability and trading volume are driven by an unobserved common variable. The seminal theoretical paper in this literature is due, however, to Tauchen and Pitts (1983), whose model assumes that the relationship between volume and volatility may be of one of two types. First, market price volatility is inversely related to the number of traders, since market prices may be considered as an average of traders' reservation prices, and increases in the number of traders represents an increase in the number of observations on which the average (market price) is computed. Second, given a certain number of traders, price variability is proportional to trading volume because higher trading volume is consistent with higher disagreement among traders. Also, the link between trading volume and volatility is stronger when new information flows to the market at a relatively higher rate.[33] In Tauchen and Pitts (1983), the joint distribution of daily price changes and transactions volumes is derived from a model of intraday equilibrium price changes and intraday volumes. Traders change their reservation prices continuously during the day in response to new information until the market reaches a new equilibrium.

Empirically, strong correlation appears to characterise the relationship between volume and volatility (see Cornell, 1981; Tauchen and Pitts, 1983; Grammatikos and Saunders, 1986). Interestingly, Frankel and Froot (1990a,b) investigate the relationships among the dispersion of survey forecasts, volatility and trading volume and find strong evidence suggesting that the dispersion parameter (the disagreement component) causes, in a Granger sense, both volatility and volume, consistent with the mixture distribution hypothesis.

Nevertheless, Jorion (1995, 1996) argues that implied volatilities may be more informative than time series models since forecasts of volatility require forecasts of parameters which are expected to be time-varying and which are typically treated as constant in the canonical MDH approach. Given that options have been traded for about fifteen years on the major stock exchanges, there is now sufficient data available for time series models to be tested with acceptable statistical power using implied standard deviations (ISDs) in the foreign exchange market. Wei and Frankel (1991) and Jorion (1995) investigate the predictive ability of ISDs by relating ISDs to future realised volatility. Their results indicate that ISDs largely outperform time series models, although they are still biased predictors.

In order to compute ISDs, some authors use stochastic volatility models which, though very appealing, have high computational costs and require estimation of a large number of parameters (see e.g. Hull and White, 1987; Scott, 1987; Wiggins, 1987; Chesney and Scott, 1989). An alternative approach, followed for example by Jorion (1996), involves deriving ISDs using Black's (1976) option-pricing model. Jorion (1996) provides strong evidence supporting the superiority of ISDs over time series models, and also shows evidence for a positive correlation between volume and volatility consistent with the MDH theory.[34]

The recent empirical contribution by Ito, Lyons and Melvin (1998) is, however, crucial in this literature. They provide evidence in favour of the private-information hypothesis using data for the Tokyo foreign exchange market, which was restricted from trading over the lunch break (12.00 to 13.30) from 1972 until 1994. Following the related study of French

---

[33] Unfortunately, the trade of information flow is an unobservable variable, implying that the estimation of this model requires an assumption about the distribution of an unobserved variable. However, an alternative model specification, which leads to similar conclusions on the relationship between volume and volatility, is provided by Richardson and Smith (1994) (see also Bessembinder, 1994). Hartmann (1999) analyses the dollar–yen bid–ask spread using a long time-series of daily spot foreign exchange trading volumes. In line with standard spread models and volume theories, Hartmann shows that unpredictable foreign exchange turnover (a measure of the rate of information arrival) increases spreads, while predictable turnover decreases them; see also Hartmann (1998a).

[34] Note that the use of ISDs on stock-market data provides less interesting results. In general, the predictive power of ISDs is very low and never higher than the predictive power of time series models (Canina and Figlewski, 1993; Lamourex and Lastrapes, 1993).

and Roll (1986) for the New York Stock Exchange, Ito, Lyons and Melvin start by noting that the three candidate explanations of the importance of trading for price determination are (a) public information arrives mainly during trading hours, (b) private information induces trades that affect prices during trading hours, and (c) errors in pricing are more likely to occur during trading hours. These authors then discriminate between these explanations using the following strategy. First, they compare volatility across regimes with an unchanged flow of public information, providing evidence that lunch return variance doubles when trading opens; given that the foreign exchange market is largely skewed towards public information, the fact that this information far from explains the whole story is an important finding in itself.[35]

Having eliminated public information as the cause of higher volatility, Ito, Lyons and Melvin (1998) then discriminate between the remaining alternatives – private information and pricing errors – by providing evidence that the volatility U-shape over the full day flattens, as predicted by private-information models on the basis that lunch-hour trading induces greater revelation during that period leaving a smaller share for the morning and afternoon. These authors also show that the U-shape over the full day tilts upwards, which suggests information whose private value is temporary: an open lunch hour reduces the incentive to trade early because it[36] reduces the likelihood that prices will reflect that information before a position can be opened. Further, there appears to be a clear U-shape in the morning when Tokyo closed over lunch but this U-shape disappears after the change to lunch opening, as predicted by private-information models. Finally, they find that the contribution of mispricing to price volatility is reduced after the lunch hour, which is inconsistent with the view that the increase in lunch variance is wholly due to mispricing. Overall, the study of Ito, Lyons and Melvin (1998) provides the strongest empirical evidence in favour of the private-information hypothesis in the literature on foreign exchange microstructure, although private information is expected to predict prices mainly over relatively short horizons and, hence, may not be 'fundamental' in that sense.[37]

Covrig and Melvin (1999) have further investigated and tested some implications of market microstructure theory along the same lines as Ito, Lyons and Melvin (1998). In particular, Covrig and Melvin identify a period in the foreign exchange market when there is a high concentration of informed yen–dollar traders active in Tokyo. Comparing the period of informed trader clustering to a similar period without the informed traders, they provide evidence that exchange rate quotes adjust to full-information levels very much faster when informed traders are active in the market than when they are not. Covrig and Melvin also find that Japanese quotes lead the rest of the market when the informed traders are active, while two-way causality is observed in quotes when the informed traders are not active. In

---

[35] Ito, Lyons and Melvin (1998) also made a number of tests to ensure that the flow of public information was unchanged.

[36] This is clear given the definition of private information used by Ito, Lyons and Melvin (1998), which includes information which is not common knowledge and which is price relevant. This definition is less stringent than in other studies (e.g. French and Roll, 1986) which typically required the price changes induced by information to be permanent.

[37] See also the related papers by DeGennaro and Shrieves (1995), Andersen and Bollerslev (1998) and Melvin and Yin (1999).

addition, the contribution of yen–dollar price discovery relative to quotes of the rest of the world is 5 to 12 percentage points higher when the informed traders are active relative to when they are not active. Covrig and Melvin conclude their study by suggesting that their results are consistent with the view that private information is at times quite important, but that 'normal' times appear to be characterised as periods where public information implies a high contemporaneous correlation across quotes, regardless of the origin. The important implication of Covrig and Melvin's study is that the results reported by Ito, Lyons and Melvin are not due to inventory rebalancing prior to the close but to private information. This line of analysis represents a very important avenue for future research.

Friedman's classic argument in favour of floating exchange rates was that rational specu-lators will, as well as imparting valuable information into the market, smooth exchange rate movements, i.e. reduce exchange rate volatility (Friedman, 1953). In a recent theoretical mi-crostructural analysis of the connection between rational speculative activity and exchange rate volatility, Carlson and Osler (1998) argue that Friedman's analysis implicitly and cru-cially excludes interest rate differentials from his interpretation of speculator behaviour. They develop a microstructural model which reveals that informed, rational speculators who consider interest differentials will tend to magnify the exchange rate effects of interest rate shocks and may thereby increase overall exchange rate volatility. This connection be-tween rational speculation and volatility, which does not rely on asymmetric information, is structural because speculators affect the exchange rate generating process. Carlson and Osler demonstrate that rational speculation will, in their framework, tend to be stabilising at low levels of speculative activity and destabilising at high levels.

9.5   Bid–ask spread determination

9.5.1   The main determinants of the spread

Modelling the bid–ask spread represents a difficult task because of the large number of institutional details which need to be accounted for. Finance theory has identified three main determinants of the bid–ask spread: the cost of dealer services, the cost of adverse selection and inventory holding costs.

The cost of dealer services has been analysed formally by Demsetz (1968), who assumes the existence of some fixed costs of providing 'predictable immediacy' as the service for which compensation is required by market-makers. This cost may include, for example, the cost of acquiring know-how and subscriptions to specialised electronic information and trading systems (e.g. Reuters in the foreign exchange market).[38]

The second argument used to justify the existence of bid–ask spreads may originally be at-tributed to Bagehot (1971). Bagehot's model includes transactors who are willing to pay the

---

[38] The determinants of the level of compensation for dealer services is still a debated issue in the relevant literature. The traditional view that centralisation of the foreign exchange market implies such economies of scale that market-makers are in a natural monopoly position (Stigler, 1964) has not received sufficient empirical support, even if, for example, in the NYSE specialists are allowed to get monopoly rents from other investors because of barriers to entry (see Smidt, 1971). In general, however, the foreign exchange market is not characterised by such barriers to entry or exit which could justify the existence of natural monopoly (see also Stoll, 1978; Black, 1991).

price of the spread to the market-maker in exchange for predictable immediacy (liquidity-motivated transactors) together with transactors who can speculate at the expense of the market-maker using some private, insider information (insiders). An adverse selection problem clearly arises because market-makers cannot distinguish between liquidity-motivated transactors and insiders, and hence they are induced to widen spreads for both categories. In other words, the bid–ask spread represents the weapon market-makers use to defend themselves against adverse selection in the form of exploitation of arbitrage opportunities. Information cost models based on the adverse selection argument have been built by, among others, Copeland and Galai (1983), Glosten and Milgrom (1985) and Kyle (1985). Although the adverse selection argument is very appealing, information cost models suffer from the same problem as MDH models, that is the empirical implementation of these models requires estimation of the rate of information arrival or the share of information trading relative to overall trading, which are unobservable variables.[39]

Finally, inventory holding costs also represent a determinant of bid–ask spreads. Inventory cost models assume that market-makers optimise their inventory holding: the desired level of inventory is zero and a constant spread is shifted continuously according to the probability of receiving a purchase or a sale order. In general, inventory cost models tend to imply that market-makers shift the spread downwards (upwards) and increase the width of the spread when a positive (negative) inventory is accumulated. The original argument of inventory holding costs as a crucial determinant of bid–ask spreads goes back to Barnea and Logue (1975), while dynamic optimisation inventory cost models are due to Bradfield (1979), Amihud and Mendelson (1980) and Ho and Stoll (1981).

9.5.2 Modelling the spread: theory and evidence

A peculiarity of the foreign exchange market is that market-making and brokerage are separated: market-makers do not operate as brokers and vice versa, suggesting that brokers' spreads need to be modelled differently from market-makers' spread. A brokered spread is usually the combination of the best bid and ask received by the broker as separate limit orders. Flood (1991) suggests modelling brokered spreads as a pair of extreme order statistics from independent distributions of purchase and sale limit orders. By definition, the k-th order statistic is the k-th number in a list containing the sample realisations of a finite number of independent random variables ranked in increasing order. Modelling limit orders also requires the derivation of the distribution of these statistics, which is conditional on volume and on the constraint that the best ask always exceeds the best bid. Given the analytical complexity of such derivation, Cohen, Maier, Schwartz and Whitcomb (1979, 1981) model limit orders assuming a 'yawl' distribution (see also Cohen, Maier, Schwartz and Whitcomb, 1986). Very little work has been done, however, on modelling brokered spreads and the underlying theory is largely still to be developed.[40]

---

[39] It also follows from the adverse selection model that predictable volume is inversely related to spreads. In fact, given that market-makers gain from transactions with liquidity-motivated transactors, spreads decrease with an increase in the expected order flow from this class of transactors and vice versa (see Easley and O'Hara, 1992).

[40] See Kubarych (1983), Burnham (1991) and Flood (1991).

The directly proportional relationship between spreads and exchange rate volatility represents a fairly stylised fact in the microstructure literature. Early studies modelled the spread as a function of transactions costs, the bank's profit from providing liquidity services and the market-maker's payoff for facing the exchange rate risk when assuming an open position. The main conclusions of these early studies are that exchange rate spreads are wider under floating exchange rate than under fixed exchange rate regimes (e.g. Aliber, 1975) and that measures of exchange rate dispersion – measuring exchange rate volatility – are followed closely by exchange rate spreads (e.g. Fieleke, 1975; Overturf, 1982).

Glassman (1987) provides a significant contribution to this literature in that she builds a model where variables representing transactions frequency are included explicitly and the non-normality of the distribution of exchange rate changes is taken into account.[41] Glassman's model not only provides additional evidence on the proportional relationship between exchange rate volatility and bid–ask spreads in the foreign exchange market, but also suggests that market-makers consider moments of the exchange rate higher than the second moment in order to evaluate the probability of large exchange rate changes. Moreover, exchange rate volatility is predicted by market-makers on the basis of the information provided by long-run trends (some sixty-five days) as well as by very recent experience (one day or one week). Glassman also provides evidence on the fact that spreads widen just before weekends and holidays. Finally, transactions costs are found to vary significantly over time in response to changes in the regime of capital controls.

Another fundamental theoretical contribution in this area is due to Admati and Pfleiderer (1988). In their model there are three types of agents: informed traders, who have relatively superior information and only trade on terms favourable to them; discretionary liquidity traders, who must trade during a day but can choose when to trade during the day in order to minimise costs; and non-discretionary liquidity traders, who must trade at a precise time during the day regardless of the cost. In this model, trading volume is explained by the concentration of trade of informed traders and discretionary liquidity traders at certain points in time: the concentrations occur because it is profitable for informed traders to trade when there are many liquidity traders who do not have the same information as themselves and because discretionary liquidity traders are attracted because the larger the number of traders the lower the cost of trading. Admati and Pfleiderer's model also predicts the increase in both volume and volatility which is typical of the open and close of a trading day, so that trading activity displays a U-shaped pattern from open to close.

The assumption of traders' risk-neutrality is, however, crucial in generating the key results of Admati and Pfleiderer's model. This is rigorously shown by Subrahmanyam (1991), who builds a model of a non-competitive speculative market where informed traders as well as market-makers are risk-averse. The main finding is that market liquidity is found to be non-monotonic in the number of informed traders, their degree of risk aversion and the accuracy

---

[41] The non-normality of the distribution of exchange rate changes has received substantial support since the late 1970s and early 1980s (see e.g. Westerfield, 1977; McFarland, Pettit and Sung, 1982; Boothe and Glassman, 1987). The distribution appears to be quite close to a leptokurtic distribution, with a higher peak and fatter tails than the normal distribution. Since non-normal distributions are not described completely by the first two moments, Glassman (1987) includes the first to the fourth moments of the distribution of exchange rate changes in her model.

of their information. The model also predicts that price efficiency is reduced by an increased concentration of liquidity traders and market liquidity may also be non-monotonic in the variance of liquidity traders.

Bollerslev and Domowitz (1993) use intradaily data to investigate the behaviour of quote arrivals and bid–ask spreads. They record quote arrivals and bid–ask spreads over the trading day, across geographical locations as well as across market participants. The evidence provided by Bollerslev and Domowitz is useful for discriminating among theoretical models of trading activity. In particular, Bollerslev and Domowitz find that trading activity and the bid–ask spreads for traders whose activity is restricted to regional markets can be described by a U-shaped distribution, consistent with the predictions of Admati and Pfleiderer's model. Nevertheless, the patterns of trading activity and spreads during the day also strongly suggest some degree of traders' risk aversion, consistent with the Subrahmanyam's model; given some degree of risk-aversion, however, the more trading activity is executed by informed participants the higher the cost of trading.

Goodhart and Figliuoli (1991) report a study of minute-by-minute spot rates (bid–ask quotes) on three days in autumn 1987 (14/15 September and 21 October) at the Reuters screen in London. They find evidence that leptokurtosis and heteroscedasticity are less pronounced at the minute-by-minute frequency than at lower frequencies. Also, leptokurtosis, skewness and heteroscedasticity are time-varying. Trading volume is also time-varying, being higher at the European and North American openings and lower at the European lunch hour. The series are also found to exhibit first-order negative serial correlation, especially pronounced immediately after jumps in the exchange rate. Time aggregation appears to reduce the first-order autocorrelation, although it does not make it disappear. Finally, multivariate analysis suggests the existence of significant relationships between lagged exchange rates (both the domestic rate and the German mark–US dollar rate) and the current spot rate.[42]

Bollerslev and Melvin (1994) use an asymmetric information model with informed traders and liquidity traders in the tradition of Glosten and Milgrom (1985) and Admati and Pfleiderer (1988) and provide empirical evidence that bid–ask spreads are proportionally related to exchange rate uncertainty. The innovation in their study is that they employ an ordered probit analysis in order to capture the discreteness in the spread distribution, with the uncertainty of the spot exchange rate modelled as a GARCH process (see also Melvin and Ramirez, 2000).

Overall, the main findings of the literature of the 1980s and early 1990s on foreign exchange market microstructure concerning bid–ask spread behaviour may be summarised by stating that spreads are directly proportional to the volatility of exchange rates and trading volume, and that they are higher on Fridays. In a more recent study, Bessembinder (1994) finds that bid–ask spreads are also proportionally related to forecasts of inventory price risk. Bessembinder confirms that spreads widen before weekends and other non-trading intervals, but explains this stylised fact using the argument that the sensitivity of spreads to risk and liquidity costs increases over non-trading intervals. Bessembinder's investigation

---

[42] See also Goodhart, Ito and Payne (1996).

of the time series behaviour of bid–ask spreads is simply based on a regression of time series of currency spreads on inventory-cost and trading-volume proxies and the estimation is executed using the generalised method of moments.[43]

Moreover, given that bid and ask prices quoted by market-makers are not necessarily symmetric around the underlying value of the asset, Bessembinder develops a simple procedure for estimating the location of bid and ask quotes with respect to the underlying value. The main innovation in this method is that it does not require the simultaneous observation of spot and forward rates, unlike previous attempts in the literature (e.g. Bossaerts and Hillion, 1991). Bessembinder's method is derived as follows. Define an unobservable value W_t as:

$$W_t = \alpha_t A_t + (1 - \alpha_t) B_t, \qquad (9.16)$$

where α_t is a location parameter for time t, A_t denotes the ask quote and B_t denotes the bid quote. Then, define the change in the underlying value of the currency as:

$$\Delta W_{t+1} = \mu_t + \varepsilon_{t+1}, \qquad (9.17)$$

where μ_t denotes the expectation at time t of the change in value over the next period and ε_{t+1} is the unexpected change. Combining (9.16) and (9.17) yields:

$$\Delta B_{t+1} = \mu_t - \alpha_{t+1} \Delta S_{t+1} + \varepsilon_{t+1}, \qquad (9.18)$$

where $S_t \equiv A_t - B_t$ denotes the bid–ask spread. Also, the two time-varying parameters μ_t and α_t are assumed to be linear functions of observable variables X_t and Z_t respectively. Hence, equation (9.18) becomes:

$$\Delta B_{t+1} = \mu_0 + \mu_1 X_t - \alpha_0 [\Delta S_{t+1}] - \alpha_1 [Z_{t+1} \Delta S_{t+1}] + \varepsilon_{t+1}. \qquad (9.19)$$

In estimating equation (9.19), Bessembinder (1994) includes in X_t the excess of 30-day Eurodollar interest rates over 30-day local currency Euro interest rates and a Monday indicator variable, and he considers in Z_t the change since the preceding day in the 30-day Eurodollar deposit rate, the change since the preceding day in the local currency Euro interest rate, a Friday indicator and a pre-holiday indicator. The results provide strong evidence that currency market-makers reduce quotes in relation to the underlying dollar value when US interest rates are rising and, less significantly, on Fridays. The results also support the existence of a Monday effect in currency values, but shifts in the placement of quotes in relation to value on the approach to weekends make it hard to detect. In addition, the evidence provided by Bessembinder 'illustrates that inference regarding asset value can be altered by allowing for variation in the placement of quotes in relation to value'.

An alternative modelling strategy for the conditional heteroscedasticity of the prediction error of foreign exchange rates is provided by Lee (1994). Under the assumption of cointegration between spot and forward rates, Lee uses a system of error correction models for GARCH-type models as a function of the spread. Estimating the system using daily series

---

[43] As proxies for inventory-carrying costs, Bessembinder uses forecasts of price risk, interest-rate based measures of liquidity costs and a non-trading indicator. As proxies for trading volume, he uses the forecastable and unexpected components of futures trading volume.

for seven exchange rates, Lee provides evidence supporting the strong correlation between spread and exchange rate volatility.[44]

Jorion (1996) uses an option implied volatility in his model specification of bid–ask spreads. His results are generally consistent with the implications of conventional spread theory. Interestingly, Jorion also shows that ISDs dominate all other risk measures for the purpose of explaining bid–ask spreads.

Bessembinder, Chan and Seguin (1996) investigate the relation between trading volume and some proxies for information flows (ratio of volatility of returns to a diversified equity portfolio) and for divergencies in opinion (the open interest of the S&P 500 Index futures contract). They find that, in both spot and futures markets, trading volume varies positively with the proxies for information flows. The choice of the trading venue largely depends, as one would expect, on the nature of information flows: traders informed on firm-specific matters trade primarily in the spot equity market, while traders with more general, market-wide information choose to trade in the spot futures market. Bessembinder, Chan and Seguin also find that trading volumes in both spot and futures markets are positively related to the proxy for divergencies of opinion when these rise, but are unrelated to the proxies when they decrease. The day-of-the-week effects appear to be asymmetric across markets, with lower futures volume relative to spot volume late in the week.[45] Bessembinder, Chan and Seguin conclude that 'additional research is warranted on identifying those circumstances under which price formation will depend primarily on order flow or on the observation of public information'.[46]

Hsieh and Kleidon (1996) stress, however, the empirical difficulties in reconciling the implications of asymmetric information models with the observed time series behaviour of stock and foreign exchange data, *unless* liquidity traders' demand to trade is very high at open and close for reasons not explainable using standard asymmetric information models. In particular, a major inconsistency lies in the fact that bid–ask spreads are observed to go up rather than down at both open and close, in contradiction to the implication of asymmetric information models that liquidity traders are trading less at these times because transactions costs are higher. Moreover, another empirical regularity which is not explained by the traditional spread theory is that trading volume as well as volatility in the New York foreign exchange market are not affected significantly at the close in London, when both volume and volatility are at a peak in that market. Hsieh and Kleidon provide two different

---

[44] Another interesting paper relating global foreign exchange markets to spreads is due to Hartmann (1998b), who estimates the long-run impact of trading activity on bid–ask spreads with a short panel containing around-the-clock Reuters quotes and global transactions volumes, allowance being made for individual and time effects in an unbalanced random effects model. In line with liquidity effect explanations, the volume parameter is found to have a (weakly) statistically significant negative sign, whereas the volatility parameter is positive. Structural parameters are found to be stable over time, while residuals are groupwise heteroscedastic.

[45] Also, Foster and Viswanathan (1990) develop a theoretical model which predicts this asymmetry.

[46] Another interesting paper in a related context is Brock and Kleidon (1992), who examine the effect of periodic stock market closure on transactions demand and volume of trade, and consequently, bid and ask prices. Their results suggest that transactions demand at open and close is greater and less elastic than at other times of the trading day. In response, a market-maker such as a NYSE specialist may effectively price-discriminate by charging a higher price to transact at these periods of peak demand. The predictions of periodic demand with high volume and concurrent wide spreads are found to be consistent with empirical evidence, while the predictions of current-information based models are not.

explanations for this empirical failure of information-based models of bid–ask spread determination. First, traders are known 'to learn the feel of the market', that is they go through a learning process. This learning process, largely ignored in spread theory until now, may help explaining the high trading volume, volatility and spreads in the morning. Also, the peaks of trading volume, volatility and spreads at the close of foreign exchange markets may be explained by inventory-related activities of traders, who become anxious to unload excess inventories. This remains an interesting area for further investigation.

9.6   Market-makers' behaviour

The microstructure literature has also been concerned with investigating how the behaviour of market-makers affects the efficiency of the market. Bid–ask spread determination and the treatment of price information represent the two most common concerns about market-makers' behaviour; while the former issue has been largely discussed earlier, the latter is the main focus of the present section. A large literature already exists for equity markets, but the foreign exchange market is receiving increasing interest. Lyons (1991, 1995, 1996, 1998b, 1999) may be considered as a pioneer in this area.

9.6.1   Private beliefs and information externalities

Lyons (1991) provides an important investigation of the importance of private beliefs and information externalities in the foreign exchange market. He argues, in fact, that the absence of different beliefs regarding the exchange rate path as well as the process of updating these beliefs in standard exchange rate determination models may represent crucial factors explaining the empirical failure of such models. Lyons makes important contributions to our understanding of the mechanism through which transactions *per se* affect the updating of private beliefs over time, the implications of the institutional characteristics of the foreign exchange market on trading volume patterns and the information transmission mechanisms of the foreign exchange markets:

Agents transact because they differ. It is important to distinguish between differences in valuation beliefs and differences that arise for other reasons. Of course, it is possible for investors to agree on valuation and still choose to transact for diversification purposes. However, in the context of the typical portfolio choice models, the trading volume that can be explained as a result of actual shifts in wealth, taxes, return second moments, etc., is minute in comparison to actual volumes, and in the simplest models is zero. The burden of explanation, then, appears almost certainly to fall on differences in beliefs regarding valuation (Lyons, 1991, pp. 1–2).

While most models in the literature describe equilibrium price determination as a one-shot outcome of the activity of traders who use both private information and the information in market-clearing prices to determine their demands for risky assets (see e.g. Diamond and Verrecchia, 1981), Lyons (1991) allows transactions *per se* to affect directly the updating process of private beliefs over time. Hence, the equilibrium is no longer a one-shot outcome, but the outcome of an interaction between private beliefs, volume and volatility. This interactive process leads, however, to a sort of information externality caused by the dual role of traders as speculators on the one hand and as an information clearing-house (intermediating customer orders which contain information) on the other.[47] Profit maximisation induces traders to underestimate important information in making their trading decisions, thereby reducing the information content of prices at any given time. A crucial implication of the model is that the greater the market power and the degree of risk aversion of traders, the less information will be revealed by market prices.

Lyons (1995) makes a number of tests on standard microstructure hypotheses in the foreign exchange market. In order to perform these tests, Lyons builds a model formulated on the basis of very realistic assumptions, in line with the institutional features of the foreign exchange market. Lyons records the transactions of one dealer and one broker in the US market for five days during August 1992. The data set includes three 'interlocking' components: the direct quotes and trades of a market-maker from a major New York bank, the position cards of the same market-maker, and the prices and quantities for third-party transactions intermediated by a major New York dealer. The main focus of the study is on testing for the effects of trading volume on quoted prices through the two channels emphasised by the literature: the information channel and the inventory-control channel. The results provide evidence that trading volume affects quoted prices through both channels, therefore giving some support to both strands of the microstructure literature.[48]

9.6.2 'Event uncertainty' versus 'hot potato'

Lyons (1996) extends the model and employs the data set previously used in Lyons (1995) in order to shed light on the statistical relationship between the intensity of trading and the informativeness of trades. In particular, Lyons (1996) attempts to discriminate between the two contrasting views of trading intensity which he describes as (a) the 'event uncertainty' (trades are more informative when trading intensity is high) view and (b) the 'hot potato' view (trades are more informative when trading intensity is low). The event uncertainty hypothesis can be traced back to Easley and O'Hara (1992) who build a model in which new information may not exist, unlike most of the asymmetric information models in this literature. In such a framework there is a probability p of new information and $(1 - p)$ of no new information; also, the new information is good news with probability q and bad news with probability $(1 - q)$. Easley and O'Hara show that trades occurring when intensity is high should induce a larger updating of beliefs than when trading intensity is low, implying that trades are more informative when trading intensity is high. The opposite view, the hot potato view, is rationalised on the basis of asymmetric information models in the tradition of Admati and Pfleiderer (1988), where there are liquidity traders who clump together in their trading in order to minimise their losses to informed traders. Hence, because of this clumping of liquidity traders, trades are more informative when trading intensity is

---

[47] Information externalities are predicted by earlier theoretical models under different mechanisms (see, for example, Stein, 1987).

[48] In modelling the price expectation formation process, Lyons uses a Bayesian model in the tradition of Amihud and Mendelson (1980), Cohen; Maier, Schwartz and Whitcomb (1981), Conroy and Winkler (1981), Glosten and Milgrom (1985) and Madhavan and Smidt (1991) (for a non-technical exposition of these models, see Flood, 1991).

low.[49] The main focus of Lyons (1996) is on examining whether currency trading volume is informative, and under what circumstances. Specifically, he uses transactions data to test whether trades occurring when trading intensity is high are more informative – dollar for dollar – than trades occurring when intensity is low. Lyons' empirical results in estimating his model are supportive of one or the other hypothesis depending upon the measure of trading intensity used in estimation, implying that 'taken together, the results highlight the potential complementarity between these seemingly polar views'.

Another recent piece of empirical evidence is due to Lyons (1998b), who examines foreign exchange trading at the dealer level. The dealer Lyons tracks averages 100,000 US dollars in profits per day on a volume of one billion US dollars per day. The half-life of the dealer's position is about ten minutes, which may be interpreted as evidence supporting inventory models. The author also identifies the dealer's speculative position over time and finds that this position determines the share of profits deriving from speculation as opposed to intermediation, with intermediation found to have a relatively more important role.

9.7 Summary and concluding remarks

This chapter has offered an overview of the recent and growing literature on the microstructure of the foreign exchange market. We provided a detailed description of the institutional features of the foreign exchange market. We then discussed the existing foreign exchange market survey data sets, followed by an exposition of the main mechanisms of expectations formation used by the relevant literature and an overview of survey data studies. We also presented a discussion of the main characteristics of chartist analysis and its role in the foreign exchange market. In the final part of the chapter, we focused on more recent issues in the foreign exchange market microstructure literature, providing an overview of theoretical and empirical contributions on modelling time-varying volatility, on the relationship between volatility, trading volumes and bid–ask spreads, on the theory of bid–ask spread determination, and also of the literature on modelling market-makers' behaviour.

We started this chapter by noting that at least a partial motivation for the development of the market microstructure literature has been the failure of standard macro fundamentals-based exchange rate models to explain or predict exchange rate movements reliably (see e.g. Flood and Taylor, 1996). To date, however, the foreign exchange market microstructure appears to shed light most strongly on related issues such as the transmission of information between market participants, the heterogeneity of agents' expectations and the implications of such heterogeneity for trading volume and exchange rate volatility.[50]

---

[49] See also Lyons (1997), who develops a simultaneous trade model of the spot foreign exchange market which produces hot-potato trading. At the outset, risk-averse dealers receive customer orders that are not generally observable. Dealers then trade among themselves. Thus, each dealer intermediates both his customers' trades and any information contained therein. This information is subsequently revealed in price depending on the information in inter-dealer trades. Lyons shows that hot-potato trading reduces the information in inter-dealer trades, making price less informative.

[50] Although, as discussed above, an important exception is the recent paper by Evans and Lyons (1999) which demonstrates that order flow may empirically explain a large proportion of nominal exchange rate movements over periods of four months or less. This clearly suggests the need for further foreign exchange market microstructure research on the relationship between order flow and exchange rate movements.

Further, there appears to be an emerging consensus in the literature that macro fundamentals are a reasonable guide to very-long-run exchange rate movements (e.g. Flood and Taylor, 1996; Lothian and Taylor, 1996) while, on the theoretical side, there is an increasing interest in exchange rate models with rigorous, stochastic general equilibrium microeconomic foundations of the kind discussed in Chapter 5 (Obstfeld and Rogoff, 1995, 1996; Lane, 2001; Sarno, 2001). For the foreseeable future, therefore, it seems that research in foreign exchange markets is likely to be dominated by these three strands – long-run empirical exchange rate modelling, the 'new open-economy macroeconomics', and foreign exchange market microstructure analysis. Synthesising these three approaches into a single unified treatment would seem to be a major challenge lying ahead for the profession.

References and further readings

Admati, A. and P. Pfleiderer (1988), 'A Theory of Intraday Patterns: Volume and Price Variability', *Review of Financial Studies*, 1, pp. 3–40.

Aliber, R.Z. (1975), 'Monetary Independence under Floating Exchange Rates', *Journal of Finance*, 30, pp. 365–76.

Allen, H. and M.P. Taylor (1990), 'Charts, Noise and Fundamentals in the London Foreign Exchange Market', *Economic Journal*, 100, pp. 49–59.

Amihud, Y. and H. Mendelson (1980), 'Dealership Market: Market-Making with Inventory', *Journal of Financial Economics*, pp. 31–53.

Andersen, T.G. and T. Bollerslev (1998), 'DM-Volatility: Intraday Activity Patterns, Macroeconomic Announcements, and Longer Run Dependencies', *Journal of Finance*, 53, pp. 219–65.

Bagehot, W. (1971), 'The Only Game in Town', *Financial Analysts Journal*, 22, pp. 12–14.

Baillie, R.T. (1989), 'Econometric Tests of Rationality and Market Efficiency', *Econometric Reviews*, 8, pp. 151–86.

Baillie, R.T. and T. Bollerslev (1989), 'The Message in Daily Exchange Rates: A Conditional-Variance Tale', *Journal of Business and Economic Statistics*, 7, pp. 297–305.

—— (1990), 'A Multivariate Generalized ARCH Approach to Modeling Risk Premia in Forward Foreign Exchange Rate Markets', *Journal of International Money and Finance*, 9, pp. 309–24.

—— (1991), 'Intraday and Inter-market Volatility in Foreign Exchange Rates', *Review of Economic Studies*, 58, pp. 565–85.

Bank for International Settlements (1998), *Central Bank Survey of Foreign Exchange and Derivatives Market Activity*, Basle.

Barnea, A. and D.E. Logue (1975), 'The Effect of Risk on the Market Maker's Spread', *Financial Analysts Journal*, 31, pp. 45–9.

Bessembinder, H. (1994), 'Bid–Ask Spreads in the Interbank Foreign Exchange Markets', *Journal of Financial Economics*, 35, pp. 317–48.

Bessembinder, H., K. Chan and P.J. Seguin (1996), 'An Empirical Examination of Information, Differences of Opinion, and Trading Activity', *Journal of Financial Economics*, 40, pp. 105–34.

Bilson, J.F.O. (1990), ' "Technical" Currency Trading', in L.R. Thomas (ed.), *The Currency-Hedging Debate*, London: International Financing Review Publishing.

Black, F. (1976), 'Studies in Stock Price Volatility Changes', in *Proceedings of the 1976 Meetings of the Business and Economic Statistics Section, American Statistical Association*, pp. 177–81.

Black, S.W. (1991), 'Transactions Costs and Vehicle Currencies', *Journal of International Money and Finance*, 10, pp. 512–26.

Bollerslev, T. (1986), 'Generalized Autoregressive Conditional Heteroscedasticity', *Journal of Econometrics*, 31, pp. 307–27.

(1990), 'Modelling the Coherence in Short-Run Nominal Exchange Rates: A Multivariate Generalized ARCH Model', *Review of Economics and Statistics*, 72, pp. 498–505.

Bollerslev, T., R.Y. Chou and K.F. Kroner (1992), 'ARCH Modeling in Finance: A Review of the Theory and Empirical Evidence', *Journal of Econometrics*, 52, pp. 5–59.

Bollerslev, T. and I. Domowitz (1993), 'Trading Patterns and Prices in the Interbank Foreign Exchange Market', *Journal of Finance*, 48, pp. 1421–43.

Bollerslev, T. and M. Melvin (1994), 'Bid–Ask Spreads and Volatility in the Foreign Exchange Market: An Empirical Analysis', *Journal of International Economics*, 36, pp. 355–72.

Boothe, P.M. and D.A. Glassman (1987), 'The Statistical Distribution of Exchange Rates: Empirical Evidence and Economic Implications', *Journal of International Economics*, 22, pp. 297–319.

Bossaerts, P. and P. Hillion (1991), 'Market Microstructure Effects of Government Intervention in the Foreign Exchange Market', *Review of Financial Studies*, 4, pp. 513–41.

Box, G.P.E. and G.M. Jenkins (1970), *Time Series Analysis: Forecasting and Control*, London: Holden Day.

Bradfield, J. (1979), 'A Formal Dynamic Model of Market Making', *Journal of Financial and Quantitative Analysis*, pp. 275–91.

Brock, W.A. and A.W. Kleidon (1992), 'Periodic Market Closure and Trading Volume: A Model of Intraday Bids and Asks', *Journal of Economic Dynamics and Control*, 16, pp. 451–89.

Burnham, J.B. (1991), 'Current Structure and Recent Developments in Foreign Exchange Markets', in S.J. Khoury (ed.), *Recent Developments in International Banking and Finance*, vol. IV, Amsterdam: Elsevier Science, pp. 123–53.

Campbell, J.Y., A.W. Lo and A.C. MacKinlay (1997), *The Econometrics of Financial Markets*, Princeton: Princeton University Press.

Canina, L. and S. Figlewski (1993), 'The Informational Content of Implied Volatility', *Review of Financial Studies*, 6, pp. 659–81.

Carlson, J.A. and C.L. Osler (1998), 'Rational Speculators and Exchange Rate Volatility', Working Paper, Federal Reserve Bank of New York.

Chesney, M. and L. Scott (1989), 'Pricing European Currency Options: A Comparison of the Modified Black–Scholes Model and a Random Variance Model', *Journal of Financial and Quantitative Analysis*, 24, pp. 267–84.

Cheung, Y.-W. and M.D. Chinn (1999), 'Macroeconomic Implications of the Beliefs and Behavior of Foreign Exchange Traders,' Department of Economics, University of California at Santa Cruz, mimeo.

Cheung, Y.-W., M.D. Chinn and I.W. Marsh (1999), 'How Do UK-Based Foreign Exchange Dealers Think Their Market Operates?', Discussion Paper No. 2230, Centre for Economic Policy Research.

Cheung, Y.-W. and C.Y.-P. Wong (1999), 'Foreign Exchange Traders in Hong Kong, Tokyo and Singapore: A Survey Study', *Advances in Pacific Basin Financial Markets*, 5, pp. 111–34.

(2000), 'A Survey of Market Practitioners' Views on Exchange Rate Dynamics', *Journal of International Economics*, 51(2), pp. 401–19.

Clark, P. (1973), 'A Subordinated Stochastic Process Model with Finite Variance for Speculative Prices', *Econometrica*, 41, pp. 135–56.

Cohen, K., S. Maier, R. Schwartz and D. Whitcomb (1979), 'On The Existence of Serial Correlation in an Efficient Securities Market', *TIMS Studies in the Management Sciences*, 11, pp. 151–68.

(1981), 'Transactions Costs, Order Placement Strategy and Existence of the Bid–Ask Spread', *Journal of Political Economy*, 89, pp. 287–305.

(1986), *The Microstructure of Securities Markets*, Englewood Cliffs, N.J.: Prentice-Hall.

Conroy, R.M. and R.L. Winkler (1981), 'Informational Differences Between Limit and Market Orders for a Market Maker', *Journal of Financial and Quantitative Analysis*, 16, pp. 703–24.

Copeland, T. and D. Galai (1983), 'Information Effects on the Bid–Ask Spread', *Journal of Finance*, 38, pp. 1457–69.

Cornell, B. (1981), 'The Consumption Based Asset Pricing Model: A Note on Potential Tests and Applications', *Journal of Financial Economics*, 9, pp. 103–8.

Covrig, V. and M.T. Melvin (1999), Asymmetric Information and Price Discovery in the FX Market: Does Tokyo Know More About the Yen?', Department of Economics, Arizona State University, mimeo.

Curcio, R. and C.A.E. Goodhart (1992), 'When Support/Resistance Levels Are Broken, Can Profits Be Made? Evidence from the Foreign Exchange Market?', Financial Markets Group Discussion Paper No. 142, London School of Economics, pp. 1–22.

(1993), 'Chartism: A Controlled Experiment', *Journal of International Securities Markets*, 7, pp. 173–86.

De Grauwe, P. and H. Dewachter (1993), 'A Chaotic Model of the Exchange Rate: The Role of Fundamentalists and Chartists', *Open Economies Review*, 4, pp. 351–79.

De Grauwe, P., H. Dewachter and M. Embrechts (1993), *Exchange Rate Theory: Chaotic Models of Foreign Exchange Markets*, Oxford: Blackwell.

De Long, J.B., A. Shleifer, L.H. Summers and R.J. Waldmann (1989), 'The Size and Incidence of the Losses from Noise Trading', *Journal of Finance*, 44, pp. 681–99.

(1990a), 'Noise Trader Risk in Financial Markets', *Journal of Political Economy*, 98, pp. 703–38.

(1990b), 'Positive Feedback Investment Strategies and Destabilizing Rational Speculation', *Journal of Finance*, 45, pp. 379–95.

DeGennaro, R.P. and R.E. Shrieves (1995), 'Public Information Releases, Private Information Arrival, and Volatility in the Foreign Exchange Markets', paper presented at Olsen and Associates conference on *High-Frequency Data in Finance*, Zurich.

Demos, A.A. and C.A.E. Goodhart (1996), 'The Interaction between the Frequency of Market Quotations, Spread and Volatility in the Foreign Exchange Markets', *Applied Economics*, 28, pp. 377–86.

Demsetz, H. (1968), 'The Cost of Transacting', *Quarterly Journal of Economics*, 82, pp. 33–53.

Diamond, D.W. and R.E. Verrecchia (1981), 'Information Aggregation in a Noisy Rational Expectations Economy', *Journal of Financial Economics*, 9, pp. 221–35.

Diebold, F.X. (1988), 'Serial Correlation and the Combination of Forecasts', *Journal of Business and Economic Statistics*, 6, pp. 105–11.

Diebold, F.X. and J.A. Nason (1990), 'Nonparametric Exchange Rate Prediction?', *Journal of International Economics*, 28, pp. 315–32.

Diebold, F.X. and M. Nerlove (1989), 'The Dynamics of Exchange Rate Volatility: A Multivariate Latent Factor ARCH Model', *Journal of Applied Econometrics*, 4, pp. 1–21.

Diebold, F.X. and P. Pauly (1988), 'Has the EMS Reduced Member-Country Exchange Rate Volatility?', *Empirical Economics*, 13, pp. 81–102.

Dominguez, K.M. (1987), 'Exchange Rate Efficiency and the Behavior of International Asset Markets', unpublished Ph.D. thesis, Yale University.

Domowitz, I. and C.S. Hakkio (1985), 'Conditional Variance and the Risk Premium in the Foreign Exchange Market', *Journal of International Economics*, 19, pp. 47–66.

Dornbusch, R. (1976), 'Expectations and Exchange Rate Dynamics', *Journal of Political Economy*, 84, pp. 1161–76.

Easley, D. and M. O'Hara (1992), 'Time and the Process of Security Price Adjustment', *Journal of Finance*, 47, pp. 577–605.

Engle, R.F. (1982), 'Autoregressive Conditional Heteroscedasticity with Estimates of the Variance of United Kingdom Inflation', *Econometrica*, 50, pp. 987–1007.

Engle, R.F. and T. Bollerslev (1986), 'Modelling the Persistence of Conditional Variances', *Econometric Reviews*, 5, pp. 1–50.

Engle, R.F., T. Ito and W.-L. Lin (1990), 'Meteor Showers or Heat Waves? Heteroskedastic Intra-Daily Volatility in the Foreign Exchange Market', *Econometrica*, 58, pp. 525–42.

Engle, R.F., D.M. Lilien and R.P. Robins (1987), 'Estimating Time Varying Risk Premia in the Term Structure: The Arch-M Model', *Econometrica*, 55, pp. 391–407.

Epps, T.W. and M.L. Epps (1976), 'The Stochastic Dependence of Security Price Changes and Transaction Volumes: Implications for the Mixture-of-Distributions Hypothesis', *Econometrica*, 44, pp. 305–21.

Evans, M.D.D. and R.K. Lyons (1999), 'Order Flow and Exchange Rate Dynamics', Working Paper No. 7317, National Bureau of Economic Research.

Fama, E. (1970), 'Efficient Capital Markets: A Review of Theory and Empirical Work', *Journal of Finance*, 25, pp. 383–417.

Fieleke, N.S. (1975), 'Exchange-Rate Flexibility and the Efficiency of the Foreign-Exchange Markets', *Journal of Financial and Quantitative Analysis*, 10, pp. 409–28.

Flood, M.D. (1991), 'Microstructure Theory and the Foreign Exchange Market', *Federal Reserve Bank of St Louis Review*, 73, pp. 52–70.

(1994), 'Market Structure and Inefficiency in the Foreign Exchange Market', *Journal of International Money and Finance*, 13, pp. 131–58.

Flood, R.P. and A.K. Rose (1995), 'Fixing Exchange Rates: A Virtual Quest for Fundamentals', *Journal of Monetary Economics*, 36, pp. 3–37.

Flood, R.P. and M.P. Taylor (1996), 'Exchange Rate Economics: What's Wrong with the Conventional Macro Approach?', in J.A. Frankel, G. Galli, and A. Giovannini (eds.), *The Microstructure of Foreign Exchange Markets*, Chicago: Chicago University Press for NBER, pp. 261–94.

Foster, F.D. and S. Viswanathan (1990), 'A Theory of the Interday Variations in Volume, Variance, and Trading Costs in Securities Markets', *Review of Financial Studies*, 3, pp. 593–624.

Frankel, J.A. and K.A. Froot (1987a), 'Understanding the U.S. Dollar in the Eighties: The Expectations of Chartists and Fundamentalists', *Economic Record*.

(1987b), 'Using Survey Data to Test Standard Propositions Regarding Exchange Rate Expectations', *American Economic Review*, 77, pp. 133–53.

(1990a), 'Chartists, Fundamentalists, and Trading in the Foreign Exchange Market', *American Economic Review*, 80, pp. 181–5.

(1990b), 'Chartists, Fundamentalists and the Demand for Dollars', in A. Courakis and M.P. Taylor (eds.), *Private Behaviour and Government Policy in Interdependent Economies*, Oxford: Clarendon Press.

Frankel, J.A., G. Galli and A. Giovannini (eds.) (1996), *The Microstructure of Foreign Exchange Markets*, National Bureau of Economic Research Conference Report series, Chicago: University of Chicago Press.

Frankel, J.A. and A.K. Rose (1995), 'Empirical Research on Nominal Exchange Rates', in G. Grossman and K. Rogoff (eds.), *Handbook of International Economics*, vol. III, Amsterdam: North-Holland, pp. 1689–729.

French, K. and R. Roll (1986), 'Stock Return Variances: The Arrival of Information and the Reaction of Traders', *Journal of Financial Economics*, 19, pp. 3–30.

Friedman, M. (1953), 'The Case for Flexible Exchange Rates', in M. Friedman, *Essays in Positive Economics*, Chicago: University of Chicago Press, pp. 157–203.

Froot, K.A. and T. Ito (1989), 'On the Consistency of Short-Run and Long-Run Exchange Rate Expectations', *Journal of International Money and Finance*, 8, pp. 487–510.

Garbade, K.D. (1978), 'The Effect of Interdealer Brokerage on the Transnational Characteristics of Dealer Markets', *Journal of Business*, 51(3), pp. 477–98.

Garbade, K.D., J.L. Pomrenze and W.L. Silber (1979), 'On the Information Content of Prices', *American Economic Review*, 69, pp. 50–9.

Garman, M.B. (1976), 'Market Microstructure', *Journal of Financial Economics*, 3, pp. 257–75.

Giovannini, A. and P. Jorion (1989), 'The Time Variation of Risk and Return in the Foreign Exchange and Stock Markets', *Journal of Finance*, 44, pp. 307–25.

Glassman, D.A. (1987), 'Exchange Rate Risk and Transactions Costs: Evidence from Bid–Ask Spreads', *Journal of International Money and Finance*, 6, pp. 479–90.

Glosten, L.R. (1994), 'Is the Electronic Open Limit Order Book Inevitable?', *Journal of Finance*, 49, pp. 1127–61.

Glosten, L.R. and P.R. Milgrom (1985), 'Bid, Ask and Transaction Prices in a Specialist Market with Heterogeneously Informed Traders', *Journal of Financial Economics*, 14, pp. 71–100.

Goldberg, L.S. and R. Tenorio (1997), 'Strategic Trading in a Two-Sided Foreign Exchange Auction', *Journal of International Economics*, 42, pp. 299–326.

Goldberg, M. and R. Frydman (1993), 'Theories, Consistent Expectations and Exchange Rate Dynamics', in H. Frisch and A. Worgotter (eds.), *Open-Economy Macroeconomics*, New York: St Martin's Press in association with the International Economic Association, pp. 377–99.

Goodhart, C.A.E. (1988), 'The Foreign Exchange Market: A Random Walk with a Dragging Anchor', *Economica*, 55, pp. 437–60.

Goodhart, C.A.E. and L. Figliuoli (1991), 'Every Minute Counts in Financial Markets', *Journal of International Money and Finance*, 10, pp. 23–52.

Goodhart, C.A.E. and M. Giugale (1993), 'From Hour to Hour in the Foreign Exchange Market', *Manchester School of Economic and Social Studies*, 61, pp. 1–34.

Goodhart, C.A.E., T. Ito and R. Payne (1996), 'One Day in June 1993: A Study of the Working of the Reuters 2000–2 Electronic Foreign Exchange Trading System', in J.A. Frankel, G. Galli and A. Giovannini (eds.), *The Microstructure of Foreign Exchange Markets*, National Bureau of Economic Research Conference Report Series, Chicago: University of Chicago Press, pp. 107–79.

Grammatikos, T. and A. Saunders (1986), 'Futures Price Variability: A Test of Maturity and Volume Effects', *Journal of Business*, 59, pp. 319–30.

Group of Thirty (1985), *The Foreign Exchange Market in the 1980s*, New York: Group of Thirty.

Hakkio, C.S. (1981), 'Expectations and the Forward Exchange Rate', *International Economic Review*, 22, pp. 663–78.

Harris, L. (1986), 'A Transaction Data Study of Weekly and Intradaily Patterns in Stock Returns', *Journal of Financial Economics*, 16, pp. 99–117.

Hartmann, P. (1998a), *Currency Competition and Foreign Exchange Markets: The Dollar, the Yen and the Euro*. Cambridge: Cambridge University Press.

(1998b), 'Do Reuters Spreads Reflect Currencies' Differences in Global Trading Activity?', *Journal of International Money and Finance*, 17, pp. 757–84.

(1999), 'Trading Volumes and Transaction Costs in the Foreign Exchange Market: Evidence from Daily Dollar–Yen Spot Data', *Journal of Banking and Finance*, 23, pp. 801–24.

Harvey, C.R. and R.D. Huang (1991), 'Volatility in the Foreign Currency Futures Market', *Review of Financial Studies*, 4, pp. 543–69.

Ho, T. and H. Stoll (1981), 'Optimal Dealer Pricing under Transactions and Return Uncertainty', *Journal of Financial Economics*, 9, pp. 47–73.

Hodrick, R.J. (1989), 'Risk, Uncertainty, and Exchange Rates', *Journal of Monetary Economics*, 23, pp. 433–59.

Hodrick, R.J. and S. Srivastava (1984), 'An Investigation of Risk and Return in Forward Foreign Exchange', *Journal of International Money and Finance*, 3, pp. 5–29.

Hogan, K.C., Jr and M.T. Melvin (1994), 'Sources of Meteor Showers and Heat Waves in the Foreign Exchange Market', *Journal of International Economics*, 37, pp. 239–47.

Hsieh, D.A. (1988), 'The Statistical Properties of Daily Foreign Exchange Rates: 1974–1983', *Journal of International Economics*, 24, pp. 129–45.

(1989a), 'Testing for Nonlinear Dependence in Daily Foreign Exchange Rates', *Journal of Business*, 62, pp. 339–68.

(1989b), 'Modeling Heteroscedasticity in Daily Foreign-Exchange Rates', *Journal of Business and Economic Statistics*, 7, pp. 307–17.

Hsieh, D.A. and A.W. Kleidon (1996), 'Bid–Ask Spreads in Foreign Exchange Markets: Implications for Models of Asymmetric Information', in J.A. Frankel, G. Galli and A. Giovannini (eds.), *The Microstructure of Foreign Exchange Markets*, National Bureau of Economic Research Conference Report series, Chicago: Chicago University Press, pp. 41–65.

Hull, J.C. and A. White (1987), 'Hedging the Risks from Writing Foreign Currency Options', *Journal of International Money and Finance*, 6, pp. 131–52.

Ito, T. (1990), 'Foreign Exchange Rate Expectations: Micro Survey Data', *American Economic Review*, 80, pp. 434–49.

Ito, T., R.F. Engle and W.-L. Lin (1992), 'Where Does the Meteor Shower Come From? The Role of Stochastic Policy Coordination', *Journal of International Economics*, 32, pp. 221–40.

Ito, T., R. Lyons and M.T. Melvin (1998), 'Is There Private Information in the FX Market? The Tokyo Experiment', *Journal of Finance*, 53, pp. 1111–30.

Jorion, P. (1995), 'Predicting Volatility in the Foreign Exchange Market', *Journal of Finance*, 50, pp. 507–28.

(1996), 'Risk and Turnover in the Foreign Exchange Market', in J.A. Frankel, G. Galli and A. Giovannini (eds.), *The Microstructure of Foreign Exchange Markets*, National Bureau of Economic Research Conference Report series, Chicago: Chicago University Press, pp. 19–37.

Kaminsky, G. and R. Peruga (1990), 'Can a Time-Varying Risk Premium Explain Excess Returns in the Forward Market for Foreign Exchange?', *Journal of International Economics*, 28, pp. 47–70.

Karpoff, J.M. (1987), 'The Relation between Price Changes and Trading Volume: A Survey', *Journal of Financial and Quantitative Analysis*, 22, pp. 109–26.

Kirman, A. (1991), 'Epidemics of Opinion and Speculative Bubbles in Financial Markets', in M.P. Taylor (ed.), *Money and Financial Markets*, Oxford: Blackwell, pp. 354–68.

Kubarych, R.M. (1983), *Foreign Exchange Markets in the United States*, New York: Federal Reserve Bank of New York.

Kugler, P. and C. Lenz (1990), 'Sind Wechselkursfluktuationen zufullig oder chaotisch?' (with English summary), *Schweizerische Zeitschrift fur Volkswirtschaft und Statistik*, 126, pp. 113–28.

Kyle, A. (1985), 'Continuous Auctions and Insider Trading', *Econometrica*, 53, pp. 1315–35.

Lamoureux, C.G. and W.D. Lastrapes (1993), 'Forecasting Stock-Return Variance: Towards an Understanding of Stochastic Implied Volatilities', *Review of Financial Studies*, 6, pp. 293–326.

Lane, P. (2001), 'The New Open Economy Macroeconomics: A Survey', *Journal of International Economics*, 54(2), pp. 235–66.

Lee, T.H. (1994), 'Spread and Volatility in Spot and Forward Exchange Rates', *Journal of International Money and Finance*, 13, pp. 375–83.

Lee, T.K. (1988), 'Does Conditional Covariance or Conditional Variance Explain Time Varying Risk Premia in Foreign Exchange Returns?', *Economics Letters*, 27, pp. 371–3.

Lui, Y.H. and D. Mole (1998), 'The Use of Fundamental and Technical Analyses by Foreign Exchange Dealers: Hong Kong Evidence', *Journal of International Money and Finance*, 17, pp. 535–45.

Lyons, R.K. (1991), 'Private Beliefs and Information Externalities in the Foreign Exchange Market', Working Paper No. 3889, National Bureau of Economic Research.

(1995), 'Tests of Microstructural Hypotheses in the Foreign Exchange Market', *Journal of Financial Economics*, 39, pp. 321–51.

(1996), 'Foreign Exchange Volume: Sound and Fury Signifying Nothing?', in J.A. Frankel, G. Galli and A. Giovannini (eds.), *The Microstructure of Foreign Exchange Markets*, National Bureau of Economic Research Conference Report Series, Chicago: Chicago University Press, pp. 183–201.

(1997), 'A Simultaneous Trade Model of the Foreign Exchange Hot Potato', *Journal of International Economics*, 42, pp. 275–98.

(ed.) (1998a), *Journal of International Financial Markets, Institutions and Money*, Special Issue on 'International Market Microstructure', 8(3–4), pp. 219–451.

(1998b), 'Profits and Position Control: A Week of FX Dealing', *Journal of International Money and Finance*, 17, pp. 97–115.

(1999), *The Microstructure Approach to Exchange Rates*, Cambridge, Mass.: MIT Press.

Madhavan, A. and S. Smidt (1991), 'A Bayesian Model of Intraday Specialist Pricing', *Journal of Financial Economics*, 30, pp. 99–134.

Malkiel, B.G. (1996), *A Random Walk Down Wall Street: Including a Life-Cycle Guide to Personal Investing*, 6th edn, New York: Norton.

Mark, N.C. (1988), 'Time-Varying Betas and Risk Premia in the Pricing of Forward Foreign Exchange Contracts', *Journal of Financial Economics*, 22, pp. 335–54.

McCurdy, T.H. and I.G. Morgan (1988), 'Testing the Martingale Hypothesis in Deutsche Mark Futures with Models Specifying the Form of Heteroscedasticity', *Journal of Applied Econometrics*, 3, pp. 187–202.

McFarland, J.W., R.R. Pettit and S.K. Sung (1982), 'The Distribution of Foreign Exchange Price Changes: Trading Day Effects and Risk Measurement', *Journal of Finance*, 37, pp. 693–715.

Meese, R.A. and K. Rogoff (1983), 'Empirical Exchange Rate Models of the Seventies: Do They Fit Out of Sample?', *Journal of International Economics*, 14, pp. 3–24.

Meese, R.A. and A.K. Rose (1991), 'An Empirical Assessment of Nonlinearities in Models of Exchange Rate Determination', *Review of Economic Studies*, 58, pp. 603–19.

Melvin, M.T. and P. Ramirez (2000), 'FOMC Days and Exchange Rate Dynamics', Department of Economics, Arizona State University, mimeo.

Melvin, M.T. and X. Yin (1999), 'Public Information Arrival, Exchange Rate Volatility, and Quote Frequency', Department of Economics, Arizona State University, mimeo.

Menkhoff, L. (1997), 'Examining the Use of Technical Currency Analysis', *International Journal of Finance and Economics*, 2, pp. 307–18.

(1998), 'The Noise Trading Approach – Questionnaire Evidence from Foreign Exchange', *Journal of International Money and Finance*, 17, pp. 547–64.

Milhoj, A. (1987), 'A Conditional Variance Model for Daily Deviations of an Exchange Rate', *Journal of Business and Economic Statistics*, 5, pp. 99–103.

Obstfeld, M. and K. Rogoff (1995), 'Exchange Rate Dynamics Redux', *Journal of Political Economy*, 103, pp. 624–60.

(1996), *Foundations of International Macroeconomics*, Cambridge, Mass: MIT Press.

O'Hara, M. (1995), *Market Microstructure Theory*, Cambridge, Mass.: Blackwell.

Oldfield, G.S., Jr and R.J. Rogalski (1980), 'A Theory of Common Stock Returns over Trading and Non-Trading Periods', *Journal of Finance*, 35, pp. 729–51.

Overturf, S.F. (1982), 'Risk, Transactions Charges, and the Market for Foreign Exchange Services', *Economic Inquiry*, 20, pp. 291–302.

Perraudin, W. and P. Vitale (1996), 'Interdealer Trade and Information Flows in a Decentralized Foreign Exchange Market', in J.A. Frankel, G. Galli and A. Giovannini (eds.), *The Microstructure of Foreign Exchange Markets*, National Bureau of Economic Research Conference Report Series, Chicago: Chicago University Press, pp. 73–99.

Pesaran, M.H. (1989), 'Consistency of Short-term and Long-term Expectations', *Journal of International Money and Finance*, 8, pp. 511–16.

Richardson, M. and T. Smith (1994), 'A Direct Test of the Mixture of Distributions Hypothesis: Measuring the Daily Flow of Information', *Journal of Financial and Quantitative Analysis*, 29, pp. 101–16.

Sarno, L. (2001), 'Toward a New Paradigm in Open Economy Modeling: Where Do We Stand?', *Federal Reserve Bank of St Louis Review*, 83, May/June, pp. 21–36.

Schwartz, R.A. (1988), *Equity Markets: Structure, Trading, and Performance*, New York: Harper and Row.

Scott, L. (1987), 'Option Pricing when the Variance Changes Randomly: Theory, Estimation, and an Application', *Journal of Financial and Quantitative Analysis*, 22, pp. 419–38.

Shiller, R.J. (1984), 'Stock Prices and Social Dynamics', *Brookings Papers on Economic Activity*, 2, pp. 457–98.

(1989), *Market Volatility*, Cambridge, Mass.: MIT Press.

Smidt, S. (1971), 'Which Road to an Efficient Stock Market?', *Financial Analysts Journal*, 27, pp. 64–9.

Stein, J.C. (1987), 'Informational Externalities and Welfare-Reducing Speculation', *Journal of Political Economy*, 95, pp. 1123–45.

Stigler, G.J. (1964), 'Public Regulation of the Securities Markets', *Journal of Business*, 37(2), pp. 117–42.

Stoll, H.R. (1978), 'The Supply of Dealer Services in Securities Markets', *Journal of Finance*, pp. 1133–51.

Subrahmanyam, A. (1991), 'Risk Aversion, Market Liquidity, and Price Efficiency', *Review of Financial Studies*, 4, pp. 417–41.

Suvanto, A. (1993), *Foreign Exchange Dealing: Essays on the Microstructure of the Foreign Exchange Market*, Sarja A 19 Series, Helsinki: Research Institute of the Finnish Economy.

Takagi, S. (1991), 'Exchange Rate Expectations: A Survey of Survey Studies', *International Monetary Fund Staff Papers*, 38, pp. 156–83.

Tauchen, G.E. and M. Pitts (1983), 'The Price Variability–Volume Relationship on Speculative Markets', *Econometrica*, 51, pp. 485–505.

Taylor, M.P. (1987) 'Covered Interest Parity: A High-Frequency, High-Quality Data Study', *Economica*, 54, pp. 429–38.

(1989) 'Covered Interest Arbitrage and Market Turbulence', *Economic Journal*, 99, pp. 376–91.

(1995), 'The Economics of Exchange Rates', *Journal of Economic Literature*, 83, pp. 13–47.

Taylor, M.P. and H. Allen (1992), 'The Use of Technical Analysis in the Foreign Exchange Market', *Journal of International Money and Finance*, 11, pp. 304–14.

Wasserfallen, W. and H. Zimmermann (1985), 'The Behavior of Intra-Daily Exchange Rates', *Journal of Banking and Finance*, 9, pp. 55–72.

Wei, S.J. and J.A. Frankel (1991), 'Are Option-Implied Forecasts of Exchange Rate Volatility Excessively Variable?', Working Paper No. 3910, National Bureau of Economic Research.

Westerfield, R. (1977), 'The Distribution of Common Stock Price Changes: An Application of Transactions Time and Subordinated Stochastic Models', *Journal of Financial and Quantitative Analysis*, 12, pp. 743–65.

Wiggins, J.B. (1987), 'Option Values under Stochastic Volatility: Theory and Empirical Estimates', *Journal of Financial Economics*, 19, pp. 351–72.

Wolinsky, A. (1990), 'Information Revelation in a Market with Pairwise Meetings', *Econometrica*, 58, pp. 1–23.

Author index

Subject index